PROVERBS

**An Explanation
With Notes and Quotes,
Illustrations and Applications**

G. Michael Cocoris

PROVERBS

An Explanation
With Notes and Quotes,
Illustrations and Applications

G. Michael Cocoris

© 2014 G. Michael Cocoris

All rights reserved. This publication may not be reproduced (in whole or in part, edited, or revised) in any way, form, or means, including, but not limited to electronic, mechanical, photocopying, recording, or any kind of storage and retrieval system *for sale*, except for brief quotations in printed reviews, without the written permission of G. Michael Cocoris, 2016 Euclid #20, Santa Monica, CA 90405, michaelcocoris.@gmail.com, or his appointed representatives. Permission is hereby granted, however, for the reproduction of the whole or parts of the whole without changing the content in any way for *free distribution,* provided all copies contain this copyright notice in its entirety. Permission is also granted to charge for the cost of copying.

Unless otherwise indicated, all Scripture quotations are taken from the New King James Version ®, Copyright © 1979, 1980, 1982 by Thomas Nelson, Inc. Used by permission. All rights reserved.

TABLE OF CONTENTS

PREFACE	1
INTRODUCTION	3
LEARNING TO LIVE WISELY	5
WHERE TO START TO LEARN WISDOM	9
OUR SECOND SOURCE OF WISDOM	13
CHOOSE YOUR COMPANIONS CAREFULLY	17
THE RESULT OF REJECTING WISDOM	21
THE BENEFITS OF LIVING WISELY	25
THE SURPRISING BENEFITS OF LIVING WISELY	29
THE VALUE OF LIVING WISELY	35
THE ULTIMATE REASON FOR LIVING WISELY	39
HOW TO LOVE A NEIGHBOR	43
GET WISDOM	47
PROTECT YOURSELF	51
WISE SEX	53
SHOULD YOU CO-SIGN FOR A LOAN?	57
LEARN ABOUT LAZINESS	61
THE TROUBLE WITH BEING A TROUBLEMAKER	67
CONSIDER THE CONSEQUENCES	71
THE STORY OF SEX	75
THE BLESSING OF GOD'S WISDOM	79
TWO INVITATIONS TO DINNER	83
INTRODUCTION TO PROVERBS 10:1-31:31	87
PROVERBS 10	89
PROVERBS 11	95
PROVERBS 12	101
PROVERBS 13	107
PROVERBS 14	113
PROVERBS 15	123
PROVERBS 16	131
PROVERBS 17	139
PROVERBS 18	147
PROVERBS 19	153
PROVERBS 20	161
PROVERBS 21	169
PROVERBS 22	177
PROVERBS 23	185
PROVERBS 24	189
PROVERBS 25	193
PROVERBS 26	201
PROVERBS 27	209
PROVERBS 28	217
PROVERBS 29	227
PROVERBS 30	237
PROVERBS 31	247
BIBLIOGRAPHY	255

PREFACE

The purpose of this commentary is to provide a practical explanation of Proverbs. The objective is a balanced exposition—explaining the passage in context and applying its truths to life with illustrations. Some commentaries are, by design, of a technical nature, delving into the meanings of words and phrases even outside their use in the book under consideration. Those types of commentaries tend to ignore the context of the book and its application. Other commentaries go to the other extreme and concentrate on the application, often not fully expounding the passage. Commentaries should do both. They should offer a contextual exposition of the book and apply the truths of that book to life. Adding illustrations facilitates clarity.

First and foremost, this is a contextual exposition. The context is not just the paragraph or the chapter but the whole book. In studying any book of the Bible, the first question that should be asked is: "What is the subject of this book?" Each natural literary unit, whether a paragraph or a narrative, develops a subject. A legitimate exposition will show how the author develops his subject. That, and only that, is contextual Bible study. All details in a book must be explained in light of the message and structure of the entire book. Words only have meaning in a context. A detailed explanation of words and phrases ripped from their sentence and the broader context is not exposition. The flow of the thought of the passage in the context of the book is the message the author intends to convey.

The Bible was written for living (2 Tim. 3:16-17). Even the most brilliant explanation that stops short of the applications is an abortion of what God intended. Thus, the practical ramifications of every passage must always be considered.

The study procedure I use is first dividing the biblical book into its natural literary units (narratives or paragraphs). Then, I analyze each unit. The analysis includes an outline of the development of thought in that unit (major points and sub-points), an explanation of each sentence, and a summary statement. After I have personally analyzed each unit, I read commentaries, deliberately reading commentaries from different theological perspectives. I credit commentators' comments by putting their names in parenthesis, even if I had seen that point in the text during my study before I read their comments. Thus, each chapter of this material expounds a natural literary unit of the book of the Proverbs.

In the study process, I also wrote a tentative title, introduction, and conclusion as if what I was working on was a sermon. If I stumble across an illustration, I include it, but, at this point, I do not search for illustrations. I write all of this for each literary unit in the book before preaching the first sermon. As a result, when I begin speaking through the book, I have the whole book in mind.

I may change the tentative title, introduction, and/or conclusion as I prepare to preach each literary unit. I rarely change the explanation of the text. It is as I preach each unit that I search for illustrations. Again, having studied the whole book first is helpful here. I sometimes found an illustration I knew would fit better later in the book.

The introduction of each chapter briefly relates that section to life and/or the context. The captions throughout the chapters are divisions of that portion of Scripture and correspond to the main points of a sermon. The italicized headings correspond to the sub-points of a sermon. Rather than footnotes, the author's name is in parenthesis in the text. While applications are made throughout the exposition, the passage as a whole is summarized and applied at the end.

I wish to thank Hunter Wood for his help and Teresa Rogers for proofreading this material.

May the Lord be pleased to use this approach to the Scripture to enlighten, encourage, and edify believers, thus glorifying His Son.

G. Michael Cocoris
Santa Monica, CA

INTRODUCTION

The Rabbinical writings called Proverbs "the book of wisdom." This book has been called "the finest and grandest collection of proverbs in the world" (Lee), "different and distinct from any other book in the Bible. It is not history, nor poetry, nor rhapsody, nor prophecy, nor law, nor ritual, nor story, nor dogma; and although it belongs to the wisdom literature, it differs from the other wisdom books, Job and Ecclesiastes" (Scroggie).

Proverbs are not laws or promises. They are proverbial maxims, general truths that technically could have an exception. A proverb is one of the most ancient forms of teaching. From the earliest times, every nation has had its proverbs. The method was particularly valuable when books were few and costly. A clear, crisp sentence was easy to memorize. Today, we use slogans.

Author

Proverbs is a collection of proverbs by different authors. Solomon is the author/editor. Proverbs 1:1 states, "The Proverbs of Solomon, the Son of David, King of Israel." Solomon was certainly qualified to write Proverbs. He asked for wisdom (1 Kings 3:5-9) and God granted it to him (1 Kings 4:29-31). According to Ecclesiastes 12:9, he pondered, searched, and arranged many proverbs. First Kings 4:32 says he spoke 3,000 proverbs and 1,005 psalms. Eight hundred of his 3,000 proverbs are recorded in the Book of Proverbs.

Otherwise, men wrote some of the proverbs. Several sections are said to be from "wise men" (see 22:17 and 24:23). In 1888, Wallis Budge discovered an Egyptian work, The Wisdom of Amenemope. The similarities between The Wisdom of Amenemope and Proverbs 22:17-24:17 are "too many and too close to be a matter of coincidence" (Kidner). Did Amenemope copy Solomon, or did Solomon copy Amenemope, or did they both copy someone else?

Many have dated Amenemope before Solomon and concluded that Solomon copied him. In the first place, dating Amenemope is difficult. Some date him from Solomon's time; others date him after, but more importantly, even if Solomon copied him, that would not undermine divine inspiration. Adaptation of pagan sources is not unknown, even in the New Testament. Paul did it several times (Acts 17:28 and Titus 1:12). If the material was borrowed, it was adapted. The polytheism of Amenemope is eliminated in Proverbs.

Some have forcefully argued that Amenemope copied Solomon. For example, Archer argues that it is possible to reconstruct the Egyptian text based on a Hebrew original but not reconstruct the Hebrew text based on an Egyptian original.

Agur wrote Proverbs 30 and Lemuel wrote Proverbs 31. Nothing is known about these two authors except that they wrote Proverbs.

Recipients

Like Psalms, Proverbs has multiple authors and was compiled after composition. Thus, pinpointing the date is complicated. At least part of the book was addressed to Solomon's son, presumably Rehoboam (1:8; 2:1; etc.; this applies to Proverbs 1:1-9:18 for sure and probably Proverbs 10:1 through 22:16; it more than likely does not apply to 25:1ff.).

The book was not "compiled" until the time of Hezekiah. Solomon lived and wrote about 950 BC, but Proverbs 25:1 says that the men of Hezekiah compiled a larger portion of the book. That was not until 725 BC. So, the book, as it is today, was not received by anyone until 725 BC. Isaiah and Micah ministered during Hezekiah's time. It has also been suggested that they were also involved in the collection of Proverbs.

Solomon's son, presumably Rehoboam, received some of the Proverbs. Yet, at the same time, the teaching was also intended for others. In Proverbs 4:1, Solomon addresses "children." Proverbs 8:1-5 indicates that Proverbs was for all humanity in general.

Message

Proverbs discusses a wide range of subjects, including types of people (such as the wise, the fool, and the simple), child discipline, sexual immorality, etc., but the book's subject is wisdom. The Hebrew word for "wisdom" means "skill." These short, pithy statements provide wisdom for living. Understanding the laws behind things gives one wisdom. The tailor has wisdom, that is, skill, when he understands the laws of fabric.

The wisdom in Proverbs is not the wisdom of men but the wisdom of God. These Proverbs are not so much popular sayings as they are distillations of wisdom by men who knew the law of God. Man's proverbs are often in opposition to each other. For example, "Look before you leap" versus "He who hesitates is lost;" "A man gets no more than he pays for" versus "The best things in life are free;" "Leave well enough alone" versus "Progress never stands still;" "A rolling stone gathers no moss" versus "A setting hen does not get fat."

Yet, while God's law is everywhere assumed, Israel is never mentioned. There is a universality in Proverbs. It is not a national Jewish book. These Proverbs apply to all people at all times in all places.

The message of Proverbs is that wise people learn skills for living from God's Word and from wise people.

Structure

The literary structure of Proverbs is discernible. There are titles heading each section. These are sometimes obscured in the English translation but are apparent in the Hebrew text. The title "The Proverbs of Solomon" appears three times. The first time (1:1), it applies to the whole book, and the other two occurrences (10:1; 25:1) apply to the sections within the book. The first nine chapters contain discourses on the value of wisdom. Then follow two collections of the Proverbs of Solomon. Two appendices supplement each collection.

I.	Introduction	1:1-7
II.	A Father's Praise of Wisdom	1:8-9:18
III.	The Proverbs of Solomon	10:1-22:16
IV.	The Words of Wise Men	22:17-24:34
	A. The Words of Wise Men	22:17-24:22
	B. The Further Words of Wise Men	24:23-34
V.	Hezekiah's Collection of the Proverbs of Solomon	25:1-29:27
VI.	The Words of Wise Men	30:1-31:31
	A. The Words of Agur	30:1-33
	B. The Words of King Lemuel's Mother	31:1-31

McGee states, "Although the book of Proverbs seems to be a collection of sayings without any particular regard for orderly arrangement, the contrary is true. The book tells a story. It is a picture of a young man starting out in life. His first lesson is given in 1:7. Two schools bid for him, and both sent their literature: one, the school of wisdom, and the other, the school for fools. In chapter 8, the young man goes to the Academy of Wisdom, where he is taught in Proverbs. From chapters 10 through 24, the young man is in the classroom of wisdom."

Purpose

Proverbs is one of the few biblical books that states its purpose (1:2-6). The opening verses give two purposes for the book. The first and foremost purpose is to impart moral discernment (1:2a, 3-5). The second purpose is to develop mental clarity and perception (1:2b, 6). The philosophy of this book is not "live and learn" but "learn and live."

Summary: Solomon and others wrote short, pithy statements to assist the wise and unwise in developing mental acumen and wisdom for living. A wise person learns wisdom for living from God's Word and wise people.

Pierson says, "What the Psalms are to the devotional life, the Proverbs are to the practical life."

LEARNING TO LIVE WISELY

The setting was a small café on the beach overlooking the Pacific Ocean. The cool breeze coming off the ocean made for a pleasant moment. The food was superb. However, the man I was having lunch with was not in a pleasant mood. He had invited me to lunch to talk. He was telling me ("confessing" would be a better word) about a decision he had made in his life that had turned out not to be very wise. As he told me the story, he kept saying, "Dumb, just dumb!" During the conversation, he must have said that a dozen times.

Have you ever felt that way about a decision or how you have lived your life? I have. We would all probably say we need to make wise decisions and learn to live a wise life. But what does that mean and how do we get it?

The subject of the book of Proverbs is wisdom. By carefully examining the book's prologue, we can discover the answers to the questions, "What is wisdom? And how does one get it?" The prologue is in Proverbs 1:1-6.

Learn Wisdom from Proverbs

Proverbs The book of Proverbs begins with "The proverbs of Solomon the son of David, king of Israel" (1:1). This is a book of "proverbs." A proverb is a general truth about life. It may be a short simile (11:22) or a longer sermon (chapter 5).

Proverbs are not laws or promises. They are general truths that could have an exception. For example, the modern proverb, "Better late than never," is certainly a general truth that a wise man should follow, but it is not a law. There could be an exception. If a man had an appointment with men who intended to kill him, the intended victim would be "better never than late."

Short proverbs are one of the most ancient forms of teaching. From the earliest times, every nation has had its proverbs. The method was particularly valuable when books were handwritten and, therefore, few and costly. A single sentence was easy to memorize. Today, we use slogans.

Wisdom It is evident from the content of the book of Proverbs that the subject of the book is wisdom (see especially 1:2). The Hebrew word translated "wisdom" means, of course, "wisdom," but it also means "skill." Concerning those who would build the Tabernacle, God says to Moses, "I have put wisdom in the hearts of all who are gifted artisans, that they may make all that I have commanded you" (Ex. 31:6). In fact, concerning one construction worker, God says, "And I have filled him with the Spirit of God, in wisdom, in understanding, in knowledge, and in all manner of workmanship, to design artistic works, to work in gold, in silver, in bronze, in cutting jewels for setting, in carving wood, and to work in all manner of workmanship" (Ex. 31:3-5).

Why does a craftsman need wisdom? By saying He had given them a spirit of wisdom, God does not mean they were of superior intellect. He means that He has given them a spirit of skill and the skill, in their case, was with wood and metal. In Proverbs, Solomon does not write to impart skills for construction. The skill that he has in mind is the skill of living.

Proverbs, then, contains wisdom, the truth about skill in living. The topics covered in Proverbs include relationships (with God, between husband and wife, between parents and children, with friends), types of people (such as the wise, the fool, the simple, the sluggard, the scoffer, etc.), use of words, money, and sex. We need to learn to live skillfully in all these areas. How do we do that?

Learn from the Wise

Solomon The opening verse appears to be announcing the book's author as Solomon (1:1). Usually when a biblical book begins with a person's name, it is the author's name. In this case, that is not precisely correct. Later in the book, we are told: "Incline your ear and hear the words of the wise" (22:17), "These things also belong to the wise" (24:23), "These also are proverbs of Solomon, which the men of Hezekiah king of Judah copied" (25:1), "The words of Agur" (30:1), and "The words of King Lemuel, the utterance which his mother taught him" (31:1). Clearly, several men wrote these poritions of Proverbs.

Solomon, however, wrote the bulk of the book and was the author of the first section. According to Ecclesiastes 12:9, he pondered, searched out, and arranged many proverbs. First Kings 4:32 says he spoke three thousand proverbs. Solomon, the author of the first part of Proverbs, was a wise man.

From His Father How did Solomon learn so much wisdom? For one thing, he asked God for wisdom (1 Kings 3:5-9) and God granted it to him (1 Kings 4:29-31), but how did God teach him? The opening verse implies Solomon learned about life from others.

Solomon is identified as "the son of David, king of Israel" (1:1). The man who wrote most of this book was the son of a man who lived a full life. David, the father of Solomon, was described as "a man after God's own heart" (1 Sam. 13:14). Surely Solomon learned much about life and about the Lord from his father. Just being the son of a man like David would teach him much about life and how to live it. Solomon himself says this was the case. "When I was my father's son, tender and the only one in the sight of my mother, he also taught me and said to me: 'Let your heart retain my words; Keep my commands and live. Get wisdom! Get understanding! Do not forget, nor turn away from the words of my mouth'" (4:3-5).

From Others Solomon, like his father before him, was also king over Israel. Solomon learned about life not only from listening to and watching his father but also from others. Being over people in any capacity will teach any observant person about life. Whether we are over other people or not, we should learn from others (5:13).

The prologue of Proverbs tells us how to obtain wisdom. We can and should learn about life from others. Don't just learn from experience; learn from the experience of others. This is how to make wise decisions. This is how to learn to live skillfully. When faced with a decision, talk to others who have been there or who have done that.

When I was growing up in Pensacola, Florida, there was a steep street near my house that all of us kids used as a playground. It was fun to ride our bikes to the top and coast down at a rapid rate of speed or to roller skate down it. One day the city decided to pave our runway. They covered it with a fresh, hot layer of tar. Needless to say, that meant we could not ride our bikes or skate down our beloved hill.

A short time after they poured the tar, one kid decided to skate across the street to see if it was dry and if he could make it. Well, he didn't. He no sooner began the trip across the street when he fell. Fortunately, he was not seriously hurt. He did have tar stuck to him, which had to be removed with gasoline. None of us felt like we had to learn from our own experiences. We decided to learn from his experience.

Learn from What the Wise Have Written

The objection to learning from others is, "I don't know anyone wise in the area I need wisdom." That may be true. Nevertheless, there is a way you can learn from wise people, namely, by reading what they have written.

Solomon states the twofold purpose of Proverbs: "To know wisdom and instruction, to perceive the words of understanding" (1:2). The first is a moral purpose and the second is a mental one.

The Hebrew word rendered "instruction" is the same Hebrew word that appears in verse 3. The Hebrew word translated "understanding" in verse 6 comes from the same root as the word rendered "understanding" in verse 2. In other words, Solomon summarizes his twofold purpose in verse 2, explains the first in verses 3-5, and picks up the second in verse 6 (see Delitzsch). Proverbs 1:3-5 expounds on wisdom and instruction. Proverbs 1:6 elaborates on understanding.

The Moral Purpose The first and foremost purpose of Proverbs is to "know wisdom and instruction" (1:2). As we have seen, the word wisdom means "wisdom," but it is talking about skillful living. To be more specific, this skill in living is, to a great degree, moral. The moral purpose of Proverbs is to develop skills in living.

Proverbs was written "to receive the instruction of wisdom, justice, judgment, and equity" (1:3). The Hebrew word rendered "instruction," the same one that appears in verse 2, means "discipline." The word here translated "wisdom," however, is not the same word translated wisdom in verse 2. The one used here means "to be prudent or have insight." It is practical wisdom. It is good sense. Proverbs was written so its readers would receive discipline or training in prudent, insightful, practical wisdom. The next three words in this verse explain what Solomon has in mind by being prudent.

The Hebrew word translated "justice" means "righteous, righteousness." Practical wisdom does what is right. "Judgment" is the social outworking of righteousness. It is dealing honestly with one another (Delitzsch). The Hebrew word rendered "equity" means "to be smooth, straight, right." It is to do what is right, true and honest without concealment. It is to do what is honorable and upright. The most basic idea in the Hebrew word is smooth. A truthful, honest, upright person is smooth without wrinkles. Proverbs is an iron that gets wrinkles out of our lives.

Thus, this skill for living is moral. For example, from Proverbs, we learn, "Dishonest scales are an abomination to the LORD, but a just weight is His delight" (11:1). I once heard a seminary professor illustrate this by saying, "Righteousness is 16 ounces to the pound. Righteousness doesn't use a 17-ounce weight to buy and a 14-ounce weight to sell."

Solomon was particularly concerned that three types of people learn this moral wisdom. He says, "To give prudence to the simple, to the young man knowledge and discretion; a wise man will hear and increase learning, and a man of understanding will attain wise counsel" (1:4-5). The three types are the simple (1:4), the young (1:4), and the wise (1:5).

Proverbs can give prudence to the simple. The Hebrew word rendered "simple" means just that, "to be simple." It also means "to be open." One commentator says that the simple is "open-hearted," that is, they are open to every influence from others, including the harmless and the good-natured as well as the foolish and the silly. They allow themselves to be easily persuaded or led astray (Delitzsch). Simple-minded people are open-minded people who are open to either wisdom or folly. Such people are inexperienced, impressionable, easily led, naïve, and gullible. The proverbs contained in this book give just such people prudence, a word which means "craftiness, prudence." In other words, Proverbs can make the gullible aware and, therefore, give them the capacity to escape the foolishness of others. The hope for the naïve is they can be made aware. Proverbs 21:11 says, "When the scoffer is punished, the simple is made wise." By seeing the consequence of sin in real life or by reading about the result of wickedness in Proverbs, the naïve can become aware of what to do or not do in life.

Proverbs can give knowledge and discretion to the young. The Hebrew word for "young" that appears here was used of infants three months old to young people seventeen years old. It is generally understood as the immature (Delitzsch). While the word "knowledge" here is the basic Hebrew word for knowledge, it carries the connotation of understanding and discernment when used in wisdom literature. Like the Hebrew word for wisdom, it can also mean "skill" (Gen. 25:27; 1 Sam. 16:16; etc.). "Discretion" not only means "discretion," it also means purpose. So, the idea of this word is the capacity to comprehend the right purpose and make the right plans. The help Proverbs can give the young is understanding. Proverbs particularly warns young men about the dangers of a harlot (see chapter 7, esp. 7:7).

Proverbs will enable the wise, who will hear and heed what it has to say, to "increase learning" and "attain wise counsel" (1:5). A wise person has not arrived at making all perfect decisions. Instead, a wise person knows that he or she has not attained all wisdom but is pressing toward more and more wisdom.

The Hebrew word rendered "counsel" comes from the root word for a ship's rope or rope pulling. It is the word used for steering and directing a ship. Hence, it means "direction." It signifies guidance and management. In other words, Proverbs will make the wise wiser (9:9). The wise are invited to learn proverbs to add learning to that which they already possess (Delitzsch). The wise come to Proverbs "to learn, not to teach; to have, not the curiosity fed, but the conscience satisfied" (Bridges).

For instance, how does a person handle someone who is angry? That can perplex even the wisest of us. Read Proverbs, and you'll discover, "A soft answer turns away wrath, but a harsh word stirs up anger" (15:1). A wise person will learn from such insight and go in that direction.

Proverbs, then, can impart awareness to the naïve, understanding to the young and direction to the wise. Each gains skill in living from Proverbs.

The Mental Purpose The second purpose of Proverbs is "to perceive the words of understanding" (1:2). The first purpose concerns wisdom, or more specifically, moral wisdom. The second purpose focuses on the ability to perceive. It has to do with developing the mind. The mental purpose of Proverbs is to develop skill in thinking.

Solomon elaborates on the second purpose, "To understand a proverb and an enigma, the words of the wise and their riddles" (1:6). In other words, the mind is exercised and developed, as it understands a proverb, an enigma and the words of the wise and their riddles. "Enigma" means "satire, mocking poem." Here, it probably refers to that which is obscure. "Riddles" means "perplexing sayings or questions." These words refer to discourse that requires interpretation. Proverbs, then, contain "wise sayings" and "perplexing sayings." Wisdom is sometimes disguised as an enigma or riddle.

Kidner says, "So the secondary purpose of Proverbs is to introduce the reader to a style of teaching that provokes his thought, getting under his skin by thrusts of wit, paradoxes, common sense, and teasing symbolism, in preference to the preacher's tactic of frontal assault."

These proverbs are like gold. Gold does not lie on the surface, waiting to be found. It is buried underground. One has to dig to get it. Only meditation will reveal what is hidden in these maxims. So, Proverbs are designed to provoke thought. Consider this passage: "There are three things which are too wonderful for me, Yes, four which I do not understand: The way of an eagle in the air, the way of a serpent on a rock, The way of a ship in the midst of the sea, And the way of a man with a virgin" (30:18-19).

Summary: Solomon wrote in Proverbs the wisdom he learned from others so his readers could develop moral skills in living and mental skills in thinking.

The way to gain wisdom is to learn from the experience and the writings of others, especially wise people. Everyone from the simple to the wise should read Proverbs to develop their minds in general and skillful living in particular.

Years ago, a speaker said, "You will be the same in five years as you are today except for the people you meet and the books you read." It seems to me that people who continue to grow and develop read. Not all readers grow, but all who grow read.

While reading what wise people have written is a good idea, the regular reading of Proverbs is a particularly prudent idea. Many have found it helpful to read one chapter of Proverbs every day beginning on the first of the month. Since there are 31 chapters, reading a chapter daily means reading the whole book every month.

There is a practical reason for reading Proverbs, namely, to develop your mind and gain skills in living. Reading, especially, what wise people have written, is one way to prevent making dumb decisions. By reading, you can learn before you make that dumb mistake and not make it. Some never learn. Some live and learn. Some learn and live. Get smart. Don't wait to learn the hard way. Read so you can learn and live.

There is also a spiritual reason for reading Proverbs. As Jesus grew up, He grew in wisdom (Lk. 2:52). So practicing the wisdom of Proverbs conforms a person to Christ.

Imagine sitting in a café at the end of your life, talking to a friend and being able to say not "dumb, just dumb," but "I read the book of Proverbs and while I didn't make all the wise decisions I could have, I can honestly say I lived a wise life." Or better yet, imagine after your life is over, standing before the Lord Himself and hearing Him say, "Well done, my good, wise, and faithful servant."

WHERE TO START TO LEARN WISDOM

After hearing me speak at a conference, a young lady asked if she could talk to me. I listened as she told me about much of what had happened in her life. When she finished, I asked, "What would you like me to do for you?" Her answer was, "After making one dumb decision after another, I want to stop making stupid mistakes in life. I want to start making wise decisions and living a more sensible life. Where do I start?"

The subject of the book of Proverbs is wisdom. The opening verses indicate that wisdom is skill in living. It is moral in nature. Wisdom can and should be learned from the experiences and the writings of others, especially wise people. Is, then, the place to begin asking others what to do or by reading what others have written? Surprisingly, the answer is "No." Well, where, then, does one start to gain wisdom, that is, to develop skills in living? Solomon says, "The fear of the LORD is the beginning of knowledge, but fools despise wisdom and instruction" (1:7). This is the theme of Proverbs. It has been called the "motto" of the book (Delitzsch; Kidner).

To Learn Wisdom, Fear the Lord

In a word, the place to start to learn wisdom is the fear of the Lord. What does that mean? When we hear the word "fear," we think of being afraid, alarmed, or terrified because of an expectation of imminent danger. Must I be afraid of the Lord or terrified of Him to obtain wisdom? Also, how is the fear of the Lord the beginning of wisdom?

The Fear of the Lord The Hebrew word translated "fear" means 1) to be afraid, terrified, 2) to stand in awe, 3) to reverence, 4) to honor. The issue is not the meaning of the word "fear;" it is the meaning of the phrase "the fear of the Lord." The way the phrase "the fear of the Lord" is used in the Bible, it is apparent that several concepts are involved.

1. Know the Lord. Part of the fear of the Lord is knowing Him. Several times in Proverbs, Solomon makes statements indicating that the fear of the Lord is synonymous with or at least very close to an intimate knowledge of the Lord. For example, "The fear of the Lord is the beginning of wisdom, and the knowledge of the Holy One is understanding" (9:10; see also 2:5). Proverbs 9:10 contains a synonymous parallelism. Parallelism utilizes a second line to reinforce the first, either by restating the first in slightly different terms (synonymous parallelism), stating the thought negatively to reinforce the positive idea (antithetical parallelism), completing the thought of the first (climactic parallelism), etc. The synonymous parallelism of Proverbs 9:10 is saying that the fear of the Lord and the knowledge of the Lord are synonymous.

Notice that Proverbs 1:7 does not mention "the fear of *God*." It says, "the fear of the LORD." In the Hebrew Old Testament, there are three words for God: Elohim, Adonai, and Yahweh. Elohim is the general term for God. God created the heavens and the earth. Adonai means Lord and is usually translated "Lord" (in English, it is translated by a capital L followed by small letters). Yahweh, translated "LORD" (in English, it is rendered in all capitals), is God's personal name. Yahweh revealed Himself to Israel and made a covenant with them. The word "LORD" in Proverbs 1:7 is Yahweh, the personal name of God. Thus, this is not fear of some vague higher power. It is the fear of someone who can be known personally because He has revealed Himself.

We get to know the Lord through faith and loving obedience. Paul told Timothy, "From childhood, you have known the Holy Scriptures, which are able to make you wise for salvation through faith which is in Christ Jesus" (2 Tim. 3:15). Jesus told the disciples, "He who has My commandments and keeps them, it is he who loves Me. And he who loves Me will be loved by My Father, and I will love him and manifest Myself to him" (Jn.14:21). He also said, "If anyone loves Me, he will keep My word; and My Father will love him, and we will come to him and make Our home with him" (Jn.14:23).

2. Reverence the Lord. The Hebrew word "fear" means "to stand in awe, to reverence." Hence, part of the fear of the Lord is reverencing Him. For example, the palmist says, "Let all the earth fear the LORD; let all the inhabitants of the world stand in awe of Him" (Ps. 33:8). The parallelism also indicates that the fear of the Lord and standing in awe are synonymous. Therefore, the fear of the Lord means awe and reverence.

Reverence for the Lord includes, or at least leads to, obedience. The Bible often links the fear of the Lord and obedience in general (Deut. 5:29; Ps. 111:10; Eccl. 12:13; Col. 3:22) and departure from evil in particular (Gen. 22:12; Ex.20:20; Job 1:1; 3:7). For example, in Genesis 22 God told Abraham to sacrifice his son Isaac. When Abraham started to do that, the Angel stopped him, saying, "Do not lay your hand on the lad, or do anything to him;

for now, I know that you fear God, since you have not withheld your son, your only son, from Me" (Gen. 22:12). A reverence and respect for God leads to obedience to God. The fear of the Lord has been called "affectionate reverence" (Bridges) and "reverential subordination" (Delitzsch),

I know a lady who, as a child, was a very obedient daughter. She once said to me that she was so obedient because she had her father on a 20-story pedestal. When we have God on His throne and revere Him, we obey Him.

3. Be afraid of the Lord. Doesn't fear also mean "be afraid?" Yes, it even means "be terrified." Unbelievers may be terrified of the judgment of God, but grace changes dread to reverence. Paul told Timothy, "For God has not given us a spirit of fear, but of power and of love and of a sound mind" (2 Tim. 1:7). Believers fear that they will not please the Lord.

A young bride described the first meal she cooked for her new husband: "I was nervous because I was afraid I would do something wrong to spoil the dinner. So, at 3:00 o'clock, I read and reread the cookbook. Then, I got everything together and put the food on the stove to cook. I was so afraid it wouldn't turn out well that I didn't leave the stove. Later, when my husband didn't arrive when I expected, I was afraid everything would either be overcooked or cold." Notice how often she used the word "afraid." She loved her husband so much she was afraid she would not please him.

However, it should be added that believers are naturally afraid of Him when they disobey Him. When Adam disobeyed the Lord, he was afraid (Gen. 3:10). Reminding us that "The LORD will judge His people," the writer to the Hebrews says, "It is a fearful thing to fall into the hands of the living God" (Heb. 10:30-31). I respect police officers. I am not afraid of them, but I would be afraid if I had broken the law.

What about love? Aren't we supposed to love the Lord? Is it possible to love and fear the same person at the same time? In the case of our relationship with the Lord, we love Him because He first loved us (1 Jn.4:19). Out of our love and deep reverence for Him comes our obedience to Him. At the same time, we fear we will not please Him. So, it is possible to love and fear the same person simultaneously. In fact, Israel was told to love and fear God all in the same verse! Moses wrote, "And now, Israel, what does the LORD your God require of you, but to fear the LORD your God, to walk in all His ways and to love Him, to serve the LORD your God with all your heart and with all your soul" (Deut. 10:12).

When we use the expression "God-fearing man," we mean someone who is devout, pious. In fact, that is the dictionary definition of "Godfearing."

The Beginning of Knowledge The Hebrew word translated "beginning" means "first, chief." It has been interpreted to mean the initial step, "the first moving influence" (Clarke), "first part, foundation" (JFB), or the "principle part" (Bridges), "the first and controlling principle" (Kidder). This verse does not refer to the first step or stage of knowledge but rather to the chief or essential factor. Of course, if it is the essential factor, it is the first step and an essential ingredient all along the way. What gas is to the car, the fear of the Lord is to knowledge. Gas is needed to get started and throughout the trip.

The word translated "knowledge" here is the same Hebrew word that appears in verse 5. As there, it is the basic Hebrew word for knowledge, but, as has been pointed out, when it is used in wisdom literature, it carries the connotation of understanding and discretion. It is also sometimes translated "skill." For example, when 1 Samuel speaks of a "man who is a skillful player of the harp" (1 Sam.16:16), the word skillful is the Hebrew word "know." When people "know" the harp, they have the skill to play it.

The fear of the Lord is not only the first principle in knowledge, it is also the first principle in wisdom. That is implied from the rest of the verse (the fool isn't said to despise knowledge, but *wisdom*) and later Solomon says, "The fear of the LORD is the beginning of wisdom" (9:10; see also Ps. 111:10).

So, a personal relationship with (knowledge of) and reverence for the Lord is the first principle of developing skillful living. How does that work? Remember, in the sense of reverence for the Lord, the fear of the Lord includes or at least leads to, obedience. When believers obey the Lord, they develop a wise, skillful way of living their lives.

Isn't that the way it is with learning any skill? If a piano student respects and, out of that respect, obeys the teacher, she will develop the skill of playing the piano. If a ball player respects and obeys her coach, she will develop baseball skills. Likewise, if believers respect and obey the Lord, they will develop skills for living.

To Be a Fool, Despise Godly Wisdom

The problem, of course, is that we don't listen and learn God's lessons and, consequently, don't develop living skills. Solomon says, "Fools despise wisdom and instruction" (1:7).

Fools have No Fear of God The root word from which the Hebrew word for "fool" comes is the word "thick," as in a thick liquid. Perhaps the implication is that a fool is thickheaded. There is no doubt that the Hebrew word for "fool" suggests stubbornness. The stubbornness of the fool is spiritual. The psalmist says, "The fool has said in his heart, 'There is no God'" (Ps. 14:1). The Apostle Paul says of sinners generally, "There is no fear of God before their eyes" (Rom. 3:18). Later in Proverbs 1, Solomon speaks of the fact that sinners do not "choose the fear of the LORD" (1:29).

Fools Despise Wisdom Since fools have no regard for God, they have no regard for His wisdom. They "despise wisdom and instruction." To despise is to have contempt. Wisdom here is the same word that occurs in verse 2. It can mean skill. This word for instruction here also occurs in verse 2. It means training, discipline. Fools regard the Lord's way of handling life with contempt.

Summary: The place to start to learn wisdom is to know and reverence the Lord, and the way to be a fool is to despise Godly wisdom. It might be said that if you don't get to know and reverence the Lord with the result that you obey Him, you will become a fool.

We can learn from the experience of others. We can and should learn from what wise people have written, but we must always remember that the first and foremost principle of wisdom is our relationship to the Lord Himself. To say the same thing another way, as we wrestle with the issues of life, we need to pray, read what God has to say, and talk to and read what wise people have written. If all we do is talk to others or just read what wise people have written, we often do not know Godly wisdom in a particular situation. So, we must start with and include the Lord all along the way. "Wisdom comes from God, and whoever fears Him receives it" (Delitzsch).

If you want to get smart, live wisely, and develop skillful living, you must do three things: 1) Get to know the Lord. Trust Him. Love Him. Reverence Him. Walk with Him, 2) Ask God for wisdom. That's what Solomon did and what we should do (Jas. 1:5). 3) Learn from the experiences of others, including reading what they have written.

My wife, Patricia, was an interpreter for deaf people in a public high school for over 12 years. At one point, she knew three deaf teenage boys who decided to break into the safe in the student bank. Watching television taught them that thieves used a stethoscope to break into a safe. So, these deaf boys broke into the nurse's office to steal a stethoscope. They then returned to the student bank to use it on the safe. They obviously did not know what they were doing. Even if they had known how to use a stethoscope to open a safe, they would not have been able to do it because they were deaf! When the safe failed to open, they began to bang on it. The noise attracted students who were practicing nearby for a school play. They called the police and the deaf (pardon the pun), dumb boys were arrested. Since they were deaf, they needed an interpreter. When asked which interpreter they wanted, they said any of them except Patricia because it would make her sad and if she came, they would feel ashamed of what we did.

Now, think about this incident. These three fellows knew Patricia. If they had just operated on their knowledge of Patricia, they would have made a wise decision and would have, therefore, been skillful in living their lives, but they ignored their relationship with Patricia and ended up doing something really stupid. Our relationship with the Lord makes us wise, and ignoring Him and His wisdom makes us foolish.

OUR SECOND SOURCE OF WISDOM

As you can learn from several sources, such as books, dictionaries, encyclopedias, and the Internet, so there are several sources of *wisdom*. According to the book of Proverbs, the first source of wisdom is the Lord. It says, "The fear of the LORD is the beginning of knowledge" (1:7). Wisdom is skill in living a moral and smooth life. If, as that verse says, a personal relationship with the Lord is the first principle of wise living, what is the second source of wisdom?

The prologue of Proverbs suggests that we can learn wisdom from others and from what wise people have written. Who are these others? The answer might surprise you. It will definitely shock some teenagers. It is in Proverbs 1:8-9.

Obey Your Parents

Solomon says, "My son, hear the instruction of your father, and do not forsake the law of your mother" (1:8). The order in this passage is significant. After the prologue (1:1-6), Solomon says the *first principle* of wisdom is knowing and obeying the Lord (1:7). The Lord is the first source of wisdom. Immediately afterward, Solomon talks about parents (1:8-9). The implication is that parents are a *second* source of wisdom. Before you react, consider carefully what this passage is teaching.

Obey Your Father The expression "my son" may be used in the literal sense of a male son. It is used that way in Proverbs (4:3; 31:2). The father and mother are the "beloved parents" of those who are addressed (Delitzsch). As David taught his son Solomon (4:3-9), Solomon now teaches his son, probably Rehoboam.

While the literal meaning is probably the primary meaning here and throughout chapters 1-9, it is also possible that this term is used in the generic sense of child. These passages don't exclude daughters. Later, Solomon says, "Hear, my children, the instruction of a father" (4:1).

Apparently, teachers commonly used this form of address for their students. A teacher calling a student "son" indicated a loving, superintending interest in the person. That is a critical point. This passage assumes a loving, caring, and wise father. That is a particularly important point today, but it is an observation that has been made long before today's widespread problem of dysfunctional parents. Two commentaries written in the nineteenth century indicate that this command assumes Godly parents (Bridges, 1846; Wardlaw, 1861). One of them also pointed out Solomon could not possibly mean that a child should obey *them* if it involved disobedience to *Him* (Wardlaw).

The word translated "hear" means "to hear with attention, to listen, to give heed, to obey." This verse is definitely commanding children to obey their parents. Wise children learn to listen to the instructions of their fathers. This admonition indicates that: 1) fathers should give instructions and 2) children should obey those instructions. In other words, fathers should teach obedience and children should learn obedience.

My mother and father were divorced when I was six years old, so I was reared in a single-parent home without a father. When I got married and had children, I felt like I didn't know how to be a father because I had never had one. I decided that being a good father meant I would never ask my children to do anything unless I explained why they should do it. Frankly, that was a tragic mistake. Whenever I asked my children to do something, they would look at me and ask, "Why"?

Then, one day, I read Dr. James Dobson's book *Dare to Discipline*. In that book, Dobson contends that the correct approach to childrearing is a balance between love and discipline. As a result of reading that book, I gathered my three children in the living room, sat them on the sofa and explained to them that their father had made a mistake and that from henceforth, I would not explain to them why they should do what I asked them to do. I would tell them what to do and expect them to obey. If they didn't, they would get punished. I would like to tell you that my simple explanation changed everything. It didn't. They had been conditioned to have me explain why they should do everything I asked them to do. It took them a while to break the habit, but eventually, we established that they were to obey me for the simple reason I was their father.

Obey Your Mother Children are told, "Do not forsake the law of your mother" (1:8). The word "forsake" means, of course, "to abandon," but it implies neglect or rejection. The question is, "What is the "law of your mother?" The Hebrew word "law" means "law, instruction, direction." It is the same Hebrew word used in the Law of Moses, but the law of mother is different than the Law of Moses. Her teachings may be based on Moses' law, but her law is not identical to it. Her law may include what Moses said but may also involve other stipulations.

It seems to me that a distinction should be made between three different sets of laws: 1) the law of God, 2) the law of society, and 3) the law of mother. The first is moral, the second deals with manners, that is, how we relate to each other, and the third is just mother. For example, eat your vegetables. That is not a moral issue. It's not even a matter of manners; it's just mother. Or, take the case of leaving the house at night. You must take a jacket. Again, that is not a violation of the legal code, but not doing so is a violation of the law of mother. Or, "I don't want you hanging around the kid down the street. I don't know why; I just don't."

The point of this proverb is that regardless of what mother's law is, it should not be forsaken. In other words, children must learn to obey their parents.

Learning Obedience is of Great Value

Young people don't like to hear this message. They sometimes feel that having to obey their parents is a burden, which has no value. So, Solomon explains, "For they will be a graceful ornament on your head, and chains about your neck" (1:9).

Wreath on Your Head Solomon says obeying your parents will be a "graceful ornament on your head." The word rendered "ornaments" means "wreath." This wreath is said to be a graceful wreath, meaning a wreath or crown that produces favor. Young people think of obedience to their parents as a heavy burden, like a load of bricks on their backs. Obedience is not a heavy load on your back. It is like a light wreath of flowers on your head.

Obedience is also of great value. Anything that would cause others to respond favorably to you is valuable.

We rent our church facilities to a congregation made up primarily of Filipinos. They have a ministry to young people and children. They also have an emphasis on respect for adults and being polite. They constantly say "Yes, sir" and "No, sir." They have the most obedient attitude of any group of young people I have seen in a long time. Their obedient attitude makes me want to grant them anything they ask of me.

In the context of the Old Testament, a wreath was probably not a reference to the Olympic games. Games were unknown in ancient Israel. The games were in ancient Greece. Nevertheless, to use the wreath in the Greek games as an illustration, it was the winner who received the wreath. In other words, learning obedience makes you a winner.

Chains About Your Neck Solomon also says obeying your parents will be "chains about your neck." The chain, of course, is a reference to a necklace. Teenagers often consider obeying their parents as a heavy burden, like a ball and chain around the ankle. A necklace of jewels is not a heavy burden. Parental obedience is a necklace of jewels around the neck, not a ball and chain around the ankle.

Jewels are valuable. Again, the point is that obedience is of great value. In this case, as jewels make a person more attractive, obedience makes a person more attractive. I once heard of a grandmother who had two sets of grandkids. One set was wild and unruly. When they came over, their parents allowed them to treat the house like a play yard, eat in the living room instead of the kitchen, and when spoken to, they would not respond. The other set of grandkids was well-mannered, polite, and obedient. If you were the grandmother, which set would you rather have come to your house? To which set would you be attracted? About which set would you brag?

Summary: The second great source of wisdom is learning to obey your parents, which is not a burden but of great personal value. In the context of Proverbs chapter 1, learning to obey your parents is the second source of wisdom. The fear of the Lord is the first and foremost source of wisdom (1:7), and immediately after that (1:8-9), Solomon says to obey your parents. That is not only wise but also a great source of wisdom, that is, a great source of gaining skills concerning how to live life. As you obey, you will learn great lessons about life, like the value of sharing, telling the truth, and working. The ultimate issue, however, is that you will learn obedience itself. It is that lesson that makes obeying parents so valuable.

Children who learn to obey their parents have an easier time obeying the Lord. A person gains eternal life by trusting Jesus Christ (Jn.3:16), but growth comes through loving obedience (Jn. 14:23). A believer in Jesus Christ must learn to obey the Lord to grow and become like Christ.

Children who learn to obey their parents will have an easier time obeying constituted authority. They will have an easier time obeying their teachers at school and later their boss at work. From a manager's standpoint, there is no more valuable lesson than the simple lesson of just following instructions. They will also have an easier time obeying the doctor and the dentist.

Years ago, I found a rental car company that, at the time, was offering the best deal, so I became a faithful customer. For years, I would not think of going to any other company to rent a car. Then, two things happened. The first was minor. An employee of my beloved company did not, in my opinion, treat me properly. It was not enough to cause me to find another car rental company, but it did irritate me. The second thing that happened was that a man backed into our car when my wife was driving and caused a small amount of damage to the car. While his insurance company was having it repaired, they sent us to their car rental company for a car. Our experience with that other car rental company was impressive. Just out of college, the young man who waited on us was polite, courteous, and well-mannered. That impressed us, so we began talking to him about him and his company. We wanted to know if he was a rare exception or if the whole company was made up of people like him. He explained to us that the company had certain standards that every employee had to follow. In other words, that company was looking for, among other things, people who knew how to follow instructions. Patricia and I were so impressed with that young man and the other employees with whom we came in contact that we switched car rental companies. When we need to rent a car, they are the first ones we call. Because of obedience, that young man got a job, the company got more business, and we got better service.

CHOOSE YOUR COMPANIONS CAREFULLY

From the mother's point of view, it was a critical time in her son's life. He was about to go through what was, for him, a major transition in life. She felt deeply that, given the circumstances, she had to talk to him and say something significant. What was the occasion? Her son was entering high school! What significant thing do you tell a 15-year-old? Do your homework? Study hard? Stay away from drugs? What *one* thing would you say she should tell her son? What she deemed critical was, in essence, "Son, choose your companions carefully." Of all the things a mother could tell a 15-year-old, why is that so important? The answer to that question is found in Proverbs 1:10-19 and is a vital bit of wisdom, not only for teenagers but for adults as well.

Solomon concludes this passage by saying, "My son, if sinners entice you, do not consent" (1:10a). Then, he gives the request that should provoke such a response. The chronological order, however, is the request first and then the response. This explanation of Proverbs 1:10-19 will follow that order, considering the request first (1:11-14), then the response (1:10, 15), and, finally, the reason for the response (1:16-19).

The Request

The Plot Solomon proposes a scenario in which a group of people invites his son to participate in something wrong. He writes, "If they say, 'Come with us, Let us lie in wait to shed blood: Let us lurk secretly for the innocent without cause: Let us swallow them alive like Sheol, and hole, like those that go down to the Pit" (1:10b-12). Their proposed plot involves murder!

He begins by saying, "If they say." "They" are the sinners mentioned in verse 11. In the Hebrew text, the word "sinners" is in an intensive form, signifying that these are habitual sinners (Delitzsch). The plan is to "lie in wait" (1:11), a word that means ambush. As a hunter lies in wait for game, so they ambush innocent people. The intended victim is "innocent," and the attack is "without cause" (1:11). This is an undeserved, groundless attack. The victim is without guilt.

The crimes committed against this innocent person begin with murder. The attackers intend to "shed blood" (1:11), an expression always used with a "reference to violent putting to death" (Delitzsch). This is further described as "let us swallow them alive like Sheol" (1:12). Sheol is an Old Testament reference to the grave. The picture is of the earth suddenly opening up and swallowing up a person. (See Num. 16:30-33, where such a thing actually happened.) The word "whole" in verse 12 indicates that what they have in mind is that the entire body of the victim will be buried in a pit. In other words, they will utterly destroy their victim "without leaving any trace behind" (Delitzsch), leaving no one left to tell the tale.

The second part of this crime is robbery. "We shall find all kinds of precious possessions, we shall fill our houses with spoil" (1:13). These killers brag that they can find all kinds of precious possessions. Precious means costly, highly valued. Furthermore, they intend to fill our houses with spoil. This is "covetousness leading to murder" (Bridges).

Invitation Having detailed their sinister plot, they conclude with an invitation, "Cast in your lot among us, let us all have one purse" (1:14). Apparently, they are suggesting that all the spoils be put into one pile and be divided among all the members of the gang (Delitzsch).

To a thinking person with any moral sense, this sinister plot is obviously evil. Murder and robbery are wrong. Be that as it may, don't overlook the allurement and appeal of what is said (see Wardlaw; Kidner). First is the possibility of profit. This is a plan that will produce immediate riches. Robbery is the "allurement of a shortcut to wealth" (Wardlaw). Second, this proposal provides an opportunity for power. The criminals picture themselves as people to be reckoned with, people of power. Third, there is the allurement of excitement. As perverse as it is, criminals sometimes get pleasure out of their crimes. The adrenaline rush is even said to be addictive.

The greatest appeal, however, is belonging. Notice they said, "Come *with us*" (1:11, italics added) and "Cast in your lot *among us*" (1:14, italics added). Wanting to belong per se is not wrong. It is a natural, God-given instinct. Belonging to the right group can be beneficial. You should have companions and belong to groups that build you up and benefit you. The problem is that some associations are detrimental, which is the case here.

This sounds like the kind of situation that a teenager would encounter and it does happen to teens all the time. It also happens to adults. People in business, in general, and sales, in particular, are confronted with individuals and groups of people who say in essence, "Come with us. We will get rich." The truth is that what they have in mind amounts to robbery and people end up getting hurt.

The Response

Solomon gives two responses to this type of request. The first is at the beginning of the paragraph and the second is in the middle.

Do Not Consent to Sin Solomon began by saying, "My son, if sinners entice you, do not consent" (1:10a). The repetition of the expression, "My son" from verse 8 either indicates a change of subjects or, as some believe, is repeated to call attention to what is said here. The word translated "entice" means "to persuade." Solomon's advice is that when habitual sinners try to persuade you to do something wrong, you should not consent, meaning you should not be willing.

The answer to an enticement to evil should be an emphatic "No." As Nancy Reagan said, "Just say no." Don't even think of sinning once and stopping later. Jesus said, "Whoever commits sin is a slave of sin" (Jn. 8:34). "The tender conscience becomes less sensitive by every compliance" (Bridges). Wardlaw says, "There must be no tampering with temptation—no compromise—no partial adoption of the practices of sinners, in the hope, or with the resolution of stopping and retracing your steps when you have advanced a certain length." Would you swallow poison by degrees to try how much your constitution would bear—how far you could go without actual suicide?

Do Not Associate with Habitual Sinners After explaining the invitation by the group of habitual sinners (1:11-14), Solomon gives a second response. "My Son, do not walk in the way with them, keep your feet from their path" (1:15). This is more than saying, "Don't do it." It is saying, "Don't walk with them. Don't even put your foot on the same path with them." In other words, do not associate with them or have no dealings with them.

Jesus, of course, loved sinners and associated with them. It is one thing, however, to associate with sinners to influence them and it is another to associate with sinners who are constantly trying to get you to sin.

My wife, Patricia, and I were in business together. Several years ago, we were introduced to a man with whom we were invited to work on a project that greatly appealed to us. It would allow us to do things that we would enjoy, help others, and possibly make a lot of money. In one of our first meetings with this man, we saw him do things that bothered us. The way he treated people was deplorable. After we left his office, I turned to Patricia and said, "If we had a brain in our head, we would get in our car head as fast as we could in the opposite direction and never look back." Did we do that? Unfortunately, no. The appeal of the possibilities was so strong that we decided to "give him a second chance."

Did he change? Of course not! We went to him privately to talk about what he was doing. Did that help? No, it did not. Did the idea work? No, it did not. The failure was not all his fault, but much of it was. Patricia wasted a great deal of time, not making any money at all and not helping anyone. It led to the waste of a lot of time, energy, and money. We learned the hard way that when people of questionable character say, "Hey, come with us," do not consent.

The Reasons

Solomon explains why he has given such advice (see "for" at the beginning of 1:16). He gives three reasons (Delitzsch) for not consenting to sin and not associating with sinners.

It is Wrong In the first place, what they are suggesting is wrong. "For their feet run to evil, and they make haste to shed blood" (1:16). They propose to do evil, more specifically, to commit murder. So, don't associate with them unless you become like them and sin yourself. The Apostle Paul told the Corinthians, "Evil company corrupts good habits" (1 Cor. 15:33).

It is Not Wise In the second place, what they suggest is not wise, because it leads to their destruction. "Surely, in vain the net is spread in the sight of any bird, but they lie in wait for their own blood. They lurk secretly for their own lives" (1:17-18). When Solomon says, "In vain the net is spread in the sight of any bird" (1:17), he means that although the birds see the net, they nevertheless fly into it. "As a bird hastens to the snare, he did not know it *would cost* his life" (7:23). Flying into a trap is not wise.

The reason lying in wait (1:11) and making haste to shed someone else's blood (1:16) are not wise is that, in reality, such people are lying in wait for their own blood (1:18). They wish to murder others but they only murder themselves (Delitzsch). "Everyone proud in heart is an abomination to the LORD; though they join forces, none will go unpunished" (16:5). "Whoever rewards evil for good, evil will not depart from his house (17:13). As the modern proverb says, "What goes around comes around," but what a vivid way to put it: you set out to shed blood and end up shedding your own. Sin eventually leads to self-destruction. Self-destruction is not smart.

Death As Solomon has been saying (1:17-18), sin results in death. It is not wise because it leads to death. He concludes, "So are the ways of everyone who is greedy for gain; it takes away the life of its owners" (1:19). The personal greed within each person made the plan of sinners attractive, but it is that very greed that leads to their death. The wages of sin is death (Rom, 6:23). Sin is "self-delusive" and "self-destructive." Ahab, Haman, and Judas are illustrations (Bridges). You become your own very worst enemy (Wardlaw).

Years ago, I heard of a practice in Alaska that may not be factual, but it is a graphic picture of this concept. It was said that Eskimos killed wolves by planting knives in the ice. When the wolves licked the ice, they cut their own tongues and drew their blood. Thinking they had come upon prey, they kept licking, which means that, thinking they were killing something else, they were actually killing themselves.

Summary: Do not associate with habitual sinners and certainly do not consent to participate in their sin because it is not only wrong, it is not wise, and sin leads to death. Choose your companions carefully because they may appeal to your sinful side to lead you to self-destruction.

At the beginning of this discussion, Solomon began this passage with a conclusion (1:10) and a chronological order was followed. Now, Solomon ends it with the ultimate cause of the problem (1:19). If the "chronological order" were followed throughout the passage, the result would look like this.

1) First, there was a bent toward some evil (1:19). In this case, it was greed.
2) Then, there is group appeal. (1:11). At first, the invitation seems harmless. They say, "Come with us" (1:11). Later, it gets serious; it is, "Cast in your lot among us (1:14). The lure is compelling. All of us want to belong to something. Group appeal is a strong attraction.
3) After the pull of our sinful side from the inside and the group appeal on the outside, we "consent" go along (1:10). The consent makes the individual responsible. Consent is the very thing Solomon tells us not to do.
4) We consent to go along and continue to participate (1:15). We walk with evil people.
5) The end of such foolish behavior is destruction (1:18).

Since that is the progression to destruction, you should 1) Know yourself. There is a bent toward evil within all of us. This bent differs from person to person, but we all have a sinful side that is bent toward various forms of evil. For some, the bent may be greed; for others, it may be violence or immorality, but all have a bent toward evil. 2) Know the character of the people you choose to associate with and do not associate with people who influence you to go in the wrong direction. As Solomon says later in the book, "The righteous should choose his friends carefully, for the way of the wicked leads them astray" (12:26). "He who walks with wise men will be wise, but the companion of fools will be destroyed" (13:20).

So, avoid those who treat evil like a sport (10:23). If someone makes light of sin, be careful. Avoid an angry man (22:24-25). Be careful, friends of an angry man, lest you become like him. Avoid a violent man (16:29). Girls, be careful. If you are dating a violent man, run. Avoid a seductive woman (2:16-18). Men, be careful. If you meet such a woman, flee.

One species of alligator is so lazy that they seldom hunt for food. They wait for their food to come to them. Acting as though they were dead, they lie on the bank with their mouths open. Soon, flies begin to light on the moist tongue of the alligator. Other insects follow. Eventually, a lizard crawls on the tongue to feed on the bugs. Then, a frog joins the party. Once the crowd has assembled, the giant jaws slam together and the alligator enjoys dinner.

Choose your friends carefully. Don't assemble with a group on the tongue of an alligator.

THE RESULT OF REJECTING WISDOM

If a friend gave you a suggestion and you did not take it, there might not be any serious consequences. Ignoring a doctor's advice could be more serious, but what about rejecting true wisdom?

According to the book of Proverbs, we should live a wise life. A wise life is a smooth, skillful, moral life. What happens if we don't do that? In the first place, isn't that a sure way to miss out on a lot of fun? Besides, if you sin, you can always get forgiven. So, why not enjoy life without worrying about restrictions and ask for forgiveness later?

To answer those questions, may I introduce you to a lady? You have heard of Lady Luck. May I introduce you to Lady Wisdom? Her address is Proverbs 1:20-33.

The Plea

Where Solomon pictures wisdom as a woman: "Wisdom calls aloud outside; She raises her voice in the open square. She cries out in the chief concourses, at the openings of the gates: in the city She speaks her words" (1:20-21). Wisdom is personified as a lady. Wisdom is not a subjective quality inside a person; wisdom exists independently of people (Delitzsch). It can be argued that this wisdom is divine. It is the personification of instruction, not just human instruction; it is divine instruction. It is not just Solomon's wisdom; it is God's wisdom. The authority of this wisdom is the authority of God. To follow wisdom is to be blessed by God and to reject wisdom is death (Wardlaw). Ultimately, Jesus is the wisdom of God (1 Cor. 1:30). At any rate, in this passage, wisdom is personified as a woman.

She calls out in the "open square" (1:20), "in the chief concourses, at the openings of the gates: in the city" (1:21). In ancient Israel, the open space near the city gate contained things like the court of justice (Deut. 16:18), business (Ruth 5:1), markets (2 Kings 8:1), councils (2 Chron. 18:9), etc. Nothing exactly like this exists today. The closest thing to it is a small town with the county courthouse in the middle of a downtown square surrounded by businesses.

Lady Wisdom is raising her voice in a crowded, noisy, public place. She is not whispering her message in the field in secret (Delitzsch); she is loudly proclaiming her message where it needs to be heard: by people in the street, the judge and jury in the courtroom, people conducting business, and people in the market. It is not for the pursuit of scholars but for the man in the street (Kidner). Wisdom must be in the courtroom, classroom, boardroom, and bedroom.

What Specifically, what does Lady Wisdom have in mind? The answer is in the context of this passage. Notice this chapter says that the *beginning* of wisdom is the fear of the Lord (1:7). Lady Wisdom has that in mind; she says so (1:29). The next primary source of wisdom is our parents (1:8-9). After our parents, we learn from our peers. In this passage, people's peers lead them astray (1:10-19), but we can and should learn from others. Lady Wisdom wants people to learn wisdom. The Lord, our parents, and wise peers give us wise counsel concerning our time, money, and relationships.

Who While everyone, everywhere, needs wisdom, Lady Wisdom specifically speaks to three groups: the simple, the scorners, and the fools. She says, "How long, you simple ones, will you love simplicity? For scorners delight in their scorning, and fools hate knowledge" (1:22). The simple are the naïve. They are inexperienced and, therefore, ignorant. They are susceptible to seduction and evil (Delitzsch). They do not weigh what they do (Bridges). Wisdom wants to know how long they will love their gullibility. The longer they persist, the greater their guilt and the more imminent their danger (Wardlaw). Of the three, these are the only ones addressed because they are the ones whom she "expects to find the soonest access" (Delitzsch).

Scorners are mockers who take pleasure in ridicule. They have no manners, remorse, or shame (Bridges). They make light of what they ought to take seriously and pleasure in what they ought to hate (Wardlaw).

The Hebrew word translated "fools" here is different than the one used in verse 7. The one here means "stupid." It comes from a word that means "to be thick, coarse, indolent" (Delitzsch). It refers to a hardened, obdurate person. The simple are ignorant, but fools know and yet hate knowledge.

The Plea Lady Wisdom pleads with these people, "Turn at my reproof; Surely, I will pour out my spirit on you; I will make my words known to you" (1:23). They are going in a wrong, unwise direction. Lady Wisdom is pleading that they will turn around and go in the way of wisdom. She promises that if people paid attention to her, a spirit of wisdom would be poured upon them; they would come to know true wisdom.

Is it possible that what is happening here is that we see the simple, the scorner, and the fools following the crowd? Remember the public square. Lady Wisdom takes to the street where they have gathered to warn them that they have the order backward. Instead of following the Lord, their parents, and then their peers, they are following their peers, who are leading them in the wrong direction; they are not following their parents and the Lord.

The Rejection

The Pause Between verses 23 and 24, there is a pause. Lady Wisdom is waiting for the people to whom she is speaking to answer. There is none. Unfortunately, instead of listening and learning, people reject wisdom.

The Rejection So Lady Wisdom continues, "Because I have called, and you refused, I have stretched out my hand, and no one regarded; because you disdained all my counsel, and would have none of my reproof" (1:24-25). She tells them she has extended her helping hand and they have refused it. She adds that they have "disdained" her counsel. The word rendered "disdained" actually means nothing more than they have let it go. She might say today, "I gave you advice and you let it go in one ear and out the other." They would have none of her reproof, that is, they would not consent.

If, as I have suggested, this is a case of these individuals following the wrong crowd, you can just hear their mother saying, "Don't hang around that fellow, he brings out the worst in you." Or, "Don't hang around that crowd; they bring out the worst side of you."

The Results

Having confronted their rejection of wisdom, Lady Wisdom now warns them of the results of rejecting her counsel. The remainder of the paragraph lists some of the results of rejecting wisdom from the viewpoint of wisdom ("I will laugh," 1:26-27; "I will not hear or help," 1:28-32). In the process, this passage also records what will happen from the fool's point of view, namely, there will be calamity, terror, and destruction.

Calamity Lady Wisdom announces, "I also will laugh at your calamity" (1:26). This is not heartless, cruel laughter at the person. Notice that the text says, wisdom will laugh at your calamity. Wisdom laughs at the absurdity of choosing foolishness (Kidner).

Rejecting wisdom leads to "calamity," a Hebrew word that means "distress." Living a foolish life will get you into trouble. Students who don't use their time wisely get distressed the night before the final examination. When the bill arrives, consumers who do not use their credit cards wisely get distressed. Married couples who do not maintain their relationship get distressed over little things that somehow become big things.

Terror Rejecting wisdom leads not only to calamity but also to terror. Lady Wisdom says, "I will mock when your terror comes, when your terror comes like a storm, and your destruction comes like a whirlwind, when distress and anguish come upon you" (1:26-27). The Hebrew word translated "terror" is much different than the Hebrew word rendered "fear" in the expression "the fear of the Lord" (1:7). The Hebrew rendered "terror" means "to be afraid, dread, terror." Those who fear the Lord end up in healthy fear. Those who don't reverence the Lord end up in terror.

The students who didn't use their time wisely and burned the midnight oil the night before the final exam felt sheer terror when they saw the exam. Consumers who do not use their credit cards wisely are terrified at how much they now owe and on which they pay interest. Married couples who do not maintain their relationship panic when they realize the rift in their relationship is becoming serious.

Lady Wisdom says she will "mock" (1:26) when terror comes like a storm, that is, suddenly (1:27), when destruction comes like a whirlwind, and when distress and anguish come (1:27). Most of what is said in verse 27 is a repetition of what has already been said, namely, that terror, distress, and anguish are coming. The only new factor is that destruction is also coming. Solomon will explain this in more detail later in the passage (1:32). The point here is that Lady Wisdom will mock when all of the results of rejecting wisdom happen. Again, the idea is not mocking the person but the absurdity of choosing foolishness.

Why are these brazen people terrified? Perhaps the explanation is in what is said next, "Then shall they call upon me, but I will not answer; they will seek me diligently, but they will not find me: Because they hated knowledge and did not choose the fear of the LORD, They would have none of my counsel and despised all my reproof" (1:28-30). Lady Wisdom says that when people who have rejected wisdom get into deep trouble, they will then call out to wisdom for help, but she "will not answer" (1:28). They will seek wisdom, even diligently seek wisdom, but they will not find her (1:28).

Wisdom will not hear them because they did not hear her. Wisdom will disregard them because they disregarded her. Solomon says these are people who hated knowledge (1:29), did not choose the fear of the Lord (1:29), rejected wisdom's counsel (1:30), and despised wisdom's reproof.

With deep emotion, they rejected wisdom. They "hated" knowledge (1:29) and despised reproof (1:29). They not only rejected wisdom, but they also did so with contempt and scorn. Their rejection is described in the strongest possible terms. They despised their only remedy (Bridges). No wonder wisdom will not hear them! Their hopelessness is their fault. They suffer the consequences of their actions.

When I was a small boy, a lady one block from our house had a backyard full of chickens and she sold eggs to her neighbors. My mother would send me to get a dozen eggs and sit on the front steps of our house to watch me as I went and returned. One day, to tease my mother, I began to swing the bags of eggs as I approached the house. My mother told me not to do that. Pardon the pun, but that just egged me on. My mother warned me that if I was swinging the eggs and dropped them, she would make me eat all the eggs that were broken, raw. Well, one day, I did, and she did. I learned that there are consequences to actions. Terror strikes when you realize you must suffer the consequences of your actions.

Destruction Rejecting wisdom ultimately leads to destruction. That was mentioned in verse 27. Now Solomon brings it up again: "Therefore shall they eat of the fruit of their own way, and be filled to the full with their own fancies. For the turning away of the simple will slay them, and the complacency of fools will destroy them" (1:31-32). Verse 31 begins with "therefore," indicating a conclusion. The conclusion picks up the theme of destruction.

Those who reject wisdom will "eat the fruit of their own way" (1:31) and they will "be filled to the full with their own fancies" (1:31). They get what they want. Still, when the simple turned away from wisdom, they were slain. The complacency of fools led to their being destroyed (1:32). The Hebrew word translated "complacency" means "quietness, ease, prosperity" ("complacency" in NASB, NIV, ESV). Despisers of wisdom destroy themselves. They commit suicide (Bridges). Their own decisions destroyed them.

This sounds hopeless. It is! Conduct has consequences. For example, money, once wasted, is gone. Time squandered is forever lost. If nothing else, it destroys the quality of life. Once it is gone, you can cry out for wisdom all you wish, but it is too late; there is nothing wisdom can do to replace that which is lost.

That doesn't mean, however, that *you* are hopeless. For one thing, God forgives. Since Christ died for all sin and rose from the dead, you can be forgiven freely by God's grace through faith in Christ. Forgiveness doesn't mean restoring all wasted opportunities or removing the consequences of sinful behavior. A man in prison for robbery can trust Christ and be forgiven, but he still has to serve his prison term.

Beyond forgiveness is the possibility of beginning to live a wise life. Isn't that the point of the whole passage? Lady Wisdom began with a plea for even fools to turn to her (1:22-23). Furthermore, Solomon ends the passage with a reminder of living a wise life: "But whoever listens to me will dwell safely, and will be secure without fear of evil" (1:33). Those who hear and heed wisdom will not experience these consequences in the future. Instead of being destroyed, they will "dwell safely" and "be secure." They will not only be free from evil but also from the fear of evil (1 33). Instead of calamity, terror, and distress, they will have safety and security. Instead of fear and terror, they will experience peace and tranquility. Instead of destruction and death, they will live.

Summary: The result of rejecting wisdom is calamity, terror, and destruction, but those who follow the way of wisdom experience peace and safety.

So, fear the Lord (1:29) and follow wisdom (1:31). We often think in terms of right and wrong. That's good. We should also think in terms of wise and unwise. That's better. Doing what is wise is always right, but doing what is wise is going beyond "right;" it's being smart.

Suppose you lived on the top of a tall mountain. The only way to the top was by stagecoach and at one point, the road was narrow, with a wall of rock on the left and a precipice falling hundreds of feet down on the right. Then imagine that you needed a driver. The first applicant drove within a foot of the precipice to demonstrate that he could control the horses. The applicant, feeling he needed to beat the first driver to get the job, drove within six inches of the edge. The third drove the rock wall, hugging it like his mother. Which one would you hire? The third driver was wise and safe. The others were unwise, flirting with danger and destruction. Be smart. Be safe. Don't be dumb and dead.

THE BENEFITS OF LIVING WISELY

A friend of mine once urged me to join a buyer's club. There was one product in particular that he was pushing. After listening to him, I said, "Thanks, but no thanks." Several weeks later, in a conversation with him, I got the distinct impression that the program had other benefits. As we talked again about this project, I wanted to say to him, "Take out a piece of paper and list the benefits of doing this."

The book of Proverbs urges us to live wisely. In our discussion thus far, we have touched on some of the benefits of living such a life. Beginning in chapter 2 and spilling over into chapter 3 and beyond, Solomon begins listing the benefits of wise living. Let's begin by looking at the top of the list in Proverbs 2:1-22. This chapter consists of two major parts: 1) the cost of wisdom and 2) the benefits of wisdom.

The Cost of Wisdom

The first four verses of Proverbs 2 reveal what must be done to obtain wisdom: "My son, if you receive my words, and treasure my commands within you, so that you incline your ear to wisdom, and apply your heart to understanding; yes, if you cry out for discernment and lift up your voice for understanding; If you seek her as silver, and search for her as for hidden treasures" (2:1-4). Three times in these four verses Solomon says "if." These mark off the three "costs" of wisdom. The first has to do with something going on *inside* a person (see "within you" in 2:1 and "your heart" in 2:2). The second deals with something *said* (see "cry" and "lift up your voice" in 2:3), and the third with actions (see "seek" and "search" in 2:4).

Passion The first thing Solomon says his son must do is *receive* (2:1) his father's words and *treasure* (2:1) his father's commands within himself. The root of the Hebrew word translated "treasure" means "hidden" with overtones of treasure in the sense of cherish. The words and commands that Solomon has in mind are words of wisdom, as the next verse makes clear.

Part of the price of wisdom is to have a passion for it. You will never be wise if you do not have a passion for wisdom.

Prayer The second thing Solomon says is that his son must "cry out for discernment" (2:3) and "lift up" his "voice for understanding" (2:3). Perhaps this is an extension of the desire described in verses 1 and 2, but Solomon has also moved from a desire within to something spoken.

To whom is this "cry" made? To whom does one lift up his or her voice? This verse does not answer that question, but Solomon cried out to God for wisdom (1 Kings 3:9-12). Later, this passage does say, "the Lord gives wisdom" (2:6). James says if we lack wisdom, we are to ask God for it (Jas. 1:5). This much is certain: the fear of the Lord is the beginning of knowledge (1:7) and wisdom (9:10).

Another part of the price tag for wisdom is prayer. To obtain Godly wisdom, one must ask God for it (Jas. 1:5). Earthly knowledge comes through study; heavenly wisdom for living comes through prayer (Bridges).

Persistence Finally, Solomon says his son must "seek" and "search" for wisdom as if he were trying to find silver or some hidden treasure (2:4). These verbs, especially in comparison to the others in this section, describe action. In chapter 1, wisdom was seeking us; in chapter 2, we must seek wisdom (Kidner).

The Lord gives wisdom (2:6) "through the medium of His word" (Delitzsch); He gives wisdom "in His word" (Wardlaw). The "starting point" of wisdom is revelation (Kidner), but it must be persistently sought. People are not born with wisdom, nor does it come naturally or easily. So, you will never obtain it if you don't have a deep craving for it. If you don't persist in the pursuit of wisdom, you will never find it.

I grew up in Pensacola, Florida, one of the oldest towns in America. Five different flags have flown over the city. To celebrate its heritage, Pensacola has an event called the Fiesta of Five Flags every year. A significant part of the fiesta is seeking a buried treasure. The treasure consists of valuable merchandise donated by merchants. Every day, a different clue, usually in the form of a vague poem, is published in the paper. As a kid, I saw people passionate about finding that treasure. Finding the treasure consumed them. They spent endless hours tracking down clues and exploring various possibilities. Since the treasure was hidden, it took passion and persistent practice to find it. It was never in a place where you might accidentally stumble upon it. Likewise, wisdom is a treasure that can only be found with passion, prayer, and persistent practice.

Benefits of Wisdom

After saying, "If" his son does this and that, Solomon says, "then," his son will obtain certain things. These benefits are listed in the remainder of the chapter (see "then" in 2:5 and again in 2:9 and "when" in 2:10).

The Knowledge of God The first and foremost benefit of seeking wisdom from God is that "then you will understand the fear of the LORD and find the knowledge of God" (2:5). As was pointed out earlier (see 1:7), the parallelism here indicates that "the fear of the Lord" is synonymous with the knowledge of God. The word rendered "knowledge" is not merely intellectual knowledge but knowledge from experience. The result of seeking and finding wisdom is personally knowing God.

As Solomon explains ("for"), "for the Lord gives wisdom; from His mouth comes knowledge and understanding" (2:6). The question is, "How does He do that?" I confess I have never heard God speak in an audible voice and I get very skeptical when I hear people say they have. Instruction, knowledge, and understanding from God for us are in words from His mouth, *which are recorded in the Scriptures* (see comments on 2:4). Notice also that wisdom comes from God (2:6) and leads to God (2:5; Wardlaw).

God does not give His wisdom to everyone. Just reading the Bible doesn't make you wise or give you godly wisdom. He gives it to those who know Him (2:5) and do what He says. "He stores up sound wisdom for the upright; He is a shield to those who walk uprightly" (2:7). This Hebrew word translated "upright" (there are others) comes from the word for "complete" and means "integrity." (The English word "integrity" means "complete, whole, sincere, honest, upright.") God gives His "sound wisdom" to those who sincerely seek it and walk in it when they hear it. The word for "sound wisdom" in Hebrew means "sound efficient wisdom, abiding success." Walking upright is regulated by right principles and directed to the right ends. It is to have the Word of God as one's rule and the glory of God as one's end (Wardlaw). God is a shield to such a person.

The kind of efficient wisdom and abiding success God gives is described next. "He guards the paths of justice, and preserves the way of His saints" (2:8). God guards those who take the path of justice. In other words, God protects His saints from evil. The way of the saint is beset with temptation, but it is safe (Bridges). Earthly knowledge, which comes through study, makes you a scholar. Heavenly wisdom, which comes through prayer, makes you a saint.

Knowledge of the Good Path Verse 5 begins with "then," and so does verse 9. These are either parallel to each other, or the second one is based on the first. In other words, either the knowledge of God and the knowledge of the good path are parallel to each other, and both come from wisdom, or the knowledge of the good path comes from the knowledge of God. Either way, directly or indirectly, the knowledge of the good path comes from wisdom.

Verse 9 says, "Then you will understand righteousness, and justice, equity and every good path." The last phrase summarizes the three virtues that precede it, that is, the good path consists of righteousness, justice, and equity (Delitzsch). The one seeking wisdom knows God and understands that the good path in life consists of righteousness, justice, and equity.

The Hebrew word translated "good" means "good, pleasing, pleasant, delightful, agreeable." Righteousness is rightness. In the context of the Scripture, rightness is measured by God's law. Justice comes from the Hebrew root word for "judge" and carries the idea of "deciding." Justice is applied rightness. Equity comes from a Hebrew root word that means "smooth, straight, level, evenness, right." The idea is "free of difficulty." The point of all of this is that one of the benefits of wisdom is taking a path of righteousness, which is not only right but good.

As a society, we have lost a sense of righteousness. This country was founded on individual freedom. We have elevated personal freedom to such a high level that anything any individual wants to do is okay, provided it doesn't hurt someone else. That idea is not all wrong. The problem is we now define what hurts someone else in the broadest possible terms. For example, we have recently decided that sexual harassment is a crime and it is, but no one can define what constitutes sexual harassment. When a six-year-old boy kissed a six-year-old girl, he was suspended from school for sexual harassment. The solution to this problem is to have God tell us what is right and wrong, wise and unwise.

Knowledge of a Guarded Path At this point in the passage, Solomon says, "When wisdom enters your heart, and knowledge is pleasant to your soul, Discretion will preserve you, understanding will keep you" (2:10-11). Although this passage does not begin with "then," it is evident from the repetition of the thought of wisdom entering the heart that these two verses introduce another benefit of wisdom. The benefit is to deliver you from evil. Actually, it is to deliver you from the perverse man (2:12-15) and the seductive woman (2:16-19; see "to deliver" at the beginning of 2:12 and 2:16).

In the opening verses of this chapter, Solomon informed us that wisdom must be in us. Repeating that idea, he now says the issue is not only that it is in your heart (see 2:2), but "knowledge is pleasant to your soul" (2:10). The

Hebrew word rendered "pleasant" means "pleasant, delightful." It is sometimes translated "lovely, beautiful." Wisdom will preserve you and keep you from evil people when it becomes your "way of thinking and your acquired taste" (Kidner). When wisdom, here described in several different ways, is your value system, it will take you down a guarded path in life. It will guard you against the perverse man (2:12-15) and the prostitute (2:16-19).

Wisdom is designed "to deliver you from the way of evil, from the man who speaks perverse things" (2:12). Who is the man who speaks perverse things? The Hebrew word for "perverse" comes from the word for "turn, overturn." Except for one reference in Deuteronomy 32:20, "perversity" is only used in Proverbs (see 2:12, 14; 6:14; 8:13; 10:31, 32; 16:28, 30; 23:33; Englishmen's, p. 1337). According to Deuteronomy, a perverse *generation* (Deut. 32:20) is one that has forsaken God (Deut. 32:15) and forgotten Him (Deut. 32:18). The perverse man, then, is one who has turned away from God. Proverbs speaks of a perverse man (16:28), of a man who has "perversity is in his heart" (6:14), who devises "perverse things" (16:30), who speaks perverse things (2:12; 8:13; 10:31-32; 23:33) and who delights in the perversity of the wicked (2:14).

These men also turn from the good path of righteousness. "From those who leave the paths of uprightness to walk in the ways of darkness" (2:13). Part of the point of this stark contrast is that those who are on the path of uprightness walk in the light. They have nothing to hide. On the other hand, those who tread the ways of darkness hide, conceal, and deceive. They walk in sin.

They also are those "who rejoice in doing evil and delight in the perversity of the wicked" (2:14). They do not just trip and fall into evil; they deliberately choose and revel in wickedness. They are "at home in it" (Delitzsch). They rejoice in sin.

Moreover, they are described as those "whose ways are crooked and who are devious in their paths" (2:15), two ways of saying that these walk in cunning and craftiness. These don't just stray from the path of righteousness; they deliberately delight in walking in darkness, depravity, and deception. They plunge deeper and deeper into sin until they lose all trace of the straightway, and all their ways become crooked (Wardlaw).

To summarize, perverse men: 1) depart from God (2: 12), 2) delight in evil (2:14), 3) declare perverse things (2:12), and 4) dwell in darkness (2:13) and deception (2:15). They are perverted, turning from righteousness spiritually, emotionally, verbally, and volitionally.

Wisdom delivers you from that type of person. How? Later, Solomon explains, "I, wisdom, dwell with prudence, and find out knowledge and discretion. The fear of the LORD is to hate; pride and arrogance, and the evil way and the perverse mouth I hate" (8:12-13). Remember, the beginning of wisdom is the fear of the Lord. If you have the fear of the Lord, if you love Him, if you get to know Him, you become like Him and one of the consequences of that is that you hate evil. Hating evil makes a perverse man who delights in it repulsive to you. Hence, you get delivered from being like him. Wisdom delivers you from the "way of evil" (2:12).

Wisdom is also designed "To deliver you from the immoral woman, from the seductress who flatters with her words" (2:16). Who is the immoral woman? Proverbs uses several different words for an immoral woman. The first is "stranger" (translated "immoral" in 2:16). It means "to be a stranger, to be estranged." In Proverbs, it is used simply of a stranger (5:10; 6:1; etc.) and of an immoral woman (2:16; 5:3, 20; 7:5; 22:14). It has been suggested the immoral woman is a stranger in the sense of being outside the circle of a man's proper relationship (Kidner).

The other common word for an immoral woman is "foreigner" (translated "seductress" in 2:16). It means "foreigner, alien" and is used in Proverbs of a foreigner and of an immoral woman (2:16; 5:20; 6:24; 7:5; 23:27). This word has been interpreted to mean an adulteress or a prostitute. The explanation for it being a prostitute is that prostitution was forbidden in Israel (Deut. 23:17) and practiced in other countries. So, a prostitute in Israel was a foreigner. In fact, in Proverbs, the word for a foreigner has been said to be a technical term for prostitutes because prostitutes were originally chiefly foreigners (Delitzsch). There is also a Hebrew word that means "to commit fornication, to be a harlot" that is used in Proverbs (6:26; 7:10; 23:27; 29:3).

Thus, the immoral woman is just that, any woman who is immoral, not necessarily a prostitute. A prostitute is, of course, immoral. So, she could be included in the category of immoral women, which is probably the case in Proverbs 6:2. There is nothing, however, in any of the major passages on the immoral woman in Proverbs (2:16-19; 5:1-23; 6:20-35, and 7:1-27) that demands that the primary reference is to a prostitute and in several of these passages there are statements that seem to suggest that such is not the case. While Proverbs 6:26 does include the "harlot" (NKJV), it also mentions "adulteress" (the Hebrew is literally "another man's wife.") and later in the passage Solomon calls the immoral woman the "neighbor's wife" (6:29). Chapter 7 refers to the "attire of a harlot" (7:10), which implies that the immoral woman in that passage is not a harlot. She is just dressed like one. Furthermore, later in the passage, she says, "My husband is not at home" (7:19). While a prostitute could be married, it is more likely that this is a reference to an immoral woman rather than a professional prostitute. So, the Hebrew words translated "immoral" and "seductress" in Proverbs 2:16 refer to an immoral woman.

This immoral, seductive woman "flatters with her words" (2:16). The Hebrew word translated "flatter" means "smooth, slippery, seductive." Immoral women use flattering words to seduce men.

This immoral woman is one who "forsakes the companion of her youth, and forgets the covenant of her God" (2:17). Companion has been taken to be a reference to her husband (Kidner), but the word companion actually means "friend" or "intimate." She forsakes her companions or "familiar associates" (Delitzsch). The covenant is not a reference to marriage; it is a reference to God's covenant with Israel (Wardlaw; Kidner). The psalmist said, "They did not keep the covenant of God; they refused to walk in His law" (Ps. 78: 10). Thus, this is a faithless woman who forgets God and His law, forsakes even her closest friends to flatter men with words to seduce them.

Spiritually, the cause of her behavior is that she forgot God and His wisdom. A twentieth-century psychologist would say that often immoral women were abused, probably sexually abused, as children. That is often true. A nineteenth-century commentator on Proverbs said that seducers have perhaps been seduced (Wardlaw).

The end is death. "For her house leads down to death, and her paths to the dead; none who go to her return, nor do they regain the paths of life" (2:18-19). Her house and what goes on in it lead to her death and the death of those who follow her. What does death mean? The basic concept of death is separation. The two most well-known forms of death are spiritual death, separation from God, and physical death, the separation of the body and the soul. In the Proverbs, death is contrasted with life in such a way that it seems to imply that it is more than either spiritual or physical death. Life is life in the fullest sense of the term. By contrast, anything less is in the sphere of "death." Rather than a single physical event, it is the *realm* that conflicts with life. It has been suggested that physical death casts a shadow over life in the form of sin (Gen. 2:17), calamity (Deut. 30:15), and sickness (Ps. 116:3; see Kidner, pp. 55-56). Immorality is in the realm of death. The people who participate in it are not "really living;" they are in the sphere of death. More specifically, it can easily be the death of a marriage, a job, a career and, of course, a life.

Is there no hope? This passage says "none" who participate "return, nor do they regain the paths of life" (2:19). This does not mean "none" in an absolute sense of not one single person. The Scripture uses this kind of language in the sense of "very few' (Isa. 64:7; see Bridges). Moreover, Proverbs is a book of general truths about life, not absolute laws. Besides, God is in the resurrection business. He resurrects people from the dead.

The point is that wisdom delivers from immorality. Dr. Laura Schlessinger, a popular radio talk show host, received a call from a distraught mother who called in to ask how to keep her teenage daughter from becoming sexually active. She explained to Dr. Laura that she had told her daughter about sexually transmitted diseases, the possibility of pregnancy, and other consequences of being promiscuous. Dr. Laura responded that none of those consequences were the issue. Teenagers have answers for all of them and, furthermore, feel that it won't happen to them anyway. Dr. Laura emphatically insisted that the issue was that God said, "Don't do it!" Her point was that was the only issue for which there was no answer. I agree with Dr. Laura. I would only add that if you don't have a fear of the Lord, that answer isn't going to stop you either. On the other hand, seeking wisdom results in knowing the Lord and following righteousness and guards you against stupid mistakes like immorality.

Solomon concludes, "So you may walk in the way of goodness, and keep to the paths of the righteous. For the upright will dwell in the land, and the blameless will remain in it; but the wicked will be cut off from the earth, and the unfaithful will be uprooted from it" (2:19-22). These verses summarize what has been said in verses 9-18, namely, that following wisdom takes you down a path of righteousness and goodness and guards you from destroying the path of sin and evil. Only here is it expressed in terms of remaining in the "land" (2:21) or being removed from it (2:22). The land is the land of Canaan (Delitzsch; see Kidner). God promised the land to Abraham and his descendants and later told the descendants that if they obeyed Him, they would remain in it and if they did not obey Him, they would be scattered. Following wisdom and, thus, the good and guarded path through life will keep you where God wants you.

Summary: If you seek wisdom, which includes asking God for it, you will know God, understand righteousness, and be delivered from evil. These are the first and foremost benefits of wisdom.

The key to gaining these benefits is the Lord. You must pray to Him for wisdom. Those who wander off into evil forget and forsake God like the perverse man or forget the word of God like the prostitute. Seeking God's wisdom leads not only to knowing Him but it also leads to a good and guarded life.

If we seek God and His wisdom, we will be blessed and benefit from knowing Him and His way of life. What a benefit! What a treasure! When I was growing up in Pensacola, I saw people with great passion persistently pursue an earthly treasure. At best, it was temporary. If we put the same emotion and energy into seeking God and His wisdom that others put into seeking fame and fortune, we would have ten thousand times the treasure they could ever hope to have. The benefits of a wise life are enormous and well worth the effort.

THE SURPRISING BENEFITS OF LIVING WISELY

Until a few years ago, I was computer illiterate. I didn't even know how to turn one on, much less operate one. Then, I entered financial services, and it became imperative that I learn how to use a computer. Finally, I decided that I needed to purchase one. At the time, I knew the benefits of having a computer at home to do financial calculations and word processing, but I had no idea how beneficial a computer could be. Once I got one, I discovered I could do all kinds of things, such as keeping my checkbook and not just typing on the computer like a typewriter but formatting a manuscript. What a computer can do with a manuscript is unbelievable. It can produce a manuscript that is ready for the printer to photocopy and print. I was surprised at the benefits of owning a computer.

The book of Proverbs not only commands us to live a wise life but also entices us by listing the benefits of living wisely. According to chapter 2, the first and foremost benefit of seeking wisdom from God Himself is that you get to know God. While that is a great treasure and would be a sufficient benefit, it is only the beginning. Chapter 2 goes on to list other benefits, such as living a righteous life, which protects you from evil, especially evil people. Chapter 3 continues to list the benefits of wise living and the list of benefits may surprise you. What are these surprising benefits?

Proverbs 3:1-12 consists of a series of admonitions: 1) Obey your father's commands. 2) Practice mercy and truth. 3) Trust the Lord. 4) Honor the Lord. 5) Endure discipline. Following each exhortation is the benefit of doing what is advised.

A Long Life

Obey Your Father Solomon once again addresses his son and this time tells him, "My son, forget not my law; but let your heart keep my commands" (3:1). Earlier, Solomon spoke of the law of mother (1:8). Here it is the law of father. As with the law of mother, the law of father is, no doubt, based on the law of God, but not identical with it (Kidner), which is obvious from the addition of "*my* commands."

The son is not to forget what his father says and, beyond that, from the heart, obey his father. The heart is the issue. This is not mere external conformity. It is internal consent. Deep inside the son, there is an agreement with and a desire to do what his father taught him. There should be an "affectionate attachment" to the father's law (Wardlaw). "The heart is the first thing that wanders from God: the first also that returns" (Bridges).

A Long Life The surprising benefit is given in the next verse, "For length of days and long life and peace they will add to you" (3:2). Does this verse mean that wholehearted parental obedience causes a person to live longer? That idea is so surprising that some commentators have said this does not apply to individuals but to the nation of Israel remaining in the land (Wardlaw). Others insist that the verse means just exactly what it sounds like it means (Delitzsch). The reward for "*hearty* obedience" is "a long and happy life" (Bridges, italics his). Actually, this kind of statement is made in the Ten Commandments (Ex. 20:12).

Today, many hearing this will likely say, "I thought that genes or diet and exercise were the reasons people live long. Furthermore, there are all kinds of stories about people who lived to be a hundred years old and did all the wrong things, such as drinking and smoking. These verses do not suggest parental obedience is the only factor in living long. There is no question but that in some cases, wicked people have lived long and godly people's lives are cut short, but as a general rule (remember this is proverbial), people who learn obedience from the heart at home live longer lives.

Perhaps the key to this verse is the word "peace." The Hebrew word translated "peace" means "complete, soundness, wellness, health, prosperity, tranquility, contentment." People who learn the critical lesson of obedience early are at peace with themselves and others. They are more likely to have all the characteristics that the Hebrew word for peace includes. They prevent the wear and tear on their bodies that hard living produces and, consequently, they live longer.

Let's get specific. In verse 1, Solomon tells his son to learn obedience. What does that mean? From the rest of the book, it is evident that if Solomon's son learned all that his father wanted him to, he would learn the virtues of control of his passions, contentment, integrity, industry, knowledge, and kindness. From a biblical point of view, these virtues produce a long and peaceful life. To say the same thing another way, modern medical science agrees that stress is hard on the body and can lead to premature death. On the other hand, a stress-free life (peace) can actually make a person live longer.

Years ago, a man told me, "I have been invited to become the pastor of a large church. The nature of the situation is such that it will be very demanding if I go. There is no doubt in my mind that if I do, it will take ten years off my life." He understood that stress can shorten your life. According to Solomon, living a wise life, which includes learning obedience early, can lengthen your life.

A Favored Life

Solomon admonishes, "Let not mercy and truth forsake you; bind them about your neck; write them on the table of your heart, and so find favor and high esteem in the sight of God and man" (3:3-4). The nature of the wisdom required for this benefit is stated in verse 3 and the benefit is given in verse 4.

Be Merciful and Truthful The required wisdom for this benefit consists of "mercy and truth" (3:3). The Hebrew word for "mercy" means "goodness, kindness." It is kindness especially extended to the lowly, needy, and miserable. This word is parallel to the word "love." The King James Version word "lovingkindness" captures the fullness of this word.

The Hebrew word rendered "truth" means "firmness, faithfulness, truth." Mercy and truth often appear together (Gen. 24:49; 32:10; 47:29; Jos. 2:14; Ps. 25:10; 85:10; 89:14, 100:5; 117:2; Prov. 14:22; 16:6; 20:28; Hosea 4:1; Micah 7:18-20). True wisdom is having both simultaneously and having mercy and truth meet together (Ps. 85:10). Mercy without truth is too soft. Truth without mercy is too hard. Both together are just right.

Solomon admonishes his son to do three things concerning mercy and truth (3:4): 1) Let them not forsake you, that is, never let them leave you. Practicing mercy and truth should not be occasional but constant. 2) Bind them around your neck. Let them not be hidden but seen. 3) Write them on the tablet of your heart. Let them not be just external conduct for show but the inward controlling principles of your life.

A Favored Life The second benefit mentioned in the passage that could, perhaps, be called a surprise is that living a life of wisdom leads to finding favor with God and man. If you consistently, from the heart, exhibit mercy and truth, you will find "favor and high esteem" with God and man (3:4). The Hebrew word rendered "favor" means just that "favor, grace" and the one translated "high esteem" means "pleasing, agreeable, good."

God's favor and grace are first and foremost obtained through faith in Jesus Christ (Eph. 2:4-8), but we are to grow in the grace and knowledge of the Lord (2 Pet.3:18). So the point of this passage is not that we obtain God's mercy for eternal salvation by being merciful, it is that after we trust in Christ for eternal salvation, and then grow in mercy and truth, we gain God's favor in this life as well as at the Judgment Seat of Christ (Jas. 2:1-13). God smiles on His children when they exercise mercy and truth. Human beings also treat people with favor who practice mercy and truth. The merciful receive mercy (Mt. 5:7).

The greatest illustration of this truth in all of history is none other than Jesus Christ. The apostle John tells us that when Jesus Christ became flesh and dwelt among us, He was "full of grace and truth" (Jn. 1:14). It is no wonder that as Jesus "increased in wisdom," He also increased "in favor with God and men" (Lk.2:52).

Years ago, a case of a barking telephone caller was reported to the police in San Diego. A woman complained that she was getting calls in the middle of the night from a man who barked like a dog and hung up. The phone company had been unable to trace the calls. Eventually, the mysterious dog man confessed. The culprit was the woman's neighbor. Whenever her barking dog awakened him, he called to make sure that she was awakened, too.

He certainly did not deal with his neighbor with either mercy or truth. The loving, mature way to deal with the barking dog was to talk with his neighbor about it. We often respond like the barking dog man. Instead of speaking the truth in love, we withhold affection, clam up and say nothing, drop hints, bark some sound that does not communicate, or do something like wake people up in the middle of the night.

A Healthy Life

Trust the Lord Solomon exhorts, "Trust in the LORD with all your heart, and lean not on your own understanding; in all your ways acknowledge Him, and He shall direct your paths" (3:5-6). Proverbs 3:5-6 is often quoted and taken to mean that if you trust the Lord, He will guide you in the sense that He will directly tell you what to do daily. Are these verses teaching that God gives direct daily guidance?

According to the authoritative Hebrew lexicon by Brown, Driver, and Briggs, the Aramaic word behind the Hebrew word for "trust" originally had the idea of "to throw one down on the ground, to lie extended on the ground." The picture shows one lying face down on the ground (see also Kidner). Trusting the Lord with "all your heart" is to "concentrate the whole inner life on the active contemplation of God" (Delitzsch).

The meaning of "our understanding" in this verse is our understanding apart from God's view of things. Later in this book, Solomon says, "There is a way which seems right to a man, but its end is the way of death" (14:12). The word for "lean" does not mean "incline" but "rely on" in the sense of support. Fallen creatures rely on their "foolish notions and false fancies." There should be no other confidence. Our trust must not only be "entire," it must also be "exclusive." Self-wisdom and self-dependence are self-idolatry (Bridges). Our understanding is the way of self-wisdom and self-will, self-sufficiency, and self-dependency. It is practical atheism (Wardlaw).

Relying on our own understanding does not mean we should not use our intelligence. The issue is what is in the mind. We are to love the Lord with our entire mind (Mt. 22:37), meaning we are to use our minds to understand how God's principles and precepts bear on our situation.

Thus, trusting the Lord with all your heart and leaning not on your understanding are two ways to say the same thing. Put positively, we are to trust the Lord. Negatively, we are not to lean on our understanding. Moreover, "acknowledge" is actually the Hebrew word "know." Thus, the thought is more than acknowledge; it is "be aware of, have fellowship with" (Kidner) the Lord in all we do. In everything we do, we are to have a personal and intimate fellowship with the Lord.

Pilots are trained to trust their instruments and not lean on their instincts or feelings. They are taught that even though they feel they are flying south, if their compass says they are flying east, they better believe their compass. During buffeting winds, they may feel like they are in a dive and be tempted to pull back on the controls, but if the instruments say they are flying level or even climbing, they better believe the instruments. Pulling back on the controls might put them in a steep climb, which would cause the plane to stall, drop off in a spin, and leave them out of control.

A Healthy Life The third benefit in this section is a surprise in that its true meaning differs from popularly thought. Including the Lord means the Lord will "direct" your path. So, what's the surprise? The Hebrew word for "direct" means "smooth, straight, right." Smooth is being free from obstacles. These verses do not promise daily direction in all the decisions we make. They are saying that if we follow the Lord, He will make our lives go straight in the sense of righteousness, smooth in the sense of removing all hindrances out of the way.

People usually quote verses 5 and 6 and stop, but the passage extends through verse 8. The next verse is obviously a continuation of the same thought (Wardlaw). "Do not be wise in your own eyes; fear the Lord and depart from evil" (3:7) is closely connected to "lean not on your own understanding; in all your ways acknowledge Him" (Bridges).

Being wise in one's own eyes indicates no room for any other wisdom. As the ancient author Seneca wrote, "I suppose that many might have attained wisdom, had they not thought they had already attained it." In Proverbs, being wise in one's own eyes indicates wisdom that leaves God and His wisdom out and practices self-reliance instead of relying on the Lord. The fear of the Lord, which, as we have seen, is a personal relationship with the Lord that includes reverential awe for Him (see 1:7), will produce a departure from evil. When God is reverence, sin is resisted (Bridges).

The result, this time, is, "It shall be health to your flesh, and strength to your bones (3:8). The expression "health to your flesh" literally translates as "healing to your navel." Navel is used here of the whole body. The Hebrew translated "strength" actually means "drink" and the expression "drink to the bones" is a figure of speech for refreshment. Following the Lord and forsaking sin results in a healthy life, if for no other reason than to avoid habits that are harmful to the body.

Wardlaw, a nineteenth-century commentator, said, "Everyone knows how a state of anxiety and care, by chasing sleep from the eyes, and depriving of appetite, and otherwise affecting the functions of the animal nature, injures the health; and, when long continued and passing heavily, may waste the vital energies, and even bring to the grave."

Another simple illustration is drinking. The book of Proverbs warns against excessive drinking. Ignoring that wisdom can cause health problems, and following it can make you healthier.

A Prosperous Life

Honor the Lord Solomon urges, "Honor the Lord with your possessions and with the firstfruits of all your increase" (3:9). This is a synonymous parallelism. To honor the Lord with your possessions, give Him some of your earnings first. In the Mosaic law, God instructed the Israelites to provide some ground produce to the Lord (Deut. 26:1-15). These "firstfruits" were to be ten percent of all they raised. The way to honor the Lord is to give Him the firstfruits, not a later share (Kidner), not the leftovers. God should have first place rather than last (Wardlaw).

Benefit This benefit may not surprise some, but it is a shock to those who have not heard it. The benefit is, "So your barns will be filled with plenty, and your vats will overflow with new wine" (3:9-10). There is no other way to interpret this: if you honor the Lord with your finances by putting Him first instead of last or not at all, you will be blessed materially. This is an often-repeated Old Testament promise. "Piety brings plenty" (Kidner).

Technically, the Old Testament teaches tithing and promises material blessings on those who do, while in the New Testament, tithing is conspicuous by its absence. The New Testament emphasizes spiritual blessings (Eph. 1), not material blessings. The law deals with us as children and prescribes an exact amount. The New Testament treats us as adults and leaves the amount up to circumstance, principle, and conscience (Bridges).

Nevertheless, the Old Testament was written for our learning (Rom. 15:4) and there is no doubt that we should honor the Lord with our finances (1 Cor. 16:1-4). If we do, we will be blessed in this life (2 Cor. 9:6-8) and the life to come (Mt. 6:19-20). Simply put, "Those who honor Me, I will honor" (1 Sam. 2:30).

When people hear this for the first time, they often object, "I can't afford to do that." Solomon might answer that by saying, "lean not on your own understanding" (3:5), "in all your ways acknowledge Him," includes acknowledging Him in the financial area of your life (3:6) and "trust in the Lord with all your heart" (3:5), because in the final analysis, all giving is by faith (Wardlaw; Kidner)

A Corrected Life

Do Not Despise Discipline Solomon commands, "My son, do not despise the chastening of the LORD; nor detest His correction" (3:11). These verses are quoted in Hebrews 12:5-11. What do they mean?

The "chastening of the Lord" is His discipline. This expression has been rendered "the school of the Lord" (Delitzsch). God's correction is His reproof and rebuke intended to correct. After pardon comes purification. God disciples and corrects His children by allowing difficulties to enter their lives.

The Hebrew word translated "despise" means "reject, refuse, despise" and the one rendered "detest" means "a feeling of loathing, abhorrence, sickening dread." These words express a "double antagonism of will and emotion" (Kidner). We should not allow ourselves to be estranged from God by an attitude of anger (Delitzsch).

When we face what we call "problems," we can respond in one of two extreme ways. We can willfully refuse the reproof and continue doing what is displeasing to the Lord, or we can be emotionally overcome with a sickening dread and be paralyzed into doing nothing, which again means continuing to do what is not pleasing to the Lord. When we willfully reject God's correction, we either treat it lightly or become bitter. When we emotionally react, we grow weary or despondent.

Knowing God's Love Solomon goes on to explain that like a father who loves and delights in his son, the Lord, our heavenly Father, disciplines us for the very reason that He loves and delights in us, "For whom the LORD loves He corrects, just as a father the son in whom he delights"(3:12). Unlike the other admonitions in this passage, this one does not give a command and the benefit of obeying that command. Nevertheless, there is a benefit implied and it will come as a surprise to most. It knows that when trials come, the Lord does not hate you; He loves you and delights in you. The point of the passage is that God's delight in us at the very time of His discipline of us.

God's discipline is family discipline, the discipline of a father to a son. It is not prison discipline, that of a warden to inmates. God does not treat His children as criminals but as children (Bridges). As a Father, He can delight in the disciple, knowing the results. The word for "delights" means to "be pleased with, accept favorably." When our heavenly Father is not pleased, like all good parents, He frowns, but His frown is the frown of love (Wardlaw).

Thus, instead of rejecting God's correction or becoming depressed over God's discipline, we can count it all joy (Jas. 1:2), knowing a gracious God who is in control of all things is allowing this trial because He loves us and is basically pleased with us. It is simply a correction. Learn from it. It is only a correction. Rejoice in it. As Job has pointed out, "For has anyone said to God, 'I have borne chastening; I will offend no more; Teach me: what I do not see; if I have done iniquity, I will do no more'" (Job 34:31-32)? Or, as so eloquently stated, the rod was sent in love. "Kiss the rod" (Bridges).

A pile of unpaid bills, a family disruption, or an unexpected stay in the hospital can be used by God to awaken a sleeping saint. God may let us be roughed up so we will grow up.

A piece of wood bitterly complained because its owner was cutting, whittling, and drilling it with holes. The craftsman said, "You may think that I am destroying you, but soon you will see what I am doing is making something of you. I am changing a worthless black stick of ebony into a lovely flute whose music will charm the souls of men."

When the father punished his little girl, she was upset at first, but later, she climbed up on his lap, hugged him tightly, and said, "Daddy, I love you." When he asked her why, she said, "Because you make me good."

Summary: The surprise benefit of wise living is if you live wisely, which includes walking with the Lord, learning obedience, and practicing mercy and truth, you will add quality and quantity to your life. You will have a healthy, prosperous, favored, corrected, and longer life.

Most of this passage talks about positive advantages like health, prosperity, being favored, and living long, but the passage also recognizes that life also consists of adversity. The surprising benefit of living wisely is that no matter what happens, you benefit. Remember to trust the Lord, honor the Lord, and practice obedience, mercy, and truth, no matter what happens.

Recently, my faithful computer, which had served me well for several years, lay down and died. So I took it to to get it fixed, but I ended up buying a new computer. In the process, I was without a computer for a week. I was surprised at how dependent I had become on a computer. After a week without one, I told my wife, "I have decided that in modern America, it is impossible for me to function without a car and a computer." I was surprised at the benefits of a computer at first. Now I'm sold. When I first started, I thought the benefits of a computer were wonderful. Now, I believe that for me, they are indispensable. Likewise, once you get accustomed to living a wise life, living without the benefits of godly wisdom becomes unthinkable. The benefits of wisdom are not just surprising; they are indispensable.

34

THE VALUE OF LIVING WISELY

When my children were small, a man and his wife, who were our friends, gave us a dog. It was their personal dog, but they were beginning to travel and could no longer care for it. It was a cute, small, white, friendly dog. He became part of our family for years until he died of dog old age. I did not then and do not now know much about dogs. I had a Cocker Spaniel when I was a kid. I knew what a German Shepherd looked like, but I had no idea what kind of dog had been given to my children. As far as I was concerned, it was just another mutt my kids loved. Its value was what it meant to them. If something happened to it, it would break their hearts, but we could replace it with another dog without a lot of expense. If, for some reason, we had wanted to get rid of it, we, like our friends, would have to find somebody to give it to as a pet or give it to the humane society. I was wrong about the value of that dog. I came to find out it was a pedigreed Chihuahua worth a great deal of money.

Our estimate of the value of living wisely could be like my estimate of the value of that dog—way undervalued. Obviously, there is value in living wisely, but just how valuable is it? While discussing the virtues of wisdom with his son, Solomon pauses to emphasize the value of wisdom. In Proverbs 3:13-18, he praises the value of wisdom and explains that wisdom is so valuable because of its virtues.

The Value of Wisdom

Happiness This passage begins with the statement that "Happy is the man who finds wisdom, and the man who gains understanding" (3:13). The Hebrew word translated "happy" means "happiness, blessedness" (more about that later). "Wisdom and understanding" are another case of synonymous parallelism. Wisdom and understanding are basically the same thing.

Because of the Value The person who gets wisdom is blessed because ("for"), "For her proceeds are better than the profits of silver, and her gain than fine gold. She is more precious than rubies, and all the things you may desire cannot compare with her" (3:14-15). Verse 14 returns to depicting wisdom as a woman (see 1:20-33). Almost every word in these two verses emphasizes the value of wisdom. The Hebrew word for "proceeds" and "profits" both come from the same Hebrew root, which means "traffic, gain," that is, gain from traffic, while the word for "better" actually means "pleasing, good, valuable, better." The Hebrew word rendered "gain" means "produce, revenue." The word in the original text translated "rubies" means "coral" and is used here as a figure of speech for value, and the word "precious" means "costly, highly valued." The Hebrew word for "desire" is actually "delight, pleasure." It is translated "delight" in Psalm 1:2. Wisdom is a priceless treasure. It will make you richer than money!

Imagine a table with two gift-wrapped boxes, one wrapped in green and the other in sky blue. Suppose you were told that you could have only one and that in the green box was a billion dollars and in the heavenly blue box was a pill that, if you swallowed it, would make you wise. Which box would you select? No doubt, Solomon thought his son and everyone else should choose the heavenly blue box. Is Solomon overstating the case? Think of all that you could buy with money: houses, cars, boats, planes, clothes, jewelry, food, financial freedom, and financial security. Think of all you could do to help others if you had the money. Maybe we should ask what exactly do we get if we take the heavenly blue box.

The Virtues of Wisdom

Wisdom is so valuable because of its virtues. In Proverbs 3:16–18, seven virtues of wisdom are listed.

Longevity "Length of days is in her right hand" (3:16a). Earlier in this chapter, Solomon said that if his son obeyed him, the son would have "length of days and long life" added to him (3:1-2). Now Solomon says that wisdom, without qualifying it as parental obedience, will give a person length of days. One of the virtues of wisdom is a longer life.

In my opinion, one of the reasons for this is that a wise life is a less stressful life. Remember, in the previous reference to "length of days," Solomon connected living longer with peace (see 3:2). Researchers have concluded that those who sleep less than six hours a night don't live as long as those who sleep seven or more. What would keep people from sleeping? Dr. Ralph Downey III of the Loma Linda University Sleep Disorder Clinic says that job stress and financial worries are the top causes of adult sleeplessness. Stress shortens life. Peace prolongs it.

Riches "In her left-hand riches" (3:16b). Though not by name, Solomon has also mentioned riches. He said that if we honor the Lord with the firstfruits of our increase, our barns would be filled with plenty (3:9-10). Apart from God's intervention, living wisely will make people financially wealthy. If you lived wisely financially, you would save money. Solomon said, "Go to the ant, you sluggard! Consider her ways and be wise which, having no captain, overseer or ruler, provides her supplies in the summer, and gathers her food in the harvest" (6:6-8). My wife and I teach a financial seminar entitled *How to Accumulate Wealth on Any Income.* In it, we teach what any financial planner will tell you: the key to accumulating wealth is not how much money you make but how much you save.

Honor "and honor" (3:16c). In a sense, this virtue has also been mentioned. Solomon said that if we practiced mercy and truth, we would find favor and high esteem with God and people (3:3-4). The Hebrew word translated "honor" means "abundance, honor, glory." People who live a wise life will have character that will give them a reputation; they will be highly regarded. We naturally respect people who live wisely and do not respect people who live foolishly. So, it should come as no surprise that one of the values of living wisely is that other people will honor you.

Pleasantness "Her ways are ways of pleasantness" (3:17a). Living wisely is to travel on a road of pleasantness. In the original text, the word for "pleasantness" means "pleasantness, delightfulness." On the one hand, pleasantness is not just the absence of pain; it is the presence of pleasure. On the other hand, the presence of pleasure does not mean that there may be no pain. Believers are disciplined by their Heavenly Father (3:11-12). Sometimes, that discipline involves pain. When the writer to the Hebrews quoted Proverbs 3:11-12, he added that God "scourges every son whom He receives." (Heb. 12:6), but he also quickly adds, "Now no chastening seems to be joyful for the present, but painful; nevertheless, afterward, it yields the peaceable fruit of righteousness to those who have been trained by it" (Heb. 12:11). Thus, living wisely does not eliminate all pain, but it leads to a much more pleasant life.

Peace "All the ways wisdom takes are paths of peace" (3:17b). Peace was listed with length of days as a benefit of wisdom (3:2). The Hebrew for "peace" is "shalom," and as we have seen, it means "complete, soundness, wellness, health, prosperity, tranquility, contentment." One commentator pointed out that wisdom brings well-being and deep inner satisfaction (Delitzsch).

Life "She is a tree of life to those who take hold of her" (3:18a). The expression "tree of life" is mentioned at the beginning and at the end of the Bible. When Adam and Eve were expelled from the Garden of Eden, they were forbidden access to the Tree of Life (Gen. 3:22-24). In the last chapter of the Bible, which describes the New Jerusalem resting on the earth out of heaven (Rev 21:2), the tree of life is present (Rev. 22:2, 14) and its leaves are said to be the "healing of the nations" (Rev 22:2). The Tree of Life, then, is a source of life (Gen. 2:9; Rev. 2:7) In Proverbs, wisdom is a source of life. As much as possible, this side of heaven, wisdom in this life is a source of life that restores and regains in some measure what was lost from the Garden of Eden and will be regained in heaven. Wise decisions renew and energize you, while stupid decisions drain and depress you.

Happiness "And happy are all who retain her" (3:18b). In the Hebrew text, this paragraph begins and ends with the word happy. The Hebrew word means "happy, blessed." Perhaps, in a sense, this word summarizes the whole process. If you live wisely, you will be blessed; you will be happy.

Summary: The virtues of wisdom make it more valuable than anything to which it can be compared.

In our society, we put a premium on wealth. If you value wealth above everything else in life so that you seek it above everything else, you may gain wealth, but you could easily do that and miss out on a lot in life. Jesus said, "Whoever desires to come after Me, let him deny himself, take up his cross, and follow Me. For whoever desires to save his life will lose it, but whoever loses his life for My sake and the gospel's will save it. For what will it profit a man if he gains the whole world and loses his own soul?" (Mk. 8:34-36).

On the other hand, if you value living wisely above everything else, which means you begin with getting to know the Lord, you may have money, but you will also have things money cannot buy. Earlier, I made this a matter of wealth versus wisdom. That is not necessarily the way it is. You may have wealth and all that it buys without having wisdom, but if you have wisdom, you may have (remember, these are proverbial statements) riches, honor, and long life. Be that as it may, if you have wisdom, you will have things money can't buy, like peace, happiness, and respect. The illustration of this is Solomon himself.

"At Gibeon, the LORD appeared to Solomon in a dream by night; and God said, 'Ask! What shall I give you?' And Solomon said: 'You have shown great mercy to Your servant David, my father, because he walked before You in truth, in righteousness, and in uprightness of heart with You; You have continued this great kindness for him, and You have given him a son to sit on his throne, as it is this day. Now, O LORD my God, You have made Your servant king instead of my father, David, but I am a little child; I do not know how to go out or come in. And Your servant is in the midst of Your people whom You have chosen, a great people, too numerous to be numbered or counted. Therefore give to Your servant an understanding heart to judge Your people, that I may discern between good and evil. For who is able to judge this great people of Yours?' The speech pleased the LORD that Solomon had asked this thing. Then God said to him: 'Because you have asked this thing, and have not asked long life for yourself, nor have asked riches for yourself, nor have asked the life of your enemies, but have asked for yourself understanding to discern justice, behold, I have done according to your words; see, I have given you a wise and understanding heart, so that there has not been anyone like you before you, nor shall any like you arise after you. And I have also given you what you have not asked: both riches and honor, so that there shall not be anyone like you among the kings all your days. So if you walk in My ways, to keep My statutes and My commandments, as your father David walked, then I will lengthen your days'" (1 Kings 3:5-14).

Solomon selected wisdom, sought it from the Lord, and he got it, plus riches, honor, and a long life.

One other observation: if it is wisdom you desire, it is not as easy as picking a box off a table. You must seek wisdom. Granted, it begins with asking the Lord for it (Ja. 1:2), but you must also put forth the effort to search it out in God's Word and you must practice what you find. Notice that you must "take hold of her," that is, wisdom. (3:18). "Take hold" comes from a single Hebrew verb, which means "take hold, seize, grasp." Actually, it comes from the word for "firm, strong." The idea is to seize firmly, to fasten on to, to bind." You are to also "retain her" (3:18), a Hebrew word which also means "grasp, support, attain," but can be translated "hold firmly." Grab her firmly and hold on tightly.

A better illustration than taking a box off a table is a lady named Wisdom with longevity in her right hand and riches and honor in her left hand with pleasantness, peace, refreshment, and happiness in walking with her through life. Grab her and don't let her go.

My wife and I have an expression for what we would like our relationship to be like. We talk about being "joined at the hip." What we have in mind is that we would go everywhere together. There is so much pleasantness, peace, refreshment, and happiness for each of us when we are together that we don't like to ever be apart.

When you experience living wisely, you will feel that way about Lady Wisdom.

THE ULTIMATE REASON FOR LIVING WISELY

It may sound strange,, but bear with me for a moment. Why should we live a wise life? Is it because we don't want to avoid doing something foolish? Is it because we want to appear wise in the eyes of others? As we have seen, there are benefits to living wisely. Is the reason for wise living to obtain the blessings it brings?

Proverbs lists all of these reasons for living wisely, but it also gives another reason, which could be called the ultimate reason for living wisely. Proverbs 3:19-26 begins with a comment concerning the Creator (3:19-20). Based on that comment, Solomon issues a command (3:21). Then, he lists the consequences of obeying the command (3:22-26).

The Creator

God Created God, who is called wise (1 Tim. 1:17; Jude 25), used wisdom when He made the universe. Solomon says, "The Lord by wisdom founded the earth; by understanding He established the heavens" (3:19). The word "founded" comes from a Hebrew verb that means "establish, found." The noun form of the word means "foundation." The Divine Builder of the universe laid the earth's foundation by wisdom. The Hebrew word translated "established" means "to be firm, set up, to establish," and here it is equivalent to "to give existence" (Delitzsch). The Divine Structural Engineer of the universe founded the earth by wisdom and set up the heavens by understanding.

God Formed Furthermore, "By His knowledge the depths were broken up, and clouds drop down the dew" (3:20). Breaking up the depths is a reference to God dividing the water from the land on the earth (Gen. 1:9-10; Delitzsch) and the dew from clouds is, of course, a reference to rain. The Divine Architect formed and fashioned the universe by wisdom.

The wisdom in Proverbs is not just from an ancient king or a mere mortal. It is from the King of Kings, God Himself. This is not human; it is Divine wisdom. This wisdom is not philosophical speculation, theoretical notions, or abstract opinions. It is practical, directed, purposeful wisdom. God created a useful universe. This wisdom gives stability and life. The description of creation is designed to convey the stability of a well-ordered world. The earth is a firm foundation. The heavens are firmly established. Of all the aspects of creation, Solomon mentions rain. Rain provides water, making all life possible in the vegetable, animal, and human worlds.

The Command

God's Wisdom Based on the fact that God used wisdom to create the universe, Solomon now gives his son a series of commands that extend to the end of the chapter. The first command is "My son let them not depart from your eyes; keep sound wisdom and discretion" (3:21). What is not to depart from the eyes ("them") are wisdom (3:19) and knowledge (3:20) and parallel to that, what is to be obeyed is sound wisdom and discretion (3:21).

Wisdom, understanding, knowledge, sound wisdom, and discretion are all synonyms for wisdom, yet slight differences exist between them. Wisdom is the normal word for wisdom in Proverbs. It is used elsewhere in the Old Testament for skill in technical work. Understanding is a noun from a Hebrew verb, which means "discern, have insight." Knowledge is not so much an informed mind as it is knowing truth and God (Kidner). "Sound wisdom" comes from a Hebrew verb, the meaning of which is uncertain. That word may mean "assist, support." The noun means "sound wisdom, efficient wisdom, abiding success." The Hebrew word for "discretion," used in Proverbs 1:4, means "purpose, discretion, devise." It has the idea of the power to form plans. The nuances of these words for wisdom are appropriate for God creating the universe. Out of His knowledge and power to form plans, He used skill to construct the heavens and the earth, which is firm support for us.

Remember God's Wisdom Based on this comment concerning the Creator, Solomon states that we are to not let such wisdom depart from our eyes. We should be reminded of God's wisdom whenever we see the sun, moon, stars, mountains, and trees. David said, "The heavens declare the glory of God" (Ps. 19:1), which includes wisdom according to his son Solomon. This is especially true of the rain. When it rains, we should be reminded again of

God's wisdom. The rain is often an aggravation, but we should be reminded of God's wisdom instead of seeing the nuisance. Being constantly reminded of God's wisdom should prompt us to live wisely.

On a recent trip, Patricia and I saw a sensational sunrise, spectacular views of mountains, striking waterfalls, and a superb sunset. As I looked at these marvelous sights, I thought to myself, God has created a beautiful earth. On occasion, I have looked at the sky, the sun, the moon, and the stars and thought to myself, God is powerful to create all of this. Without a doubt, when we see creation, we should be reminded of the beauty and God's power, but when Solomon looked at creation, he saw God's wisdom, and, he says, so should we.

The Consequences

If we use wisdom to order our lives like the Lord used wisdom to fashion the universe, we will receive life, grace, safety, and serenity.

Life Wisdom will add life. "So they will be life to your soul" (3:22). The Hebrew word translated "soul" means "soul, the inner being." Solomon has already mentioned this in this chapter (See 3:2).

Grace Wisdom will also grant grace. "And grace to your neck" (3:22). This result of wisdom has also been mentioned earlier in this chapter (See 3:4).

Safety Wisdom will supply safety. "Then you will walk safely in your way and your foot will not stumble" (3:23). The safety here is not physical but spiritual. The same Hebrew word for safety is used in Proverbs 1:33, 3:29, and 10:9, where it is used for safety from sin. When we follow wisdom, we do not stumble into sin (3:6).

Serenity Wisdom will provide serenity. "When you lie down you will not be afraid; Yes, you will lie down and your sleep will be sweet" (3:24). The word rendered "afraid" means "dread." Sin produces dread. Wisdom provides serenity. Unless you have seared your conscience if you sin, you lie down to sleep dreading getting caught. If your conscience is clear, your sleep is sweet. The Hebrew word for "sweet" means "sweet, pleasing." The adjective means pleasant (see Ps. 127:2 and Acts 12:6-7).

At this point in the passage, Solomon continues the same idea, but he changes from saying that serenity is the natural result of following wisdom (see "then" in 3:23) to a command (3:25). He now says, "Do not be afraid of sudden terror, not of trouble from the wicked when it comes" (3:25). The Hebrew word translated "afraid" is the word for fear. "Terror" is the same word that was translated "dread" in verse 24. Trouble means "devastation, ruin." Don't fear sudden dread or devastation.

To what is Solomon referring? The phrase "trouble from the wicked" can be (and is) translated "trouble of the wicked." In other words, the Hebrew expression can mean "the ruin from the wicked," that is, the ruin they cause, or "the ruin of the wicked," meaning the ruin they receive. The language here ("ruin"), as well as the previous context (3:24 and 1:27), indicates that Solomon is saying, "Don't fear the ruin that will suddenly come upon the wicked." You should not fear. They should fear. Living wisely means you need not fear sin or its consequences. If you are not—fear!

Solomon explains why those living wisely need not fear by saying, "For the Lord will be your confidence and will keep your foot from being caught" (3:26). This segment begins and ends with the Lord (see 3:19 and now 3:26). The Lord used wisdom to create the universe (3:19). The fear of the Lord is the beginning of knowledge and wisdom (1:7, 9:10). So when judgment comes, those who have trusted the Lord and followed the Lord have nothing to fear. The Lord Himself is their confidence. The Lord Himself will see to it that their foot is not caught in the trap of judgment.

There are providential benefits to living wisely. Those who live wisely naturally add life and grace to their days and sweet sleep to their nights. The Lord is also personally involved in the lives of those who are following Him and His wisdom. Those who fear the Lord first and foremost have nothing to fear from Him. They can rest in the Lord's providence, promises, and personal care.

Summary: The God who created the useful universe by wisdom gives life, grace, safety, and serenity to those who, like the Lord Himself, live wisely. We should live wisely because when we do, we are like the Lord and reap the benefits of wise living, namely life, grace, safety, and serenity.

Living wisely has benefits and blessings, but the great reason is the Lord. He used wisdom to create the useful universe. When we use wisdom to create our world, we are like God and the Lord Himself is in our life.

One summer, Patricia and I decided that we would see Yellowstone, Custer's Last Stand, and Mt. Rushmore on our vacation. Our itinerary took us through Utah and Montana. Utah has a speed limit of 75 mph on the interstate, but we wanted to make time, so I drove 85. I knew I was risking getting a ticket, so I constantly looked for a patrolman. The whole experience made me uneasy and, consequently, that part of the trip was unpleasant.

Montana has no daytime speed limit. As we entered the state, we saw signs saying the daytime speed limit for cars is whatever is "reasonable and prudent." We were behind on our schedule the day we traveled through Montana. The weather was good and there were few cars on the road. Under those conditions, 90 was reasonable and prudent. With Patricia taking a long nap on my lap, I set the car on 90 and, with a clear conscience, flew through Montana.

The next day, we visited Mt. Rushmore in South Dakota. Coming out of the park, I was on a four-lane highway. Patricia and I were reveling in our vacation and the awesomeness of Mt. Rushmore when suddenly, I saw bright flashing lights in my rearview mirror. I was pulled over for speeding. I was clocked at 40 mph on a four-lane highway! I was stunned that I would get a speeding ticket under those conditions. The officer was clear that the speed limit was 25 mph. Fortunately, he let me off with a verbal warning, but that experience had a great impact on me psychologically. It brought me back to driving wisely.

Leaving Mt. Rushmore, we traveled a few miles east and dropped south through Nebraska to return to Los Angeles through Denver. There is no interstate in that part of Nebraska, so we had to take federal highway 83, which has a speed limit of 65 and, in parts, 60, but that stretch of highway goes through barren ranch land. For miles and miles, there is not a town or even a ranch house. It would appear that even though the speed limit was 65, I could drive 80 and 90 and get away with it, but just to make sure, we stopped at a little café in Valentine, Nebraska and talked to a truck driver. He informed us in no uncertain terms that even though that stretch of road was desolate, it was patrolled. To emphasize the point, a lady at the table handed us a local newspaper to show us that speeders' names were published. Sure enough, Bruce Worth paid a $25.00 fine and $21 court costs for driving 72 in a 65-mph stretch of highway. Jenny Gideon of Nebraska was cited and fined $75 plus $21 in court costs for driving 76 mph on a highway with a speed limit of 65.

As we continued the trip, I thought about what I had seen in the newspaper and what I had experienced at Mt. Rushmore, and then I thought about something else—Patricia. She drives the speed limit and she and I get along better when I do the same. So I drove the speed limit down Highway 83. I drove the speed limit down Highway 83 for several reasons, including the newspaper and my own experience, but the ultimate reason was Patricia. There was no apprehension about being pulled over as I drove, just safety and serenity. The safety was safety from not getting a ticket and the serenity was from the inner peace about not *worrying* about getting a ticket. Sure enough, on a lonely stretch of road without a house, a car, or a cow in sight, a highway patrolman had pulled over another car, apparently for speeding.

The book of Proverbs teaches that if we learn wisdom from reading the book of Proverbs, the experience of others, our own experience, and our relationship with the Lord Himself, we will have life, grace, safety from the consequences of sin, and serenity. While it is true that we get all of this, the ultimate reason for living wisely is the Lord.

HOW TO LOVE A NEIGHBOR

A lawyer once tried to trick Jesus by asking a question he thought would be extremely difficult to answer. He asked, "Which is the great commandment in the law?" Jesus brilliantly answered, "You shall love the LORD your God with all your heart, with all your soul, and with all your mind. This is the first and greatest commandment. And the second is like it: You shall love your neighbor as yourself. On these two commandments hang all the Law and the Prophets" (Mt. 22:35-40).

According to Jesus, the second greatest commandment in the Bible is to love our neighbor. How do you do that? What specific, practical things can a person do to love a neighbor? Without ever using the phrase "love your neighbor," Proverbs 3:27-35 answers this question. This passage naturally divides into two parts: commands (3:27-32) and contrasts (3:33-35). The point of the first part concerns loving your neighbor and the second part explains why that should be done.

The Command: Love Your Neighbor

Proverbs 3:27-33 contains four negative commands, all concerning one's neighbor. The first two mention the neighbor by name. The third speaks of a "man," but the connection of ideas between the second and third commands implies that a neighbor is still in view. The fourth talks about an "oppressor." Again, the close connection of ideas between the second and now third command, namely "evil" and "harm," as well as the fact that the oppressor is close enough for one to envy, indicates that the oppressor, too, is a neighbor.

Do Not Withhold Good The first command is "Do not withhold good from those to whom it is due, when it is in the power of your hand to do so" (3:27)." The Hebrew word rendered "due" means "owner." Kindness is often thought of as something that I didn't have to do, but I do it for someone. This passage views doing good as a debt. The recipient of the kindness is portrayed as the owner. If it is within our power to do something good for someone, we are debtors to do it. Our neighbor owns any good, that is, benefit we can give them. Kindness is not an option; it is an obligation. The only exception is "when it is in the power of your hand to do so" (3:27). If it is good, within our power, and we have the means, we should do it.

Furthermore, we should do it without delay. "Do not say to your neighbor, 'Go, and come back and tomorrow I will give it,' when you have it with you" (3:28). By saying "not today, tomorrow," we can say "no" without appearing insensitive or unkind. Besides, if we put it off, perhaps someone else will do it, or the needy person will not come back and we will not have to do it. Delay is another form of denial. Delay is disobedience.

Paul says something similar in Romans, "Render therefore to all their due: taxes to whom taxes are due, customs to whom customs, fear to whom fear, honor to whom honor. Owe no one anything except to love one another, for he who loves another has fulfilled the law" (Rom. 13:7-8). Among other things, we owe others honor, help, and thanks. Honor to those in authority. Help to those in need. Thanks to those who have helped us.

Don't Do Evil The second command is "Do not devise evil against your neighbor" (3:29). The first command in this passage is against a sin of omission. The second is a probation against a sin of commission. In the first, we are not to omit doing good. In the second, we are not to devise doing evil.

If we were loving our neighbor and not withholding good, we would never devise or do evil against him or her. Even those who do not know God or His wisdom disapprove of people doing evil to others. However, what is cautioned against here is not evil against a stranger. The victim, in this case, "dwells by you for safety's sake" (3:29), meaning this neighbor knows, trusts, and feels safe with the perpetrator of the evil.

Law-abiding citizens do not plot physical harm or property damage against their neighbors. However, we sometimes dream and scheme about how to say something harmful to the person's face or behind their back. If our neighbor parks his car in front of our house, we consider putting a nail under a tire. If the next-door neighbor's dog barks too much, we would like to season his food with poison.

Do Not Strive The third command is "Do not strive with a man without cause, if he has done you no harm" (3:30). The Hebrew word rendered "strive" means "strive, dispute, quarrel" and the one for "harm" means "evil, badness," even "unpleasant" in the sense of giving pain, unhappiness, misery. Not only should we not do evil, but neither should we strive, especially if it is without cause. The rule is, "If it is possible, as much as depends on you, live peaceably with all men" (Rom. 12:18). Perhaps, under some circumstances, there is a sufficient reason to quarrel with someone, but if no such reason exists, we should never strive.

The problem is that when we become contentious, we rationalize. Contentious people insist on their rights or what they perceive is due them. The question is, "What would an impartial observer say?" Besides, among believers, there are times when rather than fight, one's rights should be abandoned, and the wrong be permitted to be done (1 Cor. 6:1-7).

We destroy relationships over insignificant issues. A listener called a counselor on a talk show to get advice concerning a dispute over a piece of jewelry. As they talked, it became apparent that the listener was going to have to choose between a relatively inexpensive piece of jewelry and a good relationship with a relative. The counselor opted for the relationship. When the listener wanted to argue with the counselor, the counselor said, "Which is more valuable, the material item or the relationship?" We often quarrel over things and damage relationships.

Do Not Envy The fourth and final command in this paragraph is "Do not envy the oppressor and choose none of his ways" (3:31). The Hebrew word for "oppressor" actually means "violence, wrong." In the Old Testament, it is used of injurious language and harsh treatment as well as physical violence. The oppressor does you wrong!

Why would anyone want to envy an oppressor? Usually, it is not the oppression that is envied; it is the power, the possessions, and the position of the oppressor we'd like to have. Solomon says don't envy such people, don't keep company with them (24:1), and certainly don't choose their lifestyle. Don't envy them or their ways, character, company, or career.

The reason is, "For the perverse person is an abomination to the Lord, but His secret counsel is with the upright" (3:32). In this passage, the oppressor (3:31) is a perverse person (3:32). The Hebrew word for "perverse" here means "turn aside, depart" and indicates a crookedness that is crafty and cunning. It is used in Proverbs 2:15, where it is translated "crooked." From our study of this person in chapter 2, we concluded that "perverse" men: 1) depart from God (2:12), 2) delight in evil (2:14), 3) declare perverse things (2:12), and 4) dwell in darkness (2:13) and deception (2:15). They are perverted, that is, turn from righteousness spiritually, emotionally, verbally, and volitionally."

Such people are repugnant and abhorred, which is the meaning of "abomination" to the Lord. He detests them, or to use the vernacular, has nothing to do with them. On the other hand, the Lord reveals His "secret counsel" to the upright. Secret counsel comes from "to be firm, compressed" and was used to being pressed together or sitting together for private conversation, which seems to be the meaning here (Delitzsch). In other words, crocked ways are contrary to the Lord, but those who follow a straight (the literal meaning of "upright") path experience intimate conversations with the Lord (see Ps. 25:14; Amos 3:7; Jn. 15:14-15). In short, God deals with the upright as friends. You can be the friend of the perverse/oppressor or the friend of God. You cannot be both (Jas. 4:4). The Lord frowned on the perverse and smiled on the upright.

The Contrast: God Will Give You Blessings, Grace and Glory

The reason for not envying the perverse consists of a contrast (3:32). The next several verses contain additional contrasts concerning how the Lord deals with various kinds of people. In the overall context of the passage, these are extensions of why we should not envy the oppressor and, therefore, reasons for neighborly love.

Blessings The first contrast is, "The curse of the Lord is on the house of the wicked, but He blesses the home of the just" (3:33). The Lord not only "has nothing to do" with the oppressor, but He also curses the house of the wicked. When a man or woman is wicked, the children pick up their ways. It is not just the individual that is affected. It is his or her family. The same is true of the just. God blesses them and their house.

You may be the type of person who plans tacks under tires and poisons pets, but you may never carry out any of your plans. You may just talk about it, but in talking about it, you have left an example for your children, who may grow up to plan and perform. Usually, when children grow up to be worse than their parents, the parents respond with, "How did that happen? I taught him better."

Grace The second contrast is, "Surely He scorns the scornful, but gives grace to the humble" (3:34). In this verse, the scorner is contrasted with the humble. The Hebrew word translated "humble" means "poor, afflicted, humble, meek." The humble person is submissive. In stark contrast, the scorner is haughty and high-minded. Later, Solomon says, "A proud and haughty man; 'Scoffer' is his name; He acts with arrogant pride" (21:24).

When James and Peter quote Proverbs 3:34, they render it, "God resists the proud, but gives grace to the humble" (see Jas. 4:6 and 1 Pet. 5:5). That is the point. God resists the proud mocker. God scorns the scorner. As they mock others, God mocks them. "He who sits in the heavens shall laugh" (Ps. 2:4). On the other hand, God gives grace to the humble. So, if you want to be resisted and rejected by God, be proud, scorn. If, however, you wish to experience God's favor, don't mock your neighbors, love them. Submit yourself to God's law of love and you will experience God's grace. Salvation is by grace through faith (Eph. 2:8), but after salvation, God gives more grace to the humble (Jas. 4:6)

Glory The third contrast is, "The wise shall inherit glory, but shame shall be the legacy of fools" (3:35). This verse contrasts the wise and the fool. The wise inherit glory, a Hebrew word that means "abundance, honor, glory." On the other hand, the fool gets shame, a Hebrew word that means "dishonor, disgrace, ignominy." While it is true that the wise obtain honor and fools receive shame in this life, the Scripture carries the concept beyond this life.

For example, Daniel says, "At that time Michael shall stand up, the great prince who stands watch over the sons of your people; and there shall be a time of trouble, Such as never was since there was a nation, even to that time. And at that time, your people shall be delivered, everyone who is found written in the book. And many of those who sleep in the dust of the earth shall awake, some to everlasting life, some to shame and everlasting contempt. Those who are wise shall shine like the brightness of the firmament, and those who turn many to righteousness like the stars forever and ever" (Dan. 12:1-3).

Notice some are raised to shame and the wise shall shine. John also reminds us to "abide in Him, that when He appears, we may have confidence and not be ashamed before Him at His coming" (1 Jn. 2:28). Foolish living has eternal consequences. These verses speak of the fact that there are eternal rewards for believers who walk with the Lord. Salvation is by grace through faith; eternal rewards are based on our loving obedience to the Lord and our love for others.

Summary: If we pay our debt to love our neighbors, God will give us grace, bless our family in time, and give us glory in eternity. The way to love your neighbor is to do good and not harm.

Think of all the debts you have. Virtually every person you see has a need. You are a debtor to help. No. Think of all the opportunities you have to invest in eternity.

My wife is one of the kindest people I know. She has spent more than 15 years helping deaf people. She has been known to take carloads of homeless people home for Thanksgiving dinner. She genuinely revels in doing the smallest kindness for anyone she can. While studying this passage, I told her we are debtors to do good.

Her response startled me. She said, "I have never heard it put like that. I always thought that we did good things for people because we wanted to, not because we owed them. If everyone understood that, it would change society. You ought to preach on that every Sunday for a month until everyone gets it." I am not sure that if I preached it every Sunday for a month, everyone would get it, but I think my wife is right. If we realized that doing good for others is a debt, it would change us.

GET WISDOM

We are drowning in information and dying of thirst for wisdom. We have access to more information than ever before in history. For example, you can get information on just about anything on the Internet. There are millions of sites on virtually any topic.

Take another example. Do you want to know something about a field of knowledge? Go to the magazine store, and you will find that someone regularly publishes a magazine there. Kids play arcade games and computer games. They can now buy a magazine to tell them how to play the game to win!

In the meantime, we have lost common sense and wisdom. Daily, we hear of educated people doing something stupid. A student on a school bus was having an asthma attack. A quick-thinking girl ran down the aisle, gave the student an inhaler, which the report I heard said saved the student's life. Guess what? The girl who saved the student's life was punished! Guess what the crime was? Wearing a short skirt that the kids saw too much when she bent over to save the student's life? No. Assault and battery because she hit someone running down the aisle? No. Her crime was drug dealing. When questioned, the school authorities said they had a no-tolerance drug rule. So, they had to put drug dealing on her record.

My thesis is we need to get wisdom. Where do we find it? How do we get it? The answers are in Proverbs 4:1-19. This portion of Proverbs contains advice from a father and a grandfather. This does not mean you should not listen to your mother and grandmother. One of the first things Proverbs says is do not forsake what your mother taught you (1:8). It does propose that under certain conditions, you should listen to your father and grandfather. What are those conditions and what should a father and grandfather say to their children and grandchildren?

A Father's Exhortation

The Exhortation Solomon admonishes his children, "Hear, my children, the instruction of a father, and give attention to know understanding" (4:1). The Hebrew word for "instruction," which is the same word used for a father's instruction in Proverbs. 1:8, means "discipline, correction, chastening." Also, as a father, Solomon gave his son "understanding," insight into life.

The Explanation The reason given for obeying your father is, "For I give you good doctrine" (4:2a). The English word "doctrine" conveys to us the idea of theological dogma. The Hebrew word used here means "teaching" and "good" means "beneficial." Solomon adds, "Do not forsake my law" (4:2b). As mother has a law (1:8), so does father.

In short, follow the beneficial wisdom of a wise, godly father. That does not mean that everything your father says you should, as an adult, follow. Some fathers give bad counsel, especially today. Augustine's father advised him to "Get wealth, worldly honor or wisdom." That is not necessarily wrong unless you make gaining wealth, not wisdom, the main pursuit of your life. According to a survey, the comment children most hear from their fathers is, "I'm too tired." Next is, "We don't have the money," and the third is, "Keep quiet."

If you wish to be successful at anything, it is a good idea to talk to someone who has done it. If they did it successfully, they can tell you what they did right; if they did not, they can tell you what they did wrong. This has been a long-recognized practice in learning a trade or business. To learn a trade, a person becomes an apprentice to a craftsman. One great way to learn a business is to be an assistant to an experienced entrepreneur. The same is true concerning life. Want to know how to live? Ask someone who has done it, meaning, among other things, an older person. The book of Proverbs admonishes us to follow this principle and tells us whom to follow. Of all the people you know, which two would you put at the top of your list to follow through life?

Children resist doing things dad's way. The point is that Dad has been down the road before, so he knows how to advise his children. Suppose a father took a trip several states away to see his son. Later, his son made the trip home to see his folks. The father might say that when you get to Phoenix, if you stay on the freeway, you will go through town, so take the bypass and save time. The father knows because the father has been there.

If you do not have a father, follow the beneficial wisdom of a wise older person who has "been there" and lived life successfully.

A Father's Example

The Positive Command After a brief exhortation, Solomon tells his son about his experience with his own father. He writes, "When I was my father's son, tender and the only one in the sight of my mother" (4:3). Solomon's father began to teach him when he was "tender" (4:3). Until this day, we speak of being "at a tender age." The expression refers to the fact that a child is not yet fully developed and is still moldable. When Solomon says that he was "the only one in the sight of my mother" (4:3), he does not mean that he was an only child because he wasn't (2 Sam. 5:13-16). It is a poetic expression for being well-beloved or perhaps even the most beloved. He was loved as if he were an only child. In other words, Solomon's training and teaching by his father began very early in his life and from his earliest days, he felt loved by his parents.

Solomon's father was, of course, none other than King David, the same David who committed adultery with Bathsheba. As a result of that affair, they had a baby who died after he was born. Notice what Scripture records happened next: "Then David comforted Bathsheba, his wife, and went in to her and lay with her. So, she bore a son, and he called his name Solomon. Now the LORD loved him, and He sent word by the hand of Nathan the prophet: So, he called his name Jedidiah, because of the LORD" (2 Sam. 12:24-25).

Bathsheba would have no doubt loved Solomon simply because he was her son, but the fact that she had just lost a son surely made her love and cling to him even more. The text also says the Lord loved him. It can be argued that the Lord loves everyone, but the Lord doesn't send a prophet to tell all parents that! On top of that, the Lord Himself gave Solomon a special name, Jedidiah, which means "beloved of the Lord." Imagine the love Solomon felt from his mother from the day he was conceived and being told all his childhood that God loved him. Solomon felt loved! All children need to feel that their parents love them and be told all their lives that the Lord loves them.

What Solomon's father taught him is recorded in verses 4 through 9. This section begins with several positive commands (4:4-5a), followed by negative commands (4:5a-6), and ends with conclusions (4:7-9).

The point of the positive commands is to ensure you get wisdom. Solomon says, "He also taught me, and said to me: 'Let your heart retain my words; Keep my commands, and live. Get wisdom! Get understanding!'" (4:4-5a). "He" is a reference to Solomon's father, David. David admonishes his son to get wisdom and assures him that if he does, he will live (3:18, 22; 4:13; 8:34-35). Wisdom is thought of as merchandise, like a diamond of great value. Years after David taught Solomon, Solomon wrote, "Buy the truth, and do not sell it, also wisdom and instruction and understanding" (23:23). Do you have something you have purchased that you would not sell at any price? I have books I have purchased that I would not sell. That should be your attitude toward wisdom.

The Negative Command The positive commands are reinforced by the negative commands, "Do not forget, nor turn away from the words of my mouth. Do not forsake her, and she will preserve you; Love her, and she will keep you" (4:5b-6). As in chapter 1, wisdom is personified as a woman. Here, Solomon is admonished to get wisdom and never forget her or forsake her. As merchandise, wisdom is to be bought and not sold. As a woman, wisdom is married and not divorced. Notice the extreme urgency of the exhortation. The benefits of doing so justify the urgency. The benefits are life (4:4) and preservation (4:6). As we have seen, the preservation is from sin (3:23-26).

The Conclusion "Wisdom is the principal thing; therefore get wisdom. And in all your getting, get understanding. Exalt her, and she will promote you; She will bring you honor, when you embrace her. She will place on your head an ornament of grace; A crown of glory she will deliver to you" (4:7-9). The Hebrew word rendered "principal thing" means "beginning, chief." The grammar of verse 7 indicates that it should be translated "The beginning of wisdom is to get wisdom" (Delitzsch; Kidner). In other words, to obtain wisdom, you must first *want* it. Or, to obtain wisdom, the first thing you must do is *make up your mind* that you want it.

The Hebrew word for beginning here is the same in Proverbs 1:7, which says, "The fear of the Lord is the beginning of knowledge." If you want wisdom, you must deeply desire it and put the Lord foremost in your life.

In his concluding statements, David points out the benefits of wisdom, such as promotion, honor, grace, glory, and deliverance. All of these benefits have been mentioned previously. To be promoted and honored is to be highly esteemed (3:4). Deliverance is deliverance from sin (2:16; 3:23-26; 4:6). Grace has been mentioned several times (1:9; 3:22). As has been pointed out, glory at least includes, and is probably, eternal rewards (3:35). One commentator says that because the Bible speaks of "a crown of glory," it is impossible for the glory here to be anything else than a reference to "the everlasting honors of heaven" (Wardlaw).

So David's advice to his son is get wisdom, buy it and never sell it; embrace her, love her, exalt her and don't ever leave her.

This is bigger than dad. It is bigger than just two people like father and grandfather. It spans generations. This is the kind of wisdom that lasts. The newspaper gives you the latest. The Bible gives you the lasting.

A Father's Explanation

Solomon concludes with an explanation of why his son should get wisdom.

The Way of Wisdom "Hear, my son, and receive my sayings, and the years of your life will be many. I have taught you in the way of wisdom; I have led you in right paths. When you walk, your steps will not be hindered, and when you run, you will not stumble. Take firm hold of instruction, do not let go; keep her, for she is your life" (Prov. 4:10-13). Solomon urges his son to hear, receive, walk, and run in his sayings to follow the way or path of wisdom. In other words, live a wise life. It is not enough to hear or even understand the way of wisdom. The objective is to walk, that is, live a wise life. Solomon also describes the results, such as long life and not stumbling into sin. Some suggest that life here is not only the duration of life but also the enjoyment of life (Delitzsch). Perhaps Proverbs 3:2 implies that, but there is no doubt that Solomon is saying that if you live a wise life, you will live longer. Not being hindered and not stumbling are references to falling into sin.

The Way of the Wicked "Do not enter the path of the wicked, and do not walk in the way of evil. Avoid it, do not travel on it; turn away from it and pass on. For they do not sleep unless they have done evil; and their sleep is taken away unless they make someone fall. For they eat the bread of wickedness, and drink the wine of violence" (4:14-17). Solomon pleads with his son not to enter, walk, or travel the path of the wicked but rather to avoid it and turn away from it. The wicked sleep and eat wickedness; they habitually sin. Not a day goes by that "they do not sleep" unless they have done evil.

Solomon describes the results. To travel the way of the wicked is to end up in violence, hurting and harming others. So, don't go that way and don't travel with those people. If you live with people who live like that, they will influence you. It is easy to emulate evil examples when they are your friends (1 Cor. 15:33).

A Comparison "But the path of the just is like the shining sun, that shines ever brighter unto the perfect day. The way of the wicked is like darkness; they do not know what makes them stumble" (4:18-19). The way of wisdom, called here "the path of the just," is like walking on a cloudless day when the sun is brightest. The "perfect day" is when the sun is at its fullest intensity. Anyone walking under such conditions will see where to walk and will not stumble over anything. On the other hand, to take the way of the wicked is to walk at night when it is so dark you cannot see where you are going. You will stumble and not even know what made you fall (see also Jn.12:35-36).

Summary: Hear and heed the exhortation and example of a wise father and get wisdom because you will benefit with a favored life and eternal reward.

We have more Bible information than ever. There are more than 70 different Study Bibles. We have all this information, and yet many believers are still stupid. We need wisdom to be smart.

Solomon says to gain wisdom is life; elsewhere, he says not to get wisdom is death. Obtaining wisdom is a matter of life and death. Imagine being on a boat that sank. If you were splashing around in the water, terrified that you would drown, the same desire, effort, and intensity you would feel about finding something to grab as a life preserver is the desire, effort, and intensity you should put into getting wisdom. Get, cling to, and don't let wisdom go. It is a matter of life and death.

PROTECT YOURSELF

You need to protect yourself. With crime as widespread as it is today, you must defend yourself physically. So, you lock your car doors. Ladies buy pepper spray, or they carry a cell phone. Some people take self-defense lessons and some even carry guns. You need to protect yourself financially. So, you buy homeowners, car, and life insurance.

Likewise, you need to protect yourself spiritually. Will church attendance protect you from falling into sin? It might help. If you learn and apply what you learn, it will definitely help, but church attendance alone will not protect you. People can go to church and still sin. They are so common that being a hypocrite is proverbial. Will reading your Bible protect you? Again, that might help, but we all have read our Bible and even prayed, and that very day, we did the very thing we decided not to do! What, then, is the answer? It is complex, but a large piece of the puzzle is in Proverbs 4:20-27. This passage gives two basic pieces of advice.

Absorb Wisdom

The Receipt Solomon says, "My son, give attention to my words; incline your ear to my sayings. Do not let them depart from your eyes; keep them in the midst of your heart" (4:20-21). In other words, listen to, look at, and learn wisdom. The Hebrew word for heart means "inner man, mind, emotions, and will. It can refer to one's inclinations, resolutions, appetites, and passions.

Educators talk about learning styles. There are several different theories. One theory says that some students are auditory learners, some are visual learners, and some are kinesthetic learners. There's no such thing as a "good" learning style or a "bad" learning style, a "right" or "wrong" approach to learning. All have their own particular way of learning new information. The important thing is to be aware of your own learning style.

To illustrate, think about how you remember a phone number. In your mind's eye, do you see how the numbers look on the phone? Or can you "see" the number on that piece of paper, picturing it exactly as you wrote it down? If so, you might be a visual learner. Or, perhaps you can "hear" the number in the way that someone recited it to you. In this case, you might be an auditory learner. If you "let your fingers do the walking" on the phone, that is, your fingers dial the number without looking at the phone, you may be a tactile/kinesthetic learner.

This is a somewhat simplistic view of a highly complex subject (the human brain). This way of looking at learning style uses the different channels of perception (seeing, hearing, touching/moving) as its model. Another theory says that some learn visually, some learn verbally, and some learn by reflection. Solomon says we can learn wisdom in several ways, but we need to learn it.

The Reason "For they are life to those who find them, and health to all their flesh" (4:22). The reason ("for") for living a life of wisdom is it will result in health, which Wardlaw defines as "a sound mind in a sound body."

Lord Byron abandoned himself to the pursuit of pleasure. When he was 35, he wrote:

> My days are in the yellow leaf
> The flowers and the fruits of love are gone
> The worm, the canker, and the grief
> Are my alone.

Adam Clarke, who wrote a commentary on the Bible at age 84, wrote, "I have passed through the springtime of my life, I have withstood the heat of its summer, I have culled the fruits of its fall. I am even now enduring the rigors of its winter, but at no great distance, I see the approach of a new eternal springtime. Hallelujah!"

Guard Yourself

As we all have painfully discovered, learning is not enough. So Solomon continues with a second piece of advice. For wisdom to guard you, you must apply wisdom to your heart, mouth, eyes, and feet. This time, he admonishes us to look at ourselves, our hearts, mouths, eyes, and feet.

Heart "Keep your heart with all diligence, for out of it spring the issues of life" (4:23). The Hebrew word rendered "keep" means "watch, guard, protect." The Hebrew word translated "diligence" is another Hebrew word that means "guard, watch." The phrase "the issues of life" means "the source of life." The concept of "heart" includes the mind (23:7), emotions (15:15), will (14:14), and the whole inner being (3:5). It has been called the "workshop" of the individual (Delitzsch). The heart, the inner self, determines the direction one takes. There may be outside influences, but the heart determines the direction. "A wound here is instant death" (Bridges).

When a group of soldiers were told they would be shooting at targets for a prize, they prepared their rifles enthusiastically. One young man showed up with a sparkling clean weapon. He positioned himself and with a steady hand and clear eye, he pulled the trigger, but his bullet swerved to one side and missed the target entirely. He later found that there was rust inside the gun barrel. For days, he had polished the outside but failed to clean his rifle's inside.

Mouth "Put away from you a deceitful mouth, and put perverse lips far from you" (4:24). The Hebrew word rendered "deceitful" means "twisted, perverted, crooked." The one translated "perverse" means "devious, crooked, crafty, cunning." In discussing spiritual growth in Colossians 3, Paul makes a major point about lying. He sets that sin apart, indicating that it is particularly important to put it away if you are to grow spiritually (see Col. 3:9).

Did you hear about the bar named The Office? The owners gave it that name so their customers could tell their wives, "I'm at the office." When people begin to practice deceitful speech, they open themselves to danger and damage. To protect yourself, put away a deceitful mouth.

Eyes "Let your eyes look straight ahead, and your eyelids look right before you" (4:25). The point is to have a "straightforward, unswerving directness toward a fixed goal" (Delitzsch). Keep your eye on the goal. Don't let anything you see distract you from moving toward your objective. Paul's attitude was "this one thing I do" (Phil 3:13). Eve (Gen. 3:3-6), Lot's wife (Gen. 19:17, 26), Achan (Jos. 7:21), and David (2 Sam. 11:2) fell because they did not keep their eyes straight ahead.

Feet "Ponder the path of your feet, and let all your ways be established. Do not turn to the right or the left; Remove your foot from evil" (4:26-27). "Ponder" means "weigh, make level, smooth." If the thought here is to make level, the meaning is to remove what is dangerous and hinders (Delitzsch). However, the translation "level" does not fit the other occurrences of this Hebrew word elsewhere in the book (Kidner). The idea here is to "weigh." Again, Solomon cautions against getting sidetracked. The writer to the Hebrews speaks of "the sin which so easily ensnares us" (Heb. 12:1). If we are to protect ourselves spiritually, we must know our weaknesses and ponder our path accordingly.

A convict told a chaplain, "All my troubles resulted from going to bars. Every time I entered a bar, I got into a fight and ended up in jail." The chaplain asked, "What do you mean every time?" The prisoner didn't get the point. So, the chaplain said, "I don't understand why you kept going. Did anyone force you to go into those bars?" The light dawned when the prisoner realized he went to bars under my own power.

Several artists were asked to illustrate their concept of temptation. One depicted man's attempt to achieve fame and fortune at any cost. Another picture shows a man's struggle against the desires of the flesh. The prize-winning canvas portrayed a pastoral scene in which a man was walking along a quiet country lane among shade trees and lovely wildflowers. In the distance, the way was divided into two roads, one leading to the right and the other leading to the left. The problem with temptation is that it is subtle. It appears as an innocent-looking fork in the road.

Summary: To protect yourself, absorb wisdom and guard your heart to ensure you follow it.

This passage mentions not speaking deceitfully, keeping your eye on the goal, and carefully considering what you do, but the issue is the heart. The issue is not your mouth, your eyes, or your feet. The issue is your heart. "Out of the abundance of the heart the mouth speaks" (Mt. 12:35). Keeping your eye on the goal is not a function of the eye but a function of the brain. Solomon says, "ponder" what you do. The issue is the heart.

The issue is not your circumstances; it's your heart. It's not others; it's you! Someone has said if you put a piece of wax, a piece of meat, some sand, some clay, and some shavings in a fire, the wax would melt, the meat would fry, the sand would dry up, the clay would harden, and the shavings would burst into flames. The issue is not the external circumstances. These materials were under the influence of identical circumstances, but they responded differently according to their inner composition. Under the same circumstances, some melt like wax, and others harden like clay.

So guard your heart. Keep it warm toward the Lord and others you love, such as your mate. Before the development of thermostatically controlled heat, greenhouses were equipped with a frost-bell, an electronic device connected to a thermostat that would warn the farmer when the mercury fell to the danger point. When the bell went off, the farmer would know to light the fires to save his crop. Believers need a frost-bell to determine when their hearts are getting cold spiritually.

WISE SEX

In the 1960s, America experienced a sexual revolution. Americans began to have free sex. Then, in the 1980s, HIV began to spread. To prevent the spread of AIDS in a free-sex society, safe sex began to be promoted. I would like to suggest that it is not free sex or safe sex but wise sex that we need. What is wise sex? The answer is in the wisdom book of the Bible, the book of Proverbs. More specifically, it is in Proverbs 5:1-23.

You may not think this message applies to you, but although the subject of this passage is sex, it is also the advice of a father to a son. So, as you think about this passage, imagine how you would use the principles here in talking to others about sex and other issues as well.

Distance Yourself from the Immoral Woman

This seamless passage consists of two parts. In the first sub-section, Solomon tells his son to distance himself from the immoral woman. The Hebrew word rendered "removed" in verse 8 means "be distant, put far away."

Listen to Wisdom Solomon begins with another appeal for his son to lend a willing ear to wisdom. "My son, pay attention to my wisdom; lend your ear to my understanding, that you may preserve discretion, and your lips may keep knowledge" (5:1-2). Solomon has pleaded for his son to lend a willing ear to wisdom before, but this time he adds specific reasons why his son should do that.

For one thing, it will "preserve discretion." The Hebrew word rendered "discretion" means "purpose, discretion, device." It is the capacity to comprehend the right purpose, the ability to make the right plans (see 1:4). Listening to wisdom will keep you on the right purpose and on the right plan. Wisdom is a moral compass. Follow it and you will go in the right direction.

For another thing, by listening to wisdom, "your lips may keep knowledge." In other words, if you listen to wisdom, you are only going to speak what is in keeping with knowledge, that is, wisdom. Lips that keep knowledge will let nothing unwise come out of them. The psalmist said, "I have purposed that my mouth shall not transgress" (Ps. 17:3). In Proverbs 5, such a practice would protect a person from an immoral woman (Delitzsch; Kidner). Wisdom protects you from saying things that will lead you to immorality.

Immorality May Sound Sweet, but in the end, it is Bitter

Solomon further explains ("for"), "For the lips of an immoral woman drip honey, and her mouth is smoother than oil; but in the end she is bitter as wormwood, Sharp as a two-edged sword. Her feet go down to death, her steps lay hold of hell. Lest you ponder her path of life; her ways are unstable; you do not know them" (5:3-6). For an explanation of the words for immoral woman, see the discussion on Proverbs 2:16.

The Beginning The words of immoral women are sweet and smooth. The Hebrew word for honey refers to honey flowing from the comb, the so-called virgin honey. Thus, it is the purest and sweetest honey. Oil, of course, is itself smooth and makes surfaces smooth. Beware! This is a case where you should not judge a book by its cover, nor should you judge a relationship by it first stages.

The End The end of the experience of an immoral woman is not sweet. It is as bitter as wormwood. Wormwood is a shrub with a very bitter taste. It is the height of bitterness. A two-edged sword cuts not just once but twice at the same time. An immoral woman may sound sweet, but the end is bitter as the bitterest and the cutting as that which cuts the most.

As Solomon says, this path is unstable and leads to death and hell. The Hebrew word for "hell" is Sheol, and it actually means "the grave." It is virtually synonymous with death. "Death," especially in Proverbs, is not just a physical and single event. It is that which is less than life at its fullest. So this idea may look like a good one, but if you go down this unstable path, you do not know what you are doing (5:6).

Solomon learned this lesson the hard way. His father committed adultery. Solomon himself had 700 wives and 300 concubines. So, Solomon is speaking from his own bitter experience.

A teenager once gave me a piece of candy as a joke. When I first put it in my mouth, it was hard but very sweet. So, I continued to suck on it. As the ball of candy got smaller, I discovered that the core was very bitter. Solomon is saying that the experience of immorality may sound sweet initially, but in the end, it is bitter.

Foolishness focuses on the beginning. Wisdom weighs the end. By the way, note that the way to teach a son the dangers of evil is to point to its consequences.

The Conclusion Solomon concludes, "Therefore hear me now, my children, and do not depart from the words of my mouth. Remove your way far from her, and do not go near the door of her house" (5:7-8). The point is obvious. Listen to wisdom; distance yourself from the immoral woman. Do not even go near the door of her house. If necessary, break off with friends. Change jobs. Move.

In order to reinforce this conclusion, Solomon gives a list of consequences of immorality: "Lest you give your honor to others, and your years to the cruel one; lest aliens be filled with your wealth, and your labors go to the house of a foreigner; and you mourn at last, when your flesh and your body are consumed, and say: 'How I have hated instruction, and my heart despised correction! I have not obeyed the voice of my teachers, nor inclined my ear to those who instructed me! I was on the verge of total ruin, in the midst of the assembly and congregation'" (5:9-14). Immorality will result in a loss of honor (5:9). Think of televangelists Jim Bakker and Jimmy Swaggart. It will result in years with a cruel one (5:9). Cruel ones are those who do not rest until their victim is ruined both bodily and financially (Delitzsch). It has been suggested that this implies possibly to a blackmailer (Kidner) or to a mocker of your misery (Bridges). It will result in a loss of wealth (5:10). I know a man who had to file for bankruptcy because of his affair with a woman. It will result in a loss of health (5:11). Just think of sexually transmitted diseases, including AIDS. It will result in a loss of peace of mind because of guilt (5:12-13) and shame (5:14). When body and soul are ruined, you will suffer self-condemnation, being condemned by your conscience. You will experience the anguish of heart, reminding yourself that you should have listened to wisdom and that you are on the verge of total ruin (5:14), which is probably a reference to the criminal punishment of adultery by stoning (see Deut. 22:22).

Not all of these results happen in every case of immorality. This passage is in the book of Proverbs, which are proverbial maxims, general truths that technically could have an exception. Nevertheless, the conclusion is clear. As Paul told Timothy, "Flee also youthful lust" (2 Tim. 2:22), or as he told the Corinthians, "Flee sexual immorality" (1 Cor. 6:18).

Years ago, I was the pastor of a church in downtown Los Angeles. One day, from my fourth-floor window, I saw a man speak to a crowd gathered during lunch. He wanted to be President of the United States and was campaigning in LA. His name was Gary Hart. He did not make it to the Presidency. He did not make it to his party's nomination. He was caught on film with a young lady on a yacht. Because of his affair, he lost honor, respect, and, no doubt, wealth. It gained him cruel treatment from others, guilt, and shame. Wise sex is distancing yourself from immorality.

Delight Yourself in Your Wife

In the second sub-section of the two-part passage, Solomon tells his son to delight in his own wife.

The Exhortation Turning his attention to his son's wife, Solomon says, "Drink water from your own cistern, and running water from your own well. Should your fountains be dispersed abroad, Streams of water in the streets? Let them be only your own, And not for strangers with you. Let your fountain be blessed, and rejoice with the wife of your youth. As a loving deer and a graceful doe, let her breasts satisfy you at all times; And always be enraptured with her love" (5:15-19). Comparing a wife to a cistern does not sound very flattering. That is not the point. In the ancient Middle East, a cistern was one of a person's most valuable possessions. A well was a prized possession. Drinking water is used here as a figure of the satisfaction of marital love.

The New King James translation makes verse 16 a question. It is better with the King James to render it as a statement. The point is that sexual relationships in marriage should be free and unrestrained (Delitzsch). The blessing of verse 18 is probably a reference to children. The deer and doe were thought of as being strikingly beautiful. The Hebrew word rendered "rejoice" means "rejoice, get pleasure from, be glad. The word translated "satisfied" means "drink to one's fill, saturated, intoxicated, drunk" and "enraptured" also refers to being intoxicated. Be wholly captivated by her so that you can no longer restrain yourself. Find contentment with your wife. Domestic contentment is the best defense against the desires of unlawful passion. You will be tempted to seek it elsewhere if there is no contentment at home.

Someone told me a cute joke that began with three couples who applied for membership in a church. They were told that in order to qualify, they had to abstain from sex for two weeks. Unfortunately, Christians have gotten the reputation of being against or down on sex. Nothing could be further from the truth. This passage demonstrates that.

The Explanation Solomon explains ("for"). "For why should you, my son, be enraptured by an immoral woman, and be embraced in the arms of a seductress? For the ways of man are before the eyes of the LORD, and He ponders all his paths. His own iniquities entrap the wicked man, and he is caught in the cords of his sin. He shall die for lack of instruction, and in the greatness of his folly he shall go astray" (5:20-23). One of the reasons men commit immorality is they think that it is done in secrecy, but there is an eye from which nothing is concealed. And they think no one will ever know. Practical atheism is the route to ruin. To a believer who knows the Lord and wants to please Him, the reminder of an all-seeing God is the ultimate safeguard. If that will not do it, remember the trouble you will bring on yourself.

Summary: Since failing to listen to wisdom and getting involved in immorality brings devastating consequences, rejoice with your wife and remember that the Lord sees everything you do. To say the same thing another way, to avoid destruction and death, distance yourself from immoral women and delight in your wife. In short, wise sex is to distance yourself from immorality and delight yourself in your wife.

Free sex is not free. There are consequences. Safe sex is not safe. No method is 100% guaranteed to work every time. Wise sex is designed to be intoxicating!

God, who designed sex, says it belongs in marriage. Put it where it was designed to be, and it will be free and safe. Put it outside of where God intended it to be and there will be damage, destruction, and death.

A bird is free in the air. Place a bird under water and the bird loses its freedom and experiences devastating consequences, even death. A fish is free in the water. Put a fish on the sand and it will lose its freedom and perish. God says the place for sex is marriage. Outside of marriage, sex is not free. It is costly with devastating consequences. Real, free, safe, wise sex is in marriage.

SHOULD YOU CO-SIGN FOR A LOAN?

Suppose you knew two men who had been friends for years. Let's call them Joe and Jim. They are genuine friends. They go hunting and fishing together. They watch ball games together. Imagine that one day, Jim says to Joe, "I need to borrow $10,000. Would you co-sign a note for me?"

What do you think Joe would say? He might say "Yes" on the spot. After all, they had been friends for years. How could he not say yes to his friend? On the other hand, Joe might say, "I have to talk to my wife first." Let's suppose that Sally, Joe's wife, is a believer but not a Southern Baptist, that group of Baptists who passed a resolution that wives should "graciously submit" to their loving husbands. She is skeptical and hesitant. In short, she does not want to do it. She remembers reading something in Proverbs that says you should never be a co-signer for a loan. Joe responds, "Well, if you are going to quote the Bible, let's remember that God wants us to be generous." Joe wants to do this and Sally does not. So they decide to go see a Pastor.

The Pastor they go see says, "I agree with Joe. You should be generous. Do it." When they leave the Pastor's office, Sally says, "That Pastor did not show us any Scripture. I want to talk to a Pastor who knows the Bible. I want a second opinion." They then go see By-the-Book Pastor. He says, "No one has ever asked me that question before, but the other day, I was reading Proverbs and Sally is right. Proverbs says, "Don't ever co-sign for a loan.""

Is the first Pastor right? Or is By-the-Book Pastor correct? If you think Pastor By-the-Book is correct, where does the Bible say that? Where does Proverbs say that?

Have you ever been asked to co-sign for a loan? If you have ever done that, did it work out satisfactorily? This hypothetical story brings up the issue of co-signing for a loan and some issues of money and friendship. Has a friend of yours ever asked to borrow money? What did you do? What does Proverbs say? Does Proverbs say that we should never co-sign for a loan? What does the Bible say about lending money to a friend? For the answer, look at Proverbs 6:1-5.

Co-signing is a Trap

There are passages in Proverbs that warn against co-signing for a loan. The first and most extensive is Proverbs 6, but there are others.

Proverbs 6 "My son, if you become surety for your friend, if you have shaken hands in pledge for a stranger, you are snared by the words of your mouth; you are taken by the words of your mouth" (6:1-2). Being surety is being a co-signer, that is, one responsible for a debt should the borrower default. The Hebrew word for "friend" has many meanings, from a close friend to a neighbor. The context determines which meaning is intended. It is "colored by context" (Kidner). Here, it just means anyone. To shake hands is to confirm a contract with a handshake. The second line of verse 1, "If you have shaken hands in pledge for a stranger," is either parallel to the first line and means virtually the same thing, namely, "If you have co-signed for anyone" (the stranger is the borrower), or stranger refers to the lender. (The KJV says "with a stranger;" this would be co-signing "to" a stranger for a friend; see Wardlaw.)

Solomon says if you co-sign for a loan, you have been snared by your own words. Co-signing is a snare. The Hebrew word for "snared" pictures being trapped by bait and the one for "taken" means "captured." If you co-sign for a loan, you are in a trap. You have been trapped like an animal. You have made your own possessions and possibly your freedom dependent on someone else paying his or her debts. You could be putting stress on your family and damaging your credit.

There is an old joke about three guys who died in an accident and went to hell. As the story goes, Satan told them that he didn't have enough room and he offered to let them buy their way out (this is a joke; no one can do that; see Acts 8:20). The first fellow, who was known for writing bad checks, wrote a bad check for $10,000 and left. Later, someone asked him what happened to the two others. He said, "I don't know, but when I left, one had negotiated him down to $8000 and the other was looking for a co-signer." The point is some people are looking for a co-signer. It's that person about whom Solomon is warning us.

Solomon continues, "So do this, my son, and deliver yourself; for you have come into the hand of your friend: Go and humble yourself; plead with your friend. Give no sleep to your eyes, nor slumber to your eyelids. Deliver yourself like a gazelle from the hand of the hunter, and like a bird from the hand of the fowler" (6:3-5). Since surety is a snare, do everything possible to withdraw as quickly as possible. The words used to describe what you should do are vivid. "Humble" means "to stamp, tread." It is used to describe throwing oneself to the ground in a stamping manner, that is, violently to trample upon oneself or let oneself be trampled upon. In other words, place oneself in an attitude of a most humble position (Delitzsch). "Plead" means "to act stormily, boisterously." Furthermore, this should be done immediately (don't go to sleep until it is done) and with all that is within you like a trapped animal, use your strength and skill to disentangle yourself from the snare.

Other Passages Other passages in Proverbs echo this warning. Proverbs 11:15 says, "He who is surety for a stranger will suffer, but one who hates being surety is secure." The Hebrew word for "suffer" means "evil, distress, misery, injury, harm, calamity." Proverbs 17:18 states, "A man devoid of understanding shakes hands in a pledge and becomes surety for his friend." Proverbs 22:26 warns, "Do not be one of those who shakes hands in a pledge, one of those who is surety for debts."

A young man decided to get married and buy a mobile home. He could not qualify for the loan without a co-signer, so he saw an elderly lady who agreed to help this young couple get started. Well, the wife ran off with another man and her husband could not stand the memories of their home together, so he ran off by joining the army. The lender, of course, came after the co-signer. She said, go see the young man. He said, "I don't want anything to do with that place." Now, the creditors are hounding the elderly lady. Co-signing can get you in a mess.

So, does that mean that you should never co-sign for a loan?

Co-signing Needs Collateral

There are also passages in Proverbs that seem to be saying that it is all right to co-sign for a loan.

Passages Proverbs 11:15 says, "He who is surety for a stranger will suffer, but one who hates being surety is secure," but the next verse says, "A gracious woman retains honor, but ruthless men retain riches" (11:16). In other words, co-signing for a loan might make you suffer, but be generous.

Proverbs 17:18 says, "A man devoid of understanding shakes hands in a pledge, and becomes surety for his friend," but the verse before it says, "A friend loves at all times, and a brother is born for adversity" (17:17). Again, the point is practice love. Be generous. Help a friend in need, but to co-sign for a loan is not wise.

Proverbs 20:16 says, "Take the garment of one who is surety for a stranger, and hold it as a pledge when it is for a seductress." The Hebrew words translated "stranger" and "seductress" (they both are the same Hebrew word) mean "foreigner." In Proverbs, it is sometimes a technical word for prostitute, perhaps because prostitutes were originally chiefly foreigners. The person referred to here is either a foreigner or a prostitute, maybe even a mistress (Delitzsch). If you co-sign for a loan, make sure you get collateral. It is foolish to co-sign for a loan without a pledge, that is, a promise of repayment. (Exodus forbids doing this to a fellow Israelite.) Don't loan money without security. Proverbs 27:13 repeats this: "Take the garment of him who is surety for a stranger, and hold it in pledge when he is surety for a seductress." As in Proverbs 20:16, the Hebrew words translated "stranger" and "seductress" (they both are the same Hebrew word) mean "foreigner."

Proverbs 22:26-27 says, "Do not be one of those who shakes hands in a pledge, One of those who is surety for debts. If you have nothing with which to pay, why should he take away your bed from under you?" He refers to the creditor (Delitzsch). If you can't repay the loan, don't co-sign for it. You may lose your bed!

Conclusion Well, what is the solution? Is co-signing permitted, or is it not? As you can imagine, there are different opinions. One view says the prohibition is general. It is proverbial. It is not to be taken as an unqualified prohibition to which no exceptions exist (Wardlaw). Another opinion is that the warning is against rash decisions to which the young and inexperienced are exposed (Bridges). Perhaps the warnings are against the backdrop of the fact that in Solomon's day, a co-signer who could not pay could lose all he had and be reduced to slavery. A co-signer could lose his or her independence.

Those who allow exceptions say to do this only if you are willing and able to pay the loan yourself. In fact, the famous commentator Matthew Henry cautioned not to be bound for more than you knew you could pay or for more than you would be willing to pay if the borrower failed.

So, how does all this apply today?

Be Generous, but Be Guarded

To get a complete picture of what the Bible says about this and related subjects concerning money and your friends, you must consider several passages in and outside Proverbs.

Lend Compassionately Exodus 22:25-27 says, "If you lend money to any of My people who are poor among you, you shall not be like a moneylender to him; you shall not charge him interest. If you ever take your neighbor's garment as a pledge, you shall return it to him before the sun goes down. For that is his only covering, it is his garment for his skin. What will he sleep in? And it will be that when he cries to Me, I will hear, for I am gracious." In other words, lend money to the poor (and all fellow Israelites, Deut. 23:20) without interest. Do not take any goods needed for survival as collateral.

On the other hand, Deut. 23:20 says, "To a foreigner, you may charge interest, but to your brother, you shall not charge interest, that the LORD your God may bless you in all to which you set your hand in the land which you are entering to possess." As a business transaction, you can charge interest, but not to a brother. Amos pronounced judgment on Israelites who loaned money to their fellow Israelites, charged interest, and foreclosed. Amos 2:8 says, "They lie down by every altar on clothes taken in pledge, and drink the wine of the condemned in the house of their god." The picture is of a ruthless foreclosure because of debts. So, the Mosaic Law taught that you could lend money but should be generous. When you loan money to a brother, do not charge interest.

Bob Hope, the famous comedian, said, "If you haven't got any charity in your heart, you have the worst kind of heart trouble."

Co-sign Cautiously Proverbs sanctions co-signing (see 20:16; 27:13). It also warns against it (6:1-5; 11:15; 22:26-27). The conclusion is co-sign cautiously. Make sure you can repay the loan if you have to. get collateral.

I know of a financial planner who advises his clients to consider it a gift if they lend money or co-sign for a loan. If you can afford that gift, do it. If not, don't.

Frankly, I'm glad that co-signing is permitted. When I was young, someone co-signed for me to buy a car. It is how I got started. I do not know what I would have done had someone not done that for me.

Give Generously Proverbs recognizes the wisdom of giving generously. "The generous soul will be made rich, and he who waters will also be watered himself" (11: 25). "He who has pity on the poor lends to the LORD, and He will pay back what he has given" (19: 17). "He who has a generous eye will be blessed, For he gives of his bread to the poor" (22:9). "He who gives to the poor will not lack, But he who hides his eyes will have many curses" (28:27). "The righteous considers the cause of the poor, But the wicked does not understand such knowledge" (29:7).

Jesus taught that it was all right to loan money, but He, too, wants us to be generous. Luke 6:34-35 records what He said on the subject, "And if you lend to those from whom you hope to receive back, what credit is that to you? For even sinners lend to sinners to receive as much back. But love your enemies, do good, and lend, hoping for nothing in return; your reward will be great, and you will be sons of the Most High. For He is kind to the unthankful and evil." Losses suffered will be rewarded a hundredfold, that is, 10,000 percent (Mt. 19:28-29).

Be generous. Proverbs would say, "Start with the Lord." "Honor the LORD with your possessions, and with the first fruits of all your increase; so, your barns will be filled with plenty, and your vats will overflow with new wine. (3:9-10).

The nineteenth-century French author Victor Hugo wrote, "As the purse is emptied, the heart is filled." Be generous and have a happy heart.

Summary: Be generous, but when it comes to co-signing for a loan or lending money, be guarded, that is, do not do it without security or if it will put you or your family in danger financially.

God is generous and He wants us to be generous. In a sense, God co-signed for us. (Job was too bad a risk for anyone but God; Job 17:3; see also Ps. 119:122.)

You should give money to the Lord and others. Loan money, in some cases, without interest. That is part of being gracious and generous.

God is wise and He wants us to be wise. Loan money and make sure you get collateral. In some cases, you should not loan money at all. If you can't afford to lose the amount you are co-signing for, do not do it.

LEARN ABOUT LAZINESS

My assignment today is rather difficult. I have been teaching through Proverbs and I have come to a passage that describes a person for whom I have a message. My problem is that I know before I begin that I will have an extremely difficult time finding the person for whom this message is intended. It is not because this is a small congregation. If I were speaking to an audience of several thousand, I suspect that no one present would feel the message was for him or her. In fact, I imagine that if I were on national TV with millions watching, very few would think the message was meant for them. Today's message is on laziness and it is how hard to find someone who will admit to the problem.

So let me suggest that we can all learn from this type of person. Do you know someone who is lazy? What is that person like? What would it take to solve that person's problem? Has anyone ever told you that you are lazy, perhaps when you were young? Have you ever thought to yourself, "I'm lazy?" What exactly are the characteristics of a lazy person? A look at all the proverbs on this subject will answer that and other questions about laziness. For our lesson on laziness, let's begin with Proverbs 6:6-11.

Characteristics of Laziness

In Proverbs 6:6, Solomon addresses the sluggard. It has been suggested that the connection between the previous passage and this one is that this is another way poverty may be induced (Wardlaw). The Hebrew word translated "sluggard" means "lazy, sluggish." The noun, the verb, and the adjective form of this Hebrew word for laziness occur eighteen times in the Old Testament (sixteen of these are in Proverbs) and they are translated "sloth" and "idle." As we shall see from Proverbs, the lazy person resists work or exertion, is disposed to idleness, and moves very slowly. The old song speaks of a lazy river, which slowly moves down by the old millstream. Proverbs 6 and other passages in the book provide the characteristics of a lazy person.

They Do Not Start Things The first characteristic of lazy people is that they do not start things. Solomon asks, "How long will you slumber, O sluggard? When will you rise from your sleep?" (6:9). Apparently, the answer to those questions is in the next verse, "A little sleep, a little slumber, a little folding of the hands to sleep" (6:10). Some suggest that verse 10 is the sluggard's answer to the questions of verse 9 (Delitzsch; Bridges). "The folding of the hands," that is, to cross them over the chest or put them into the bosom, denotes the idler (Delitzsch). A person can have busy hands doing work, wringing hands with worry, or folded hands waiting to fall asleep. Elsewhere, Solomon wrote, "The fool folds his hands," meaning that he is idle (Eccl. 4:5). If confronted with their laziness, they plead for a little more sleep. Notice the sluggard in this passage says, "a little … a little … a little." They want to do as little as possible. Their only concern is present comfort. The future is of no concern.

A soldier entered his barracks and shouted, "I'll give ten dollars to the laziest man here!" Nearly everyone scrambled to his feet and rushed to tell him how lazy he was. One recruit, who did not move from his bed, said, "Gracious. Just roll me over and slip it in my back pocket."

Later, Proverbs says, "A lazy man buries his hand in the bowl, and will not so much as bring it to his mouth again" (19:24). Proverbs 26:15 repeats this almost exactly. Kidner calls this "comically extreme." Lazy people would rather sleep than eat. Eating is work. So they sleep when they eat. They are so lazy that they do not do even necessary things for themselves. They would rather suffer the cravings of hunger than make the effort of putting food in their mouth. The slightest exertion, however necessary, is an "insufferable annoyance" (Wardlaw).

Lazy people are not going to do anything. Some people are workaholics; they burn out. Others are work-allergic; they rust out. Some love work. Others loathe it.

They are certainly not going to start anything. I once heard someone say to a person, "Are you working hard?" The reply was, "I'm working hard to keep from working." That is the characteristic of a lazy person.

They Do Not Finish Things If lazy people ever manage to begin something, they do not finish it. Solomon put it like this, "The lazy man does not roast what he took in hunting, but diligence is man's precious possession" (12:27). Technically, the Hebrew word for "lazy" here is different than the word used most often in Proverbs. This one basically means "deceitful," but it also means "laxness, slackness" and is translated "slothful" and "idle" in Proverbs. Both Hebrew words are used of the lazy people in the same verse (see 19:15). Lazy people hunt, catch prey, and bring it home. Then they do not prepare it for a meal. All that labor was wasted. So was the food. From sheer laziness, it becomes useless.

Lazy people do not finish what they start. They sometimes have a burst of energy. They may even have a successful effort. Then, they relapse into their former state. I know of a man who took a week off work to paint his house. He only worked a few hours each day and was not done at the end of the week. Twenty years later, it was still not finished.

They Rationalize Their Laziness You would think that they would get the point. After all, nothing gets done. It is so bad that others ask about when they will get busy, but they do not get the point. They make excuses. For example, "The way of the lazy man is like a hedge of thorns, but the way of the upright is a highway" (15:19). To the lazy, the future is like a field with a fence around it that contains thorns. Their perception paralyzes them. They see hindrances and difficulties everywhere. They fancy innumerable obstacles, anything as a reason for sitting still. Every effort is like forcing through a hedge of thorns where thorns tear at the flesh. The hedge is not only annoying; it is impenetrable. However, the difficulty is in their minds and hearts, not their path. Lazy people are not contrasted with the diligent but with the upright. The contrast between them indicates that the sluggard is not upright. Kidner says there is an "element of dishonesty in laziness" in that lazy people try to sidestep their share of the load. Jesus spoke of a "wicked and lazy servant" (Mt. 25:26). The straight course is the easiest.

Take another excuse: "The lazy man will not plow because of winter; He will beg during harvest and have nothing" (20:4). "Because of" is literally "from." Kidner points out that it can be used causally ("by reason of") or temporally ("from"). The former (KJV; NKJV; Kidner; Wardlaw) has the lazy person using the cold weather as an excuse. The latter rendering (Delitzsch) makes it simple procrastination, that is, from the beginning of winter. The former view is probably the correct one. In Israel, the farmer waited for the "early rain" in October or November to begin plowing and planting for the winter crop. The sluggard uses the weather as an excuse and does not bring in a harvest.

The excuses get more absurd: "The lazy man says, 'There is a lion outside! I shall be slain in the streets!'" (22:13). Luther translated this "I might be murdered on the streets." Lions do not frequent streets. They roam the forest. Lazy people imagine difficulties and dangers that are not there. They invent excuses for avoiding work and risk. They will do anything to avoid anything. Any excuse will do: any "fancy of danger", any "pretense of fear" (Wardlaw). Life is difficult enough without having "imaginary difficulties" (Bridges). How many imaginary lions are on your mental streets?

In describing her lazy husband to me, a lady said she left the house early one morning, knowing that her husband had a list of repairs to do around the house. When she returned in the early afternoon, he was watching TV on the sofa. He said when she entered the room, "I plugged the electric screwdriver in and I'm waiting for it to charge."

The Consequences of Laziness

Poverty There are consequences to laziness. The book of Proverbs lists a number of them. First, there is poverty. Solomon warns, "So shall your poverty come on you like a prowler, and your need like an armed man" (6:11). "Prowler" comes from the Hebrew word for "walk" and here means "highwayman." "Armed man" comes from the Hebrew word for "shield" and means "warrior." Here it probably means armed man in the sense of a robber. In other words, the coming of poverty and need will be unforeseen, a surprise that catches the sluggard without defense.

This result of laziness is echoed elsewhere in Proverbs. "The soul of a lazy man desires, and has nothing, but the soul of the diligent shall be made rich" (13:4). Lazy people have a desire, but as an old maxim says, "If wishes were horses, every man would ride." The problem is that they have desire without diligence. Consequently, they have nothing. One of the maxims of Proverbs is "nothing without labor." The lazy long for gain without pain. They want wealth without work. They fancy being a scholar without studying. They dream of the crown but are not willing to carry the cross. To expect the reward without the race is a delusion. In Proverbs 13:4, the Hebrew word translated "rich' is literally "fat." It is used here figuratively of prosperity (BDB) or possibly being "abundantly satisfied" (Ryrie). The lazy have nothing; the diligent prosper.

Proverbs 20:4 says, "The lazy man will not plow because of winter; He will beg during harvest and have nothing." At first glance, it appears that this verse is saying that lazy people do not work and, as a result, they have nothing, so they beg. The verse, however, does not say they have nothing and beg. It says they beg and have nothing. They will have nothing, even when they beg. It was said of the prodigal son in the parable Jesus told that "no one gave him anything" (Lk. 15:16). Because of their laziness, no one has compassion for lazy people.

Proverbs 10:4, which uses a Hebrew word for laziness that basically means deceitful, says, "He who has a slack (deceitful, margin) hand becomes poor, but the hand of the diligent makes rich." Ryrie takes slack as "negligent, idle." The lazy are deceitful. They pretend to work when, in truth, they are doing nothing. Laziness leads to poverty. While it is spiritually dangerous to set one's heart on wealth as the chief pursuit, diligence still leads to riches.

Hunger Secondly, there is hunger. It is not that lazy people end up with nothing. They end up hungry. Proverbs 19:15 says, "Laziness casts one into a deep sleep, and an idle person will suffer hunger." The Hebrew word translated "laziness' is the adjective form of the word for sluggard, which basically means deceitful and it only appears here and in Ecclesiastes 10:18. The lazy grow in laziness. They sit. They sleep. They fall into a deep sleep. This has been called "the creeping spread of laziness." It is not static like its victims (Kidner). The idle suffer hunger. Proverbs call for compassion on the poor and weak (19:17) but only contempt for the lazy.

Servitude Then there is servitude. Proverbs 12:24 says, "The hand of the diligent will rule, but the lazy man will be put to forced labor." The Hebrew word rendered "lazy" is the one that basically means deception and the Hebrew word translated "forced labor" means just that, "forced service." It was used for conquered people subject to forced labor (see Judges 1:30; Isa. 31:8). It signifies "service rendered to a master" (Delitzsch). Slothfulness results in servitude. The diligent will rise to a position of authority, but the lazy will be under authority. The diligent will rule. The lazy will be ruled.

Lazy people also irritate their bosses. Proverbs 10:26 says, "As vinegar to the teeth and smoke to the eyes, So is the lazy man to those who send him." Lazy people irritate those who are over them. If you send people to do something, you expect them to do it. When they listlessly linger and trifle away the time, you get irritated, disappointed, impatient, fretful, and even angry. Those kinds of servants (employees) are bitter and painful.

Death Finally, there is death. Proverbs 21:25-26 says, "The desire of the lazy man kills him, For his hands refuse to labor. He covets greedily all day long, But the righteous gives and does not spare." The desire of the lazy is the desire not to work and just do nothing. Their desire is for rest, enjoyment, and pleasure. Lazy people obtain nothing because they refuse to work. Furthermore, as this verse points out, it is worse than not obtaining something; the refusal to work is so bad that it leads to death. Their desire destroys them. People who will not help themselves commit suicide. "The fool folds his hands And consumes his own flesh" (Eccl. 4:5). Lazy people also have other desires. They desire things. In fact, as verse 26 points out, they are covetous of what others have. Verse 26 contracts the lazy person's insatiable greed with the righteous's generosity. The sluggard lives in a "world of wishing," which is a substitute for work (Kidner). It destroys him materially (verse 25) and enslaves him spiritually (verse 26). He has "insatiable desires," but he lives "by wishing" (Bridges). The goal is not out of sight, just out of reach for lack of labor. Sir Thomas More prayed, "Lord, make me to bestow pains in getting those things, for the obtaining of which I am used to pray unto thee." Lazy people desire, resolve, yawn and do nothing. The contrast in verse 26 between the lazy and the righteous indicates that the righteous 1) work hard, 2) have an abundance, and 3) gladly give.

Proverbs 18:9 adds, "He who is slothful in his work is a brother to him who is a great destroyer." The Hebrew word rendered "slothful" is a third word in Proverbs for lazy people. It comes from the Hebrew word for "sink, relax." The slothful person is the slack one. Delitzsch says it means "to show one's self slack, lazy, negligent." The Hebrew word translated "destroyer" means "ruin, destruction." (Wardlaw renders it "waster.") The word rendered "business" means "occupation, work, business." Delitzsch says "business" is actually a commission for another, as a king has a messenger, ambassador, or commissioner, but here, it refers to any business, whether for another or oneself. One can be slack in business or diligent in business. To be relaxed long enough is to destroy. A house that is not maintained will eventually be destroyed. Lazy people destroy themselves and the things around them.

Cure for Laziness

If laziness ends in death, is there no cure? As we have seen, pain, which usually causes most to change, does not work. The lazy suffer hunger (19:15). Shame will not do it. They beg (20:4). There is not much chance that lazy people will change as long as they make excuses. Solomon says, "Do you see a man wise in his own eyes? There is more hope for a fool than for him. The lazy man says, 'There is a lion in the road! A fierce lion is in the streets!' As a door turns on its hinges, So does the lazy man on his bed. The lazy man buries his hand in the bowl; It wearies him to bring it back to his mouth. The lazy man is wiser in his own eyes Than seven men who can answer sensibly" (26:12-16). Those who are wise in their own eyes think they have the right answer and, therefore, see no need for additional information. The delusion of the self-conceited is that there is no need for change. They hold themselves fit to be the standard (Bridges). They think they are wise because they do not know what it is to be wise.

Moreover, the false persuasion that they have gained wisdom precludes them from gaining it. They have to unlearn what they think they know before learning true wisdom. Those who possess high regard of their superior wisdom will listen to nothing. They are so trapped in their own self-sufficiency that no advice, correction, or reproof will reach them. There is more hope for fools who are aware that they lack something. Lazy people are an example of those who are wise in their own eyes. They say they see lions in the streets (see 22:13). "Street" is "a broad open place, a plaza or square."

As was pointed out in Proverbs 22:13, lions roam the forest, not the streets. Lazy people imagine difficulties and dangers that are not there. They turn on their bed like a door on a hinge. A door turns on its hinges without going beyond the narrow space of its motion. So lazy people are attached (glued) to their bed, turn in it, but never get beyond it. Like a door on hinges, lazy people move but make no progress. They work all right; they work from one excuse to another. Like a hinged door where they were a year ago, they are today. In their view, they are not lazy; they are just not their best in the morning (26:14). They just do not have the energy (26:15). Lazy people are too lazy to feed themselves (26:15; see also 19:24). For the lack of the most trivial effort, they starve. Yet they are wise in their own eyes. Lazy people are so lazy that they do not leave the house. They stay in bed and are even lazy at the table, but they have no idea that they are lazy. In their view, they are "realists;" there is a valid reason why they do not work (26:13), why they stay in bed (26:14) and why they do not feed themselves (26:15). Seven (the number of perfection) truly wise men could not persuade them otherwise. They bless themselves, think their way is better and with inward self-congratulations, turn over in bed and lie still (Wardlaw). (See Bunyan's picture of Ignorance in *Pilgrim's Progress*.)

The solution for laziness is for lazy people to go to the ant. Solomon says, "Go to the ant, you sluggard! Consider her ways and be wise" (6:6). Solomon sends the sluggard to the school of the ant to learn a lesson about laziness. That means that the process of recovery begins with humility. People who are created in the image of God, made a little lower than the angels and built to be wiser than the creation, are not sent to the greatest or the noblest animal, but to the least and most insignificant, to the lowly ant. Ants are often considered pests. The virtuous woman is not lazy (31:27), but Solomon does not send lazy people to look at people who labor hard. He sends them to the ant. As long as lazy people think they are smarter than seven truly wise people, they will not change. They must have enough humility to be willing to learn from the ant. These know-it-alls must learn from the lowly ant. They can learn all they need to know from the ant.

Notice that Solomon did not say, "Be like the ant." Ants are workaholics. Lazy people are to learn from the ant. Like the ant, the wise person works hard.

Solomon continues, "Which, having no captain, Overseer or ruler, Provides her supplies in the summer, and gathers her food in the harvest" (6:7-8). "Captain" means "ruler, have dominion over." "Overseer" means "official, a subordinate officer, judicial, civil or military." "Ruler" means "chief, ruler" and is used by commanders in war and dictators. Bees have levels of workers, culminating with a queen bee; they have government. Ants have no superiors to tell them what to do or how to do it. They have no guide to direct their work, no overseer to inspect it, and no ruler to call it into account (Bridges). They differ in size and color, but they are all hard-working. They are industrious. They perform unwearied and well-planned labor. They carry and gather. They push what they cannot carry. Some can build anthills as high as a man is tall. The type mentioned here is called the "harvester" ant, which is common in Palestine. (See 30:25.) The point is that no one has to tell the ant what to do. Ants work hard without outside motivation or supervision. The only hope for lazy people is that they see the problem and they decide to do something about it. Lazy people must contemplate the consequences of laziness and decide for themselves that "I am going to get busy because I do not want these consequences; I want other results."

Summary: Lazy people resist work and consequently, they have nothing but poverty, servitude, hunger, and death. Lazy people are captive to leisure, addicted to creature comforts, and have lost all interest in work. Be wise; work.

Two groups need to learn about laziness. The lazy need to learn from the ant. The lesson is simple enough. Ants do not need to have anyone to tell them what to do. They do it on their own.

All of us need to learn from the lazy. For one thing, all of us are lazy sometimes. We all have our moments – some longer than others. For another, Proverbs was written for all who are interested in learning wisdom. People who are not lazy can learn wisdom by studying the lazy. That is the point made in Proverbs 24: "I went by the field of the lazy man and by the vineyard of the man devoid of understanding; and there it was, all overgrown with thorns; its surface was covered with nettles; Its stone wall was broken down. When I saw it, I considered it well; I looked on it and received instruction: A little sleep, a little slumber, A little folding of the hands to rest; So shall your poverty come like a prowler, And your need like an armed man" (24:30-34). To some degree, this is a repetition of Proverbs 6:9-10. The account here describes a lingering look at a neglected field. Lazy people don't cultivate their field to enrich themselves! For lack of attention, the field is not only unproductive; it is unsightly.

Moreover, procrastination brings unexpected disaster. The same could be said of a neglected family or a neglected business. A proverb says, "Wise men profit more by fools than fools by wise men: for wise men will learn to avoid the faults of fools, but fools will not learn to imitate the virtues of wise men."

In ancient Greece, between 620 and 560 BC, a writer of fables named Aesop lived. One of his fables is entitled "The Ant and the Grasshopper." One version goes like this: In a field one summer's day, a Grasshopper was hopping about, chirping, and singing to its heart's content. An Ant passed by, bearing along with great toil an ear of corn he was taking to the nest. "Why not come and chat with me," said the Grasshopper, "instead of toiling and moiling in that way?" "I am helping to lay up food for the winter," said the Ant, "and recommend you to do the same." "Why bother about winter?" said the Grasshopper; we have plenty of food now." But the Ant went on its way and continued its toil. When the winter came, the Grasshopper had no food and found itself dying of hunger, while it saw the ants distributing, every day, corn from the stores they had collected in the summer. Then the Grasshopper knew: It is best to prepare for the days of necessity.

Another version says, "The ants spent a fine winter's day drying grain collected in the summertime. A Grasshopper, perishing with famine, passed by and earnestly begged for a little food. The ants asked him, 'Why did you not treasure food during the summer?' He replied, "I had not leisure enough. I passed the days in singing.' They then said in derision: 'If you were foolish enough to sing all the summer, you must dance supperless to bed in the winter.'"

THE TROUBLE WITH BEING A TROUBLEMAKER

My job gets harder by the week. Last week, my assignment was to find a lazy person. In going through Proverbs, the next passage dealt with the sluggard. So I had a message for a sluggard, that is, a lazy person, and I felt that it would be difficult to find someone who would admit to being lazy. Well, that was easy compared to what I have to do now. The passage after sluggard deals with another type of person who will be hard to find. It is about a troublemaker! Who is going to admit to that? There are some things all of us can learn by looking at the troublemaker. So, let's consider what Proverbs says about being a troublemaker.

Have you ever known a troublemaker? It seems that every family has one. Unfortunately, many churches have one or, God forbid, two. What are they like? There is a massive problem with being a mischief-maker. What is it? Proverbs 6:12-19 offers insights into the troublemaker.

At first glance, this passage seems to describe a worthless person and a list of sins God hates, but a closer look reveals the subject is the troublemaker. Granted, the word "troublemaker" is not used, but an analysis of the passage indicates that is the person Solomon has in mind. At the end of the description portion, it says this individual "sows discord" (6:14) and at the end of a list of sins God hates, it speaks of the one who "sows discord among the brethren" (6:19). Hence the conclusion that this passage is describing a troublemaker.

Their Description

This description of a troublemaker begins by saying that such an individual is "A worthless person" (6:12). The Hebrew word translated "worthless" means "useless, worthless, good for nothing" (BDB). It appears three times in Proverbs (6:12, 16:27, and 19:28) and in other places in the Old Testament. It implies wickedness as well as worthlessness (1 Sam. 2:12; 1 Kings 21:10) and sometimes destructiveness (Nah. 1:11, 15; Ps. 18:4). Eventually, it became a name for the Devil ("And what accord has Christ with Belial?" 2 Cor. 6:15) who is the father of such qualities (Kidner). The heart of a troublemaker is worthless. Today, useless means unproductive financially. Spiritually it means there is no love there (1 Cor. 13:1-3). This person is useless to God and others.

The troublemaker is "a wicked man" (6:12). "Wicked" means "trouble, sorrow, wickedness" and occurs in Proverbs 6:12, 18, 10:29. 11:7, 12:21, 17:4, 19:28, 21:15, 22:8, 30:20 and in many other places outside Proverbs. Delitzsch says it denotes the "want of all moral character." The heart of the troublemaker is not only worthless, it is wicked. An ancient author wrote, "In a time of discord, bad men have the most power" (Tacitus).

The troublemaker "walks with a perverse mouth" (6:12). This individual not only has a perverse month, he or she walks with one, meaning it is their life. "Perverse" means "crookedness" and is used here for speaking falsely. It is also used in Proverbs 4:24. The wicked, worthless person "practices deceit with his mouth, that is, who makes language the means of untruthfulness and uncharitableness" (Delitzsch). In describing a troublemaker to me, a lady said, "He told one person one thing and another something else." Troublemakers pervert the truth.

The troublemaker uses body language to communicate. "He winks with his eyes, He shuffles his feet, He points with his fingers" (6:13). "Winks" here implies winking maliciously. As is stated later, "He who winks with the eye causes trouble" (10:10) and, still later, it is said that a violent man "winks his eye to devise perverse things" (16:30). "Shuffles" means "scrape" and here refers to making a sign with the feet (BDB). Delitzsch says that it means drawing one's feet backward and forwards on the ground to give others a sign. The Hebrew word for "points" is a word that means "throw, shoot, point out, show." "Points" is a good translation here, but it is interesting that this word also means "direct, instruct, teach." The noun form of this verb means "teacher." In fact, the King James Version of this verse says, "He winketh with his eyes, he speaketh with his feet, he teacheth with his fingers." All of this suggests sly, covert communication. Once troublemakers draw you into their circle, they share their "insights" with you, often secretly as if to say, "You are in the know with me." Body language is then used to communicate confirmations of "what I've been telling you." There are lying looks and lying gestures as well as lying words. Experts today often say that communication is 7% words, 38% tone of voice, and 55% non-verbals. Non-verbal body language can be a powerful means of communication. If Solomon were writing this today, he might add, "They used every means including phone calls, letters, faxes, e-mail or whatever means are at their disposal."

The troublemaker's real problem is on the inside. "Perversity is in his heart, He devises evil continually" (6:14). The Hebrew word for "perverse" comes from the word for "turn, overturn." As we saw in Proverbs 2:12, the perverse man has turned away from God. Later, Proverbs says, "A perverse man sows strife, and a whisperer separates the best of friends" (16:28). Here, the perverse man habitually plans evil.

Finally, "He sows discord" (6:14). "Discord" means "strife, contention." He sows discord instead of love. Troublemakers stir up strife by telling everyone their perverse points of view. They often begin by telling everyone except the people directly involved.

I have seen troublemakers divide families and split churches. They often do it in the name of being right when they are wrong about what they say. I have also seen troublemakers who just had an agenda or wanted to control the church. One of the saddest stories I read occurred many years ago in a small town in North Dakota. A young man with a wife and two small children was, from all appearances, happily married. When he came home from work, his wife and children greeted him at the door with hugs and kisses. They were often seen having a good time enjoying each other's company. Then, one day, a whispered rumor spread through the small town that this man was having an affair. It was without foundation, but it spread rapidly. When the man's wife heard it, she went into a deep depression. One day, when the man returned home, there was no family to meet him at the door. When he entered his home, he found that his wife had committed suicide and killed their two children. The man was beside himself with grief. According to the story I read, the man was later proven innocent of having an affair, but the damage was already done by some troublemaker who whispered an untrue rumor.

Their Destruction

"Therefore his calamity shall come suddenly; suddenly he shall be broken without remedy. Like a pest he will be destroyed suddenly" (6:15). Perhaps the greatest illustration of this is in the book of Acts. Chapter four says, "Now the multitude of those who believed were of one heart and one soul; neither did anyone say that any of the things he possessed was his own, but they had all things in common" (Acts 4:32). There was unity among the believers. They sold their possessions and gave the money to the church, so no one had a need (Acts 4:34-35). After these general statements, Luke gives two examples: Barnabas (Acts 4:36-37) and Ananias and Sapphira (Acts 5:1-11). Barnabas sold everything and gave it to the church. Ananias and Sapphira sold everything and "kept back part of the proceeds" (Acts 5:2). As a result, when they were confronted, they both died on the spot. It is usually suggested that they died because of their lying, or lying was, no doubt, part of their sin. Nevertheless, the passage begins with the fact that there was unity. Is it possible that this is a case of troublemakers being suddenly destroyed?

Their Detestableness

The next paragraph in Proverbs sounds like it is about another subject. It is not. Proverbs 6:12-15 ends with a reference to the one who "sows discord" (6:14). The next paragraph (6:16-19) also concludes by talking about "one who sows discord among brethren" (6:19). Thus, the two paragraphs are a unit both dealing with the troublemaker.

Solomon says, "These six things the LORD hates, Yes, seven are an abomination to Him" (6:16). Six ... seven (see also three ... four in 30:15, 18, etc.) is a literary device to show that the list is not complete (Kidner). It also builds to a climax, with the last item being the most important. "Abomination" means "abhorred." It is used of something that is repugnant and detestable.

The Lord detests "a proud look" (6:17). This is reminiscent of the body language spoken in the previous section. Apart from the troublemaker, the Lord hates pride. He resists the proud (see 3:34; Jas. 4:6) and hates their proud smirk.

The Lord detests "a lying tongue" (6:17). This echoes what was said about the troublemaker. Besides the troublemaker's use of lies, the Lord hates lying, period.

The Lord detests "Hands that shed innocent blood" (6:17). The first innocent bloodshed was the blood of a brother. Troublemakers are not said to shed blood literally, but they hurt people as much as they did. Beyond troublemakers, God hates hands that hurt others.

The Lord detests "a heart that devises wicked plans" (6:18). It was said explicitly of troublemakers that they devise evil continually (6:14). God hates the heart that is used to plan wickedness.

The Lord detests "feet that are swift in running to evil" (6:18). Troublemakers shuffle their feet (6:13). Here, the feet do more than shuffle; they run to carry out the plans of the heart. God hates the planning and the execution of evil (see 1:16).

The Lord detests "a false witness who speaks lies" (6:19a). Lying is mentioned twice in this list. First, it mentions a lying tongue (6:17); now, it mentions a witness who speaks lies. The first is informal and the second is formal. Troublemakers speak lies (6:12) and, if necessary, will do so under oath. God hates this one so much that it made it to the top ten list, called the Ten Commandments (Ex. 20:16).

The Lord detests "one who sows discord among the brethren" (6:19b). This is the climax of the whole passage. The first section ended with "he sows discord" (6:14). The last section ended with the same issue. Furthermore, this time, it is not just one of the activities of a wicked person; it is the ultimate sin that God hates. On top of all of that, Solomon adds, "among brethren." By making the one who sows discord among brethren the crowning abomination, this passage clinches the indictment of the troublemaker. No vice is a greater abomination to God than causing strife between two who are related and who love each other. This has been called the "*non plus ultra* (Latin for "none greater") of all that God hates" (Delitzsch).

Notice all the various aspects of a person that are again mentioned here: attitude (proud look), thoughts (heart), speech (lying tongue, unofficial and official), and actions (hands and feet). God hates for people to use all of themselves to sin, especially sowing strife.

Summary: Troublemakers will suddenly be destroyed because God detests those who sow discord among brethren. The trouble with being a troublemaker is that they will end up in trouble because God detests troublemakers. From God's point of view, it is good and pleasant for brethren to dwell together in unity (Ps. 133).

The troublemakers use all of their being to cause trouble. They use their mouth (6:12, 19), eyes (6:13), fingers (6:13), feet (6:6, 13), heart (6:14, 18), look (6:17), tongue (6:17), hands (6:17) and feet (6:18). They use their minds and their mouth, their eyes and their ears, their fingers, and their feet. Paul says, "Do not use your members as instruments of unrighteousness ... but as instruments of righteousness" (Rom. 6:13). In this case, the unrighteousness is sowing strife. Instead of the malicious wink, the pointing finger, and the scuffling feet, you need the closed eye, the lifted hand, and the bent knee in the petition.

There are two choices. You can use your members as instruments of unrighteousness, or you can use your members as instruments of righteousness. You can sow discord, or you can sow peace. You can make trouble or you can make peace. If you do the former, you will be called all sorts of unpleasant things. If you do the latter, you will be called "sons of God" (Matt. 6:8). God is pleased with the latter and detests the former. Unrighteousness is repugnant to Him.

Some time ago, I was told about a small quaint restaurant in Santa Monica that would be nice to visit. According to the person who told me about the place, they had good Italian food that was not expensive. Once, Patricia, her father, and I decided to eat there. The location was great. It was near the ocean. The place itself was not fancy, just basic. I ordered Fettuccine Alfredo. It was served hot and looked delicious. It was good. There was only one problem. After I had eaten at least a third of what was on my plate, I discovered a roach right in the middle of my food. I almost threw up. That was as repugnant to me. That is how God feels about someone who sows discord among brethren, and you know what happens to roaches.

CONSIDER THE CONSEQUENCES

All of us would like to make wise decisions. How do you do that? There are many answers to that question. Listen to the Lord. Learn from others. Look at your own past mistakes. Another powerful way to make wise decisions is to consider the consequences. The wisdom book of the Bible, the book of Proverbs, teaches that indirectly by repeatedly pointing out the consequences of various decisions. For example, in Proverbs 6:20-35, some of the consequences of immorality are given as a reason for avoiding immorality.

Listen to Your Parents

Solomon again addresses his son and admonishes him to listen to his parents. He says, "My son, keep your father's command, and do not forsake the law of your mother" (6:20). Solomon has spoken before about the father's command (1:8; 2:1; 3:1; 4:1; etc.) and the mother's law (1:8; 6:20). These passages assume that godly parents are giving godly advice, that they are giving their instruction based on God's Law (see verse 23 below). Later in the passage, it becomes clear that the command and law here have to do with what God said about sex. Also, both parents should be involved in the sex education of the child.

Solomon's son is urged to keep and not forsake the instruction of his parents. In language reminiscent of what Moses said we should do with the Word of God (see Deut. 6:4-9), Solomon continues, "Bind them continually upon your heart; tie them around your neck." (6:21). Godly wisdom should be the inward controlling principle ("heart") and it should be seen by others ("tie them around the neck"). Being bound to the heart and tied around the neck, godly wisdom should be a constant companion. In Proverbs 3:4, Solomon admonishes his son to bind mercy and truth around his neck, that is, let them not be hidden, but seen, and write them on the tablet of your heart. Let them not be just external conduct for show, but the inward controlling principles.

Solomon goes on to say, "When you roam, they will lead you; when you sleep, they will keep you; and when you awake, they will speak with you" (6:22). Notice Solomon speaks of roaming, sleeping, and being awake. The Hebrew word translated "roam" means "walk" (NASB; NIV). Solomon talks about leaving the house, being asleep at night, and being awake during the day. In addition, note that godly parental wisdom is personified as a guide, guard, and governess. When godly wisdom is a constant companion, it directs, protects, and instructs.

This is not a new idea. Solomon said before, "When wisdom enters your heart, and knowledge is pleasant to your soul, Discretion will preserve you, understanding will keep you" (2:10-11). Solomon has made the point that wisdom will supply safety. "Then you will walk safely in your way and your foot will not stumble" (3:23). The safety here is not physical but spiritual. The same Hebrew word for safety is used in Proverbs 1:33, 3:29, and 10:9, where it is being used for safety from sin. When we follow wisdom, we do not stumble into sin (3:6).

American Express says, "Don't leave home without it." They are talking about their credit card, but there are other things you should not leave home without. What do you not leave home without? What do you go back home for if you forget? For me, it is my wallet, my glasses, and my cell phone. Solomon says don't leave home without godly wisdom.

Don't leave home without godly wisdom, whether you got it from your human parents or from your heavenly Father, who used some other means. Let wisdom be your constant companion. If you do, you will be safe; if not, you will be sorry.

Solomon explains ("for"), "For the commandment is a lamp, and the Law a light; reproofs of instruction are the way of life" (6:23). It now becomes clear that the parental rules of verse 20 are expressions of the divine law (Kidner). God's Law, here received through parents, is a spiritual light in a morally dark world. Its light may expose our own misdirection, but such reproof is life because to continue down the wrong path is death.

Let wisdom be your constant companion, a guide by day and a guard by night. If you do that, you will be safe; if not, you'll be sorry.

Stay away from the Immoral Woman

Verses 23 mentions the commandment. The specific command is, "To keep you from the evil woman, from the flattering tongue of a seductress" (6:24). For an explanation of the immoral woman, see the discussion about her on Proverbs 2:16. The Hebrew noun rendered "flattering" means "smoothness."

Solomon's son is warned, "Do not lust after her beauty in your heart, nor let her allure you with her eyelids" (6:25). On Mount Sinai, Moses received the commandment, "Do not covet" (Ex 20:17) and in the Sermon on the Mount, the Master said, "But I say to you that whoever looks at a woman to lust for her has already committed adultery with her in his heart" (Mt. 5:28). From the point of view of the one tempted, the problem begins in the heart. Wisdom advises, "Keep your heart with all diligence, for out of it spring the issues of life" (4:23).

The Hebrew word for "eyelids" comes from a Hebrew word for fluttering and has been interpreted here as a reference to "winking" (Delitzsch), "eyelashes" (RSV), and even "glances" (Kidner). Whatever the specifics, it refers to a woman's seductive use of her eyes.

Immorality Destroys You

Some young men like the one to whom Solomon is addressing might think, "But sex is fun. My parents are just trying to restrict me. What harm can come from a little fun?" There are consequences to adultery. This passage lists some of the possible results.

Destitution Solomon explains, "For by means of a harlot a man is reduced to a crust of bread; and an adulteress will prey upon his precious life" (6:26). Harlot and adulteress could be synonyms. If so, the whole passage is a warning against the lure of a prostitute. More likely, Solomon has two different types of women in mind; one is a prostitute and the other is a simple, seductive, married woman. A "crust of bread" is the "smallest piece of bread" (Delitzsch). A piece of bread describes poverty (1 Sam. 2:36). The adulterer squanders his money until he is poverty-stricken. "A companion of harlots wastes his wealth" (29:3). Not long after I graduated from seminary, I counseled a fellow who was many thousands of dollars in debt because of visiting massage parlors.

Death The adulterer loses more than money. He loses his life! As Solomon says, "And an adulteress will prey upon his precious life" (6:26). A seductress will seek a man like a hunter seeking wild prey; she will pursue him to death. The man loses his life, his purity, and his dignity.

Solomon points to fire as an illustration of the life-threatening damage that can be done. "Can a man take fire to his bosom, and his clothes not be burned? Can one walk on hot coals, and his feet not be seared? So is he who goes in to his neighbor's wife; whoever touches her shall not be innocent" (6:27-29). The Hebrew word rendered "innocent" means "to be clean, free from, exempt" and is used for being exempt from punishment. Punishment is inescapable. It is impossible to participate in immorality without suffering the consequences.

Many young men are like a forest of dry timber. A small spark will ignite a large fire.

Dishonor The adulterer loses honor. "People do not despise a thief if he steals to satisfy himself when he is starving Yet when he is found, he must restore sevenfold; He may have to give up all the substance of his house" (6:30-31). This does not condone stealing. It simply observes that people generally do not condemn those who steal food because of starvation. Nevertheless, there are consequences for stealing. The Mosaic Law speaks only of a twofold, fourfold, and fivefold restoration (Ex. 21:37; 22:1-3, 8; see Lk. 19:8). A thief, however, could go beyond the law. He could give up all of his possessions, including his house, to satisfy the law, appease the one he had wronged, and gain an honorable name. So, people may have compassion for some thieves, but they still must pay the consequences. They may have to pay sevenfold. If they make restitution, they regain at least some of their honor.

In contrast to stealing, which under some circumstances is understandable, immorality never makes sense. A thief may obtain compassion, but an adulterer gets contempt (Delitzsch). A person has to eat to survive, but a person is expected to have self-control. The sin of immorality claims no sympathy. With immorality, the issue is not a lack of bread but a lack of understanding.

Damage The next four verses mention several things that could be listed as separate consequences of adultery. They could also be taken to refer to a jealous husband. He is not mentioned explicitly until verse 34, but verse 32 could refer to him. Hence, it could be said that all four verses do.

Solomon says, "Whoever commits adultery with a woman lacks understanding; He who does so destroys his own soul" (6:32). The adulterer lacks understanding because he does not remember what wisdom says about adultery and does not act accordingly. The mention of "destroying his own soul" can be interpreted in two ways. It could be a reference to the Mosaic Law, which says, "If a man is found lying with a woman married to a husband, then both of them shall die; the man that lay with the woman, and the woman; so you shall put away the evil from Israel" (Deut. 22:22). Proverbs 6:32 has been taken to be "corporal punishment inflicted on the adulterer by the husband" (Delitzsch). If so, the husband of the unfaithful wife will demand the death of the adulterer. On the other hand, the next three verses contemplate his continued existence. So maybe "destroys his own soul" refers to a living death (see 2:18; 1 Tim. 5:6).

Solomon continues, "Wounds and dishonor he will get, and his reproach will not be wiped away" (6:33). In a healthy society, adultery is "social suicide" (Kidner). With a thief, restoration is possible (30-31), but with adultery, it is not (34-35). If a thief pays heavily, at least some of the reproach is removed. Not so with an adulterer. He has disgraced himself forever. One stolen from may be appeased, but not the betrayed husband.

Solomon explains, "For jealousy is a husband's fury; therefore he will not spare in the day of vengeance. He will accept no recompense, nor will he be appeased though you give many gifts" (6:34-35). The word "for" indicates that this is an explanation of the previous verse, which is another indication that verses 32-35 all refer to the jealous husband. Jealousy knows no mercy. Vengeance allows no atonement. No gift, no recompense, no restoration will satisfy. Elsewhere, Proverbs says, "Wrath is cruel and anger a torrent, but who is able to stand before jealousy?" (27:4) and Solomon wrote, "Jealousy as cruel as the grave; its flames are flames of fire, A most vehement flame" (Song of Solomon 8:6).

I once saw a bumper sticker that read, "Sex Instructor. First lesson free." That is what foolishness would like for you to think. The truth is that immorality has a price tag and the price is high.

Summary: If you listen to wisdom and do not participate in immorality, you will live, but if you don't, you will suffer many damaging consequences.

Immorality has consequences. People who commit this sin learn that the hard way. Augustine, who, as a young man, lived an immoral life, later became not only a Christian but a great theologian. He wrote, "Oh! How great iniquity is this adultery! How great a perverseness! The soul, redeemed by the precious blood of Christ, is thus for the pleasures of an hour given to the devil; a thing much to be lamented and bewailed; when that which delights is soon gone, that which torments remains without end" (Augustine, cited by Bridges).

It should be pointed out that while some, like the jealous husband in this passage, will not forgive the sin of immorality, God does. Christ died for all sins, including this one. All who trust Him for the gift of eternal life are forgiven. All believers who confess their sins are forgiven (1 Jn. 1:9).

I began by pointing out that there are many ways to make wise decisions. Listen to the Lord. Learn from others. Look at your own past mistakes. All of these and more teach us to avoid immorality. In the Ten Commandments, God said, "Do not commit adultery" (Ex. 20:14). In the book of Proverbs, others tell us to avoid immorality (5:1-23, 6:20-35). You may have learned from your own experience. This passage focuses on considering the consequences. In any area of life, but especially in the area of sexual immorality, consider the consequences.

The great objection, especially from young people, is that sex is natural and fun. Everyone does it, so why not? Sex is natural and fun in its proper place. God says that place is marriage. Put sex where it belongs and it is constructive. Take it out of its proper place and it is destructive. Consider the consequences. God said there are destructive consequences. You may not see them. They may not be immediate, but they are there. Outside of where God intended, sex results in damage, destruction, and death.

Fire is an illustration. Fire is a good thing. Think of all the places where fire exists in your house and of all the beneficial things it does for you. In the furnace, it warms your house in the cold winter. In the hot water heater, it prepares the water for a comfortable shower. In the gas stove, it cooks your food. In the fireplace, it provides not only warmth but a warm atmosphere. Fire is good and beneficial in its place, but take it out of its place and it is dangerous, damaging, and destructive. If the fire in the fireplace got out of the fireplace into the living room, it would damage or destroy everything it touched. It could conceivably burn down the whole house. It could also mar and scar people. It is not too much to say that it could literally kill people as well; that happens all the time. Sex is like fire. In its place, it is good and beneficial; out of place, it is destructive and even deadly. Consider the consequences and put sex in its proper place.

THE STORY OF SEX

There is more than one way to communicate a truth. You could simply make a statement, or you could tell a story. In the first ten chapters of Proverbs, Solomon informs his son about a seductive woman four times (2:16- 19; 5:1-23; 6:20- 35; 7:1-27). The first three times, he makes statements. The fourth time, he tells a story. What is the story behind seduction? When a woman decides to seduce a man, what does she do? Everyone needs to know about this: young people should avoid the trap, and parents should tell their children. Consider the story of sex as recorded in Proverbs 7:1-27.

The Prologue people

The prologue of this passage is like a father saying to his son, "Let me give you the point of the play before it begins." Solomon says, "My son, keep my words, and treasure my commands within you. Keep my commands and live, and my law as the apple of your eye. Bind them on your fingers; Write them on the tablet of your heart. Say to wisdom, 'You are my sister,' and call understanding your nearest kin" (7:1-4).

The Plea The father begins with an exhortation for the son to listen to him, but as it becomes clear, the father's law is God's law; his wisdom is God's wisdom. So this is an exhortation to do what is wise. Much of this exhortation is a repetition of, or something similar to, what has already been said. Solomon has said, "keep my commands" (3:1, 4:4), "treasure my commands within you" (2:1), "keep my commands, and live" (4:4), "bind" your father's command and your mother's law "continually upon your heart" (6:21; see also 3:3), "write" mercy and truth "on the tablet of your heart" (3:3). The figure that has not been used is making the father's law "as the apple of your eye" (7:2). The Hebrew word translated "apple" means "pupil of the eye." As you would be sensitive to your eye and guard it, so be sensitive to and guard wisdom.

Solomon has personified wisdom as a woman (1:20-33), but now he goes further and makes wisdom a sister, a nearest of kin. In other words, wisdom should be near and dear, an intimate companion.

The Purpose The purpose of the plea is to protect from immorality, "That they may keep you from the immoral woman, from the seductress who flatters with her words" (7:5). This is an almost exact repetition of Proverbs 2:17.

The Drama

The drama begins by introducing the characters. This drama has three people: a perceptive father, a young man, and a woman, but there are only two main characters.

The Characters "For at the window of my house I looked through my lattice, and saw among the simple, I perceived among the youths, a young man devoid of understanding, Passing along the street near her corner; and he took the path to her house In the twilight, in the evening, In the black and dark night" (7:6-9). The story begins with the father standing in his house, looking out his window through a lattice. A lattice is a framework of crossed wood that serves the same purpose as our Venetian blinds, excluding the sun but letting cool air into the house.

1. An Inexperienced Man. As the father looked out his window, he observed a young man he describes as "simple." The Hebrew word for simple means just that, to be simple. It also means to be open. A simple-minded person is an open-minded person who is open to either wisdom or folly. Such a person is inexperienced, impressionable, easily led, naïve, and gullible. This young, inexperienced fellow also lacked wisdom.

He passed the house of the immoral woman (7:8) and deliberately passed her house repeatedly. He went backward and forwards. He went past at twilight as the day was coming to a close, in the evening after it was dark and "in the black and dark night" (7:9), that is, in the middle of the night.

2. An Immoral Woman. "And there a woman met him, with the attire of a harlot, and a crafty heart. She was loud and rebellious, her feet would not stay at home. At times she was outside, at times in the open square, lurking at every corner" (7:10-12). The immoral woman is not necessarily a prostitute (see the discussion of the immoral woman in Proverbs 2:16). Still, she is dressed like one. We would say today "she was dressed to kill." Her heart is crafty, a Hebrew word that means "guard, keep secret." She guarded her heart in the sense of concealing what was in it (Delitzsch). Her clothes were revealing. Still, she was not. She kept her thoughts and feelings to herself. She was

"loud," that is, boisterous, and rebellious, a word that means "stubborn" and can mean "resentful." She could not sit still or stay at home (see 1 Tim. 5:13).

The Come-On The immoral woman used at least four different tactics to seduce this inexperienced young man.

1. Kisses. "So she caught him and kissed him" (7:13a). It is unlikely that she kissed him before she said anything to him. Perhaps Solomon put the kiss first as if to say, "This is an issue of the utmost importance." When there is a romantic kiss, the seductive process has begun.

A married man once told me, "My wife buried herself in her business. Being lonely, I became good friends with a lady. Before I knew it, I kissed her." This man had no intention of being unfaithful, but he was now on the way. I suspect he should have figured that out a long time before the kiss, but surely, when the kiss happened, he should have known. In his case, the kiss was a wake-up call. He told his wife all about the incident and they decided to seek counseling concerning their marriage.

2. Flattery. "With an impudent face she said to him: 'I have peace offerings with me; today I have paid my vows. So I came out to meet you, diligently to seek your face, and I have found you'" (7:13b-15). "With her enticing speech she caused him to yield, with her flattering lips she seduced him" (7:21). The Hebrew word translated "impudent" means "strong, mighty."

This woman was religious! She had made a peace offering, a religious activity in ancient Israel. It has been said, "She durst not play the harlot with man till she had played the hypocrite with God, and stopped the month of her conscience with her peace offering" (cited by Bridges). The favorite mistress of Louis XIV was so rigid in her religious duties that she weighed her bread during Lent for fear she would violate the fast. It is possible to meet an immoral woman at church.

The immoral woman used flattery to seduce the young man. Verses 13-15 relate how she did it. Verse 21 says that is what she did. She tells him about making the peace offering and paying her vows. The meat from the peace offering had to be eaten the same day (Lev. 7:15). So she flatters him, telling him that she had diligently sought his face until she found him. With flattering words, she made him feel special.

Flattery should be a sign that seduction has begun. Compliments are legitimate. Flattery from someone interested in you should be a warning sign.

3. Sensuality. "I have spread my bed with tapestry, colored coverings of Egyptian linen. I have perfumed my bed with myrrh, aloes, and cinnamon. Come, let us take our fill of love until morning; Let us delight ourselves with love" (7:16-18). The bed was inviting. It looked expensive, soft, pleasant, and beautiful. It smelled great! Here, the sensuality was in the way she prepared her bed. It could also be how she moves, talks, or dresses. In fact, she does use sensual talk. Today, it is over the phone or even on the internet.

4. Reassurance. "For my husband is not at home; He has gone on a long journey; He has taken a bag of money with him, and will come home on the appointed day" (7:19-20). The young man was apprehensive for fear of being caught. So, the immoral woman assures him that her husband is not going to return. He is a long way from home. He has taken enough money to stay a long time and does not plan to return for a long time.

Men on the prowl are proverbial. Young men and some older men need to be aware that there are also seductive women on the loose. I know of a young lady who went to see a photographer to have her picture taken. After the first visit, she decided to seduce him and said so. She told another lady that she would do it and she succeeded. The one who told me the story said, "She did everything mentioned in Proverbs 7."

Conclusion "Immediately he went after her, as an ox goes to the slaughter, or as a fool to the correction of the stocks, till an arrow struck his liver. As a bird hastens to the snare, he did not know it would cost his life" (7:22-23). The word rendered "immediately" means "suddenly, all at once." It implies that the young man was indecisive and then impulsively yielded to the temptation. He is oblivious to his fate. He had no idea what would happen to him. An ox goes to the slaughterhouse unaware that he is going to be slaughtered. A criminal does not realize what is happening to him until he is in jail. Then, the painful realization hits him like an arrow to a sensitive part of his body. A bird flies into a trap, not knowing it means his death.

She was dressed as a harlot; she was dressed to kill. Her kiss was the kiss of death.

THE EPILOGUE

After the drama, Solomon gives his son advice on how not to make the mistake of the gullible young man. He begins with another plea to listen, "Now therefore, listen to me, my children; Pay attention to the words of my mouth" (7:24). Of course, Solomon has more in mind than just listening to what he has to say. He wants his son to hear and heed.

Solomon gives a threefold defense for protecting oneself from the immoral woman.

Guard Your Heart As Solomon has said before, the first step is to guard the heart (4:23). Here, he puts it like this, "Do not let your heart turn aside to her ways." (7:25a). Immorality begins in the heart. If you would resist this temptation, the minute the thought crosses your mind, abort it!

Years ago, I had an appointment to see Dr. J. Vernon McGee, the teacher on the *Thru the Bible* radio broadcast. As I pulled into the parking lot of the broadcast center, I saw Dr. McGee's parking place. It had a sign that read, "Don't even think about parking in this space." That is the message. Don't even think about it.

Stay Away from Immoral Women Solomon adds, "Do not stray into her paths" (7:25b). Not only should you not think about it, but you also should not go anywhere near it. Don't just stay away from her. Stay away from her path. The young man deliberately walked up and down her street many times, just asking for trouble (7:8-9). If the Bible has any one solution to sexual immorality, it is "flee" (1 Cor. 6:18; 2 Tim. 2:22).

Consider the Consequences Next, Solomon gives the reason for fleeing ("for"), "For she has cast down many wounded, and all who were slain by her were strong men. Her house is the way to hell, descending to the chambers of death" (7:26-27). While this is the for fleeing, it is also a third defense: consider the consequences. The consequences of immorality are wounds and death. As Solomon points out, this sin has wounded and slain strong men. Remember Samson and David, Solomon's own father.

A night of pleasure can result in days of torment. Thinking you are drinking a cup of pleasure can result in drowning in a sea of trouble. Just ask former president Bill Clinton.

Summary: Since being snared by the seductive tactics of an immoral woman results in death, guard your heart and steps, and consider the consequences.

Watch out for immoral women. Beware of kisses and flattery. All of this sounds too restrictive to a generation that has experienced the sexual revolution. Solomon is trying to convince everyone to be a conscientious objector in the sexual revolution.

God is not trying to restrict people. He is putting limits on them so they can have the maximum freedom. God has said that sex is for marriage. If you abide by His "limitations," you will soar. If you don't, you are doomed to destruction.

A little boy tied a string onto his kite and ran against the wind. The kite soon soared higher until the boy released all of his string. The kite then began to object. The string is restricting me. If it weren't for the string, I could fly higher. So, the kite tugged and tugged against the string until it broke. It appeared that the kite would fly even higher, but it soon dashed to the ground and was totally destroyed. Rather than restricting the kite, the string was the means of keeping it up in the air.

THE BLESSING OF GOD'S WISDOM

There are different kinds of wisdom. For example, there is something we call "conventional wisdom." All mothers of newborn babies are told when they lay a baby down, they should always place it on its stomach. Some medical authorities have questioned conventional wisdom, but that is what conventional wisdom dictates. Another example of conventional wisdom is, "Early to bed, early to rise, makes one healthy, wealthy, and wise."

There is also something called street wisdom. A streetwise person will tell you always to watch your backside. As one man told me, "Sleep with one eye open."

Which kind of wisdom should we follow and why should we follow it? I want to introduce you to a lady who has the answer to that question. She resides in Proverbs 8.

The Call of Wisdom

In Proverbs chapter 1, wisdom was personified as a woman pleading for people to listen to her. In this chapter, Solomon again personifies wisdom. The passage begins with wisdom calling from everywhere to everyone.

From Everywhere "Does not wisdom cry out, and understanding lift up her voice? She takes her stand on the top of the high hill, beside the way, where the paths meet. She cries out by the gates, at the entry of the city, at the entrance of the doors: 'To you, O men, I call, And my voice is to the sons of men'" (8:1-4). Lady Wisdom calls from the top of a high hill (8:1), possibly from the summit of a hill outside the city. She calls along the way, where roads intersect, perhaps on the way to the city (8:2). At any rate, she is shouting her invitation publicly in the great outdoors. The immoral woman in chapter 7 spoke privately. Lady Wisdom publicly broadcasts her intentions. She calls at the gates, that is, at the entrance to the city where business was conducted (8:3) and at the doors of every house in the city (8:3). She invites men (8:4) to be wise.

In short, wisdom calls from everywhere, from the great outdoors, on every road and intersection, at work and at home. Wisdom is needed everywhere: in the shopping malls, sports arenas, and schoolhouses.

To Everyone Lady Wisdom calls to everyone. She cries out to men in general (8:4) and to the simple and the fool in particular (8:5). She says, "O you simple ones, understand prudence, and you fools, be of an understanding heart" (8:5). The simple person is open to either wisdom or folly. Such a person is inexperienced, impressionable, easily led, naïve, and gullible (see comment on 1:4). The slut privately seduces the simple in the street. The "daughter of heaven" (Delitzsch) publicly speaks to the simple in the highways and the hallways. Fools are thickheaded and full of stubbornness. They reject God and His wisdom (see comment on 1:7).

The call of wisdom is universal. It is for all, regardless of race or rank. Whoever you are, wherever you are, you need wisdom.

The Command of Wisdom

In the next section, wisdom issues two commands.

Listen "Listen, for I will speak of excellent things and from the opening of my lips will come right things; for my mouth will speak truth; wickedness is an abomination to my lips. All the words of my mouth are with righteousness; nothing crooked or perverse is in them. They are all plain to him who understands and right to those who find knowledge" (8:6-9). Wisdom speaks truth and righteousness. The words translated "crooked or perverse" both mean "to twist." Wisdom does not twist or pervert the truth. It does not deceive.

The exhortation is to listen to wisdom because it is the truth. Recently, a lady in trouble came to talk to me. At first, I just listened. As long as I listened, she continued to come to talk. Then, one day, I said, "You said you wanted to know that truth. So I am going to tell you the truth." When I did that, she didn't talk to me anymore. I felt like saying to her, "The reason you need to hear me is that I am telling you the truth." That is what wisdom is saying.

Receive "Receive my instruction, and not silver, and knowledge rather than choice gold; for wisdom is better than rubies, and all the things one may desire cannot be compared with her" (8:7-11). I once heard a young man say that when he was a little boy, a relative asked him, "Would you rather have friends or money?" He had heard that this person believed that the answer was money. So he said money. It was the wrong answer. Later, another family member asked that question. This time he said "friends" and again, he was told that he had the wrong answer. He then decided the right answer was "have friends with money."

The friend with wealth is not greater than wisdom. Receive wisdom because it offers something of inestimable worth.

The Companions of Wisdom

Who is this Lady Wisdom? Why is she so valuable? What do we receive if we listen to her? After issuing a command to listen, Lady Wisdom describes her companions. We need to look at Lady Wisdom's companions, because this is a case of being known by the company you keep.

Prudence This section begins with Lady Wisdom saying, "I, wisdom, dwell with prudence and find out knowledge and discretion. The fear of the LORD is to hate evil; pride and arrogance and the evil way and the perverse mouth I hate. Counsel is mine, and sound wisdom; I am understanding, I have strength" (8:12-14). Like any smart woman, Lady Wisdom chooses her companions carefully.

Lady Wisdom dwells with prudence. The Hebrew word translated "prudence" means "to be shrewd, crafty, sensible" (see 1:4). She finds knowledge. This word means "perception, discernment, understanding" and discretion, that is, "purpose, devise and plan" (see 1:4). Discretion "denotes well-considered, carefully thought out designs, plans, conclusions" (Delitzsch). Lady Wisdom resides with those who are "canny and resourceful" (Kidner).

Lady Wisdom does not dwell with evil. Instead of saying that wisdom abides with prudence and does not dwell with foolishness, Solomon says wisdom dwells with prudence and speaks about the fear of the Lord, saying, "The Lord fears to hate evil" (8:13). In other words, instead of stupidity being the opposite of prudence, hating evil is the opposite, meaning that wisdom not only cannot live with evil, but she also hates evil. If you fear God, you will hate evil. If you don't fear God, you will hate evil. Yea, not fearing God is the greatest of all evils. It is the sin of Satan. It is pride (1 Tim. 3:6).

Pride is the root and the fruit is arrogance, a perverse mouth, and an evil way. "The virtue of all virtues is humility; therefore, wisdom hates self-exaltation in all its forms" (Delitzsch).

Lady Wisdom, then, associates with those who fear the Lord and possess prudence, knowledge, discretion, and understanding. She shuns pride, arrogance, a perverse mouth, and evil ways.

More specifically, Lady Wisdom's companions are kings, rulers, and judges who love her. She says, "By me kings reign, and rulers decree justice. By me princes rule, and nobles, all the judges of the earth. I love those who love me, and those who seek me diligently will find me. Riches and honor are with me enduring riches and righteousness. My fruit is better than gold, yes, than fine gold, and my revenue than choice silver. I traverse the way of righteousness, In the midst of the paths of justice, that I may cause those who love me to inherit wealth, That I may fill their treasuries" (8:15-21). Not all rulers are wise, but the proper use of authority requires wisdom. Some, like Solomon, love and seek wisdom. The Hebrew word rendered "diligently" means "look early, diligently." To seek and find wisdom, let the search be early in your life (Eccl. 12:1), early in your day (Ps. 5:2), and early in your thoughts about an issue. Seek her early and seek her earnestly.

When William McKinley took the oath of office as President of the United States, he prayed, "Give me now wisdom and knowledge, that I may go out and come in before this people, that is so great." All who rule at any level should recognize their need for wisdom and look to the Lord to give it to them. Rulers who fall in love with and marry Lady Wisdom have children called riches and righteousness.

God "Lady Wisdom is not only the companion of great men. She is the companion of God. Wisdom says, 'The LORD possessed me at the beginning of His way, before His works of old'" (8:22). In a poetic sense, it can be said that wisdom is the companion of God. Actually, wisdom is one of the attributes of God. Paul put it like this: "Now to the King eternal, immortal, invisible, to God who alone is wise, be honor and glory forever and ever. Amen" (1 Tim. 1:17). So it can be said that God, who is eternal, possesses wisdom, which means that there is eternal wisdom. The word "possessed" means "to bring forth, create" (Gen. 14:19). As one of God's characteristics, wisdom always existed (8:23). It had a beginning, that is, it was "brought forth" or "created" "only in the sense that God singled it out for special display at the time" (Nelson).

Hence, wisdom can say, "I have been established from everlasting, from the beginning, before there was ever an earth. When there were no depths I was brought forth, when there were no fountains abounding with water. Before the mountains were settled, before the hills, I was brought forth; while as yet He had not made the earth or the fields, or the primeval dust of the world. when He prepared the heavens, I was there, when He drew a circle on the face of the deep, when He established the clouds above, when He strengthened the fountains of the deep, when He assigned to the sea its limit, So that the waters would not transgress His command, when He marked out the foundations of the earth, then I was beside Him as a master craftsman; and I was daily His delight, rejoicing always before Him, rejoicing in His inhabited world, and my delight was with the sons of men" (8:22-31). Wisdom is older than creation. In fact, this wisdom assisted in creation and rejoiced in it. In other words, there is an eternal wisdom.

The reference to the deep (8:27-28) refers to the ocean. To draw a circle on the deep (8:27) is to mark out the circle of the horizon. The expression "marked out the foundations of the earth" is probably a reference to the landmass (8:29). The word "daily" (8:30) is an allusion to the creation week of Genesis 1. Delitzsch says it means "during the whole course of creation."

This section has been interpreted as a reference to the pre-incarnate Christ. In fact, it has been used to argue that the word "possessed" in verse 22 means "create" and, therefore, Christ was a created being. Christ is the revelation of God's wisdom (1 Cor. 1:24) and He possesses all wisdom and knowledge (Col. 2:3), but there is no clear indication that this passage refers to Christ. In fact, there are indications that the passage does not refer to Christ. In this passage, wisdom is not a person but a personification. Wisdom is personified as a woman! Proverbs 8 is simply describing the eternal character of wisdom. It is older than creation (8:23). Wisdom is not Christ, the Eternal Word, but wisdom is eternal.

The point of this portion of Proverbs 8 is that wisdom is eternal. There is a wisdom that comes from above (Jas. 4:17). God displayed His wisdom in creation (Prov. 8) and God manifested His wisdom in redemption (1 Cor. 1). That is the kind of wisdom we should seek.

The Counsel of Wisdom

Lady Wisdom concludes her discourse with an exhortation that reveals why all should seek this kind of wisdom. "Now therefore, listen to me, my children, For blessed are those who keep my ways. Hear instruction and be wise, and do not disdain it. Blessed is the man who listens to me, watching daily at my gates, waiting at the posts of my doors. For whoever finds me finds life, and obtains favor from the LORD; But he who sins against me wrongs his own soul; all those who hate me love death" (8:32-36). The Hebrew word for "soul" means "life."

Those who seek, find, and listen to (with a view to obedience) the eternal wisdom of God will be blessed with life and favor with the Lord. The one who refuses to seek, find and obey God's eternal wisdom sins, wrongs his soul, and loves death. To take a path other than wisdom is to commit suicide. If you hate wisdom, you love death because wisdom is life. People who hate wisdom are bent on self-destruction.

Blessing and life belong to those listen and cursing and death to those who do not. Be wise and live. Be otherwise and die.

Summary: The eternal wisdom of God calls from everywhere to all, saying that those who know the Lord, obey Him, and hate evil are blessed with life, and those who don't will die.

God did not create the universe without His eternal wisdom, yet you think you can live without it! Don't seek the latest; search for the lasting.

The fear of the Lord is the critical issue. It knows the Lord (9:10), reverencing Him and fearing not to obey Him (see comments on 1:7). It is that relationship with the Lord that is the beginning of wisdom (1:7, 9:10). If you want the wisdom spoken of here, you must know the Lord, because this wisdom only dwells with those who know Him.

If you find wisdom from the Lord, you will live. If you don't, something dies. The result of not following wisdom is death.

I began by talking about different kinds of wisdom. I once violated a bit of street wisdom and almost got into serious trouble that could have gotten me killed. I was teaching a class in South Central Los Angeles at the time. A couple invited me to their house to help them with their finances. On the way there in the evening, I got lost. So I stopped at a well-lit phone to call for directions. I violated a cardinal rule of street wisdom: I did not watch my backside. Three teenagers came up behind me and said, "Give us your money." I then violated another rule of street wisdom. I refused. One of them whacked me in the head with a blackjack. Fortunately, I was not seriously hurt. I could have easily been killed.

If you do not listen to wisdom, you will die. If you do listen to wisdom, you will live.

82

TWO INVITATIONS TO DINNER

Every day we are faced with decisions that we have to make. Some decisions are simple and easy. Others are complicated and difficult. What decision are you facing this week?

Perhaps the simple ones are how to spend your evenings this week. Maybe you are thinking about more major stuff like moving to another location, leaving your present job, or leaving your spouse. In the past week, I have talked to people who are trying to decide all those issues and more.

How do you make decisions? My experience is that making decisions can get complicated quickly. Granted, some are simple, but many decisions involve two appealing options, at least at the moment. It's like deciding what to eat for dinner when you have an appetite for two things. When you are faced with a decision that contains two attractive options, what basis do you use to make up your mind? Also, why is it that we so often make the wrong decision?

I do not want to oversimplify the decision-making process, but there is a principle that I would like to suggest you constantly keep in mind when making many of the decisions you have to make. Consider the two invitations to dinner in Proverbs 9:1-18.

The Feast of Wisdom

Lady Wisdom prepares a meal and invites several guests.

The Preparation The preparation for this meal includes a house, a table, and a meal. "Wisdom has built her house, she has hewn out her seven pillars; she has slaughtered her meat, she has mixed her wine, she has also furnished her table" (9:1-2).

Lady Wisdom's house is built with seven pillars. The seven pillars indicate that it is well-built and large. With seven pillars, the house is solidly and substantially built. It is enduring. The seven pillars (seven is the number of perfection) also indicate the ideally constructed house. It is spacious and grand.

Lady Wisdom's table is furnished, indicating that it is orderly and beautiful.

Lady Wisdom's meal is healthy. It consists of meat. Freshly butchered meat meant a feast. The wine was mixed either with water to make it palatable or with spices to improve the taste (see Song of Solomon 8:2). Wine was a staple at a meal, but for special feasts, spices were added to it.

Everything is prepared to make the meal appealing, appetizing, and healthy, not only nurturing but also pleasant. This meal was made to make one strong and happy.

In this passage, eating and drinking symbolize the assimilation of wisdom. God has prepared us a table of appealing, appetizing, and healthy food called wisdom, and He invites us to come and dine. If you eat at this table, you will be healthy and strong.

The principle that you need to keep in mind constantly is wisdom (9:6). The wisdom we are to assimilate begins with "the fear of the Lord" (9:10). It consists of knowing the Lord (9:10) and doing what is right and just (9:9).

The People After the feast is prepared, an invitation is sent out for various people to come and dine. The focus is not on the invitation but on the people who are invited.

1. The Simple. At the top of the guest list is the simpleton. Solomon says, "She has sent out her maidens, she cries out from the highest places of the city, 'whoever is simple, let him turn in here!' As for him who lacks understanding, she says to him, 'Come, eat of my bread and drink of the wine I have mixed. Forsake foolishness and live, And go in the way of understanding'" (9:3-6). As has been pointed out, the simple are those who are inexperienced. They have not yet decided. In this passage, the simple and the person devoid of understanding are one and the same. The only qualification for attending this feast is "deficiency" (Kidner).

Earlier in the passage, meat and wine were said to be on the menu (8:2). Now it is said to be bread and wine (8:5). The expression "bread and wine" was the "most common, all-comprehensive name for nourishment" (Delitzsch).

2. The Scoffer. At this point in the passage, Solomon discusses the scoffer and the wise. What he says almost seems out of place. In fact, verses 7 through 12 have been considered parenthetical. These two groups are not invited to the banquet so much as they are described. Perhaps that is because the wise are already at the table and the scoffer will not come.

"He who corrects a scoffer gets shame for himself, and he who rebukes a wicked man only harms himself. Do not correct a scoffer, lest he hate you" (9:7-8a). The scoffer is the mocker, one who mocks God or morality (1:22). The parallelism indicates that the scoffer and the wicked person are the same individual. The wicked would "shun restraint by God and give himself up to the unbridled impulse to evil" (Delitzsch).

Wisdom's teaching method includes correction and even rebuke. The problem is some will not listen. If you correct a scoffer, you will be disgraced and he will hate you. If you rebuke a wicked person, you will be hated and harmed. As one commentator has said, "The incorrigible replies to goodwill with insult" (Delitzsch).

There is no need to invite some because they will not respond (see Mt. 7:6, 13:12).

3. The Wise. "Rebuke a wise man, and he will love you. Give instruction to a wise man, and he will be still wiser; teach a just man, and he will increase in learning. The fear of the LORD is the beginning of wisdom and the knowledge of the Holy One is understanding. For by me your days will be multiplied, and years of life will be added to you. If you are wise, you are wise for yourself, and if you scoff, you will bear it alone" (9:8b-12). Wisdom and righteousness are intertwined (9:9). It is wise to do what is right and doing what is right is wise. Wisdom is not just an intellectual quality; it is a moral attribute. Wise people are humble (11:3). Therefore, they accept correction with gratitude. They even welcome constructive criticism. If you rebuke wise people, they will love you (9:8) and learn (9:9). They will learn about the Lord (9:10) and live longer (9:11). Both the scoffer and the wise are personally responsible for themselves (9:12).

These verses sum up the book of Proverbs. The wise choose wisdom. The scoffer mocks wisdom and the simpleton is caught in the middle, being pulled in the opposite directions of wisdom and folly. These three types of people represent the three types of responses to wisdom. You will either receive, reject, or be caught in the middle, trying to decide what to do.

For the past several months, I have lost my wife to a book. She has been studying for a securities exam. Actually, she had to take two exams. She no sooner passed the first test than she buried herself in the books again to pass the second one. The second one was last week. I must confess that I had a vested interest in her passing this exam. If she passed it I would get my wife back. If she failed it, I would lose her for another 30 days. In the providence of God, she made it! She was as relieved as a criminal facing the death penalty when he heard that he was pardoned. I was thrilled for her that she passed, but I was also thrilled for me that she passed. At any rate, we decided that we should celebrate. We carefully weighed three options: our favorite burrito, our secret barbecue ribs place, or filet mignon at home. I choose the latter. My wife cooked one of the most delicious meals I had in years. It was filet mignon and all the trimmings. She set a gorgeous table in the most pleasant surroundings. The meal was appealing, appetizing, and healthy. In this case, we had, as it were, two invitations to dinner and we made the wise choice. It was beneficial and we felt good about the decision.

The Feast of Folly

To complicate matters, there is another invitation. This one is from a foolish woman who appears in contrast to the wise lady.

The Clamorous Woman This woman is not a lady. She is "degraded womanhood." (Delitzsch). Solomon describes "Female Folly," saying, "A foolish woman is clamorous; She is simple, and knows nothing. For she sits at the door of her house, on a seat by the highest places of the city" (9:13-14).

Female Folly is not working; she is sitting. Instead of preparing an inviting, appealing meal, she is sitting at the entrance of her house, causing trouble.

Female Folly is clamorous, loud, boisterous, and brash. She is undisciplined. She knows nothing. Neither her mouth nor her mind contains anything appealing. Perhaps the appeal of her appearance overcomes her appalling loudness.

Female Folly is near Lady Wisdom. Lady Wisdom and Female Folly are in the city's high places (9:3 and 9:14). They are in the same vicinity. Others, who are described as going "straight on their way" (9:15), are said to be passing by Female Folly (9:15). Perhaps those passing by are headed for Lady Wisdom. At least, some of them were. If so, on the way to Lady Wisdom is Female Folly. Folly's purpose is to prevent those who pass by from eating at Lady Wisdom's table.

The Call Like Lady Wisdom, Female Folly gives an invitation. She sits "To call to those who pass by, who go straight on their way: 'whoever is simple, let him turn in here;' and as for him who lacks understanding, she says to him, 'stolen water is sweet, and bread eaten in secret is pleasant'" (9:15-17).

This woman is a harlot. "Drink water out of one's own cistern" was used as a symbol of sex in marriage. Here, stolen water is sex outside marriage. It is illicit sex (5:15-20; 30:20), but there is more than illicit sex here. There is an invitation to folly.

This woman only makes sense to those who lack understanding! Women, you need to attend one instead of putting on a banquet!

The Consequences The passage concludes with, "But he does not know that the dead are there, that her guests are in the depths of hell" (9:18). Instead of a marvelous meal consisting of wine and meat, there is a meager meal of bread and water and the water is stolen and the bread is eaten in secret. Nevertheless, it is sweet. There is pleasure in sin. It is sweet. The temporary sweetness is the lure.

The simpleton who responds to folly invitation has "sunk to the deepest destruction" and become like "wandering corpses" (Delitzsch). Those stolen waters contain deadly poison. The bread is only pleasant to the taste. Ultimately, it is bitter. The house of Female Folly has been described as the "vestibule of hell" (Wardlaw).

When I was a kid growing up in Florida, we had a Krispy Kreme donut shop in town. I grew up on Krispy Kreme donuts. I had no idea how unique they were. I just knew that they were the sweetest, most unbelievably delicious donuts I had ever had, especially when they were hot. In fact, Krispy Kreme donut shops hang a red neon sign in their window that says "Hot." When they make donuts, that sign flashes on and off, alerting everyone to come get hot, fresh donuts. Recently, when a Krispy Kreme donut shop opened in La Habra, people lined up for a block just to get one of these donuts. It made the evening news.

At the beginning of June, I decided to lose a few pounds. For 25 days, I really behaved myself and I lost six pounds.

My wife and I try to spend one evening a week alone. One evening at the end of June, Patricia and I spent our evening together by going out to eat. We were very proud of ourselves for how we behaved ourselves. We ate low-calorie, low-fat, boring food. As I sat there eating that healthy food, I thought about the fact that there was now a Krispy Kreme donut shop in Southern California. I thought about how those donuts melted in your mouth. I thought about how sweet they were, but it wasn't much of a problem because we were in Santa Monica, and the Krispy Kreme donut shop was in La Habra, which was better than 50 miles away.

We finished our meal and headed for the car. Somewhere in the middle of the parking lot, the donut demon attacked. He twisted my arm. He held the sweet-smelling aroma of a Krispy Kreme donut under my nose and I followed it to La Habra. As determined to stay on my diet, as faithful as I had been, I succumbed to the donut demon. It was the sweetness that got me. Those donuts destroyed my diet. I gained two pounds!

Satan makes sin pleasurable and we simpletons follow folly to our death instead of eating at the table of wisdom and living a long healthy life.

Summary: The simple are called both to wisdom (9:4) and foolishness (9:16) and the wise respond to wisdom and get wiser (9:8b-12), but the wicked (9:7 and 9:16b) follow foolishness to their own destruction (9:18).

There are two banquets in life. One serves life and the other death.

If you are within sight of the house of Female Folly, there is still time to look the other way. If you consider entering that house, there is still time to turn toward Lady Wisdom. If you are on the porch, you can still turn around and go to the house of wisdom. If you are sitting at the table of Female Folly, you can always leave. You can change your diet if you have drunk her water and eaten her bread.

INTRODUCTION TO PROVERBS 10:1-31:31

In the introduction to Proverbs, Solomon explains that one of the reasons he writes is "To understand a proverb and an enigma, the words of the wise and their riddles" (1:6). By "enigma," he means that which is obscure and "riddles" are "perplexing sayings or questions." In other words, Solomon writes Proverbs "to introduce the reader to a style of teaching that provokes his thought, getting under his skin by thrusts of wit, paradoxes, common sense and teasing symbolism, in preference to the preacher's tactic of frontal assault" (Kidner). These proverbs are designed to make us think.

As in other written material, Proverbs 1:1-9:18 consists of paragraphs. Beginning with Proverbs 10:1, the development of thought is usually in two lines (one verse) instead of a paragraph. Occasionally, two or more consecutive verses are linked together by a common subject or word. It has been suggested that the frequent change of subject from one verse to another intentionally forced readers to grapple with or meditate on the one verse before going to the next (Buzzell).

The heading "The Proverbs of Solomon" in Proverbs 10:1 introduces a large section of Solomon's proverbs extending to Proverbs 22:16. Proverbs 10:1-22:16 contains 375 sayings. They are not systematic in arrangement and are frequently unconnected.

In the commentary on the part of Proverbs, the text, as usual, is highlighted. Also, as in the first part of Proverbs, the names in parentheses are the names of commentators. The sentence that is underlined is my summary statement of the meaning of the proverb(s) under consideration.

PROVERBS 10

Proverbs 10:1 "A wise son makes a glad father, but a foolish son *is* the grief of his mother." This proverb sounds like a wise son affects the father and a foolish son affects the mother. Elsewhere, Proverbs states that a wise child affects both parents (23:24-25) and a foolish son affects the father (17:21, 25; 19:13). A wise son brings joy to his father (10:1; 15:20; 23:15, 24; 27:11; 29:3).

A wise son knows the Lord and has spiritual insight (1:7; 9:10). A foolish son disregards the Lord. He is insensitive to God's instruction and is insensible (1:7). The grief caused by a wayward son falls primarily on the mother.

The way children choose to live their lives has an emotional impact on their parents.

Proverbs 10:2 "Treasures of wickedness profit nothing, but righteousness delivers from death." The "treasures of wickedness" are those things obtained by immoral means (Delitzsch; Ryrie). This proverb teaches that wickedly obtained wealth profits nothing, but that does not seem to be true. Some people profit from stealing. The second half of the verse indicates how "nothing" should be interpreted. The parallelism indicates "death as a judgment is meant" (Delitzsch), including temporal death (Wardlaw). Wickedness leads to death, premature physical death.

On the other hand, righteousness delivers from death. In the context of the Scripture, righteousness is measured by God's Law. Living by God's Law (His Word) delivers from death. In the context of Proverbs, it is not likely that death means eternal death because life after death is beyond the scope of Proverbs (Kidner, p. 56). Death here refers to temporal death.

Kidner claims that death in Proverbs does not mean a single, merely physical, event but a realm in conflict with life. It includes sickness, calamity, and sin. He refers to the opinion of A. R. Johnson, who thinks that "life" in Proverbs is "life in its fullness" and that any weakness in life is a form of "death." In support of this is the parallelism of Proverbs 5:23, which says of the wicked, "He shall die for lack of instruction, and in the greatness of his folly he shall go astray." Dying is going astray.

Wickedness leads to premature physical death, but righteousness delivers from death. This is a major point in the book of James. In chapter 1, he writes, "Each one is tempted when he is drawn away by his own desires and enticed. Then, when desire has conceived, it gives birth to sin; and sin, when it is full-grown, brings forth death" (Jas. 1:14-15). In short, sin leads to death. He goes on to explain that righteousness saves a person's physical life (Jas. 1:21). At the end of his book, James says, "Let him know that he who turns sinner from the error of his way will save a soul from death and cover a multitude of such sins" (Jas. 5:20).

Wickedness, such as obtaining material possessions by immoral means, leads to premature physical death, but righteousness leads to a full and satisfying life.

Proverbs 10:3 "The LORD will not allow the righteous soul to famish, but He casts away the desire of the wicked." Because the Hebrew word translated "famish" means "to be hungry, have famine," this proverb probably means that the Lord does not allow the righteous to experience famine. As a general rule (this is a proverb, not a law), God does not allow righteous saints to experience famine (Ps. 37:25; Mt. 6:33). "He who gives life to the soul, will not neglect the body" (Wardlaw). Bridges says that to exercise their faith, God may allow believers to be hungry (1 Cor. 4:11; 2 Cor. 11:27), but not to famish (Ps. 37:3; Isa. 33:16; Mt. 6:32).

Perhaps the point is spiritual. The word "soul" includes the whole person (Buzzell). The Lord does not allow the righteous to be *spiritually* famished. That interpretation fits the second line of the proverb.

God casts away the desire of the wicked. Delitzsch says the Hebrew word rendered "desire" refers to desire without limits and without restraint. God "disappoints the strong desire of the wicked" (Barnes); He repels "the greedy desires of the wicked" (JFB). "They never get the enjoyment they thirst after" (Tantalus, cited by Barnes).

The righteous are satisfied spiritually, but the wicked are never fully satisfied.

Proverbs 10:4 "He who has a slack hand becomes poor, but the hand of the diligent makes rich." The Hebrew word translated "slack" means "laxness, slackness, neglect, idle" (BDB). The hand that is lax or idle is not engaged in work. Such a hand belongs to a lazy person. Lazy people become poor people. The hands of lazy people are empty and so are their pockets! No one ever became the man of the hour by watching the clock. On the other hand (pardon the pun), the diligent hand, the one engaged in hard work, makes the owner rich. The hands that are full of work belong to people whose wallets are filled with money. The way to wealth is not wishing; it is work. For an illustration of this principle, see the next verse.

Lazy people become poor and hard workers become rich.

The way to wealth is work. Wealth is the result of working, not wishing.

Proverbs 10:5 "He who gathers in summer *is* a wise son; he who sleeps in harvest *is* a son who causes shame." It has been suggested that this verse illustrates the previous verse (Buzzell). One example of a diligent (10:4) and wise son (10:5) is working hard during the summer harvest, while an example of laziness is a son who sleeps rather than works during harvest. Sleeping during the harvest is the most extreme form of laziness (Barnes). Sloth brings shame. "How great the shame of doing nothing, where there is so much to be done!" (Bridges). Such a son not only ends up poor (10:4), but he causes shame to himself and his parents. The parents of lazy children ought to be ashamed of themselves!

A wise son works, but a lazy son brings shame on himself and his parents.

The work habits of children are ultimately a reflection on their parents.

Proverbs 10:6 "Blessings *are* on the head of the righteous, but violence covers the mouth of the wicked." This proverb has three contrasts: one between the righteous and the wicked, one between the head and the mouth, and one between blessings and violence. The primary contrast is the righteousness of the righteous and the violence of the unrighteous.

The opposite of violence is kindness. In other words, in this proverb, the righteous person is a good person, one who not only does what is right but also does what is good and beneficial to others (Wardlaw). Such individuals are blessed temporally and spiritually by God and others (Bridges). Blessings hover over their head (NKJV Study Bible). Their blessings are on public display for all to see.

In contrast, violence covers the mouth of the wicked. The last half of this proverb is repeated in Proverbs 10:11. The word "covers" has been taken to mean that their face is covered for condemnation (Esther 7:8; Job 9:24; Delitzsch; Wardlaw; Bridges; Barnes; Clarke), that their mouth is characterized by violence (Buzzell; Ryrie Study Bible), or that the mouth of the wicked conceals or deceptively hides violence (JFB; Buzzell). Such individuals speak words of blessing, but violence lurks behind their words (Bertheau; Elster; and Zöckler, cited by Delitzsch, who also lists Prov. 10:11, 10:18, 19:28).

The blessings of the righteous are on public display; they speak that which blesses, but the violence of the wicked is concealed by what they say.

Proverbs 10:7 "The memory of the righteous *is* blessed, but the name of the wicked will rot." After death, the remembrance of the righteous provokes praise (JFB). Thinking about the righteous triggers thankfulness (Delitzsch). After the wicked are deceased, the mere mention of their name produces the same reaction as the sight of a decayed tree. Their name becomes as corrupt as their bones. Their name becomes loathsome, offensive, and exciting disgust "as the putrid carcass of a dog" (Wardlaw).

A righteous life is a sweet-smelling fragrance, but a wicked life evokes a stench (MacDonald). We want to remember the righteous; we want to forget the wicked (Buzzell). Parents name their son John, not Judas.

The memory of the kind of life we live lingers long after we are gone, provoking either praise or disgust.

King Jehoram wasn't mourned when he passed from this earthly scene, for he was unscrupulous, cruel, and bloodthirsty. He inaugurated his reign by murdering his seven brothers and all others who might possibly become rivals to the throne. Things went from bad to worse, and finally, the Lord smote him with a loathsome disease. When his life came to an end, people were glad!

Proverbs 10:8 "The wise in heart will receive commands, but a prating fool will fall." Wise people are willing to receive instruction to which they willingly submit themselves. Thus, they gain knowledge and set limits on themselves (Delitzsch). They humbly submit to legitimate authority (Wardlaw). Instead of listening, fools talk. The Hebrew word rendered "prating" means "lip, speech" and the one translated "fall" means "to thrust down," that is, to ruin (BDB). A "fool of lips" has been tagged "a braggart blunderer, one pleasing himself with vain talk" (Delitzsch). Since fools think they know everything, they do not receive instruction. Instead, they boast about their superior knowledge and, as a result, they fall; they come to ruin.

Wardlaw suggests that since they do not like being dictated to, fools become skilled in fault-finding. There is no rule, proposal, or order that they do not find something to which they cannot submit. They have much talk and little substance.

Comments on this proverb also include, "Inward self-contained wisdom is contrasted with self-exposed folly" (Barnes). The wise listen to sound advice, but because of their unwillingness to learn and obey, loudmouthed fools are hurled down to their ruin (MacDonald). A wise person is teachable, but a fool does not stop chattering long enough to learn anything (Buzzell).

The wise listen and learn; the fool talks and falls to ruin.

Proverbs 10:9 "He who walks with integrity walks securely, but he who perverts his ways will become known." In this context, living life with integrity is the opposite of living a perverted life. The Hebrew word translated "perverts" means "twisted, crooked, perverted." Some walk down the straight road of a wise, righteous life and some walk down the crooked road of a foolish and wicked life.

Furthermore, walking securely is the opposite of becoming known. The idea of becoming known indicates deception. In other words, people who have integrity have nothing to hide, so they have nothing to fear (Delitzsch); they are not afraid of detection (Clarke), whereas those who practice deception (JFB; MacDonald) shall be exposed (Barnes; MacDonald; Buzzell). Be sure your sin will find you out (Num. 32:23)!

<u>Those who have integrity do not fear detection, but those who practice deception will be exposed.</u>

Proverbs 10:10 "He who winks with the eye causes trouble, but a prating fool will fall." This proverb contrasts between people who cause others trouble and those who bring it on themselves (Bridges; Wardlaw). The winking of the eye indicates cunning (Barnes; MacDonald), suggesting sinful intent (JFB; Buzzell). The Hebrew word translated "trouble" means "hurt, injury, pain." The last half of this verse is a repetition of the last half of Proverbs 10:8, which means that instead of listening and learning, the fool talks and falls to ruin. Fools fall victim to their own folly.

<u>Cunning, sinful people hurt others, but those with foolish tongues hurt themselves.</u>

Proverbs 10:11 "The mouth of the righteous *is* a well of life, but violence covers the mouth of the wicked." Like a well of water, the words of the righteous benefit others. They are "words of wisdom" that are "as refreshing as a cool spring to a weary desert traveler" (Buzzell). They are "morally strengthening, intellectually elevating, and inwardly quickening" in their effect on others (Delitzsch). They are healing and helpful.

The last half of Proverbs 10:11 is the same as the last half of Proverbs 10:6. The words of the wicked conceal the violence they intend to do to others. They are "deceitful words" (Delitzsch). They are hurtful and harmful. "From one proceeds the words of comfort, truth, and joy; under the tongue of the other lies concealed cursing and bitterness, wrath, and clamor, and evil speaking" (Wardlaw).

<u>The words of the righteous help others, but the words of the wicked conceal intended harm.</u>

Proverbs 10:12 "Hatred stirs up strife, but love covers all sins." Hatred stirs up feuds and factions, dissension and division, strife and splits. Love covers all kinds of sin (1 Pet. 4:8). It does not expose sin; it forgives sin (Barnes). It "covers, overlooks, speedily forgives, and forgets" (Bridges).

"A hateful spirit isn't satisfied to forgive and forget; it insists on raking up old grudges and quarrels. A heart of love draws a curtain of secrecy over the faults and failures of others. These faults and failures must, of course, be confessed and forsaken, but love does not gossip about them or keep the pot boiling" (MacDonald).

<u>Hatred stirs up conflict, but love forgives and forgets the sins of others.</u>

Proverbs 10:13 "Wisdom is found on the lips of him who has understanding, but a rod *is* for the back of him who is devoid of understanding." The Hebrew word translated "understand" means to "be discerning, have insight" (BDB, p. 106). When insight is in the mind, wisdom is found on the lips.

Some lack discernment. They have been described as those who will not listen to wisdom because they are self-sufficient and full of themselves (Wardlaw). The rod is for them, which has been taken to mean it takes the rod for them to "get it" (Talmud; Delitzsch; Clarke; Kidner; Waltke), or the rod is the result of them not getting it (Barnes; MacDonald; Buzzell). The first of these options is correct ("for"). The Talmud says, "That which a wise man gains by a hint, a fool only obtains by a club." Clarke explains, "The rod is a most powerful instrument of knowledge. Judiciously applied, every twig has a lesson of profound wisdom." Some don't "get it." They need discipline to help them see. They have to feel the pain of failure.

<u>Those with insight have wisdom on their lips, but those who lack discernment need to be disciplined to gain wisdom.</u>

Proverbs 10:14 "Wise *people* store up knowledge, but the mouth of the foolish *is* near destruction." It is true that wise people gather and store knowledge in general, but the contrast in this proverb seems to suggest that the knowledge here is the knowledge that is destructive. The contrast also indicates that those who store such knowledge either do not talk about it or only talk about it when it is not destructive.

Since fools babble "without discretion—with reckless inconsideration and rashness" (Wardlaw), they say what is destructive. They speak when they should be silent and they are silent when they should speak. They babble out secrets, forgetting until it is too late that what they know was given to them in confidence (Wardlaw).

In other words, wise people store up destructive knowledge, but because foolish people speak when they should be storing up knowledge, they are always near destruction, either of themselves or others. Clarke captures the concept when he says the wise "keep secret everything that has a tendency to disturb domestic or public peace; but the foolish man blabs all out, and produces much mischief. Think much, speak little, and always think before you speak. This will promote your own peace and that of your neighbor."

<u>The wise store up, rather than speak, knowledge that is destructive, but because fools speak without thinking they are always near harming themselves and/or others.</u>

Proverbs 10:15 "The rich man's wealth *is* his strong city; the destruction of the poor *is* their poverty." The first half of this proverb is repeated in Proverbs 18:11, which adds, "and like a high wall in his own esteem." Since

money does not protect against everything (for example, disease and death), some say that Proverbs 10:15 should be interpreted in light of Proverbs 18:11. In other words, the security provided by wealth is a "state of mind" (Wardlaw). Granted, a rich man's wealth may make him think he is protected behind a high wall, but at the same time, it is also true that there is protection in wealth. Here, the point is that wealth protects compared to poverty. Changes and adversities cannot so easily overthrow the rich (Delitzsch).

In the previous proverb, words brought destruction. Here, it is poverty. The same Hebrew word for destruction appears in both verses. Poverty exposes the poor to misfortune (Ryrie Study Bible). People with low incomes are overthrown by a little misfortune (Delitzsch).

<u>Wealth protects; poverty destroys.</u> So, save money!

Proverbs 10:16 "The labor of the righteous *leads* to life, the wages of the wicked to sin." The kind of work the righteous do (MacDonald) and the money the righteous make from work serve to establish life (Ryrie) to elevate their life-happiness (Delitzsch), but the money the wicked makes results in sin, the ruin of life (Delitzsch). The revenue earned by the wicked only enlarges their means of sinning, increases the amount of their selfishness, and increases their worldly indulgence (Wardlaw).

<u>The wages earned by the righteous support and sustain life, whereas the wages earned by the wicked are used for sin, which leads to death (Jas. 1:15).</u>

Proverbs 10:17 "He who keeps instruction *is in* the way of life, but he who refuses correction goes astray." Like the previous proverb, this one speaks about life. People who hear and heed wise (Bridges), godly (MacDonald) instruction stay on a road of life, that is, a route that leads to being "truly and fully alive" (Kidner, p. 55), but those who refuse to obey correction stray from the road of life (Bridges). They are like travelers who refuse to listen when they are told they have taken a wrong turn. They wander farther and farther from the right road (Bridges).

<u>Obeying wise instruction keeps people on the road to being fully alive, but refusing to obey correction causes people to stray from the road of life.</u>

Proverbs 10:18 "Whoever hides hatred *has* lying lips, and whoever spreads slander *is* a fool." The next four proverbs (Prov. 10:18-21) refer to some speaking aspects.

Those who hate to hide their hate by lying and those who spread slander are fools. "The first is a hypocrite and the second is a fool" (MacDonald). Perhaps it is the same person who is first a hypocrite and a fool (Wardlaw). Buzzell says that the second half of this proverb begins with "and" rather than "but," "to show that the two thoughts of hatred and slander are not opposites. Such lying and slandering, born out of hatred, characterize a fool." Some who have hate in their heart have flattery on their lips in front of the one they hate, but they slander that individual behind his or her back. Such a person is a fool because the slander is almost sure to reach the ear of the hated yet flattered one (Wardlaw).

<u>Those who hate are hypocrites when they lie about it, and they become fools when they spread slander about that person.</u>

Charles Haddon Spurgeon said, "When you hear an ill report about anyone, halve it, quarter it, and then say nothing about the rest."

A wealthy, elderly grandfather, who was not quite deaf, decided to buy a hearing aid. Two weeks after the purchase, he stopped at the store where he had bought the device and reported to the delight of the manager that he could now pick up conversations quite easily, even in the next room. "Your relatives must be very happy to know that you can hear so much better," beamed the proprietor. "Oh, I haven't told them yet," the man chuckled, "I've just been sitting around listening and you know what? I've changed my will twice!"

Proverbs 10:19 "In the multitude of words sin is not lacking, but he who restrains his lips *is* wise." Those who talk a lot often sin by what they say, including speaking lies and slander (10:18). "Incessant conversation often leads to exaggeration, breaking of confidences, and associated sins. Trying to top someone else's joke often mushrooms into off-color stories" (MacDonald).

By contrast, the wise restrain their words. Jerome said, "Let us first learn not to speak, that afterward, we may open our mouths to speak wisely." Someone has said, "Either keep silent or give that which is better than silence."

<u>Those who do not control their speech often sin with what they say, but the wise practice self-control in what they say.</u>

John Wesley tells of a wagonload of Methodists who were brought before the magistrate. "What have they done?" asked the judge. Before their persecutors could formulate charges, someone in the back of the crowd spoke up in their defense. "Please, Sir, let me say a word in their favor. They converted my wife. Before she belonged to their group, she had such an evil tongue, but now she is as quiet as a lamb!" "Release them at once," said the magistrate, "Let us hope that they convert all the souls in the entire parish!"

Proverbs 10:20 "The tongue of the righteous *is* choice silver; the heart of the wicked *is worth* little." What the righteous say is of great value, but what the wicked think and, therefore, what they say is of little or no value (see the lying, slander, and sins mentioned in 10:18-19).

This proverb indicates that what people are is reflected in what they say (see the contrast between "heart" and "tongue"). Sterling character produces sterling speech (MacDonald). "If the tongue is precious, how much more the mind! If the heart is worthless, how much more the speech!" (Barnes).

Like a valuable piece of silver, what the righteous say is of great value, but what the wicked think is worthless.

Proverbs 10:21 "The lips of the righteous feed many, but fools die for lack of wisdom." One of the reasons that the righteous are valuable (10:20) is that they benefit others (Buzzell). The Hebrew word translated "feed" means "pasture, tend, graze." It was used of a ruler and a teacher's guide. Delitzsch says that it contains partly the idea of leading and partly of feeding.

Since the first part of this proverb refers to talking, the second part probably includes speaking (Buzzell). Because of their lack of wisdom, fools cause themselves, and probably others, destruction (Barnes).

With their wise words, the righteous feed and guide others, but because of their lack of wisdom, fools involve themselves and others in destruction.

Proverbs 10:22 "The blessing of the LORD makes *one* rich, and He adds no sorrow with it." The Hebrew word translated "sorrow" means "hurt, pain, grief." When God blesses "the righteous and diligent" (Buzzell) with wealth, there is no grief that comes with it, as there is wealth obtained apart from the blessing of God. In short, "Riches from God are without the sorrow of ill-gotten wealth" (JFB).

When God blesses people with riches, there is no grief with it, as there is with riches gained illegally.

Proverbs 10:23 "To do evil *is* like sport to a fool, but a man of understanding has wisdom." Most of Proverbs 10:23-32 contains contrasts between righteousness and evil. The Hebrew word translated "sport" means "laughter, derision, sport." Fools find enjoyment in doing evil, but those who understand righteousness find "refreshment and delight" (Barnes), and "pleasure" (JFB) in wisdom. MacDonald says this: "A fool amuses himself by getting into trouble; it's his favorite sport. A man of understanding gets his pleasure in conducting himself wisely."

Fools find enjoyment in doing evil, but those who have understanding delight in wisdom.

Proverbs 10:24 "The fear of the wicked will come upon him, and the desire of the righteous will be granted." What the wicked fear, getting caught, will come and what the righteous desire, namely to do what is right and be of benefit to others, happens. It has been suggested that what the wicked fear, that is, "sickness, bankruptcy, and the loss of reputation" (Delitzsch) is often what happens to them, and what the righteous desire, that is, "the will of God in this life and the presence of God in the next" (MacDonald) is granted to them.

In Proverbs, Solomon is seeking to convince the naïve that in the long run, not necessarily in the immediate future, disaster comes to the wicked and the righteous are rewarded (Buzzell). The ultimate consequences of righteousness and wickedness should be considered.

The wicked get what they dread and the righteous get what they desire.

Proverbs 10:25 "When the whirlwind passes by, the wicked *is* no *more*, but the righteous *has* an everlasting foundation." When the storms of life come, the wicked are no more; storms destroy them (Buzzell). The righteous are secure, firmly fixed on a foundation of eternal truth. An everlasting foundation is a foundation incapable of being shaken (Delitzsch). As Jesus said, when the rain, flood, and wind come, the house built on a rock does not fall, but the house built on sand does (Mt. 7:24-27). Jesus is a rock (1 Cor. 10:4). There is "no other foundation" (1 Cor. 3:11).

The storms of life destroy the wicked, but the righteous rest on a sure foundation that enables them to weather the storms.

Proverbs 10:26 "As vinegar to the teeth and smoke to the eyes, so *is* the lazy *man* to those who send him." The Hebrew word translated "lazy" means "sluggish, lazy." As vinegar is sour to the taste (Buzzell) and as smoke irritates the eyes, so sending a lazy man to do something "causes vexation" (JFB), is annoying (MacDonald), and aggravating because he fails to carry out his responsibilities (Buzzell). The sender of the sluggish will experience sorrow.

The one who sends a lazy person to do something will be irritated.

Proverbs 10:27 "The fear of the LORD prolongs days, but the years of the wicked will be shortened." This is one of those passages many commentators skip. Some who do comment suggest that it is true from the perspective of eternity (Buzzell). This proverb and others clearly claim that the fear of the Lord (10:27; 14:27), obeying the Lord (3:1-2), and living a wise life (3:13-16; 4:10; 9:11) will add years to your life. It is common sense. The fear of the Lord "makes men content and satisfied in God" and "is truly the right principle of longevity," whereas "vice destroys body and soul" (Delitzsch).

This proverb, like all proverbs, is not an absolute law. By definition, proverbs are pithy statements that are generally true, meaning there are exceptions. In this case, martyrdom may be an exception, but as a general rule, "Wicked men are cut off prematurely, e.g., gangland slayings, reprisal killings, deaths caused by drunkenness, drugs, and dissipation" (MacDonald).

The fear of the Lord, which leads to righteous and wise living, adds days to a person's life, but living a wicked life can shorten one's life.

Proverbs 10:28 "The hope of the righteous *will be* gladness, but the expectation of the wicked will perish." The next five proverbs contrast the blessings of the righteous and the result of being wicked (if the previous proverb is included, six proverbs contrast the righteous and the wicked). The righteous experience longer life (10:27), joy (10:28), safety (10:29), security (10:30), and speech filled with wisdom (10:30-31).

Being righteous, the righteous look forward to things that are righteous. When their expectations are realized, there is joy. The wicked hope for evil things, which, even if obtained, do not produce joy.

"G. S. Bowes illustrates: 'Alexander the Great was not satisfied, even when he had completely subdued the nations. He wept because there were no more worlds to conquer, and he died at an early age in a state of debauchery. Hannibal, who filled three bushels with the gold rings taken from the knights he had slaughtered, committed suicide by swallowing poison. Few noted his passing, and he left this earth completely unmourned. Julius Caesar, 'dyeing his garments in the blood of one million of his foes,' conquered 800 cities, only to be stabbed by his best friend at the scene of his greatest triumph. After being the scourge of Europe, Napoleon, the feared conqueror, spent his last years in banishment'" (MacDonald).

The expectations of the righteous will be realized and bring joy, but the expectation of the wicked for joy will not be realized.

Proverbs 10:29 "The way of the LORD *is* strength for the upright, but destruction *will come* to the workers of iniquity." The Hebrew word translated "strength" means "place of safety, protection, refuge" (BDB), a "fortress, bulwark, defense" (Delitzsch), a "refuge of safety" (Buzzell). The upright, who follow the way of the Lord, have security, "a strong protection and safe retreat" (Delitzsch), but the workers of wickedness do not. In the providence of God, He watches over the upright, but He offers no such protection to the wicked.

The upright, those following the way of the Lord, are protected, but the wicked are not.

Proverbs 10:30 "The righteous will never be removed, but the wicked will not inhabit the earth." The righteous will never be removed from the land of promise (JFB), but the wicked will not abide in the land. "The history of Israel in their exile, which was a punishment of their national apostasy, confirms this proverb and explains its form" (Delitzsch; see also MacDonald). The righteous are secure; the wicked are not (Buzzell). The righteous might appear to be struggling now and the wicked might appear to be secure, but ultimately, the reverse will be true (NKJV Study Bible).

The righteous are secure in the will of God, but the wicked are not secure.

Proverbs 10:31 "The mouth of the righteous brings forth wisdom, but the perverse tongue will be cut out." The Hebrew word translated "brings forth" means to "bear fruit." As a tree naturally bears fruit, so the righteous naturally bear the fruit of wise words (Buzzell). The unrighteous have a perverse tongue, which will be cut down (Gill), "as an unproductive plant" (JFB). Every idle word will be judged (Mt. 12:36). "The abuse of God's gift of speech will lead ultimately to its forfeiture" (Barnes). "Were the tongue of every shrew or scold to be extracted, we should soon have much less noise in the world" (Clarke).

The righteous bear fruit of wise words, but the wicked speak perverse words that will be judged.

Jesus taught that it is out of the heart that we speak (Mt. 12:34). Good people speak good things and evil people speak evil things (Mt. 12:35). A tree is known by its fruit (Mt. 12:33). When you see apples, you know there is an apple tree. Likewise, when you hear wise words, you know there is a wise person; when you hear perverse words, you know they come from a perverse heart. The point is not to mask a perverse heart with wise words but to be righteous. Be righteous; wise words will follow. The problem is not our tongue; it is our heart.

Proverbs 10:32 "The lips of the righteous know what is acceptable, but the mouth of the wicked *what is* perverse." The Hebrew word translated "acceptable" means "goodwill, favor, acceptance." Because of what is in their heart ("know"), the righteous speak words of goodwill; they know what is "most pleasing and most profitable" (Clarke). The wicked speak "mere falsehood" (Delitzsch); they "distort the facts" (MacDonald). "As the love of God is not in his heart, so the law of kindness is not on his lips" (Clarke).

Because of what is in their hearts, the righteous speak words of goodwill, but the wicked speak falsely.

PROVERBS 11

Proverbs 11:1 "Dishonest scales *are* an abomination to the LORD, but a just weight *is* His delight." (20:23; 20:10; 16:11; Deut. 25:13-14). Dishonesty in business is an abomination to the Lord, but honesty in business dealings is His delight. Crooked merchants used two sets of stone weights when weighing merchandise. When buying, they used stones heavier than the standard, and when selling, they used stones lighter than the standard. Thus, with the use of "dishonest scales," merchants got more than they paid for and the customers received less (MacDonald; Buzzell). Today's version is the butcher who holds his hand on the steak when he weighs it, the farmer who feeds his cow salt to fill it up with water before he sells it, and the salesman who pads his expense account. Be honest.

In business transactions, dishonesty is an abomination to the Lord and honesty is His delight.

M. R. De Haan says, "Too often people have two standards-one for private use and one for public application to others. We measure ourselves by a different standard than we do our neighbor."

Proverbs 11:2 "When pride comes, then comes shame; but with the humble *is* wisdom." The Hebrew word translated "shame" means "dishonor, disgrace." Pride goes before a fall (16:8); it also goes before disgrace (pride→fall→dishonor), but humility goes before wisdom (humility→wisdom→honor). The proud evidently come to be discredited, disgraced, and dishonored. Being wise reduces the danger of stumbling (MacDonald) and being shamed. A rabbinic proverb says, "Lowly souls become full of wisdom as the low place becomes full of water" (cited by Barnes).

Pride produces dishonor, but humility results in wisdom and (implied) honor.

Proverbs 11:3 "The integrity of the upright will guide them, but the perversity of the unfaithful will destroy them." The integrity of the righteous guides them on the right track to safety (*cf.* the contrast "destroy"), like a shepherd leading sheep (JFB; Buzzell). It "guards them against the danger of erring" (Delitzsch). The unrighteous, who twist and pervert the truth, will be destroyed. "The disfiguring of truth avenges itself against them" (Delitzsch).

The integrity of the righteous guides them to keep them from danger, but the twisting of truth of the unrighteous leads to their destruction.

Proverbs 11:4 "Riches do not profit in the day of wrath, but righteousness delivers from death." The Hebrew word translated "profit" means "profit, benefit." The "day of wrath" refers to death (*cf.* the contrast between "day of wrath" and "death;" see Buzzell). The backdrop of this proverb is the "sin unto death" (1 Jn. 5:16), that is, the sin that leads to premature physical death (1 Cor. 11:30). When God judges, money will not buy off the judge or buy the judged out of the judgment of premature physical death. Wealth cannot avert the wrath of God, but "righteousness is a safeguard against premature death" (MacDonald).

Wealth cannot prevent the judgment of God, which includes premature physical death, but righteousness does.

Proverbs 11:5 "The righteousness of the blameless will direct his way aright, but the wicked will fall by his own wickedness." "Blameless" is "more in the negative sense of moral spotlessness than of moral perfection" (Delitzsch). Those who keep their conscience and character pure (Delitzsch) have an internal moral compass that helps them stay on the right path in life. Righteousness directs them. In contrast to the wicked, they do not stumble and fall. On the other hand, the wicked are directed by their wicked desires, which cause them to fall. Their desire to "do it my way" results in their destruction.

The blameless are directed by righteousness and thus take the right path, but the wicked are directed by their wickedness and thus fall.

Proverbs 11:6 "The righteousness of the upright will deliver them, but the unfaithful will be caught by *their* lust." The Hebrew word translated "unfaithful" means "to act or deal treacherously, faithlessly, deceitfully." Those who live a righteous life are delivered from moral dangers and damage, but those who "mask their intentions ever so cunningly, are ensnared in their passionate covetousness; the mask is removed, they are convicted and are caught" (Delitzsch). The righteous are directed (11:5) and delivered (11:6). These are but two of the benefits of righteous living. The wicked fall and are exposed.

The upright are delivered from moral damage, but unfaithful deceivers are caught by their own evil desires.

Proverbs 11:7 "When a wicked man dies, *his* expectation will perish, and the hope of the unjust perishes." When wicked and unjust people, those who only live for this life, use unjust means to get what they want, all they hope for comes to naught. They have no expectations beyond the grave. One Hebrew scholar put it like this: "A godless man to whom earthly possessions and pleasure and honor are the highest good, and to whom no means are too base, in order that he may appease his threefold passion, rocks himself in unbounded and measureless hopes; but with his death, his hope, *i.e.*, all that he hoped for, comes to naught" (Delitzsch). It has been said that a fool is a man whose plans end at the grave.

When wicked and unjust people die, all they had hoped to accomplish dies with them.

Proverbs 11:8 "The righteous is delivered from trouble, and it comes to the wicked instead." There are times when God not only delivers the righteous *from* trouble, He delivers trouble *to* the wicked. In the Book of Esther, God delivered Mordecai from trouble and delivered it to Haman. Instead of Mordecai being hanged, as Haman had planned, Haman was hanged (Esther 3-7)! In the book of Daniel, the three Hebrews were delivered out of the fiery furnace and the fire consumed their would-be executioners (Dan. 3:22-26). In these cases, the wicked received the trouble they planned to give to the righteous.

God delivers the righteous *from* trouble and delivers it *to* the wicked.

This is a proverb, not an absolute law.

Proverbs 11:9 "The hypocrite with *his* mouth destroys his neighbor, but through knowledge the righteous will be delivered." The Hebrew word translated "hypocrite" means "profane, irreligious, godless" ("godless" in the NASB and the NIV). With doubts and denials spewing out of their mouths, the godless destroy their neighbors. Their unbelief destroys the faith of their neighbor.

The righteous are delivered from destruction by knowledge. "Knowledge of the truth enables the righteous to detect the counterfeit and to save himself and others from subversion" (MacDonald). "The just is saved by superior discernment" (JFB).

What the godless say destroys their neighbor, but what the righteous know delivers them from destruction.

Proverbs 11:10 "When it goes well with the righteous, the city rejoices; and when the wicked perish, *there is* jubilation." This proverb, and the next one, talk about life in the city. When the righteous prosper, the whole city rejoices. In the righteous, a city has good examples that help keep the city morally healthy (Buzzell).

When the wicked perish, the city is jubilant. In the wicked, a city has bad examples who hurt the city morally. "Men breathe freer when the city is delivered from the tyranny and oppression which they (the wicked) exercise, and from the evil example which they gave" (Delitzsch). When those who "lie, slander, deceive, rob, and murder die," the city is "safer" (Buzzell).

A city joyfully celebrates when the righteous prosper and when the wicked perish.

Proverbs 11:11 "By the blessing of the upright the city is exalted, but it is overthrown by the mouth of the wicked." This proverb confirms the previous one (Delitzsch). Explanations of the "blessing of the upright" include the prayers of the upright for the city (Barnes), the benefits of the godly influence of the upright on the city (MacDonald), and the active benevolence of the upright in the city (JFB). Believers are the salt of the earth (Mt. 5:13).

On the other hand, "the deceit, broken promises, fraud, and profanity of the wicked are enough to ruin any local government" (MacDonald).

The beneficial activities of the upright exalt a city, but the words of the wicked wreck it.

Proverbs 11:12 "He who is devoid of wisdom despises his neighbor, but a man of understanding holds his peace." The Hebrew word translated "despises" means "despise, contempt." It refers to the contemptuous treatment of another person. One Hebrew scholar says no English word completely covers it. He suggests that it conveys what is derisive, degrading, or insulting (Delitzsch). Another commentator says it means to belittle someone (Buzzell). Those who lack wisdom despise others and say so (*cf.* those who have understanding hold their peace).

The wise keep their judgments to themselves. They abstain from "arrogant criticism" (Delitzsch). If they cannot find something admirable, they at least know how to be silent (Barnes). If you know something unpleasant about your neighbor, it is wise to keep quiet because slander creates friction and dissension (Buzzell).

Those who lack of wisdom have contempt for others and belittle them, but those with understanding remain silent.

Proverbs 11:13 "A talebearer reveals secrets, but he who is of a faithful spirit conceals a matter." The nature of talebearers is to tell what they know. Their propensity to talk leads them to break confidences (JFB). So, be on guard (Delitzsch). Those who tell tales about others will reveal your secrets too (Barnes).

Faithful friends know how to keep a confidence and how to refrain from telling tales (MacDonald). They do not betray trust (Buzzell).

Talebearers tell tales, even secrets, but the faithful do not reveal secrets told to them in confidence.

Proverbs 11:14 "Where *there is* no counsel, the people fall; but in the multitude of counselors *there is* safety." The Hebrew word translated "counsel" means "direction, counsel, guidance." Because this proverb speaks about the guidance of "people," it is generally considered a reference to the government of people, not necessarily individuals. The idea is, "Without wise leadership and statesmanship, the people are bound to fall into trouble" (MacDonald).

The Hebrew word translated "safety" means "deliverance, salvation." It is used for national success in war (24:6) and deliverance from personal trouble (Ps. 37:39).

"In the region of ecclesiastical and political affairs, and in general, it is found to be true that it is better with a people when they are governed according to the laws and conclusions which have resulted from the careful deliberation of many competent and authorized men than when their fate is entrusted unconditionally to one or to a few" (Delitzsch). The church is to be governed by a group of elders (Acts 14:23).

<u>When there is no wise counsel in the government of people, they fall into trouble, but when a multitude of counselors governs people, they are delivered from trouble.</u>

Seeking counselors (plural) is mentioned four times in Proverbs (11:14; 15:22; 20:18; 24:6).

Proverbs 11:15 "He who is surety for a stranger will suffer, but one who hates being surety is secure." The Hebrew word translated "suffer" means "evil, distress, misery, injury, calamity." Those who co-sign for someone they do not know, that is, guarantee a debt or a promissory note (MacDonald) for a stranger, may suffer financial loss, misery and distress, but those who hate the idea will be secure (Delitzsch: will have "good rest") from financial loss and other problems. This is a proverb, not a law. In other words, it is a generally true principle but not necessarily true in every case.

<u>As a general rule, those who secure the debt of someone they do not know will suffer calamity, but those who refuse to do so, because they hate the idea, will avoid all kinds of trouble.</u>

Proverbs 11:16 "A gracious woman retains honor, but ruthless *men* retain riches." The Hebrew word translated "gracious" means "favor, grace, elegance" (BDB), "kind, pleasant" (Strong). A gracious lady gains honor (e.g., Abigail in 1 Sam. 25). "Her company is sought, she finds her way into the best society, they praise her attractive, pleasant appearance" (Delitzsch).

The Hebrew word translated "ruthless" means "terror-striking" (BDB), "oppressor, violent" (Strong). A man strikes terror "because of his wickedness" (Buzzell). Such a man may gain wealth, but he will not get a "good name" (MacDonald); he does not enjoy honor, respect, or peace of mind (Buzzell).

<u>A gracious, kind woman gains honor, whereas a violent man may gain riches but not honor.</u>

Proverbs 11:17 "The merciful man does good for his own soul, but *he who is* cruel troubles his own flesh." Being merciful helps our mental and emotional health. Those who do good to others are good to themselves. An article in the *Los Angeles Times* reported that researchers have found that doing good for others has mental and physical benefits (*Los Angeles Times*, August 10, 2009, p. E3).

On the other hand, being cruel hurts our bodies. "A cruel disposition takes its toll on the body" (MacDonald). "Cruelty boomerangs, harming both its recipient and its giver" (Buzzell). Clarke cites a proverb that says, "He frets his flesh off his bones."

In other words, our disposition affects our health (MacDonald). "Both kindness and cruelty are reciprocal" (Buzzell). As reported in the *British Medical Journal,* no human body tissue is wholly removed from the spirit (cited by MacDonald).

<u>Those who are merciful do good things for their own mental and emotional health, but those who are cruel bring trouble to their physical health.</u>

Proverbs 11:18 "The wicked *man* does deceptive work, but he who sows righteousness *will have* a sure reward." The wicked deceive to get what they want, but what they actually get is not sure (*cf.* contrast). The expression "sows righteousness" means to live a righteous life, to do what is right. The Hebrew word translated "sure" means "faithfulness, reliable." The righteous do what is right and receive a reliable reward.

<u>The wicked deceive to obtain gain, but what they want, they do not always get, whereas the righteous are rewarded for doing what is right.</u>

Proverbs 11:19 "As righteousness *leads* to life, so he who pursues evil *pursues it* to his own death." Righteousness leading to life and wickedness leading to death are "frequent themes" in Proverbs (Buzzell). The life and death spoken of here are physical, not spiritual. "Righteousness delivers from death" (11:4). The evil that wicked people pursue slays them, like a man who pursues a serpent, captivated by its beauty but ignorant of its venom, overtakes it, only to be bitten by it, and killed (Wardlaw). To paraphrase Clarke, who captures the essence of this proverb, true godliness promotes health and is the best means of lengthening life, but wicked men do not live half their days.

<u>Righteousness leads to a healthier, longer life, but evil leads to premature physical death.</u>

Proverbs 11:20 "Those who are of a perverse heart *are* an abomination to the LORD, but *the* blameless in their ways *are* His delight." The Hebrew word translated "perverse" means "twisted, perverted, crooked" and the one rendered "abomination" means "repugnant, abhorrent, disgusting." The Lord detests distorted attitudes and actions (Buzzell). As far as the Lord is concerned, people with a "false" heart are "loathsome" (MacDonald). On the other hand, those who think straight and walk straight are a delight to the Lord.

The Lord is disgusted with those who don't think straight, but He delights in those who not only think straight, but walk straight.

Proverbs 11:21 "*Though they join* forces, the wicked will not go unpunished; but the posterity of the righteous will be delivered." Literally translated, the phrase "join forces" is "hand to hand." It is a reference to "clasping hands over an agreement" (Buzzell). The wicked may join in a confederation, but they will not go unpunished. "The combined power of the wicked cannot free them from just punishment, while the unaided children of the righteous find deliverance because of their pious relationship" (JFB).

The wicked who form a confederation will be punished, but the descendants of the righteous, who follow righteousness, will be delivered from punishment.

Proverbs 11:22 "*As* a ring of gold in a swine's snout, *so is* a lovely woman who lacks discretion." This is the first of many Proverbs that use the word "like" or "as" to make a comparison, called emblematic parallelism.

Like earrings today, a gold ring attached to the right nostril and hanging down over the mouth was a female ornament used since the time of the patriarchs (Gen. 24:47; Delitzsch). In this proverb, what is considered a lovely piece of jewelry on a lady is in the snout of a pig. A gold ring in a pig's nose is inappropriate, incongruous, and incompatible.

The Hebrew word rendered "discretion" means "taste, judgment, discernment." A lovely lady without good judgment and discernment is as unbecoming, unappealing, and unattractive as a gold ring in a pig's nose. Her outward beauty is lost in her lack of inward beauty. Instead of retaining honor (11:16), she only brings disgrace on herself (Bridges). As a gold ring does not make an ugly pig beautiful, so physical beauty does not make a woman who lacks good judgment and discernment attractive.

A lovely lady, who lacks good judgment and discernment, is as incongruous as a pig with a gold ring in its nose.

Proverbs 11:23 "The desire of the righteous *is* only good, *but* the expectation of the wicked *is* wrath." The righteous desire only what is good; thus, it is attainable and well-pleasing to God (Delitzsch), but the wicked hope for wrath. The last part of this proverb has been taken to mean either that God's wrath comes on the wicked or that the wicked desire only to vent their wrath (Buzzell). Since the expectation of the wicked is in contrast to the desire of the righteous, the meaning is that the wicked want to vent their wrath.

The righteous only desire what is good, but the wicked want to vent their wrath.

Proverbs 11:24 "There is *one* who scatters, yet increases more; and there is *one* who withholds more than is right, but it *leads* to poverty." This proverb and the next two are about generosity. This one is a paradox. Those who give gain and those who do not give lose. The farmer who scatters seed ends up with more, but the farmer who hoards seed ends up in poverty. As for giving, be generous (2 Cor. 9:6-8). "The bountiful man, who gives to the poor, never turning away his face from anyone in distress, the Lord blesses his property and the bread is multiplied in his hand" (Clarke). Spiritually, as Jim Elliot said, "He is no fool who gives what he cannot keep to gain what he cannot lose."

The generous gain, but the stingy end up in poverty.

Years ago, two young men were working their way through Stanford University. At one point, their money was almost gone, so they decided to engage the great pianist Paderewski for a concert and use the profits for board and tuition. Paderewski's manager asked for a guarantee of $2,000. Unfortunately, the concert was during the Lenten season, a bad time for concerts. The box office receipts totaled only $1,600. In great anguish, the students turned over the entire amount to Paderewski's secretary, saying that they were very sorry, but it would be necessary for the renowned pianist to wait for the rest of his fee. It appeared that their college days were over.

When the great artist heard about what happened, he directed that the two students pay all their expenses for the auditorium and advertising from the fund on hand and deduct 20% of the gross receipts for themselves. The small remainder would be his fee. His liberal attitude greatly impressed the two students. They determined that if they could ever return the favor somehow, they certainly would do so.

Years passed. Following World War I, Paderewski became the premier of Poland. Thousands of his countrymen were starving. Paderewski appealed to the head of the U.S. Food and Relief Bureau. As a result, thousands of tons of food were delivered to Poland. Later, he met the American statesman to thank him. "That's all right," replied Herbert Hoover. "Besides, you don't remember, but you helped me once when I was a student in college."

Paderewski's generosity resulted in great gain—for a whole country!

Proverbs 11:25 "The generous soul will be made rich, and he who waters will also be watered himself." The Hebrew word translated "generous" means "blessing" and the one rendered "rich" means "fat," a "figure for prosperity" (Barnes). Watering was a common figure for blessing (JFB). People who bless others, that is, give "freely and fully" (Barnes), prosper and are blessed (Delitzsch).

People who bless others prosper and are themselves blessed.

Proverbs 11:26 "The people will curse him who withholds grain, but blessing *will be* on the head of him who sells *it*." Many commentaries conclude that the backdrop of this proverb is selling or not selling grain during a time of famine (Delitzsch; Barnes; MacDonald; Buzzell; et al.). The point is that some withhold their stores of corn in times of scarcity, speculating on receiving a higher price as the famine grows worse. People curse such selfishness and bless those willing to accept a modest gain to help others.

Proverbs 11:24-26 is about generosity. Farmers who are generous with their sowing of seed gain more materially (11:24). Generous people end up blessing themselves (11:25) and receiving the blessing of others (11:26).

<u>People curse selfish commercial gain, but bless those who use their business to help others.</u>

Proverbs 11:27 "He who earnestly seeks good finds favor, but trouble will come to him who seeks *evil*." Those who seek the good of others will find favor in their eyes, but those who seek evil will not find favor; instead, they will find trouble. Be careful what you seek, for what you seek will find you (Delitzsch). MacDonald puts it like this: "When a man's motives are pure and unselfish, he wins the esteem of others. But the man who is out to cause trouble for others will get it for himself."

<u>Those who seek the good of others will find favor from them, but those who seek to do evil to others will find trouble for themselves.</u>

Proverbs 11:28 "He who trusts in his riches will fall, but the righteous will flourish like foliage." Riches are uncertain and therefore not worthy of our trust (1 Tim. 6:17-19). The rich who trust their money, rather than the Lord, to be free from danger will go to their ruin (Delitzsch). Samuel Johnson said, "The lust of gold, unfeeling and remorseless, is the last corruption of degenerate man."

The righteous, who trust the Lord rather than riches, will flourish like green leaves on a tree.

<u>Those who trust riches rather than the Lord will fail, but the righteous, who trust the Lord rather than riches, will flourish like the green leaves on a beautiful tree.</u>

Proverbs 11:29 "He who troubles his own house will inherit the wind, and the fool *will be* servant to the wise of heart." Various suggestions of what a man does to trouble his house include denying his servants sufficient food and necessary recreation (Delitzsch), worrying to the point of making those around him miserable (Barnes), being a drunkard, a crank, or an adulterer (listed by Buzzell) and being greedy of gain (JFB; MacDonald; Buzzell). The one who troubles his family because he is greedy for material gain obtains the wind, that is, he does not get what will satisfy his greed. Instead of being a fool, he ends up a servant to the wise (MacDonald). Buzzell suggests this means "to bring trouble on one's own family members means that such a person will be disinherited from the estate; he will receive only wind or nothing. And rather than being wealthy and having servants, such a fool becomes a servant!"

<u>By troubling your family, you not only gain nothing but end up being a fool who serves the wise in the family.</u>

Proverbs 11:30 "The fruit of the righteous *is a* tree of life, and he who wins souls *is* wise." Fruit is that which a tree produces for others, not for itself. One of the results of living a righteous life is the benefit to others. A righteous life impacts other people. The words and actions of a righteous person exert a refreshing, happy influence on others (Delitzsch). "A righteous life is like a fruit-bearing tree that brings nourishment and refreshment to others" (MacDonald). By this means, the righteous and wise person wins others, not for himself, but for righteousness and wisdom (Delitzsch; MacDonald).

<u>One of the results of living a righteous and wise life is making an impact on others who are won to living a wise, righteous life.</u>

Richard Gibbs, an old Puritan doctor, wrote *The Bruised Reed*. A copy fell into the hands of a boy named Richard Baxter, resulting in his conversion. In later years, Baxter authored a large number of tracts and books. His *Saints' Rest* and *Call to the Unconverted* was translated into many languages. Through them, multitudes of sinners were led to Jesus—including Philip Doddridge, who became a famous preacher, hymn writer, and the president of a theological seminary. Doddridge wrote the well-circulated book *The Rise and Progress of Religion in the Soul*, which proved a rich blessing. William Wilberforce read it and came to Christ. After being instrumental in freeing a great number of slaves in the British colonies, Wilberforce penned *A Practical View of Christianity*. This changed the life of Leigh Richmond, who became a world-famous writer of tracts that influenced thousands to seek the Lord.

Proverbs 11:31 "If the righteous will be recompensed on the earth, how much more the ungodly and the sinner." Many commentators consider the word "recompense" a reference to discipline for sin (Barnes; MacDonald; Buzzell). The second half of the proverb seems to suggest that is the meaning. Moses was excluded from the Promised Land. The point of the proverb is that if the righteous are punished, surely the ungodly will much more be. If the righteous reap what they sow, how much more do the ungodly! Peter quotes the Septuagint translation of this verse: "If the righteous one is scarcely saved, where will the ungodly and the sinner appear?" (1 Pet. 4:18).

<u>If the righteous are disciplined, how much more will the ungodly be punished.</u>

PROVERBS 12

Proverbs 12:1 "Whoever loves instruction loves knowledge, but he who hates correction *is* stupid." The Hebrew word rendered "instruction" means "discipline, correction." Those who love, that is, desire (Buzzell) discipline, want to learn. The Hebrew word translated "correction" means "correction, reprove, rebuke" and the one rendered "stupid" comes from the Hebrew word for "beast" and means "brutishness." It is the idea of being dumb, stupid, and unreceptive, like an animal. Those who resent, refuse, and reject reproof and rebuke are just plain dumb. They get no more benefit from correction than the ox does from the goad (Clarke).

Those who desire to learn and grow welcome knowledge that will help them do that, but those who resent reproof are stupid.

Proverbs 12:2 "A good *man* obtains favor from the LORD, but a man of wicked intentions He will condemn." Proverbs uses many words to describe the righteous and wise, such as upright (11:3), blameless (11:5), a man of understanding (11:12), he who is of a faithful spirit (11:13), merciful (11:17), generous (11:25), etc. In this proverb, the righteous are described as "good." The Hebrew word translated "good" means "pleasant, agreeable, good." It can also mean "kind" (BDB). The Hebrew word translated "favor" means "goodwill, favor, acceptance, pleasure." The Lord accepts, favors, and even takes pleasure in those who are kind to others. The Lord condemns the wicked.

The Lord accepts with pleasure and favors those who are kind to others, but He condemns the wicked.

Proverbs 12:3 "A man is not established by wickedness, but the root of the righteous cannot be moved." The wicked are like seeds on top of a rock (MacDonald); they have no roots. Thus, they do not have stability. Because the righteous have roots in righteousness, they are not uprooted when the storms of life come.

The wicked are not established because they do not have roots, but since the righteous have roots in righteousness, they cannot be uprooted.

Proverbs 12:4 "An excellent wife *is* the crown of her husband, but she who causes shame *is* like rottenness in his bones." The Hebrew word translated "excellent" means "strength, ability, efficiency," often involving moral worth (BDB). It is translated "virtuous" (KJV), "excellent" (NASB), "of noble character" (NIV). It implies "strength of character" (Barnes). Such a wife makes her husband proud and honored, like a king who wears a crown. "She adds dignity to him" (Buzzell). For the Jews, the crown was also a sign "not of kingly power only, but also of joy and gladness" (Barnes; also see 3:11). In other words, a wife's strength of character (Buzzell) is a source of pride and joy for her husband. He holds his head high.

Conversely, a wife who is "not noble or strong morally" is a source of shame (Clarke), which, like rotten bones, gives her husband inner pain (Buzzell). He bows his head in shame. "An unhappy marriage gnaws at the marrow of life, it destroys the happiness of life, disturbs the pursuit, and undermines the life of the husband" (Delitzsch). It has been suggested that rottenness of the bones is an "an incurable evil" (JFB).

A wife, who is a strong, virtuous woman, makes her husband feel like an honored, joyful king, but a wife, who is not a strong, virtuous woman, brings shame and personal pain to her husband.

Mary Wesley was not a crown to her husband but a cross. Someone said, "How you accept your new role; how you adjust to your new situation; how you adapt to your husband's new work becomes very important."

Proverbs 12:5 "The thoughts of the righteous *are* right, *but* the counsels of the wicked *are* deceitful." The Hebrew word translated "thoughts" means "device, plan, purpose" (BDB). The purposes and plans of the righteous "for themselves and others" (Buzzell) have "an objective rule, namely, that which is right in the sight of God and of men" (Delitzsch). Their goals are "honorable and just" (MacDonald), "fair and honest" (Buzzell).

The wicked "have only a selfish purpose, which they seek to attain by deceiving and at the cost of their neighbor" (Delitzsch). Their advice is "dishonest and self-serving" (Buzzell), designed to "trick and defraud their neighbors" (Gill). Bridges cites biblical examples such as Daniel's enemies under the pretense of honoring the king, Sanballat under the guise of friendship, Haman under the cover of patriotism, and Herod under the profession of worshipping the infant Savior.

In other words, "A man's aims are a mirror of his character" (MacDonald). "One's thoughts and words are usually consistent with his character" (Buzzell). The actions of the righteous reveal their thoughts, but the wicked think one way and act another. Their words and their deeds are not a "fair index" of their thoughts (Wardlaw).

The objectives of the righteous are right, but because the wicked are selfish, they deceive others.

Proverbs 12:6 "The words of the wicked *are*, 'Lie in wait for blood,' but the mouth of the upright will deliver them." The wicked use words "to lay fatal traps for the innocent and unwary" (MacDonald), to destroy people (Buzzell). To accomplish their aims, they use deceitful words (12:5).

The expression "the mouth of the upright" implies speaking truth, not entreaty (Wardlaw). The upright deliver others by speaking the truth (Delitzsch). They rescue "victims attacked by gossipers and slanderers" (Buzzell). Some suggest that the second half of this proverb means the upright deliver themselves and others by speaking the truth (MacDonald).

The wicked use words of deceit to hurt and harm others, but the upright speak words of truth to rescue others from danger.

Proverbs 12:7 "The wicked are overthrown and *are* no more, but the house of the righteous will stand." Wicked people eventually meet a situation that overwhelms and overthrows them. When that happens, "it is all over with them" (Delitzsch). "They are no more; they cease to exist." They are "overthrown in death" (Buzzell). In the book of Esther, Haman illustrates the wicked being overthrown to be no more (Bridges).

Righteous people are not overwhelmed or overthrown; they overcome. They are standing on a rock when all around them is sinking sand. "When justice catches up with the wicked, that's the end of them. Godly people have a good foundation; they are not swept away by calamity" (MacDonald).

It has been suggested that Solomon had an example of this proverb in the case of Saul and his father David. Saul seemed to be the master of the situation and David seemed to be forsaken, but Saul was overthrown, while David and his house were established (Wardlaw).

Eventually, the wicked are overthrown in death, but the righteous and their house overcome the overwhelming calamities of life.

Proverbs 12:8 "A man will be commended according to his wisdom, but he who is of a perverse heart will be despised." The first half of this proverb could mean that wise people are commended either by others, by God, or by both (Wardlaw). The second half indicates that Solomon has others in mind. Perverse people, not poor people or uneducated people, are despised by others. The Hebrew word rendered "despised" means "contempt." "People speak well of one who has insight and acts wisely, but they have nothing but contempt for one who has no principles" (MacDonald).

The wise receive commendation, but the perverse receive contempt from others.

Proverb 12:9 "Better *is the one* who is slighted but has a servant, than he who honors himself but lacks bread." This is the first of 19 verses in Proverbs that use the "better… than" formula (see 12:9; 15:16-17; 16:8, 16, 19, 32; 17:1, 12; 19:1, 22; 21:9, 19; 22:1; 25:7; 25:24; 27:5; 27:10; 28:6). The Hebrew word translated "slighted" means "dishonored, held of little account" (BDB). This proverb is used to describe one who has a low position (Barnes), one who is obscure (JFB), one who is unknown, or a nobody (Buzzell). This unknown is not poor (Clarke); he has a slave. By contrast, some self-conceited people (JFB) honor themselves and do not have enough bread to eat.

It is better to be of low rank with food on the table than to pretend to have status with starvation (MacDonald). "Respectable mediocrity is better than boastful poverty" (Barnes). "What good is boasting if one cannot put food on the table?"(Buzzell).

It is better to be unknown and have some material possessions than to honor oneself and have nothing.

It is better to be humble with something than proud with nothing.

Proverbs 12:10 "A righteous *man* regards the life of his animal, but the tender mercies of the wicked *are* cruel." God cares about animals and includes compassion toward them in His Law (Ex. 20:10; 23:5; Deut. 22:6; see Jonah 4:11).

Therefore, kindness extends to animals. The righteous do not inflict "unnecessary pain" on them (Delitzsch). The modern proverb says, "Be kind to dumb animals." It has been said, "You can tell a lot about a person's character by the way he treats creatures that cannot defend themselves or fight back." Beyond animals, the point is that people who do what is right in God's sight are concerned about more than themselves. "He deserves not the designation of a 'righteous man,' who is destitute of mercy. He is without one of the most important features of resemblance to God" (Wardlaw).

The second half of this proverb is an oxymoron: compassionless compassion (loveless love). A wicked man is cruel to animals, even when he thinks he is being gentle (MacDonald). "The kindest thing a sinner does is really cruel. He does not know how to treat his livestock properly" (Clarke).

The righteous have compassion, even to animals, but the wicked are cruel to animals, even when they think they are being compassionate.

In 1846, a commentator on this proverb observed, "The delight of children in putting animals to pain for amusement, if not early restrained, will mature them in cruelty, demoralize their whole character, and harden them against all the sympathies of social life." He goes on to quote another of his day who said, "They who delight in the suffering and destruction of inferior creatures will not be apt to be very compassionate and benign to those of their own kind" (Bridges). Twenty-first-century psychologists say something similar.

Proverbs 12:11 "He who tills his land will be satisfied with bread, but he who follows frivolity *is* devoid of understanding." This proverb is similar to Proverbs 12:19. Obviously, this contrasts the industrious and the idle. The first fellow is a hardworking man; he plows, sows, reaps, thrashes, and grinds to produce his bread (Wardlaw).

The second fellow is frivolous. The Hebrew word translated "frivolity" means "empty, vain, and worthless" and is used of unprofitable things (BDB). Here, it describes an idle, frivolous, time-killing person (Wardlaw). Based on the first half of the proverb, it would be expected that the second half would say that the fellow who pursues unprofitable ventures would lack bread, but instead, it says he lacks understanding, which is the root of his problem.

In the words of one commentator, "A man who engages in positive, constructive work, like farming, will have his needs supplied. But the man who spends his time in worthless pursuits has an empty cupboard and an empty head" (MacDonald). Another says, "The proverb recommends the cultivation of the field as the surest means of supporting oneself honestly and abundantly, in contrast to the grasping after vain, *i.e.*, unrighteous means of subsistence, windy speculations, and the like" (Delitzsch).

<u>Those who work have their needs met, but those who pursue worthless ventures lack having their most basic needs met and lack understanding.</u>

Proverbs 12:12 "The wicked covet the catch of evil *men,* but the root of the righteous yields *fruit.*" The Hebrew word translated "catch" means "net" (see "net" in the KJV; "booty" in the NASB; and "plunder" in the NIV). The wicked covet what evil men catch in a net, implying things gained by illegitimate or fraudulent means (Wardlaw), what is taken from others unjustly (MacDonald). When wicked people see the devices of evil people succeed, they are envious and try to imitate what the evil people do (Wardlaw). The wicked emulate each other in wickedness; if they see wicked men more successful than themselves, they desire to discover their plans to imitate them (Bridges). They have no inward principles of righteousness.

On the other hand, righteous people are like a plant whose secure roots cause it to bear fruit (Buzzell). They have deep-seated principles that produce righteous acts.

<u>Wicked people covet the devices of evil people, but the righteous have a root desire that produces righteous fruit.</u>

Proverbs 12:13 "The wicked is ensnared by the transgression of *his* lips, but the righteous will come through trouble." In various ways, Proverbs 12:13-20 and 12:22-23 speak of right and wrong speech (10:11-14, 18-21, 31-32; 11:9, 11-13).

Their own words often trap the wicked. In the previous verse, the wicked trap others; in this verse, they trap themselves. Those who lie and deceive will be discovered sooner or later (Clarke). Flatterers fall by their own words (JFB). By failing to tell a consistent story, the wicked trip themselves up (MacDonald). The righteous avoid trouble by telling the truth.

<u>The wicked are trapped by their own words, but because the righteous speak the truth, they avoid trouble.</u>

Proverbs 12:14 "A man will be satisfied with good by the fruit of *his* mouth, and the recompense of a man's hands will be rendered to him." The fruit of a person's mouth is his or her words. When people use their words for good, it is good for them. A blessing bestowed on others benefits you. When commentators expand on what is spoken, they say things like right guidance, comforting exhortation, peace-bringing consolation for others (Delitzsch), wholesome advice, expressions of encouragement, consolation, kindness (Wardlaw), and wise, gentle, pure speech (Buzzell).

What is true of words is also true of their work. Hard work is compensated. In short, "Good speech and good behavior carry their own reward with them" (Buzzell).

<u>Good words and hard work benefit the speaker and the worker.</u>

Proverbs 12:15 "The way of a fool *is* right in his own eyes, but he who heeds counsel *is* wise" (see 16:2; 21:2). Fools are proud, high-minded, and self-sufficient (Wardlaw). Their standard for determining right from wrong is their own opinion (Delitzsch). "You can't tell a fool anything. He knows everything and will not listen" (MacDonald).

The wise are humble (Wardlaw). They have a teachable spirit (Bridges). They are not so wise in their own eyes that they are unwilling to listen to others; they do not consider their judgment unerring (Delitzsch). They welcome advice (MacDonald). "O God, save me from myself—from my own self-deceitfulness" (Bridges).

<u>Since fools think they are right, they do not receive instruction, but the wise hear and heed the wise counsel of others.</u>

We tend to listen to those who tell us what we want to hear. If you are bent on doing it "my way," you will seek advice from someone who will reinforce your decisions. Don't be a fool; be wise. Seek counsel from someone who will tell you the truth.

The pastor of a small church sensed he needed guidance in determining what to do concerning a situation in his church. He turned to his uncle, Dr. M. R. De Haan, the nationally-known Bible teacher. The young pastor said at the time, "I went to him because he was older and wiser. I also knew he wanted the best for me and would tell me the truth—even if it hurt! His advice, for which I am deeply grateful, was just what I needed" (*Our Daily Bread*, 4/19/1983).

Proverbs 12:16 "A fool's wrath is known at once, but a prudent *man* covers shame." The Hebrew word rendered "shame" means "dishonor, disgrace." In this proverb, it refers to "any affront" (Wardlaw). This proverb is talking about being dishonored. When annoyed, perhaps by an insult, fools immediately show it (Buzzell). They blow up at the slightest provocation (MacDonald). They are easily angered and generally speak whatever comes first to their mind (Clarke). They cannot restrain their wrath (Barnes). Not controlling their passions, they allow their anger to "burst forth in whatever place, time or circumstance; and no matter in whose presence" (Wardlaw).

On the other hand, those who are prudent control their response (Buzzell). They know "how to ignore the insult and to exercise self-control" (MacDonald). As Delitzsch explains, when an injury is done to a fool, he immediately shows his vexation in a passionate manner, while those who are prudent maintain silence as to the dishonor done to them, repressing their displeasure so as not to increase their vexation to their injury.

<u>When offended, fools do not control their anger, but the prudent exercise self-control.</u>

Proverbs 12:17 "He *who* speaks truth declares righteousness, but a false witness, deceit." The meaning of this proverb seems obvious. In fact, a number of commentators skip it, but there is more here than lies on the surface (Bridges).

The Hebrew word translated "speak" means "breathe, utter" (BDB). The idea here is that when people speak, they are breathing out (uttering) what is inside. A Hebrew scholar says the point is a "causal connection (between) the internal character of men and their utterances." He adds that those with character speak the truth, but those who speak that which is not true confirm their "impure character" by what they say (Delitzsch). Those without character not only reveal who they are, they also conceal the truth, misrepresent the truth, and deceive people (Bridges).

Focusing on the word "witness," this proverb has been interpreted to mean witnessing in court. "A witness who tells the truth in court gives righteous evidence. A false witness tells lies" (MacDonald; NIV). Those who "tell the truth, the whole truth, and nothing but the truth" serve the interest of righteousness, contributing to a just result, but false witnesses mislead and deceive, "drawing judge and jury, and audience into a wrong train, and producing a false and unrighteous verdict, which acquits the guilty or condemns the innocent" (Wardlaw).

<u>People with character speak the truth in court and everywhere else, but people who lack character lie and deceive.</u>

One of the striking traits in the character of Ulysses S. Grant was his absolute truthfulness. He seemed to have an actual dread of deception. One day, while sitting in his bedroom in the White House, where he had retired to write a message to Congress, word of an unscheduled visitor was brought in by a servant. Seeing that the President did not want to be disturbed, an officer said to the attendant, "Just tell him the President is not in." Overhearing the remark, Grant swung around in his chair and cried out, "Tell him no such thing. I don't lie and don't want anyone else to do so for me."

Proverbs 12:18 "There is one who speaks like the piercings of a sword, but the tongue of the wise *promotes* health." The Hebrew word translated "speaks" means "speak rashly, thoughtlessly," and the one rendered "health" means "healing, cure, health." It has been translated "medicine" (see Delitzsch) and "means of healing" (Delitzsch; NASB; NIV). Thus, the point of this proverb is that thoughtless words are like a sword that *wounds* others, but the words of the wise *heal*. Harsh words hurt; the gentle words of the wise heal.

Jibes, jests, and jokes can cut to the core. Sarcasm and sometimes silliness can pierce the heart. "This is especially the case when the words are from the lips of a friend, or one we love, when heated by sudden passion. The utterance of the moment can embitter the future of a lifetime" (Wardlaw).

On the other hand, the words of the wise can calm and comfort. What they say can be a means of support and encouragement. Their word "soothes the sorrowful, comforts the afflicted, cheers the drooping and despondent in spirit, promotes peace and concord, justice and piety, personal and social happiness" (Wardlaw).

<u>Thoughtless words wound; wise words heal.</u>

This ancient proverb puts the lie to the modern proverb: "Sticks and stones may break my bones, but words cannot hurt me." As someone has said, "Words break no bones, but they do break hearts." Saying to children such things as "You are a failure" or "You are no good" can do great damage.

Proverbs 12:19 "The truthful lip shall be established forever, but a lying tongue *is* but for a moment." Spoken words that are true live forever. "How important is it to eye eternity in all of our words!"(Bridges).

Lies soon die. Some commentators say that the Hebrew phrase rendered "for a moment" is an idiom, which is literally "a twinkling of the eye" or "a wink of the eye" (Delitzsch; MacDonald; Buzzell). One explanation of the second half of this proverb is that lies do not last long because they are soon detected and exposed (Clarke; JFB).

Another goes like this: "Should it (a lie) escape our detection for a whole life, yet for eternity before us, what a moment is that!"(Bridges). This view takes into account that the second half of the proverb is in contrast to the first.

<u>Truth is eternal; lies do not last long.</u>

Proverbs 12:20 "Deceit is in the heart of those who devise evil, but counselors of peace have joy." People who plan evil have malicious deceit in their hearts. The contrast with those seeking peace implies that the ones planning evil are also preparing sorrow for themselves (Delitzsch).

The Hebrew word translated "peace" means "soundness, welfare" as well as "peace." People who think about how to promote the peace and welfare of others have joy in their hearts. Also, as the deception is not self-deception, so the joy is not only for the ones contemplating peace but also for others (Barnes; Delitzsch).

<u>Deceit fills the hearts of those who plan evil, but joy fills the hearts of those who pursue peace.</u>

Two slick "con" men boarded a train that ran between New York and Boston and singled out a prosperous-looking individual. Sitting next to him, they invited him to play a game of cards. Soon, the "prosperous-looking individual" was several hundred dollars in the red. The winner agreed to take a check, but once he had it in his hands, he acted conscience-stricken and tore it up. "I never thought you'd lose so much money. Let's call the whole thing off," he said. Impressed with their generosity, the loser insisted on writing a new one. Later, when his checks returned from the bank, he found that the second and first checks had been cashed! The crook had quickly slipped the first one into his pocket and had torn up a blank one instead. The loser was hooked twice. We would never think of deceiving anyone like that, would we? No, we would not, but we do deceive others. What is the form you use?

Proverbs 12:21 "No grave trouble will overtake the righteous, but the wicked shall be filled with evil." Compared to the previous proverb, the righteous experience joy and protection (Buzzell). The Hebrew word translated "grave trouble" means "trouble, sorrow, wickedness." Delitzsch says that although it may be used for any misfortune in general, this proverb signifies evil as ethical wickedness. The contrast indicates that this conclusion is correct. In other words, the kind of wickedness sin produces does not fall on the righteous (Delitzsch). "The just are preserved from the evil consequences that follow the behavior of the wicked" (MacDonald).

Conversely, "the wicked experience trouble" (Buzzell). The wicked are "hurt, grieved, and wounded, by every occurrence; and nothing turns to their profit" (Clarke).

<u>The righteous are protected against the evil and trouble caused by sin, but the wicked are filled with evil and trouble.</u>

Proverbs 12:22 "Lying lips *are* an abomination to the LORD, but those who deal truthfully *are* His delight." MacDonald says it all: "God hates liars. How careful we should be about shading the truth, white lies, exaggerations, and half-truths! A sure way of bringing delight to His heart is by being absolutely honest and trustworthy." The God of truth is pleased and delighted with His children when they tell the truth, but He hates lies.

<u>God hates lies, but He delights in those who tell the truth.</u>

During a Sunday School class, the teacher discussed what the Bible says about lying. She concluded by asking one of the boys, "Would you tell a lie for a penny?" "No, I certainly would not," he quickly replied. "For a dime?" "Not for a dime!" "How about a quarter?" "Nope!" he responded with emphasis. "Supposing you could get a thousand quarters by telling a fib," the teacher questioned. "Would you do it for that?" The boy thought for a moment. "A thousand quarters! That's a lot of money!" Just then, another one of the pupils spoke up. "Teacher, I wouldn't do it even for a thousand quarters!" "Well, why not?" the instructor asked. "Because," the boy answered, "When the quarters have all been spent, and the things bought with them are gone too, the lie would still be there. You see, teacher, a lie sticks!"

Proverbs 12:23 "A prudent man conceals knowledge, but the heart of fools proclaims foolishness." The Hebrew word translated "prudent" means "crafty, shrewd, sensible." Sensible people do not go around showing off how much they know. They modestly conceal their knowledge (MacDonald).

Fools blurt out their folly (Buzzell). "You aren't long in the presence of fools before they reveal their foolishness" (MacDonald).

<u>Sensible people do not parade their knowledge, but fools cannot wait to proclaim their folly.</u>

"I have known men of some learning, so intent on immediately informing a company how well cultivated their minds were that they have passed … for insignificant pedants" (Clarke).

Wise are the people who know when to share their wisdom.

Proverb 12:24 "The hand of the diligent will rule, but the lazy *man* will be put to forced labor." When one nation conquers another, the conqueror rules and the conquered serve. This proverb indicates that beyond political divisions, there lies an ethical law (Barnes). The diligent rise to a position of leadership (MacDonald). They rise to be in charge (Clarke; Buzzell).

The lazy end up being forced to do the hard labor. Solomon had firsthand experience with compulsory labor (1 Kings 9:21).

Diligence leads to leadership; laziness leads to forced labor.

Proverbs 12:25 "Anxiety in the heart of man causes depression, but a good word makes it glad." The Hebrew word translated "depression" means "to be bowed down" and is used figuratively of being depressed. Having a "down day" may be caused by anxious care.

A "good word" is a word of sympathy, kindness, encouragement, and a word from God (Wardlaw). "Friendly encouragement from a sympathizing heart cheers the sorrowful soul" (Delitzsch). A "sympathetic word works wonders in perking someone up again" (MacDonald). An empathetic, kind word can cheer up an anxious, depressed person (Buzzell).

A heavy heart bows people down, but an encouraging word cheers them up.

Speak an encouraging word to someone today.

Proverbs 12:26 "The righteous should choose his friends carefully, for the way of the wicked leads them astray." Righteous people choose their friends carefully because they are aware that wicked friends can lead them astray. The wicked are unconcerned about who becomes their friend (Buzzell).

The righteous select their friends with care, aware that how the wicked live their lives can lead them astray.

Parents should have their children memorize this proverb—the earlier the better, but it applies to adults as well.

Proverbs 12:27 "The lazy *man* does not roast what he took in hunting, but diligence *is* man's precious possession." The Hebrew word translated "roast" only appears here in the Old Testament. Its meaning is obscure. Thus, this proverb may mean the lazy man does not even go after food (Vulgate) or that he hunts but is too lazy to cook what he gets (Buzzell). The latter is the traditional translation (see KJV; NASB; and NIV). The lazy man does not cook what he catches. He may make some effort and may even have some success, but he does not finish the job. He goes hunting, catches prey, and brings it home, but because of sheer laziness, the loafer lets it lie until it becomes useless. "His fit of exertion is soon over" (Bridges). "His labor is lost" (Wardlaw).

The diligent value what they have worked for (MacDonald) suggests they turn their substance to good account (Wardlaw). It also implies that the lazy do not value what they own (Buzzell).

The lazy do not finish what they start, but the diligent value their possessions, thus making the best use of them.

Proverbs 12:28 "In the way of righteousness *is* life, and in *its* pathway *there is* no death." This proverb is not talking about eternal life at the end of life (see "way" and "pathway"). "Life after death lies beyond the horizon of Proverbs" (Kidner, p. 56). It is talking about temporal life (Buzzell). The *way* of righteousness promotes real life. There is no death in living a righteous life.

In the Bible, "death" is not always what we normally think of when we hear the word. It is not necessarily physical, spiritual, or eternal death. In Proverbs 5:23, the fate of the wicked, "He shall die," is explained in the second line as "he shall go astray.'" Paul speaks of a widow who is "dead while she lives" (1 Tim. 5:6). The fact that Paul mentions her in the context of supporting widows indicates she is a believer. In other words, it is possible for a believer to be dead, not in the sense of being unregenerate, but in the sense of not having an active spiritual life. Revelation speaks of a church being "dead." (Rev. 3:1). The church at Sardis had some works but no vital spiritual life (see also the "dead" womb of Sarah in Rom. 4:17).

In his commentary on the Gospel of John, Barclay says, "A man can become so selfish that he is dead to the needs of others. A man can become so insensitive that he is dead to the feelings of others. A man can become so involved in the petty dishonesties and the petty disloyalties of life that he is dead to honor" (Barclay, *John*, vol. 2, p. 110). Sin kills reputations, health, marriages, relationships, etc.

Living righteously is real life—life that does not result in the kinds of death sin produces.

PROVERBS 13

Proverbs 13:1 "A wise son *heeds* his father's instruction, but a scoffer does not listen to rebuke." A wise son is receptive to parental instruction (Buzzell), but a scoffer refuses to hear not only instruction, but also "the much stronger rebuke" (Barnes). Scoffers think they have all the answers and refuse to be corrected (MacDonald). "The proud spirit does not easily bend" (Bridges). "The child that is permitted to fulfill its own will and have its own way, will jest at the reproofs of its parents" (Clarke).

Wise sons listen to and learn from instruction, but scoffers not only do not listen but also ridicule instruction and rebuke.

Those who are blessed do not sit in the seat of the scorner (Ps. 1:1).

Proverbs 13:2 "A man shall eat well by the fruit of *his* mouth, but the soul of the unfaithful feeds on violence." The expression "the fruit of his mouth" refers to edifying, encouraging, and comforting words. Such speech not only benefits others, but it is also food to the one who speaks. Speakers of edifying words are rewarded when they see the results of their words (MacDonald). "What he gives, he receives" (Buzzell).

Then, some do not desire to help others but harm them with their words (Buzzell). The Hebrew word translated "unfaithful" means "to act or deal treacherously, deceitfully" (BDB; NASB). Those who speak deceitfully and act treacherously end up eating their words in the sense that their intended violence is turned on them. They bear the consequences of their evil intent (Delitzsch). They are repaid in kind (Barnes).

Those who speak words that help others are themselves benefitted and those who speak and act in such a way as to hurt others are repaid in kind.

Proverbs 13:3 "He who guards his mouth preserves his life, *but* he who opens wide his lips shall have destruction." People who control what they say prevent damage to themselves (MacDonald). Being careful about what you say will keep you out of trouble (Buzzell).

Those who do not exercise self-control over their speech will have trouble (MacDonald). Opening your lips wide to let all come out is fearful (Bridges). "By his reckless words, he makes promises he can't keep, divulges private information, offends, or misrepresents. People learn not to depend on what he says and do not want to be around him. He may also suffer physically or financially" (Buzzell).

Exercising self-control over what one says prevents getting into trouble, but those who lack self-control over their speech are headed for ruin.

"God has given us two eyes that we may see much; two ears, that we may hear much; but has given us, but one tongue, and that fenced in with teeth, to indicate that though we hear and see much, we should speak but little" (Clarke). David prayed, "Set a guard, O LORD, over my mouth; keep watch over the door of my lips" (Ps. 141:3).

Proverbs 13:4 "The soul of a lazy *man* desires, and *has* nothing; but the soul of the diligent shall be made rich." Those who are lazy have a *desire* for things, but because they are lazy, they end up with nothing. Desire is not enough. An old adage says, "If wishes were horses, beggars would ride." "To expect the blessing without diligence is delusion" (Bridges). Simply put, the desires of the lazy are not satisfied because they are not willing to work (Buzzell). "He would be wise without study and rich without labor" (Bridges).

On the other hand, those who are *diligent* end up rich. Work is the key to wealth. "The industrious gain, and that richly, what the slothful wishes for, but in vain" (Delitzsch).

Although lazy people desire things, they end up with nothing, but the diligent end up wealthy.

The message of this proverb is be diligent. "Adam Clark is reported to have spent 40 years writing his commentary on the Scriptures. Noah Webster labored 36 years, forming his dictionary; he crossed the ocean twice to gather the material needed to make the book absolutely accurate. Milton rose at 4 o'clock every morning to have sufficient hours to compose and rewrite his poetry, which stands among the best of the world's literature. Gibbon spent 26 years on his book *The Decline and Fall of the Roman Empire*, but it towers as a monument to careful research and untiring dedication to his task. Bryant rewrote one of his poetic masterpieces 100 times before publication to attain complete beauty and perfection of expression. These men enjoyed what they were doing, and each one threw all of his energy into his effort no matter how difficult the job" (Bosch, cited by MacDonald).

Proverbs 13:5 "A righteous *man* hates lying, but a wicked *man* is loathsome and comes to shame." The Hebrew word translated "lying" means "deception, falsehood." The righteous hate all that is "tainted by falsehood" (Delitzsch), "any kind of dishonesty" (Buzzell), even simple truth colored by exaggeration (Bridges).

The Hebrew word rendered "loathsome" means "to have a bad smell, stink" and the one rendered "shame" means "abased, ashamed." As compared to the righteous, who give the pleasant smell of truth, the wicked stink and will eventually come to shame. Because they prefer falsehood, the wicked end up abased, being distrust, shunned, nicknamed, and scorned (Wardlaw).

<u>The righteous hate all forms of falsehood, but because the wicked practice falsehood in general and lying in particular, they end up being shamed, shunned, and scorned.</u>

J. Allen Blair says of Abraham Lincoln that "he would accept no case in which the client did not have justice on his side. One time, a man came to employ him. Lincoln stared at the ceiling yet listened intently as the facts were given. Abruptly, he swung around in his chair. 'You have a pretty good case in technical law,' he said, 'but a pretty bad one in equity and justice. You will have to get someone else to win the case for you. I could not do it. All the time while pleading before the jury, I'd be thinking, Lincoln, you're a liar! I might forget myself and say it out loud'" (Blair, cited by MacDonald).

Proverbs 13:6 "Righteousness guards *him whose* way is blameless, but wickedness overthrows the sinner." The Hebrew word rendered "blameless" means "integrity" and the one translated "overthrows" means "turned upside down, ruin." People with integrity live a righteous life, which guards them against the damage and destruction caused by sin. On the other hand, people with sinful lives eventually experience ruin. People who walk with an untroubled pure mind stand under the shield and the protection of righteousness, but those who live a sinful life will be brought to destruction (Delitzsch).

<u>Living a righteous life protects people from the damage caused by sin, but people living a sinful life are destroyed by their wickedness.</u>

Proverbs 13:7 "There is one who makes himself rich, yet *has* nothing; *and* one who makes himself poor, yet *has* great riches." The primary meaning of this proverb concerns material riches. Some people try to create the impression that they are wealthy, but the truth is that they are poor. On the other hand, some people make themselves look poor when they are rich.

<u>Some appear rich, who are actually poor, and some appear poor, who are actually rich.</u>

This proverb is often applied to the spiritual side of life. "There is a seeming wealth behind which there lies a deep spiritual poverty and wretchedness. There is a poverty which makes a person rich for the kingdom of God" (Barnes). "The godless millionaire actually is a spiritual pauper, whereas the humblest believer, though financially poor, is an heir of God and a joint heir with Jesus Christ" (MacDonald).

Proverbs 13:8 "The ransom of a man's life *is* his riches, but the poor does not hear rebuke." Rich people are kidnapped and held for ransom because they have money. The contrast in this proverb indicates that the point of the word "rebuke" is being threatened with the loss of life (Delitzsch; Barnes; MacDonald). Poor people are not threatened with the loss of their lives for the simple reason there is nothing to be obtained from them. They have nothing.

This could be applied to litigation (Barnes), blackmail (MacDonald), or even theft (Buzzell). "Being poor has at least one advantage" (Buzzell).

<u>Rich people are threatened with the loss of their lives because they have money, but poor people do not have to hear such threats because they do not have money.</u>

Proverbs 13:9 "The light of the righteous rejoices, but the lamp of the wicked will be put out." The issue in this proverb is the meaning of the figures of speech, namely light and lamp. They have been explained as life (Buzzell), prosperity (Clarke; JFB; Ryrie Study Bible), testimony (Unger; MacDonald), and expectations (Kidner). They probably mean something like character, reputation, or testimony. The character of the righteous is like a light that burns brightly. What little light may come from the lamp of the wicked is soon put out.

<u>The character and reputation of the righteous radiate like a light and causes joy to themselves and others, but any good reputation the wicked may have will not last long.</u>

Proverbs 13:10 "By pride comes nothing but strife, but with the well-advised *is* wisdom." The contrast in the second half of this proverb indicates that Solomon is saying the proud do not listen to others; they do not take advice. Their know-it-all attitude results in strife. "Nothing good ever comes from pride: only bitter feuding" (MacDonald). An unyielding arrogance, an inflated, know-it-all attitude, leads to quarreling, in contrast to a humble, wise spirit that makes one willing to take advice from others (Buzzell).

<u>A proud, know-it-all attitude produces strife, but a wise spirit is willing to take advice, avoiding the pride and the conflict that goes with it.</u>

"Perhaps there is not a quarrel among individuals in private life, nor a war among nations, that does not proceed from pride and ambition. Neither man nor nation will be content to be less than another; and to acquire the wished-for superiority all is thrown into general confusion, both in public and private life" (Clarke).

C. S. Lewis writes: "It is pride which has been the chief cause of misery in every nation and every family since the world began. Other vices may sometimes bring people together; you may find good fellowship and jokes and friendliness among drunken people or unchaste people. But pride always means enmity—it is enmity. And not only enmity between man and man, but enmity to God" (Lewis, cited by MacDonald).

Proverbs 13:11 "Wealth *gained by* dishonesty will be diminished, but he who gathers by labor will increase." The Hebrew word translated "dishonesty" means "vapor, breath." The Hebrew lexicon suggests that the meaning here is wealth gained out of vanity, that is, "not by solid toil" (BDB). In other words, it is wealth gained by "a windfall, or sudden stroke of fortune, not by honest labor" (Barnes). It is wealth that "comes in haste or without exertion. This would include the money won by gambling, sweepstakes, or stock market speculation. This kind of wealth has a way of leaking out of a man's hands" (MacDonald). Such material gain is "seldom permanent. All fortunes acquired by speculation, lucky hits, and ministering to the pride or luxury of others, etc., soon become dissipated" (Clarke). "Easy come, easy go" (Kidner).

On the other hand, wealth gained by honest labor "accumulates instead of dwindling" (MacDonald).

Wealth gained without working for it is soon gone, but wealth made by hard work not only does not disappear, it will increase.

Proverbs 13:12 "Hope deferred makes the heart sick, but *when* the desire comes, *it is* a tree of life." The Hebrew word translated "sick" means "weak, sick." "Extended waiting" (Delitzsch) and "repeated postponement of expectations" is disheartening (MacDonald). Delayed gratification pains the mind, but the increase of the delay sickens the heart (Clarke).

In this proverb, the expression "the tree of life" is "used purely psychologically of the reviving of drooping spirits" (Kidner). When a wish, a desire, or a hope comes to pass, it is a tree of life, a quickening and strengthening influence, like that tree of paradise that was destined to renew and extend the life of man (Delitzsch). Fulfilled hope refreshes and encourages (Buzzell).

Repeated disappointment is discouraging, but realized expectation is encouraging.

Proverbs 13:13 "Who despises the word will be destroyed, but he who fears the commandment will be rewarded." The Hebrew word rendered "despises" means "despise, contempt." It is a contempt that "springs from pride and wickedness" (BDB). Some say the "word" is advice or instruction (JFB). If that is the case, the meaning is, "Whoever despises advice rushes into destruction" (Joel, cited by Delitzsch). Others say it is a reference to the Word of God (Wardlaw; Kidner; MacDonald; Clarke), "the expression of the divine will" (Delitzsch). He who despises the Word "destroys himself" (Luther). To fear God's commandment is to have "reverential child-like obedience" (Bridges).

The Hebrew word translated "rewarded" is the well-known word "shalom." It means to be "complete, sound, made whole, recompense, rewarded, peace." Those who respect God's commands so that they obey what He says will be rewarded (Clarke). Obedience pays (Kidner).

Those who despise God's Word will be destroyed, but those who respect and obey God's commandments will be rewarded.

"God as a God of holiness will not be trifled with. As a God of grace, none serve Him for naught" (Bridges).

Proverbs 13:14 "The law of the wise *is* a fountain of life, to turn *one* away from the snares of death." The Hebrew word translated "law" means "direction, instruction, law." It is used of the Torah, God's Law, but here it is the instruction of the wise. Drinking from the fountain of wise instruction is refreshing (MacDonald); it is life-sustaining (Buzzell). Wisdom is a fountain of life to the thirsting and teachable (Bridge).

Wise counsel heard and heeded also protects from premature physical death, "pictured here as an animal trap that ensnares suddenly" (Buzzell).

Listening to wise counsel provides life and protects from premature physical death.

For example, listening to wise advice concerning not driving too fast or too recklessly could save your life, preventing your premature death.

Proverbs 13:15 "Good understanding gains favor, but the way of the unfaithful *is* hard." People with sound judgment are valued and loved (Wardlaw). "Right perception and action secure goodwill" (JFB).

The Hebrew word translated "unfaithful" means "deal treacherously, deceitfully." (The translation of the KJV is the well-known statement "the way of the transgressors is hard.") Those who do not have good judgment and are deceitful and disloyal will not find favor but will have a hard road to travel. They dream of an easy street but end up on a hard road. The hard road is not described other than it is the opposite of finding favor.

Good understanding gains goodwill, but taking the way of deception and disloyalty is a hard road of ill will.

Proverbs 13:16 "Every prudent *man* acts with knowledge, but a fool lays open *his* folly." Prudent people conduct themselves according to knowledge. They do not act rashly; they deliberate, gathering information before they proceed (Wardlaw).

Fools do not think; they live foolish lives for all to see. They expose their folly "like a peddler who openly spreads his wares before the gaze of all men" (Toy, cited by Buzzell).

In other words, behavior indicates whether or not a person is prudent or foolish. Conduct reveals character (MacDonald; see also Kidner). "Normally, a person's conduct is consistent with his character" (Buzzell).

<u>As is usually plain to see, prudent people conduct themselves based on information, but fools expose their foolishness.</u>

Proverbs 13:17 "A wicked messenger falls into trouble, but a faithful ambassador *brings* health." Wicked messengers betray their trust; they do not follow their instructions (Wardlaw). Their disobedience will be detected and they will be disgraced.

In contrast, trustworthy messengers accomplish their mission, benefiting themselves (they do not fall into trouble), as well as those they serve. "Faithfulness is the servant's glory and his master's gain. He brings and receives a blessing" (Bridges).

<u>Unreliable messengers get themselves into trouble, but reliable messengers benefit themselves and others.</u>

Faithful ambassadors for Christ have the joy of delivering a message from the Lord that benefits and blesses others.

Proverbs 13:18 "Poverty and shame *will come* to him who disdains correction, but he who regards a rebuke will be honored." Those who disdain discipline are doomed to shame and even poverty. Delitzsch puts it like this: "He who rejects the admonition and correction of his parents, his pastor, or his friend, and refuses every counsel to duty as a burdensome moralizing, such a one must at last gather wisdom by means of injury if he is at all wise: he grows poorer in consequence of missing the right rule of life and has in addition thereto to be subject to disgrace through his own fault."

Wardlaw suggests that if the origin of the poverty of multitudes were traced back to its origin, it would be discovered that it originated in the neglect of "instruction, admonition, and advice, in the morning of life." He speaks of the "early disobedience to parental counsel" and the "disregard of the fathers and a mother's entreaties and tears." Bridges concurs, admonishing young people to "learn to dread the liberty of being left to your own choice." He also says, "Man's pride deems it a degradation to receive reproof."

Those who listen and learn from a rebuke are honored. Delitzsch points out that such people are disgraced at first because they deserve the rebuke, but their disgrace becomes honor when they receive the rebuke. He says that not rejecting reproof "shows self-knowledge, humility, and goodwill; and these properties in the judgment of others bring men to honor."

<u>Those who disdain discipline are headed for shame and poverty, but those who receive rebuke are honored.</u>

Proverbs 13:19 "A desire accomplished is sweet to the soul, but *it is* an abomination to fools to depart from evil." When a desired goal is reached, it is sweet to the soul. Since that is the case, fools abhor ceasing to seek evil because they think they will be pleased when they get what they want. Since there is pleasure in sin (even though the pleasure is short-lived), fools continue to sin for the momentary pleasure it brings. They do not consider the ultimate consequence of their actions. Wesley says, "Whatsoever men earnestly desire, the enjoyment of it is sweet to them; therefore sinners rejoice in the satisfaction of their sinful lusts and abhor all restraint of them."

<u>Since reaching a desired goal is sweet to the soul, fools abhor departing from their pursuit of evil, believing that what they desire will satisfy them.</u>

"It (evil) must be had, at all costs, not because of its worth but because you have promised it to yourself" (Kidner).

Proverbs 13:20 "He who walks with wise *men* will be wise, but the companion of fools will be destroyed." If you walk with the wise, you will become like the wise. If you follow fools, you become like them, ending up in ruin. Someone has said, "A wicked companion leads his associate into hell" (cited by Delitzsch).

You have heard it said, "A man is known by the company he keeps." Solomon says it is not just that "a man is known by the company he keeps," he *becomes like* the company he keeps. Paul warns, "Do not be deceived: evil company corrupts good habits" (1 Cor. 15:33). Clarke observes, "To walk with a person implies love and attachment; and it is impossible not to imitate those we love. So we say, 'Show me his company, and I'll tell you the man.' Let me know the company he keeps, and I shall easily guess his moral character." (For the influence of associations in Proverbs, see 1:10-11; 2:12; 4:14-17; 16:29; 22:24-25; 23:20-21; 28:7.)

<u>You will become wise if you walk with the wise, but if your companions are fools, you will end up like them—in ruin.</u>

Proverbs 13:21 "Evil pursues sinners, but to the righteous, good shall be repaid." "Sinners are dogged by the hounds of misfortune, physical harm, bad reputation, loss of possessions" (MacDonald). The Hebrew word translated "good" means "good, pleasant, agreeable, benefit." The righteous enjoy the good things of life (Buzzell). God is not named; He is in the background, but He is the One who rewards the righteous (Delitzsch).

<u>Sinners are pursued by evil, which will catch them eventually, but the righteous are rewarded with good, not evil.</u>

Proverbs 13:22 "A good *man* leaves an inheritance to his children's children, but the wealth of the sinner is stored up for the righteous." Good people not only leave money to their children, but they also leave money to their grandchildren. The wealth accumulated by sinners eventually ends up in the hands of the righteous. As someone has said, "Ill-gotten gain has a way of finding better hands."

This proverb also indicates that wealth gained by legitimate means lasts long after the good people who earned it pass away, while the wealth obtained by illegitimate means does not last long. Well-gotten gains are permanent; ill-gotten gains seldom reach the third generation.

In addition, this proverb implies that good people leave an inheritance of living a wise life.

<u>Good people obtain wealth by legitimate means, which they leave as an inheritance to their grandchildren, but the illegitimate gain of sinners evidentially lands in the hands of the righteous.</u>

Proverbs 13:23 "Much food *is in* the fallow *ground* of the poor, and for lack of justice there is waste." The first half of this proverb is saying that the poor peasant, who cultivates his plot of ground industriously, will produce an ample supply of food for himself and his family (Wardlaw). In the second half, the Hebrew word translated "justice" means "judgment" and the one rendered "waste" means "sweep or snatched away" (KJV: "destroyed for want of judgment"). By hard work, a man is able to gain support from a small plot, while fertile estates may be destroyed for lack of judgment (Barnes). By bad management, by careless neglect, by excess, some squander what they have (Wardlaw).

If the second half refers to the same people mentioned in the first half, the meaning is poor people, who work hard in their small fields, manage to grow much food, but because of *their* mismanagement, their gain is swept away. "The size of your resources matters less than the judgment with which you handle them" (Kidner). Clarke exclaims, "O, how much of the poverty of the poor arises from their own want of management! They have little or no economy and no foresight. When they get anything, they speedily spend it." At any rate, the second half is saying some waste what they have because of their mismanagement.

<u>By hard work, the poor have abundant food, but because of a lack of judgment what some have is swept away.</u>

Proverb 13:24 "He who spares his rod hates his son, but he who loves him disciplines him promptly." This is one of several proverbs on disciplining children (19:18; 22:15; 23:13-14; 29:15; 29:17). The "rod" is a reference to corporal punishment, which is one form of discipline.

Parents may think that withholding discipline is the loving thing to do. God says it is not love; it is hate. Why is withholding discipline hate? Delitzsch explains, "A father who truly wishes well to his son keeps him under strict discipline, to give him while he is yet capable of being influenced the right direction, and to allow no errors to root themselves in him; but he who is indulgent toward his child when he ought to be strict, acts as if he really wished his ruin." MacDonald puts it like this: "To withhold punishment from a child when it is deserved is to encourage the child in sin and thus to contribute to his eventual ruin." Thus, parents "could not do him a greater disservice than not to correct him when his obstinacy or disobedience requires it" (Clarke).

The loving thing to do is discipline disobedience promptly. The Hebrew word translated "promptly" means "look early, diligently." Delitzsch says it is a reference to "the morning of life." While it is true that discipline ought to start early, this probably means that the discipline should be promptly after the disobedience (MacDonald). Solomon says, "Because the sentence against an evil work is not executed speedily, therefore the heart of the sons of men is fully set in them to do evil" (Eccl. 8:11). At any rate, the point is the "loving parent inflicts temporary discomfort on his children (by spanking with a rod) to spare them the long-range disaster of an undisciplined life" (Buzzell).

<u>To withhold discipline from a child who deserves it is tantamount to hate, but to discipline disobedience promptly is loving.</u>

Several observations are in order.

Corporal punishment can be carried too far. "Ephesians 6:4 warns against undue severity, but the obligation remains" (Kidner). This is not talking about a "harsh severity, but a wise, considerate, faithful exercise" (Bridges). Bridges adds, "The rod without affection is revolting tyranny."

The backdrop of this proverb is: "Foolishness is bound up in the heart of a child; the rod of correction will drive it far from him" (22:15). The problem is that our children are the children of Adam; they are born with a sinful nature. "Every vice commences in the nursery. The great secret is to establish authority in the dawn of life; to bend the tender twig, before the knotty is beyond our power" (Bridges). Holden says, "By the neglect of early correction, the desires (passions) obtain ascendancy; the temper becomes irascible, peevish, querulous. Pride is nourished, humility destroyed, and by the habit of indulgence, the mind is incapacitated to bear with firmness and equanimity the cares and sorrows, the checks and disappointments, which flesh is heir to" (Holden, cited by Clarke).

"Among the many modern theories of education, how often is God's system overlooked!" (written in 1846 by Bridges). MacDonald says, "The Bible teaches corporal punishment, whether the modern 'experts' agree or not. He goes on to say, "For years. Dr. Benjamin Spock encouraged parents to be permissive. After living to see a generation of bratty, pesky children, he admitted that he had been wrong. He said, 'Inability to be firm is, to my mind, the commonest problem of parents in America today.' He placed the blame, at least in part, on the experts—'the child psychiatrists, psychologists, teachers, social workers, and pediatricians, like myself.'"

Proverbs 13:25 "The righteous eats to the satisfying of his soul, but the stomach of the wicked shall be in want." This proverb is a good example of a proverb that is designed to make us think, which Solomon says is one of the reasons he wrote Proverbs (1:6).

Proverbs 13:25 has been taken as a reference to being contented versus being discontented. According to this view, the righteous are content with their circumstances; they are "pleased with the lot which God is pleased to send" (Clarke), but the wicked are always dissatisfied with their portion. "A contented mind is a continual feast. At such feasts he eats not" (Clarke; see also Wardlaw). Bridges says the righteous are satisfied because their desires are moderate, whereas "no abundance can satisfy" the wicked.

Delitzsch, however, declares that this proverb is not a "commendation of temperance and moderation in contrast to gluttony, but a statement regarding the diversity of fortune of the righteous and the godless." He adds, "That God richly nourishes the righteous, and on the contrary, brings the godless to want and misery." MacDonald concurs, "God ensures that the needs of the righteous will be supplied, but wicked men are equally assured of an empty stomach." So does Buzzell, who says, "God supplies the physical needs of the righteous." JFB also agrees, "The comparative temporal prosperity of the righteous and wicked, rather than contentment and discontent, is noted."

Unger seems to combine the two. He suggests that the righteous are satisfied because they are content with God's provision, but the wicked are never satisfied because the Lord punishes them "by giving them up to their insatiable lust without the means of gratifying it."

<u>The righteous are satisfied with their food because they are content, whereas the wicked eat, but they are never fully satisfied because they are discontented; they want more and more.</u>

Proverbs 14

Proverbs 14:1 "The wise woman builds her house, but the foolish pulls it down with her hands." In this proverb, "builds her house" does not refer to constructing a physical house but to caring for a household (family) and causing it to flourish (Buzzell; Wardlaw). Thus, a wise woman cares for her household, but a foolish woman neglects her household.

Clarke says, "By her prudent and industrious management, she (the wise woman) increases property in the family, furniture in the house, and food and raiment for her household. This is the true building of a house. The thriftless wife acts differently, and the opposite is the result. Household furniture, far from being increased, is dilapidated; and her household are ill-fed, ill-clothed, and worse educated." MacDonald says, "A sensible housewife attends to her house and family. The foolish woman goes gallivanting off to card parties, bingo games, fashion shows, and other empty amusements. She neglects her husband and children and wonders why her family goes to ruin. Is it possible for a woman to tear down her home by too much religious activity too?" (MacDonald).

A wise woman takes care of her household, but a foolish woman neglects her household to the point of its ruin.

A foolish woman may be "building" something outside the family to the neglect of the family. So she builds up something while she tears down her own family.

Bridges points out that a wife can either be a blessing or a curse to her husband. He adds, "What responsibility then belongs to the marriage choice, linked with the highest interest of unborn generations!" and, "To err once, maybe the undoing of ourselves and our house. An old adage says, 'A fortune *in* a wife is better than a fortune *with* one.'"

Obviously, this proverb relates only to the wife's side of the household responsibility. As Wardlaw observes, "It is at once the duty and the interest of husband and wife to co-operate in promoting the common benefit of the family. They must be *one in principle and in aim*. If not, while the one is 'building,' the others will be 'pulling down;' the one will overturn what the other has reared: while the one gathers, the other will scatter" (Wardlaw, italics his).

Proverbs 14:2 "He who walks in his uprightness fears the LORD, but *he who is* perverse in his ways despises Him." One's behavior reflects one's attitude toward the Lord. Those who live their lives according to the will of God walk in His way because they reverence and respect Him.

The Hebrew word translated "perverse" means "turn aside, depart" and the one rendered "despises" means "despise, regard with contempt." Those who live their lives departing from the will of God do not care what the Lord says (MacDonald), which is tantamount to despising Him personally. Wardlaw puts his finger on the pulse of this proverb when he says, "Actually, 'perverseness' or disobedience is contempt of God's *authority*; contempt of God's *glory*; contempt of God's *threatenings*; and contempt of God's *promises*. It shows a scornful disregard of *all*. They who despise God's will despise God Himself" (Wardlaw, italics his). Kidner observes: "The 'despising' may be unconscious, but nonetheless, it is real. Every departure from God's path is a pitting of one's will, and a backing of one's judgment, against His; but the contempt it spells is too irrational to acknowledge."

Those who walk in the will of God show their reverence and respect for Him, but those who depart from the will of God demonstrate their contempt for Him.

Proverbs 14:3 "In the mouth of a fool *is* a rod of pride, but the lips of the wise will preserve them." Fools are proud. They are arrogant, hardened, and thickheaded in their ways (Buzzell). What they say is like a rod that strikes them. "The rod in the mouth is often sharper than the rod in the hand" (Bridges).

The contrast suggests that the wise are humble. They are meek, gentle, and kind (Wardlaw). The wise say things that preserve them from the self-inflicted punishment of the fool.

What fools say is like a rod that strikes them, but the words of the wise protect them from such self-inflicted punishment.

Proverbs 14:4 "Where no oxen *are,* the trough *is* clean; but much increase *comes* by the strength of an ox." The Hebrew word translated "trough" means "crib, "feeding trough" (BDB). When people do not have work animals, they do not have the added burden of having to feed them. The feeding trough is clean.

On the other hand, having work animals, while it involves work, also provides more income. "Labor has its rough, unpleasant side, yet it ends in profit" (Barnes). "The rewards of toil more than compensate for its disagreeable aspects" (MacDonald). "Meaningful results of any kind require investing time, money, and work" (Buzzell).

Not having work animals is less work for you, but having them is more profitable.

This proverb is sometimes interpreted as if the point is a clean barn. Some preachers say there are people who choose a clean barn rather than the profit of having a work animal to clean up after. They prefer having a living room that looks like a museum than having people over who would mess up their living room. They prefer a pristine church building to a thriving youth ministry.

One pastor illustrated it like this: "One summer during my college years, I was an intern for a church in Kansas that had a booming children's and youth program. While I was there, they remodeled their parlor to make it more beautiful for the women's group to use. Since the hall in front of it was where the kids went to their youth rooms, the kids tended to hang around and look into the parlor. It was pretty impressive! So, the ladies decided to padlock the door. After all, they didn't want kids to be tempted to come in and mess up their beautiful parlor. In the years after that, I kept track of things that were going on in that church. I heard that one day, someone forgot to lock that parlor door. Some kids went in and bounced around on the furniture and broke a lamp. Well, the women's group had an emergency meeting and decided that they would pay to have a new entrance made for the children's department. From that time on, the children entered from an outside entrance and were banned from ever stepping foot in the wing of the church where the parlor stood. But things didn't stop there. They also padlocked the kitchen, the office suite, and a few other parts of the church to protect them from those messy kids. I don't think it's a coincidence that within two years, their booming children's and youth programs had dwindled to almost nothing. The parlor was clean, tidy, beautiful … and usually empty. As it turned out, the children's classrooms were also clean and tidy … and usually empty. In the tension between clean and filled, clean won, and the church lost sight of its purpose" (K. Edward Skidmore).

All of that is true, but it is not exactly what Solomon is saying. Solomon is saying that having a work animal is more work, but it is worth the effort because there is more profit.

As is common with commentators, some make a point that misses the point of the passage. Clarke points out that the oxen are the most profitable of all the beasts. Except for speed, the ox is almost in every respect superior to the horse. As compared to a horse: 1) The ox lives longer. 2) It is less likely to get sick. 3) It is steady and always pulls fair in its harnesses. 4) It lives, fattens, and maintains its strength on what a horse will not eat, and, therefore, is supported on one-third the cost. 5) Its manure is more profitable. 6) When it is worn out, its flesh is good for the nourishment of man, its horns of great utility, and its hide almost invaluable. Clarke goes on to say, "He is little or no expense in shoeing and his gears are much simpler and much less expensive than those of the horse. In all large farms, oxen are greatly to be preferred to horses. Have but patience with this most patient animal, and you will soon find that there is much increase by the strength and labor of the ox."

All of that is interesting, but it has nothing to do with what Solomon is saying. Commentators and Bible teachers do this kind of thing, thinking they are digging deep when all they are doing is digging in the wrong place.

The point of this proverb is not about a clean barn or the superiority of the ox over the horse. The point is that not having work animals means less work, but having them is more profitable. To put this in modern terms, where there is no car, there is a clean garage, but having a car enables you to get more done.

Proverbs 14:5 "A faithful witness does not lie, but a false witness will utter lies." This proverb sounds like it is saying the obvious, but there is more here than first meets the ear. A faithful witness has been proven to tell the truth. Therefore, such a witness can be trusted not to lie. "The man of sterling integrity and truthfulness will adhere to truth and all of the statements, at whatever risk and at whatever cost. Nothing will tempt him to depart from it—neither the fear of threatened suffering nor the hope of promised reward" (Wardlaw). "*A faithful witness* is moved neither by entreaties nor bribes, promises nor threats, to swerve from the truth. He is the man to trust. *He will not lie*" (Bridges, italics his).

On the other hand, those who make a habit of lying lie, even in court. "A man addicted to falsehood, regarding merely what is expedient—and what at the time promises more benefit, whether negative or positive,—such a man *will* utter lies, let the temptation be ever so small;—something from the very pleasure he has in deceiving others" (Wardlaw, italics his). "*A false witness* has lost all principle of truth" (Bridges, italics his).

<u>People who habitually tell the truth can be trusted not to lie, but those addicted to lying lie.</u>

Proverbs 14:6 "A scoffer seeks wisdom and does not *find it,* but knowledge *is* easy to him who understands." "The Hebrew word translated "scoffer" means "scorner." Solomon says that such people are proud, haughty, and arrogant (21:24). They have a know-it-all attitude. They recognize no authority except themselves (Delitzsch). Because of their pride, they scorn authority and truth (Wardlaw). They even "reject divine revelation" (Wardlaw; see also Delitzsch, Clarke, Buzzell, et al.). A lack of desire is not their problem; they seek wisdom. Their problem is their attitude; they are scoffers. By continually refusing to listen, they lose the capacity to hear (MacDonald). They shut themselves out from the capacity to recognize truth (Barnes). With that kind of attitude, when they do seek wisdom, they do not find it. They can never find true wisdom as long as they reject the Lord (MacDonald).

On the other hand, people who understand that finding truth presupposes a "humble, teachable spirit" (JFB), discover that finding knowledge is easy. "They know where to look for true knowledge" (Buzzell).

The proud scoffer does not find true wisdom, but knowledge is easy to find for those who understand that a teachable spirit is necessary.

"There is a certain spirit and frame of mind necessary to the understanding and successful investigation of divine truth" (Wardlaw).

Proverbs 14:7 "Go from the presence of a foolish man, when you do not perceive *in him* the lips of knowledge." When you perceive by what is being said that a person is foolish, do not stick around to be influenced by him or her. "Don't cultivate the friendship of a foolish man" (MacDonald). "Since one's associations can influence him for good or bad (13:20), he ought to steer clear of being with the foolish for they speak without knowledge. They cannot offer the young anything of value" (Buzzell). "Never associate with a vain, empty fellow, when you perceive he can neither convey nor receive instruction" (Clarke). Since the company and conversation with a foolish man does not profit you, your time spent in his presence is wasted (Wardlaw).

Do not become friends with foolish people.

Proverbs 14:8 "The wisdom of the prudent *is* to understand his way, but the folly of fools *is* deceit." Wise people understand their own behavior. They consider their conduct, choosing to do what is right (Delitzsch).

Fools do not consider their ways and, consequently, they act foolishly, deceiving themselves (Bridges). They think they are right, which trips them up (Buzzell). Some take this self-deception to be the deception of others (Delitzsch; Barnes). Some want to have it both ways. "The essence of that folly is deceiving others, which eventually results in self-inflicted deceit" (MacDonald). The contrast suggests that the deception is self-deception.

Wise people think about their conduct and its consequences, but fools act foolishly, which deceives them.

Proverbs 14:9 "Fools mock at sin, but among the upright *there is* favor." In the Hebrew text, the first half of this proverb is obscure (MacDonald). The fact that the word "favor" in the second half is used elsewhere in the context of sacrifices has led some to say that the point is, "Fools mock making amends for sin" (NIV; Buzzell). Kidner calls such a rendering "far-fetched," adding that "favor" speaks of a relationship *among* people, not *for* people.

The traditional understanding is preferred. It says the meaning is that fools mock sin; they make a sport of sinning (Wesley; Clarke; MacDonald). People who mock sin cannot be trusted, "neither word nor deed being trustworthy" (Wardlaw).

The second half of this proverb "contrasts the unconcern of fools for the damage they do" and "the care of the upright to preserve goodwill" (Kidner).

Since fools mock sin, they cannot be trusted, but the upright seek favor among themselves and others.

To mock sin is "to despise God's holiness, to set at naught God's authority, to abuse God's goodness, to disregard and slight God's glory, to make light of God's curse and threaten vengeance, which implies a denial of God's truth and a scornful defiance of God's power" (Wardlaw). Bridges adds, "Go to Calvary. Learn there what sin is."

Proverbs 14:10 "The heart knows its own bitterness, and a stranger does not share its joy." The person who really knows what you think and feel, is you. You know what troubles you. This proverb does not say you should not share your bitterness. It simply says you know how you feel. To share or not to share is another issue.

While the word "stranger" might imply you would only share your joy with a friend, it probably only signifies "another" (Kidner, who points to Job 19:27b). In other words, others do not share your joy unless, of course, you choose to share it with them.

Individuals know the pain and joy that they experience and others don't unless they share their feelings.

This proverb is often misinterpreted. Many commentators conclude that it says, "You and only you understand how you feel." MacDonald says, "There are sorrows in the human heart that no other human being can share (though the Lord can and does). There is also joy that can be enjoyed only by the person directly involved." Buzzell puts it like this, "One's inner pain (bitterness) and joy cannot be fully experienced by anyone else. There are individual, private feelings in one's own soul" (see also Barnes).

I disagree. All this proverb says is that you know and others do not. Whether or not you share how you feel is not addressed. A few observations are in order.

This proverb does not say we should not share our joys and sorrows with others. As the old adage reminds us, "Distributed joy is doubled joy; distributed sorrow is half sorrow."

This proverb is not saying that no one can understand what we experience. Just as "No temptation has overtaken you except such as is common to man' (1 Cor. 10:13), you have no experience that others have not also experienced. Indeed, perhaps this proverb implies that only someone who has gone through the same experience can know what you are going through. "Who but a widow can realize the exquisite 'bitterness' of a widow's agony" (Wardlaw)?

This proverb is simply saying that you know your own bitterness and joy. "Each one knows the plagues of his own heart" (1 Kings 8:38). "For what man knows the things of a man except the spirit of the man which is in him?"(1 Cor. 2: 11). As the adage says, "Everyone knows where the shoe pinches him."

This proverb indicates that "we are not competent judges of either the happiness or unhappiness of others" (Wardlaw). We don't know what others are experiencing until they tell us. So be careful of jumping to conclusions about how others think and feel.

Proverbs 14:11 "The house of the wicked will be overthrown, but the tent of the upright will flourish." The major contrast in this proverb is between the house and the tent. "We think of a *house* as permanent and a *tent* as temporary" (MacDonald, italics his; see also JFB). A tent is easily destroyed, but in this proverb, it is the house that is overthrown, while the tent not only stands, it flourishes. The difference is the moral character of the occupants.

<u>The apparent stability and prosperity of the wicked will be overthrown, but the seeming instability and poverty of the upright will not prevent them from flourishing.</u>

"The lowly mud-walled cottage of the pious poor, with the blessing of heaven abiding under its roof and resting on its inmates, (is) incomparably better than the splendid and spacious mansion of a man of the world, who is living without God, and enjoys not His favor and love" (Wardlaw). "The feeble state of the *upright* is more stable than the prosperity of the *wicked*" (Bridges).

Proverbs 14:12 "There is a way *that seems* right to a man, but its end *is* the way of death." This proverb is repeated in Proverbs 16:25 (see also 12:15 and 21:2). The man who thinks the wrong way is the right way has been described as one who has no regard for God and His Word; he follows his own opinion (Delitzsch). He is self-indulgent and self-willed (Barnes). He is impatient and looks for a shortcut (Kidner). Delitzsch says death includes the sentence of a judge, slow decay, disease, suicide, or the sorrow of living a dishonored life. Buzzell says it is the way of sin and folly.

<u>There is a way that seems to be the right way to go, but it is a road to damage and death.</u>

This proverb can be applied to practical decisions in life, such as taking the wrong road and ending up going over an embankment to one's death. It can also be applied to the spiritual decision about salvation. As MacDonald says, "The way which seems right to men is salvation by good works or good character. More people go down to hell laboring under that misconception than under any other."

It is possible to be completely sincere and yet badly mistaken. It's the kind of mistake that doctors sometimes make. One physician administered a controlled mixture of oxygen and anesthetic gas to a patient in a New York Hospital. When one of the tanks was empty, the doctor used a new one marked "oxygen." The patient immediately died. The autopsy revealed carbon dioxide poisoning. Upon investigation, the second tank was found to contain carbon dioxide. Somehow, it had been mislabeled. The manufacturer denied any wrongdoing. No one else knew how it could have gotten the past the inspectors. The doctor had no doubt that he was using oxygen when he administered the lethal gas. No one wanted the tragedy to happen. All thought they were doing something right. Good intentions are not enough.

Proverbs 14:13 "Even in laughter the heart may sorrow, and the end of mirth *may be* grief." People can be laughing and have sorrow in their hearts. Sorrow can mingle with joy (Barnes). "By his laughter, a person may give the impression that he is enjoying life when actually in his heart he is hurting emotionally" (Buzzell). In fact, the laughter may not last long. It will end when something happens that causes grief. Knox says, "Joy blends with grief, and laughter marches with tears" (Knox, cited by MacDonald).

<u>People may be laughing on the outside and hurting on the inside, or they may be laughing now and grieving later.</u>

Some commentators draw conclusions that go too far: "There is no such thing in life as pure, unadulterated joy. Sorrow is always mixed to some extent" (MacDonald). No mood is permanent (see Kidner). It has been suggested that, as in Ecclesiastes 7:6, the laughter here is the "laughter of the fool" (Wardlaw). "Could you look within; could you see the inner depths of the sinner's heart—you might find there something widely different from what outward appearances indicate" (Wardlaw).

While some such statements may be true, the issue here is more the story of the sad clown. External appearance may camouflage the hurt in the heart, and the joy of the moment may end with the coming of grief.

Proverbs 14:14 "The backslider in heart will be filled with his own ways, but a good man *will be satisfied* from above." The Hebrew word translated "backslider" means "one who moves away, turns back, backslides." It indicates a "willful step" (Bridges). The first half of the proverb implies that backsliders move away from God's *ways* (Wardlaw). The second half indicates they turn away from *God* (Jer. 2:19; Delitzsch; Barnes). When people withdraw from God, they withdraw from His ways as well. The Hebrew word rendered, "be filled" means "be satisfied." Some backsliders not only turn away from the Lord but are satisfied with doing things their way and not God's. They enjoy the reward of wandering in estrangement from God (Delitzsch).

By contrast, good people "cleave" to the Lord (Bridges) and faithfully walk in His way. "A man is so called whose manner of thought and action has as its impulse and motive self-sacrificing love" (Delitzsch). The Lord satisfies such people; they are satisfied with Him.

<u>Backsliders are satisfied with their ways, but good and godly people are satisfied with the Lord and His ways.</u>

We tend to think that when we sin, we backslide. That is backward; we backslide, then we sin. First, we slide back from the Lord. Then, we become satisfied with our own way. After that, we sin. The process looks like this: satisfied with the Lord and His ways → sliding away from the Lord → satisfied with my way → sin (not sin → backslide).

J. C. Ryle said, "It is a miserable thing to be a backslider. Of all the unhappy things that can befall a man, I suppose 'backsliding' is the worst. A stranded ship, a broken-winged eagle, a garden overrun with weeds, a harp without strings, a church in ruins—all these are sad sights. But a backslider is a sadder sight still."

Proverbs 14:15 "The simple believes every word, but the prudent considers well his steps." The Hebrew word translated "simple" means "simple, open." The simple are so open-minded their brains fall out. They believe everything they hear without thinking. They are "easily persuaded" with no principles or judgments of their own (Delitzsch). "A naïve, gullible person is susceptible to every new idea or fad" (MacDonald).

The prudent think before they act. They take "no step without thought and consideration" (Delitzsch).

<u>The simple believe everything they hear, but the prudent think before they act.</u>

When Paul says, "Love believes all things" (1 Cor. 13:7), he is simply saying that love gives people the benefit of the doubt. That is a vast difference between being naïve and gullible. Do not be thoughtless; think! Don't react; reflect.

Bridges illustrates. "We do not thus sit down to our food blindfold, not knowing whether we take food or poison. But here are men ready to drink of any cup that is presented to them, like children, who think everything sweet is good."

This proverb applies to everyday decisions, business dealings, and biblical doctrine. When it comes to things spiritual, think, don't be a Kool-Aid drinker, like the crowd that followed Jim Jones in the Guyana massacre.

Proverbs 14:16 "A wise *man* fears and departs from evil, but a fool rages and is self-confident." The fear mentioned in this proverb could be the fear of consequences or the fear of the Lord. Most say it is a reference to the fear of the Lord (Bridges; Delitzsch; etc.). Because wise people fear the Lord, they depart from evil.

The Hebrew word translated "rages" means "to be arrogant, to put oneself in a fury" and the one rendered "self-confident" means "trust, confident" (see "arrogant and careless" in the NASB and "hotheaded and reckless" in the NIV). Instead of being filled with "reverential awe of God" (Delitzsch), fools, trusting themselves and being full of rage, plunge headlong into sin. Fools are arrogant and careless; they throw off restraint (MacDonald). Being driven by their impetuous (hotheaded) nature, fools are wild (reckless) with regard to evil (Buzzell). They are proud and conceited (JFB), overconfident (Kidner). "The voice of God is unheard amid the uproar of passion" (Bridges).

<u>Because the wise fear the Lord, they depart from evil, but because fools are arrogant, full of fury, and trust themselves, they plunge into evil.</u>

Proverbs 14:17 "A quick-tempered *man* acts foolishly, and a man of wicked intentions is hated." Compare this proverb with the previous one. Both speak of an angry man. The contrast in this proverb is between a quick-tempered, foolish man and a wicked man who is intentionally evil. The contrast is between "sudden passion" and "deliberate purpose" (Bridges).

The quick-tempered man "flies off the handle." He "has no time for reflection; he is hurried on by his passions, speaks like a fool, and acts like a madman" (Clarke). In anger, he "does things without stopping to consider the consequences. He slams doors, throws whatever handy, yells curses and insults, breaks furniture, and walks out in a rage" (MacDonald). His outburst is quickly over; he often apologizes (Wardlaw).

The Hebrew word translated "intentions" means "purpose, device." In contrast to the hot-headed man, the wicked man thinks about his evil acts. He plans them! He is willful (Bridges), crafty (NIV), and cunning (Kidner). He is a man of "wicked devices" (KJV). He "contrives secret vengeance against those with whom he is angry;" he is a "deceitful man" (Delitzsch). He has also been described as "vindictive and insidious" (Barnes).

This proverb implies that both the hot-headed and the cool-headed are angry. Without thinking, one blows up and "gets over it." The other clams up to think about how to get even.

The ultimate contrast is the reaction of others to these two. The first is considered foolish; the second is hated. The quick-tempered man is more easily tolerated than the man who acts in cold-blooded treachery (MacDonald). Not controlling one's temper is bad; it causes people to do and say ridiculous things, which they may later regret (Buzzell). "The deliberate evildoer is more hated than the rash" (JFB).

<u>The quick-tempered man is considered foolish, but the man who plans evil is hated.</u>

There is a difference between crimes of passion and crimes that are premeditated.

Proverbs 14:18 "The simple inherit folly, but the prudent are crowned with knowledge." The simple believe "every word" (14:15). They believe everything they hear without thinking. They are naïve, gullible people (see notes on 14:15). They do not think or listen to wise counsel. Therefore, they inherit foolishness. "If they refuse to listen to sound teaching, they thereby choose to become more stupid" (MacDonald). Those who are prudent acquire more and more knowledge (MacDonald).

Delitzsch explains that those who are swayed by the "first influence" become habitual fools; folly is their possession. He says the prudent have thoughtfully pondered their steps to gain knowledge as a crown. "Knowledge is to them not merely an inheritance, but a possession won, and as such remains with them a high and as it were a kingly ornament."

Being gullible, the simple make one foolish decision after another, but the prudent make wise decisions, gaining more and more knowledge.

Proverbs 14:19 "The evil will bow before the good, and the wicked at the gates of the righteous." Evil often wins over good. That will not always be the case. Eventually, good will triumph over evil. There will come the day when evil bows before good and the wicked will bow before the righteous at the gate. "Submitting at the gate meant an inability to overcome its defenses" (NKJV Study Bible).

Eventually, evil and wickedness will bow before goodness and righteousness.

This proverb is proverbial in time, but it is certain in eternity. Kidner says, "The Old Testament in its own terms, and the New Testament in full of detail, promises complete vindication" (of goodness). He is right. "The upright shall have dominion over them (the foolish) in the morning" (Ps. 49:14). "For behold, the day is coming, burning like an oven, and all the proud, yes, all who do wickedly will be stubble. And the day which is coming shall burn them up," says the LORD of hosts, "that will leave them neither root nor branch" (Mal. 4:1). "Do you not know that the saints will judge the world?" (1 Cor. 6:2). "Therefore God also has highly exalted Him and given Him the name which is above every name, that at the name of Jesus every knee should bow, of those in heaven, and of those on earth, and of those under the earth, and *that* every tongue should confess that Jesus Christ *is* Lord, to the glory of God the Father" (Phil. 2:9-11). The superiority of righteousness over wickedness will appear in the "judgment of the great day" (Wardlaw). "The grand consummation will set all things right" (Bridges).

Proverbs 14:20 "The poor *man* is hated even by his own neighbor, but the rich *has* many friends." This is a proverb, not a law. It is a general truth, not a universal truth (see the next proverb; Ruth stayed with poverty-stricken Naomi). As a general rule, people avoid the poor. "Besides the economic frustrations that come with poverty, poor people suffer socially as people often refuse to associate with them" (Buzzell).

On the other hand, people want to associate with the rich. "Many people form friendships on the basis of self-interest. They avoid the poor and cultivate the rich for selfish ends" (MacDonald). Other ancient authors made similar observations. People are "like swallows, who fly off during the winter, and quit our cold climates; and do not return till the warm season, but as soon as the winter sets in, they are all off again" (Cicero). "As long as you are prosperous, you shall have many friends: but who of them will regard you when you lose your wealth?" (Horace).

When it comes to making friends, people often shun the poor, which is tantamount to hating them, but they befriend the rich.

If you are rich, beware. It is hard to know who your real friends are. "In one sense, the rich man has many friends, but in another sense, he never knows how many true friends he has, that is, friends who love him for who he is rather than for what he has" (MacDonald).

Don't be surprised. Delitzsch suggests, "One should take notice of it (this proverb), so that when it goes well with him, he may not regard his many friends as all genuine, and when he becomes poor, he may not be surprised by the dissolution of earlier friendship but may value so much the higher exceptions to the rule."

Don't be a fair-weather friend.

Proverbs 14:21 "He who despises his neighbor sins; but he who has mercy on the poor, happy *is* he." This proverb and the previous one speak of reaction to the poor. The Hebrew word translated "despise" means "despise, contempt," which the Hebrew lexicon suggests comes from pride. Buzzell says it means "to hold in contempt, to belittle, to ridicule;" see "scorns." God commanded people to love their neighbor (Lev. 19:18). So to despise one's neighbor is a sin against God (Jas. 2:5). People who despise their neighbors raise themselves "proudly and unwarrantably" above others; they measure others "not by the rule of duty and of necessity, but according to that which" pleases them.

People who have mercy on the poor not only please God but also make themselves happy. God blesses him who divides his bread with the hungry (Clarke).

People who despise others, even others close by, sin against God, but those who show mercy to others, especially the poor, are personally happy and are blessed by God.

Proverbs 14:22 "Do they not go astray who devise evil? But mercy and truth *belong* to those who devise good." This is the first question in the section of Proverbs that begins with Proverbs 10:1. Note it is stated in the negative. "As usual, interrogative negative strengthens the affirmative" (JFB). Some take the word "devise" in this proverb to mean plot or plan (NIV; Buzzell), but this Hebrew word means "engrave, plough" and according to the Hebrew lexicon, here it means "practices" (BDB). Those who practice evil stray from truth and mercy.

On the other hand, those who plan and execute things that benefit others will experience love from them, as well as the Lord (Wardlaw). "God shows kindness to them and is true to His promises of protection and reward. It also means that people repay them with loyalty and faithfulness" (MacDonald). Being guided and guarded by that which is good, they reach a glorious end (Delitzsch).

Those who practice evil stray from mercy and truth, but those who practice doing what is good are recipients of mercy and truth.

Proverbs 14:23 "In all labor there is profit, but idle chatter *leads* only to poverty." All work produces some results; nothing but talk gains nothing. Idle chatter includes "vain promises and plans" (JFB). For those who talk without toil, "there is only loss, for by it one only robs both himself and others of time, and wastes strength, which might have been turned to better purpose" (Delitzsch). "Hard work pays off, whereas people who merely talk about work become poor" (Buzzell). With some people, all that is in motion is their tongue instead of their hands and feet.

Work produces profit, but words without work lead to poverty.

Some need to be told to talk less and work more. "We all know people who talk by the hour about their problems but never lift a little finger to solve them. They talk up a storm about world evangelism but never move from their Lazy-Boy reclining chair to witness to their neighbor. Without coming up for air, they tell you what they plan to do in the future, but they never do it" (MacDonald).

Proverbs 14:24 "The crown of the wise is their riches, *but* the foolishness of fools *is* folly." The crown, the "ornament" (Delitzsch), the glory (Barnes) of the wise is their wealth. The wise work (14:23); they are diligent (Buzzell). Consequently, they have some riches. "They have something to show for their wisdom, whether we think of that wealth as spiritual or material" (MacDonald).

The foolishness of fools is of no value; it is not to their benefit (JFB). They have nothing but folly "to show for their lives and labors" (MacDonald).

The wise work and, as a result, gain some wealth, which is to their credit and benefit, but fools produce foolishness, which is of no value or benefit to them (or anyone else).

Proverbs 14:25 "A true witness delivers souls, but a deceitful *witness* speaks lies." In court, witnesses who speak the truth deliver innocent people from being "framed" (MacDonald).

Because the first half of this proverb speaks of *delivering* people, it would be expected that the second half would say people are *destroyed*. Instead, it only says that the deceitful witness lies, but deception leads to destruction (Barnes). Deceitful witnesses tell lies with "ruinous results" (MacDonald), such as "wrongly acquitting the guilty" or sending the innocent to prison (Buzzell).

When testifying in court, those witnesses who speak the truth prevent the innocent from being found guilty, but those who deliberately deceive lie with destructive results.

"If the responsibility is so great to the witness in court, how much more to the witness in the pulpit!" (Bridges). True witnesses deliver souls from eternal death; cultists are deceitful witnesses who speak lies and lead souls astray (MacDonald).

Proverbs 14:26 "In the fear of the LORD *there is* strong confidence, and His children will have a place of refuge." The Hebrew word translated "fear" means 1) to be afraid, terrified, 2) to stand in awe, 3) to reverence, 4) to honor. The fear of the Lord includes standing in awe of Him, reverencing Him (Ps. 33:8), and, yes, being afraid to disobey Him. Those who respect and reverence the Lord trust Him, obey Him, and have a healthy fear of disobeying Him.

The Hebrew noun translated "confidence" comes from a Hebrew verb that means "security." Those who so reverence the Lord that they trust and obey Him feel secure. They have a strong confidence that the Lord will protect them (see "place of refuge" in the second half).

The second half begins with the word "His," which can be a reference to either God (NKJV; notice the capital "H") or the children of the ones who fear the Lord (KJV; NASB; NIV; see the small "h"). Although some take "Him" to mean the Lord (Bridges; Wardlaw), as Kidner points out, most commentaries take it as a reference to the children of the one who fears the Lord (Barnes; Delitzsch; JFB; MacDonald; Buzzell; et al.). Parents who fear the Lord provide an example and influence their children to have great confidence in the Lord as a place of refuge.

Those who so respect and reverence the Lord that they trust Him, obey Him, and have a healthy fear of disobeying Him, are confident the Lord will protect them and they also influence their children to have strong confidence in the Lord as a place of refuge.

The fear of the Lord is a strong ground of confidence and has an inheritance which is enduring and unwavering (Delitzsch).

Proverbs 14:27 "The fear of the LORD *is* a fountain of life, to turn *one* away from the snares of death." In Proverbs 13:14, the law of the wise is said to be a fountain of life. Here, the fear of the Lord is a fountain of life. The fear of the Lord is the beginning of wisdom (9:10). Thus, the fear of the Lord is a source of wisdom and life.

As was mentioned in the previous proverb, the Hebrew word translated 'fear' means 1) to be afraid, terrified, 2) to stand in awe, 3) to reverence, and 4) to honor. The fear of the Lord includes standing in awe of Him, reverencing Him (Ps. 33:8) and, yes, being afraid to disobey Him. Those who respect and reverence the Lord trust Him, obey Him, and have a healthy fear of disobeying Him.

That relationship with the Lord is the source of life, real life, not just an existence. Wardlaw calls the fountain of life "waters of joy." That relationship with the Lord, especially the healthy fear of disobeying Him, keeps people from sin, which is a death trap. Delitzsch says that in those who fear the Lord, there springs up a life that is "strong of will to escape the snares which death lays." MacDonald also includes strength in the concept of the fear of the Lord. He paraphrases this proverb: "Trust in God is a source of spiritual strength and vitality, enabling one to avoid the snares of death." Buzzell concludes that the "fear of the Lord assures longevity, for it protects from the snares of death."

<u>Those who so respect and reverence the Lord that they trust Him, obey Him, and have a healthy fear of disobeying Him have a joyful, prolonged life that prevents their premature physical death.</u>

In Proverbs 14:26, the fear of the Lord protects from danger; Proverbs 14:27 prevents premature physical death.

Proverbs 14:28 "In a multitude of people *is* a king's honor, but in the lack of people *is* the downfall of a prince." The subject of this proverb is the glory of a ruler. The glory of a ruler is the number of people he serves. "Not conquest, or pomp, or gorgeous array, but a happy and numerous people form the true glory of a king" (Barnes). The size, contentment, and loyalty of the populace determine a king's honor.

"There is little prestige for a prince to hold the title if he has few or no people over whom to rule" (MacDonald). "Having no one over whom to rule would make his high title and position worthless. A pompous title with no meaningful responsibilities draws little respect" (Buzzell).

<u>The glory of a ruler is the number and prosperity of the people he serves, but having the title and not having people to serve is the downfall of a ruler.</u>

As political "rulers" know, their "glory" is in the number of people who support them. Their downfall is when they have few supporters. This is true of our national, state, and local political leaders, as well as the leader of any group of people, such as the elected leader of the homeowners association.

Proverbs 14:29 "*He who is* slow to wrath has great understanding, but *he who is* impulsive exalts folly." Those who explode with anger need to meditate on this proverb. It says two things about such explosions. First, those who do not explode are the ones who have great understanding. They have insight (MacDonald). So, to control outbursts, think! Second, those who express their wrath exalt, that is, lift up their folly; they expose it to the gaze of others (14:17; Luther; Barnes; MacDonald). So to control outbursts, think about how foolish it makes you look.

<u>Those who are slow to get angry reveal their great insight, but those who explode expose their lack of wisdom and their foolishness.</u>

Do not allow rage to rule; let reason reign.

Proverbs 14:30 "A sound heart *is* life to the body, but envy *is* rottenness to the bones." The Hebrew word rendered "heart" refers to the inner person, including the mind, emotions, and will (BDB). The Hebrew word translated "sound" means "healing, cure, health" (BDB). In contrast to envy, a healthy heart is free from the evil passions of the fallen nature (Wardlaw). Delitzsch calls it a "quiet heart" and adds it is "like a calm and clear water mirror, neither interrupted by the affections nor broken through or secretly stirred by passion." Barnes says that a "heart of health" is one in which all emotions and appetites are in a healthy equilibrium. Buzzell calls it a "healthy disposition." A healthy heart, that is, a positive mental attitude and healthy emotions, gives life to the body.

On the other hand, "To nurse resentment is bad for the body as well as the soul" (Kidner). Socrates said, "Envy is the daughter of pride, the author of murder and revenge, the father of secret treason, the perpetual tormenter of virtue. Envy is the filthy slime of the soul; a venom, a poison, a quicksilver, which consumes the flesh and dries up the marrow of the bones."

Simply put, emotions affect the body (Buzzell).

<u>A healthy heart, a calm disposition free from negative passions such as envy, promotes health in the body, but negative emotions such as envy affect one's physical health.</u>

The mind-body connection is not new. In 1861, a commentator remarked on this proverb, "The connection is imminent between mind and body—between the spirit and the tabernacle in which it resides. They mutually affect each other." He goes on to say that the expression "rottenness to the bones" describes "not a mere surface sore, but a deep-seated disease; like caries or inflammation in the substance of the bone itself. It burns and destroys inwardly" (Wardlaw).

Proverbs 14:31 "He who oppresses the poor reproaches his Maker, but he who honors Him has mercy on the needy." The first line of this proverb is repeated in Proverbs 17:5 (see also Prov. 19:17). The Hebrew word translated "oppresses" means "oppress, wrong, extort." Those who "take advantage of" poor people "insult" their Creator (MacDonald), since God is the Maker of all (Buzzell).

The Hebrew word translated "honors" means to "honor, glorify." To glorify someone is to reveal what that person is like (Jn.16:14). Thus, showing mercy on the needy glorifies God because God is merciful.

Those who glorify God not only refrain from oppressing the poor and needy but also show mercy on them because the poor are made in God's image and because God is merciful.

Proverbs 14:32 "The wicked is banished in his wickedness, but the righteous has a refuge in his death." The Hebrew word rendered "banished" means to "thrust, cast down" (see "thrust down" in the NASB and "brought down" in the NIV). The wickedness of the wicked is their downfall. Unlike the righteous, they have no refuge, but the righteous have a refuge even in death because they commit themselves to God (Kidner). "The godless in his calamity is overthrown, or he fears in the evils which befall him the intimations of the final ruin; on the contrary, the righteous in his death, even in the midst of extremity, is comforted in God in whom he confides" (Delitzsch). This proverb implies that there is life after death. "The hope which abides even 'in death' must look beyond it" (Barnes).

Their wickedness brings down the wicked because they have no refuge; the righteous have refuge in the Lord not only when they encounter trouble but even in death.

Proverbs 14:33 "Wisdom rests in the heart of him who has understanding, but *what is* in the heart of fools is made known." The key that unlocks this proverb is the word "rest." The Hebrew word rendered "rest" means "rest, remain, repose, be quiet." As Delitzsch explains, wisdom in the heart of those who have understanding "remains silent and still, for the understanding feels himself personally happy in its possession" (Delitzsch).

On the other hand, whatever is in the heart of fools comes out of their mouth. "They are not able to keep to themselves the wisdom which they imagine they possess. They discredit and waste their little portion of wisdom (instead of thinking on its increase) by obtrusive ostentatious babbling" (Delitzsch).

Others agree. "Wisdom is "reserved and reticent in the one, noisy and boastful in the other" (Barnes). Wisdom is "preserved in quietness for use, while fools blazon their folly" (JFB). "He (the wise) chooses his time and company, unfolding his mental treasures in appropriate seasons, to appropriate persons, in appropriate circumstances. The fool has little and that little he has he is anxious to show, ever seeking to be thought of as wise as possible" (Wardlaw).

Those who have understanding let wisdom remain in their hearts until it is appropriate to speak, but whatever fools think they say.

The wise do not parade their wisdom.

Proverbs 14:34 "Righteousness exalts a nation, but sin *is* a reproach to *any* people." Righteousness lifts up and benefits a nation (Buzzell). This proverb applies to Israel (Deut. 26:16-19), but it also includes all nations, not just Israel (Delitzsch, a Hebrew scholar, who bases that observation on the meaning of the Hebrew word translated "nation").

The Hebrew word translated "reproach" means "reproach, shame." It is a strong word used only here and in Leviticus 20:17, where it is translated "a wicked thing." "People may seem to be getting away with sin, but ultimately it catches up with them and shames them" (Buzzell). "In order for a nation to be great, its leaders and people must have upright, moral characters known for their righteousness. Corruption, graft, bribery, 'dirty tricks,' scandal, and all forms of civil unrighteousness bring disgrace to a country" (MacDonald).

"History everywhere confirms the principle, that not the numerical, nor the warlike, nor the political, nor yet the intellectual and the so-called civilized greatness, is the true greatness of a nation, and determines the condition of its future as one of progress; but this is its true greatness, that in its private, public, and international life, conduct directed by the will of God, according to the norm of moral rectitude, rules and prevails. Righteousness, good manners, and piety are the things which secure to a nation a place of honor, while, on the contrary, sin, viz., prevailing, and more favored and fostered than contended against in the consciousness of the moral problem of the state, is a disgrace to the people, *i.e.*, it lowers them before God, and also before men who do not judge superficially or perversely, and also actually brings them down" (written in 1872 by Delitzsch, a German Hebrew scholar).

Righteousness benefits the nation, but sin is a shame to a nation.

"The true honor of a nation, like that of an individual, lies in *character*" (Wardlaw, italics his).

Proverbs 14:35 "The king's favor *is* toward a wise servant, but his wrath *is against* him who causes shame." A ruler (boss) deals favorably with a wise servant. The Hebrew word translated "wrath" means "overflow, fury, outburst." Wrath is an outburst of anger, an overflow of fury (BDB; Buzzell). A king blows up at a servant who causes shame. "The king favors an able minister; his anger is for the incompetent" (Moffatt).

<u>Those who manage others deal favorably with a wise servant, but managers get angry and even explode at servants who cause shame.</u>

"The king should have an intelligent man for his minister; a man of deep sense, sound judgment, and of a feeling, merciful disposition. He who has not the former will plunge the nation into difficulties; and he who has not the latter will embark her in disastrous wars" (Clarke). "The same is true of employees today: prudence pays off and lack of it causes employers problems" (Buzzell).

Proverbs 15

Proverbs 15:1 "A soft answer turns away wrath, but a harsh word stirs up anger." The obvious backdrop of this proverb is experiencing someone's wrath. Virtually every word in this proverb has nuances that offer insight to the point. For example, the Hebrew word translated "wrath" comes from the word for "heat" and means "heat, rage." It "denotes anger in the highest degree" (Delitzsch).

What do you do when someone explodes in a rage? Do you "answer" them? That is not exactly the point of this proverb. The Hebrew word translated "answer" means "answer, respond." In other words, the focus is on responding, not answering the argument. The point is to respond with "soft" words. The Hebrew word rendered "soft" means "tender, delicate, soft." Here, the idea is "mild, gentle words" (BDB).

Responding to wrath with soft-spoken, gentle words turns away the wrath. "A mild, gentle word turns away the heat of anger" (Delitzsch). A response of "conciliating" words prevents wrath from increasing (MacDonald).

On the other hand, a single word (note the singular) that hurts is enough to make anger arise (Kidner). The Hebrew word translated "harsh" means "hurt, pain" and the one rendered "anger" comes from the Hebrew word for "nostril, nose, face" and means "anger." "A wounding word makes anger arise" (Delitzsch). Bridges observes, "We yield to irritation; retort upon our neighbor; have recourse to self-justification; insist upon the last word; say all that we could say; and think we 'do well to be angry.'" He adds, "There is the self-pleasing sarcasm; as if we had rather lose a friend than miss a clever stroke."

<u>Responding with gentle words defuses wrath, but using a single word that wounds inflames anger.</u>

"The *soft answer* is the water to quench—*Grievous words* are the oil to *stir up* the fire" (Bridges, italics his).

Spurgeon relates: "I once lived where my neighbor's garden was divided from me only by a very imperfect hedge. He kept a dog, and his dog was a shockingly bad gardener, and did not improve my plants. So, one evening, while I walked alone, I saw this dog making mischief and being a long way off, I threw a stick at him with some earnest advice as to his going home. Instead of going home, this dog picked up my stick and came to me with it in his mouth, wagging his tail. He dropped the stick at my feet and looked kindly at me. What could I do but pat him, call him a good dog, and regret that I had spoken roughly to him?"

Proverbs 15:2 "The tongue of the wise uses knowledge rightly, but the mouth of fools pours forth foolishness." Out of the mouths of wise people comes knowledge, that is, "helpful information" (MacDonald). The wise not only have knowledge, they know "when to speak, and when to be silent; what to speak, and what to leave unspoken; the manner that is best and most suitable to the occasion, the subject, the circumstances, and the persons" (Clarke; see also Wardlaw).

What comes out of the mouth of fools is foolishness. Foolishness "gushes" out of their mouth "like a torrent" (MacDonald). "The character of their words corresponds with the character of their minds" (Wardlaw).

<u>The wise speak what they know at the appropriate time in an appropriate way, but foolishness erupts and pours forth from the mouth of a fool.</u>

Proverbs 15:28 says something very similar to this, only different: "The tongue shows the man. The *wise* commands *his* tongue. *The fool*—his tongue commands him" (Bridges, italics his).

Proverbs 15:3 "The eyes of the LORD *are* in every place, keeping watch on the evil and the good." God sees everything. Nothing is hidden from His all-seeing eyes. "He is keeping watch over every word, act, thought, and motive, both on the evil and the good" (MacDonald).

"The proverb seeks first to warn, therefore it speaks first of the evil" (Delitzsch). The Lord sees evil, whether it is the king in his palace or the servant indulging in his secret sins (Bridges).

"This universal inspection, this omniscience of God, has an alarming but also a comforting side" (Delitzsch). Since God sees everything, He is able to judge evil and reward good justly. This truth should convict those who do evil and comfort those who do good.

<u>The Lord sees everything, including evil and good.</u>

"When a child of God wanders, it is not from God's ceasing to see *him*, but from his, for a short time, ceasing to see God" (Wardlaw, italics his).

Proverbs 15:4 "A wholesome tongue *is* a tree of life, but perverseness in it breaks the spirit." The Hebrew word translated "wholesome" means "healing, cure, health" and is used here in the sense of a "soothing tongue" (BDB). The wholesome tongue has been explained as one that is "gentle" (Delitzsch), "gracious" (MacDonald), "pacifying and soothing" (JFB), etc. Such words sustain life. "Gracious speech refreshes, soothes, and revives" (MacDonald).

"Gentleness characterizes the tongue when all that it says to a neighbor, whether it be instruction or correction, or warning or consolation, it says in a manner without rudeness, violence, or obtrusiveness, by which it finds the easiest and surest acceptance because he feels the goodwill, the hearty sympathy, the humility of him who is conscious of his own imperfection. Such gentleness is a tree of life, whose fruits preserve life, heal the sick, and raise up the bowed down" (Delitzsch).

The Hebrew word translated "perverseness" means "twist, pervert, overturn." It implies that which is false (Kidner). Perverse speech has been described as "a lying tongue" (Luther), "malicious talk" (MacDonald), "deceitful" (Buzzell), "cross, ill-natured language" (JFB), et al. Such talk breaks the spirit. It wounds deeply, making the heart sorry (Delitzsch; Bridges), depresses one's morale (Buzzell; Kidner), "grieves, instead of appeasing" (JFB).

In other words, "Words can encourage or depress an individual;" they can bring "healing that contributes to a person's emotional health," being a "source of strength and growth" or they can "crush the spirit" (Buzzell). Wholesome words soothe the anguish of the afflicted, but perverse words stir and irritate the spirit, destroying tranquility and peace of mind (Wardlaw).

<u>Gentle, soothing words refresh, but malicious words wound, depress and break one's morale.</u>

"When there is grace in the heart, there will be *healing in tongue*" (Bridges, italics his).

Proverbs 15:5 "A fool despises his father's instruction, but he who receives correction is prudent." The Hebrew word translated "despises" means "to view with contempt, spurn" and the one rendered "instruction" means "discipline, correction." "A fool views his father's correction with contempt; he spurns it. He rejects restraint" (Bridges). "He considers his father outdated, his ideas old-fashioned, and his instruction worthless" (MacDonald).

The Hebrew word translated "correction" means "rebuke, correction, reprove." The contrast between the two parts of this proverb suggests that the second half means a prudent *son* receives parental correction. Taken by itself, the second half indicates that prudent *people* receive correction, whether it comes from a father or a friend.

<u>The fool views his father's correction with contempt, but a prudent son listens to his father's correction.</u>

Those who despise their earthly father's instruction will not listen to their Heavenly Father either (Bridges).

Proverbs 15:6 "*In* the house of the righteous *there is* much treasure, but in the revenue of the wicked is trouble." Righteous people are usually disciplined, hardworking folks who make money that benefits their family. Many take "treasure" figuratively. "For though *his house* may be destitute of money, yet is there *much treasure*" (Bridges, italics his).

On the other hand, money earned through wicked means brings trouble to themselves and their households. "Far from enriching the house, such gain is the cause of nothing but ruin" (Delitzsch). "The ill-gotten gain of the unscrupulous man brings trouble on himself and his family" (MacDonald).

<u>The righteous enrich their family, but money earned through unrighteous means brings trouble to the family.</u>

Proverbs 15:7 "The lips of the wise disperse knowledge, but the heart of the fool *does* not *do* so." Wise people dispense knowledge; fools do not because the *heart* of the fool is different from the *heart* of the wise. "A wise man's conversation is full of helpful knowledge. The foolish man can't edify anyone else because his own mind is empty" (MacDonald). The heart of the fool is "not right;" it is "crooked and perverse" and does not have a "mind for wisdom" (Delitzsch). Fools "can *dispense* nothing from their empty storehouse" (Bridge, italics his). "What comes out of the mouth reveals what is in the heart!

<u>The wise disperse helpful knowledge to others, but fools do not because they do not have wisdom.</u>

Proverbs 15:8 "The sacrifice of the wicked *is* an abomination to the LORD, but the prayer of the upright *is* His delight." (21:27). The subject of this proverb is what is pleasing to the Lord. In the Old Testament, for a wicked person to offer an animal sacrifice was displeasing to the Lord; it was an abomination! The Hebrew noun translated "abomination" comes from the Hebrew verb, which means to "abhor." Obviously, the point is that God is more concerned about the life of the person offering the sacrifice than the external act of the sacrifice itself. "The sacrifices of God are a broken spirit, a broken and a contrite heart" (Ps. 51:17).

It is prayer that comes from the heart of an upright person that delights the Lord. In the words of others: "Sacrifices well-pleasing to God, prayers acceptable to God depend on the relations in which the heart and life of the man stand to God" (Delitzsch). "No religious acts will do in place of holiness to the Lord" (Clarke). Ritual without reality is worthless (MacDonald).

<u>The Lord is disgusted with the rituals of religion performed by those who live a wicked life, but He delights in those who live a righteous life and seek Him in prayer.</u>

The Lord is more interested in the way we live during the week than He is in our church attendance on Sunday. "To obey is better than sacrifice" (1 Sam. 15:22).

Proverbs 15:9 "The way of the wicked *is* an abomination to the LORD, but He loves him who follows righteousness." In the previous proverb, Solomon said the sacrifices of the wicked are an abomination to the Lord.

In this proverb, it is the *way* of the wicked that the Lord abhors. In the previous proverb, Solomon said the Lord delights in the prayers of righteous people. In this proverb, the Lord is said to *love* those who live a righteous life. Kidner points out that the Hebrew word translated "follows" appears here in the intensive form, implying a strong purposefulness. The Lord delights in those who are dedicated to righteousness.

The Lord detests the way the wicked live, but He loves those who live a righteous life.

Proverbs 15:10 "Harsh discipline *is* for him who forsakes the way, *and* he who hates correction will die." In this proverb, "the way" is the way in which God would have people go (JFB). The Hebrew word translated "harsh" means "bad, evil;" that is, bad in the sense of "unpleasant, painful, unhappiness, misery" (BDB). *Those who forsake the godly way of wisdom* will experience painful discipline, but that discipline is short of physical death.

Those who hate correction have been described as "unteachable" (MacDonald). They will not only have a painful time, but they will also die a premature physical death. In Proverbs, going God's way leads to life and forsaking it is "visited with the punishment of death," that is, "temporal death" (Delitzsch).

MacDonald points out that this proverb could be talking about the two different types of people or referring to the same person. He says the Hebrew parallelism favors the second interpretation. Buzzell agrees. He says the second line expands the first. He adds that those who refuse moral correction will "pay for it (13:13) with poverty, shame (13:18), and death (15:10)." "There is no surer step to ruin than this *hatred of reproof*" (Bridges, italics his).

Those who forsake the godly way of wisdom will encounter painful discipline, and if they are so unteachable that they refuse to learn from the correction, they will experience premature physical death.

Of course, the point is to learn from discipline. As the writer to the Hebrews says, "Now no chastening seems to be joyful for the present, but painful; nevertheless, afterward it yields the peaceable fruit of righteousness to those who have been trained by it" (Heb. 12:11).

Proverbs 15:11 "Hell and destruction *are* before the LORD; so how much more the hearts of the sons of men." The Hebrew word translated "hell" is *sheol*, a Hebrew word that means "underworld." The one rendered "destruction" means "destruction, ruin, Abaddon" and is used of the place of ruin in Sheol (BDB). In Revelation 9:11, Abaddon is a title for the devil. These words refer to the "unseen world beyond the grave" (MacDonald).

This proverb is based on the concept that there is no further distance from God in all creation than Sheol and Abaddon. Thus, the point is that if Sheol is open before the Lord, how much more will the hearts of the children of men be open (Delitzsch)? "If God knows all about what transpires in death and in the hereafter, how much more does He know the thoughts and secrets of the sons of men on earth?" (MacDonald). "Since God can see the dead in their graves, surely He can see living people's hearts; that is, their motives, thoughts, and desires" (Buzzell). In the words of the New Testament, "There is no creature hidden from His sight, but all things are naked and open to the eyes of Him to whom we must give account" (Heb. 4:13).

Since the Lord can see what happens after death, even the place of destruction in the underworld, surely He can see the thoughts and intents of people's hearts.

"No depth is there then, he cannot fathom; no manner of deceit so complicated, he cannot track them. Words are not necessary with him to lay open the heart" (Bridges). What is hidden from the eye is of man is open before the Lord (Wardlaw).

Proverbs 15:12 "A scoffer does not love one who corrects him, nor will he go to the wise." The Hebrew word translated "scoffer" means "scorn, deride" and the one rendered "corrects" means "to reprove, chide" (BDB). Buzzell says "corrects" should be rendered either rebuke or reprove. Deriders of God and divine things cannot bear reproof (Wardlaw). Scorners who deride that which is holy do not love those who rebuke them. That is an understatement. Scoffers "resent being corrected" (MacDonald). They count their truth-telling friends as enemies (Bridges).

Scorners do not go to the wise for instruction (JFB) or advice (MacDonald). Mockers of religion and virtue prefer people who respond to their frivolity (Delitzsch). They go to people who will tell them what they want to hear (MacDonald).

Scorners of that which is holy and right resent being rebuked and they do not go to the wise for advice.

"Men loved darkness rather than light because their deeds were evil" (Jn. 3:19).

Proverbs 15:13 "A merry heart makes a cheerful countenance, but by sorrow of the heart the spirit is broken." A happy heart is manifested in a cheerful countenance. A heavy heart breaks the spirit. "A merry heart is reflected in a smiling face, but a broken heart has deeper effects. It causes despondency and despair" (MacDonald).

A happy heart reveals itself with a smile, but a hurting heart breaks the spirit and can be seen in a sad countenance.

"A man's countenance is the index of his spirit" (Barnes). People do not naturally smile when angry or frown when happy (Wardlaw).

A happy heart puts a smile on the face, but the process does not work in reverse. "If anything, the excruciating effort of insincere smiling may make a sad heart even sadder and will drive a wandering soul farther than ever from the truth (Mason, *The Gospel According to Job*, p. 122).

Proverbs 15:14 "The heart of him who has understanding seeks knowledge, but the mouth of fools feeds on foolishness." People with "discernment" (Buzzell) seek knowledge. "The most knowledgeable people never stop in their pursuit of knowledge" (MacDonald). Delighted with every new discovery, yet never tiring of the old, people with understanding seek more and more knowledge (Wardlaw). Fools feed on folly (Buzzell). "The wise grow wiser, the fools more foolish" (JFB). "The wise grow wiser, the foolish more dense" (cited by MacDonald from an unspecified source).

<u>People with sense constantly seek knowledge, but fools feed on foolishness.</u>

People of "natural understanding" are "ready to learn from any quarter, even from a child." They are never satisfied with their knowledge, but a "fool is fully satisfied with folly." He "feeds on foolishness as his meat and his drink" (Bridges). Wise people have an appetite for knowledge; they feast on wisdom. Fools have no hunger for wisdom; they feed on folly. There is a proverb that says, "Wise men talk about ideas. Ordinary men talk about things. Fools talk about each other."

Proverbs 15:15 "All the days of the afflicted *are* evil, but he who is of a merry heart *has* a continual feast." The Hebrew word translated "afflicted" means to be "bowed down, afflicted" and the one rendered "evil" means "bad, evil, distressed, misery." Those who are bowed down with affliction are miserable.

Those with a merry heart are happy, like being at a continual feast, regardless of the external circumstances. "The true and real happiness of a man is thus defined, not by external things, but by the state of the heart, in which, in spite of the apparently prosperous condition, a secret sorrow may gnaw, and which, in spite of an externally sorrowful state, may be at peace, and be joyfully confident in God" (Delitzsch). "The state of the heart governs the outward condition" (JFB). "One's temperament has a considerable effect on one's circumstances" (Ryrie Study Bible).

"This (proverb) seems to contrast the pessimist and the optimist. The first is always down in the mouth. He is gloomy, fearful, and negative. The optimist always seems to be on top. He enjoys life to the full" (MacDonald). In this proverb, sadness is contrasted with the cheerfulness of a feast.

<u>Those who are bowed down with affliction are miserable, but those who have inner happiness enjoy life in spite of adverse circumstances.</u>

Those with a happy heart can sing in prison as well as in the palace (see Bridges).

Proverbs 15:16 "Better *is* a little with the fear of the LORD, than great treasure with trouble." The contrast in this proverb indicates that "fearing God gives peace, not confusion" (Buzzell). "Where the fear of God is, there are moderation and contentment of spirit" (Clarke). Thus, those who fear the Lord are better off with a little materially than those who have great material possessions but who at the same time have trouble.

The Hebrew word translated "trouble" means "tumult, confusion, disturbance, turmoil." It is "restless, covetous-care and trouble" in contrast to the "quietness and contentment proceeding from the fear of God" (Delitzsch). "A poor believer is better off than a wealthy worrywart. Wealth has trouble attached" (MacDonald). Better is godliness with contentment (1 Tim. 6:6) than wealth with worry.

<u>People who are at peace because of their relationship with the Lord but do not have much materially, are better off than those who have trouble, tumult, and turmoil and, at the same time, have great material wealth.</u>

Jesus said, "Take heed and beware of covetousness, for one's life does not consist in the abundance of the things he possesses" (Lk. 12:15). "Riches and poverty are more in the heart than in the hand" (Bridges).

Wardlaw says trouble "may be understood in various senses, either of which yields a meaning to the verse in harmony with truth. It may signify *bodily affliction:* in which case, the explanation of the verse will be, that poverty with health and cheerfulness is better than wealth with such corporeal trouble as incapacitates for its enjoyment. It may signify trouble *of mind and conscience,* and then the sentiment will be, that poverty with peace of mind is far preferable to riches with the disquietude of conscious guilt and self-dissatisfaction;—poverty with a good conscience better than wealth with an accusing and evil conscience; poverty with a conscience pacified by the blood of sprinkling, better than abundance with a conscience to which that peace-speaking blood has never been applied. Or it may signify the trouble of *domestic discord* and *broils:* and then the lesson will be that poverty with domestic union and peace, springing from and hallowed by the influence of true religion, is incomparably superior to riches the most profuse connected with the absence of such love and harmony,- with alienation, hostility, and strife. What a wretched compensation are 'thousands of gold and silver' for the want of affection and peace—the absence of what the poet calls 'that only happiness which has survived the fall'—domestic happiness!" Wardlaw also says that those who have godliness with contentment have a treasure in the heart, a treasure in the house, and a treasure in heaven—a treasure for time and eternity.

Proverbs 15:17 "Better *is* a dinner of herbs where love is, than a fatted calf with hatred." (17:1) A dinner of herbs was the meal of the poor and the fatted calf indicates "stately magnificence" (Barnes). In modern terms, "A plate of vegetables in an atmosphere of love is better than a filet mignon roast where there is strife" (MacDonald). "*Love* sweetens the meanest food. *Hatred* embitters the richest feast" (Bridges, italics his).

<u>Poverty with love is better than prosperity with hate.</u>

"Normally, people would choose luxury over privation, but love is more important. Many people have found that a home where material possessions are few but love for each other is present is far better than a house of great opulence where people hate each other. Love endures one's difficult circumstances, whereas hatred undoes all the enjoyments that good food might otherwise bring" (Buzzell).

Joseph R. Sizoo says, "In a nearby city, I visited one of the most luxurious estates I've ever seen in America. Within the house were Italian fireplaces, Belgian tapestries, Oriental rugs, and rare paintings. I said to a friend, 'How happy the people who lived here must have been!' 'But they weren't,' he replied. 'Although they were millionaires, the husband and wife never spoke to each other. This place was a hotbed of hatred! They had no love for God or for one another.'"

Putting Proverbs 15:16 and 17 together, Bridges observes, "Here is the source of *the merry heart—the fear of the Lord*, and *love* to man" (Bridges, italics his).

Proverbs 15:18 "A wrathful man stirs up strife, but *he who is* slow to anger allays contention." The Hebrew word translated "wrathful" comes from the word for "heat" and means "burning anger, rage, wrath" and the one rendered "strife" means "strife, contention." Hotheaded people who blow up ignite contention.

The Hebrew word translated "contention" means "strife, dispute, quarrel." People who control their anger "quiet quarrels" (Buzzell). They "carry about with them an atmosphere in which quarrels die a natural death" (Archibald, cited by Kidner).

<u>People full of wrath and rage excite contention, but those who are slow to anger quiet quarrels.</u>

Quotes of note: "Anger is an ill wind that can quickly blow out the lamp of reason and good judgment." "People who fly into a rage always make a bad landing." "Bring water, not fuel, to the fire" (Bridges). "Staying calm is the best way to take the wind out of an angry man's sails."

An ancient legend says that Hercules became irritated by a strange-looking animal that blocked his path in a threatening manner. In anger, he struck it with his club. As he went on his way, he encountered the same creature again several times, and in each instance, the beast grew larger and more fearsome than before. At last, a "heavenly messenger" appeared and warned Hercules to stop his furious assaults, saying, "The monster is Strife and you are stirring it up. Just let it alone and it will shrivel and cease to trouble you."

Proverbs 15:19 "The way of the lazy *man is* like a hedge of thorns, but the way of the upright *is* a highway." A hedge of thorns in the path of life depicts problems that keep people from moving forward. For lazy people, life is filled with "obstructions" (Buzzell). They do not make much progress. Their path is thick with "thorns, briars, fences," through which they do not force their way (Barnes). They do not go forward because they see hindrances and difficulties everywhere (Delitzsch). Because they are slothful, they imagine ten thousand difficulties in the way that cannot be surmounted, but they are all the creatures of their own imagination, and that imagination is formed by their sloth (Clarke).

The fact that the lazy are contrasted with the upright, not the diligent (Bridges) indicates that there is an element of dishonesty in laziness (Kidner; Bridges). Jesus speaks of the "wicked and lazy servant" (Mt. 25:26). For the upright, the same path "is as the broad raised causeway of the king's highway" (Barnes). They go forward "unhindered and quickly" (Delitzsch).

<u>Lazy people do not make much progress because they see problems, difficulties, and hindrances in their path, but the upright move forward because they work through problems, making their path seem like a smooth highway.</u>

Here are some additional comments concerning the sluggard: "The sluggard is *wiser* in his own conceit than seven men that can render a reason" (Wardlaw, italics his). "*The slothful* fancies, as apologies for lazy inaction, innumerable obstacles and difficulties—anything as a reason for sitting still" (Wardlaw, italics his). "He plants his own *hedge*, and then complains of its hindrance" (Bridges, italics his). "Indecision, delay, and sluggishness, add to his difficulties, and paralyze his exertion; so that after a feeble struggle of conscience, with much to do, but no heart to do anything, he gives up the effort" (Bridges). "The slothful man may have a fit—sometimes an astonishing fit—of exertion; but he relapses to his former state" (Bridges, who cites 12:27).

Proverbs 15:20 "A wise son makes a father glad, but a foolish man despises his mother." The choices of a son affect his parents. The wise son gives "great satisfaction to his dad" (MacDonald). The foolish son callously disregards his mother's counsel, which is tantamount to contempt for her. The wayward son disobeys her will and disregards her tears (MacDonald). The contrast between the father and the mother suggests that the foolish conduct of a son grieves the mother (10:1; Kidner).

<u>The wise son brings joy to the heart of his father, but the foolish son, who by his conduct shows contempt for the "upbringing" by his mother, grieves her deeply.</u>

Proverbs 15:21 "Folly *is* joy *to him who is* destitute of discernment, but a man of understanding walks uprightly." Those who are destitute of discernment and even understanding enjoy their folly! Those with understanding and discernment walk uprightly and rejoice in doing so. The empty-headed go the wrong way, rejoicing in folly, but those with understanding go the right way, rejoicing in wisdom (Barnes). "A stupid man enjoys his stupidity. He has never known anything better. The wise man gets his joy out of a life of sobriety and morality. A pig enjoys wallowing in the mire, whereas a sheep wants the clean pasture" (MacDonald). Departing from the path of one's duty gives joy to the fool, but he is wasting time and strength; "while, on the contrary, a man of understanding, who perceives and rejects the vanity and unworthiness of such trifling and such nonsense, keeps the straight direction of his going, *i.e.*, without being drawn aside or kept back, goes straight forward" (Delitzsch).

<u>Those who lack discernment of what is important enjoy their folly, but those who understand live an upright life and enjoy doing what is right.</u>

Proverbs 15:22 "Without counsel, plans go awry, but in the multitude of counselors they are established." The Hebrew word translated "awry" means "break, frustrate" ("frustrated" in the NASB and "fail" in the NIV). When people act solely on their own without consulting others, their plans are often frustrated, but when they ask advice from several others, their plans are more likely to work. "It is safer to get a broad range of information and advice. Men who have had the experience can warn against dangers to be avoided, can suggest the best methods, etc." (MacDonald). "Designs not well weighed shall miscarry; but when many have well deliberated, they shall succeed" (Wardlaw). Do not stubbornly follow your own heart (or head); listen to the counsel of intelligent and honest friends, not merely to one counselor, but to many (Delitzsch). "Get all the advice you can" (Kidner).

<u>When people rely on their judgment without seeking wise advice from others, they and their plans are often frustrated, but asking for counsel from a number of different counselors makes it more likely that their plans will succeed.</u>

Seeking counselors (plural) is mentioned four times in Proverbs (11:14; 15:22; 20:18; 24:6). Applying this bit of wisdom to government officials (as does Solomon in Prov. 11:14), Bridges says, "A *multitude of counselors* is an indispensable advantage to the Sovereign for his own *purposes*" (Bridges, italics his).

Proverbs 15:23 "A man has joy by the answer of his mouth, and a word *spoken* in due season, how good *it is!*" People who give helpful answers at the appropriate time experience personal joy and benefit others. The word spoken must be good and at the right time (Wardlaw). "There is genuine satisfaction in being able to give an honest, helpful answer at just the right time to meet a particular need" (MacDonald). "Saying the right thing at the right time delights not only the hearer but also the one who says them. Timely words (whether of love, encouragement, rebuke, or peacemaking) are beneficial" (Buzzell). "Good advice blesses the giver and receiver" (JFB).

<u>To say the right thing at the right time satisfies the speaker and benefits the hearer.</u>

"Obviously, a moment of irritation is out of season. We must wait for the return of calmness and reason" (Bridges).

Proverbs 15:24 "The way of life *winds* upward for the wise, that he may turn away from hell below." The Hebrew word translated "hell" is *sheol*, which means "underworld." Living a wise life is a road that leads to the "highest life" and rescues the wise from the downward road that leads to the "gloom of Sheol" (Barnes), "to death and destruction" (MacDonald), to "a premature physical death" (Buzzell). There are three great contrasts in this proverb: 1) the way of the wise and (implied) the way of the fool, 2) above and below, and 3) life and death.

<u>Living a wise life is a road that leads to the highest life and delivers the wise from premature physical death.</u>

Buzzell says see Proverbs 3:2, 3:16, 4:10, 9:11, 10:27, 14:27 for other references to premature physical death in Proverbs; to that list I would add Proverbs 10:2, 11:4, 11:19, 13:14, 14:27, 15:10.

Proverbs 15:25 "The LORD will destroy the house of the proud, but He will establish the boundary of the widow." The major contrast in this proverb is between the *house* of the proud and the *boundary* of the widow. The house of the proud is "the estate of the haughty and highhanded" (MacDonald).

Buzzell explains the importance of the boundary: "Land, a precious commodity to the Israelites, was marked by boundaries to preserve its original parameters (Deut. 19:14). Land was kept in a family and its boundaries were important (Deut. 22:28, 23:10-11). The vulnerability of widows made them easy prey to thieves who would seek to steal their land, so the Lord Himself promised to keep widow's boundaries from being moved." The Lord will "protect the boundary of the oppressed widow's little farm" (MacDonald). "The most desolate who have God's aid have more permanent good than the self-reliant sinner" (JFB).

<u>The Lord will destroy the estate of the proud, but He will protect the property of the defenseless widow.</u>

Proverbs 15:26 "The thoughts of the wicked *are* an abomination to the LORD, but *the words* of the pure *are* pleasant." The Hebrew word rendered "thoughts" means "thought, devise, plan, purpose." Not just wicked actions but also wicked attitudes are an abomination, a Hebrew word that means "repugnant, abhorrent, disgusting." The plans of the wicked are "hateful to God even before they issue in words and deeds" (Kidner).

The pure thoughts and words of the pure are "pleasing to God" (JFB; Wardlaw). "The LORD detests the wicked plans of unscrupulous men, but He is pleased with the words of the pure" (MacDonald).

The Lord detests the wicked's thoughts, schemes, and plans, but He delights in the thoughts and words of the pure.

Many think lightly of their thoughts! Thoughts are the seeds that yield the fruit of words. When Jesus said "You will know them by their fruits" (Mt. 7:16) and "by their fruits you shall know them" (Mt. 7:20), He was talking about the *words* of false prophets (Mt. 7:15; Mt. 12:32-37). "Out of the abundance of the heart the mouth speaks" (Mt. 7:34). "Out of the heart proceeds evil thoughts" (Mt. 15:19). Thoughts are the "index of character" and "evil thoughts are the first bubbling of the corrupt fountain" (Bridges). "Your most secret imaginings; your most momentary wishes and purposes; ideas never uttered; designs never executed—all are naked to his view—that circumstances have prevented the execution of any purpose, does not in the least interfere with or mitigate the criminality of the *intention*" (Wardlaw, italics his).

Proverbs 15:27 "He who is greedy for gain troubles his own house, but he who hates bribes will live." The Hebrew word for "greedy" means "unjust gain" (BDB; Buzzell). The second half of the proverb suggests that the subject of the whole proverb is a bribe (Wardlaw). In other words, the greed mentioned in the first half is a greed stimulated by a bribe. Some say this proverb refers to public officials. "This proverb may refer primarily to a judge or other public officer who swells his bank account by accepting bribes" (MacDonald; Barnes).

The contrast between "his own house" and "will live" indicates that those who are greedy for unjust gain trouble themselves as well as their family (Kidner). People who refuse bribes enjoy life (MacDonald) and live in "domestic harmony" (Wardlaw).

The people who are so greedy that they accept bribes bring trouble, not just to themselves, but to their whole household, but those who hate bribes enjoy life and domestic harmony.

Proverbs 15:28 "The heart of the righteous studies how to answer, but the mouth of the wicked pours forth evil." The Hebrew word rendered "heart" refers to the inner person, including the mind, emotions, and will (BDB), and the one rendered "studies" means "muse, mediate" (it also appears in Josh. 1:8 and Ps. 1:2). The righteous think before they speak. "A righteous person weighs his answers before giving them rather than blurting out the first thing that comes to his mind" (Buzzell). The tongue of the righteous "never runs before his wit, he never speaks rashly, and never unadvisedly; because he studies—ponders, his thoughts and his words" (Clarke). "It is the characteristic of the righteous that he does not give the reins to his tongue" (Delitzsch). The fear of God and the love of neighbor dictate that the righteous consider what they say (Wardlaw).

The heart of the wicked is full of evil, so evil pours forth from their mouth. "An ungodly man opens his mouth and out comes a torrent of profanity, filth, and vileness" (MacDonald). What is said of the wicked implies "rashness" (JFB) and "recklessness" (Wardlaw).

The righteous think before they speak, but when the wicked, who have hearts full of evil, speak, they pour out evil.

Wardlaw points out, "What is before said of the *wise and the foolish* is said here of the *righteous and the wicked*; and what is before said of the utterance of *wisdom and folly*, is here said of the utterance of *good and evil*" (Wardlaw, italics his; 15:2).

Bridges's comments are insightful: "Consideration is an important part of the Christian's character." Think twice before you speak once. Many stumble by speaking from the moment's impulse rather than "a well-balanced and considered judgment." The wicked do not care what they say; it is of little consequence to them, "whether it be true, or well-timed, or whom it wounds."

Proverbs 15:29 "The LORD *is* far from the wicked, but He hears the prayer of the righteous." The second half of this proverb indicates that the subject is prayer. "The Lord has withdrawn Himself from the wicked so that if they pray, their prayers do not reach Him" (Delitzsch). "He is neither near to hear nor near to help" (Clarke).

The Lord is near the righteous; He hears their prayers. "Believers have an instant audience with the Sovereign of the universe in the throne room of heaven" (MacDonald).

Bridges clarifies, "He is equally near to them both in his essence. But in his favor, he *is far from the wicked* and rejects their prayers. He is near to *the righteous and hears* them (Bridges, italics his).

Regarding prayer, the Lord is far from the wicked and near the righteous; He does not hear the wicked but does hear the righteous.

Proverbs 15:30 "The light of the eyes rejoices the heart, *and* a good report makes the bones healthy." (See 16:24.) A twinkle in the eye, a smile on the face, brings joy to the heart of others. The brightness shines in the eyes of one whose heart and face are full of joy and "acts with a healing and quickening power" (Barnes). "A person's beaming countenance is contagious. It gladdens the heart of everyone he meets" (MacDonald). A radiant face is heartwarming (Kidner). Hearing good news is good for the body. It makes a man's whole being feel good (MacDonald).

"A positive person's encouragement, whether nonverbal (by a cheerful look, lit., 'bright eyes') or verbal (good news; 25:25), is helpful and uplifting" (Buzzell). The eyes of a friend glisten with gladness when he or she is the bearer of pleasant news, and having such an experience cheers the spirit and contributes to the vigor of the body itself (Wardlaw).

This proverb implies that "emotional health contributes to physical well-being" (Buzzell).

<u>A smile on the face and an encouraging word coming out of the mouth bring joy to the heart and health to the bones of others.</u>

Proverbs 15:31 "The ear that hears the rebukes of life will abide among the wise." The expression "rebukes of life" means "the reproof that leads to, or gives life, rather than that comes from life and its experience" (Barnes; JFB). Nothing teaches like experience; and no experience is more useful than rebuke (Bridges).

<u>Those who hear and heed the rebukes that lead to life will be numbered among the wise.</u>

Someone has said, "Never fear criticism when you're right; never ignore it when you're wrong."

Proverbs 15:32 "He who disdains instruction despises his own soul, but he who heeds rebuke gets understanding." The previous proverb spoke of those who hear and heed a rebuke. This one addresses those who disdain instruction. They may think that all they are doing is rejecting instruction, but in reality, they are despising their own soul. The unteachable are not just despising the instruction of others; they are despising themselves. Those who listen to rebuke gain insight, which is good for them.

<u>Those who reject instruction harm themselves, but those who listen to rebuke help themselves.</u>

Wisdom honors those who deal faithfully with our faults (Bridges).

Proverbs 15:33 "The fear of the LORD *is* the instruction of wisdom, and before honor *is* humility." The Hebrew word translated "instruction" means "discipline, chastening, correction" (BDB), "training" (Kidner). The fear of the Lord is the discipline that leads to wisdom (Barnes; MacDonald). "The fear of the Lord is not merely the gateway but the whole path of wisdom" (Kinder). "The fear of the Lord is not only the beginning of knowledge, but it also teaches wisdom. By fearing (reverencing, trusting, obeying, serving, and worshiping) the Lord a person learns wisdom" (Buzzell). "He who fears God much, is well taught" (Clarke). The fear of the Lord also produces humility (see Wardlaw), which is the way to honor.

<u>The fear of the Lord is the way to wisdom and humility, and humility is the way to honor.</u>

Proverbs 16

Proverbs 16:1 "The preparations of the heart *belong* to man, but the answer of the tongue *is* from the LORD" (see 16:9). Proverbs 10:1-22:16 contain the proverbs of Solomon (Prov. 22:17*ff* records the proverbs of wise men *et al.*). Solomon's proverbs can be divided into two parts. The first half of Solomon's proverbs (10:1-15:33) consists mostly of contrasting proverbs. As Buzzell points out, "Most of the 191 verses in this section (16:1-22:16) are either comparisons (synonymous parallelism) or completions (synthetic parallelism), and only a few are contrasts (antithetic parallelism)." In other words, most proverbs in Proverbs 10:1-15:33 contain a contrast, and most proverbs in Proverbs 16:1-22:16 are comparisons or completions.

The Hebrew word translated "preparation" in Proverbs 16:1 means "order, row, arrange" (BDB) "plans" (see Kidner). Godly people prepare, arrange, and plan in their heads before they speak.

Sometimes, we arrange our thoughts but think one thing and then say another. All experience that, but for the godly, there are times when it is as if the Lord puts words in their mouth. For example, Balaam wanted to curse the Children of Israel, but a blessing came out of his mouth (Num. 22:38, 23:7-12). "God's persecuted people often plan in advance what to say at their trial, but God gives the proper words at the suited time (Mat. 10:19)" (MacDonald). "Man may plan his thoughts in advance, but the Lord is sovereign and overrules all man's words for the accomplishment of His purposes. 'Man proposes, but God disposes'" (MacDonald; JFB). Every preacher has experienced this. Praying for the Lord to give you the right words is appropriate.

<u>There are times when godly people plan to say one thing, but the Lord sees to it that something different comes out of their mouths.</u>

"It is a matter of experience which the preacher, the public speaker, the author, and every man to whom his calling or circumstances present a weighty, difficult theme can attest. As the thoughts pursue one another in the mind, attempts are made and again abandoned; the state of the heart is somewhat like that of chaos before the creation. But when, finally, the right thought and the right utterance for it are found, that which is found appears to us, not as if self-discovered, but as a gift; we regard it with the feeling that a higher power has influenced our thoughts and imaginings" (Delitzsch).

Proverbs 16:2 "All the ways of a man *are* pure in his own eyes, but the LORD weighs the spirits." (21:2 is almost identical; see also 12:15.) People ponder their chosen path and pronounce themselves pure. God not only looks at our actions, but He also considers our thoughts, desires, and motives. A man judges himself by his outward acts and pronounces himself pure, but God sees the motives and intentions of the heart (MacDonald; Buzzell). "We are blind to our own faults, do not see ourselves as others see us. There is One who tries not the 'ways' only, but the 'spirits' (Heb. 4:12): this is the true remedy against self-deceit" (Barnes). Self-justification is a form of "subtle self-deception," but God's judgment "excludes all deception, so that thus a man can escape the danger of delusion by no other means than by placing his way, *i.e.*, his external and internal life, in the light of the word of God, and desiring for himself the all-penetrating test of the Searcher of hearts and the self-knowledge corresponding to the result of this test" (Delitzsch).

<u>People judge themselves based on their actions, but God also considers their motives.</u>

"But the LORD said to Samuel, 'Do not look at his appearance or his physical stature, because I have refused him. For *the* LORD does not *see* as man sees; for man looks at the outward appearance, but the LORD looks at the heart'" (1 Sam. 16:7). "Now the Pharisees, who were lovers of money, also heard all these things, and they derided Him. And He said to them, 'You are those who justify yourselves before men, but God knows your hearts. For what is highly esteemed among men is an abomination in the sight of God'" (Lk. 16:14-15).

Proverbs 16:3 "Commit your works to the LORD, and your thoughts will be established." Committing what you do to the Lord assumes that what you are doing is acceptable to the Lord (Wardlaw). Thoughts are "the plans or counsels out of which the works spring" (Barnes). They will come to pass when we commit our plans to the Lord. "The best way to ensure that our dreams and goals will be achieved is to dedicate our works to the LORD" (MacDonald).

"Committing one's plans (see 16:1 and 16:9) to the Lord is essential to success. This verse, however, does not offer divine assistance to *all* plans" (Buzzell, italics his). Clarke says when your schemes "are agreeable to the Divine will," when your thoughts and meditations are "right," when you "begin and end" your work in the Lord, "all issues well." Or put simply, "Rely on God for success to your lawful purposes" (JFB). Look to the Lord for guidance and strength; "look to Him for success in all" (Bridges).

<u>Commit your God-pleasing plans to the Lord and they will come to pass.</u>

"The act of committing all things into the hands of God to be regarded as He may see fit reserves the spirit from corroding anxiety; from carefulness, and sleeplessness, and torturing apprehension about the results. It 'keeps the soul in peace'" (Wardlaw). "We should roll on God all matters which, as obligations, burden us, and on account of their weight and difficulty cause us great anxiety, for nothing is too heavy or too hard for Him who can overcome all difficulties and dissolve all perplexities; then will our thoughts, *viz.*, those about the future of our duty and our life-course, be happy, nothing will remain entangled and be a failure, but will be accomplished, and the end and aim be realized" (Delitzsch).

Proverbs 16:4 "The LORD has made all for Himself, yes, even the wicked for the day of doom." The translation "for Himself" is misleading (Kidner). This proverb does not mean God has created some to be damned; people are "damned by their own deliberate choice, not by God's decree" (MacDonald). The phrase "for Himself" means "its own ends" (Buzzell), or purpose (JFB; see "for its own purpose" in the NASB). As Barnes says, "The Lord has done everything for its own end; and this includes the appointment of an 'evil day' for 'the wicked' who deserve it." God has an end or purpose for everything; "He has ordained a day of trouble or evil for the wicked" (MacDonald).

Delitzsch explains, "God has not indeed made the wicked as such, but He has made the being which is capable of wickedness, and which has decided for it, viz., making His holiness manifest in the merited punishment, and thus also making wickedness the means of manifesting His glory." Bridges says, "When they (the wicked) sin and by their own free will, he ordains them to punishment, as the monuments of his power, his justice, and his longsuffering."

<u>The Lord does everything for its purpose, including appointing a day of doom for the purpose of punishing the wicked.</u>

"The general meaning is that there are ultimately no loose ends in God's world: everything will be put to some use and matched with its proper fate. It does not mean God is the author of evil: James 1:13, 17" (Kidner).

Proverbs 16:5 "Everyone proud in heart *is* an abomination to the LORD; *though they join* forces, none will go unpunished." The Hebrew word translated "abomination" means "repugnant, abhorrent, disgusting." Pride is repugnant to the Lord. He resists the proud (Jas. 4:6; 1 Pet. 5:5). He punishes people who are proud. Even if they band together, none of them will go unpunished. In other words, their punishment is certain (MacDonald). "The day of wrath shall come on the wicked, whatever means he may take to avoid it" (Clarke).

<u>Pride is disgusting to the Lord; He will punish it.</u>

Proverbs 16:6 "In mercy and truth atonement is provided for iniquity; and by the fear of the LORD *one* departs from evil." In the context of the Old Testament, the point here is that iniquity is atoned for by God's mercy and truth (Wardlaw; JFB; Clarke), "not by sacrifices and burnt offerings" (Barnes). As the New Testament explains, by His mercy, God provided the atonement for our sins by sending His Son to die for our sins and be raised from the dead (1 Cor. 15:3-4). By the "fear of the Lord," that is, by "trusting the Lord," people depart from evil (MacDonald).

<u>By His mercy and truth, God provides atonement for sin and those who trust and fear the Lord depart from evil.</u>

Proverbs 16:7 "When a man's ways please the LORD, He makes even his enemies to be at peace with him." When people live in ways that please the Lord, which includes pursuing peace (see the second half of the proverb; Heb. 12:14), they may still have enemies, but the Prince of Peace makes their enemies at peace with them. This is a proverb, not a law; there are exceptions, such as persecution (JFB). "God is the guardian and defense of all that fear and love him, and it is truly astonishing to see how wondrously God works in their behalf, raising them up friends, and turning their enemies into friends" (Clarke). Perhaps this proverb implies, "Goodness has power to charm and win even enemies to itself" (Barnes). "A righteous life disarms opposition" (MacDonald). Kidner suggests this proverb is an encouragement to fearlessness. He says, "Consult God's wishes, not man's; He can handle the people you fear!"

<u>When the path people take pleases the Lord, the Prince of Peace makes even their enemies be at peace with them.</u>

MacDonald illustrates, "Stanton treated Lincoln with utter contempt. He called him a 'low cunning clown' and 'the original gorilla.' He said there was no need to go to Africa to capture a gorilla when one was available in Springfield, Illinois. Lincoln never retaliated. Instead, he made Stanton his war minister, believing that he was the best qualified for the office. Years later, when an assassin's bullet killed Lincoln, Stanton looked down on his rugged face and said tearfully, 'There lies the greatest ruler of men the world has ever seen.'"

Proverbs 16:8 "Better *is* a little with righteousness, than vast revenues without justice." It is better not to have much in terms of material wealth and be righteous than to have a huge income without being righteous (15:16). "It is better to have a modest income which is earned honestly than to have vast revenues without justice or with fraud" (MacDonald). One who amasses revenue dishonestly will eventually be punished. "So righteous living—even if it means having little—is certainly better" (Buzzell).

It is better to have a small income and be righteous than be have a large income and not be righteous.

Proverbs 16:9 "A man's heart plans his way, but the LORD directs his steps" (see 16:1). People make plans, but the Lord "alone determines whether these plans ever come to pass" (MacDonald). An old proverb says, "Man proposes; God disposes."

"Man deliberates, calculates, reflects on how he will begin and carry on this or that; but his short-sightedness leaves much out of view which God sees; his calculation does not comprehend many contingencies which God disposes of and man cannot foresee. The result and issue are thus of God, and the best is that in all his deliberations, one should give himself up without self-confidence and arrogance to the guidance of God, that one should do his duty and leave the rest, with humility and confidence, to God" (Delitzsch).

"Saul of Tarsus planned to persecute the Christian saints in Damascus but ended up becoming one of them! Onesimus planned to leave Philemon forever, but God brought him back on better terms than ever" (MacDonald). This proverb implies that the Lord not only has the last word, He has the soundest (Kidner). This proverb also "exposes the folly and presumption, on man's part, of *self-confidence*—of his thus assuming himself of success, as if he had the future under his eye and at his bidding (Wardlaw).

People plan, but the Lord determines what actually happens.

Bridges says, "As rational agents, we think, consult, and act freely. As dependent agents, the Lord exercises his own power in permitting, overruling, or furthering our acts. Thus, man proposes; God disposes. *Man devises; the Lord directs*. He orders our will, without infringing our liberty or disturbing our responsibility" (Bridges, italics his). Bridges adds, "Inscrutable indeed is the mystery, how He accomplishes His fixed purpose by free-willed agents."

Proverbs 16:10 "Divination *is* on the lips of the king; his mouth must not transgress in judgment." The subject of this proverb is the words of a king (see "lips" and "mouth"). Also, this proverb should be understood first and foremost in light of the Old Testament. God gave Israel His law. Kings were to speak what was in line with that law (Deut. 17:18-20). When a king of Israel spoke an oracle, he was to do so as God's representative (Buzzell). This proverb is "what the king *ought to be* and what *good kings always are*" (Wardlaw, italics his).

Barnes says, "Here is a manual for kings; showing not what they are, but what God requires them to be, that they may be a blessing to their people, and benefactors to the world (2 Sam. 23:3-4)." He adds, "When God's law is his law, *a divine sentence is in his lips*" (Barnes, italics his).

The words of rulers, especially their official decisions, should be in line with the Word of God and certainly not contrary to justice.

Lord, may we be that kind of ruler as parents and bosses, and may You give us those kinds of rulers at every level of government.

Proverbs 16:11 "Honest weights and scales *are* the LORD's; all the weights in the bag *are* His work." In this proverb, Solomon says that the *Lord*, not just the king, has weights and measures. It is said that standard weights and measurements were kept in the Temple (Wardlaw). Business transactions are not outside of God's concern; He desires that truth and righteousness prevail there (Bridges). "God maintains a Bureau of Standards. He determines honest weights and scales. When men deal in accordance with His standards, He approves and blesses them" (MacDonald).

So, using honest weights honors the Lord. To use dishonest weights and measurements is to disobey God (Buzzell). It is not just criminal; it is sinful.

Since business transactions are sacred, we should be honest in them in order to honor the Lord.

Proverbs 16:12 "*It is* an abomination for kings to commit wickedness, for a throne is established by righteousness." The Hebrew word translated "abomination" means "repugnant, abhorrent, disgusting." For a ruler to commit wickedness is repugnant to the Lord. Delitzsch defines wickedness as kings placing themselves "in despotic self-will above the law." God established government to see to it that righteousness rules (see Rom. 13:4-5). When righteousness rules, government is established, but corruption is the downfall of a government.

Righteousness establishes a government, but the Lord detests wicked rulers.

Proverbs 16:13 "Righteous lips *are* the delight of kings, and they love him who speaks *what is* right." Good rulers want people to tell them the truth and what is right. They love such advisors. "Good kings don't appreciate those who flatter and speak hypocritically. They want men whose word is trustworthy, who are frank and sincere" (MacDonald).

Good rulers delight in advisers who tell them what is right.

It has been suggested that this proverb is a more specific form of the previous one (JFB), which speaks of righteousness establishing a nation. Thus, the idea is that rulers should value honesty because it is how their rule is established (Buzzell). This can also be applied to advice we get from others personally. The wise delight in friends who tell them the truth.

Proverbs 16:14 "As messengers of death *is* the king's wrath, but a wise man will appease it." When a ruler is full of wrath, he punishes those with whom he is angry, but a wise man will appease the ruler's wrath. With the "despotic monarchies of the East, punishment, even death, follows royal displeasure" (Barnes).

"If the king is angry, it is as if a troop of messengers or angels of death went forth to visit with death him against whom the anger is kindled; but if he against whom the wrath of the king has thus broken forth is a wise man, or one near the king who knows that he will seek to discover the means (and not without success) to cover or to propitiate, *i.e.*, to mitigate and appease, the king's anger" (Delitzsch). We possess the power to bring misery on others and "may play the appalling role of petty tyrant" (Kidner).

<u>Since enraged rulers punish people, even pronouncing death (being fired), the wise pacify them.</u>

Proverbs 16:15 "In the light of the king's face *is* life, and his favor *is* like a cloud of the latter rain." This proverb is in contrast to the previous one, which speaks of the king's wrath. The expression on the king's face indicates whether or not he has life or death in mind. Some say that "life" means "prosperity and joy—(a) happy life" (Wardlaw). When the king is happy, the expression of joy on his face "spreads gladness through the realm" (MacDonald).

The "latter rain" came in March/April, just before the harvest. The clouds that brought the latter rain screened people from the scorching sun (Barnes). The king's favor is like that refreshing cloud. "Like a cloud which discharges the rain that mollifies the earth and refreshes the growing corn, is the king's favor" (Delitzsch).

<u>A joyful expression on the king's face indicates life instead of death, and his favor is like the refreshing rain just before the harvest.</u>

Proverbs 16:14-15 can be applied to people in general, not just kings. We all possess the power to bring misery or happiness to others (Kidner).

Proverbs 16:16 "How much better to get wisdom than gold! And to get understanding is to be chosen rather than silver." Obtaining spiritual wisdom and understanding is better than obtaining material wealth. Remember who penned this proverb—Solomon, who had both wealth and wisdom! "Riches often disappear overnight but divine wisdom remains throughout eternity" (MacDonald). Wisdom is "more valuable, more abiding, more fruitful, more satisfying. It is inexpressibly *better*" (Bridge, italics his).

<u>Having wisdom is better than having wealth.</u>

"Multitudes labor night and day for *gold*; yet miss the treasure. But who was ever disappointed in the effort to *get wisdom*?" (Bridges, italic his).

Proverbs 16:17 "The highway of the upright *is* to depart from evil; he who keeps his way preserves his soul." People who live a righteous life obviously depart from evil, but what may not be so immediately observed is that such people preserve their "soul."

Since the Hebrew word translated "soul" means "soul, life, self, person, desire, emotions," some say that what is preserved is the inner life. Buzzell says preserving one's soul "is a means of guarding one's soul (inner life with its drives, appetites, and desires) from sin." Others take preserving one's soul to mean avoiding damage. MacDonald says, "The righteous follow the highway of holiness without turning off on the tangents of sin. The one who keeps straight on this highway preserves his life from damage and misfortune." Preserving the soul is more than preserving one's inner life or avoiding damage. It is preserving one's very life, which is the point in the context of Proverbs. Solomon says, "He who keeps the commandment keeps his soul, *but* he who is careless of his ways will die" (19:16; Jas. 1:14-15). In Proverbs, sin leads to premature physical death (10:2, 10:27, 11:4, 11:19, 13:14, 14:27, 15:10, 15:24).

<u>Those who live an upright life not only depart from evil, they preserve their life from premature physical death.</u>

Proverbs 16:18 "Pride *goes* before destruction, and a haughty spirit before a fall." The Hebrew word translated "pride" means "exaltation." Those who are proud exalt themselves. The Hebrew word translated "destruction" means "to break, fracture, crush, crash." It was used of the breaking of pottery (Isa. 30:14) and the fracturing of a lamb (Lev. 21:19; 24:20; Delitzsch). Satan fell and was destroyed because of pride. "So far as any man is proud, he is kin to the devil, and a stranger to God and himself" (Baxter, cited by Bridges).

The Hebrew word rendered "haughty" contains a similar idea to pride, namely being high and exalted and the one translated "fall" means "to stumble." Those who exalt themselves are so self-confident they are careless (JFB), which causes them to stumble and break a bone or something worse, like a piece of pottery crashing to the ground (see "destruction" in the first part of the proverb). "Stuck-up people usually suffer some humiliating experience designed to deflate their ego. It takes only a small pin to prick a large balloon" (MacDonald).

<u>Those filled with pride fall and are eventually destroyed.</u>

Many Hebrew Bibles have a note that says "the middle of the book." This verse is the middle verse in the book of Proverbs. Pride is the opposite of the first principle of wisdom, which is the fear of the Lord (Kidner). Pride produces personal destruction (Prov. 16:18), interpersonal division (Prov. 13:10), and divine disgust (Prov. 16:5).

Quotes on pride: "None have more pride than those who dream that they have none" (Spurgeon). "Be humble lest you stumble" (D. L. Moody). Pride is "self-exultation, in direct disregard of God's word." It is the "deification of self. It always wants to be in the limelight, wants to attract attention, a conceit of one's superiority. But the Bible says: 'For if a man think himself to be something when he is nothing, he deceives himself' (Gal. 6:3)" (M. R. De Haan).

Proverbs 16:19 "Better *to be* of a humble spirit with the lowly, than to divide the spoil with the proud." It is better to be humble among people "who have experience of the vanity of earthly joys, than (be) intoxicated with pride, to enjoy oneself amid worldly wealth and greatness" (Delitzsch). It is better to have a humble spirit and "be a companion of the lowly than to share the seeming advantages of the proud" (MacDonald). "More happy, more honorable, more acceptable to God and man is a *humble spirit*, companying *with the lowly, than the spoils* of the haughty conqueror" (Bridge, italics his). The spirit of the humble is content, cheerful, submissive, and happier by far than the spirit of the proud, who may have the temporary advantage obtained by the plunder of their fallen rivals. Their riches and glory are no more than meteors in the midnight sky that glitter for a while and die (Wardlaw). Conclusion: "Avoid the society of the proud" (JFB).

It is better to have a humble spirit and be with people who do not have much than to be with the proud, who are willing to divide the spoils of conquest with you.

Most strive to rise; few desire to lie low (Bridges). Jesus humbled Himself (Phil. 2:8).

Proverbs 16:20 "He who heeds the word wisely will find good, and whoever trusts in the LORD, happy *is* he." The Hebrew word translated "word" means "speech, word," but it can also mean "matter, affair (things about which one speaks), business" (BDB). Hence some say the meaning here is "matter" (Wardlaw; Bridges; NIV). Others say the "word" is God's Word (Delitzsch; JFB; Kidner), which the second part of the proverb seems to support.

The Hebrew word translated "good" means "benefit, welfare, prosperity." "To give heed to God's Word is the way to true prosperity" (Delitzsch). Those who trust the Lord are happy.

Those who obey the Word of God prosper and those who trust the God of the Word are happy.

"So, the proverb says, 'Read your Bible; heed it; and trust the One who wrote it'" (MacDonald).

Proverbs 16:21 "The wise in heart will be called prudent, and sweetness of the lips increases learning" (16:23). Those who are wise will be recognized as prudent. "A person who is wise is known for his discernment, his ability to see to the heart of issues" (Buzzell).

The wise have wisdom and a way of expressing it that is "pleasing" (Delitzsch). "The pleasant manner in which he speaks will make others more willing to listen to him and to learn" (MacDonald). "Eloquent discourse persuades and instructs others" (JFB).

Wise people not only have wisdom but also a pleasant way of expressing it that makes people want to listen and learn.

"Harsh words do the opposite" (Buzzell).

Proverbs 16:22 "Understanding *is* a wellspring of life to him who has it. But the correction of fools *is* folly." Those who "get it" have "a fountain of strength, a source of guidance, and a counsel which make life secure" (Delitzsch). Understanding refreshes its possessor (MacDonald).

Since fools do not have understanding, correcting them is folly. They not only do not have understanding, they do not learn from correction.

People with understanding have a source of life within themselves, but fools not only do not "get it," correcting them is folly because they do not learn from correction.

Proverbs 16:23 "The heart of the wise teaches his mouth, and adds learning to his lips" (16:21). Wise people teach their mouth what to say. They exercise self-control over their speech. They do not blurt out whatever comes to their mind (Buzzell). Those with a wise hearts speak with wisdom. As a result, what they say is beneficial to others.

Those who have wisdom in their hearts have knowledge on their lips, which benefits others.

Proverbs 16:24 "Pleasant words *are like* a honeycomb, sweetness to the soul and health to the bones" (15:30). For the ancient Israelites, honey was a luxury and a medicine (Barnes; Wardlaw). There are people today who claim that honey heals some ailments. "Words of comfort, sympathy, or encouragement are medicinal" (Bridges). "Appropriately spoken words that encourage, soothe, or commend can be most pleasant and even uplifting to the point of helping a person feel better physically" (Buzzell). "Gentle, kind words, by soothing the mind, give the body health" (JFB). "To say nice things when we can is a simple benefit we may bring a person, in mind and thence in body" (Kidner).

Pleasant words are sweet to the soul and healing to the bones of the hearers.

Pleasant words should be distinguished from flattering words. The latter may be palatable at the time but are otherwise injurious, for they are not words of truth (Wardlaw).

Proverbs 16:25 "There is a way *that seems* right to a man, but its end *is* the way of death." This proverb is a repeat of Proverbs 14:12. The repetition is for emphasis (MacDonald; Buzzell; Kidner).

People who see their way as the right way and do not see that the consequence of going their own way is death are self-deceived. "The judgment is perverted because the heart is blinded" (Bridges). "The way of a fool *is* right in his own eyes" (12:15). "All the ways of a man *are* pure in his own eyes" (16:2). The danger of self-delusion is so great that "we are only safe by warning upon warning" (Bridges).

<u>There is a way that seems right, but it is a road to damage and death.</u>

There is a way of strict discipline without love that seems right to parents but destroys their children. There is a way of dishonest dealings that seems right to business people that ends in destroying their business. There is a way of law-keeping that seems right to religious people that leads to eternal death.

MacDonald makes the same application here as he did in Proverbs 14:12: "It seems logical and reasonable that the way to heaven is by being good and doing good. But the fact is that the only people who will ever get to heaven are sinners saved by grace" (MacDonald). There are many ways to death, but only one way to eternal life (Jn. 14:6; Bridges).

A man whose bathtub was filthy was having little luck getting it clean with normal bathroom cleansers, but he had heard that gasoline was a solvent. So he took a rag with gasoline to the tub. It worked! It also stank up the bathroom. So, he decided to do something to take care of the odor. He set out aromatic candles and he lit them. He survived… but his apartment didn't.

Proverbs 16:26 "The person who labors, labors for himself, for his *hungry* mouth drives him *on."* People work because they want to eat. "Hunger is the incentive to labor" (Wardlaw). "Hunger of some kind is the spring of all hearty labor. Without that, the man would sit down and take his ease" (Barnes). In plain English, "He knows that if he doesn't work, he won't collect his paycheck, and without money, he can't go to the supermarket to buy food. So if he is ever tempted to stop working, his appetite urges him on" (MacDonald).

<u>People are motivated to work because they want something, even something as basic as food.</u>

Of course, this is not the only motivation for work. Paul says, "Let him who stole steal no longer, but rather let him labor, working with *his* hands what is good, that he may have something to give him who has need" (Eph. 4:28). Nevertheless, it is proverbial: people work because they want to eat.

Proverbs 16:27 "An ungodly man digs up evil, and *it is* on his lips like a burning fire." Proverbs 16:27-30 contains four proverbs about troublemakers: "Those who plot evil (Prov. 16:27), stir up strife (Prov. 16:28), lead others into violence (Prov. 16:29), and persist in sin (Prov. 16:30)" (Buzzell). Kidner says plots (16:27), a mere whisper (16:28), toughness (16:29), and subtlety are ways of spreading damage.

The Hebrew word translated "ungodly" in Proverbs 16:27 means "worthless, useless, good-for-nothing" (BDB; "worthless" in the NASB and "scoundrel" in the NIV). "A worthless man (is) a man whose disposition and conduct are the direct contrast of usefulness and piety" (Delitzsch). The word rendered "digs" is the Hebrew word for digging a pit and is used figuratively of "digging a calamity" (BDB) and "plotting" (Kidner). The worthless dig "an evil pit for others to fall into" (Barnes). They dig a calamity, which suggests the effort they put forth to dig a pit to trap others (Buzzell). "A wicked man labors as much to bring about an evil purpose as the quarryman does to dig up stones" (Clarke). "His pleasure is to *dig up evil*; pursuing his *evil* projects within intense activity, as if he were 'searching for hidden treasure.' The tongue is usually the chief instrument of mischief" (Bridges, italics his).

<u>Worthless, good-for-nothing scoundrels plot evil against others and scorch them with burning words.</u>

Acknowledging this proverb probably means taking pains to plan evil. Wardlaw suggests that it may include another idea, namely, taking "pains to *retrieve it* after It has been buried and forgotten. He goes down into the very graves of old quarrels; brings them up fresh; puts new life into them; wakes up grudges that have long slept; and (stirs people up) again, who have abandoned their enmities, and had for years been living in reconciliation and peace" (Wardlaw, italics his). In other words, the worthless scoundrel digs up dirt that had been dealt with decades ago.

Proverbs 16:28 "A perverse man sows strife, and a whisperer separates the best of friends." Perverse people distort the truth by withholding it, shading it, or lying, thus spreading strife (Buzzell). A talebearer not only spreads strife but he or she can also actually separate the best of friends. Bridges points out that in 1 Peter 4:15, the "mischievous gossiper" is classed with the murderer and the thief.

<u>Distorting the truth spreads strife and bearing tales can break up even the best of friends.</u>

Who is the whisperer in this proverb? Could it be one of the friends? Wardlaw suggests that insinuation, intended to engender suspicion and jealousy, is spoken by one concerning his friend. Then he says, "Mutual coolness ensues, and neither can understand why." Thus, he says, "Confiding attachments—the source of life's sweetest joys—are broken up, perhaps forever." Be careful what you say, especially about your friends behind their back. What you say could destroy a cherished friendship.

Proverbs 16:29 "A violent man entices his neighbor, and leads him in a way *that is* not good." A violent man is not content to sin himself; he wants to lead others with him in his wicked way (Buzzell). The way that is "not good" is "one altogether evil and destructive" (Delitzsch). The violence encourages others "to be a partner in crime" (MacDonald).

<u>A violent man not only wants to harm people, he also wants to have others join him in his wicked ways.</u>

Proverbs 16:30 "He winks his eye to devise perverse things; he purses his lips *and* brings about evil." The Hebrew word translated "winks" means "shuts" (BDB; KJV). Based on that rendering, some older commentators say the shutting of the eyes denotes "deep thought" (JFB). Thus, this proverb is referring to shutting the eyes "to meditate deeply upon ways and means to commit sin. He shuts his eyes that he may shut out all other ideas, that his whole soul may be in this" (Clarke). People shut their eyes to prevent outward distractions and move their lips as if engaged in deep thought (Bridges). When the "ungodly" close their eyes to think without being distracted, they're doing so for the purpose of planning "mischief devices" (Wardlaw).

More modern translations interpret "shut" to mean "wink" (NKJV; NASB; NIV). According to this rendering, a wink can send a signal of a sinister scheme. In addition, compressed lips can communicate commitment to commit evil. These "facial gestures" communicate intentions to be involved in perversity and evil (Buzzell).

<u>Facial expressions, such as a wink or compressed lips, can be an indication of perverse and evil intentions.</u>

Proverbs 16:31 "The silver-haired head *is* a crown of glory, *if* it is found in the way of righteousness." The silver hair stands for long life (MacDonald). Notice that the word "if" is in italics, indicating that it is not in the Hebrew text. Thus, this proverb is saying that silver hair comes as a reward for righteousness (Barnes; see Kidner). "Whoever would reach an honored old age attains to it in the way of a righteous life and conduct" (Delitzsch). Young men glory in their strength (20:29), but old men can take pride in their gray hair; "Longevity is a result of righteous living, but not all who are aged have lived righteously" (Buzzell).

<u>The silver hair indicates living a long life because living a righteous life is glory.</u>

Proverbs 16:32 "*He who is* slow to anger *is* better than the mighty, and he who rules his spirit than he who takes a city." People who control their anger are a "greater hero than a military conqueror. Victory in this area is more difficult than capturing a city" (MacDonald). Indulging passion is easy; bridling passions requires strenuous effort or the grace of God. Wardlaw says, "The truly great man (is) not one who destroys and wastes cities, and desolates kingdoms, and wades through the fields of bloody carnage to the utmost point of his ambitious aspiring; but (he) who succeeds in subjugating his passions; who by meekness and gentleness, diffuses peace and happiness around him; who loves his enemies, does good to them that hate him, praise to them but who despite fully use him and persecute him."

<u>People who control their anger or any other passion are mightier than generals who conquer a city.</u> If you don't believe it, try it!

For David to control his temper when being maligned by Shimei (2 Sam. 16:5-13) was a greater victory than slaying Goliath. Although one of the mightiest of the Czars of Russia, Peter the Great, failed here. In a fit of temper, he struck his gardener, and a few days afterward, the gardener died. "Alas," said Peter sadly, "I have conquered other nations, but I have not been able to conquer myself!"

Bridges says, "The heart is the field of battle. All its evil and powerful passions are deadly foes, and they must be met and triumphed over in the strength of God." He also says, "The glory of this victory is indeed far above *the mighty. The taking of the city* is child's play, compared with this 'wrestling with flesh and blood.' That is only the battle of the day. This the weary, unceasing conflict of a life. There, the enemy be mastered with a single blow. Here, he is to be chained up and kept down with unmitigated perseverance" (Bridges, italics his).

> Yet he who reigns within himself, and rules
> Passions, desires, and fears is more a king
> Which every wise and virtuous man attains.
> (Milton's *Paradise Regained*, ii. 466-8)

Proverbs 16:33 "The lot is cast into the lap, but its every decision *is* from the LORD." Casting lots consisted of writing options on stones, placing the stones in a vessel (or, as here, the lap, that is, in the fold of a garment) and shaking the vessel until one fell out. This proverb is saying that the one that falls out is not the result of mere chance; it is the result of the hand of the Lord. In the Old Testament, the Lord used this method for people to determine His will (1 Sam. 14:37-42). "The process here described would seem to have been employed ordinarily in trials where the judges could not decide on the facts before them" (Barnes).

<u>When casting lots, the one that falls out of the shaken vessel is not the result of mere chance but God's choice.</u>

The question is, "Should we use casting lots today to determine God's will?" The last incident of casting lots in the Bible is in Acts 1. It was used to determine who should replace Judas. Thus, Matthias was not appointed by the apostles or the church but directly by the Lord. It is critical to note two things. First, notice what they did. They looked at the Scripture, prayed, and agreed as a group. The Lord had opened their minds to understand the Scripture (Lk. 24:45) and the Lord had breathed on them, imparting to them the Holy Spirit until Pentecost (Jn. 20:22), at which time they were baptized by the Holy Spirit (Acts 1:5). In other words, Peter was not referring to the Psalms on his own; he was being guided into all truth by the Spirit of God. Second, after the coming of the Holy Spirit, there is no other case of casting lots. So, to determine the will of God, do not cast lots. Ask God for wisdom. Search the Scripture and consult a group of godly people.

Proverbs 17

Proverbs 17:1 "Better *is* a dry morsel with quietness, than a house full of feasting *with* strife" (15:17). The Hebrew word translated "strife" means "strife, dispute, quarrel." A dry toast with peace and quiet is better than a sumptuous meal with "bickering and unhappiness" (MacDonald). "Harmony in one's relationships is to be desired over a sumptuous supply of food" (Buzzell).

Having dry toast with quietness is better than filet mignon with a quarrel.

Proverbs 17:2 "A wise servant will rule over a son who causes shame, and will share an inheritance among the brothers." It is better to be a wise slave than a foolish son because a wise servant will be put in charge of a son who causes disgrace, and a wise servant will even be given an inheritance as if he were a son. "The fool will be servant to the wise of heart" (11:29). The Hebrew word translated "wise" here is not the normal word translated "wise" in the book of Proverbs. This one means "prudent."

Wardlaw says, "The servant whose character has been long tried and proved will be highly respected and valued, and will obtain the most important trust" and "Such a servant is a treasure in the family to which he or she belongs." Solomon's servant, Jeroboam, rose over Solomon's disgraceful son, Rehoboam, and became the leader of ten of the twelve tribes (MacDonald; Buzzell).

A wise servant will be given charge over a son who causes shame and will be given an inheritance as if he were a member of the family.

"Folly naturally tends to shame; wisdom to honor" (Bridges). Living a wise life has its rewards.

Proverbs 17:3 "The refining pot *is* for silver and the furnace for gold, but the LORD tests the hearts." The first line of this proverb is identical to Proverbs 27:21. It simply points out that refiners put silver and gold in a furnace to separate the pure metal from the dross. The second line seems to be saying only that the Lord examines the heart ("test"), but the first line implies that the Lord uses trials not to find people out but to sort them out (Kidner).

Wardlaw says, "*Trying* is more than simple *discerning*. The Lord does not need to try to make any discovery from Himself" (Wardlaw, italics his). Wardlaw goes on to say that the Lord tries the heart to bring to light what may be concealed, especially to the individual himself. Thus, through fiery trials, the Lord *refines* the heart of His children (Zech. 3:9). Barnes puts it like this: "Divine discipline *purifies* the good that lies hidden, like a grain of gold, even in rough and common natures, and frees it from all admixture of evil" (Barnes, italics added). In order for the process to work, we must respond properly (1 Pet. 1:6-7). Wardlaw exclaims, "O how sad to suffer, and not to profit!"

Refiners put silver and gold in the furnace to refine them, but the Lord uses fiery trials to purify the hearts of His children.

Bridges makes several interesting comments, including the following: Were it not for the furnace, the dross would "cleave inseparably to the metal." Until the metal is refined, it is "unfit for use." The process is painful, but "no milder remedy would accomplish the purpose." The refining process may be slow, but it is sure and when it is finished, only the dross will perish; the pure metal will be left.

Proverbs 17:4 "An evildoer gives heed to false lips; a liar listens eagerly to a spiteful tongue." The Hebrew word translated "gives heed" means "give attention." Evildoers pay attention to lies. The Hebrew word translated "spiteful" means "destruction, ruin." Liars like to listen to talk that is destructive. "The more ill they can hear of others, the better" (Wardlaw).

What people like to listen to says something about their character. "Whoever gives ear with delight to words which are morally reprobate, and aimed at the destruction of neighbors, thereby characterizes himself as a profligate. 'A wicked man gives heed to wicked mouths and a false man listens willingly to scandalous tongues'" (Delitzsch). Evildoers "welcome lies, unfounded rumors, false accusations. Liars, in turn, like to listen to scandal, slander, and a spiteful tongue. In that sense, the kind of talk a man feeds on is a barometer of what he is at heart" (MacDonald). "If he did not 'love a lie,' he would not listen to it" (Bridges).

Evildoers delight in liars and liars are eager to listen to destructive talk.

"If I cannot stop other men's mouths from speaking evil, I will either open my mouth to reprove it, or else I will stop my ears from hearing it, and let him see in my face that he has no room in my heart" (Bishop Hall, cited by Bridges).

Proverbs 17:5 "He who mocks the poor reproaches his Maker; he who is glad at calamity will not go unpunished" (see 14:31). The Lord is the "maker" of all, including the rich and the poor (22:2). Therefore, to mock the poor, who are made in God's image, is to "speak against" God (Buzzell).

"Equally bad is being glad when other people experience calamities (Prov. 24:17). A person who gloats over the misfortunes of others will himself experience misfortune (he will be punished)" (Buzzell). "The book of Obadiah pronounces doom on Edom for rejoicing when Jerusalem fell" (MacDonald).

<u>Mocking the poor is a reproach against God because all are made in God's image and being glad at another's calamity will be punished by God.</u>

"To pour contempt upon the current coin with the king's image on it, is treason against the sovereign" (Bridges).

"Compassion and pity, not joy, are appropriate in the presence of misfortune" (Delitzsch).

Proverbs 17:6 "Children's children *are* the crown of old men, and the glory of children *is* their father." Prior to this proverb, another crown of old age has been mentioned. Proverbs 16:31 speaks of living a righteous life being a crown of old age.

This proverb assumes that the individuals involved are "properly related to God and to each other" (Buzzell). Godly grandchildren are the result of a grandfather who has ruled ("crown") well. He taught his children how to teach their children. The grandchildren can glory in having a godly extended family.

<u>The glory of old age is having children who have reared wise, godly children, and the glory of being young is having a wise, godly father.</u>

Bridges says, "Gracious children and parents reflect honor upon each other" and "What a *crown* of thorns to each other are an ungodly prodigy and graceless parents!" (Bridges, italics his).

Proverbs 17:7 "Excellent speech is not becoming to a fool, much less lying lips to a prince." People expect consistency between what a person is and what a person says. Hence, excellent speech does not fit a fool. The incongruity of words of wisdom coming from an unwise person "shocks, discuss, and revolts the hearer" (Wardlaw).

Since people expect honesty from rulers, lying is "inappropriate" (Buzzell). Excellent speech "seems out of place" coming from a fool and lies are "unsuitable" for a prince because people "expect more from a prince" (MacDonald).

<u>It is incongruous for excellent speech to fall from the lips of a fool, and even more so for lies to come out of the mouth of a ruler.</u>

Proverbs 17:8 "A present *is* a precious stone in the eyes of its possessor; wherever he turns, he prospers." The Hebrew word translated "present" means "present, bribe" (BDB; NASB; NIV). It is "a gift by which one seeks to purchase for himself preference on the part of a judge" (Delitzsch). From the giver's perspective, a bribe is a precious stone that "performs wonders for him, opening doors, obtaining favors and privileges, or getting him out of trouble" (MacDonald).

The proverb is not commending bribes. It is simply expressing "a fact of experience" (Delitzsch). Bribes are condemned (Prov. 17:23; Ex. 23:8; Deut. 16:19; 27:25).

<u>To the giver, a bribe is a precious stone that works wonders.</u>

Bribes work. Money talks. For the rest of the story, keep reading. A few verses later you will find God's view of a bribe (17:23).

Proverbs 17:9 "He who covers a transgression seeks love, but he who repeats a matter separates friends." The one who "refuses to remember" an offense "seeks love and friendship" (MacDonald). He does not dwell on the offense; he buries it in oblivion (Barnes). He does not "make much ado" about the offence; he "endeavors by a reconciling, soothing, rectifying influence, to mitigate the evil, instead of making it worse" (Delitzsch). "When we learn to love, we also learn to cover, to forget, and to overlook many faults in others" (MacDonald).

On the other hand, those who keep repeating the offense lose their friend. One who "insists on digging up past grievances only succeeds in alienating friends" (MacDonald). Do not be a tale-bearer; be a peace-maker.

<u>People who are seeking love forget an offense, but those who repeatedly tell it alienate friends.</u>

Wardlaw says, "Be slow to take offense," and suggests that in the spirit of love, we throw a veil of concealment over offenses. MacDonald cites several illustrations. One woman to another: "Don't you remember the mean thing she said about you?" The other woman: "I not only don't remember; I distinctly remember forgetting!" George Washington Carver was refused admission to a college because he was black. Years later, when someone asked him for the name of the college, he answered, "It doesn't matter!"

Proverbs 17:10 "Rebuke is more effective for a wise *man* than a hundred blows on a fool." Verbal rebuke is effective for the wise. They get it.

Since the Mosaic Law only allowed for no more than forty lashes (Deut. 25:2-3), a hundred lashes is severe physical punishment. Severe physical punishment is not effective on fools. Even after that, they still do not get it. "*Stripes* only scourge the fool's back. They never reach his heart. He is, therefore, a fool still" (Bridges, italics his). "The '*fool*' clings pertinaciously to whatever is his own—his own thoughts, his own projects, his own ways—

simply because they *are* his own. He possesses neither a genuine love of truth nor a candid and humble solitude to know and do what is right" (Wardlaw, italics his).

"The wise are sensitive and learn readily, but a thickheaded fool is unresponsive even after extreme measures of correction" (Buzzell). "Usually, people who are sensitive do not need harsh forms of discipline. But those who are unfeeling and indifferent require the sledgehammer treatment. It is hard for them to think that they are ever wrong" (Barnes).

<u>The verbal rebuke of the wise is more effective than severe physical punishment is on a fool.</u>

"Criticism is always difficult to accept, but if we receive it with humility and a desire to improve our character, it will be very helpful. Only a fool does not profit when he is reproved for his mistakes" (*Our Daily Bread*, 8/18/1981).

Proverbs 17:11 "An evil *man* seeks only rebellion; therefore a cruel messenger will be sent against him." This proverb is usually understood to be about a rebellious citizen refusing to submit to governmental authority. Evil people refuse to submit to lawful authority; they are determined to have their own way (MacDonald; see also Barnes; etc.). These evil people have been described as "unprincipled, discontented, intractable, indomitable" troublemakers who seek to disturb the public peace (Wardlaw).

The "cruel messenger" is "the king's officer dispatched to subdue and punish" (Barnes), the "arresting officer sent by the king, or it may be the messenger of death sent by God" (MacDonald).

<u>Since evil people only seek rebellion against authority, they will be punished by the authorities.</u>

Those who refuse to listen to their parents, peers, and pastor, usually end up dealing with the police. Submission to authority is one of the fundamental principles of life.

Proverbs 17:12 "Let a man meet a bear robbed of her cubs, rather than a fool in his folly." The contrast is "designed to express real danger" (Wardlaw; Buzzell). The rage of the "large brown bear of Syria" (Barnes) over the loss of her cubs was "fierce and unmanageable" (MacDonald). Such an angry, raging bear is not as dangerous as "a fool in a fit of temper. Once he gets some crazy idea into his head, nothing will stop him" (MacDonald; Kidner, p. 40). "They (fools) are less rational in anger than wild beasts" (JFB).

<u>An angry, raging bear over the loss of her cubs is not as dangerous as a fool in his folly.</u>

"Consider meeting a fool with a knife, or gun, or even behind the wheel of a car; a mother bear could be less dangerous" (Alden, cited by Buzzell).

Proverbs 17:13 "Whoever rewards evil for good, evil will not depart from his house." The Hebrew word translated "evil" means "badness, evil, distress, misery, injury, calamity" (BDB) and can also mean "grief, harm, hurt, trouble" (Strong). It is one thing to not respond to a kindness, but to react by harming the person who was been good to you is particularly bad. Anyone who receives good and responds with injury will be not only suffering injury himself, but will bring "calamity" (Buzzell) on his family ("house"). To pay kindness with unkindness is to be guilty of the sin of ingratitude (Clarke). MacDonald says, "A curse rests upon the house of any man who repays a kindness with an injury. David repaid his loyal general, Uriah, with treachery, bringing misery upon his house (2 Sam. 12:9-10)."

<u>Those who receive good and respond with injury bring grief, trouble, and hurt to their family.</u>

It has been said, "To render evil for good is devil-like; to render evil for evil is man-like; to render good for evil is God-like." To return blessing for evil is Christ-like (1 Pet. 3:9).

Proverbs 17:14 "The beginning of strife *is like* releasing water; therefore stop contention before a quarrel starts." The release of water refers to the first crack in the mouth of a reservoir used to store water for a city. First, a few drops ooze out. Then the water gushes out with fury, causing no telling how much destruction (Barnes). It is a hole in a dike that enlarges rapidly (MacDonald). Disputes are like that. They begin small and rapidly enlarge, causing great destruction. So it is a good idea to stop minor contention before it becomes a major quarrel. Refuse to let an issue fester; stop before a dispute starts (Buzzell).

<u>Since minor disagreements are like a small leak in a dam that grows until it breaks forth with a destructive amount of water, they should be stopped at the beginning.</u>

Wardlaw describes how this might work: "A single word, the motion of a finger, the glance of an eye, happens to be noticed; and being interpreted as conveying a certain meaning, is resented;—the measure of the retaliation is, of course, excessive, and it provokes a return; the quarrel rises; the breach is widened; irreconcilable alienation ensues; and the alienation of the individual spreads to families, to circles of friends, neighborhoods, to communities!" He adds, "Rather let the offense pass than risk the consequences. When the fissure in the embankment appears, let the first drop of oozing water be the signal to stop the leak, and prevent the threatening flood."

Proverbs 17:15 "He who justifies the wicked, and he who condemns the just, both of them alike *are* an abomination to the LORD." To justify is to declare righteous (Barnes). As has been pointed out in these studies, the

Hebrew word rendered "abomination" means "repugnant, abhorrent, disgusting." Justifying the guilty and condemning the innocent is repugnant to the Lord.

Delitzsch says this proverb is "against the partisan judge who is open to bribery." This is a warning "against an unjust acquittal, no less than against unjust condemnation" (Barnes). Simply put, "God hates miscarriages of justice" (MacDonald).

<u>Judges who declare the wicked righteous and condemn the just are abhorrent to the Lord.</u>

This proverb provokes several thoughts.

What would cause a human judge to do this? Wardlaw answers, "There may be various motives by which individuals are tempted to this crime: the fear of evil from the power and influence of the wicked man, or the hope of benefit from his favor; self-interest, in one or another of its various forms; and in the other case, spite, and envy; malicious dislike of principles or of conduct by which their own are condemned; the revenge of fancied injury; considerations of expediency; and others of a similar kind."

God justifies the ungodly, but He does not do it by simply declaring the guilty innocent. He does it by declaring the wicked guilty, assessing the penalty (death), and having His Son pay the penalty. In other words, we are declared righteous because Jesus died for our sins and rose from the dead when we trust Him for the gift of eternal life. Thus, God is "just and the justifier of the one who has faith in Jesus" (Rom. 3:26).

Proverbs 17:16 "Why *is there* in the hand of a fool the purchase price of wisdom, since *he has* no heart *for it?*" Fools pay to go to school to get wisdom, but they do not learn. The reason that is given is that they have no heart for wisdom. The Hebrew word translated "heart" means "the inner man, mind, will, heart" (BDB). Kidner says that here it probably has the double meaning of "will" and "mind." In other words, the reason the fools do not gain wisdom is they do not have "understanding" (Barnes; Delitzsch; MacDonald). They just don't get it. They have "no mind to learn" (Moffett, cited by Kidner). They do not "really mean business" (Buzzell).

<u>Fools pay to purchase wisdom, but they do not get it because they do not really have a mind to learn.</u>

"A young man will spend a large income at the university in the *professed* purchase of wisdom, and yet idle away all this time!"(Bridges, italics his). Wardlaw says, "If you 'have *no heart for it*,' the work is all *uphill*; you begin with reluctance; you yawn and nod over it." He adds if you are of the mind, "You then set about it in earnest; you pursue it with energy and perseverance; you let no difficulties deterred you, nor cease application until you have mastered them;—it is your pleasure" (Wardlaw, italics his).

Proverbs 17:17 "A friend loves at all times, and a brother is born for adversity." The two halves of this proverb are not in contrast to one another, as if to say that a friend loves at all times, *but* a brother is born for times of trouble. It is true that there are some situations where a friend sticks closer than a brother (18:24), but it is also proverbial that "A true friend loves in adversity as well as in prosperity. Often it takes hard times to show which friends are genuinely loyal" and a brother is "at your side when you need him most" (MacDonald).

In this proverb, "both the friend and the brother are valued" (Buzzell). So, while in some cases, a friend is more faithful than a brother (18:24), that is not always the case. A brother can be just as loyal as a faithful friend. So the point of this proverb is a true friend loves you—at all times, "through (an) evil as well as (a) good report. He does not change when circumstances change" (Bridges). "He is not ashamed of poverty or of a prison" (Bridges). Brothers are "born to help each other in need. This is the will and purpose of God in placing them in their near relationship. It is sad when it fails; and beautiful when it is displayed" (Wardlaw). "In the troubled, you see what family ties are for, and you'll also see who are your friends" (Kidner). D. L. Moody's Bible says, "A true friend is like ivy—the greater the ruin, the closer he clings."

<u>A faithful friend is a friend during good times and bad and a brother is especially made to be there in time of trouble.</u>

A personal note: I have such a brother. A suggestion: see the notes on the next proverb.

Proverbs 17:18 "A man devoid of understanding shakes hands in a pledge, *and* becomes surety for his friend." MacDonald observes, "This verse modifies the previous one by showing that love should not be without discernment." Buzzell spells out the details when he says, "Being a reliable friend in times of adversity (17:17) is different from a foolhardy agreement to provide financial security for a high-interest loan."

Shaking hands in a pledge was an ancient form of signing a contract (Clarke). Solomon is saying that people who co-sign for a loan lack understanding. In co-signing for a loan, other factors besides friendship must be understood. As Wardlaw explains, as great a claim as friendship may be, the claims of wife and children and the claims of obvious justice must not be disregarded. In the words of Bridges, "There is no true benevolence in rash engagements, which may involve our name and family in disgrace or ruin." The point is, "It would be a case of bad judgment to agree to guarantee a friend's debts in the event that he should default. Any man who needs a surety is a bad credit risk" (MacDonald).

<u>Only people who lack understanding co-sign for others—even their friends.</u>

Earlier in Proverbs, Solomon discussed this concept in great detail. "My son, if you become surety for your friend, *If* you have shaken hands in pledge for a stranger, you are snared by the words of your mouth; you are taken by the words of your mouth. So do this, my son, and deliver yourself; for you have come into the hand of your friend: Go and humble yourself; plead with your friend. Give no sleep to your eyes nor slumber to your eyelids. Deliver yourself like a gazelle from the hand *of the hunter,* and like a bird from the hand of the fowler" (6:1-5; see also 11:15).

An observation: This is not a law; it is a proverb. It is not an absolute; it is a general truth.

A suggestion: If your friend needs financial help, give him or her a gift; if you co-sign, consider your potential liability a possible gift.

Proverbs 17:19 "He who loves transgression loves strife, and he who exalts his gate seeks destruction." Both halves of this proverb refer to this same person (Delitzsch). Those who love transgression are the same as those who exalt themselves at their gate.

The phrase "exalt his gate" is a reference to building "a stately house" and indulging in "arrogant ostentation" (Barnes). Such people are proud (Buzzell; Clarke) and arrogant (Kidner) and loudly proclaim their wealth (MacDonald).

These proud transgressors love to stir up strife. They also court destruction. "Sooner or later, their day will come and their name, glory, and honor will be swept away" (Bridges). They made their gate so large their estate went out of it (Matthew Henry).

Proud rebels who love strife court destruction.

Proverbs 17:20 "He who has a deceitful heart finds no good, and he who has a perverse tongue falls into evil." The Hebrew word translated "deceitful" means "twisted, perverted" (see "crooked" in the NASB and "perverse" in the NIV). People whose motives are distorted will not prosper (Buzzell). The Hebrew word translated "evil" means "evil, misery, distress." People with a perverted tongue fall into "trouble" (Buzzell; NIV).

People with a perverted heart will not prosper and people with a perverted tongue will get into trouble.

Proverbs 17:21 "He who begets a scoffer *does so* to his sorrow, and the father of a fool has no joy." The Hebrew word rendered "scoffer" means "stupid, dullard" and the one rendered "fool" means "senseless, foolish." Buzzell says the first refers to the "dull and thickheaded" and the second to the one who "lacks spiritual perception and sensitivity." Jamieson-Fausset-Brown (JFB) say that both denote "stupidity and impiety."

Fathers have no joy, only sorrow, over stupid, senseless children. Fathers grieve over disappointing children (Buzzell). Foolish children also affect the mother (10:1).

The father of stupid children lives with sorrow and the father of senseless children does not have joy.

P. W. Philpott related a story about a British Christian who was successful in business and had a well-educated son who was highly respected and honored like his father. Then, to everyone's surprise, the young man was charged with embezzlement. At his trial, he appeared nonchalant and arrogant. When the judge told him to stand up for sentencing, he still seemed unrepentant. Hearing a slight scuffle on the other side of the room, he turned to see that his aged father had also risen. The once erect head and straight shoulders of his father were now bowed low with shame. He stood to be identified with his son and to receive the verdict as though it were being pronounced upon himself. That is the way the father of a wayward son feels. Wardlaw suggests that the meaning here is more than the father has no joy *in his son*. He says, "The character and conduct of that son serve to infuse 'bitterness' into everything else."

Proverbs 17:22 "A merry heart does good, *like* medicine, but a broken spirit dries the bones." Pointing out that the word "like" is in italics, which means that it is not in the Hebrew text, Barnes says the first part of this proverb should be translated "a merry heart works good healing." "A cheerful disposition is a powerful aid to healing. A broken, disconsolate spirit saps a person's vitality" (MacDonald).

There is a mind/body connection. "One's inner life affects his physical well-being" (Buzzell). A cheerful heart is good for the soul and the body, and a broken spirit adversely affects the body. "Nothing has such a direct tendency to ruin health and waste out life as grief, anxiety, fretfulness, bad tempers, etc. All these work death" (JFB).

A cheerful heart has a healing effect on the body and a broken spirit has an adverse effect on the body.

MacDonald says, "Today's doctors tell us that a hearty laugh is great exercise. When you emit an explosive guffaw, they say, your diaphragm descends deep into your body and your lungs expand, greatly increasing the amount of oxygen being taken into them. At the same time, as it expands sideways, the diaphragm gives your heart a gentle, rhythmic massage. That noble organ responds by beating faster and harder. Circulation speeds up. Liver, stomach, pancreas, spleen, and gall bladder are all stimulated—your entire system gets an invigorating lift. All of which confirms what that sage old Greek, Aristotle, said about laughter more than 2000 years ago: 'It is a bodily exercise precious to health.'"

MacDonald quotes Blake Clark, who says: "Emotions can make you ill. They can make hair fall out by the handful, bring on splitting headaches, clog nasal passages, make eyes and nose water with asthma and allergies, tighten the throat with laryngitis, make skin break out in a rash, even cause teeth to drop out. Emotions can plague one's insides with ulcers and itises, give wives miscarriages, make husbands impotent—and much more. Emotions can kill."

The man credited with bringing the study of humor into the medical mainstream is Norman Cousins, the former editor of the *Saturday Review* and later a faculty member at UCLA Medical School. In his *Anatomy of an Illness*, Cousins described an unusual approach to his own self-treatment. Diagnosed with the connective tissue disease ankylosing spondylitis, Cousins determined that large doses of vitamin C and a steady diet of watching his favorite Marx Brothers movies and "Candid Camera" episodes gave him extended periods of pain relief. It became his quest to prove a biochemical link between laughter and fighting serious disease.

There is a link between laughter and levels of stress hormones and immune cell activity. Samples taken from subjects watching self-selected comedy videotapes showed decreased levels of stress hormones and increased immune cell activity.

Having a sense of humor doesn't mean knowing how to tell a joke. It is being able to see the humor around us. It is seeing humor rather than horror. It is using humor to keep a positive perspective.

Proverbs 17:23 "A wicked *man* accepts a bribe behind the back to pervert the ways of justice" (see 17:3). The expression "behind the back" (Heb. "out of the bosom") indicates that the bribe was given and received covertly (Bridges; Wardlaw). The one who pays the judge a bribe purchases an unjust verdict, and the one accepting the bribe renders an unjust sentence. Bridges makes several interesting observations: "Not even a good cause will justify the evil practice" and "even a corrupt world is ashamed of this sin."

Wicked judges who secretly accept bribes pervert justice.

Proverbs 17:24 "Wisdom *is* in the sight of him who has understanding, but the eyes of a fool *are* on the ends of the earth." The Hebrew word translated "understanding" means "discernment." The Hebrew text reads "in front of a man of discernment' (Buzzell; Kidner). People who have discernment see wisdom before their very eyes. For them, wisdom is near at hand and "ready for immediate use in all circumstances" (Wardlaw).

Fools look to the ends of the earth for wisdom and never find it. In the words of Clarke, "Wisdom is within the sight and reach of every man: but he whose desires are scattered abroad, who is always aiming at impossible things, or is of an unsteady disposition, is not likely to find it." Bridges puts it like this: "He who has understanding fixes his eyes on wisdom and is content with it, but the eyes of the fool are "rolling and wandering from one object to another. His thoughts are scattered. He has no definite object, no subtle principle, no certain rule."

People who "get it" see wisdom before their very eyes, but fools who do not "get it" look to the ends of the earth and still do not "get it."

Proverbs 17:25 "A foolish son *is* a grief to his father, and bitterness to her who bore him." (see 10:1; 17:21.) Proverbs 10:1 says, "a foolish son *is* the grief of his mother" and Proverbs 17:21 says that a foolish son brings sorrow to his father. Buzzell says this proverb is a repetition of Proverbs 17:21, using a stronger word for grief (see also Kidner). Parents are emotionally affected by their children's actions.

A foolish son causes his parents grief and bitterness.

Proverbs 17:26 "Also, to punish the righteous *is* not good, *nor* to strike princes for *their* uprightness." This is the first of six proverbs with the words "is not good" (17:26, 18:5, 19:2, 24:23, 25:27, 28:21).

The Hebrew word translated "prince" means "noble, princely." It can refer to those who are noble in character or those who are princely in rank (BDB). Barnes thinks this refers to those who are *noble in character* rather than those who are princely in rank. If so, the same group is being mentioned in both halves of the proverb.

Buzzell says this is another reference to injustice in court (17:5), adding that the princes here are officials and only kings or judges could order the punishment of an official. If that is the correct explanation, two different groups are in view: the ruler and the ruled (Wardlaw).

Either way, "perversion of justice takes place every day" (MacDonald). Actually, to say that punishing the righteous and striking princes is not good is an understatement. Earlier in this chapter Solomon said, "He who justifies the wicked, and he who condemns the just, both of them alike *are* an abomination to the LORD" (17:15).

It is not good to punish people or officials for doing what is right.

Proverbs 17:27 "He who has knowledge spares his words, *and* a man of understanding is of a calm spirit." (see "In the multitude of words sin is not lacking, but he who restrains his lips *is* wise" in Prov. 10:19). Those who have knowledge bridle their tongue, "in contrast to inconsiderate and untimely talk" (Delitzsch). Those who have understanding have a "calm" spirit. The Hebrew word translated "calm" means "cool" in the sense of "calm" (BDB). They "keep their cool" (Buzzell), "in contrast to passionate heat" (Delitzsch). The wise think before they speak (Buzzell). "Rash speech and quick temper betray a shallow character" (MacDonald).

<u>People with knowledge and understanding restrain their words and keep their cool.</u>
Proverbs 17:28 "Even a fool is counted wise when he holds his peace; *when* he shuts his lips, *he is considered* perceptive." Fools who are silent can be mistaken for people who are wise. Just keeping their mouths shut makes them appear perceptive.

"He cannot be known as a fool who says nothing" (Bridges). "Folly, to be known, must be *uttered*" (Wardlaw, italics his). An Arab proverb says, "Silence is the covering of the stupid" (cited by Delitzsch). James G. Sinclair suggests, "At times, it is better to keep your mouth shut and let people wonder if you're a fool than to open it and remove all doubt" (Sinclair, cited by MacDonald).

<u>A fool who is silent comes across as wise and perceptive.</u>
The problem with a fool is that he cannot control his tongue and, thus, his folly is discovered (Wardlaw). "A man may be golden-mouthed and silver-tongued in eloquence, but to know when and where to speak and to be silent is better than diamonds" (Clarke).

Proverbs 18

Proverbs 18:1 "A man who isolates himself seeks his own desire; he rages against all wise judgment." This proverb has been interpreted in several different ways. Some say that the one who isolates himself separates himself from folly (Jewish commentators), which is "improbable" (MacDonald). Others say the one who isolates himself separates himself from all hindrances to seek wisdom (Bridges; Wardlaw).

Another explanation is that the one who isolates himself separates himself from people. "This is the nonconformist who is going to have his own way even if it conflicts with tested knowledge or approved methods. He flies in the face of sound wisdom by his self-assertion" (MacDonald). "He who separates himself from others seeks his own desire and rushes forward against all wise counsel: a warning against self-will and the self-assertion which exults in differing from the received customs and opinions of mankind" (Barnes).

<u>Those who isolate themselves from others seek to do what they want to do and they rage against wise judgment.</u>

Proverbs 18:2 "A fool has no delight in understanding, but in expressing his own heart." Barnes suggests this is another form of egotism. He says the fool finds no pleasure in self-knowledge but "self-assertion, talking about himself and his own opinions is his highest joy." He refuses to listen to people with understanding; he is only interested in "expressing his own heart or displaying what he is" (MacDonald). He does not want to gain knowledge; he only wants to share his views (Buzzell). This fool has a "closed mind" and an "open mouth" (Kidner).

<u>Fools are not interested in gaining understanding; they are only interested in expressing their opinions.</u>

Proverbs 18:3 "When the wicked comes, contempt comes also; and with dishonor *comes* reproach." The Hebrew word translated "wicked" should be translated "wickedness" (JFB; Kidner). Kidner calls this proverb "sin's traveling companions." Ryrie says, "Contempt, dishonor, and reproach are the three companions of wickedness."

<u>With wickedness come contempt, dishonor, and reproach.</u>

Proverbs 18:4 "The words of a man's mouth *are* deep waters; the wellspring of wisdom *is* a flowing brook." As a general rule, what people say is like a pool of deep water. As the surface of the deep water does not reveal what is in the depths, people's words do not reveal their deepest thoughts and feelings. "Their meaning does not lie on the surface but can be perceived only by penetrating into the secret motives and aims of him who speaks" (Delitzsch). "Generally speaking, the words of a man's mouth don't give him away. They are deep waters hiding his true thoughts and motives" (MacDonald).

On the other hand, the words of the wise are a flowing brook. They are heard and they refresh the hearers. Gushing forth like a flowing brook, their "message is clear and transparent" (MacDonald). "A wise person's words are helpful and encouraging" (Buzzell). "Wise speech is like an exhaustless stream of benefit" (JFB). This proverb contrasts "our human reluctance or inability to give ourselves away with the refreshing candor and clarity of the true wisdom" (Kidner).

<u>What people say usually does not reveal the depth of what they think and feel, but the words of the wise not only are obvious, they refresh others.</u>

Tennyson wrote, "For words, like Nature, half reveal and half conceal the Soul within" (Tennyson, *In Memoriam*, V).

Proverbs 18:5 "*It is* not good to show partiality to the wicked, *or* to overthrow the righteous in judgment." This is the second of six proverbs with the words "is not good" (17:26; 18:5; 19:2; 24:23; 25:27; 28:21).

In dealing with the wicked, showing partiality is not good. "To show partiality to the wicked is, in effect, condoning their wickedness" (MacDonald). In judicial cases, we must not "pay any attention to a man's riches, influence, friends, offices, etc., but judge the case according to its own merits" (Clarke).

Nor is it good to oppose the righteous in judgment (Delitzsch). To deprive the righteous of justice is "putting truth on the scaffold and wrong on the throne" (Lowell, cited by MacDonald). The point of this proverb is the distortion of justice (see NKJV Study Bible).

<u>It is not good to distort justice by practicing partiality with the wicked or overturning a just judgment of the righteous.</u>

Proverbs 18:6 "A fool's lips enter into contention, and his mouth calls for blows." The Hebrew word translated "contention" means "strife, controversy, dispute, strife, quarrel." The words of fools start strife. After the contention has begun, their words escalate to calling for physical violence. "A loudmouthed fool is always trying to pick a fight or start trouble" (MacDonald). Fools are fond of fights.

<u>The words of a fool start strife and then call for physical violence.</u>

Some people love to say things that will stir up strife. God calls them fools. "If it is possible, as much as depends on you, live peaceably with all men" (Rom. 12:18).

Proverbs 18:7 "A fool's mouth *is* his destruction, and his lips *are* the snare of his soul." In a sense, this proverb further develops the previous one. In Proverbs 18:6, Solomon said that a fool's words result in contention and could call for physical violence. Now, he says that the words of a fool result in his destruction. It has been suggested that verse 6 is the immediate result, and verse 7 is the remote result of the fool's temper (Barnes). Thus, first, there is contention, then calls for physical violence, and after that, the destruction of the fool. His speech is his "downfall;" it is his "eventual ruin" (MacDonald).

The words of a fool ensnare him, eventually resulting in his destruction.

Proverbs 18:8 "The words of a talebearer *are* like tasty trifles, and they go down into the inmost body." This proverb is repeated in Proverbs 26:22. The Hebrew word translated "tasty trifles" means "to swallow greedily" (BDB; see Kidner). People gladly swallow gossip as if it was a delicious dessert and it settles into their inmost being, their "mind or heart" (JFB). "The words of a talebearer are like delicious tidbits; they are eagerly devoured by the listeners. It is almost as if the listeners say, 'Yum, yum. I like that. Tell me more!'"(MacDonald). Gossip is like eating a delicacy and like food being digested, it assimilated in one's innermost parts, that is, it is retained and remembered (Buzzell).

People eagerly swallow gossip like they do a delicious dessert and like a digested dessert, it affects their inner most parts, their hearts.

Proverbs 18:9 "He who is slothful in his work is a brother to him who is a great destroyer." The lazy are akin to great destroyers. They cause "great havoc or devastation" (MacDonald). "A poor or unfinished job differs little from a project that someone demolished; both projects are valueless" (Buzzell). "He who leaves work undone is next of kin to him who destroys it" (Oesterley, cited by Kinder).

Those who are lazy at their job are like those who destroy work.

"We know today that it is shoddy workmanship in cars, airplanes, buildings, and the like which is the cause of fatal accidents. This is also true in some offices and leadership in the church, where negligence of responsibility may lead to a breakdown of fellowship. A church may be disintegrated through foolish negligence and laziness as well as by satanic attack" (Griffiths, cited by MacDonald).

Proverbs 18:10 "The name of the LORD *is* a strong tower; the righteous run to it and are safe." The expression "the name of the Lord" refers to the Lord Himself (Delitzsch; MacDonald). A common idiom in the Scripture is using a person's name for the person (Wardlaw). Also note that, as the psalmist says, "Those who know Your name will put their trust in You" (Ps. 9:10).

Like a strong tower, the Lord is a place of protection (MacDonald), but not everyone takes shelter there. The righteous, those who trust the Lord, are those who run to Him for safety in a time of danger. "By putting their trust in Him they are as safe as a person hiding from the enemy in a strong tower" (Buzzell; also Clarke).

Those who trust the Lord are safe, like people in a strong tower are safe from an enemy.

In "temptation, trial, difficulty, and danger" (Wardlaw) run, do not walk, to the Lord.

Proverbs 18:11 "The rich man's wealth *is* his strong city, and like a high wall in his own esteem." (10:15) This proverb is in stark contrast to the previous one, which teaches the righteous trust the Lord for protection. The rich trust money as if it were a strong city with a high wall to guard them "from danger of every kind" (MacDonald). They fancy themselves in the midst of their "treasures as if surrounded by an inaccessible wall" (Delitzsch).

"Such is a vain trust" (JFB). Money is not a shield from many problems (Buzzell). "Trouble will find an entrance into his castle. Death will storm, and take it. And judgment will sweep both him and it into perdition" (Scott, cited by Bridges). Money is "a wall of no real strength, and no real safety—either from the ills of time, or from the woes of eternity" (Wardlaw).

Wealthy people trust their money to protect them like a city with a high wall protects its inhabitants from an enemy.

Pointing out that the first line here is identical with the first line of Proverbs 10:15, Buzzell says, "Wealth is more desirable than poverty and does help keep a person from disaster (10:15)," but he adds "money cannot replace the Lord as a base of security."

Proverbs 18:12 "Before destruction the heart of a man is haughty, and before honor *is* humility." The first line is a variation of Proverbs 16:18 and the second line is similar to Proverbs 15:33 (Delitzsch; see also 11:2). The proud are headed for destruction. Pride goes before a fall. People who think they are superior will experience a downfall (Buzzell). They walk on the brink of a precipice (Bridges). On the other hand, people who are humble are honored.

The proud are headed for destruction, but the humble are headed for honor.

The Lord repeated this basic concept several times (Mt. 23:12; Lk. 14:11; 18:14; see also Jas. 4:6). The repetition underscores the importance of this concept.

Proverbs 18:13 "He who answers a matter before he hears *it*, it *is* folly and shame to him." "To not get the facts before giving an opinion is folly and shameful. Since there are two sides to every story, you will be embarrassed if you agree with a person before you have heard the other person's side" (MacDonald). "Hasty speech evinces self-conceit and ensures shame" (JFB).

Wardlaw says this is very common in ordinary conversation, where people interrupt and answer you before you are finished, and is no less common in arguments, where your opponent will not allow you to complete your thought but answers you long before you are finished or could possibly be understood. Clarke says, "Before a man can tell his story, another will begin his. Before a man has made his response, the other wishes to confute piecemeal, although he has had his own speech already. This is foolishness to them. They are ill-bred. There are also many who give a judgment before they hear the whole of the cause and express an opinion before they hear the state of the case. How absurd, stupid, and foolish!"

To form an opinion and state it before you have all the facts is folly and shameful.

Get the facts first (Deut. 13:14). Don't jump to conclusions (Kidner). Don't interrupt to give your own answer before the other person has finished speaking.

Proverbs 18:14 "The spirit of a man will sustain him in sickness, but who can bear a broken spirit?" The nuances of several Hebrew words in this proverb add helpful details. The Hebrew word translated "sustain" means "support, endure." The one rendered "bear" means "lift, carry, endure" and the one rendered "broken" means "smite, scourge." In other words, this proverb asks, "If the body is sick, the spirit can support people, but if the spirit is smitten, who can endure that, who can lift that person?

"A man's spirit can bear up under all kinds of physical infirmities, but a broken spirit is far more difficult to endure. Emotional problems are often more serious than physical ailments" (MacDonald). "A physically ill person can be borne along by his spirit, but if his spirit is down too, if he is depressed, what or who can lift him out of his illness?"(Buzzell).

People's spirits can support and sustain them when they are sick, but if the spirit is smitten, who can endure that; who can lift that person?

MacDonald gives examples: "Dr. Paul Adolph tells of an elderly patient who was recovering satisfactorily in the hospital from a broken hip. When it was time for her to go home, her daughter told her that arrangements had been made for her to go to an old people's home. Within a few hours, the patient showed general physical deterioration and she died in less than a day—'not of a broken hip but of a broken heart.' A man who had faced the horrors of a concentration camp with gallantry discovered after his release that it was his own son who had informed on him. 'The discovery beat him to his knees and he died. He could bear the attack of an enemy, but the attack of one whom he loved killed him.'"

This proverb asks a question, "Who can lift a broken spirit?" The answer is, "No support is left, except, as implied, in God" (JFB). Delitzsch says, "If the spirit is borne down to powerless and helpless passivity, then within the sphere of the human personality, there is no other sustaining power that can supply its place." He also says, "But is not God the Most High the lifter up and the bearer of the human spirit that has been crushed and broken? The answer is that the manly spirit, 14a, is represented as strong in God; the discouraged, 14b, as not drawing from God the strength and support he ought to do."

Clarke agrees: "A man sustains the ills of his body, and the trials of life, by the strength and energy of his mind. But if the mind be scoundrel, if this be cast down, if slow-consuming care and grief have shot the dagger into the soul, what can then sustain the man? Nothing but the unseen God. Therefore, let the afflicted pray."

"Now David was greatly distressed, for the people spoke of stoning him, because the soul of all the people was grieved, every man for his sons and his daughters. But David strengthened himself in the LORD his God" (1 Sam. 30:6).

Proverbs 18:15 "The heart of the prudent acquires knowledge, and the ear of the wise seeks knowledge." The repetition of the word "knowledge" is for emphasis (Kidner; Buzzell). "The wise, who are already in possession of such knowledge, are yet at the same time constantly striving to increase this knowledge: their ear seeks knowledge, eagerly asking where it is to be found, and attentively listening when the opportunity is given" (Delitzsch). "The wise man never comes to the place where he ceases to learn. His mind is always open to instruction, and his ear is receptive to knowledge" (MacDonald). "The discerning and the wise are eager to increase their knowledge. They desire it with their hearts and they listen for it with their ears" (Buzzell). Some have a mind with an appetite (Kidner).

Prudent people have a heart for knowledge and the wise have an ear for knowledge.

Bridges says, "Clearer knowledge sweeps away many clouds." He adds that a better view of your work will make it easier, and more knowledge of the road makes it more pleasant. You not only guide yourself, but you will be able to "admonish one another (Rom. 15:14)."

Proverbs 18:16 "A man's gift makes room for him, and brings him before great men." This proverb has been interpreted several different ways. Some have explained the "gift" as a simple or generous gift. Delitzsch says, "By liberal giving where duty demands it, and prudence commends it, one does not lose but gains, does not descend but rises; it helps a man over the difficulties of limited, narrow circumstances, gains for his affection, and helps him up from step to step."

Others have understood the word "gift" as a bribe. Barnes says the bribe is personified, appearing as a powerful "friend at court." MacDonald says the gift is a bribe or gratuity. Buzzell says it is "close to bribery." JFB (Jamieson, Fausset & Brown) say it is a bribe and disapproval is implied. Although the Hebrew word translated "gift" in this verse is used of a bribe (15:27), there is another Hebrew word for bribe (17:8, 23). The one used here is "a more neutral word," which can simply refer to an "innocent courtesy" (Kidner).

Then some take this proverb to reference spiritual gifts (see Bridges). MacDonald says this proverb is sometimes used to teach that those who exercise their spiritual gift "will have plenty of openings, but that is not the meaning of this verse."

<u>Giving gifts opens doors and can enable a person gain a meeting before great men.</u>

Giving money to a political campaign could gain you a meeting with a politician. A generous tip to the maître' may make room for you at a crowded restaurant.

Proverbs 18:17 "The first *one* to plead his cause *seems* right, until his neighbor comes and examines him." This proverb is taken to be "an exhortation to be cautious in a lawsuit" because the second party may show the arguments of the first were untenable (Delitzsch; Barnes; Clarke). The judge needs to hear both sides before making a decision (Buzzell).

Even if that is only the primary meaning, it is still generally true (Wardlaw). Hence, some say, "When a man tells his side of the story, it seems very convincing and you are apt to believe him. But when his neighbor comes and asks him a few leading questions, then it may appear that he was not so right after all" (MacDonald). "One-sided statements are not reliable" (JFB).

<u>The first to plead a cause may seem to be right, until what he said is examined.</u>

This proverb certainly applies to cases in court, but is also applies to disputes outside of court. "The same is true of parents when their children argue" (Buzzell). "Hear both sides" (Kidner). Do not form hasty opinions (see 18:13). Let all the evidence be "sifted" (Bridges). When the first person speaks, what is said may be false, partial (not the whole truth), or the truth with additions (Wardlaw). So get the facts—all the facts.

Proverbs 18:18 "Casting lots causes contentions to cease, and keeps the mighty apart." As was explained earlier (16:33), casting lots consisted of writing options on stones, placing the stones in a vessel or in the fold of a garment, and shaking the stones until one fell out. Proverbs 16:33 says the one that fell out was not the result of mere chance; it was the result of God's choice. In the Old Testament, the Lord used this method for people to determine His will (1 Sam. 14:37-42).

Proverbs 18:18 says casting lots settles disagreements among people. Barnes says, "A tacit appeal to the Divine Judge gave a fairer prospect of a just decision than corruption (Prov. 18:16) or hasty one-sidedness (Prov. 18:17)." Appealing to the Lord to settle matters provided a peaceful settlement between powerful contenders who might otherwise have resorted to force (MacDonald).

<u>Letting the Lord settle disagreements stops contentious disputes and prevents further conflict.</u>

In Acts 1, the last use of casting lots in the Bible, they looked at the Scripture, prayed, and agreed as a group. After the coming of the Holy Spirit, the way the will of God is determined is by searching the Scripture, praying, and seeking wise advice from mature believers (see notes on 16:33).

When difficulties arise, let the Lord be the final Judge (MacDonald). Of course, this assumes that the contentious parties agree to abide by God's Word.

Proverbs 18:19 "A brother offended *is harder to win* than a strong city, and contentions *are* like the bars of a castle." Some disagreements degenerate to the point that one party is offended. If the offended person is a brother, not an enemy (Bridges), nor a stranger (Wardlaw), mending the relationship is more difficult than the conquest of a strong city. Contention is like bars on a castle gate that prevent others from entering. "The nearer the relation, the wider the breach" (Bridges). MacDonald reminds us: "Quarrels between close relatives are often the hardest to mend," and, "Civil wars are always the bitterest."

<u>An offended brother is hard to win than conquering a fortified city, and having contentions is as difficult to get past as the bars on a castle gate.</u>

The caution here is against offending, as well as being offended (Wardlaw). Remember, the invisible walls of estrangement are easy to erect and hard to demolish (Kidner).

Proverbs 18:20 "A man's stomach shall be satisfied from the fruit of his mouth; *from* the produce of his lips he shall be filled." People are affected by what they say. If what they say is good, they are satisfied and filled. "A man has to eat his words. If they have been good words, they will yield satisfaction to him" (MacDonald). Words bear fruit, not only for others, but also for the speaker (Delitzsch). People's words can give them inward satisfaction. Their conscience can have peace and their heart enjoyment (Wardlaw).

People who speak that which is good are personally satisfied and filled.

Proverbs 18:21 "Death and life are in the power of the tongue, and those who love it will eat its fruit." What is spoken has the power of life and death. This applies to all (Clarke), but the focus here is on those who love to talk; their words are seeds that will bear fruit, fruit they themselves will eat.

Everyone, particularly those who are talkative, have the power of life and death in what they say and they will reap the consequences of their speech.

In court, the words of a witness can determine whether a defendant lives or dies (Buzzell). In ordinary conversation, what is said can be helpful or harmful. With words, people can save others by exhorting them or destroy others by abusing them (Bridges).

"There is an ancient fable about a monster known as Proteus who had the power of assuming many shapes and appearances. He could become a tree or a pebble, a lion or a dove, a serpent or a lamb. He seemed to have little difficulty in passing from one form into another. That fabled creature reminds me of the human tongue. It can bless or curse; it can express praise or whisper slander; it can speak a word of encouragement or spread the poison of vindictive hatred" (Leonard Greenway).

Proverbs 18:22 "*He who* finds a wife finds a good *thing,* and obtains favor from the LORD." The Hebrew word translated "good" means "good thing, benefit, welfare." A man who finds a wife has found something beneficial for himself and has also received a blessing from the Lord.

Some add "good" before "wife" (MacDonald) and the Greek translation of the Old Testament adds, "He that puts away a good wife puts away happiness; and he that keeps an adulteress, is foolish and ungodly" (Delitzsch; Barnes), but these additions to the Hebrew text are not justified (Clarke).

Nevertheless, this proverb is to be taken "with limitations" (Bridges). It is implicit here and explicit elsewhere that not every kind of wife is a good thing (19:13-14; 21:9; Kidner). Some men find a crown for the head (a "jewel") and other men get "rottenness in [their] bones" (12:4).

The man who finds a good and godly wife has found something beneficial for himself and has received a blessing from the Lord.

When they read this, some women will scream sexism, but remember, Solomon is writing to his son (1:8). Obviously, a good and godly husband is beneficial to a wife and a blessing from the Lord. The simple truth of this proverb is that even with all of its troubles, marriage is a blessing from God (Clarke). Marriage is a blessing from a benevolent God; it is meant for "the happiness of His creatures" (Wardlaw).

Proverbs 18:23 "The poor *man* uses entreaties, but the rich answers roughly." Poor people often speak gently, compared to rich people, who answer harshly. "Note the paradox. The poor man, of whom one might expect roughness, supplicates; the rich, well nurtured, from whom one might look for courtesy, answers harshly and brusquely" (Barnes). "The well-bred man of the world, who is all courtesy and refinement to his own circle, to those under his feet is often insufferably rude and unfeeling" (Bridges). While it is true that rich people can "respond roughly and be overbearing, not all rich people have bad manners" (MacDonald). Actually, there are exceptions to both sides of this statement (Wardlaw).

Poor people usually speak humbly, but arrogant rich people often respond roughly.

Recognizing our poor, needy state, we come humbly before the Lord, but we often speak roughly (and wrongly) to the homeless.

Proverbs 18:24 "A man *who has* friends must himself be friendly, but there is a friend *who* sticks closer than a brother." This proverb has "many interpretations" (MacDonald). Friendliness wins friends, but some friends stay closer than a brother (the LXX, the Greek translation of the OT; KJV; NKJV; Bridges; Wardlaw; Clarke). A man of many friends may come to ruin, but there is a friend that sticks closer than a brother. The point is it is better to have one loyal friend than many friends who will lead you astray (Hebrew text; NASB; NIV; Barnes). "There are friends who pretend to be friends, but there is a friend who sticks closer than a brother" (RSV). This explanation contrasts fair-weather friends with those who are loyal through thick and thin.

The Hebrew text is to be preferred. It contains a play on words (Kidner). The Hebrew word translated "friends" is related to the Hebrew word for "break" (come to ruin) and the one rendered "friendly" above is the word for "break." The point of this play on words is that friends can break you, bring you to ruin, lead you astray. The Hebrew text also contains a contrast ("but"). The contrast is between friends who can lead you to ruin and a friend who is loyal. Thus the proverb is saying that those who have "numerous friends, chosen indiscriminately" may find themselves in trouble; that is, "broken into pieces" (Buzzell).

All agree on the interpretation of the second line. In some cases, genuine friends are more attached than a natural brother (Clarke). That is not to say that a natural brother is not as loyal as a friend. In fact, Proverbs 17:17 says, "A friend loves at all times, and a brother is born for adversity." So while *in some cases* a friend is more faithful than a brother (18:24), that is not *always* the case. A brother can be just as loyal as a faithful friend.

<u>Having many friends chosen indiscriminately can lead to trouble, but there is a friend who clings closer than a natural brother.</u>

Some apply this proverb to the Lord. G. Campbell Morgan writes: "All consideration of this great verse leads us at last to one place, to One Person. He is the Friend of sinners. There comment ceases. Let the heart wonder and worship." It is true that the Lord is a Friend of sinners (Mt. 11:19; Lk. 7:34), but this proverb "has no such meaning" (Clarke; Wardlaw). It could be applied to the Lord, but that is not the primary interpretation of the proverb.

Proverbs 19

Proverbs 19:1 "Better *is* the poor who walks in his integrity than *one who is* perverse in his lips, and is a fool." (The first line is repeated in 28:6.) The contrast between the two halves of this verse suggests that the second half is about someone who is rich. The contrast is between the upright poor and the perverse rich (Barnes). The Hebrew word translated "perverse" means "twisted, distorted, crooked, perverse, perverted" (see "perverse" in the NASB and NIV; "crooked" in the ESV). The poor who are honest are better off than the rich who distort the truth (MacDonald). Simply put, "Integrity is better than riches" (Clarke). "Better be in the wilderness with God, then in Canaan without Him" (Reynolds, cited by the Bridges).

<u>It is better to be poor and have integrity than to be a rich fool who is perverse in lip and life.</u>

Being poor with integrity is better than being a perverse, rich fool because the poor have personal honor and happiness and because they are better citizens in society. "The perverse *lips* and perverse *life* of the unprincipled fool do incomparable more harm to society, then his wealth can ever do it to good" (Wardlaw, italics his).

Proverbs 19:2 "Also it is not good *for* a soul *to be* without knowledge, and he sins who hastens with *his* feet." This is the third of six proverbs with the words "is not good" (see also 17:26; 18:5; 19:2; 24:23; 25:27; 28:21). The word "also" connects this proverb with the previous one (Kidner), which says it is better to be poor with character than to be a rich, perverse fool.

It is not good to act without knowledge. In fact, acting hastily usually leads to sin. "This man knows what he wants to do, but he doesn't know how to do it, so he goes off half-cocked. Haste only adds to his misery. He is in too much of a hurry to ask for directions or to follow them if given, so he misses the way and goes around in circles" (MacDonald). "Ambitious drive without adequate knowledge may lead to hasty blunders" (Buzzell). "Rashness, the result of ignorance, brings trouble" (JFB).

<u>To act without adequate information is not good; it often leads to sin.</u>

Haste makes sin. Slow down. No, stop. Think. Get the facts. Then act.

Proverbs 19:3 "The foolishness of a man twists his way, and his heart frets against the LORD." Fools end up ruining their lives and blaming the Lord! After "having brought about disasters by (their) own perverseness," they turn round and "angrily complain against the Providence of God" (Barnes; MacDonald). People blame God for their failure (JFB).

<u>After fools ruin their lives, they blame the Lord.</u>

One example of this foolishness is the man who undertakes a business venture for which he is not qualified or he neglects his business. Then when the business fails, he blames the Lord (Wardlaw). Another illustration is the person goes against the will of God. "It is monstrous to charge the providence of God with the consequences of actions that He has forbidden" (Adeney, cited by MacDonald).

Proverbs 19:4 "Wealth makes many friends, but the poor is separated from his friend" (see 14:20). Buzzell says Proverbs 19:4-6 speak of false friendship and suggests that the first line of Proverbs 19:4 is developed in Proverbs 19:6, and the second line of Proverbs 19:4 is expanded in Proverbs 19:7. Proverbs 19:4 is another indication of the selfishness of people (Bridges).

People make friends with rich people who can benefit them and separate themselves from the poor who cannot benefit them (MacDonald). Thus, as a general rule, the rich make many friends and the poor lose friends. Perhaps it is because "many people, unfortunately, want to avoid the embarrassment of associating with poor people" (Buzzell). At any rate, when foul weather destroys people's wealth, they discover which friends are their fair-weather friends. "Let wealth become poverty; then comes the test of friendship. Let 'riches make themselves wings and fly away' and the selfish friends find wings too" (Wardlaw).

<u>Money makes friends, but the loss of money means the loss of friends.</u>

On the other hand, the psalmist declared, "I *am* poor and needy, *yet* the LORD thinks upon me. You *are* my help and my deliverer" (Ps. 40:17).

Proverbs 19:5 "A false witness will not go unpunished, and *he who* speaks lies will not escape." This proverb is virtually repeated a few verses later (19:9; see also 21:28). Wardlaw points out that our sinful nature makes taking an oath necessary and when an oath is taken, falsehood becomes perjury. Perjury will eventually be punished (Buzzell). Be sure your sin will find you out (Num. 32:23). Perjurers in court will be punished and liars will not escape punishment.

<u>Perjurers are punished; liars do not get away with it.</u>

Again, it needs to be pointed out that this is a proverb, not a law. It is like parents saying to their teenager who is about to take the car out for the night, "Speeders pay fines." That does not mean that all speeders are caught, but that is a truth about life that law-breakers need to remember.

Proverbs 19:6 "Many entreat the favor of the nobility, and every man *is* a friend to one who gives gifts." This proverb is similar to the first half of Proverbs 19:4. The Hebrew word translated "nobility" means "noble, generous." In this proverb, it refers to a generous person (NASB; MacDonald). When people are generous gift-givers, many seek their favor and everyone is their friend. "People tend to befriend those from whom they hope to benefit" (MacDonald). Buzzell, however, says that "entreat favor (literally, 'stroke the face') refers to blatantly insincere flattery."

<u>Many seek favors from the generous, and everybody is a friend to those who give gifts.</u>

Proverbs 19:7 "All the brothers of the poor hate him; how much more do his friends go far from him! He may pursue *them with* words, *yet* they abandon *him.*" In contrast to the rich (see 19:6), the poor cannot find friends (Buzzell). The relatives and friends of the poor detest and desert him. They give him the "cold shoulder" and when he appeals for help they abandon him (MacDonald). "They will have nothing to do with him" (Clarke).

<u>The relatives of the poor people detest them; their friends disregard them, and even when they pursue relatives and friends, they desert them.</u>

Proverbs 19:8 "He who gets wisdom loves his own soul; he who keeps understanding will find good." It is in people's best interests to get and keep wisdom. Those who find wisdom find life and obtain favor from the Lord (8:35). Those who gain wisdom benefit themselves, but they must also keep it. It takes as much effort to keep it as to get it (Bridges). Those who keep it are on "a sure road to success" (MacDonald). They will prosper spiritually and emotionally as well as materially (Buzzell).

<u>Those who gain and keep wisdom benefit themselves.</u>

Proverbs 19:9 "A false witness will not go unpunished, and *he who* speaks lies shall perish." This proverb is virtually a repetition of Proverbs 19:5. Buzzell says it is identical to it, except for the last verb. MacDonald says, "We should not be surprised at the frequency with which this is repeated. After all, one of the Ten Commandments deals with perjury (Ex. 20:16)." Buzzell suggests that the "thought is repeated because of the seriousness of lying in court." The slight difference between this proverb and Proverbs 19:5 is that Proverb 19:5 says liars will not escape punishment and this one says they will perish, which is a reference to physical death.

<u>Perjurers are punished; liars will perish.</u>

Proverbs 19:10 "Luxury is not fitting for a fool, much less for a servant to rule over princes." Fools do not handle luxury well. They do not "know how to act in the midst of culture and refinement" (MacDonald). They do what fools do. They handle it foolishly. They become "more foolish" (Delitzsch). Their good fortune renders them vain, self-sufficient, and overbearing (Wardlaw).

Servants who become rulers do not do well either. They do not know how to act in a position of authority. Their treat their "former superiors arrogantly" (MacDonald). Their habits make them unfit to rule (Bridges). It is not that slaves are naturally inferior; it is that their education and habits of life render them unfit for governing (Wardlaw).

<u>Fools do not know how to handle abundance and servants do not know how to handle authority.</u>

Fools who receive an inheritance or win the lottery spend their money foolishly, ending up with nothing. People who have been servants all their life and who are suddenly elevated to a position of authority do not automatically know how to handle authority just because they are now in a position of authority.

Proverbs 19:11 "The discretion of a man makes him slow to anger, and his glory *is* to overlook a transgression." The Hebrew word translated "discretion" means "prudence, insight, understanding." Prudent people are patient, slow to anger. Discretion defers anger (Bridges). When provoked, people with discretion restrain resentment (Wardlaw).

The glory of people who have understanding is that they overlook a transgression done to them. "A man of good sense knows how to control his temper. He can graciously overlook it when somebody wrongs him" (MacDonald). "A prudent, patient man is not easily upset by people who offend him; in fact he overlooks offenses, knowing that to harbor resentment or attempt revenge only leads to more trouble. Overlooking them is his glory, that is, it is honorable" (Buzzell). "A quick and touchy irritability is the mark of the weak and foolish, rather than of a vigorous and sensible, mind" (Wardlaw).

<u>People with insight are slow to give anger and their honor is overlooking transgressions against them.</u>

Solomon saw this demonstrated in the life of his father David, whose attitude toward Saul "illustrates the proverb well" (MacDonald; Kidner). Those who have insight are slow to get angry and when they do, they do not hold on to it. They replace anger, resentment, and malice with forgiveness and forbearance. When it comes to anger, practice self-control, not self-indulgence.

Proverbs 19:12 "The king's wrath *is* like the roaring of a lion, but his favor *is* like dew on the grass." (see 20:2) The roar of a lion precedes its falling upon its prey (Delitzsch). Amos says, "A lion has roared! Who will not fear?" (Amos 3:8). "There is nothing more dreadful than the roaring of this tyrant of the forest. At the sound of it all other animals tremble, flee away, and hide themselves. The king who is above law, and rules without law, and whose will is his own law, is like the lion" (Clarke).

Dew on the grass is a picture of refreshment (Delitzsch). The king's wrath is a warning of danger ahead and his favor is gentle and refreshing (MacDonald).

When those in authority get angry, there is danger ahead, but when they are favorable, refreshment is about to come.

Proverbs 19:13 "A foolish son *is* the ruin of his father, and the contentions of a wife *are* a continual dripping." For the adverse effects of a foolish son on his father, see Proverbs 17:21 and Proverbs 17:25 (see also 10:1).

Barnes says the Hebrew word rendered "ruin" is in the plural, which "seems to express the multiplied and manifold sorrow caused by the foolish son." Pointing out that it means "chasm," Buzzell says "a foolish son is like an overwhelming catastrophe that sucks a person into a deep pit. Fathers with foolish sons can testify to the engulfing agony that sinks them into depression and despair."

This is the first of five proverbs concerning a contentious wife (21:9; 21:19; 25:24; 27:15). The Hebrew word translated "contentious" means "strife, contention, quarrelsome." It comes from the Hebrew verb for "judge." A judging, contentious wife is like "the irritating, unceasing, sound of the fall, drop after drop, of water through the chinks in the roof" (Barnes). A nagging wife is "as annoying as a continual dripping of water on metal" (MacDonald). "The man who has got such a wife is like a tenant who has got a cottage with a bad roof through every part of which the rain either drops or pours. He can neither sit, stand, work, nor sleep, without being exposed to these droppings. God help the man who is in such a case, with house or wife!" (Clarke).

Wardlaw makes several interesting observations. First, continual dripping is very destructive to the house, rotting its timbers, loosening its cement, and endangering its stability. Thus the contentious wife is ruinous to the family's interests as well as its comfort and peace. "They dishearten, dispirit, and paralyze exertion." Second, if a man only had to deal with a foolish son, he might be sustained and comforted by his wife. If a man had to live with a contentious wife, he might receive sympathy from an affectionate son. But when the same man is both wretched father and wretched husband, neither relationship alleviates the other; each aggravates the affliction of the other. Third, "many a wife leads a life of daily irksomeness and grief from the behavior of the hasty and furious, or selfish and sullen, and unreasonable husband."

The two things that make home life miserable for a man are a foolish son, who causes deeply-felt sorrow, and a contentious wife, who is an incessant irritation, an unceasing annoyance.

An Arab proverb says that there are three things which make a house intolerable: a leaking roof, a nagging wife, and bugs.

Proverbs 19:14 "Houses and riches *are* an inheritance from fathers, but a prudent wife *is* from the LORD." (see 18:22.) The previous proverb talks about a contentious wife. This one speaks of a prudent wife. This proverb is a contrast between men's gifts and God's gifts. A father may give his son houses and riches as an inheritance, but the Lord gives a prudent wife. "House and riches, which in themselves do not make men happy, one may receive according to the law of inheritance; but a prudent wife is God's gracious gift" (Delitzsch). For Paul's description of a prudent wife see 1 Timothy 5:14 and 1 Timothy 5:10.

Wealth may come from an inheritance, but a wise wife is a gift from God.

The fact that a wise wife is a gift from God does not mean that the human will is not involved. The wife is prudent because she seeks God's wisdom. The man selects such a wife. In the providence of God, they get married. Thus, in the final analysis, a prudent wife is "by His providence, and therefore (is) His special gift" (Bridges). So young man, be wise in your wife selection. As Wardlaw says if you err here, your inheritance will little avail to your happiness.

The same, of course, could be said of a prudent husband. It must be remembered that Solomon wrote Proverbs to his son, not his daughter, but the principles apply to both.

Proverbs 19:15 "Laziness casts *one* into a deep sleep, and an idle person will suffer hunger." Laziness is like a sleeping pill. "Laziness can cause a person to be so inactive that he easily falls into a deep sleep, totally oblivious to the precious time he is losing" (Buzzell). Lazy people are "unconscious" (Clarke) of even their own interests. They are in "a state of utter indifference" (JFB).

Laziness has consequences. For one thing, idleness leads to hunger and poverty.

Lazy people are unaware of what is going on and their idleness will lead to hunger.

These are people who persuade themselves that all is well, because they will not trouble themselves to open their eyes to the truth and content themselves to let things run their course (Bridges). Does this proverb apply to personal Bible study?

Proverbs 19:16 "He who keeps the commandment keeps his soul, *but* he who is careless of his ways will die." Keep God's command to do what is right (Delitzsch); it is a matter of life and death. Going God's way leads to life.

The Hebrew word translated "careless" means "despise, regard with contempt, to be careless." The second half of this proverb refers to people who disregard, despise, and disobey God's command to do what is right. When they hear that they are to do what is right, they roll their eyes, grin, and walk away. When people go their careless way, they prematurely die physically. Premature physical death is a repeated theme in Proverbs (see 3:2, 16; 4:10; 9:11; 10:2, 27; 11:4, 19; 13:14; 14:27; 15:10, 24).

"The one who obeys the commandment of the Lord is doing what is best for himself in the long run, both physically and spiritually. The person who lives recklessly and carelessly will die" (MacDonald). "To keep, that is, to obey instructions, is self-preserving; to do the opposite is self-destructive" (Buzzell).

<u>Keeping God's command to do what is right enables people to keep their life, but those who go their way experience premature physical death.</u>

Proverbs 19:17 "He who has pity on the poor lends to the LORD, and He will pay back what he has given." The pity in this proverb is not the pity of words (see "Depart in peace, be warmed and filled" in Jas. 2:16). It is practical "pity that acts—the pity that visits, and comforts, and relieves" (Wardlaw). The word "lends" also indicates that more than compassion is involved. In this proverb, pity on the poor involves giving money (Buzzell). "Giving to the poor is lending to the Lord" (MacDonald).

"O what a word is this! God makes himself debtor for everything that is given to the poor! Who would not advance much upon such credit? God will pay it again. And in no case has he ever forfeited his word" (Clarke). "God will not only pay back the amount loaned but will pay good interest as well. Even a cup of cold water given in His name will be rewarded (Mat. 10:42)" (MacDonald). Giving is "an investment God will reward. God blesses people's generosity with His generosity" (Buzzell).

<u>Giving to the poor out of compassion is like giving a loan to the Lord; He will repay.</u>

Remember: Love is essential. "Though I bestow all my goods to feed the poor, and give my body to be burned, but have not love, it profits me nothing" (1 Cor. 13:3). If there is love, there is profit. The Lord rewards the compassion of believers at the Judgment Seat of Christ (Jas. 2:12-13). He may even do that here and now.

"Henry Bosch illustrates: A father once gave his boy a half dollar, telling him he could do with it as he pleased. Later when he asked about it, the little fellow said he had lent it to someone. 'Did you get good security?' inquired his father. 'Yes, I gave it to a poor beggar who looked hungry!' 'O how foolish you are. You'll never get it back!' 'But Dad, I have the best security; for the Bible says, he that gives to the poor lends to the Lord!' Thinking this over, the Christian father was so pleased that he gave his son another half-dollar! 'See!' said the boy. 'I told you I'd get it again. Only I didn't think it would come so soon!'" (Bosch, cited by MacDonald).

> We lose what on ourselves we spend,
> We have, as treasures without end,
> Whatever, Lord, to Thee we lend,
> Who givest all.
> —*Christopher Wordsworth*

Proverbs 19:18 "Chasten your son while there is hope, and do not set your heart on his destruction." The Hebrew word translated "chasten" means "discipline, chasten, admonish." Children should be disciplined when they are young because when they are young, there is still hope that they will learn. If discipline is not applied when they are young, they will destroy their lives.

Discipline children while they are young and "capable of being reformed," because not to do so is to expose them to "a far worse penalty" (Barnes). Discipline children while they are "young and teachable," for refusing to do so, will ruin their lives (MacDonald). The issue is timing—do it while there is hope; "the cure of the evil must be commenced in infancy" (Bridges). "To withhold discipline is neither a compliment nor a kindness" (Kidner). "Permissiveness is cruelty" (MacDonald).

<u>Children should be disciplined while they are young and teachable because for parents to be passive will lead to the destruction of their children.</u>

"Though a son shows obstinacy, and manifest a bad disposition, yet there is hope in the training of the youth of being able to break his self-will, and to wean him from his bad disposition; therefore his education should be carried forward with rigorous exactness, but in such a way that wisdom and love regulate the measure and limits of correction" (Delitzsch). "This is a hard precept for a parent. Nothing affects the heart of a parent so much as a child's cries and tears. But it is better that the child may be caused to cry, when the correction may be healthful to his soul, than that the parent should cry afterward, when the child is grown to man's estate, and his evil habits are sealed for life" (Clarke).

Proverbs 19:19 "*A man of* great wrath will suffer punishment; for if you rescue *him,* you will have to do it again." Anger harms the people who are angry. Someone has said, "The acid of anger harms the one in whom it is stored more than the one on whom it is poured."

Moreover, trying to rescue angry people from their anger is usually a fruitless and frustrating endeavor. "The connection between wrath and punishment is so invariable that all efforts to save the passionate man from the disastrous consequences which he brings on his own head are made in vain" (Barnes). "A hot-headed man will suffer punishment for it. Even if you rescue him from the consequences of his vile temper, he will soon be at it again, and you will have to do it again" (MacDonald). A hot-tempered person does not learn. He does not gain from his experience (Bridges). "Like many undisciplined sons, he is incorrigible" (Buzzell). "Repeated efforts of kindness are lost on ill-natured persons" (JFB).

People with great anger, those who do not just get angry once in a while, but those who are angry individuals, will suffer the consequences of their anger, and those who attempt to rescue such people will find themselves having to do it again and again.

Implications: 1) Angry people like to hold on to their anger. 2) Angry people can be rescued from the consequence of their anger, but just dealing with consequences does not solve the problem. 3) Angry people have to personally deal with their anger. Outside help will not solve their inside problem.

Proverbs 19:20 "Listen to counsel and receive instruction, that you may be wise in your latter days." Young people should listen to and accept sound advice so that they may be wise in their old age. As someone has said, "Wisdom is a long-term investment." "In youth, prepare for age" (JFB). When it comes to gaining wisdom, start early.

Young people should listen to wise counsel and accept wise instruction so that they can live wisely all their lives, even when they are old.

"Remember now your Creator in the day of your youth" (Eccl. 12:1), so you can say at the end of your life, "I have fought the good fight, I have finished the race, I have kept the faith" (1 Tim. 4:7). It is wise to start young, the younger the better, but it is never too late to start.

Proverbs 19:21 "There are many plans in a man's heart, nevertheless the LORD's counsel—that will stand." People make many plans, some of which come to pass and some of which do not, but the Lord's counsel is sure to come to pass.

"Man makes all kinds of plans; nevertheless, it is the LORD's purposes that come to pass" (MacDonald). "A person may and should make plans (see 16:1, 9), but God can sovereignly overrule and accomplish His purpose through what one seemingly plans on his own" (Buzzell). "Man proposes; God disposes" (Kidner). "All this is clear above, however cloudy it be below. All is calm in heaven, however stormy it may be on earth" (Bridges).

People make many plans, some of which work and some of which do not, but the Lord's counsel will stand no matter what people think or do.

Psalm 2 is an illustration. The heathen rage against the Lord and against His anointed, thinking they will cast off God's restraints (Ps. 2:1-3). He who sits in the heaven will laugh. God's plan will prevail (Ps. 2:4-9).

Proverbs 19:22 "What is desired in a man is kindness, and a poor man is better than a liar." The Hebrew word translated "kindness" means "goodness, kindness." It is used of men benefiting others, especially by extending favors to the needy and miserable. Hence, there are shades of "mercy" in this word, which is sometimes translated "loving kindness" (BDB). Kidner says it means "loyal love."

When someone has a need, what they want is goodness, kindness, and mercy. They would rather have a poor man be honest and give nothing than have a rich man make them a promise that is a lie. The poor are better than liars who say and do not (JFB). "The quality that endears a man to you is kindness. That's what makes him to be desired as a friend. A poor man who has nothing but sympathy to offer is better than a rich man who promises help but doesn't deliver it" (MacDonald). Buzzell, who adopts "unfailing love" as the meaning of kindness, says, "Loyalty is a virtue people desire in others. But lying, evidence of the absence of loyalty is so despicable that poverty is preferred to it (see 19:1)."

When people have a need, they want a friend to be merciful and kind and they would rather have a poor friend who cannot help or be honest with them than have a rich friend make a promise that is a lie.

"Let us be of those who say the little and do much, rather than those who say much and do little" (Wardlaw).

Proverbs 19:23 "The fear of the LORD *leads* to life, and *he who has it* will abide in satisfaction; he will not be visited with evil." The first half of this proverb is a variation of Proverbs 14:27. The fear of the Lord includes standing in awe of Him, reverencing Him (Ps. 33:8), and, yes, being afraid to disobey Him. Those who respect, reverence, trust, obey, and have a healthy fear of disobeying the Lord (see notes on 14:26) have life, a life that is "enduring, free from care, and happy" (Delitzsch). They have "every reason to be satisfied" and "will not be overtaken with calamity" (MacDonald). There is "tranquility, settled repose, and serenity of spirit from confidence in God's wisdom, faithfulness, and power, and an assurance sense of His love" (Wardlaw). "Instead of being cast from waves to wave, here is quiet rest" (Bridge).

Those who fear the Lord will not be visited with evil. JFB say that "visit" is often used of being visited with judgment.

<u>Those who so respect and revere the Lord that they trust and obey Him live a life of satisfaction, serenity, and security.</u>

Proverbs 19:24 "A lazy *man* buries his hand in the bowl, and will not so much as bring it to his mouth again." This proverb is repeated in almost the same words in Proverbs 26:15. It is a hyperbole (Delitzsch). It is "comically extreme" (Kidner).

The lazy man is so lazy he does not feed himself. "He reaches into the bowl of potato chips but is too lazy to lift them to his mouth" (MacDonald). "He will yawn, and wish, and resolve, but do nothing" (Wardlaw).

<u>Some people are so lazy that they do not even use the energy it takes to put food in their mouth.</u>

This proverb vividly *describes* lazy people. It *implies* that laziness hurts and harms the people who are lazy; they have less and less strength from a lack of eating. It *applies* to believers who eat only once a week (or once a month) when the pastor feeds them but are too lazy to feed themselves on the Word during the week. Don't just snack on this proverb today. Take time to feast on the Word yourself.

Proverbs 19:25 "Strike a scoffer, and the simple will become wary; rebuke one who has understanding, *and* he will discern knowledge." This rich proverb describes three types of people: the scoffer, the simple, and the understanding (Kidner suggests that it describes three varieties of mind: closed, empty, and open) and two types of punishment: a physical strike and a verbal rebuke.

The scoffer, even if he were physically punished with a slap on the face, would not change. The simpleton, who is an impressionable fellow, will learn from the scoffer being punished. (One purpose of punishment is to warn others; see Deut. 21:21.) Those with understanding do not need physical punishment. They will gain knowledge from verbal rebuke (for the same thought, see 21:11).

Others say "Even if you strike a scoffer, he won't change, but at least some impressionable onlookers might learn a lesson. You don't have to strike one who has understanding. A word of rebuke will make him correct his error and grow wiser in the process" (MacDonald). "When a mocker is flogged, the simple learn prudence. But mockers do not learn. 'The simple' are the untaught, uninitiated, open-minded, who here are warned by the public punishment of another. Whereas flogging is needed for mockers, a mere verbal rebuke is enough for a discerning person" (Buzzell). "Such is the benefit of reproof; even the simple profit, much more the wise" (JFB).

<u>Scoffers do not learn, even if they receive physical punishment, but the simple will learn from the punishment of others and those with understanding will learn from verbal rebuke.</u>

"While the punishment of the 'scorner' benefits *others*, the reproof of the wise man benefits *himself*" (Wardlaw, italics his).

Proverbs 19:26 "He who mistreats *his* father *and* chases away *his* mother *is* a son who causes shame and brings reproach." The Hebrew word translated "mistreats" means "deal violently with, devastate, ruin" ("assaults" in the NASB and "robs" in the NIV). A son who physically attacks his father and evicts his mother causes shame to himself and his family.

Others say: "A son who treats or slanders (Berkeley) his father and evicts his mother from home is shameful and disgraceful himself and brings disgrace and reproach to his heartbroken parents" (MacDonald). "A grown son who robs (assaults or mistreats) his father and drives his mother off their property brings shame and disgrace to himself and his society. To disregard the instruction of one's parents is bad enough, but to abuse them physically (or to curse them, Prov. 20:20) is despicable" (Buzzell). Such a son is "without natural affection" (2 Tim. 3:3; KJV).

<u>A son who assaults his father and evicts his mother brings shame and reproach to himself and his parents.</u>

These monsters are a scandal to their parents and a nuisance to society; this is the extreme of evil (Wardlaw).

Proverbs 19:27 "Cease listening to instruction, my son, and you will stray from the words of knowledge." (19:20). Some say this proverb means, "Avoid whatever leads from truth" (JFB; see KJV, which adds the words "that causeth"), but the Hebrew text does not say that (Kidner).

The Hebrew text means if you, my son, stop listening to wise instruction, you will stray from it. To stop listening is to stop learning. "The man who stops hearing and obeying will soon go astray" (*Ryrie Study Bible*). "Being wise is not a static state" (Buzzell). Don't trifle with truth (Kidner).

Fathers should warn their sons that if they stop listening to wise instructions, they will sooner or later stray from wisdom.

Proverbs 19:28 "A disreputable witness scorns justice, and the mouth of the wicked devours iniquity." The Hebrew word translated "disreputable" means "worthless." The words of a worthless witness scorn justice itself.

For the speakers, the words of their wicked witness are devoured like a delicacy. They enjoy lying against the truth! Their wickedness, "that which is morally perverse, is a delicious morsel for the mouth of the godless, which he eagerly devours; to practice evil is for him a true enjoyment" (Delitzsch). "The wicked gulp down evil, that is, they pursue sin with an insatiable appetite" (Buzzell). They devour iniquity with greediness (Bridges).

Witnesses who practice deliberate distortion mock justice and devour wicked words as if they were a delicious dessert.

Proverbs 19:29 "Judgments are prepared for scoffers, and beatings for the backs of fools." Delitzsch says that the Hebrew word translated "judgments" "never means punishment which a court of justice inflicts, but is always used of the judgments of God, even though they are inflicted by human instrumentality." "While scoffers and fools play to the balconies from the stage of human history, punishment and judgments are waiting in the wings. As soon as the curtain is drawn, the inevitable meeting will take place" (MacDonald).

Scoffers and fools will be punished.

Proverbs 20

Proverbs 20:1 "Wine *is* a mocker, strong drink *is* a brawler, and whoever is led astray by it is not wise." A word about the various words for wine in the Bible is in order. The Hebrew word translated "wine" is the usual word for wine. It almost invariably denotes the fermented juice of the grape and, of course, when consumed in excess, is an intoxicating beverage (Wardlaw says it signifies fermented or intoxicating wine). Another Hebrew word rendered "new wine" means "fresh wine" (BDB), that is, the fruit of the vine that had not fully aged but was intoxicating (Hos. 4:11). The Hebrew word for "strong drink" means "intoxicating drink," but it was not the distilled liquor of today. It was an intoxicating drink from a source other than grapes, such as grain (ISBE).

The Hebrew word translated "brawler" means "growl, boisterous." In this proverb, wine and strong drink are personified as doing what they make people do (Barnes). Wine and strong drink are a mocker because those who are intoxicated scoff at that which is holy and because those who are inebriated break the limits of propriety (Delitzsch).

Since wine and strong drink cause people who get intoxicated to mock and be boisterous, it is not smart to get drunk.

The Bible does not require total abstinence. It forbids drunkenness (Eph. 5:18).

Proverbs 20:2 "The wrath of a king *is* like the roaring of a lion; *whoever* provokes him to anger sins *against* his own life" (see 19:12). It is dangerous to arouse a lion to a roar. Wardlaw says the roar of a lion here is his roaring after his prey when famished with hunger. Those who provoke a hungry lion put their lives in danger.

Likewise, "the terror which a king spreads around is like the growling of a lion which threatens danger" (Delitzsch). So don't provoke a king to anger. "Whoever provokes the king to anger takes his own life in his hands" (MacDonald). "It is dangerous to anger a ruler because he has the power to take an offender's life. In fact, making *any* person angry may pose problems" (Buzzell, italics his).

Provoking those with great authority is dangerous because, like a hungry, angry lion, they can threaten your very life.

Proverbs 20:3 "*It is* honorable for a man to stop striving, since any fool can start a quarrel." If honorable people get into a quarrel, they stop before it escalates, knowing that any fool can start and maintain an argument. "He who is prudent, and cares for his honor, not only breaks off strife when it threatens to become passionate but does not at all enter into it; he keeps himself far removed from it" (Delitzsch). "An honorable person makes a point of keeping aloof from strife" (MacDonald). "Arguments can be avoided by overlooking insults (Prov. 12:16), by dropping issues that are potentially volatile (Prov. 17:14), and by getting rid of mockers (Prov. 22:10)" (Buzzell).

People of honor stop a quarrel before it escalates, knowing that fools start quarrels.

An implication of this proverb is that "folly is fed by man's pride" (Bridges). Because of our pride, we want the last word. The wise are humble enough to not need to have the last word. Wardlaw says it is an honor for people to have control over their passions. It is an honor for people to not tamper with the passions of others. It is an honor for people to keep their ears open to reason and, when convinced, to yield to truth. He goes on to say that fools with a litigious spirit, who instituted the process, feel "honor-bound" (the honor not to high principles, but of pride) to prosecute it to the uttermost. They risk all they are worth rather than giving in; they would rather be ruined than yield because for them to yield is dishonor.

Proverbs 20:4 "The lazy *man* will not plow because of winter; he will beg during harvest and *have* nothing." The key words in the first half of this proverb are "will not" and "because." The lazy *will not* plow. The reason they give is the weather conditions. They use the cold weather (MacDonald), the "pretense of unfavorable weather" (Clarke), the discomfort of plowing a muddy field in the cold (Buzzell) to excuse their inaction.

The natural consequence of a lack of planting is a lack of harvest. "Without effort and advance planning, there are few results; lack of work leads to lack of benefits" (Buzzell). So when the harvest comes, the lazy have nothing.

Actually, the situation is worse. Notice carefully the text does not say the lazy have nothing and, thus, they beg. It says they beg and have nothing! The lazy, who refuse to work, and have nothing, do not get sympathy from others (Wardlaw).

Lazy people use excuses for not working and so they beg, but even then, they have nothing.

What is your excuse for not doing what you need to do—today? Is it too cold? Is it too hot? The problem is not the *external* circumstances. The problem is the *internal* condition of the heart. If you keep putting off what you need to do, you will end up not accomplishing what you should have done—even when you beg for help.

Proverbs 20:5 "Counsel in the heart of man *is like* deep water, but a man of understanding will draw it out." People have secrets they conceal carefully, craftily misleading those who seek to draw them out (Delitzsch). "A man's thoughts and intentions are often hidden deep in his mind. He will not generally bring them to the surface"

(MacDonald). The depths of the human heart are not easily fathomed (Bridges). The heart is like deep water. The casual observer only sees what is on the surface, not what is buried deep below the surface.

People who have discernment, however, can help people bring to the surface their "true thoughts, intentions, or motives" (Buzzell). People of discernment know how to draw them out by wise questions (MacDonald).

People's thoughts are buried deep within, but people of discernment can help bring those thoughts to the surface.

Today, this proverb is often applied to counselors. "A good counselor can help a person bring crooked thinking to the light and thus remedy it" (MacDonald). "Often a wise counselor can help a person examine his true motives—thoughts he may not fully understand otherwise" (Buzzell). Older commentaries applied it to the skillful general who studies his opponent's tactics, the shrewd politician who understands his adversary's secret strategies, and the insightful ordinary citizen who discerns the intentions of others (see Wardlaw).

Proverbs 20:6 "Most men will proclaim each his own goodness, but who can find a faithful man?" The Hebrew word translated "goodness" means "goodness, kindness" (see "loyalty" in the NASB and "unfailing love" in the NIV). The idea here is people proclaim their kindness, love, and loyalty. The Hebrew word rendered "faithful" means "faithfulness, trust, fidelity." The idea is being truthful and trustworthy.

In other words, the point of this proverb is that people proclaim their kindness (love and loyalty), but it is hard to find those who are truly faithful to their proclamation. Barnes said this is a contrast between promise and performance. MacDonald says, "It is not hard to find those who *profess* to be loyal, but it is another thing to find those who really *are* faithful" (MacDonald, italics his). Buzzell puts it this way: "Loyalty (Heb. unfailing love) and faithfulness are desirable qualities (Prov. 3:3; Prov. 19:22), but not everyone who claims to have them actually does."

People proclaim their love and loyalty, but who can find those who are truly trustworthy?

Proverbs 20:7 "The righteous *man* walks in his integrity; his children *are* blessed after him." Righteous people who consistently do what is right live lives of integrity and, as a result, their children benefit from their "life and example" (MacDonald). The children who come after them are not children after their death but those who follow the example of their parents while the parents are still alive (Delitzsch, who cites Deut. 4:40). Their children, seeing their example of integrity, are encouraged to be the same kind of people (Buzzell). Kidner calls this the father's best legacy.

Righteous people, those who consistently do what is right, live lives of integrity, giving their children the benefit of an example of how to live a righteous life.

Proverbs 20:8 "A king who sits on the throne of judgment scatters all evil with his eyes." An ancient king often served as chief judge (Buzzell). The Hebrew word translated "scatters" means "scatter, fan, winnow" (see "winnows out all evil" in the NIV; Kidner). When kings function as judges, they sift out evil with their eyes. By carefully examining people, they can detect evil motives and actions; they are not easily fooled (Buzzell). "The practiced eye of a true ruler sifts the chaff from the wheat" (Kidner).

Judges can detect all kinds of evil by carefully observing the people before them.

Some apply this to the Lord (Kidner). "When Christ sits upon His throne of judgment, His all-seeing eyes, like flames of fire, will see through pretense and sift all evidence" (MacDonald).

Proverbs 20:9 "Who can say, 'I have made my heart clean, I am pure from my sin'"? The question, of course, implies a negative answer (JFB). Some say this proverb's point is that no one can claim to be perfect. Delitzsch says no one can claim this because sin is so deeply rooted in human nature "that the remains of a sinful tendency always still conceal themselves in the folds of his heart, sinful thoughts still cross his soul, sinful inclinations still sometimes by their natural force overcome the moral resistance that opposes them, and stains of all kinds still defile even his best actions" ("Who can say, 'I have kept my heart pure; I am clean and without sin'?" in the NIV; see also Barnes; Buzzell). In short, all have sinned. Others go a step further and say the point is that people are sinful and cannot cleanse their own hearts (NJKV; NASB; Buzzell).

Perhaps both points are here. Thus, MacDonald says, "By his own efforts, no one can cleanse himself from sin. If a man thinks he is pure, he is a victim of pure delusion." This is where self-help fails (Kidner). The answer to the question of this proverb humbles us. "The sinner in his self-delusion may conceive of himself to be a saint. But that a saint should believe that he *made himself so*, is impossible" (Bridges, italics his).

People cannot say they have made their hearts clean from sin.

This proverb provokes probing the possibility of being pure. Consider:
1. All have sinned. Bridges says, "The more we search the heart, the more will its impurity open upon us" and "the boast (of goodness) proves, not the good, but the blindness."

2. People cannot cleanse themselves from sin. All have sinned and all do good things, but the good things we do, do not erase the bad things we have done. The penalty for sin must be paid. Imagine telling a judge you are not guilty of running a stop sign because you have stopped at other stop signs!

3. What we cannot do for ourselves, the Lord can do for us. Jesus Christ died for our sins (1 Cor. 15:3). In other words, the penalty of sin is death and Jesus Christ paid it.

4. Those who trust Jesus Christ for the gift of eternal life are cleansed from sin (1 Tim. 1:16; Jn. 1:29; Col. 2:13; Clarke; MacDonald).

5. So we cannot make ourselves clean and pure, but we can be made clean by the grace of God.

Proverbs 20:10 "Diverse weights *and* diverse measures, they *are* both alike, an abomination to the LORD" (see 11:1). Diverse weights and diverse measures refer to weights and measures of different sizes. In other words, one was small and another was large (Delitzsch). One weight was used to buy and another was used to sell (Wardlaw; Bridges; Clarke). Thus, the customer was deceived and the merchant made money dishonestly (Buzzell).

The Hebrew word translated "abomination" means "repugnant, abhorrent, disgusting." Unequal measurements are repugnant to the Lord.

Dishonest business dealings are disgusting to the Lord.

"God hates deceitful weights and measurements. This includes any dishonest device to benefit self at the expense of others. It includes the butcher's trick of resting his finger on the scales when he is weighing the meat. And it even includes the practice of demanding stricter standards from others than we do from ourselves" (MacDonald). It includes "all fraudulent dealings" (Wardlaw). For the buyer's deceptive practice, see Proverbs 20:14.

Proverbs 20:11 "Even a child is known by his deeds, whether what he does *is* pure and right." First and foremost this proverb is about children (Kidner; Buzzell). Children's character is known by their conduct. What they do is an indication of their disposition, whether they are kind or cruel, open or deceitful, selfish or generous (Wardlaw).

Many, however, suggest that this proverb is about what children will become as adults. The early actions are prophecies of the future (Barnes). "The child is father of the man." People's basic nature is revealed early and they carry their character into adulthood. "Some children are downright ornery, others are pleasant" (MacDonald). Behavior is a reflection of character, even in children.

Children's good and evil character is known by their conduct and is usually carried into their adult life.

Clarke says, "A child is easily detected when he has done evil; he immediately begins to excuse and vindicate himself, and profess his innocence, almost before accusation takes place." Clarke adds, "This proverb also teaches that "we may easily learn from the child what the man will be. In general, they give indications of those trades and callings for which they are adapted by nature. And, on the whole, we cannot go by a surer guide in preparing our children for future life, than by observing their early propensities. The future engineer is seen in the little handicraftsman of two years old."

Bridges says, "Let parents watch their children's early habits, tempers, and *doings*. Generally the discerning eye will mark something in the budding of this young tree, by which the tree in maturity *may be known*. The child will tell what the man will be. No wise parent will pass over little faults, as if it was only a child doing childish things." Bridges goes on to say, "If a child is deceitful, quarrelsome, obstinate, rebellious, selfish, how can we help trembling for its morals? A docile, truth-loving, obedient, generous child—how joyous is the prospect of a blossom and fruit from this hopeful budding" (Bridges, italics his).

Proverbs 20:12 "The hearing ear and the seeing eye, the LORD has made them both." This proverb states a single, simple truth. The Lord has given us eyes to see and ears to hear. So keep your eyes and ears open.

The implications are many and varied. We should thank God for these gracious gifts (Wardlaw). "*Seeing and hearing* are the two senses by which instruction is conveyed to the mind" (Bridges, italics his). Since the Lord has given us hearing ears and seeing eyes, we should use them to do His will (Clarke; MacDonald). The Lord has given us sight to see His world and ears to hear His Word (Delitzsch). Since the Lord is the Giver of these gifts, we are accountable to Him for their use (Barnes). God sees and hears all we do (Delitzsch; Wardlaw; JFB).

The Lord created both the hearing ear and the seeing eye for us to learn especially His will.

Proverbs 20:13 "Do not love sleep, lest you come to poverty; open your eyes, *and* you will be satisfied with bread" (see 6:9-11; 10:4; 19:15). The people described in the first part of this proverb are not just asleep, they *love* sleep. They are lazy (Buzzell). As a result, they will end up in poverty.

So Solomon advises his son to open his eyes, which is more than waking up from sleep. In this proverb, it involves going to work to at least earn enough money to eat. It is being "vigilant and active" (Barnes). "Don't overindulge in sleep, lest you land in the poorhouse. Get up and go to work. You'll earn money to pay your rent, buy your groceries, and give to the work of the Lord" (MacDonald).

Since laziness leads to poverty, wake up and go to work so you can eat.

Clarke says sleep "is like food; a certain measure of it restores and invigorates exhausted nature; more than that oppresses and destroys life."

Proverbs 20:14 "'*It is* good for nothing,' cries the buyer; but when he has gone his way, then he boasts." The Hebrew word translated "good for nothing" means "bad." Here is means "of low value" (BDB), "worthless" (Delitzsch; Barnes). The buyer tells the seller what he is selling is worthless, but once he buys it for a lower price, he boasts to his buddies that he got a bargain.

"This is an old buyer's trick. As he looks over the used car, he squawks about its dents, worn tires, noisy engine, and hideous color. 'It is good for nothing.' The seller hadn't realized it was such a junk-heap; he naively lowered the price. The buyer gives him the money, then he goes and boasts to his friends about his tremendous bargain'" (MacDonald).

Buzzell says this proverb "implies that this action is wrong and that a person who sells products needs to be on guard against dishonest bargain hunters." Delitzsch agrees, saying, "It is customary for the buyer to undervalue that which he seeks to purchase, so as to obtain it as cheaply as possible; afterward, he boasts that he has bought that which is good, and yet so cheap. That is an everyday experience, but the proverb indirectly warns against conventional lying and shows that one should not be startled and deceived thereby." We lie to get a bargain (Wardlaw).

Beware of the buyer who says what is being sold is of a lower value than the posted price; he knows better and will boast that he got a bargain when he buys it at the lower price.

Augustine tells of a "mountebank published, in the full theater, that at the next entertainment, he would show to every man present what was in his heart. The time came, and the concourse was immense; all waited, with deathlike silence, to hear what he would say to each. He stood up, and in a single sentence redeemed his pledge: 'You all wish to buy cheap, and sell dear'" (Clarke). For the seller's deceptive practice, see Proverbs 20:10.

Proverbs 20:15 "There is gold and a multitude of rubies, but the lips of knowledge *are* a precious jewel." This proverb is obviously a contrast between gold and a multitude of rubies on the one hand and lips that speak knowledge on the other, but what exactly is the contrast?

One possibility is that, like gold and a multitude of rubies, lips that speak knowledge are also precious jewels. Another explanation is that the contrast is between abundance and scarcity (see Wardlaw). "Gold and rubies, though rare and valuable, are in abundance compared with the rare and valuable ability to speak knowledge, to speak wise, appropriate words that fit the occasion" (Buzzell).

Many commentators, however, say the point is that lips that speak knowledge are of "greater value" than gold and rubies (JFB). Delitzsch puts it like this: "The proverb rises to a climax: there is gold, and there are pearls in abundance, the one of which always has a higher value than the other; but intelligent lips are above all such jewels—they are a precious treasure, which gold and all pearls cannot equal." Clarke says, "Gold is valuable, silver is valuable, and so are jewels, but the teachings of sound knowledge are more valuable than all." MacDonald writes, "A person may wear gold jewelry and precious gems, but the best adornment is wise speech. Wear this!"

Wise words are more valuable than gold and a multitude of rubies.

"To be justly admired, study to catch the ear, not the eye, and offer things of more than scarcity-value" (Kidner). In the morning, as you put on your gold watch and jewelry with precious stones, remember that wearing wise words is more valuable than all material accessories. A simple illustration is telling someone the good news of the gift of eternal life, which is obtained by trusting Jesus Christ.

Proverbs 20:16 "Take the garment of one who is surety *for* a stranger, and hold it as a pledge *when it* is for a seductress." This proverb, repeated in Proverbs 27:13, warns against lending money to someone who cosigns for a stranger. If you are going to loan money to such an unwise person, take his outer garment as collateral (Barnes; Wardlaw; Delitzsch; Buzzell).

That is especially true if the stranger is a seductress. "Any man who is foolish enough to make financial guarantees for people he doesn't know is a bad credit risk. If you have any dealings with him, be sure that he puts up plenty of collateral to protect you in case he reneges or goes bankrupt. The advice is especially true if the stranger is an immoral person" (MacDonald). "Here a creditor is commanded to take the garment of a person who cosigns for a stranger, especially if the stranger is a wayward woman" (Buzzell). "Don't lend him without security; he is a bad risk!"(Kidner).

If you are going to loan money to someone who is a cosigner for a stranger, be sure to obtain collateral, especially if the stranger is a person of questionable character.

Proverbs 20:17 "Bread gained by deceit *is* sweet to a man, but afterward, his mouth will be filled with gravel." "Bread gained by deceit" is material obtained dishonestly. At first, there is something satisfying about ill-gotten gain, but ultimately, such sin brings dissatisfaction to the soul. At first, it is like eating a sweet pastry, but in the end the pastry tastes like gravel. This proverb contrasts the short-range pleasure of sin and its long-range consequences (Buzzell).

"There is a pleasure in the sense of cleverness felt after a hard bargain or a successful fraud, which must be met by bidding men look on the after consequences" (Barnes). "Any form of wealth gained dishonestly might yield momentary satisfaction, but eventually, it will prove as unpleasant and aggravating as a mouthful of gravel. This condemns falsifying tax returns, fudging on expense accounts, bribing inspectors, labeling dishonestly, and advertising product differences that don't exist" (MacDonald).

Wealth gained by deceit is satisfying at first, but in the end, it is not.

There is pleasure in sin—for a season (Heb. 11:25 KJV).

Proverbs 20:18 "Plans are established by counsel; by wise counsel wage war." When making plans, it is wise to seek the wise counsel of others, but that is especially true in planning to go to war. So seek the counsel of others in times of peace as well as war.

"A pooling of advice is desirable before making any plans. No general makes war without consulting with other military experts" (MacDonald). War should not be entered into "rashly and inconsiderately;" it should only be engaged in after the "utmost deliberation" and sound advice (Wardlaw).

When making plans seek wise counsel, especially if the issue is going to war.

Seeking counselors (plural) is mentioned four times in Proverbs (11:14; 15:22; 20:18; 24:6).

Proverbs 20:19 "He who goes about *as* a talebearer reveals secrets; therefore do not associate with one who flatters with his lips." The Hebrew word translated "flatters" means "to be open, simple, open-minded." Here the idea has open lips. Since talebearers reveal secrets, do not associate with them; they do not know when to keep their mouths shut.

"A gossip betrays confidences. Therefore, do not associate with a blabber, because if he talks against others to you, you can be sure that he will talk against you to others" (MacDonald). Buzzell says, "Since gossiping betrays confidence, a person ought to be careful with whom he shares secrets." He adds, "So people who talk too much should be avoided because they will probably divulge information that should be kept confidential." Beware of gossips; it may be your secrets next (Kidner).

Since gossips reveal secrets, do not associate with them.

"We would not wish him to look over our wall, much less to enter into our houses; least of all, to associate with our family circle" (Bridges). Carefully select those to whom you reveal your secrets. If they reveal the secrets of others to you, they will reveal your secrets, too.

Proverbs 20:20 "Whoever curses his father or his mother, his lamp will be put out in deep darkness." According to the Mosaic Law, cursing one's parents was punishable by death (Ex. 21:17; Lev. 20:9; see also Prov. 30:17). The expression "his lamp will be put out" has been explained as describing a "failure of outward happiness" (Barnes), as having "no prosperity" (Clarke), as a reference to being "forsaken by divine protection" (Delitzsch), and as a picturesque way of referring to death (Buzzell; Barnes).

Wardlaw suggests that the word "lamp" was sometimes used by a son who preserved a man's name and memory. Thus, the point is that the name and memory of the son will be extinguished and forgotten. Wardlaw also says that the figure of the lamp being put out was used in connection with "outward prosperity." If that is the case here, the meaning is the son who curses his father or mother will not prosper. In addition, Wardlaw suggests the "lamp" may signify "life itself" (see also the Ryrie Study Bible). In other words, those who curse their parents will have their temporal life shortened.

While other things may be involved, in light of the Law (Ex. 21:17; Lev. 20:9) and in the context of Proverbs (10:27; 11:19; 14:27), having one's lamp be put out includes physical death.

Those who curse their father or mother will suffer dire consequences, including death.

Cursing your earthly father results in being cursed by the heavenly Father (Wardlaw).

Proverbs 20:21 "An inheritance gained hastily at the beginning will not be blessed at the end." Some says this proverb is about money gained dishonestly (13:11; Barnes; Bridges; Kidner). Others say it is simply talking about quickly gaining money (MacDonald; Buzzell; Clarke). Then, of course, there are those who say it could be either (JFB).

The word "blessed" suggests that *God* is involved. Hence, Clarke says, "All such inheritances are short-lived; God's blessing is not in them, because they are not the produce of industry; and they lead to idleness, pride, fraud and knavery." Not all, however, thinks that God's involvement is required.

The point may be that "such wealth may be squandered and often squelches initiative and work. As a result, the recipient is not blessed at the end" (Buzzell). What is gained freely is spent freely. The prodigal son is an illustration. He gained his inheritance quickly and lost it just as quickly (MacDonald).

When money is gained quickly without working for it, it is not blessed; it is often squandered.

The proverb is often proven true when people get an inheritance, a windfall, or win the lottery. "Easy come, easy go" (MacDonald).

Proverbs 20:22 "Do not say, 'I will recompense evil'; wait for the LORD, and He will save you." This proverb assumes that an injustice has been committed against you, an injustice that might stir up revenge (Delitzsch). When you have been treated unjustly, do not seek revenge (24:29). Take the injustice to the Lord and He will deliver you. Note, this proverb does not say that the Lord will punish the evil person (Paul says that in Rom. 12:19; Barnes). It says the Lord will *deliver you*. Commit your deliverance out of the distress and your vindication to the Lord and He will deliver you (Delitzsch).

When treated unjustly, do not retaliate; wait for the Lord to deliver you from the situation.

Proverbs 20:23 "Diverse weights *are* an abomination to the LORD, and dishonest scales *are* not good" (see 11:1; 20:10). As was explained in the notes on Proverbs 20:10, "diverse weights" are weights of different sizes. One was used to buy and the other was used to sell, enabling the merchant to deceive the customer. As compared to Proverbs 20:10, this proverb adds dishonest scales to diverse weights. Also, as has been explained before, the Hebrew word translated "abomination" means "repugnant, abhorrent, disgusting." Thus, this proverb is saying that deceptive weights and dishonest scales are not only not good but also repugnant to the Lord.

Deceptive and dishonest business practices are not only not good, they are disgusting to the Lord.

Proverbs 20:24 "A man's steps *are* of the LORD; how then can a man understand his own way?" (see Ps. 37:23.) The point of the first part of this proverb is "man proposes; God disposes" (Delitzsch). In other words, "God is sovereign over human affairs" (MacDonald). Since God has the ultimate 'say,' it is often difficult for people to know their own way (Buzzell).

This proverb does not deny free will; it just recognizes divine sovereignty (both are true). People choose, but just because they choose to do something does not mean it will come to pass. In the final analysis, God is in control. So, sometimes human plans "work out" and sometimes they do not. Wardlaw asks how a man can "form and carry forward his plans, with any assurance of success, or of things turning out in accordance with his wishes and designs?" Wardlaw answers his own question: "He *cannot*" (Wardlaw, italics his).

Since what happens in life is ultimately in God's control, people do not always understand what is happening in their lives.

Bridges points out that people often act as if they were the masters of their fate, but Providence is an over-ruling agency. Pharaoh's daughter went to bathe where the infant Moses was committed to the water (Ex. 2:1-5). Bridges asks, "Was this the working of chance, or some fortunate coincidence? Who can doubt the finger of the leading of God?" Bridges adds, "The humble, heaven-taught Christian exercises free agency in the spirit of dependence." James teaches that we should make plans (Jas. 4:13), acknowledging we will do it if the Lord wills (Jas. 4:15). That is what Paul did (Rom. 15:32).

Proverbs 20:25 "*It is* a snare for a man to devote rashly *something as* holy, and afterward to reconsider *his* vows." For people to suddenly dedicate something to the Lord is a snare (Delitzsch), if they reconsider their vow later. "It is dangerous to dedicate something to the Lord and to have second thoughts about it. Before making a vow, a man should be sure that he can fulfill it and that he intends to" (MacDonald).

"Making a vow rashly and *then* considering what he did can get a person in as much trouble as if he stepped into an animal trap. It is better to think before acting" (Buzzell, italics his). This proverb describes an impulsive man, pledging more than he seriously intends" (Kidner). The sin is not in spontaneously making a vow. The sin is in making it and not paying it (Wardlaw).

For people to impulsively dedicate something to the Lord and afterward reconsider it, is a trap.

In Ecclesiastes, Solomon wrote, "When you make a vow to God, do not delay to pay it; For *He has* no pleasure in fools. Pay what you have vowed—better not to vow than to vow and not pay" (Eccl. 5:4-5). People in a crisis make promises to the Lord. If He delivers them, they will do _____, but if after the crisis is over, they reconsider, they are in a trap—a trap of conscience.

Proverbs 20:26 "A wise king sifts out the wicked, and brings the threshing wheel over them" (see 20:8). The threshing wheel passed over the grain and separated the grain from the chaff (Barnes). Using the figure of the threshing wheel, Solomon says the wise king separates the wicked from the righteous and punishes the wicked (Barnes; Delitzsch; MacDonald; Buzzell). Since the threshing wheel was armed with teeth, it has also been suggested that the figure denotes severity (Wardlaw; JFB, who cite Amos 1:3).

A wise government separates the wicked from the righteous and punishes the wicked.

Proverbs 20:27 "The spirit of a man *is* the lamp of the LORD, searching all the inner depths of his heart." The spirit of man in this proverb is the conscience (Wardlaw; Clarke; MacDonald). The Lord gives us the conscience to serve as a lamp. It enables us to search out the "darkest recesses of the heart" (Barnes). It throws "light on our thoughts, motives, affections, and actions. It approves and reproves the innermost thoughts and intents of our lives (see Rom. 2:14-15)" (MacDonald).

<u>Our conscience is a light from the Lord that searches even the dark depths of our hearts.</u>

The conscience does not always work as God intended. Some have a good conscience (1 Tim. 1:5) and some have a conscience that has been seared (1 Tim. 4:2). When the conscience is aligned with the Word of God, it is good. It is functioning as it should. The conscience can be seared by constant violation or, as some suggest, by a radical act of perverting the truth. Therefore it is essential that we keep the lamp of our conscience properly trimmed so that is sheds light on the darkness of our soul.

Proverbs 20:28 "Mercy and truth preserve the king, and by lovingkindness he upholds his throne." A king who practices mercy and truth is preserved in his position and the one who exercises lovingkindness ("loyal love") maintains his power.

People respect leaders who are characterized by mercy and truth and they support those who are characterized by lovingkindness; they do not respect or support tyrants (MacDonald). Love and loyalty keep a leader in leadership, and disloyalty and unreliability causes people to replace leaders (Buzzell). "A wise king will follow the example of the Great Sovereign and 'make judgment his strange work' and mercy his 'delight'" (Bridges). Mercy and truth are "the brightest jewels in the royal crown;" and those kings who are most governed by them have a stable government (Clarke). Tyrants maintain their throne by terror; they try to preserve their power by force and fear (Wardlaw).

<u>Those in a position of authority who practice mercy and truth are preserved, and those who exercise lovingkindness maintain their power.</u>

The ideal leader (ruler) unites truth and mercy. Truth without mercy is rigid justice. Mercy without truth is undisciplined leniency. Someone has said that "a God of all mercy is a God unjust." Mercy must be righteous mercy; righteousness must be merciful. "Justice must be tempered by clemency and clemency must be restrained by justice. What would a father be without mercy? But, at the same time, a father is required to be firm and impartial" (Wardlaw).

Proverbs 20:29 "The glory of young men *is* their strength, and the splendor of old men *is* their gray head" (see 16:31). The gray hair in this proverb indicates "wisdom, experience, prudent counsels, etc." (Clarke). Thus the contrast is between the strength of youth and the wisdom of old age. The glory of young men is their physical strength (muscles) and the glory of old men is their spiritual wisdom (gray hair).

<u>The glory of youth is physical strength, and the glory of age is wisdom.</u>

"Every church needs both strength for service and age for wise counsel" (MacDonald). Of course, it is possible for youth to turn their glory to shame (Wardlaw).

Robertson McQuilkin wrote, "God planned the strength and beauty of youth to be physical, but the strength and beauty of age to be spiritual. We gradually lose the strength and beauty that is temporary so we will sure to concentrate on the strength and beauty that is forever."

Proverbs 20:30 "Blows that hurt cleanse away evil, as *do* stripes the inner depths of the heart." Physical punishment that causes pain cleanses the evil in the heart. "The purpose of corporal punishment is not to inflict pain but to veer one's conduct from sin. Such punishment, however, is not merely to change a person's conduct out of fear of physical pain but to help him mature" (Buzzell). Although stripes hurt for a time, they become the means of correcting the vice of the heart (Clarke). Punishment provides healing of soul by deterring it from evil (JFB). Blessed are the stripes that break the proud will (Wardlaw).

<u>Painful physical punishment can cleanse the evil in the depth of the heart.</u>

"A child remembers the pain of the last spanking when he is tempted to steal from his mother's purse" (MacDonald). Of course, there are those who do not learn, even after suffering the pain of the consequences of their actions, but that is not the point of this proverb.

Proverbs 21

Proverbs 21:1 "The king's heart *is* in the hand of the LORD, *like* the rivers of water; He turns it wherever He wishes." The backdrop of this proverb is the Eastern method of watering the land. From one stream, several canals are dug, enabling the farmer to direct the water where he wills (Clarke; JFB; Kidner). Likewise, the Lord directs the thoughts of kings "that his favors may fall, not at random, but in harmony with a divine order" (Barnes). Just as a canal directs the flow of water, so "the Lord rules and overrules a king's thoughts and actions" (MacDonald; Buzzell).

Bridges says this reminds us that God acts providentially. Then he adds that God turns political projects to His own purposes "without interfering with the moral liberty of the king's will."

As farmers channel water where they will, the Lord directs rulers' thoughts where He wishes.

God has often moved officials to make decisions that favored His people. He turned the heart of Pharaoh to Joseph (Gen. 41:37-45). He induced a Babylonian officer to show special favor to Daniel and his three friends (Dan. 1:9). He gave Nehemiah, who had "prayed to the God of heaven," favor 'with the king (Neh. 2:4-6).

"This is an encouragement to Christians under oppressive governments or to missionaries taking the gospel to hostile lands" (MacDonald).

Proverbs 21:2 "Every way of a man *is* right in his own eyes, but the LORD weighs the hearts." Pointing out that this proverb virtually repeats Proverbs 16:2, Kidner says, "The contrast between our guessing and God's knowing is important enough for re-emphasis." People justify their actions, but the Lords weights the "thoughts and motives" of their hearts (MacDonald). "Man looks at the outward appearance, but the Lord looks at the heart" (1 Sam. 16:7).

"The proverb indirectly admonishes us of the duty of constant self-examination, according to the objective norm of the revealed will of God, and warns us against the self-complacency of the fool, of whom Proverbs 12:15 says: 'all fools live in the pleasant feeling that their life is the best,' and against the self-deception which walks in the way of death and dreams of walking in the way of life, Proverbs 14:12 and Proverbs 16:25" (Delitzsch).

People justify their actions, but the Lord examines their thoughts and motives.

During World War II, E. V. Darling wrote, "The German viewpoint is: When Nazi flyers bomb England, that is war, but when British flyers bomb Germany, that is murder. Following is a translation of an account in a Berlin newspaper of a British air raid: 'If the English pilots could only see in the gray light of dawn the effect of their ruthless and indiscriminate bombings of Berlin's residential districts, they might possibly, if they have even a trace of human heart left in them, be overwhelmed by the horrors of the great crime they have committed.'"

Someone has written, "Have you noticed that: When the other fellow acts that way, he is ugly; when you do, it is nerves? When the other fellow is set in his way, he's obstinate; when you are, it is just firmness? When the other fellow doesn't like your friends, he's prejudiced; when you don't like him, you are simply showing that you are a good judge of human nature? When the other fellow tries to treat someone especially well, he's toadying; when you try the same, you are using tact? When the other fellow takes time to do things, he's dead slow; when you do it, you are deliberate? When the other fellow spends a lot, he's a spendthrift; when you do, you are generous? When the other fellow picks flaws in things, he's cranky; when you do, you are discriminating? When the other fellow is mild in his manner, he is a mush of concession; when you are, it is being gracious? When the other fellow dresses extra well, he's a dude; when you do it, it is simply a duty owes to society? When the other fellow runs great risks in business, he's foolhardy; when you do, you are a great financier? When the other fellow says what he thinks, he's spiteful; when you do, you are being frank? When the other fellow won't get caught in a new scheme, he's backwooday when you won't, you are conservative?"

Proverbs 21:3 "To do righteousness and justice *is* more acceptable to the LORD than sacrifice." It is more acceptable to the Lord to do what is right than to perform some religious ritual. "God is not a ritualist. What He wants is inward reality" (MacDonald). "The Lord detested the hypocrisy in a wicked person who brought an animal sacrifice to Him (Prov. 15:8; Prov. 21:27)" (Buzzell). There is a danger of being satisfied with the outward rituals of religion (Wardlaw).

It is more acceptable to the Lord to do what is right and just than just to practice the rites of religion.

Proverbs 21:4 "A haughty look, a proud heart, a*nd* the plowing of the wicked *are* sin." This proverb lists three sins. The first two are easy to explain. The haughty look is the outward expression of the inward sin, which is pride. Pride is the root; a haughty look is the fruit.

The explanation of the third is more difficult. The Hebrew word translated "plowing" means "lamp" (BDB), but with a slight change of vowels points it means "the fallow field" (Barnes). It is used figuratively of "happiness, delight" (BDB). Hence this third sin has been interpreted a number of different ways.

If the translation "plowing" is taken (KJV; NJKV), the meaning is that the very plowing of the wicked is sin. Where pride prevails, there sin will be the first-fruit on the field of action (Ewald and Elster, cited by Delitzsch) or where there is pride, "the whole of the field cultivated by them, with all that grows thereon, is sin" (Delitzsch). Bridges says, "The motive determines the act." He goes on the explain that those who acknowledged God as they plow, seeking His strength and blessing, glorify God, but those who work without regard for God, their work in sin.

If the translation "lamp" is taken (NASB; NIV), the meaning is that the "outwardly bright prosperity" (Barnes; Clarke) of the wicked, their "prosperity, happiness, life, or hope" (MacDonald), their "life" (Buzzell), their "joy or delight" (JFB) is sin. Wardlaw says the light, the joy, of the wicked is sin, because it is all about self; there is no recognition of God. The wicked supply their own oil for their lamp. They trim it. They keep it burning.

<u>Pride, which produces a haughty look and a life that leaves God out, is sin.</u>

Proverbs 21:5 "The plans of the diligent *lead* surely to plenty, but *those of* everyone *who is* hasty, surely to poverty." In this proverb, the contrast is between the diligent and the hasty, rather than the diligent and the lazy. The Hebrew word translated "plans" means "thought, devise, plan." The diligent think through what they're going to do and they do it. As a result, their plans lead to plenty.

On the other hand, because those who are hasty do not carefully plan; they do not succeed. The diligent plan their work and work their plan, whereas the hasty make decisions and act without thinking them through (Buzzell). "Undue hurry is as fatal to success as undue procrastination" (Barnes).

<u>Those who plan their work and work their plan will produce plenty, whereas those who hastily work without planning will surely end up in poverty.</u>

Those who seek to get rich overnight end up in poverty (MacDonald).

Proverbs.21:6 "Getting treasures by a lying tongue *is* the fleeting fantasy of those who seek death." Seeking to get rich by defrauding others is a fleeting fancy that leads to death. Those who seek riches through fraud are "chasing the wind. They are pursuing that which will elude them, and they will perish in the process. Their position is like that of a desert traveler chasing a mirage; it proves to be a snare of death for him" (MacDonald). "Seeking money dishonestly is like seeking or pursuing death" (Buzzell).

<u>Getting wealth by ensnaring others with a lying tongue ensnares people in a fleeting fancy and, ultimately, death.</u>

Proverbs 21:7 "The violence of the wicked will destroy them, because they refuse to do justice." Wicked people's violence destroys them, because when they *refuse* to do what is right, they bring judgment on themselves. Their problem is not ignorance; it is willingness (Bridges). "There is a moral principle at work in the universe which guarantees that violence, wickedness, and injustice will never escape unpunished. Never!"(MacDonald). Violence done to others will boomerang (Buzzell). "Their own sin is the seed of destruction" (Bridges).

<u>Wicked people who refuse to do what is right and are violent will be destroyed.</u>

In the end, there will be justice. So if you have had an unjust act of violence done against you, do not worry, stay angry, or get bitter. (Someone has said that being bitter is like drinking poison thinking the other person will die.) You do not have to fret; Justice is coming (note the capital J).

Proverbs 21:8 "The way of a guilty man *is* perverse; but *as for* the pure, his work *is* right." Guilty people live perverse lives. Guilt causes them "to hide, to masquerade, to fear, and to act deceitfully" (MacDonald).

On the other hand, people with pure motives, free from guilt, live righteous lives. They have nothing to hide; they walk in the light (MacDonald). Where there is a clear conscience, there is a clear path (Kidner).

<u>Guilty people live perverse lives, but those with pure motives live righteous lives.</u>

This is a critical concept. A pure conscience is fundamental and essential to living a righteous life, which is a loving life (Rom. 13:8-10). Paul explains that love comes "from a pure heart, *from* a good conscience, and *from* sincere faith" (1 Tim. 1:5).

In the Greek text of 1 Timothy, one preposition unites these three as a unit. A pure heart, good conscience, and sincere faith work together to produce love. The Greek word translated "pure" means "pure, clean." Out of a *clean heart*, believers are to love one another. Those who have trusted Jesus Christ for eternal life have been cleansed from their sins (1 Jn. 1:7). A *good conscience* is one that has been freed from guilt and thus contains no impure motives. Such a conscience will only approve thoughts, words, and deeds that are in harmony with love. *Faith*, of course, is foundational to this process, which looks like this: faith→ pure heart→ good conscience→ love.

If we feel guilty, we will not be loving; we will be focused on ourselves. It is when we have pure motives that we are free to love another.

Proverbs 21:9 "Better to dwell in a corner of a housetop, than in a house shared with a contentious woman." This proverb is repeated in Proverbs 25:24. There are five proverbs concerning a contentious wife (19:13; 21:9, 19; 25:24; 27:15).

Houses in ancient Palestine had a flat roof. The flat roof "was often used for retirement by day, or, in summer, for sleep by night. The corner of such a roof was exposed to all changes of weather, and the point of the proverb lies in the thought that all winds and storms which a man might meet with there are more endurable than the tempest within" (Barnes).

The Hebrew word translated "contentious" means "strife, contention, quarrelsome." It comes from the Hebrew verb for "judge." This proverb is saying it would be "better to live alone in a cramped corner of one of those roofs, exposed to heat, cold, rain, snow, wind, and hail, than to live in a house shared with a nagging, cantankerous woman" (MacDonald). Living with an argumentative and contentious woman who causes strife "makes a home unpleasant and undesirable" (Buzzell).

Some suggest that since the Hebrew word translated "women" can mean either "woman" (NKJV; NASB) or "wife" (KJV; NIV) and houses were large enough for several families (Bridges; JFB), this proverb can be about a quarrelsome mother-in-law, or other females (Delitzsch). While it could apply to any contentious woman, it is primarily about an argumentative wife (see the references to other proverbs listed above). A wife can make life so bitter for her husband that, in order to have rest, he would rather sit alone on the edge of the roof, exposed to danger and storm (Delitzsch).

<u>Living alone in uncomfortable surroundings is better than living in a house with a contentious wife.</u>

As has been pointed out, Solomon is speaking to his son, hence, the reference to contentious wives. If he were discoursing with his daughters, he would no doubt say that it is better to better to dwell in a corner of a housetop, than in a house shared with a contentious (controlling, abusive) husband.

In his book *Love and Survival: The Scientific Basis for the Healing Power of Intimacy*, Dr. Dean Ornish tells of researchers from Case Western Reserve University in Cleveland who studied almost 10,000 men who had no prior history of angina. "Men who had a high level of risk factors such as elevated cholesterol, high blood pressure, age, diabetes, and electrocardiogram abnormalities were over twenty times more likely to develop new angina during the next five years. However, those who answered 'yes' to the simple question, 'Does your wife show you her love?' had significantly less angina even when they had high levels of these risk factors. Men who had these risk factors but did not have a wife who showed her love had substantially increased angina—almost twice as much. The greater the cholesterol and blood pressure and the greater the anxiety and stress the more important was the love of the spouse in buffering against these harmful effects."Ornish adds, "Men who also had anxiety and family problems, especially conflict that their wives and children, had even more chest pains" (Ornish, *LAS*, p. 25). Ornish concludes that diet, blood pressure and other risk factors, can be "significantly moderated by a loving relationship" (Ornish, *LAS*, p. 26).

Proverbs 21:10 "The soul of the wicked desires evil; his neighbor finds no favor in his eyes." The second half of this proverb indicates that the evil spoken of in the first half is evil to others (Wardlaw). These wicked people are bend on evil; they sin "not merely from weakness but eagerly and ruthlessly" (Kidner). In their innermost heart, evil people desire to do evil to others. Even those close to them are "not spared" (Delitzsch).

These evil people are "always plotting some new evil," and they show no mercy to their neighbor in perpetuating it. Thus their sin is both "deliberate and ruthless" (MacDonald). Wicked people crave evil as if they are addicted to it; they are even mean to those near them (Buzzell). So strongly do they desire evil that they will not spare their friends if their friends get in their way (JFB).

<u>Some people are so wicked that deep within their hearts, they desire to do evil to others and those close to them are not exempt.</u>

Wardlaw elaborates: "Whenever 'his neighbor' stands at all in the way of his own gratification,—of the acquisition of any object on which he has set his heart,—no consideration of his interest will be allowed for a moment to interpose an obstacle to its persecution and attainment. SELF is his idol; SELFISHNESS his grand principle and impulse. He views 'his neighbor' in no other light than as, on the one hand, the means of thwarting, or, on the other, the instrument of promoting his own ends."

It goes without saying that you should stay away from such people. Earlier in Proverbs, Solomon warned his son to stay from these types of people (1:28-33). All wise parents instruct their children to stay away from people bend on evil. "Do not be deceived: 'Evil company corrupts good habits'" (1 Cor. 15:33).

Proverbs 21:11 "When the scoffer is punished, the simple is made wise; but when the wise is instructed, he receives knowledge." (see 19:25.) This proverb features three kinds of people: the scoffer, the simpleton, and the wise. The story begins with the scoffer, the one who mocks spiritual things (Delitzsch; Clarke) and laughs at all principles and restraint (Wardlaw) being punished.

The simpleton, the naïve one (MacDonald), the inexperienced one (Wardlaw), sees the punishment of the scoffer and learns not to do what the scoffer did.

The wise also learn, but they learn from instruction, not seeing someone punished. "That which the simple learn by the terrors of punishment, the wise learn by teaching" (JFB).

<u>The naïve learn by seeing scoffers punished, but the wise gain knowledge by simple instruction.</u>

This proverb is about "teachability" (Kidner). Wise people are teachable. They "get it" when they hear it taught. Naïve people need more than instruction; they "get it" when they see others punished. At least they learn. Scoffers do not learn from instruction or from seeing others suffer the consequences of their actions. Thus they end up punished.

Proverbs 21:12 "The righteous *God* wisely considers the house of the wicked, overthrowing the wicked for *their* wickedness." The all-wise, all righteous God carefully considers the ways of the wicked and overthrows them for their wickedness. "God keeps close watch on all the affairs of ungodly men; at the proper time He throws the switch which brings their doom upon them" (MacDonald).

<u>In His righteousness and wisdom, God considers the ways of the wicked and overthrows them for their wickedness.</u>

Eventually, justice will be done (Kidner). Those who struggle with injustice done to themselves or others must remember this.

Proverbs 21:13 "Whoever shuts his ears to the cry of the poor will also cry himself and not be heard." The point of this proverb seems simple. Those who do not hear the cry of the poor will not be heard when they cry. There is, however, a question. Is it God or people who will not hear those who do not listen to the poor?

Many say it is God (Delitzsch; Bridges; Clarke; MacDonald; Jas. 2:13). Since the proverb does not specify who does not hear those who do not listen, it could be God, people, or both. At any rate, the point is what goes around comes around. Those who have "heartless disregard" for the poor will be disregarded when they are in need (Buzzell).

<u>Those who deliberately disregard the pleas of the poor will be disregarded when they cry for help.</u>

Wardlaw says when it comes to helping those who cry for help, discretion is needed. There are times when shutting the ears is a virtue. The sin here is "unfeeling hardness of heart," "gripping selfishness." He has a valid point. Not all cries for help are legitimate.

Proverbs 21:14 "A gift in secret pacifies anger, and a bribe behind the back, strong wrath." This proverb assumes that the gift-giver has offended someone to the point that the person is angry (Wardlaw) and seems to indicate that the offence was known publically. A monetary gift given in secret pacifies such an angry person and a bribe can even clam wrath. "An angry man will quiet down if the offender slips him a gift, and a man who is in a rage is appeased by a bribe tucked in his pocket" (MacDonald).

<u>A secret gift pacifies anger and a secret bribe clams wrath.</u>

This proverb does not condone brides (Ex. 23:8; Deut. 16:19). It simply states a fact (Buzzell)—money talks. Bribes work. Gifts can pacify anger.

Proverbs 21:15 "*It is* a joy for the just to do justice, but destruction *will come* to the workers of iniquity." The second half of this proverb appears in Proverbs 10:29. Also note that the words "it is" and "will come" are in italics, indicating that they have been supplied by the translators.

There are a number of explanations of this proverb (see Wardlaw). 1. The righteous delight in doing good, but the wicked delight in mischief and ruin. 2. The righteous find happiness in doing what is right, but doing what is right is irksome to the wicked (Kidner, who says doing what is right is "dismay" to the sinner). 3. Doing what is right is joy to the righteous, but to the workers of wickedness, judgment is anything but joy (Wardlaw).

The third explanation is correct. The point is when the righteous do what is right, they experience joy, but when the wicked do what is wrong, they will ultimately experience ruin. "The wicked at last meet destruction" (JFB). It is either joy or judgment.

<u>When the righteous do what is right, they experience joy, but when the workers of wickedness do what is wrong, they will ultimately be judged.</u>

Proverbs 21:16 "A man who wanders from the way of understanding will rest in the assembly of the dead." Wandering out of understanding implies once having it (Bridges; Wardlaw). Also note that "every journey (has) a goal, whether it be one that is self-appointed or which is appointed for him" (Delitzsch). Thus, those who willfully wander away from wisdom end up in the assembly of the dead.

"An unwise person leaves the company of the wise only to find himself in the company of dead people!"(Buzzell)."The rebel, who must roam at will, is only hastening to lose his mobility, his independence and his life" (Kidner).

<u>Those who know better but wander from it end up among the dead.</u>

Bridges describes the wanderer: "Novelties have been preferred; self-confidence indulged; self-pleasing delusions cherished." Every journey begins with a first step. Beware of taking that first wandering step away from wisdom.

Proverbs 21:17 "He who loves pleasure *will be* a poor man; he who loves wine and oil will not be rich." The reference to oil is about a fragrance poured over the head and clothes at festivals (Delitzsch). Barnes says that the price of the oil was about equal to the 300 days' wages of a field laborer (Mt. 20:2). He adds, "Indulgence in such a luxury would thus become the type of all extravagance and excess" (Barnes).

Those who love extravagant parties will not be rich: they will end up poor (MacDonald). "Costly luxuries impoverish" (JFB). "Money is squandered, debt is incurred, credit is lost, (and) the divine blessing is forfeited" (Wardlaw).

<u>Living for pleasure produces poverty, not wealth.</u>

The Hebrew word translated "joy" in verse 15 is the same one that is translated "pleasure" in this verse. Righteous people seek to do what is right and find joy. Pleasure-lovers live for joy and find poverty (Kidner). Although this proverb does not speak about spiritual issues (poverty is financial), it is true that people who live for pleasure are not rich spiritually in time or eternity. "Heavenly pleasures will lose its sweetness, as earthly pleasures are relished" (Bridges).

Proverbs 21:18 "The wicked *shall be* a ransom for the righteous, and the unfaithful for the upright." The same thought is in Proverbs 11:8 (Delitzsch), which teaches that there are times (this is a proverb, not an absolute law) when God not only delivers the righteous *from* trouble, He delivers their trouble *to* the wicked.

The wicked and the unfaithful are a *ransom* for the righteous and upright. That does not mean that the wicked *redeem* the righteous. It means the wicked are a *substitute* for the righteous (Bridges). Isaiah says that God gave "Egypt for your (Israel) ransom and Ethiopia and Seba in your place" (Isa. 43:3). Notice that "in your place" is synonymous with "ransom." (The NASB adds "in the place of" to the second half of Proverbs 21:18). Cyrus possessed Egypt, Ethiopia, and Seba as a ransom, that is "in place of Israel" (Wardlaw; MacDonald). By suffering what they had devised for the righteous, the wicked became their ransom in the sense of substitute (JFB).

<u>The wicked and the unfaithful are sometimes substitutes for the righteous and the upright; they suffer what they did or plan to do to the righteous.</u>

The great illustration of this truth is in the book of Esther. Instead of Mordecai being hanged, as Haman had planned, Haman was hanged! (Esther 3:7).

Proverbs 21:19 "Better to dwell in the wilderness, than with a contentious and angry woman." Earlier Solomon said, "It is better to dwell in a *corner of a housetop* than in a house shared with a contentious woman" (21:9, italics added). Five proverbs concern a contentious wife (19:13; 21:9; 19; 25:24; 27:15). The Hebrew word translated "contentious" means "strife, contention, quarrelsome." It comes from the Hebrew verb for "judge."

In this proverb, he looks further out for a lonely seat (Hitzig, cited by Delitzsch). He would "prefer the discomfort, distance, and *loneliness of a desert* to being cooped up with an angry, quarrelsome woman" (MacDonald, italics added). Under such circumstances, even the rooftop is too near! The man is off to the wilderness, which is as far away as possible (Wardlaw). It is better to be destitute of social life than to be with one whose contentions turn every comfort into bitterness (Bridges).

<u>It is better to be alone in the wilderness than to live in a house with a contentious woman.</u>

"The number of suffering wives is greater than that of the suffering husbands" (Wardlaw).

In his book *Love and Survival: The Scientific Basis for the Healing Power of Intimacy*, Dr. Dean Ornish says, "Almost 8500 men with no history or symptoms of duodenal ulcers were given a questionnaire before they developed ulcers. Over the next five years, 254 developed ulcers. Those who had reported a low level of perceived love and support from their wives when they entered the study had over twice as many ulcers as other man. Those man who answered, 'my wife does not love me' had almost three times as many ulcers as those who said their wives showed their love and support. This factor was more strongly associated with ulcers than smoking, age, blood pressure, job stress, and other factors. Man who also had anxiety and family problems had more ulcers" (Ornish, *LAS*, p. 26).

Proverbs 21:20 "*There is* desirable treasure, and oil in the dwelling of the wise, but a foolish man squanders it." The contrast in this proverb is between the house of the wise and the house of the foolish. In the house of the wise are desirable treasure and oil. In other words, there is a "plentiful supply of all good things" (MacDonald), which has been taken to mean wealth (JFB; Wardlaw), or food (Buzzell). The wise man "gains uprightly, spends moderately, never exhausts himself" (Barnes).

By contrast, the fool has nothing because he has squandered what he has gained. His "sin, waste, and extravagance lead to scarcity" (MacDonald). "Caring only for the pleasures of the present time, he does not save for the future; he consumes all his food and therefore has nothing to eat between harvests" (Buzzell)." Drunkenness, wasteful expenditure, idleness, (and) gambling, devours it all" (Bridges).

<u>In the house of the wise, there are desirable treasures and stored food, but in the house of fools, there are no valuables and a scarcity of food because they have squandered everything they get.</u>

Do you have a saving account? You should. If you cannot save much, save something, even if it is only a few dollars a month. Then as you are able, increase it. Financial planners teach that you should save 10% and have six months living expenses in a liquid account. Saving is the wise thing to do. Are you wise or foolish?

Proverbs 21:21 "He who follows righteousness and mercy finds life, righteousness and honor." The Hebrew word translated mercy is *hesed*. In the Old Testament, this is one of those special words, like the Greek word *agape* in the New Testament. The Hebrew word *hesed* means "goodness, kindness, loving-kindness," especially to the needy and miserable (BDB), "devoted love, fidelity" (Kidner), "loyal love" (Buzzell). It appears elsewhere in Proverbs (11:17; 19:22; 20:6; etc.).

"Three good things are promised to those who are zealous in the works of love: a prosperous life, enduring righteousness, true honor" (Delitzsch). Those who do what is right and who show mercy to others get more than they bargained for; in addition to being righteous, they receive life and honor (MacDonald). When people simply seek to do what is right and are merciful, they find what they are *not* seeking, life and honor (Barnes).

<u>Those who pursue doing what is right and who is merciful find more than just being righteous and merciful; they find a full, satisfying life and honor.</u>

This proverb speaks of being both righteousness and loving. These two virtues are the two great virtues in the Bible. On the one hand, there is truth, righteousness, and justice, and on the other, there is love, grace, mercy, and kindness. God is holy (Lev. 11:44) and God is love (1 Jn. 4:8). God is both (Ex. 34:5-8; Ps. 108:4). As God's children, believers are to be God-like, which includes developing both of these kinds of virtues (Micah 6:8; Prov. 14:22; Mt. 23:23). Jesus is full of grace and truth (Jn. 1:14). To have Christ-like maturity, believers must be righteous (Heb. 5:13) and loving (Eph. 4:15; see also 1 Tim. 6:11; 2 Tim. 2:22). "Righteousness and mercy are the two great divisions of moral duty between man and man" (Wardlaw). Those who pursue both find life and honor.

Proverbs 21:22 "A wise *man* scales the city of the mighty, and brings down the trusted stronghold." Mighty men defend the city, but one wise man can cause it to fall, if he knows where to scale the wall (Eccl. 9:14-15). "If a city is defended by ever so many valiant men, the wise man knows the point where it may be overcome, and knows how to organize the assault so as to destroy the proud fortress" (Delitzsch).

The wise conquer the mighty (Buzzell). Wisdom succeeds where brute force fails (Kidner).

<u>One wise man can defeat a city defended by mighty men because he knows where to scale the wall of their stronghold.</u>

One wise man defeated the mighty ancient city of Babylon. Babylon was considered unconquerable because of two massive, impenetrable walls around the city. The outer wall was 85 feet high (comparable to an eight story building). Nevertheless, Babylon fell quickly and without a major battle. In 539 BC, Cyrus, the king of Persia, diverted the waters of the Euphrates River, which ran through the city, and the Persian soldiers used the riverbed to enter and capture the city (the story is told by Herodotus, the ancient historian; see also Dan. 5).

In 2 Corinthians 10:4, Paul probably has the Septuagint version (the Greek translation of the OT) of this proverb in mind as he writes. He was being accused of walking according to the flesh (2 Cor. 10:2), which is probably the charge that he was only thinking of himself when he didn't come to them as promised (see 2 Cor. 1:15-17, esp. "according to the flesh" in 2 Cor. 1:17). Paul insists that he did not "war according to the flesh" (2 Cor. 10:3). He did not conduct his ministry in a self-serving way that was opposite to what God Himself is like.

Paul explains (see "for" in 2 Cor. 10:4), "For the weapons of our warfare are not carnal but mighty in God for pulling down strongholds casting down arguments and every high thing that exalts itself against the knowledge of God, bringing every thought into captivity to the obedience of Christ" (2 Cor. 10:4-5). Paul is using the image of a conquering a fortified city. The stronghold (the fortress itself), and the "high thing" (the tower) are figures for arguments (Greek: reasonings, rationalizations) and thoughts (Greek: perceptions, intentions) against the knowledge of God. He does not identify his spiritual weapons. He simply says these reasonings and rationalizations, these perceptions and intentions of his own heart that are against God must be pulled down, cast down, and taken into captivity. In other words, believers have a sinful side that argues for living a selfish, sinful life. In order to combat that and not walk or war in the flesh, they must talk to and debate with themselves until those ideas and concepts are defeated and ideas that honor the Lord win out in their life. Paul says that's what he did. He brought his thought life into obedience to Christ.

No matter how mighty the city (a sinful rationalization and/or intention), wise believers can be victorious by using the spiritual weapon of the Word of God.

Proverbs 21:23 "Whoever guards his mouth and tongue keeps his soul from troubles." This proverb resembles Proverbs 13:3. The difference between guarding the *mouth* and guarding the *tongue* is guarding the mouth means not speaking when it is better to remain silent and guarding the tongue is saying what is fitting (Delitzsch). It is the different between knowing the time to be silent and the time to speak—and in the time to speak, knowing what to say (Wardlaw).

In the Hebrew text, the word translated "guards" is the same as the one rendered "keeps." Those who *guard* what they say *guard* themselves against trouble. To say the same thing another way, not controlling what you say gets you into trouble.

Those who control their speech so that they know when to be silent and what to say when they do speak, keep themselves from trouble.

Proverbs 21:24 "A proud *and* haughty *man*—"scoffer" *is* his name; he acts with arrogant pride." Delitzsch describes the scoffer: "Not only does he inwardly raise himself above all that is worthy of recognition as true, of faith as certain, of respect as holy; but acting as well as judging frivolously, he shows reverence for nothing, scornfully passing sentence against everything."

When you meet someone like that, you want to ask, "What is your problem?" Solomon's answer is that the problem is pride. Such people think they are superior to others (Buzzell), even God. They think all should yield to their will and wishes. That is why they become the object of disgust and get for themselves a name of reproach—scoffer (Wardlaw).

Scoffers are proud, haughty, arrogant sorts who earn the disgusting name of scoffer.

Proverbs 21:25 "The desire of the lazy *man* kills him, for his hands refuse to labor." The desire of the lazy man is to rest and not work. That will kill him because if he refuses to work, he will not have anything to eat.

Delitzsch says the lazy man's "inordinate desire after rest and pleasure," his "always seeking only enjoyment and idleness," will bring him to ruin. Simply put, by refusing to work, the sluggard eventually staves (Buzzell; JFB).

The desire of lazy people to rest and not work prompts them to refuse to work and refusing to work leads to their ruin.

Being a sluggard is a sure way to suicide. Elsewhere, Solomon says, "The fool folds his hands and consumes his own flesh" (Eccl. 4:5).

Proverbs 21:26 "He covets greedily all day long, but the righteous gives and does not spare." This proverb continues the discussion of the previous proverb. The "he" of verse 26 is the lazy man of verse 25. The lazy not only refuse to work (verse 25), they lay around all day greedily coveting what others have. "The sluggard lives in his world of wishing, which is his substitute for working" (Kidner). He lives in "a dream world of unfulfilled hopes" (MacDonald). Wishing without working is worthless. The righteous, however, work enough to have money to give to others.

Lazy people spend their days greedily coveting what others have, but the righteous spend their days working and consequently have money to give to others.

Proverbs 21:27 "The sacrifice of the wicked *is* an abomination; how much more *when* he brings it with wicked intent!" The first half of this proverb is repeated in Proverbs 15:8. As has been pointed out several times in these explanations of Proverbs, the Hebrew word translated "abomination" means "repugnant, abhorrent, disgusting." A religious act, such as a sacrifice in the Old Testament, performed by wicked people is disgusting to the Lord. Remember, He looks at the heart. What is *really* repugnant to Him is a religious act done with a wicked motive, such as giving money "to 'buy Him off' or induce Him to condone, approve, or bless some wicked scheme" (MacDonald).

A religious act performed by a wicked person is disgusting to the Lord, but what is even more repugnant is a religious act performed by a wicked person with wicked intent.

The solution, of course, is for believers to confess their sins (1 Jn. 1:9) and serve the Lord with a clean heart (1 Tim. 1:5).

Proverbs 21:28 "A false witness shall perish, but the man who hears *him* will speak endlessly." This proverb is about being a witness in court (see "witness;" MacDonald; Buzzell, who points out that Proverbs speak repeatedly against perjury in court; he lists 6:19, 12:17, 14:5, 14:25, 19:5, 19:9, 25:18).

Note that in the second half of this proverb, the word translated "him" is in italics, indicating that it has been supplied by the translators. The Hebrew word rendered "endlessly" means "enduring, everlasting."

The meaning of this proverb is that in court, the testimony of a witness who heard, that is, who has "personal knowledge of the case" (Wardlaw; Bridges) will last. "The man who listens carefully and answers honestly gives testimony that can never be shaken" (MacDonald).

On the other hand, the testimony of a false witness will ultimately be exposed (Wardlaw).

The testimony of false witnesses in court will perish, but the testimony of those who honestly tell what they heard will endure.

Proverbs 21:29 "A wicked man hardens his face, but *as for* the upright, he establishes his way." The explanation of this proverb hinges on the meaning of the expression "hardens his face." Some say that it signifies determined self-will (Wardlaw). The hardened face is a manifestation of a hard heart (Bridges). As someone has said, "There is an invisible sculptor who chisels the face into conformity with the attitude of the soul." In other words, the wicked refuse to listen. The upright, however, not only listen; they establish their ways; they change their conduct. The wicked are obstinate (JFB). The upright are teachable (MacDonald).

Another suggestion is that the hardened face is a "bold front." In order to persuade people to believe him, the wicked put on a bold front, but the upright concentrates on his conduct in order to establish his way (Buzzell). "This proverb shows that a bold front is no substitute for sound principles" (Kidner).

The wicked harden their face which is an indication of a hard heart, but the upright take wisdom to heart and establish their behavior.

Proverbs 21:30 "*There is* no wisdom or understanding or counsel against the LORD." No human wisdom, insight, or counsel can outsmart the Lord. Human wit and wisdom cannot outwit Him (MacDonald). The reason no human wit outwits the Lord is not stated here, but the Scripture is clear that God is sovereign. What He plans to do will get done. No human strategy will can stop Him.

No human wisdom, insight, or advice can prevail against the Lord.

Proverbs 21:31 "The horse *is* prepared for the day of battle, but deliverance *is* of the LORD." The military develops elaborate plans to ensure victory on the day of battle, but on that day, the Lord gives the victory.

"Soldiers may use horses in battle, but the superiority of a cavalry unit against foot soldiers is no guarantee of victory. That comes only from the Lord, who can turn battles His way in spite of man's efforts" (Buzzell). This proverb does not condemn the use of resources; it just condemns reliance on them (Kidner). "The *horse* indeed may be legitimately employed as a means of defense. But never let the material of warfare be our confidence. Use the means, but idolize them not. They who 'trust in them fall'" (Bridges, italics his). David learned this lesson. He said, "Some trust in chariots, and some in horses; but we will remember the name of the Lord our God" (Ps. 20:7).

No amount of military might guarantee victory; victory comes from the Lord.

Comparing the previous proverb with this one, some observe: nothing avails against God (verse 30) and nothing avails without God (verse 31; Plumptre, cited by MacDonald). "It is useless to fight against God (Prov. 21:30), or without Him (Prov. 21:31)" (Buzzell; Kidner).

Proverbs 22

Proverbs 22:1 "A good name is to be chosen rather than great riches, loving favor rather than silver and gold." To fully appreciate this proverb, several observations need to be made. First, a good name is the fruit of good character (Wardlaw; MacDonald; Buzzell). Character is the root; a good name is the fruit. A "good name" is a good reputation for such things as integrity, wisdom, generosity, etc. (Wardlaw). Loving favor is not just admiration. It is affection (Wardlaw).

So, putting all of this together, if you had to choose between godly character and a good reputation versus great riches, it would be better to choose the former. It is better to have good character that produces a good reputation and the affectionate favor of friends than to have great riches in silver and gold.

It is better to choose to be rich in a good reputation and the affection of people than to choose great wealth in the form of material possessions.

Better to have character and all that goes with it, than to have billions of dollars. Some people sacrifice the former to gain the latter. Shakespeare paraphrased Solomon with these words, "The purest treasure mortal times afford is a spotless reputation."

Before he made his now-famous flight to Paris, Colonel Charles Lindbergh said that he would not sell his name for the movies or any other like project. When he returned, he had offers galore for making money. William R. Hearst thought he could get him to lend his name to a story of his life that would inspire the youth of America. Hearst's motives may have been pure, but Lindbergh had given his word. When Hearst offered Lindbergh a check for $500,000, he refused to take it. Surprised, Hearst handed the famous flier the check asking him to destroy it. Hearst thought that would weaken Lindbergh's resolve. Lindbergh, however, took the check, tore it up, and tossed it into the fire in the fireplace. He chose character over cash.

Proverbs 22:2 "The rich and the poor have this in common, the LORD *is* the maker of them all." Economic diversity and class distinctions cause divisions among people, but all humans have one thing in common that ought to unite them; namely, they are created by God. Common ground is not achieved by eliminating economic differences. It is established by acknowledging common origin.

"All enter the world naked, helpless, unconscious beings; all stand in the same natural relation to their God; dependent on him for their birth; the children of his Providence; the creature of his moral government. All are subject to the same sorrow, sickness, infirmities, and temptations. At the gate of the invisible world, the distinction of riches and poverty is dropped" (Bridges).

<u>The rich and the poor are vastly different economically, but they are very much alike in that God creates both.</u>

"Every attempt to prevent this diversity is vain" (Wardlaw). Jesus said the poor would always be here. The solution is not to erase the economic differences. The solution is spiritual.

Proverbs 22:3 "A prudent *man* foresees evil and hides himself, but the simple pass on and are punished." This proverb is repeated "with insignificant variations" in Proverbs 27:12 (Delitzsch). A similar thought is stated in Proverbs 14:16 (Buzzell).

The prudent person is one who is "shrewd in a good sense" (Buzzell) and the simple person is one who is inexperienced (Clarke), "naïve, untaught" (Buzzell). The word "punished" here seems to mean injury or damage rather than judicial punishment (Wardlaw). Thus, the point of the proverb is that the prudent person is aware of the danger and avoids it, but the naïve person does not see it, makes no effort to avoid it, and consequently suffers the consequences (see Buzzell).

"A prudent man arises from his perceiving an evil standing before him; he sees, *e.g.*, the approaching overthrow of a decaying house in a sudden storm or fearful flood, and takes himself to a place of safety; the simple, on the contrary, go blindly forward into the threatening danger, and must bear the punishment of their carelessness" (Delitzsch).

<u>The wise are aware of danger and take steps to protect themselves, but the naïve are not aware of danger, do not protect themselves, and as a result are hurt or punished.</u>

Proverbs 22:4 "By humility *and* the fear of the LORD *are* riches and honor and life." As has been pointed out (14:26, 27; 19:23), the Hebrew word translated "fear" means 1) to be afraid, terrified, 2) to stand in awe, 3) to reverence, 4) to honor. The fear of the Lord includes standing in awe of Him, reverencing Him (Ps. 33:8), and, yes, being afraid to disobey Him. Those who respect and reverence the Lord trust Him, obey Him, and have a healthy fear of disobeying Him.

This proverb points out that humility and a healthy fear of the Lord are inseparable. There is no humility without the fear of the Lord and there is no fear of the Lord without humility (Wardlaw). People cannot fear God and be filled with pride.

Furthermore, those who have humility before the Lord, faith in the Lord, and fear of disobeying the Lord will be "rewarded" (Barnes; MacDonald) with riches, honor, and life. Earlier Solomon said, "The fear of the LORD *is* a fountain of life, to turn *one* away from the snares of death" (14:27) and "He who follows righteousness and mercy finds life, righteousness and honor" (21:21). A relationship with the Lord is the source ("fountain") of real living, living that includes doing what is right and merciful, which is rewarded with being materially prosperous, socially honored, and personally fulfilled.

<u>Those who humble themselves before the Lord, who trust Him, and fear disobeying Him are rewarded with personal riches, life, and honor from others.</u>

Proverbs 22:5 "Thorns *and* snares *are* in the way of the perverse; he who guards his soul will be far from them." The Hebrew word translated "perverse" means "twisted, crooked, perverted." Here is it describing people who do not live "straight" lives. In this proverb, it does not refer to any particular sin. It is a reference to living a life that deviates from the straight path of righteousness delineated in God's Word.

The path of perverse people is filled with thorns and snares, figures for "hindrances and dangers" (Delitzsch), "all kinds of difficulties and troubles" (MacDonald), "various difficulties, trials, and sufferings" (Clarke). "Like thorns, their conduct keeps them from getting ahead, and like snares, they are stopped like a trapped animal" (Buzzell).

Those who guard their lives by taking the "path of straightforward, single-eyed integrity" (Wardlaw) avoid the problems of the perverse. Being aware of those consequences, the wise avoid the path of the wicked (Buzzell).

<u>The path of perverse people is paved with problems, but those who guard their lives avoid the problems of the wicked.</u>

The path of the perverse is not pleasant. Wardlaw describes the experience: "The man who makes his way through the thicket of 'thorns' is vexed, fretted, and wounded; and when there are 'snares' besides, by which he is rendered insecure at every step, whether his foot may not be taken unawares, and even the troublesome progress he is making be thus arrested, great is the addition to his distress and perplexity" (Wardlaw).

Proverbs 22:6 "Train up a child in the way he should go, and when he is old he will not depart from it." There are two interpretations of this proverb. One contends it is about training a child according to *God's way*. The Hebrew word translated "train up" can mean "dedicate" and "the way" in Proverbs is "basically the way of wisdom" (Buzzell). Thus the point is, dedicate children to God according to the Scripture (Wardlaw). Lange says that although this interpretation has been generally adopted, it has the least support from the Hebrew idiom.

The other explanation claims that this proverb is talking about the *child's way*. The Hebrew phrase rendered "in the way, he should go" literally translated means "according to his way" (Archer). Hence, the point is to train children according to their individual characteristics.

Many commentators have concluded that this is the correct interpretation. Barnes says this proverb "enjoins the closest possible study of each child's temperament." *The Pulpit Commentary* says the injunction is to consider the child's nature, faculties, and temperament in the education given to him. MacDonald says parents should train their children along the lines of their natural talents. Delitzsch says the manner of instruction ought to be according to the child's stage in life. Kidner says that the verse teaches respect for the child's individuality and vocation, though not for his self-will. Ryrie says a child's training should be according to his "habits and interest." He adds, "The instruction must take into account his individuality and inclinations and be in keeping with his degree of physical and mental development."

<u>When children are trained according to their individuality, they will not depart from their training when they are adults.</u>

Keep in mind that this is a proverb, not a law. Proverbs are not absolute guarantees. Proverbs are not promises; they are statements that are generally true (Buzzell). There may be exceptions to a proverb.

Proverbs 22:7 "The rich rules over the poor, and the borrower is servant to the lender." To appreciate the point of the first half of this proverb, just think how often you have seen the poor rule the rich. In this world, the golden rule is "The one with the gold rules." To make matters worse, those who borrow are the servants of their lender because, when they are working, they are not working for themselves; they are working to pay off their debt.

"Debt is a form of bondage. It keeps a man's nose to the grindstone. It limits his mobility and his ability to take advantage of opportunities" (MacDonald).

<u>While it is generally true that the rich rule over the poor in society, it is the borrower who really becomes the servant of the rich person who loans him money.</u>

The English preacher Rowland Hill deplored the longing for luxuries that pushes even Christians head-over-heels into debt. Seeking to impress his congregation on the importance of spending wisely, Hill preached a sermon stating, "I never pay any debts." After pausing, he added, "But I have the best reasons. I never pay any debts because I never have any!"

Proverbs 22:8 "He who sows iniquity will reap sorrow, and the rod of his anger will fail." The Hebrew word translated "sorrow" means "trouble, sorrow, wickedness." Those who sow seeds of wickedness will reap a harvest of trouble. "The crop must be according to the seed. If a man sow thistle seed, is it likely he shall reap wheat?" (Clarke).

The Hebrew word rendered "anger" means "overflow, fury." It is used of an outburst of rage. The rage used as a rod to "smite others" (Barnes) will fail. "The attempt to beat others into submission by anger will be thwarted" (MacDonald). "What the wicked achieve through their fury or wrath will not last; their manipulative techniques will be exhausted" (Buzzell). Oppressors may prosper for a time, but their abusive power will fail and they will reap the harvest of their injustice (Bridges).

Those who sow sin reap a harvest of sorrow and trouble and those who fly into a rage of fury as a rod to smite others will fail and reap the harvest of their sin.

Remember, there is a lapse of time between sowing and reaping.

There are repeated references in the Bible to the law of sowing and reaping. Those who sow righteousness reap a reward (11:18; Hosea 10:12; see also Ps. 126:5-6; 2 Cor. 9:6). Those who sow evil reap evil (Job 4:8). "Do not be deceived. God is not mocked; for whatever a man sows, that he shall also reap" (Gal. 6:7).

Proverbs 22:9 "He who has a generous eye will be blessed, for he gives of his bread to the poor." (See 11:25 for the same thought.) Those who see a need and generously meet it will be blessed because they share *their* substance with the poor.

The phrase "his bread" suggests this generous person is not giving a "small portion of his superfluities" but is sharing his own provisions (Wardlaw). The willingness to share food with the poor indicates a desire to help, not take advantage of, the poor (Buzzell).

Those who see a need to feed the hungry and share their substance to meet that need will be blessed.

Proverbs 22:10 "Cast out the scoffer, and contention will leave; yes, strife and reproach will cease." A scoffer is one who "treats religious questions without respect, moral questions in a frivolous way, serious things jestingly, and in his scornful spirit, his passion for witticism, his love of anecdote, places himself above the duty of showing reverence, veneration, and respect" (Delitzsch). Such people cause "ceaseless contentions and conflicts" (Delitzsch).

"When a scoffer fails to respond to instruction, correction, and admonition, the next step is eviction. When Ishmael was put out of the house, contention, quarreling, and abuse ceased (Gen. 21:9-10)" (MacDonald). Removing the troublemaker removes the trouble (Buzzell). When the cause of contention is cast out, peace prevails.

When mockers are made to leave, contention, conflict, and reproach leave with them.

Commenting on this proverb, in 1861, Wardlaw said, "There are persons who sometimes make their appearance in churches,—persons who are full of spiritual pride and self-consequences,—'wise in their own conceits'—'O how lofty are their eyes, and their eyelids are lifted up!'—'no doubt they are the people, and wisdom shall die with them!' They 'trust in themselves that they are *right,* and despise others.' They are supercilious '*scorners*' of all opinions but their own; and they treat all others with the sneer of self-sufficient derision. They thus produce 'contention, strife, and reproach'—envies, resentments, charges and recriminations, uncharitable conjectures and surmises, schisms and divisions, wherever they go. And from church to church, sometimes they *do* go, carrying their tinder-box and steel with them:—and woe to each in succession!" (Wardlaw, italics his).

Paul told Timothy to withdraw himself from proud, argumentative people because they are "of corrupt minds and destitute of the truth" (1 Tim. 6:3-6). He told Titus to admonish contentious, divisive people twice and if they did not respond after the second admonition, reject them because such people are warped (Titus 3:9-11).

"Disagreement and bad blood sometimes arise not from the facts of the situation but from a *person* with the wrong attitude, who makes mischief. That is to say, an institution sometimes needs not reforms, but the expulsion of a member" (Kidner, italics his). When scoffers do not respond to admonition, do not argue with them; cast them out.

Proverbs 22:11 "He who loves purity of heart *and has* grace on his lips, the king *will be* his friend." People who have pure motives and speak with grace are the kind of people wise kings want for friends. Pure motives and gracious words are appreciated by a king. "A counselor and associate who is governed by a pure intention, and connects therewith a gentle and amiable manner of speech and conversation, attaches the king to himself" (Delitzsch). "So purity and graciousness are advantageous; they help give a person a friendship with leaders in high positions" (Buzzell).

People with pure motives and gracious words are the kind of people leaders want as friends and advisors.

This proverb speaks of a rare "equal partnership," namely integrity and charm (Kidner).

Proverbs 22:12 "The eyes of the LORD preserve knowledge, but He overthrows the words of the faithless." The expression "the eyes of the Lord" describes His "searching omniscience" (Bridges; for another appearance of "the eyes of the Lord," see 15:3). Knowing everything enables the Lord to preserve the knowledge of the truth "so that it will never perish from the earth in spite of the rage of demons and men" (MacDonald).

The Hebrew word translated "faithless" means "to act or deal treacherously, faithlessly, deceitfully." God "makes vain the words of the deceitful" (Delitzsch). He "overthrows false teaching and exposes lies" (MacDonald).

"To be wise, then, is to be under God's protection. To be unwise and treacherous, even in what one says, is to be on a path that will end in frustration" (Buzzell).

<u>Since the Lord sees everything, He can preserve the knowledge of the truth and overthrow the false words of the deceitful.</u>

The Lord sees to it that truth is preserved in the world, including preserving His Word (Bridges, who points to 2 Chron. 34:14-18 as an illustration).

Proverbs 22:13 "The lazy *man* says, '*There is* a lion outside! I shall be slain in the streets!'" Virtually the same proverb appears again in Proverbs 26:13. When people do not want to do something, they use an excuse as a reason. Here it is lazy people who do not want to work, so they come up with an outlandish excuse.

As one commentator points out, "If a lazy man can't find an excuse for not going to work, he will make one up, no matter how ridiculous it is." He suggests that the lion is probably nothing more than a cat (MacDonald). It has been suggested that "frivolous excuses satisfy the indolent man's conscience" (JFB), but such ridiculous reasoning does not fool others.

<u>Lazy people invent absurd excuses for not doing what they are supposed to do, such as there is a danger involved that will harm them.</u>

Proverbs 22:14 "The mouth of an immoral woman *is* a deep pit; he who is abhorred by the LORD will fall there." (See also 23:27.) The first half of this proverb is simple enough. A man who listens to the seductive words of an immoral woman will fall into a deep pit. The seductive words of an immoral woman conceal a trap from which it is difficult to escape (MacDonald; Buzzell). This deep pit is easy to fall into and hard, sometimes next to impossible, to get out of (Bridges).

The second half sounds a bit strange. The man's fall into the snare of the immoral woman seems to be the consequence of the Lord's anger. Upon reflection, it becomes apparent that the immoral man has got away from the Lord and the Lord allowed him to fall. In other words, the anger of the Lord is the result of a previous sin. These are men who "have turned away from instruction, hated reproof, (and) resisted conviction" (Bridges). "The man is left to himself, and sin becomes the penalty of sin" (Barnes).

<u>Men who reject God and His wisdom are repulsed by the Lord, who allows them to fall into the snare of the seductive words of an immoral woman.</u>

Writing to his young son in Proverbs, wise Solomon repeatedly warns him about the dangers of the immoral woman (2:16-19; 5:1-14; 6:24-29; 7:1-27; 29:3; etc.). Wardlaw exclaims, "O! Let youth hear this and tremble!" Older men and women also need to hear and heed this bit of wisdom.

In Romans 1, Paul teaches that those who reject God are under His wrath, which means God gives them over to immorality (see Rom. 1:18-25). "God often abandons men to sin when those men reject the knowledge of God" (MacDonald). "God makes their own sin their punishment" (JFB).

Proverbs 22:15 "Foolishness *is* bound up in the heart of a child; the rod of correction will drive it far from him." The foolishness that is bound in the heart of a child is not "childishness" or "harmless play" (Bridges). It is "not merely frivolity, levity, and nonsense" (Wardlaw). It is "mischief and self-will" (MacDonald), "an arrogant, flippant, hardened" attitude (Buzzell), "the principles of moral evil" (Wardlaw). It is self-will and "proud independence" that includes all the sins a child is capable of, including lying, deceit, willfulness, perverseness, and a lack of submission to authority (Bridges).

This tendency toward sin is "bound" in the heart of the child. Children are born with a sinful nature (Eph. 2:3; Ps. 51:5; 58:3). They are sinners by nature (Isa. 53:6a) and by choice (Isa. 53:6b). That little child has a little heart full of sin, even before the child is capable of speaking or of observing and imitating those around him or her (Bridges). The sinful nature is "bound up" in the heart; it is "firmly fixed" (Clarke). It is not only on the surface and easily corrected; it is held firmly in the heart (Bridges). It is inbred and not easily dislodged (Wardlaw).

The solution is "the rod of correction." The Hebrew word translated "correction" means "discipline, correction." There are various forms of discipline, including verbal correction and the rod (29:15). The "rod" is spankings (13:24; 23:13-14; 29:15; Buzzell). When properly applied, it will drive a sinful habit "far" from a child. "By applying the board of education to the seat of learning, you can rid him of these vices" (MacDonald). "If the child is punished for falsehood, to avoid future punishment, he abstains and speaks the truth" (Bridges).

The tendency towards sin is firmly fixed in the heart of a child, but the proper use of a rod will break a sinful habit.

Spanking is not the only form of discipline. Wardlaw says that nothing could be more "preposterous" them to suppose that the rod is the only means of discipline.

Spanking can be done improperly. Wardlaw says, "Injudicious chastisement, ill-timed, ill-tempered, ill-adapted to the case, and ill-proportioned in measurement, may effectually frustrate the end in view and may even serve to promote its opposite, confirming, instead of expelling folly."

Spanking should be done properly. Wardlaw says it should be accompanied by "instruction, admonition, counsel, example, and prayer." When done properly, it does not have to be done often.

Proverbs 22:16 "He who oppresses the poor to increase his *riches, and* he who gives to the rich, *will* surely *come* to poverty." This proverb describes two types of people who will come to poverty. First are those who extort the poor to enrich themselves (Delitzsch). "Ill-gotten gains do not prosper and only expose the oppressor to extortion and violence" (Barnes). "The employer who gets rich by paying starvation wages will himself suffer want" (MacDonald).

The second group gives to the rich. The fact that the first half of this proverb describes people oppressing the poo*r to gain something for themselves* implies that the same type of thing is going on in the second half of the proverb. In other words, some give to the rich "presumably in order to court their favor" (MacDonald; Bridges; Clarke).

"These two vices pertain to the same selfish feeling. Both are deservedly odious to God and incur punishment" (JFB).

Those who extort the poor to enrich themselves and those who give to the rich to gain something for themselves will come to poverty.

This proverb may be the reverse of Robin Hood. Instead of robbing the rich to give to the poor, this proverb seems to be speaking about people who extort money from the poor to give to the rich to gain favors for themselves. Wardlaw put it like this: "The one also furnished the means of the other; the wealth obtained by the oppression of the poor, being employed in courting, by gifts and accommodations, the favor of the rich."

Proverbs 22:17 "Incline your ear and hear the words of the wise, and apply your heart to my knowledge." It might not be immediately apparent, but this verse marks a major division in Proverbs (Delitzsch; Wardlaw; Kidner; et al.). Starting with this verse and extending through Proverbs 24:34 are the words of wise men. However, the expression "my knowledge" suggests that some of the proverbs in this section were Solomon's (MacDonald). Proverbs 22:22-24:12 generally express the proverbs in two verses instead of one (JFB). The proverbs of Solomon begin again with Proverbs 25:1.

Proverbs 22:17-21 is an introduction to this collection of proverbs (Delitzsch). These verses form a unit that is a general exhortation to seek wisdom (see also 3:1, 21; 4:1; 7:1).

The threefold exhortation in Proverbs 22:17 is to incline your ear, hear, and apply the words of wisdom. As you hear words of wisdom, be alert. Pay attention. Concentrate (Kidner). You are not hearing ordinary words; you are hearing the words of the wise (Bridges) and, in the case of the Scripture, the very Word of God. Hence, there ought to be earnest, eager listening. Wardlaw illustrates this exhortation by describing what happens when an audience hears something they are really interested in hearing. There is breathless silence. Every ear is erect. Every effort is made to hear what is being said. After you have understood the words of wisdom, apply them from the heart, that is, give serious thought as to how this applies to you.

If the words of wisdom are to make you wise, you must deeply desire to hear, understand, think about how to apply, and do what is being taught.

Proverbs 22:18 "For *it is* a pleasant thing if you keep them within you; let them all be fixed upon your lips." Proverbs 22:17-21 is a unit that serves as an introduction to the collection of the proverbs of the wise men recorded in Proverbs 22:22-24:12.

The first verse in this introduction (22:17) exhorts readers to hear and heed words of wisdom. Now, the author explains ("for") that the reason for doing that is wisdom is a pleasant thing to keep in the mind and heart. It is satisfying to the soul (Clarke). The words of wisdom should also be firmly fixed on the lips "so as to be ever ready" (Barnes; JFB) to be spoken to others (Wardlaw; Kidner). MacDonald puts it like this: "A person should keep these proverbs in his mind (to remember and obey) and let them all be fixed upon his lips (to pass them on to others)."

We should hear and heed the words of wisdom because they are satisfying to our own soul and we should always have them firmly fixed on our lips so that we will always be ready to share them with others.

Proverbs 22:19 "So that your trust may be in the LORD; I have instructed you today, even you." In the introduction to the collection of the proverbs of the wise men (22:22-24:12), the readers are exhorted to hear and hear the words of wisdom (22:17) and have them firmly fixed on their lips (22:18) so that *they* can trust the Lord

(22:19; MacDonald) and encourage *others* to trust the Lord ("lips" in verse 18 followed by "so that" in verse 19; Buzzell). In the second half of this line, the author emphasizes that these proverbs are to be taken personally.

<u>We should hear and heed the words of wisdom so that we learn to trust the Lord and so we can encourage others to do the same.</u>

Proverbs 22:20-21 "Have I not written to you excellent things of counsels and knowledge that I may make you know the certainty of the words of truth, that you may answer words of truth to those who send to you?" Proverbs 22:20-21 form the conclusion to the introduction of the collection of the proverbs of the wise men (22:22-24:12). The concluding statement is a question. The author asks if he has not written excellent counsel that the readers may know the certainty of what is written and the counsel ("answer;" see Wardlaw) to be given to others.

<u>Be assured that these written words of wisdom are true and that they are the answer you should give to those you instruct.</u>

The message of the introduction to Proverbs 22:22-24:12 (contained in Proverbs 22:17-21) is that we should hear and heed the words of wisdom so that we learn to trust the Lord, be assured they are true and be able to instruct others with them.

Technical note: there are several interpretations of the word "excellent" in verse 20, including 1) "three" (LXX; Vulgate; Delitzsch; Barnes), 2) "thirty" (RSV; NIV; Buzzell; Kidner), 3) "previously" ("today" in verse 19; Berkley Bible; JFB), and "excellent" (KJV; NKJV; NASB; Bridges; Wardlaw). Also, some claim that the words of the wise in Proverbs 22:17-23:14 are dependent on the ancient Egyptian book the *Wisdom of Amenophis* (Erman; see also Kidner).

Of all the possibilities, "thirty" (NIV) is the one that is definitely *not* correct. That explanation *amends* the Hebrew text! As for the connection between Proverbs and the *Wisdom of Amenophis*, the supposed parallel is simply not there (see Gleason L. Archer, Jr., *A Survey of the Old Testament Introduction*, p. 458 and R. K. Harrison, *Introduction to the Old Testament*, pp.1014-15). Wardlaw points out that in the final analysis, "In all the views given of it (excellent) there is still the idea, more plain or covert, of superiority or excellence."

Proverbs 22:22-23 "Do not rob the poor because he *is* poor, nor oppress the afflicted at the gate. For the LORD will plead their cause, and plunder the soul of those who plunder them." Proverbs 22:22-23 go together ("for" at the beginning of verse 23). The exhortation is not to rob the poor because they are poor, that is, because they are without defense (Delitzsch). "Do not be tempted by the helplessness of the poor man to do him wrong" (Barnes). Do not take advantage of the defenseless poor (MacDonald; Buzzell). In addition, do not oppress the afflicted "at the gate," that is, in the courts (Barnes; Delitzsch). The reason for not robbing or oppressing the helpless is that the Lord is on their side and will plunder the souls of those who plunder them.

<u>Do not take advantage of the helpless in life or the defenseless in court because the Lord is the defense attorney for the defenseless.</u>

Proverbs 22:24-25 "Make no friendship with an angry man, and with a furious man do not go. Lest you learn his ways and set a snare for your soul." Proverbs 22:24-25 go together ("lest" at the beginning of verse 25). The Hebrew word translated "angry" comes from the Hebrew word for nose and means "anger." It is the picture of the rapid breathing of a passionate person. It has been translated "passionate" (Delitzsch). The Hebrew word rendered "furious" comes from the Hebrew word for "hot" and means "burning anger, rage." We speak of people being "hotheaded."

It is wise not to be friends with people filled with anger or rage because you might learn to be angry and, in so doing, damage yourself. Those in a close relationship with a furious person can be easily influenced by their manner of handling life and begin to express outbursts of anger, which has "ruinous complications" (Delitzsch). Buzzell says that even associating with hot-tempered people leads to taking on their ways "which are foolish" (14:17, 29), "divisive" (15:18), and "sinful" (29:22) and also leads to "becoming ensnared" (29:6), that is, "caught up in a situation which is hard to get out of." People become like the company they keep (MacDonald). Bad company is bad business (MacDonald; Kidner). "Sin is contagious;" it never loses its "infectious character" (Bridges).

<u>Do not be friends with people filled with anger and rage because you will learn to be like them, which has damaging consequences for you.</u>

Association with an angry, furious person is like living in a house that is on fire. "One fire kindles another" (Bridges).

Proverbs 22:26-27 "Do not be one of those who shakes hands in a pledge, one of those who is surety for debts. If you have nothing *with which* to pay, why should he take away your bed from under you?" Proverbs 22:26-27 go together, as is obvious from their content. "Shaking hand in a pledge" is equivalent to signing a contract. In this case, it is entering into a binding agreement for someone else's debt. Hence, the first half of this pair of proverbs is saying do not be the guarantor for someone else's debt (Delitzsch; Barnes; MacDonald).

The second part of the pair gives the reason, namely that if the debtor defaults and you are not able to pay, you could lose the very bed on which you sleep. It would not only be embarrassing, it would be uncomfortable. As Buzzell explains, "If a debtor fails to pay, the creditor will hound the cosigner, and if the cosigner cannot pay, then his furniture may be taken as payment. This serious consequence results from becoming foolishly entangled in others' financial problems."

<u>It is not wise to be the guarantor for other people's debt because if they default and you are not able to pay, you could suffer serious consequences.</u>

Buzzell points out, "The high risks in putting up security for debts is mentioned several times in Proverbs." He cites Proverbs 6:1-5, 11:15, 17:18, 20:16, and 27:13.

Proverbs 22:28 "Do not remove the ancient landmark which your fathers have set." In ancient Israel, families were initially given land passed down from one generation to another, like family farmers today. Landmarks marked off each family's land. Landmarks were literally marks (stones) that established land boundaries.

This proverb talks about boundaries established long ago by people's ancestors. It is saying honor those ancient land agreements; do not move them. Buzzell says that the Bible mentions the sin of moving boundary stones six times (Deut. 19:14; 27:17; Job 24:2; Prov. 22:28; 23:10; Hosea 5:10). Today, we would say, "Don't move the surveyor's stake." MacDonald says dishonest people often moved landmarks at night to increase the size of their farm at their neighbor's expense. In other words, this proverb is talking about "grasping covetousness" (Barnes), "highhandedness" (Kidner), "detestable deceit and fraud" (Wardlaw), a form of stealing (Buzzell).

<u>Do not move land markers established long ago by your forefathers to take land away from a neighbor to get more for yourself.</u>

This proverb has been used to teach that *doctrine* should not be changed. For example, MacDonald says, "Spiritually, the ancient landmarks would be 'the faith which was once for all delivered to the saints' (Jude 3). The fundamental doctrines of Christianity should not be tampered with" (see also Wardlaw; Clarke). The Roman Catholics even used this verse to charge that the Protestants had changed ancient doctrine (Bridges)! While it is true that biblical doctrines should not be changed, that is not what this proverb is saying (23:10-11). Barnes notes, "The not uncommon reference of the words to the 'landmarks' of thought or custom, however, natural and legitimate, is foreign to the mind of the writer." This proverb is about a form of stealing.

Proverbs 22:29 "Do you see a man *who* excels in his work? He will stand before kings; He will not stand before unknown *men*." The issue in this proverb is the meaning of the word "stand." Most say that it indicates that people who excel in their work will *serve* kings (Delitzsch; Buzzell; etc.). It probably includes the idea they will be promoted to a *place of honor* (MacDonald). They will not serve before obscure people (Buzzell). Cream rises to the surface.

<u>People who excel in their work will be honored by and serve those in high places.</u>

> The heights by great men reached and kept
> Were not attained by sudden flight,
> But they, while their companions slept,
> Were toiling upward in the night.
> —*Longfellow*

Proverbs 23

Proverbs 23:1-3 "When you sit down to eat with a ruler, consider carefully what is before you; and put a knife to your throat if you are a man given to appetite. Do not desire his delicacies, for they are deceptive food." Proverbs 23:1-3 is a unit. As the remainder of this exhortation makes clear, the expression "put a knife to your throat" is not a reference to suicide; it means "restrain your appetite" (Barnes; Clarke; MacDonald; Buzzell). Eat as if a knife were at your throat, that is, as if you were in imminent danger, because your reputation may be at risk (Wardlaw). Delicacies can be deceptive in that they are being served to influence the guest (MacDonald). "The banquet may be a 'buttering-up' occasion" (Buzzell). So put a knife to your throat, not just to your food. Beware of eating to excess (Barnes). Beware of gluttony (MacDonald; Buzzell; JFB).

Since delicacies might be a deceptive way of influencing you, when dining with an influential person, carefully consider the menu, do not desire the delicacies, and restrain your appetite.

Not bad advice: when not dining with dignitaries, just eating alone, carefully consider the menu, do not desire sweets, and consume small portions. This is the proverb we should take to the table!

Proverbs 23:4-5 "Do not overwork to be rich; because of your own understanding, cease! Will you set your eyes on that which is not? For riches certainly make themselves wings; they fly away like an eagle toward heaven." Proverbs 23:4-5 is not saying, "Don't work hard." The book of Proverbs teaches that work is the way to wealth. For example, "He who has a slack hand becomes poor, but the hand of the diligent makes rich" (10:4).

Proverbs 23:4-5 is a warning against living just to gain riches. It speaks of setting the eyes. To set one's eyes on something is to set one's heart on it. It speaks of using your understanding just to gain wealth. "The ceaseless struggle to be rich is a form of 'wisdom' to be avoided" (MacDonald). It speaks of not just work, but overwork.

Thus this passage is saying, "Do not give yourself (your desire, thoughts, and efforts) to just accumulating riches." The reason is that riches have a way of sprouting wings and flying away like a bird. These verses are not speaking against being industrious, but against being consumed with gaining money, because "ironically, flying after wealth results in wealth flying away like an eagle" (Buzzell).

Do not use all your desires, thoughts, and efforts to the point of overworking to gain riches, because riches have a way of flying away like a frightened bird.

Chasing riches is like chasing pigeons in the park. Riches can suddenly take flight. The company you work for can go bankrupt. The bottom can fall out of the stock market (for example, your 401k). "The accumulations of half a life-time vanished in an hour!"(Wardlaw).

Proverbs 23:6-8 "Do not eat the bread of a miser, nor desire his delicacies; for as he thinks in his heart, so *is* he. 'Eat and drink!' he says to you, but his heart is not with you. The morsel you have eaten, you will vomit up, and waste your pleasant words." Proverbs 23:1-3 warns against eating with an influential person. Proverbs 23:6-8 warns against eating with a miser, a "purse-proud rich" man (Barnes). He begrudges every bite of the food you eat; he counts every spoonful you take (MacDonald). Oh, he says, "Help yourself; have more," but his thoughts are not with you. He is thinking of the cost of the food (the Hebrew word rendered "thinks" means "calculate;" see Kidner; Buzzell). He is only "hypocritically feigning generosity" (Buzzell). When you realize what is really going on, you will be so repulsed that you will want to throw up. Your pleasant words, that is, your compliments (Bridges; Buzzell), will be wasted.

Don't dine with a miser who will tell you to eat all you want but will begrudge every bite you eat because it will not be a pleasant experience; you will be nauseated.

The price is too high and the food is too distasteful to eat with the wrong kind of person. When choosing a dinner date, choose a loving person (see 15:17).

Proverbs 23:9 "Do not speak in the hearing of a fool, for he will despise the wisdom of your words." This proverb is not talking about a fool *overhearing* your words of wisdom; it is talking about speaking directly to a fool (Kidner). In this proverb, the fool is one who "willfully and persistently" refuses to hear wisdom (Barnes). The Hebrew word translated "despised" means "despised, contempt." If you try to give words of wisdom to such willful fools, they will not only not hear what you say, they will despise what you say. So "don't try to teach a dull, stupid fool. You are wasting your time" (MacDonald). Trying to teach a "thickheaded, stubborn fool" is "useless" (Buzzell). "Do not give what is holy to the dogs; nor cast your pearls before swine, lest they trample them under their feet, and turn and tear you in pieces" (Mt. 7:6).

Do not give wisdom to fools, because they will despise what you say.

As long as there is hope, speak, but there is a time to keep silent (Eccl. 3:7). You will know when that time comes by the reaction of the people to whom you are speaking.

Proverbs 23:10-11 "Do not remove the ancient landmark, nor enter the fields of the fatherless; for their Redeemer *is* mighty; He will plead their cause against you." The first part of this proverb appears in Proverbs 22:28. It means do not remove property markers established long ago by the forefathers. In other words, do not steal property by moving the boundaries. This proverb also mentions *entering* the field, that is, entering it to plunder it (Wardlaw).

Stealing the property itself or taking something off of the property is wrong, but doing that to defenseless orphans is worse. In this case, the reason for not stealing from the defenseless ("for") is the defenseless have a Redeemer. According to the Mosaic Law, a kinsman could perform several functions for a relative, such as redeeming a piece of land (Lev. 25:25), redeeming the relative himself from slavery (Lev. 25:47-49), or even avenging a murder (Num. 35:19). Thus the point of these two verses is, do not steal from defenseless orphans, because a strong relative will come to their defense.

<u>Do not take advantage of the defenseless because others will come to their defense.</u>

Many commentators apply this proverb to the Lord (the capital "R" in Redeemer;" Barnes; Bridges; Wardlaw; MacDonald; etc.). For example, Buzzell says, "The Lord, in His concern for the fatherless (Deut. 10:18; Ps. 10:14; Ps. 10:17-18; Ps. 68:5; Ps. 82:3; Ps. 146:9), opposes all who mistreat and steal from fatherless children. He is their Defender."

Proverbs 23:12 "Apply your heart to instruction, and your ears to words of knowledge." Since this proverb is an "echo" of Proverbs 22:17-12, which was an introduction to a new section, this proverb is probably an introduction to a new series of proverbs (Delitzsch; Buzzell).

The expression "apply your heart" suggests desire and diligence in seeking instruction and applying your ears is "another way of saying 'pay attention and listen' (see 22:17)" (Buzzell). "There is no easy way to gain instruction. It requires discipline and application. Disregard the ads that promise it in 'three easy lessons'" (MacDonald). "Godly wisdom is not lightly picked up" (Kidner).

<u>In order to gain wisdom, desire instruction and pay attention to words of knowledge.</u>

A listless heart produces a careless ear, but an opened heart instantly fixes the attention of the ear (Bridges).

Proverbs 23:13-14 "Do not withhold correction from a child, for *if* you beat him with a rod, he will not die. You shall beat him with a rod, and deliver his soul from hell." The Hebrew word translated "correction" means "discipline, chastening, correction" and the one rendered "beat" means "smite" (see "strike" in the NASB and "punish him with a rod" in the NIV). There are many ways to discipline a child. This proverb is talking about corporal punishment.

Do not withhold physical punishment as part of discipline for fear that the child will suffer some harmful physical affect, such as physical death. Actually, physical punishment may deliver the child from premature physical death (MacDonald; Delitzsch says that "hell," which is the Hebrew *Sheol*, in this proverb is not a reference to death in general, "but to death falling upon a man before his time"). "The child will not only survive it, he will survive *because* of it" (Kidner, italics his). Corporal punishment will not kill a child; withholding it may (Barnes). "The pain caused by spankings may make the parent and the child think the child will die, but that is not so. The punishment will actually *deliver* him from physical death not *cause* his death" (Buzzell, italics his). By learning obedience, the child will not do things that would put life and limb in danger.

<u>Do not withhold physical punishment (spanking) from a child for fear it will cause physical harm; it may actually deliver the child from physical harm, perhaps even premature physical death.</u>

MacDonald says, "Instead of disciplining his wicked sons, Eli rebuked them with a mild 'Why do you do such things?' (1 Sam. 2:22-25). He fostered a permissiveness that brought ruin on his house, on the priesthood, and on the nation. David failed in the area of parental discipline too. He never displeased Adonijah by correcting him (1 Kings 1:6). After making two treasonable attempts to seize the throne, Adonijah was killed by Solomon."

Proverbs 23:15-16 "My son, if your heart is wise, my heart will rejoice—indeed, I myself; Yes, my inmost being will rejoice when your lips speak right things." Foolishness is bound up in the heart of a child (22:15). Wisdom does not come naturally. An Arab proverb says, "The wise knows how the fool feels, for he himself was also once a fool." It is the responsibility of the father to teach his children wisdom. The great goal is that the child not only understands wisdom, but is wise and speaks the truth. The ultimate goal is that the child teaches others. When a child "gets it," the father is overjoyed.

"A father rejoices when his son has a heart that is wise and lips that speak the truth" (MacDonald). "The teacher rejoices when the disciple's heart receives wisdom, and yet more when his lips can utter it" (Barnes).

<u>When the heart and the mouth of a son is filled with wisdom, the father's heart is filled with joy.</u>

The point of this proverb applies to the parent, the teacher, the pastor, and the friend who shares truth with another. John said, "I have no greater joy than to hear that my children walk in truth" (3 Jn. 4). Want joy? Take the time to teach truth.

Proverbs 23:17-18 "Do not let your heart envy sinners, but *be zealous* for the fear of the LORD all the day; for surely there is a hereafter, and your hope will not be cut off." As has been pointed out, Proverbs 22:17-24:34 is a division of Proverbs written by wise men. In that division, there are three warnings against being envious of evil people (see 23:17; 24:1, 19; see also 3:31).

In your innermost being, rather than envying the prosperity of sinners, envy the fear of the Lord. "Make communion with God the aim of our life" (MacDonald). Two reasons ("for") are given for this counsel.

The first is that there is a hereafter. The "hereafter" may be a reference to what happens in the future in this life. "The prosperity of the wicked is short" (JFB). Some stretch it into eternity. Barnes says immorality is implied. MacDonald says "hereafter looks past death and resurrection to a glorious future in heaven."

The second is that your hope in the Lord will not be disappointed. "The immediate pleasure of sin cannot be compared with the ultimate hope associated with the fear of the Lord" (Buzzell). "There is a future day of reckoning for the wicked and a bright hope of reward for the righteous which shall never be disappointed" (MacDonald). Do not be preoccupied with yourself and the present; instead, look up and look ahead (Kidner).

<u>In your innermost being, do not envy the prosperity of the wicked, envy knowledge of and trust in the Lord, because of what will happen in the future, namely the end of the sinner is destruction and hope in the Lord will not be disappointed.</u>

Proverbs 23:19 "Hear, my son, and be wise; and guide your heart in the way." Fathers should admonish their sons to listen to instruction so they can become wise and direct their thoughts in the way they should go, namely the way of wisdom. Buzzell puts it like this: "By listening and heeding his father's instruction and desiring the right path (proper conduct), a son is wise."

<u>In order to be wise, a son needs to listen to a wise father, desire to be wise, and decide to go in the way of wisdom.</u>

Listening is the first step in becoming wise. As faith comes by hearing (Rom. 10:17), so wisdom comes by hearing (Bridges).

Calvin Coolidge told a young man, "You are starting out in life. When you begin any journey you chart your course, you plan which direction and which road will lead to your desired destination. Have a predetermined chart, and then follow it." General Foch told his troops, "Battles are won the day before." Fathers should teach their children to chart their course.

Proverbs 23:20-21 "Do not mix with winebibbers, *or* with gluttonous eaters of meat; for the drunkard and the glutton will come to poverty, and drowsiness will clothe *a man* with rags." Do not keep company with those who drink too much or eat too much because drunkenness and gluttony lead to drowsiness and poverty. Shun their company lest you learn their ways and share their doom (Wardlaw). "Intemperance takes its toll. The drunkard and the glutton are headed for poverty. The stupor which results from surfeiting will clothe a man in rags" (MacDonald).

<u>Do not keep company with drunkards and gluttons because those two vices lead to drowsiness, which leads to poverty.</u>

Proverbs 23:22 "Listen to your father who begot you, and do not despise your mother when she is old." Some suggest that Proverbs 23:22-25 are a unit (Delitzsch; Buzzell). This subsection begins with an admonition to young people to listen to the instruction of their biological father and not to despise the advice given to them by their elderly mother. "Old folks have years of experience behind them. Young people should recognize this and try to benefit as much as possible from their experience" (MacDonald). "Wise children respect their parents when they are old" (Buzzell).

<u>People should listen to, not despise, the advice of their wise elderly parents.</u>

Heeding parental instruction and advice is repeatedly encouraged in Proverbs, apparently because children tend to go their own ways (Buzzell).

Proverbs 23:23 "Buy the truth, and do not sell *it, also* wisdom and instruction and understanding." If you want to obtain an understanding of truth, that is, instruction on how to live a wise life, it will cost. Pay the price and once you have it do not sell it for any price. Wisdom is exceedingly valuable (see 3:13-15). It is a bargain at any price.

Commentators explain and expand the imagery. One says spare no expense, effort, or privation to attain it and do not place it over "any earthly possession, worldly gain, sensual enjoyment; nor to let it be taken away by any intimidation, argued away by false reasoning, or prevailed against by enticements into the way of vice" (Delitzsch). Another says, "We should spare no pains to acquire them, but never surrender them for anything in this world" (MacDonald). Still another says spend "whatever energy or financial resources are necessary to acquire truth" (Buzzell).

<u>Pay whatever price it costs to obtain truth, that is, instruction for wise living, and do not sell it for any price.</u>

People will spend a fortune to learn how to make a living and nothing to learn how to live. Should we not study God's Word, like a student in college studies to get all As?

Proverbs 23:24-25 "The father of the righteous will greatly rejoice, and he who begets a wise *child* will delight in him. Let your father and your mother be glad, and let her who bore you rejoice." In the book of Proverbs, being wise means being righteous (Buzzell). Proverbs 23:24 is one demonstration of that. The father who has reared a wise, godly child will greatly rejoice and delight in his child. So children should let their parents rejoice and be glad. "Wise, godly living, in obedience to the parents' discipline, not only benefits the child; it also benefits the parents" (Buzzell).

<u>Since parents delight in godly, wise children, children should live so that they are glad and rejoice.</u>

Proverbs 23:26-28 "My son, give me your heart, and let your eyes observe my ways. For a harlot *is* a deep pit, and a seductress *is* a narrow well. She also lies in wait as *for* a victim, and increases the unfaithful among men." The book of Proverbs contains a number of warnings about sexual immorality. In Proverbs 1-9, there are several "extended discourses" (Delitzsch) on the subject (2:16-19; 5:1-23; 6:24-29; 7:1-27; see also 22:14; 23:17; 29:3).

In this case, a father begins with an appeal that his son listen carefully to what he is being told and observes the ways his father lives. Then, the father explains ("for") there are two kinds of immoral women: the prostitute and the wayward wife ("seductress;" Buzzell). The prostitute is like a deep well and wayward wife is like a narrow well—"easy to fall into and hard to get out of" (MacDonald; JFB). Like a hunter setting a trap, she waits for a victim and she is successful in catching unfaithful men.

<u>Fathers should warn their sons that prostitutes and wayward wives are traps that are easy to fall into and hard to escape and that unfaithful men constantly fall into these tarps.</u>

This also applies to daughters, who should be on the lookout for men who seduce women.

Proverbs 23:29-35 "Who has woe? Who has sorrow? Who has contentions? Who has complaints? Who has wounds without cause? Who has redness of eyes? Those who linger long at the wine, those who go in search of mixed wine. Do not look on the wine when it is red, when it sparkles in the cup, when it swirls around smoothly; at the last it bites like a serpent, and stings like a viper. Your eyes will see strange things, and your heart will utter perverse things. Yes, you will be like one who lies down in the midst of the sea, or like one who lies at the top of the mast, saying: They have struck me, but I was not hurt; they have beaten me, but I did not feel it." When shall I awake, that I may seek another drink?" Proverbs 23:29-35 is an extended discourse. It begins with a series of questions (23:29) followed by an answer to those questions (29:30) and an exhortation to avoid drunkenness (29:31-35). These verses are "the longest and most articulate warning in Proverbs against drunkenness (see also 23:20-21, 20:1, 31:4-5)" (Buzzell).

The father (23:26) asks who has these six characteristics: woe, sorrow, contentions, complaints, wounds, and bloodshot eyes. These people have "emotional problems (woe and sorrow), social problems (strife and complaints), and physical problems (bruises from beatings or bumping into things while staggering and bloodshot eyes)" (Buzzell).

The father's answer is those who linger long at the wine and search for mixed wine (23:30). As was noted earlier (20:1), the Hebrew word translated wine means "fermented juice of the grape." The Hebrew word rendered "mixed wine" is a reference to wine mixed with spices (BDB), which increases "its stimulating properties" (Barnes) "to make it more inebriating" (Clark).

The father admonishes his son not to be "fascinated" (MacDonald; Kidner) with wine when it is red, sparkling in the cup, and swirling around smoothly (29:31). He explains that drunkenness is like a snake's bite and a viper's sting (23:32). It is poisonous and painful, possibly deadly. It makes people perceive strange things, speak perverse things (23:33), and do dangerous things, like lying down to sleep in the midst of the sea or on top of a mast (23:34) and waking up saying, "I was not hurt; I want to drink again (23:35). Some suggest that seeing "strange things" is hallucinations (Buzzell) or the "horrors of delirium tremens" (MacDonald).

<u>People who get drunk end up with emotional problems (sorrow), social problems (conflict), physical problems (wounds), and they put themselves in the place of physical danger, possibly even physical death, yet they want to do it again.</u>

"*Habitual* intoxication is the worst state of the vice, but *occasional* intoxication is still the vice" (Wardlaw, italics his). "Do not be drunk with wine, in which is dissipation; but be filled with the Spirit" (Eph. 5:18).

Wine bites like a serpent. There is a fable about a serpent who found himself surrounded with a ring of fire, who asked a man standing nearby, "Lift me out." The answer was, "If I do, you will bite me?" Over and over the serpent said he would not do it, and finally, as the fable goes, the man reached over and lifted the serpent from his perilous position. No sooner was the serpent safe than he made ready to strike with the sting of death. "You promised that you would not do that," protested the rescuer. To which the serpent replied, "I know I did, but it is my nature to sting and I can't help it."

Proverbs 24

Proverbs 24:1-2 "Do not be envious of evil men, nor desire to be with them; for their heart devises violence, and their lips talk of troublemaking." As has been pointed out, Proverbs 22:17-24:34 is a division of Proverbs written by wise men. In this section, there are three warnings against being envious of evil people (23:17; 24:1, 19; see also 3:31). In the other two proverbs, the reason for not envying sinners is that they will be destroyed in the end.

Here we are advised not to envy evil people or even desire to be with them. The reason given is that they plan violence and talk about the trouble they will cause others. Evil people have a way of dragging others down to their level (MacDonald).

Do not envy evil people or even desire to be their friend because they plan violence and talk of causing others trouble.

Proverbs 24:3-4 "Through wisdom a house is built, and by understanding it is established; by knowledge the rooms are filled with all precious and pleasant riches." The term "house" has been taken as a figure of speech for the home (see JFB), the whole of life (Barnes), or a particular endeavor (Kidner). The rooms are the various parts of whatever the house represents.

A "great life" is not built on wickedness; it is built on wisdom. Wickedness leaves life "empty;" knowledge of wisdom fills it with "precious and pleasant furnishings" (MacDonald). By wisdom, understanding, and knowledge a life is "established" and "filled with treasures" (Buzzell).

By understanding and applying wisdom a good and godly life (home) is established and filled with many valuable treasures of true riches.

The previous pair of proverbs urged us not to be envious of evil men (24:1-2). Why be envious of the wicked when it is wise, godly people who have lives filled with the treasures of precious and pleasant riches?

Proverbs 24:5-6 "A wise man *is* strong, yes, a man of knowledge increases strength; for by wise counsel you will wage your own war, and in a multitude of counselors *there is* safety." Wise people are strong. "Knowledge is power" (Lord Bacon). The primary point of this proverb pertains to kings going to war. The Hebrew word translated "safety" means "deliverance, salvation" and is used hash here of national success in war. Wisdom gained from a multitude of advisors delivers from defeat in battle. "A wise person is not self-reliant; he looks to others for counsel on how to win a battle" (Buzzell). In short, "strategy is strength" (Kidner). The last part of this proverb appears in Proverbs 11:14.

When rulers wage war, knowledge and wisdom gained from a multitude of counselors make them strong and give them victory.

We may not be kings trying to decide whether or not to go to war, but we all have decisions to make and battles to fight. Don't be self-reliant or just rely on the advice of a few friends. Seek knowledge and wisdom from a number of wise, godly people.

Seeking counselors is mentioned four times in Proverbs (11:14; 15:22; 20:18; 24:6).

Proverbs 24:7 "Wisdom *is* too lofty for a fool; he does not open his mouth in the gate." Wisdom is beyond the grasp of fools (MacDonald). To say they have no desire for it or make no effort to obtain it (Wardlaw) is an understatement. They despise wisdom (1:7). They "cannot appreciate, comprehend, or say anything wise" (Buzzell).

Therefore, they do not say anything in the gate, which is where legal decisions were made (Delitzsch; Kidner). They have babbling tongues in the street, but they are utterly unfit to give their judgment in the presence of the wise (Bridges).

Since wisdom is beyond fools, they usually do not open their mouths in the presence of wise people, or, at least, they have nothing of value to contribute.

Proverbs 24:8-9 "He who plots to do evil will be called a schemer. The devising of foolishness is sin, and the scoffer is an abomination to men." Proverbs 24:8-9 are two proverbs with the "same thought" (JFB); the expression is different (Wardlaw). Scheming is the root idea (Kidner).

Verse 8 speaks about those who *plot* evil. Verse 9 talks about those who *devise* foolishness and who scoff. Both verses 8 and 9 give the consequence of planning such wickedness. Those who do it are schemers, sinners, and an abomination to others. The Hebrew word translated "abomination" means "repugnant, abhorrent, disgusting." People who plan and plot evil are repugnant individuals. "People detest" them (Buzzell). They "earn the "contempt of others" (MacDonald).

Those who plot evil, devise foolishness, and scoff are not just schemers, they are sinners before God and an abomination to people.

Proverbs 24:10 "If you faint in the day of adversity, your strength is small." The English word "faint" implies something that is beyond a person's control, but the *Hebrew* word translated "faint" in this proverb means "sink, relax." The Hebrew lexicon renders it "has shown yourself slack" (BDB).

Also in the Hebrew text, there is a play on words (Buzzell). The Hebrew word translated "adversity," a noun, means "straits, distress." The adjective form of that word is rendered "small" and means "narrow, tight." A literal translation is "If you fail in the day of straits (adversity), strait (small) is your strength" (JFB). The Hebrew word translated "strength" means "strength, power."

Clarke puts it like this: "If you give way to discouragement and despair in the day of adversity, (a) time of trial or temptation, your strength is small. In times of trial, we should endeavor to be doubly courageous." MacDonald puts it bluntly: "If he gives up when the going is rough, he doesn't have what it takes." In other words, this proverb is about the quitter (Kidner). Buzzell says, "This may subtly suggest that person is not wise, because, as stated in Proverbs 24:5, wisdom gives strength."

<u>If you slack off in days of distress, your (will) power is weak.</u>

Believers do not need to slack off, claiming they have no strength. "The LORD *is* my strength and my shield; my heart trusted in Him, and I am helped; therefore my heart greatly rejoices, and with my song I will praise Him" (Ps. 28:7).

Proverbs 24:11-12 "Deliver *those who* are drawn toward death, and hold back *those* stumbling to the slaughter. If you say, "Surely we did not know this," Does not He who weighs the hearts consider *it*? He who keeps your soul, does He *not* know *it*? And will He *not* render to *each* man according to his deeds?" The Hebrew word translated "drawn" means "take, lead" ("being taken" in the NASB and "being led away" in the NIV). Verse 11 is describing someone being taken to their death, probably "victims of unjust oppression rather than guilty people" (Buzzell) and is saying "rescue" them (BDB).

Verse 12 describes people making excuses for not helping. They claim ignorance. Verse 12 is also saying that God knows what is going on in the heart and will judge people according to their works. In other words, this is not just simple ignorance; it is "willful ignorance" (Buzzell). It "denounces the tendency to hush up a wrong with the false plea of ignorance" (Barnes).

<u>If you claim ignorance when you know better rather than trying to rescue innocent people being taken to their death, God, who knows the heart, will judge you according to your works.</u>

"God is concerned about the plight of the poor and the helpless (Prov. 22:22-23; Prov. 23:10-11)" (Buzzell).

MacDonald puts these verses in a modern context: "When innocent people are being led off to gas chambers, ovens, and other modes of execution—when unborn babies are destroyed in abortion mills—it is inexcusable to stand by and not seek to rescue them. It is also useless to plead ignorance. As Dante said, 'The hottest places in hell are reserved for those who in a time of great moral crisis maintain their neutrality.'"

Proverbs 24:13-14 "My son, eat honey because *it is* good, and the honeycomb *which is* sweet to your taste; So *shall* the knowledge of wisdom *be* to your soul; If you have found *it,* there is a prospect, and your hope will not be cut off." Honey is mentioned six times in Proverbs [5:3; 24:13 (twice); 25:16, 27; 27:7]. The Hebrew word translated "honeycomb" means "flowing honey, honey from the comb" (BDB). The honey flowing from the honeycomb, the "virgin-honey," is the purest honey (Delitzsch).

Honey is good for you and tastes great. What honey is to the body, wisdom is to the soul. Those who find wisdom have found a "bright future" (MacDonald) and hope.

<u>As honey is good for the body and sweet to the taste, so wisdom is good for the soul and will benefit one's future prospects.</u>

Proverbs 24:15-16 "Do not lie in wait, O wicked *man,* against the dwelling of the righteous; Do not plunder his resting place; for a righteous *man* may fall seven times and rise again, but the wicked shall fall by calamity." The wise advise the wicked not to plunder the home of the righteous. The warning is against coveting the house of the righteous and driving them out of it "by cunning and violence" (Delitzsch).

The reason the wicked should not do this is "God's providential care over them" (Barnes). "An unscrupulous victory is never permanent; you are fighting against God" (Kidner). The righteous may experience calamity over and over, but they will rise up from it. The wicked, however, fall and do not rise up again. The righteous recover "from robberies and attacks" (Buzzell); the wicked stumble into ruin, even "in a single misfortune" (MacDonald; see also Barnes and Bridges). The wicked have "no strong arm to uphold them" (Clarke).

<u>Do not plunder the home of the righteous because although they may fall into calamity over and over, they will recover, in contrast with the wicked, who fall into calamity and do not recover.</u>

Proverbs 24:17-18 "Do not rejoice when your enemy falls, and do not let your heart be glad when he stumbles; lest the LORD see *it,* and it displease Him, and He turn away His wrath from him." The point of this proverb is plain

enough. Do not rejoice when your enemy falls. Clarke claims that the Hebrew word translated "falling" is never used for falling into sin. According to him, it is used of falling into trouble.

The reason ("lest") for not rejoicing is perplexing. Is this proverb suggesting that if we rejoice when our enemies fall, the Lord will be so displeased with *us* that He stops being angry with our enemy?

Some say, "Yes." Buzzell says, "Gloating may cause God to side with one's enemy and to withdraw His wrath… from that enemy." That cannot be the meaning, however, because that would be the same spirit. "It would be the continuance of the divine displeasure, and taking care to avoid whatever would remove it" (Wardlaw).

Some say, "No." They say the point is simply that God will punish you for your gloating. Delitzsch says one ought to abstain from this joy so as not to experience God's displeasure. Barnes says, "Your joy will be suicidal, the wrath of the righteous Judge will be turned upon you, as the greater offender, and you will have to bear a worse evil than that which you exult in." MacDonald says, "If the Lord sees anyone harboring a gloating, vindictive spirit, He will consider that spirit more punishable than the guilt of the enemy." Kidner says, "Your glee may well be a more punishable sin than all the guilt of your enemy." The point here is the same as Solomon noted earlier: "He who is glad at calamity will not go unpunished" (17:5).

<u>Do not rejoice when your enemy falls into trouble, lest the Lord punish you for your attitude.</u>

To rejoice in the fall of an enemy is to fall deeper than the enemy; it is to fall into sin, not trouble (Bridges). Rejoicing over the calamity of an enemy is the "propensity of our corrupt nature." It is that "inward feeling of satisfaction" from an enemy falling into trouble. It is "the very spirit of revenge" (Wardlaw).

In the final analysis, this is a "warning against a vindictive disposition" (Delitzsch). "God hates gloating because it suggests a superior attitude over others. The proverb extends the duty of love even to an enemy; for it requires that we do good to him and not evil, and warns against rejoicing when evil befalls him" (Buzzell). When David's enemy fell, David wept (1 Sam. 1:11-12).

Proverbs 24:19-20 "Do not fret because of evildoers, nor be envious of the wicked; for there will be no prospect for the evil *man;* the lamp of the wicked will be put out" (24:19-20). In the section of Proverbs written by wise men (22:17-24:34), there are three warnings against being envious of evil men (23:17; 24:1, 19; see also 3:31).

Do not be bothered by the success of sinners. As MacDonald says, do not get "all upset over the apparent success of evildoers." The reason for not being envious of evildoers has to do with their future. They will not have a "life worthy of being called life" (Barnes). They will not have a blessed life (Barnes; Clarke).

The figure of their lamp going out has been interpreted as a reference to their prosperity. Their prosperity will "finally cease" (Clarke), "come to an end" (JFB). It has also been explained as death, that is, their lamp will be put out; "they will die" (Buzzell).

<u>Do not be bothered by nor envious of the prosperity of evildoers because their prosperity will not last.</u>

In the end, one way or another, sinners lose!

Proverbs 24:21-22 "My son, fear the LORD and the king; do not associate with those given to change; for their calamity will rise suddenly, and who knows the ruin those two can bring?" The Hebrew word translated "change" was "a common name of a particular class of men (dissidents, oppositionists, or revolutionaries), who recognize neither the monarchy of the Lord, the King of kings, nor that of the earthly king" (Delitzsch). It refers to those who "seek to set aside the worship of the true God, or the authority of the true king, who represents Him" (Barnes). It is about "those who are out to change divine institutions or to overthrow civil governments" (MacDonald). The word "two" refers to the Lord and the king (JFB; Wardlaw; Buzzell).

Thus the proverb says we are to fear the Lord and the king, His representative, and not associate with those who oppose the Lord or the king because rebels and revolutionaries experience sudden calamity and unimaginable ruin.

<u>Reverence the Lord, respect the king and refuse to associate with those who rebel against the Lord and leaders in society because people who rebel will suddenly experience calamity and unimaginable ruin from the Lord and civil authorities.</u>

In the process of commenting on this proverb, several authors give a detailed description of troublemakers. These are the kinds of people who periodically appear in church ("fear the Lord") and in society ("king").

Bridges notes that such men "would prefer a storm which would bring them into note than to a calm in which they were already quietly secure. They are more eager to fish for a name in troubled waters than to cultivate those quiet and social virtues, which, if generally cultivated, would restrain the commotion."

Wardlaw observes, "The men against whom we are here warned are men of a discontented, unsettled, fractions, turbulent, revolutionary spirit; men who can be satisfied with nothing as it is; who, with a mighty conceit on their own wisdom, talk and act as if they thought the world would never be right but under *their* domain and boast of what a world would be, could they but get all of their own way" (Wardlaw, italics his).

Proverbs 24:23-26 "These things also belong to the wise: It is not good to show partiality in judgment. He who says to the wicked, 'You are righteous,' Him the people will curse; Nations will abhor him. But those who rebuke the wicked will have delight, and a good blessing will come upon them. He who gives a right answer kisses the lips." This first part of Proverbs 24:23 indicates the beginning of a new section. This small subsection is written by wise men, not Solomon (Barnes). This new subsection extends through verse 34 (MacDonald). This is the first of four proverbs with the words "it is not good" (17:26; 18:5; 19:2; 25:27; see also "is not good" in 24:23; 28:21). Also, verse 23 is the fourth of six proverbs with the words "is not good" (17:26; 18:5; 19:2; 24:23; 25:27; 28:21).

When judging matters of right and wrong, it is "despicable" to show partiality (MacDonald). Judges who say the wicked are righteous will be cursed by the people and abhorred by the nation (24:24). "The judge who blurs moral distinctions by acquitting the guilty will be cursed by the people and hated by nations" (MacDonald).

On the other hand, judges who rebuke the wicked will have the delight of the people and they will be blessed (24:25). Those who render just verdicts will "win the kiss of approval from the people. Judges who rebuke sin will be rewarded by God and blessed by men" (MacDonald). Just judges are "respected and appreciated" (Buzzell).

Judges should not practice partiality because unjust judges will be cursed and abhorred, but just judges will have the delight, blessing, and affection of the people.

This applies to judges in court, politicians in public service, pastors in the pulpit, believers in the pew, and to us all in private life.

Proverbs 24:27 "Prepare your outside work, make it fit for yourself in the field; and afterward build your house." The word "house" in this proverb has been taken literally and figuratively. If taken literally, the point is, clear the land before your build the house.

If taken figuratively, to "build a house" is equivalent to "founding a family" (Kidner). Thus, this is "a warning against a hasty and imprudent marriage. The young man is taught to cultivate his land before he has to bear the burdens of a family" (Barnes). It may be "a warning against rushing into marriage with all its responsibilities before a person is spiritually, emotionally, and financially prepared" (MacDonald).

Buzzell observes, "Whether house should be taken literally (constructing a house) or figuratively (getting married and having a family), the principle is the same: it is important to have one's priorities straight." "One begins at the wrong end when he begins with the building of his house" (Delitzsch).

As you would clear the land before you would build the house, do the prerequisite preparation before getting married, starting a family, or any other project.

Proverbs 24:28-29 "Do not be a witness against your neighbor without cause, for would you deceive with your lips? Do not say, 'I will do to him just as he has done to me; I will render to the man according to his work.'" The word "witness" in verse 28 indicates that the primary reference is to being a witness in court. Proverbs 24:23-26 spoke of judges; Proverbs 24:28-29 comments on the witnesses in court (Buzzell).

The expression "without cause" means "groundless." In other words, the witness "has no substantial reason for his testimony" (Delitzsch). Do not give a testimony in court for which you have no proof. Do not be deceptive. Do not use your testimony as an opportunity for revenge (Clarke; Buzzell).

When testifying in court, do not bear false witness, be deceptive, or use your testimony to get revenge.

The motive of the thief is money. The motive of the adulterer is sex and the motive of the murderer is sometimes revenge. Revenge wants to kill one's enemy, hurt one's enemy, or at least damage the reputation of one's enemy. Do not take the sword of revenge out of God's hand (Rom. 12:19; Bridges). Our job is to speak the truth, the whole truth, and nothing but the truth publicly in court and privately in conversation.

Proverbs 24:30-34 "I went by the field of the lazy *man,* and by the vineyard of the man devoid of understanding; and there it was, all overgrown with thorns; its surface was covered with nettles; its stone wall was broken down. When I saw *it,* I considered *it* well; I looked on *it and* received instruction: a little sleep, a little slumber, a little folding of the hands to rest; so shall your poverty come *like* a prowler, and your need like an armed man." The description of the lazy man given here also appears in Proverbs 6:10-11. Looking at the field of a lazy man, one who lacks understanding, the wise (24:23) see it overgrown with thorns and nettles and its stone wall in disrepair. Pondering the picture, the wise see that laziness leads to poverty, like an encounter with an armed robber.

The lazy man lacks understanding; he thinks he is wise (26:16)! This passage seems to suggest that the lazy man is as *surprised* at his poverty as he would be if a robber attacked him (Buzzell). At a distance, a robber appears harmless. Then when he is close, it is too late to resist (Wardlaw). Likewise, the lazy see poverty as a harmless possibility until it *suddenly* overtakes them.

The lazy may lack understanding and be surprised, but the wise should not be. They should receive instruction by looking at the lazy. It has been said, "Wise men profit more by the fool than the fool by wise men; for wise men will learn to avoid the faults of fools, but fools will not learn to imitate the virtues of the wise."

If you consider carefully the lot of the lazy, you will learn that laziness leads to poverty.

Proverbs 25

Proverbs 25:1-2 "These also *are* Proverbs of Solomon which the men of Hezekiah king of Judah copied. *It is* the glory of God to conceal a matter, but the glory of kings *is* to search out a matter." Proverbs 25:1 marks the beginning of the fourth division of the book of Proverbs [A Father's Praise of Wisdom (1:8-9:18), the Proverbs of Solomon (10:1-22:16), the Words of Wise Men (22:17-24:34), and now Hezekiah's Collection of the Proverbs of Solomon (25:1-29:27)].

The proverbs in this division were composed by Solomon (1 Kings 4:32 says he spoke 3000 proverbs) and copied by Hezekiah's men (Wardlaw says "in all likelihood," including Isaiah) about 250 years after Solomon wrote them (Buzzell; Clarke says about 270 years). The Hebrew word translated "copied" means "move, transcribe (from one book or scroll to another)." In other words, these proverbs were not written down from oral tradition or "from memory" (JFB). "The first collection of Proverbs is a book for youth, and this second a book for the people" (Delitzsch). Many of the proverbs in this division are grouped in units of similar thoughts (Buzzell; 25:2-7 are about the king).

It is the glory of God to conceal some things; He does not reveal everything. He conceals things "to place before men mystery upon mystery, in which they become conscious of the limitation and insufficiency of their knowledge so that they are constrained to acknowledge, that 'secret things belong to the Lord our God'" (Delitzsch; Deut. 29:29).

In contrast, in order to make proper decisions, kings must investigate matters fully (Buzzell). "A wise king will keep himself informed of important developments affecting his kingdom and will make full investigation in order to render true judgments and formulate sound policies" (MacDonald).

<u>Solomon, a king, wrote proverbs that were later added to this collection by the men of Hezekiah, including the one that says, whereas it is the glory of God to conceal some things, the glory of a king is to fully search out an issue in order to make a good decision.</u>

In order to make good and wise decisions, all of us ought to thoroughly research an issue before we make up our minds. Get the facts first.

Proverbs 25:3 "*As* the heavens for height and the earth for depth, so the heart of kings *is* unsearchable." The height of the heavens and the depth of the earth are unsearchable, meaning they are unknowable. Likewise, as the height of the heavens and the depth of the earth are unsearchable, so are the thoughts of kings. "No one knows exactly what they are thinking" (MacDonald). "God hides some of His knowledge from kings, and kings hide some of their knowledge from their subjects" (Buzzell).

<u>As the heavens' height and the earth's depth are unknowable, the thoughts of political leaders are inscrutable.</u>

"The proverb is a warning against the delusion of being flattered by the favor of the king, which may, before one thinks of it, be withdrawn or changed even into the contrary" (Delitzsch).

Proverbs 25:4-5 "Take away the dross from silver, and it will go to the silversmith *for* jewelry. Take away the wicked from before the king, and his throne will be established in righteousness." The last line of Proverbs 25:5 is nearly identical to that of Proverbs 16:12.

When silver is melted, the dross (impurities) rise to the top. After the impurities are removed, the silver is suitable for jewelry. Likewise, when the wicked counselors are removed from the king's court, the king's rule is established in righteousness. "Getting rid of wicked assistants enables a king to have a righteous reign" (Buzzell). When all bad counselors are banished from the court and cabinet and the wise and good only are the king's ministers and advisers, the king's administration will be established in righteousness (Clarke).

<u>As removing the impurities from silver makes it suitable for jewelry, so removing wicked counselors from the cabinet of rulers makes their administration more righteous.</u>

What is good for the rulers is good for the citizens. This is a warning about taking advice from the wrong people. Refusing the counsel of the ungodly makes for a righteous life.

Proverbs 25:6-7 "Do not exalt yourself in the presence of the king, and do not stand in the place of the great; for *it is* better that he say to you, 'Come up here,' than that you should be put lower in the presence of the prince, whom your eyes have seen." These verses are "a warning against arrogance before kings" (Delitzsch). In the presence of the king, do not gab to promote yourself or grab the place of honor because it is better for the king to elevate you than for you to be humiliated in the presence of the prince.

Observations by commentators include: "It is far better to be invited to a place of honor than to seize it and then be publicly humiliated" (MacDonald). "It is far better for the king to promote him than for the king to humiliate him in front of others whose position the status seeker is desiring" (Buzzell). It is better to "take the lower place at first in humility, than to take it afterward with shame" (Barnes). "The elevation of the humble is honorable, but the humbling of the proud disgraceful" (JFB).

Do not promote yourself or seek a place of honor before those who rule, such as your boss, because it is better for those in authority to promote you than for you to be demoted in the presence of others.

Jesus said, "When you are invited by anyone to a wedding feast, do not sit down in the best place, lest one more honorable than you be invited by him; and he who invited you and him come and say to you, 'Give place to this man,' and then you begin with shame to take the lowest place. But when you are invited, go and sit down in the lowest place so that when he who invited you comes, he may say to you, 'Friend, go up higher.' Then you will have glory in the presence of those who sit at the table with you. For whoever exalts himself will be humbled, and he who humbles himself will be exalted" (Lk. 14:8-11).

Proverbs 25:8-10 "Do not go hastily to court; for what will you do in the end, when your neighbor has put you to shame? Debate your case with your neighbor, and do not disclose the secret to another; lest he who hears *it* expose your shame, and your reputation be ruined." Do not hastily go to court to settle a dispute with a neighbor because what the neighbor says in court may embarrass you. "The Bible condemns the litigious spirit, that is, the desire to rush to the law court to settle every grievance" (MacDonald). It is risky business to accuse others publicly in court (Buzzell). Instead, go to your neighbor privately (Mt. 18:15) and do not reveal to others what was said lest the one you tell exposes your shame and ruins your reputation.

Instead of going to court hastily, which may end up embarrassing you, privately go to the one with whom you have a dispute, and when you do, do not reveal secrets of that meeting to others, lest your shame be exposed and your reputation ruined.

The following is taken from Sir John Hawkins's *Life of Dr. Johnson*, who quotes from Mr. Selwin of London: "A man who deliberates about going to law should have,

1. A good cause;
2. A good purse;
3. A good skillful attorney;
4. Good evidence;
5. Good able counsel;
6. A good upright judge;
7. A good intelligent jury; and with all these on his side, if he have not,
8. Good luck, it is odds but he miscarries in his suit."
O the glorious uncertainty of the law!

Proverbs 25:11 "A word fitly spoken *is like* apples of gold in settings of silver." An appropriate word is like gold apples on a silver tray. They are not only valuable, but they are also attractive (Buzzell) and demonstrate craftsmanship (Kidner). The right word spoken at the right time is a delightful gift "which heightens its impression and its influences" (Delitzsch). A word fitly spoken is one that is well-suited, well-timed, and well-expressed (Wardlaw). The next proverb suggests that a fitly-spoken word may be a rebuke.

Appropriate words are attractive as well as valuable.

Proverbs 25:12 "*Like* an earring of gold and an ornament of fine gold *is* a wise rebuker to an obedient ear." Gold jewelry is valuable and attractive. As gold earrings and jewelry are physically valuable and attractive, the one who wisely rebukes is valuable and appealing to the obedient hearer.

Kidner says the association is "attractiveness, value, and craftsmanship." MacDonald focuses on beauty: "An earring of gold and an ornament of fine gold enhance physical beauty; so a wise rebuker adds moral beauty to the one who is willing to learn." Reproof well-timed and well-taken is a profitable hearing of reproof (Bridges). When reproof is administered in wisdom and received in humility, there is the prevention or correction of evil and the beginning or confirmation of friendship (Wardlaw).

As gold jewelry is valuable, so is a wise rebuker to an obedient hearer.

The psalmist said, "Let the righteous strike me; *it shall be* a kindness. And let him rebuke me; *it shall be* as excellent oil; let my head not refuse it" (Ps. 141:5).

Proverbs 25:13 "Like the cold of snow in time of harvest *is* a faithful messenger to those who send him, for he refreshes the soul of his masters." The first part of this proverb does not refer to snow falling on the crops during the harvest (Buzzell). That would be a "calamity" (Delitzsch), "a disaster" (MacDonald). Harvest time was a time of oppressive heat (Wardlaw). Thus, this proverb refers to snow brought from the mountains of Lebanon or Hermon during the harvest for cool drinks (Delitzsch; Barnes; MacDonald; et al.). The point is, "Just as an iced drink refreshes a man on a hot day, so a faithful messenger refreshes those who sent him" (Buzzell).

<u>Like an iced drink on a hot day refreshes, so a faithful messenger refreshes the one who sent him.</u>

Proverbs 25:14 "Whoever falsely boasts of giving *is like* clouds and wind without rain." Growing up in Florida and living in Texas for a number of years, I remember seeing dark clouds and concluding it is about to rain. I also know there can be ominous clouds, even with lightning and thunder, that don't produce rain. Solomon uses that phenomenon to illustrate people who boast about giving something but don't give it.

Barnes graphically describes the situation, applying it to promises in general (see also Bridges). He writes: "The disappointment caused by him who promises much and performs little or nothing, is likened to the phenomena of an eastern climate; the drought of summer, the eager expectation of men who watch the rising clouds and the freshening breeze, the bitter disappointment when the breeze dies off, and the clouds pass away, and the wished for rain does not come."

MacDonald applies this proverb to those who promise a gift but fail to deliver it (see JFB; Buzzell). Bridges applies it to the Devil, called "the Great Deceiver." Peter and Jude use this figure to describe false teachers who promise but do not deliver (2 Pet. 2:19; Jude 12; see also Bridges).

<u>Some people are like clouds and wind without rain; they promise something, but their promise is false, because they do not do what they said they would do.</u>

MacDonald quotes Indians who say, "Heap big wind—no rain." Buzzell says, "A person ought not promise something if he knows he cannot follow through."

Proverbs 25:15 "By long forbearance a ruler is persuaded, and a gentle tongue breaks a bone." The Hebrew word translated "ruler" denotes "a judge or a person occupying a high official position" (Delitzsch). The issue in this proverb is how to persuade someone in authority.

When people feel that an injustice has been done, they get upset, angry, and passionate. "Boisterous passion injures even a just cause" (Delitzsch). Solomon says it is long forbearance that will persuade someone in authority. The Hebrew word rendered "forbearance" means "anger." Long forbearance is being slow to get angry (JFB). It is "dispassionate calmness, not breaking out into wrath" (Delitzsch). "Gentleness and patience will often persuade a prince more than if a person becomes provoked and excited" (MacDonald).

The Hebrew word translated "gentle" means "tender, delicate, soft." "The soft, gentle tongue is the opposite of a passionate, sharp, coarse one" (Delitzsch). A softly spoken word can break a bone; that is, do that which seems impossible. It can "accomplish difficult things" (Buzzell). It "overcomes obstacles" (Barnes). A German proverb says, "Patience breaks iron;" another says, "Patience is stronger than a diamond."

To sum up: "A patient and gentle tongue can accomplish far more than the loss of temper and harsh words" (Buzzell). "A quiet, composed, thoughtful behavior, which is not embarrassed by injustice, either experienced or threatened, in the end, secures a decision in our favor" (Delitzsch).

<u>Being slow to get angry and speaking softly can work wonders in persuading someone in authority.</u>

The next time you speak to the service department about a compliant or grievance, remember this proverb.

Proverbs 25:16 "Have you found honey? Eat only as much as you need, lest you be filled with it and vomit." Eat honey sparingly because too much is unwholesome (Delitzsch). "Honey is good when taken in moderation, but too much of a good thing is sickening" (MacDonald).

Barnes says honey is a symbol of pleasure. Clarks says the point is to make moderate use of all enjoyments. Delitzsch applies this proverb to the overloading of the mind, saying there should be the right distribution of enjoyment and labor. Bridges says the principle is the temperate enjoyment of our earthly blessings. He goes on to say that in excess, the most elevated pleasures of earth become distasteful, injurious, and fraught with disappointment. He adds "Satisfy the wants, but mortify the lusts of the flesh." The next proverb, "Seldom set foot in your neighbor's house, lest he become weary of you and hate you" (25:17), is also about moderation.

<u>As one should only eat sweets in moderation because too much makes one nauseous, too much of any good thing can be a bad thing.</u>

Larry Christenson illustrates: "Some friends of ours have eight children, and they all love ice cream. On a hot summer day, one of the younger ones declared that she wished they could eat nothing but ice cream! The others chimed agreement and to their surprise, the father said, 'All right. Tomorrow you can have all the ice cream you want—nothing but ice cream!' The children squealed with delight and could hardly contain themselves until the next day. They came trooping down to breakfast, shouting their orders for chocolate, strawberry, or vanilla ice cream—soup bowls full! Mid-morning snack—ice cream again. Lunch—ice cream, this time in slightly smaller portions. When they came in for a mid-afternoon snack, their mother was just taking some fresh muffins out of the oven, and the aroma wafted through the whole house.

'Oh, goody!' said little Teddy. 'Fresh muffins! My favorite!' He made a move for the jam cupboard, but his mother stopped him.

'Don't you remember? It's ice cream day—nothing but ice cream.'

'Oh yeah.'
'Want to sit up for a bowl?'
'No thanks. Just give me a one-dip cone.'
By suppertime, the enthusiasm for an all-ice-cream diet had waned considerably. As they sat staring at fresh bowls of ice cream, Mary—whose suggestion had started this whole adventure—looked up at her daddy and said, 'Couldn't we just trade in this ice cream for a crust of bread?'" (Christenson, cited by MacDonald).

Proverbs 25:17 "Seldom set foot in your neighbor's house, lest he become weary of you and hate you." Like the previous proverb, this one is about moderation. "Moderation applies not only to honey but to visiting. It is important to know when to leave. You can overstay your welcome" (MacDonald).

The Hebrew word translated "seldom" means "be precious, prized, appraised;" it is equivalent to "highly valued" (BDB; Buzzell). In other words, visits should be valuable and limited in order to avoid being a nuisance (Buzzell). "Let our visits neither be unseasonably paid, nor unduly prolonged, nor too frequently repeated" (Wardlaw).

<u>Make visiting your neighbor valuable to your neighbor and don't overdo it because that will weary your neighbor and could even make him hate you.</u>

This is about visiting your neighbor's house. "Familiarity breeds contempt."

This proverb also applies to friendship. "Even the close bond of friendship requires its measure of prudent restraint" (Bridges).

Frankly, "Overdoing anything can be a problem" (Buzzell).

Thank God, this does not apply to God. "His gates are always open" (Bridges).

Proverbs 25:18 "A man who bears false witness against his neighbor *is like* a club, a sword, and a sharp arrow." This proverb is about bearing false witness in court (Buzzell; JFB). The Hebrew word translated "club" means "club, hammer" (BDB). Bridges says it means "a heavy sledgehammer."

The club, the sword, and the arrow would at least cause damage. A false witness ruins his neighbor's estate, takes away his honor and even murders him (Delitzsch). "Lying can wound a person's character and even destroy his life as effectively as weapons" (Buzzell). "A *false witness* is as destructive to reputation as such weapons to the body" (JFB, italics theirs). The lying witness wounds and injures his neighbor by lying. He may inflict wounds that cannot be cured on his person, substance, credit, character, happiness, and life (Wardlaw). "Would you shrink with horror at the thought of beating out your neighbor's brains with a hammer or of piercing his bowels with a sword or a sharp arrow! Why then do you indulge in the like barbarity, destroying as far as you can that reputation, which is dear to men as their life, and wounding all their best interests by mangling their character?" (Bridges).

The club, the sword, and the arrow have been described as instruments of murder, some being gross and others refined, some being slow and others working more quickly (Delitzsch). Wardlaw says these are "lethal weapons" (see also Buzzell). Bridges says this is a picture of cruelty, malice, and even intentional murder! He adds, "The tongue intended as 'a tree of life' becomes a weapon of death."

<u>People who bear false witness in court against their neighbor do great damage and can even cause death.</u>

Proverbs 25:19 "Confidence in an unfaithful *man* in time of trouble *is like* a bad tooth and a foot out of joint." "If you bite down hard with a broken tooth, you'll wish you hadn't. If you put your weight on a foot that's out of joint, it will let you down" (MacDonald). Trusting an untrustworthy person in time of trouble is like having a bad tooth and a foot out of joint; it is "useless" (Barnes; Bridges), "painful and disappointing" (MacDonald), "disappointing and troublesome" (Buzzell). It will cause "intolerable agony" (Wardlaw). Citing the previous proverb which speaks of a false witness in court, Buzzell says, "An example of an unreliable person is one who lies in court."

<u>Trusting an untrustworthy person in times of trouble is like a painful toothache and an out-of-joint foot; it will be painful and disappointing.</u>

However, the Lord is a "very present help in trouble" (Ps. 46:1). Trust Him; He is trustworthy.

Proverbs 25:20 "*Like* one who takes away a garment in cold weather, *and like* vinegar on soda, *is* one who sings songs to a heavy heart." Taking away a person's coat on a cold winter day is irritating. Pouring vinegar on soda causes a "violent agitation" (MacDonald). Thus, "Trying to perk up by songs a person who is discouraged or depressed (a heavy heart) is as cruel as stealing his garment in cold weather. It is also like pouring vinegar on soda; it is useless and it causes a violent reaction. Being insensitive and unsympathetic does much harm" (Buzzell). Singing to someone with a heavy heart is like taking off his coat in cold weather and pouring vinegar on soda; it is unsuitable, unwelcome, and annoying (MacDonald). "To be joyful to one with a heavy heart is not only incongruous, it demonstrates a lack of sympathy" (JFB).

<u>To sing a cheerful song to a person with a sad heart is like taking off his coat on a cold winter day and pouring vinegar on soda; it is inappropriate, irritating, and could initiate a violent reaction.</u>

"Keith Weston told of a fellow minister who was making his first hospital visit. He found a poor patient with both legs strung up to pulleys, both arms in plaster, and an intravenous in one of them. And he said with his big evangelical smile and taking out his big evangelical Bible, 'Brother, are you rejoicing?' Weston said, 'The minister never told me what the patient said, but it wasn't very polite'" (Weston, cited by MacDonald).

What is needed is "sympathetic tenderness" (Wardlaw; Jesus is sympathetic, Heb. 4:15). We ought to weep with those that weep (Rom. 12:15).

Upon reading this, a friend of mine wrote, I needed that! I made that mistake a couple of weeks ago. I made light of a woman trying to account for a lost $50 in her cash register. I tried to say that $50 is small compared to whatever I said. It didn't go over well, and I had to apologize to her afterward. Seeing it in scripture like this will hopefully prevent me from making that mistake again. Having said that, it's interesting how suffering people will feel somewhat consoled by a song that speaks to their pain."

Proverbs 25:21-22 "If your enemy is hungry, give him bread to eat; and if he is thirsty, give him water to drink; for *so* you will heap coals of fire on his head, and the LORD will reward you." Proverbs 25:21 and Proverbs 25:22 go together. Verse 22 explains ("for") verse 21. Paul quotes these verses in Romans 12:20 and goes on to say, "Do not be overcome by evil, but overcome evil with good" (Rom. 12:21). Paul's point is, "We can overcome evil with good by repaying every offense or discourtesy with a kindness" (MacDonald).

The first part of this proverb is simple enough. If your enemy is hungry and thirsty, give him food and water. In other words, do not seek vengeance; be kind. "We are the disciples of him, who died for his enemies" (Bridges). Solomon goes on to give two reasons for doing good, not evil, to an enemy.

First, it will heap coals of fire on his head. "Heaping coals of fire" on someone's head has been explained in a number of different ways.

Some see "coals of fire" as a reference to the fire on the Day of Atonement. The high priest put coals of fire in a censer. Then, he put incense, a symbol of prayer, on the coals. As Barnes explains it, "The first emotion in another caused by the good done to him may be one of burning shame, but the shame will do its work and the heart also will burn, and prayer and confession and thanksgiving will rise as incense to the throne of God. Thus, 'we shall overcome evil with good.'" In this case, the coals first produce shame, then repentance and prayer.

Another explanation of the "coal of fire" is that it refers to the enemy's fire, which, when it went out, meant he needed to borrow live coals to restart his fire. Buzzell explains, "Giving a person coals in a pan to carry home 'on his head was a neighborly, kind act; it made friends, not enemies. Also, the kindness shown in giving someone food and water makes him ashamed of being an enemy and brings God's blessing to the benefactor. Compassion, not revenge, should characterize believers (Pro. 24:29). Alternately, light on this passage may come from an Egyptian expiation ritual, in which a person guilty of some wrongdoing would carry a pan of burning coals on his head as a sign of his repentance. Thus, treating one's enemy kindly may cause him to repent." The conclusion is that the coals produce shame, repentance, and even friendship.

Still another explanation of "coals of fire" is a metaphor taken from smelting ore. "As metals are melted by heaping coals upon them, so is the heart softened by kindness" (JFB). Kindly treatment melts down the enemy "to conciliation, as fuel heaped on the ore fuses it from its hardness, and sends it forth in liquid streams, to take the features and impress of the mold" (Wardlaw). The point is not to consume the enemy but to melt him into kindness (Clarke). Bridges points out that too often, showing love to our enemy is only ceasing to quarrel with him. He adds, "Love is of too substantial a nature to be made up of mere negatives" and "Few hearts are so obdurate as not to melt under the mighty energy of patient, self-denying, burning love." Kindness is a fire that melts hard hearts.

The second reason for doing good, not evil, to an enemy, is that the Lord will reward you for it. If the enemy does not respond to your kindness, be kind anyway because the Lord will reward you (Bridges). "God is well-pleased in such practical love toward an enemy and will reward it" (Delitzsch).

Whatever the exact explanation of the coals, this much is clear: we are to show kindness to our enemies, which will have some kind of effect on them (shame them, make them repent, melt them, make a friend of them, cause them to pray, etc.) and will be rewarded by the Lord. There is a double victory here: one over ourselves and one over our enemy (Wardlaw).

<u>If we are kind to our enemies, it may melt them, perhaps even making them friends instead of enemies, and the Lord will reward us.</u>

Wardlaw tells of a prince who, when leading his army, declared that he would not leave a single enemy alive. He then made allies out of his enemies. When confronted with his failure to fulfill his promise, he said, "I have not failed. I have kept my word. I engaged not to leave a living enemy, nor have I. They are enemies no longer; they are friends." Wardlaw concludes, "He had 'heaped coals of fire on their head.'"

Proverbs 25:23 "The north wind brings forth rain, and a backbiting tongue an angry countenance." This proverb assumes that when the wind came out of the north, you would know that rain was coming (Kidner says that since rain did not normally come from the north in Palestine, perhaps this saying originated outside Palestine; Buzzell cites Kidner). At any rate, this proverb assumes that the north wind brings rain.

The Hebrew word translated "backbiting" means "covering, hiding place, secrecy" and when use of the tongue, it means "tongue of secrecy, i.e., slanderous" (BDB; JFB; Buzzell). As the north wind produces rain, so slander produces an angry look (Moffatt, cited by Kidner; Buzzell). "The angry looks almost surely come from the victim of gossip and they should also come from anyone else who hears it. If people would rebuke the backbiter, he would soon go out of business" (MacDonald).

<u>As the north wind produces rain, so slander produces an angry look.</u>

Proverbs 25:24 "*It is* better to dwell in a corner of a housetop, than in a house shared with a contentious woman." This proverb is repeated in Proverbs 21:9 (21:19 is similar). Repetition shows the "deep importance of the matter" (Bridges). This proverb is repeated to emphasize the point of "the unpleasantness of living with a nagging woman" (MacDonald). Five proverbs concern a contentious wife (19:13; 21:9, 19; 25:24; 27:15). The Hebrew word translated "contentious" means "strife, contention, quarrelsome." It comes from the Hebrew verb for "judge." As explained in the comments on Proverbs 21:9, houses in ancient Palestine had flat roofs, which were often used for retirement by day or in summer for sleep at night. The corner of such a roof was exposed to all changes of weather. Thus the point of the proverb is that all the annoying changes in weather are more tolerable than living with a cantankerous woman. A wife can make life so bitter for her husband that, to have rest, he would rather sit alone on the edge of the roof, exposed to danger and storm (Delitzsch on 21:9). "Solitude in cramped quarters with peace is better than living in a spacious house with a cantankerous, contentious wife" (Buzzell).

<u>Living alone in uncomfortable surroundings is better than living in a house with a contentious wife.</u>

As has been pointed out, Solomon is speaking to his son, hence the reference to contentious wives. If he were discoursing this with his daughters, he would no doubt say that it is better to better to dwell in a corner of a housetop than in a house shared with a contentious (controlling, abusive) husband.

Some wives (and some husbands) are chronic complainers. In 1900, comedian W. C. Fields married a chorus girl named Harriet "Hattie" Hughes. By 1907, he and Hattie had separated. They were never divorced and they rarely saw each other, but for forty years until his death, Fields supported his wife. In 1933, he sent Hattie a typical letter: "I received your complaint No. 68,427."

Proverbs 25:25 "*As* cold water to a weary soul, so *is* good news from a far country." Proverbs 15:30 is a similar proverb concerning the effect of good news. It says, "A good report makes the bones healthy."

In the ancient world, news traveled slowly. "Thus, long periods of anxious waiting usually followed the departure of a loved one or friend to a distant land. The impact of receiving good news from a friend or relative who lives far away is like a refreshing drink of water to a tired person" (Buzzell). Good news is particularly refreshing when it comes after a long delay, "when day after day, week after week, and month after month, we have waited and longed, and sighed, and prayed, for favorable accounts" (Wardlaw).

<u>Good news from someone near, dear and far away is refreshing, like a drink of cold water to someone weary.</u>

MacDonald applies this proverb to the gospel. He says, "The gospel is God's good news from a far country—heaven. Like cold water to a thirsty soul, the gospel is refreshing and thirst quenching" (see also Wardlaw and Bridges).

Proverbs 25:26 "A righteous *man* who falters before the wicked *is like* a murky spring and a polluted well." The Hebrew word translated "falter" means "totter, shakes, slip." It has been taken to refer to failing to stand up for what is right (MacDonald), yielding to the wicked (Barnes), letting one's reputation be compromised (Buzzell), being oppressed by the wicked (JFB). Delitzsch says it "may be understood as a spontaneous as well as of a constrained, forced, wavering and yielding." "The verse, one of the most profound of the whole book, does not speak of the misfortunate, but of the fall of the righteous, whose sin compromises the holy cause which he serves" (Lagarde, cited by Delitzsch).

A pure spring and an unpolluted well are a benefit to people. A muddy spring and a contaminated well are of benefit to no one. "You go looking for purity and cleanliness and are disappointed" (MacDonald). "A righteous person who defects to sin disappoints others who look to him" (Buzzell).

Delitzsch puts his finger on the pulse of this proverb when he says, "From the fear of man, or the desire to please man, or from a false love of peace, he (the righteous) yields before it, and so gives way, then he becomes like to a troubled fountain, a ruined spring; his character, hitherto pure, is now corrupted by his own guilt, and now far from being a blessing to others, his wavering is a cause of sorrow to the righteous and an offense to the weak; he is useful no longer, but only injurious."

<u>When the righteous fall, they are like a contaminated water fountain; they disappoint others and do not benefit them.</u>

Proverbs 25:27 "*It is* not good to eat much honey; so to seek one's own glory *is not* glory." This is the fifth of six proverbs with the words "is not good" (17:26; 18:5; 19:2; 24:23; 25:27; 28:21).

In the Hebrew text, the second half of this proverb is obscure. In the first place, "not" is not in the Hebrew text; it is supplied (notice "not" is in italics, which is an indication the translators inserted it). The second difficulty is the meaning of the word "glory." Some change the Hebrew text slightly and render the Hebrew word translated "glory" as "heavy, weighty, difficult."

If "not" is omitted and "glory" is taken to mean "weighty," the second half of this proverb can mean either "to search into weighty matters is itself a weight" (Barnes, who says "possibly a warning against an over-curious searching into the mysteries of God's word or works") or "to search into weighty matters is glory" (Delitzsch, who says the meaning is, "To overdo oneself in eating honey is not good; on the contrary, the searching into difficult subjects is nothing less than an eating of honey, but an honor"; see also Clarke).

If the traditional Hebrew text is followed, "not" will be inserted (Wardlaw says it is a Hebrew idiom according to which the negative in the former part of a sentence is carried forward) and the Hebrew word translated "glory" means "glory, honor." Thus the meaning is, "Seeking to exalt oneself (seeking one's own honor; Pro. 25:6; Pro. 27:2) is as bad as overeating honey (Pro. 25:16; Pro. 27:7)" (Buzzell; see also JFB). "To be puffed up by our own endowments; to listen to our praise; to force ourselves upon public attention, thus to search out our own glory, is not glory, but shame" (Bridges).

<u>As eating too much honey is not good, so seeking one's glory is not good.</u>

Proverbs 25:28 "Whoever *has* no rule over his own spirit *is like* a city broken down, without walls." See Proverbs 16:32. People who lack self-control are like a city without walls; they are defenseless. Such people are "vulnerable to trouble" (Buzzell). They are "open to every kind of attack, exposed to every temptation" (MacDonald). "Such are exposed to the incursions of evil thoughts and successful temptations" (JFB).

A city without walls "can be plundered and laid waste without trouble, so a man who knows not to hold in check his desires and affections is in constant danger of blindly following the impulse of his unbridled sensuality, and of being hurried forward to outbreaks of passion, and thus of bringing unhappiness upon himself. There are sensual passions (*e.g.*, drunkenness), intellectual (*e.g.*, ambition), mingled (*e.g.*, revenge); but in all of these a false ego rules, which, instead of being held down by the true and better ego, rises to unbounded supremacy" (Delitzsch).

<u>People who lack self-control are like a city whose walls are broken, subject to attack and defeat.</u>

"What then is to be done? On the first assault, fortify the walls by prayer. Never dare trust the strength of the citadel. Have not repeated defeats taught us the need of calling in better strength than our own?" (Bridges).

Proverbs 26

Proverbs 26:1 "As snow in summer and rain in harvest, so honor is not fitting for a fool." Except for verse 2, Proverbs 26:1-12 are about a fool. What is the point of the comparison between summer snow, a rainy harvest time, and honoring a fool? A number of suggestions have been made.

As snow in the summer is "contrary to nature" and rain during the harvest is "contrary to what is usually the case" in Palestine, so honor and a fool are incongruous (Delitzsch; Wardlaw). Snow is out of place in the summer, rain is out of place during the harvest, and honor is out of place with a fool. "It is morally unfitting and only encourages them in their folly" (MacDonald). As snow in the summer and rain during the harvest are unsuitable and unwelcome, so for a fool to be honored is unbecoming (Clarke). Snow in the summer and rain during are "inappropriate, highly unusual, and potentially damaging to crops. Putting a fool in a position of honor is inappropriate and may injure others who follow him as a model" (Buzzell). "The fool's unworthiness is also implied" (JFB). Fools neither deserve honor, nor do they know how to use it (Bridges).

To sum up: as snow in the summer and rain during the harvest are incongruous (Delitzsch), out of place (MacDonald), unbecoming (Clarke), and potentially damaging to crops (Buzzell), so honor given to a fool is incongruous, inappropriate, and injurious.

<u>As snow in the summer and rain during the harvest are incongruous, inappropriate, and injurious to crops, so honor bestowed on a fool is inappropriate and injurious.</u>

Wardlaw makes an interesting observation: "In the land of Israel, 'snow in summer and rain in harvest' would have been regarded as indications of the displeasure of Jehovah. Such appearances were fitted to fill them with the fear that God was about to visit them with famine. So the advancement to honor and authority of wicked men—men devoid of principle—would have been with them, and is indeed with all, a presage of impending calamities."

Proverbs 26:2 "Like a flitting sparrow, like a flying swallow, so a curse without cause shall not alight." A groundless curse (Delitzsch) is like a flitting sparrow and a flying swallow that never land on you. "An undeserved curse will never land on a person" (MacDonald). The causeless curse will not reach its goal (Barnes). The groundless curse fails to have any effect (Delitzsch; Clarke).

Bridges puts it like this: "A curse flies out of an angry mouth undeserved, unprovoked. What if it should come to pass? But we need no more fear the causeless curse, than the birds wandering over our heads. The swallow flying up and down never lights upon us; so the curse causeless shall not come to hurt us. Powerless was the curse of Moab, though attempted to be strengthened with the divination of the wicked prophet Goliah's curse against David was scattered to the winds. What was David the worse for the curse of Shimei or Jeremiah for the curse of his hateful persecutors?"

<u>A groundless curse is like a flitting sparrow and a flying swallow; it will not land on you.</u>

Balaam tried to curse Israel but couldn't (Num. 23:8; Deut. 23:5).

Proverbs 26:3 "A whip for the horse, a bridle for the donkey, and a rod for the fool's back." Before analyzing this proverb, look at a Psalm: "Do not be like the horse *or* like the mule, *which* have no understanding, which must be harnessed with bit and bridle, else they will not come near you" (Ps. 32:9). Since horses and mules do not understand spoken instruction, they need external force to get them to obey. "The horse needs a whip to accelerate his speed" and the donkey needs a bridle to guide him (Bridges).

Hence Solomon, who learned this from his father David (who wrote Psalm 32), says as the horse and the donkey need a whip and bridle, so a fool needs a rod applied to his back. In other words, as brute beasts have no internal motivation and need external motivation, so the fool does not understand and must have external discipline. "Sharp correction is the only language a fool seems to understand" (MacDonald). The fool "will be ruled neither by reason nor persuasion. A rod therefore is for the fool's back" (Bridges). "Nothing else [can] bring him to his senses, or drive his folly from his heart" (Wardlaw).

<u>As dumb animals are not motivated internally, but must have external motivation, so the fool needs external discipline.</u>

"The believer should be so sensitive to the Lord's leading that he does not need the harsher disciplines of life to bring him into line" (MacDonald).

Proverbs 26:4-5 "Do not answer a fool according to his folly, lest you also be like him. Answer a fool according to his folly, lest he be wise in his own eyes." These verses are not contradictory; they are complementary. The second half of each verse explains the difference (MacDonald; Bridges; Wardlaw).

MacDonald explains, "Do not answer a fool in such a manner that you become a fool in the process. Don't lose your temper, or behave rudely, or speak unadvisedly. But answer a fool. Don't let him off with his folly altogether.

Reprove and rebuke him, as his folly deserves, so he will not be wise in his own eyes." The Jewish Talmud says that verse four pertains to foolish comments that can be ignored and verse five refers to erroneous ideas that must be corrected (Buzzell). "On the one hand, it means 'avoid the temptation to stoop to his level'; that is, don't use his methods, lest you also be like him. On the other hand, it means 'avoid the temptation to ignore him altogether'; that is, respond in *some* way, or else he will become wise in his own eyes and his folly will get worse" (NKJV Study Bible).

<u>Do not answer a fool in such a way that you become like him, but answer him lest he thinks he is right in his folly.</u>

"Taken together these verses illustrate the point that no proverb is intended to cover every possible situation. The apparent contradiction in the two proverbs indicates that proverbs must be appropriately applied" (Reformation Study Bible*)*.

As a truck driver was driving along on the freeway, a sign came up that read "low bridge ahead." Before he knew it the bridge was right ahead of him and he got stuck under the bridge. Cars were backed up for miles. Finally, a police car comes up. The cop gets out of his car and walks around to the truck driver, puts his hands on his hips and says, "Got stuck, huh?" The truck driver says, "No, I was delivering this bridge and ran out of gas." Is that joke an illustration of answering a fool according to his folly and becoming like the fool?

Jesus said, "I give them eternal life, and they shall never perish; neither shall anyone snatch them out of My hand" (Jn. 10:29). Some say it is possible for a believer to jump out of His hand. Solomon says, "Answer a fool according to his folly, lest he be wise in his own eyes" (Prov. 26:5). Here is an answer to a fool according to his folly: according to the New Testament, believers are part of His body; a finger cannot jump out of the hand.

Proverbs 26:6 "He who sends a message by the hand of a fool cuts off *his own* feet *and* drinks violence." Notice that the words "his own" are in italics, indicating they are not in the Hebrew text. In other words, the feet could be a reference to the sender's feet (Delitzsch; MacDonald; Buzzell) or the fool's feet (Barnes; Bridges).

"To cut off the feet means to render oneself helpless" (MacDonald), "that is, the message does not get delivered; it is as if the sender tried to take it himself by walking the distance without feet" (Buzzell). The one sending the message "thinks to supplement his own two legs by those of the messenger, but in reality he cuts them off" (Delitzsch).

Most commentators take the former position (see also NKJV; NASB; NIV). In either case, the message does not get delivered.

Wardlaw suggests that in this case, the fool "may signify either a weak and incompetent man, who has not capacity for the discharge of the trust committed to him, or one who is unprincipled, on whose integrity and honor little chance can be placed; either the senseless man, or the worthless man, or a combination of both."

Sending a fool to deliver a message is useless (Clarke; Buzzell). "The fool is utterly unfit for service. When a message is sent by his hands, he makes so many mistakes, careless or willful, that it is like bidding him go, when we have cut off his legs" (Bridges).

Drinking violence is to do damage to one's self (Buzzell). To send a message by a fool is "against your own best interests. The fool won't deliver the message properly. He will only cause you grief" (MacDonald).

<u>To send a fool to deliver a message is as useless as cutting off one's legs and as potentially damaging to the sender as drinking violence.</u>

In short, the message does not get delivered and the sender gets damaged. Maybe the two consequences are related. The sender of the message is damaged because the message did not get delivered. Spare yourself a lot of trouble; select (hire) competent people to do a job. As Bridges says, "Entrust important business to trustworthy persons! Fools are either unqualified for their mission, or they have their own interests to serve, at whatever cost to their masters."

Proverbs 26:7 "*Like* the legs of the lame that hang limp *is* a proverb in the mouth of fools." As limp legs are useless to a lame man, so is a proverb in the mouth of a fool. The fool cannot make use of "an intelligent proverb, or moral maxim" (Delitzsch). "A fool does not know what to do with a proverb; he does not understand it or apply it" (Buzzell). "He does not know when, where, or how to apply it" (MacDonald).

<u>As limp legs are useless to a lame man, so is a wise proverb in the mouth of a fool.</u>

Proverbs 26:8 "Like one who binds a stone in a sling *is* he who gives honor to a fool." The key to understanding this proverb is the word "binds." To bind a stone to a sling means the stone will go nowhere. As binding a stone to a sling renders the sling ineffective, so giving a fool honor is a useless waste (Delitzsch; Barnes). It is absurd (MacDonald), senseless, and possibly harmful in that it may "damage the reputation of the one giving the honor. His wisdom will be questioned" (Buzzell). As binding a stone to a sling is "nonsensical" (Kidner) because it is there to be thrown out, so giving honor to a fool is nonsense.

<u>As it is senseless to bind a stone to a sling, so it is nonsense to give honor to a fool.</u>

Proverbs 26:9 "*Like* a thorn *that* goes into the hand of a drunkard *is* a proverb in the mouth of fools." In Proverbs 26:7, a proverb in the mouth of a fool was said to be useless. In this proverb, the idea is that a proverb in the mouth of a fool is dangerous (Delitzsch; MacDonald; Buzzell; et al.)

A proverb rightly used "instructs and improves," but in the mouth of a fool, who misuses it, it wounds and grieves others (Delitzsch). It does "mischief to the man himself or to others" (Barnes). It is "misapplied and distorted. He might use it to justify his folly and to draw false conclusions concerning others" (MacDonald).

<u>As a thorn is dangerous in the hand of a drunk man, so is a wise proverb in the mouth of a fool.</u>

Proverbs 26:10 "The great *God* who formed everything gives the fool *his* hire and the transgressor *his* wages." The Hebrew text of this proverb has been called "obscure" (Delitzsch), "very obscure" (MacDonald). For one thing, notice that the word "God" is in italics, indicating that it is not in the Hebrew text. Furthermore the Hebrew word rendered "great" can mean "great one" or "archer." In others words, it can refer to the great God (KJV; NKJV), a great man (see Clarke), or an archer (Barnes; NASB; NIV). The Hebrew word translated "formed" means "bring forth, wounding." "Since several of the words have more than one meaning, numerous combinations have been tried" (Kidner).

Many conclude that the word "God" is "improperly supplied" (JFB). They prefer translating the Hebrew word "great" as "archer" (NASB; NIV). Barnes says the best interpretation is: "As the archer that wounded everyone, so is he who hires the fool, and he who hires every passerby. Acting at random, entrusting matters of grave moment to men of bad repute, is as likely to do mischief as to shoot arrows at everyone." Buzzell also takes the translation "archer." He says, "The absurdity of an employer hiring a fool or any passer-by is like a berserk archer (Prov. 26:18) indiscriminately shooting without aiming. Hiring "just anybody" will actually harm the hirer."

A few prefer translating the Hebrew word "great" as "a great man." For example, Clarke says this proverb could be rendered, "A great man grieves all, and he hires the fool, he hires also transgressors."

If the translation of the NKJV is followed (see also the KJV), the meaning is the great God, who formed all things, rewards both the fool and transgressors (see Bridges; Wardlaw).

Since having to supply the word "God" is "very unusual" (Wardlaw), it is best to translate the Hebrew word "great" as a reference to a "great man" (a master or employer) or as a reference to an "archer." The second half of this proverb seems to mean that "a fool and a casual laborer make equally poor employees" (Kidner). Thus the meaning of the proverb is either: a master grieves all when he hires a fool or a transgressor (see Matthew Henry; Bridges) or as an archer who shoots at random wounds everyone, so is he who hires a fool or a transgressor.

Wardlaw says the meaning is probably, "When a prince takes into his service ministers without capacity and without principle, the fool and the transgressors, it is to his subjects matter of universal concern and trouble; both because it is a sad indication of his own character; and because the administration of such men ensures to the country so many and so grievous evils. The sentiment, in this view of it, quite harmonizes with those in preceding and following verses."

<u>When people hire fools and transgressors, everyone is grieved.</u>

"The French translation is 'Great men cause offense, or grief, to all, and take into their service the foolish and the wicked'" (cited by Wardlaw).

Matthew Henry suggests, "We should therefore *pray for kings and all in authority,* that, under them, our lives may be quiet and peaceable."

Proverbs 26:11 "As a dog returns to his own vomit, *so* a fool repeats his folly." (Peter quotes this proverb in 2 Pet. 2:22). As a dog returns to its vomit, so fools repeat their folly. They "return again in word and in deed to their past folly" (Delitzsch).

Wardlaw says there are two ideas conveyed by the comparison, the tendency of fools to return to their folly and "the loathsomeness—the vileness—of the thing itself, when it does take place." Fools go back to that which is "repulsive and disgusting" (MacDonald; see also Buzzell). "Though disgusting to others, the fool delights in his folly" (JFB).

<u>As dogs revisit their vomit, so fools revisit their disgusting behavior.</u>

Fools do not learn from their folly.

Proverbs 26:12 "Do you see a man wise in his own eyes? *There is* more hope for a fool than for him." The second half of this proverb is repeated in Proverbs 29:20.

People who are wise in their own eyes think they are wiser than other people. Buzzell says self-conceit (pride) blinds people to their sense of need. MacDonald says conceited people put themselves above correction, instruction, and rebuke. Bridges says they think themselves to be wise because they do not know what it is to be wise.

There is more hope for fools than for people who are wise in their own eyes. The book of Proverbs does not seem to hold out much hope for fools. They "despise wisdom and instruction" (1:7) and "hate knowledge" (1:22). They mock sin (14:9) and consider departing from sin an abomination (13:19). They repeat their folly (26:11). They die for lack of wisdom (10:21). A simple rebuke to the wise is more effective than a hundred blows to a fool (17:10). Yet there seems to be a glimmer of hope for them because Solomon does say, "Answer a fool according to his folly, lest he be wise in his own eyes" (26:5). There is only a little hope for fools, but there is more hope for them than those who are wise in their own eyes.

Thus, MacDonald says an ignorant fool can sometimes be helped, (but) a conceited man is "impervious to advice." Buzzell says, "At least a fool may sense his need for correction." Bridges declares, "There is more hope of the fool, who knows himself to be one. The natural fool has only one hindrance—his own ignorance. The conceited fool has two—ignorance and self-delusion."

<u>When you see people who are wise in their own eyes, remember, there is more hope for fools than for them.</u>

Wardlaw underscores the utter hopelessness of the self-conceited man by pointing out that in the previous verse Solomon said that fools are prone to return to their folly. He goes on to say it is hard to imagine a stronger rebuke. "The man who is thoroughly possessed with a high notion of his own superiority in wisdom and excellence will listen to nothing."

Proverbs 26:13 "The lazy *man* says, '*There is* a lion in the road! A fierce lion *is* in the streets!'" Proverbs 26:13-16 are about lazy people. Proverbs 26:13 is virtually identical to Proverbs 22:13. In this version, there is a dramatic progression. First, there is a lion. Then there is a fierce lion.

The point is that a lazy man says the fierce lion outside prevents him from going to work (MacDonald). Kidner thinks the lazy man has come to believe his own excuses (Kidner, p. 42). He "has no idea that he is lazy: he is not a shirker but a realist." Whatever is going on in his head, he is "utterly reluctant to his work. When therefore his indolence is disturbed, he is ingenious in inventing excuses and fancying dangers, which have no real existence" (Bridges). He goes to bizarre measures to avoid leaving his house (Buzzell).

<u>Lazy people invent more and more absurd excuses for not doing what they are supposed to do, such as saying there is a danger involved that will harm them.</u>

Proverbs 26:14 "*As* a door turns on its hinges, so *does* the lazy *man* on his bed." "The door turns itself on its hinges, on which it hangs, in and out, without passing beyond the narrow space of its motion" (Delitzsch). "Now he lies on his back, now on his front. Back and forth he swings with plenty of motion but no progress toward getting up" (MacDonald). A lazy man is anchored to his bed as a door is "joined to the jamb. He will not even exert the energy needed to get up" (Buzzell). He turns himself, as the door upon his hinges "moving indeed, but making no progress."

<u>A lazy man lying in bed is like a door turning its hinges; he turns from side to side without making any progress.</u>

The modern version of a lazy man is the one lying of the sofa channel-surfing.

See similar proverbs: "How long will you slumber, O sluggard? When will you rise from your sleep? A little sleep, a little slumber, a little folding of the hands to sleep" (6:9-10). "A little sleep, a little slumber, a little folding of the hands to rest" (24:33).

Proverbs 26:15 "The lazy *man* buries his hand in the bowl; it wearies him to bring it back to his mouth." This proverb is virtually identical to Proverbs 19:24.

The lazy man "dips his hand in the bowl but can't muster up enough energy to lift the food to his mouth. Even something as pleasurable as eating is an exhausting effort" (MacDonald). He starves because he refuses to feed himself (Buzzell).

<u>Some people are so lazy that lifting food to their mouth wears them out.</u>

In the previous proverb, the lazy man was too lazy to get out of bed. Here he is too lazy to feed himself. The lazy are not only lazy at work; they are lazy in bed and at the table (Wardlaw).

Proverbs 26:16 "The lazy *man is* wiser in his own eyes than seven men who can answer sensibly." A lazy man thinks he is wiser than seven intelligent men who are unanimous in their insistence that he is wrong (MacDonald). Barnes says that the number seven is the definite number used for the indefinite." Clarke states that seven here means "perfection, abundance, or multitude. He is wiser in his own eyes than a multitude of the wisest men." He "prides himself upon his superior wisdom" (Bridges). In other words, no one can change his mind. He sticks to his guns (Kidner).

<u>A lazy man thinks he is wiser than everyone else; you cannot convince him of anything.</u>

Proverbs 26:17 "He who passes by *and* meddles in a quarrel not his own *is like* one who takes a dog by the ears." One who grabs a dog by the ears may expect to be bitten. The degree of the damage depends on the fierceness of the dog (Wardlaw). To meddle in a quarrel that is none of your business is like grabbing a dog by the ears; it is to bring trouble on oneself (Bridges; Buzzell). Involvement in another man's strife is "a useless risk of reputation, does no good, and may do us harm" (JFB).

<u>To meddle in a quarrel that is none of your business is like grabbing a dog by the ears; you will get bitten.</u>

Wardlaw wisely writes, "Are we never then to meddle? Are we, in all cases, just to let strife go on, to let the combatants fight it out, come what will? Assuredly not. There is no proverbial saying that has no exceptions. We must take the general lesson without pushing it to extremes. That lesson is sufficiently plain that we should beware of taking part in quarrels with which we have nothing to do,—of thrusting ourselves in between angry disputants; of zealously interfering between those who have expressed no wish for an umpire in their strife,—for advice or mediation." In other words, there may be a situation where you should step in a quarrel.

Proverbs 26:18-19 "Like a madman who throws firebrands, arrows, and death, *is* the man *who* deceives his neighbor, and says, 'I was only joking!'" What is involved in deceiving a neighbor? Suggestions include thoughtlessness (Bridges; Ryrie Study Bible), lying to them (Barnes) or about them (Delitzsch), "false or distorted representations" (Wardlaw), defrauding them, slandering them, cheating them (Delitzsch), or dealing treacherously with them (MacDonald). Whatever the specifics, it is done intentionally (Bridges).

The result of the deception is like an irrational man throwing firebrands, arrows, and even causing death. Notice the progression leading to a climax. The firebrand causes property damage; the arrow causes personal damage and maybe even death.

The deceiver's excuse is that he meant no harm (Wardlaw); he was only joking. He says, "It was all in fun" (Barnes), "I was only kidding" (MacDonald). "I meant no harm" (Kidner). "It is like excusing murder as a joke" (MacDonald). "His deception, like a deadly arrow, has already done its damage" (Buzzell). What he regards as sport, the Lord considers the "the work of the madman, scattering murderous mischief firebrands, arrows and death" (Bridges). "The serious damage done by deceit cannot be dismissed as a joke" (MacArthur Study Bible).

<u>To deceive a neighbor and say it was only a joke still causes damage and even death.</u>

Behind her friend's back she said, "She is not a good mother" and when found out, she said, "I was just joking," but the damage was already done. The mother was hurt and her reputation was harmed. "The person who makes a joke of his thoughtlessness is a dangerous person to be around" (Ryrie Study Bible).

Proverbs 26:20 "Where *there is* no wood, the fire goes out; and where *there is* no talebearer, strife ceases." This proverb and the next one relate fire to strife. In the next proverb a contentious man kindles strife and in this one where there is no talebearer, the strife ceases. The next proverb speaks of starting the fire; this one talks about putting it out.

If wood is not added to a fire, it goes out. Likewise, if there is no gossip, strife ceases. "Just as fuel feeds a fire, so gossip feeds trouble. Unless a troublemaker keeps adding aggravations and gossip and lies, strife will soon die out" (MacDonald). To say the same thing another way, "A quarrel dies down without gossip" (Buzzell).

"To quench the flame we must take away the fuel. We must remove the talebearer; stop him in his words; compel him to produce his authority; face him, if possible, with the subject of his tales. This decisive course will prevent a mass of slander, and put him to shame" (Bridges).

<u>A lack of wood makes a fire go out, so a lack of gossip ceases strife.</u>

Proverb 22:10 says the same thing about mockers: "Cast out the scoffer, and contention will leave; yes, strife and reproach will cease."

Clarke adds, "The tale-receiver and the tale-bearer are the agents of discord. If none received the slander in the first instance, it could not be propagated. Hence our proverb, 'The receiver is as bad as the thief.' And our laws treat them equally; for the receiver of stolen goods, knowing them to be stolen, is hanged, as well as he who stole them."

Wardlaw observes, "It requires no ordinary exercise of Christian discipline to maintain the silence of charity and to regulate both the tongue and the ear within its well-advised limits."

Proverbs 26:21 "*As* charcoal *is* to burning coals, and wood to fire, so *is* a contentious man to kindle strife." This proverb and the previous one relate fire to strife. In the previous proverb, a lack of gossip causes strife to cease and in this one a contentious man kindles strife. The previous proverb speaks of putting out the fire; this one talks about kindling it.

Delitzsch says that coal nourishes the fire and wood sustains it. Buzzell says "kindle" means "to heat up." Thus as coal and wood sustain a fire, so contentious people sustain strife. "It is the whisperer or quarreler himself, not (as he would claim) the truth, that feeds the fires; for his mind refashions facts into fuel' (Kidner).

<u>As charcoal and wood keep a fire burning, so contentious people keep the strife going.</u>

"I am more deadly than the screaming shell of a howitzer. I win without killing. I tear down homes, break hearts, and wreck lives. I travel on the wings of the wind. No innocence is strong enough to intimidate me, no purity pure enough to daunt me. I have no regard for truth, no respect for justice, no mercy for the defenseless. My victims are as numerous as the sands of the sea, and often as innocent. I never forget and seldom forgive. My name is Gossip!" (*Atlanta Journal*, cited by MacDonald).

Proverbs 26:22 "The words of a talebearer *are* like tasty trifles, and they go down into the inmost body." This proverb is an exact repetition of Proverb 18:8. As was pointed out in the comments on Proverbs 18:8, the Hebrew word translated "tasty trifles" means "to swallow greedily" (BDB; see also Kidner). "Fallen human nature eats up gossip as if it were tasty trifles" (MacDonald).

"Soft as they (the words of a talebearer) are, sweet and gentle and the very opposite of injurious as they seem, they are pernicious. Like many poisons, they are tempting to the taste; but they are deadly. They destroy the mental peace and enjoyment of him to whom they are uttered: they destroy the reputation and the interest of him of whom they are uttered; and they destroy the friendship and the social happiness of both" (Wardlaw).

<u>People eagerly swallow gossip like they do a delicious dessert; like a digested dessert, gossip affects their innermost parts, their hearts.</u>

Proverbs 26:23 "Fervent lips with a wicked heart *are like* earthenware covered with silver dross." Proverbs 26:23-26 are talking about people who deceive others by what they say (the word "deceit" appears in verse 24; the other verses speak of it without using the word).

The Hebrew word translated "fervent" means "burning." Fervent lips are those that speak warm words. They have been described as: "lips glowing with affection, uttering warm words of love" (Barnes), lips of "pretended love" (MacDonald), lips of "warm affection" (Bridges), lips making "great professions of friendship" (Clarke), and "lips burning with affection" (Wardlaw).

In this case, the flattery (verse 28; Bridges) covers a wicked heart, which has been called a heart of hate (MacDonald; verse 24), a "malignant heart" (Barnes), and "a heart filled with malice and wickedness" (Bridges).

Silver dross (solid impurities formed on top of molten silver) covering a clay vessel may look good, but underneath is a worthless vessel. As Delitzsch explains, "One may regard a vessel with the silver gloss as silver, and it is still earthen; and that also which gives forth the silver glance is not silver, but only the refuse of silver." In other words, a shining, silvery finish *disguises* the pottery underneath" (MacDonald, italics added). "A person who tries to disguise his evil motives and character by zealous speech is like an attractive glazed-over jar" (Buzzell). Clarke makes the interesting point that a vessel "plated over with base metal to make it resemble silver" is "only a vile pot, and *even the outside is not pure*" (Clarke, italics added).

<u>Warm words of friendship that are used to disguise a heart of hate are like a clay vessel covered with silver dross; both the inside and the outside are worthless.</u>

Wardlaw says, "A worthless deceiver; a silver vessel in appearance, but a potsherd in reality," one having "lips of honey, but a heart of gall," one "glowing with love, and a heart burning with enmity" is dangerous.

"The pretended affection of Judas, the betrayer, illustrates the point" (MacDonald).

Proverbs 26:24-26 "He who hates, disguises *it* with his lips, and lays up deceit within himself; when he speaks kindly, do not believe him, for *there are* seven abominations in his heart. Though his hatred is covered by deceit, his wickedness will be revealed before the assembly." Proverbs 26:24-26 expand the idea expressed in Proverbs 26:23 (Buzzell; Kidner).

Those who hate disguise their hate with their words. So when they speak kindly, do not believe them because their heart is filled with seven abominations. Although they may "speak graciously," you cannot trust them (MacDonald). The seven abominations are not necessarily literally seven. Seven indicates "numerous" (Buzzell), "many" (JFB), "a whole host of abominable thoughts and designs" (Delitzsch), being "full of evil and malice" (MacDonald; Clarke), a "great variety of abominations" (Bridges).

Hatred may camouflage itself behind deception, but the wickedness will become public (Delitzsch). Scoundrels can hide their feelings through deceit temporarily, but they will eventually be known (Buzzell). Their "falsehood and hypocrisy will come to light" (Wardlaw). The heart filled with hate will be exposed.

<u>Do not trust people who camouflage hate-filled hearts with kind, gracious words because their heart is full of all kinds of wickedness, which will be exposed eventually.</u>

"Cain talked with his brother in the field while murder was in his heart. Saul pretended to honor David, while he was plotting his ruin. Absalom dissembled with his brother, by seeming to let him alone, and for two years laying up deceit within him. Joab covered his murderous intentions with peaceable profession" (Bridges).

Proverbs 26:27 "Whoever digs a pit will fall into it, and he who rolls a stone will have it roll back on him." In this proverb, the digging of a pit and the rolling of a stone are for the destruction of others (Delitzsch). They are "the planning schemes of evil" against others (Wardlaw). Thus the point is "attempts to trap or destroy others will eventually turn on the schemer" (Buzzell). Designing destructive devices for others boomerangs.

<u>Their own devices often destroy those who design destructive devices for others.</u>

Bridges points out, "Moab, in attempting to curse Israel, fell himself under the curse of God. Haman's gallows for Mordecai was his own 'promotion of shame.' The enemies of Daniel were devoured in the ruin, which they plotted against him."

MacDonald says, "Man's evil recoils upon himself, just as Louis the Strong's workmanship did. He was asked to make chains that would hold the most desperate prisoners during one of the early French wars. He tempered some very fine steel and made chains that were unparalleled for strength. Later, Louis himself was found guilty of treason and sent to prison. He was heard to moan, 'These are my own chains! If I had known I was forging them for myself, how differently I would have made them!'"

This concept is echoed in many passages (Ps. 7:15-16; 9:15-16; 35:8; 57:6; Prov. 12:13; 28:10; Eccl. 10:8).

Proverbs 26:28 "A lying tongue hates *those who are* crushed by it, and a flattering mouth works ruin." Anyone who lies about someone hates that person. "They desire to harm others by slandering their reputations" (Buzzell). Those who flatter someone works ruin, may refer the ruin of themselves (Delitzsch), their victims (MacDonald), or both (Gill). "The flattering tongue worked the ruin of the world" (Wardlaw).

The slanderer and the flatterer cause great harm.

Proverbs 27

Proverbs 27:1 "Do not boast about tomorrow, for you do not know what a day may bring forth." This proverb and the next one form a pair dealing with "unseemly boasting" (Delitzsch).

The Hebrew word translated "boast" means "be boastful, praise." It is translated "praise" in the next verse. In this proverb, it has the connotation of "self-confident boasting" (BDB). It describes people who are "thinking confidently, talking confidently, and acting confidently" (Wardlaw). People boast about tomorrow when they say what they will do (Delitzsch). They talk as if they are *certain* that what *they* plan to do will *actually happen*, like the politician who says, "When I am President…." "A person should not praise himself about what he will do the next day" (Buzzell).

People should not boast about what they will do tomorrow because they have no way of knowing what will happen tomorrow. "No one is sure of tomorrow" (MacDonald). The future is uncertain.

<u>Do not praise yourself about what you will do tomorrow because you do not know what will happen tomorrow.</u>

This does not mean people should not plan. Alluding to this proverb (Jas. 4:14), James says, "You boast in your arrogance" (Jas. 4:16). He says the solution is to say, "If the Lord wills, we shall live and do this or that" (Jas. 4:15). Notice, he speaking about planning ("do this or that"), but he also talks about acknowledging the Lord's will in the process.

Proverbs 27:2 "Let another man praise you, and not your own mouth; a stranger, and not your own lips." The previous proverb spoke of praising yourself about what you will do tomorrow. This one speaks of praising yourself for what you have done (Buzzell) or who you are. This proverb makes two points.

First, do not praise yourself. Praising yourself is not only in poor taste (MacDonald), it is evidence of pride (Buzzell). It is certainly no commendation (Clarke). So "avoid self-praise" (JFB).

Second, let others praise you. Let your neighbor praise you or, better yet, let a stranger be the one to praise you. For praise to be of value, it must be independent (Barnes). A German proverb says, "Self-praise stinks, a friend's praise is lame, a stranger's praise sounds." The ultimate, of course, is to have the praise of God (1 Cor. 4:5).

<u>Do not praise yourself; let others do that.</u>

Some commentators suggest that in rare cases, praising yourself may be necessary, but in general it is improper to applaud yourself (Delitzsch; Wardlaw). When Paul found it necessary to boast about what he had done (2 Cor. 11:18), he called what he was doing "a little folly" (2 Cor. 11:1, 16; 12:11). For example, he says "Are they ministers of Christ—I speak as a fool—I more" (2 Cor. 11:23). Paul goes on to say, "If I must boast, I will boast in the things which concern my infirmity" (2 Cor. 11:30) "that the power of Christ may rest upon me" (2 Cor. 12:9).

Paul also said, "God forbid that I should boast except in the cross of our Lord Jesus Christ, by whom the world has been crucified to me, and I to the world" (Gal. 6:14).

Proverbs 27:3 "A stone *is* heavy and sand *is* weighty, but a fool's wrath *is* heavier than both of them." A stone and sand are the "heaviest material burdens" (Barnes). The fool's wrath has been called an "unreasonable passion" (Barnes), "unreasonable and excessive" (JFB), and "disproportionate, ungovernable, furious, destructive" (Wardlaw).

"The persistent, provocative remarks of a fool are harder to put up with than a heavy physical burden. A man would rather carry stone or sand than be constantly annoyed by a loudmouthed fool" (MacDonald). Such words of wrath are more grievous because they are "without cause, without measure, and without end" (Wesley; Bridges).

<u>A fool's unreasonable wrath is a heavier burden to carry than a heavy stone or a large load of sand.</u>

Proverbs 27:4 "Wrath *is* cruel and anger a torrent, but who *is* able to stand before jealousy?" "There is a passion which is worse than uncontrolled anger" (Wardlaw). People filled with wrath can be cruel and people filled with anger can be overwhelming like a torrent (Heb.: flood) of water, but jealousy is worse "because it may include anger and fury and merciless revenge" (Buzzell, who cites Prov. 6:32-25). "Wrath and anger are often short-lived, but jealousy continually gnaws away at a person and is, therefore, more grievous" (MacDonald). "As cruel as anger may be, it may be appeased, but envy is an implacable passion" (Bridges). "Jealousy is more unappeasable than the simpler bad passions" (JFB). "Who can stand before jealousy? is one of the few rhetorical questions in Proverbs" (Buzzell).

Delitzsch put it like this: "Let one imagine the blind, relentless rage of extreme excitement and irritation, a boiling over of anger like a water-flood, which bears everything down along with it—these paroxysms of wrath do not usually continue long, and it is possible to appease them, but jealousy is a passion that not only rages, but reckons calmly; it incessantly ferments through the mind, and when it breaks forth, he perishes irretrievably who is its object."

<u>Dealing with jealousy is worse than having to deal with wrath or anger.</u>

Proverbs 27:5 "Open rebuke *is* better than love carefully concealed." A rebuke for a fault, whether from a friend or foe, is better than love that never shows itself in rebuking a fault (Barnes). Open rebuke benefits the recipient, but love that refuses to point out one's failings benefits no one (MacDonald). Love not manifested in acts is useless (JFB; Kidner). "In other words, correcting a person's fault is evidence of love, but failing to correct his shows one's love is withdrawn" (Buzzell).

<u>A straightforward rebuke is more beneficial than love, which says nothing about a fault.</u>

"Open" does not mean "publicly." Open rebuke should be done in private.

Proverbs 27:6 "Faithful *are* the wounds of a friend, but the kisses of an enemy *are* deceitful." The Hebrew word translated "faithful" means "reliable, faithful, trusty;" the one rendered "wounds" means "bruise, wound by bruising," and the Hebrew word "friend" means "one who loves. The "constructive criticism" (MacDonald) of a friend, who genuinely loves, may sting like a bruise, but what is said can be trusted.

The Hebrew word translated "deceitful" means "abundance." In this proverb, it means "excessive" or even "hypocritical" (BDB). Enemies can "lavish" (Barnes) kisses. These kisses are "frequent and hence deceitful" (JFB). The Hebrew word rendered "enemies" means "one who hates." The kisses of an enemy, who really hates, may be abundant, but they only cover up a harmful intent.

Rebukes that wound are to be preferred to the kisses of an enemy (JFB). Buzzell captures the nuances of this proverb when he says, "An enemy (lit., 'one who hates') may seem to be a friend by his many kisses, and a true friend (lit., 'one who loves') may seem to be an enemy by the wounds he inflicts (probably inner hurts that come from being rebuked or criticized; see Prov. 27:5). Yet, ironically, the rebukes may actually be more genuine expressions of friendship."

<u>Constructive criticism from someone who loves you may hurt like a bruise, but the criticism can be trusted, while the abundant kisses from someone who hates you cannot be trusted.</u>

A kiss can be deceptive. "And Joab took Amasa by the beard with his right hand to kiss him. But Amasa did not notice the sword that *was* in Joab's hand. And he struck him with it in the stomach, and his entrails poured out on the ground and he did not *strike* him again. Thus he died" (2 Sam. 20:9-10).

Christ being kissed by Judas is the ultimate example of being kissed by an enemy. Matthew records, "Now His betrayer had given them a sign, saying, 'Whomever I kiss, He is the One; seize Him.' Immediately he went up to Jesus and said, 'Greetings, Rabbi!' and kissed Him'" (Mt. 26:48-49). The Greek word translated "kiss" in Matthew 26:48 is the simple Greek word for kiss, but the one that appears in verse 49 is a compound form of the word for "kiss." It means "to kiss fervently, kiss affectionately." It is the same one that is used of the father's reception of his prodigal son (Lk. 15:20). Barclay says it was the word for lover's kiss and it means "to kiss repeatedly, passionately, and fervently." Instead of an expression of honor or affection, this kiss was "the lowest depths of insincerity" (McNeile). "The universal symbol of love was to be prostituted to its lowest use" (MacDonald).

Proverbs 27:7 "A satisfied soul loathes the honeycomb, but to a hungry soul every bitter thing *is* sweet." The Hebrew word translated "loathes" means "tread down, trample." Satisfied people have no appetite for the sweetest of food; they trample it. But to hungry people, even something bitter is sweet. MacDonald says that overfed people lose their "appreciation of the choicest, sweetest foods," while hungry people are "grateful for the slimmest pickings."

Commentators tend to extend this proverb beyond food. Kidner states, "This is not a truism about food, but a parable about possessions." Buzzell says, "This verse may be teaching that one's attitude toward material possessions is influenced by how much he possesses. Those who have much do not appreciate or value a gift as much as do those who have little." MacDonald says this proverb is "true of material possessions and of spiritual privileges" (see also Bridges and Wardlaw).

<u>Those who are satisfied reject even the sweetest of food, while for those who are hungry even bitter food is sweet.</u>

Proverbs 27:8 "Like a bird that wanders from its nest *is* a man who wanders from his place." The key to unlocking this proverb is the meaning of a bird wandering from its nest. One common suggestion is that a wandering bird shirks responsibility (MacDonald; Kidner; Wardlaw, who points out that birds build nests to lay eggs in them). Another proposal is that a wandering bird exposes itself to danger (Fleischer, cited by Delitzsch; Bridges; Clarke). Then there are those who say both ideas are involved: "Such is not only out of place but out of duty and in danger" (JFB; Buzzell). Likewise, a man with wanderlust abandons his responsibilities at home and exposes himself to danger.

<u>People who wander from where they are supposed to be are like birds wandering far from their nest; they are abandoning their responsibility and are exposing themselves to danger.</u>

Proverbs 27:9 "Ointment and perfume delight the heart, and the sweetness of a man's friend *gives delight* by hearty counsel." The Hebrew word translated "delight" means "rejoice, be glad." As ointments and perfumes gladden the heart, so "the sweet exhortation" (Delitzsch), the "loving advice" (MacDonald), of a friend rejoices the heart. "A friend's earnest counsel is as sweet or pleasant as the fragrance emanating from perfume and incense" (Buzzell). "There is something truly heartwarming about fellowship with a friend" (MacDonald).

As ointments and perfumes gladden the heart, so the encouraging counsel of a dear friend rejoices the heart.

Wardlaw says, "The comparison is, plainly, that of the influence of good counsel, kindly administered, upon the mind, to the refreshing and cheering effect of the fragrance of rich perfumes upon the sense and upon the spirit. This is especially felt in times of trouble and in seasons of difficulty and perplexity. When the heart is heavy and depressed, and the mind troubled with conflicting and distracting thoughts—how soothing is the salutary counsel of a judicious and affectionate friend!—how does it sweeten the embittered and settle the agitated spirit!"

Proverbs 27:10 "Do not forsake your own friend or your father's friend, nor go to your brother's house in the day of your calamity; better *is* a neighbor nearby than a brother far away." Do not forsake your personal friends or your family's friends by neglecting or undervaluing their counsel or in their time of need (Wardlaw). Be a faithful friend. "Adhere to tried friends" (JFB).

The Hebrew word translated "calamity" means "calamity, distress." The reason for not forsaking your friends is that when you experience trouble or tragedy, it is better to have a neighbor who is near than a brother who is far away. Delitzsch puts it like this: When you need consolation and help, go to the nearby neighbor rather than the brother who lives at a distance. Buzzell points out, "Normally in times of adversity, a brother (relative) is helpful (Prov. 17:17). But if the brother lives a great distance away, a neighbor may be far more helpful (Prov. 18:24)."

Some commentators say that the brother who is far away is "far off in feeling" (Barnes), who "keeps himself at a distance" (Clarke), who is "far off in affection" (Bridges), who is "estranged from you" (MacDonald; see also Wardlaw).

Be a faithful friend to your personal and family friends because when trouble comes, it is better to have a friend nearby than a brother who is far away.

Proverbs 27:11 "My son, be wise, and make my heart glad, that I may answer him who reproaches me." A father should exhort his son to be wise so that the father can have joy and an answer to "critics who may accuse him of being an incompetent father" (Buzzell; see Delitzsch). A wise son brings joy to his father (10:1; 15:20; 23:15, 24; 29:3). "A son's behavior reflects on his father's instruction" (MacDonald).

Some commentators apply this to the teacher/student relationship (Kidner). For example, Barnes says the teacher is pleading with his disciple "that the uprightness of the scholar will be the truest answer to all attacks on the character or teaching of the master." Berkeley says, "The teacher's one defense—the success of his students" (Berkeley, cited by MacDonald). Wardlaw says the principle applies to the pastor and his people.

Fathers should exhort their children to live wise lives so that, among other things, the father can have a happy heart and a hearty answer to critics of his child-rearing.

Parents should teach their children to live wise, godly lives, not only because it is good for the children but also for the parents.

Proverbs 27:12 "A prudent *man* foresees evil *and* hides himself; the simple pass on *and* are punished." This proverb is "nearly identical" to Proverbs 22:3 (Buzzell). As pointed out in the comments on Proverbs 22:3, the prudent man is "shrewd in a good sense" (Buzzell). Prudent people are aware of danger and avoid it.

The simple are inexperienced and, as a result, are naïve. The word "punished" here seems to mean injury or damage rather than judicial punishment (Wardlaw). The naïve do not see the evil and, as a result, are damaged by it.

Bridges puts it like this: Every intelligent man foresees coming evil and provides himself shelter. The man who has never realized evil is without a hiding place.

The wise are aware of danger and take steps to protect themselves, but the naïve are not aware of danger and do not protect themselves, and, as a result, they are hurt or punished.

In his comments on Proverbs 27:13, Bridges suggests that Proverbs 27:13 may be an illustration of Proverbs 27:12. He says the prudent are "foreseeing evil, and, instead of rushing into it, avoiding it. What can be more imprudent than trusting a man who is surety for a stranger or a strange woman? Such folly is utterly unworthy of confidence. And therefore take his garment full security for a debt."

"Noah was a prudent man, hiding himself and his family in the ark. The rest of the people went on their way carelessly and indifferently and suffered for it" (MacDonald).

Proverbs 27:13 "Take the garment of him who is surety for a stranger, and hold it in pledge *when* he is surety for a seductress." This proverb is "a near repetition of Proverbs 20:16" (Kidner).

As pointed out in the comments on Proverbs 20:16, this proverb warns against lending money to someone who cosigns for a stranger. If you loan money to such an unwise person, take his outer garment as collateral (Barnes; Wardlaw; Delitzsch; Buzzell). That is especially true if the stranger is a seductress, that is, an immoral person.

MacDonald says, "In modern idiom, the first line means that the man who is surety for a stranger will 'lose his shirt.'" He says the second line means, "Be sure you have a legal claim on the property of anyone who will guarantee the debts unworthy of strangers, for if the debtor can't pay, the surety will have to."

If you are going to loan money to someone who is a cosigner for a stranger, be sure to obtain collateral, especially if the stranger is a person of questionable character.

Proverbs 27:14 "He who blesses his friend with a loud voice, rising early in the morning, it will be counted a curse to him." When a person blesses his or her friends with a loud voice early in the morning, it will be considered more of a curse than a blessing. "To a man of any real modesty, this will be painfully irksome,—insufferably offensive. It is putting him on the rack,—torturing his spirit" (Wardlaw).

Some commentators take this proverb at face value. They say the one who blesses with a loud voice early in the morning is simply inappropriate. "The picture (is) of the ostentatious flatterer going at daybreak to pour out blessings on his patron. For any good that he does, for any thanks he gets, he might as well utter curses" (Barnes). "A man doesn't appreciate loud, flattering greetings early in the morning when he is trying to sleep. They are more of a nuisance than a blessing" (MacDonald). "Blessing (i.e., praising or commending) a neighbor is commendable, but not early in the morning. Timing and sensitivity to others who are sleeping are important. The wrong time for the right action causes it to be received as a curse" (Buzzell).

Other commentators claim that the one who blesses with a loud voice early in the morning is selfish. "This salutation of good wishes, the affected zeal in presenting which is a sign of a selfish, calculating, servile soul, is reckoned to him as (a curse) before God and everyone who can judge correctly of human nature, also before him who is complimented in so ostentatious and troublesome a manner, the true design of which is thus seen" (Delitzsch). "He who makes loud and public protestations of acknowledgments to his friend for favors received subjects his sincerity to suspicion. Extravagant public professions are little to be regarded" (Clarke). "Excessive zeal in praising raises suspicions of selfishness" (JFB). "A loud voice and extravagant praises bring sincerity into question. When a man exceeds all bounds of truth and decency, affecting pompous words and hyperbolical expressions, we cannot but suspect some sinister end" (Bridges). "The flatterer, instead of being liked and encouraged, will be disliked, and held at a due distance, as one who is to be suspected of unworthy motives,—one who in praising others is only looking after his own interests" (Wardlaw).

People who bless their friends with a loud voice early in the morning will be considered more of a curse than a blessing.

Proverbs 27:15-16 "A continual dripping on a very rainy day and a contentious woman are alike; whoever restrains her restrains the wind, and grasps oil with his right hand." Verse 15 is similar to Proverbs 19:13, which says, "A foolish son *is* the ruin of his father, and the contentions of a wife *are* a continual dripping." There are five proverbs concerning a contentious wife (19:13; 21:9, 19; 25:24; 27:15-16). The Hebrew word translated "contentious" means "strife, contention, quarrelsome." It comes from the Hebrew verb for "judge."

The backdrop behind this proverb is "the flat, earthen roof of Eastern houses, always liable to cracks and leakage" (Barnes; see comments on 21:9). On "a very rainy day" (Hebrew: "a day of showers," JFB), the roof leaks. "The continual drip, drip, drip of water through the roof on a very rainy day has this in common with a scolding, nagging wife. They are both enough to 'drive a person up the wall!'" (MacDonald). "Like water dripping on a rainy day, she is annoying and never stops quarreling" (Buzzell).

Trying to restrain a contentious woman is like restraining the wind or holding oil in your hand. "The point is the impossibility of concealment or restraint" (Barnes). "No matter what you say, she will evade, excuse, blame others—and go right on nagging" (MacDonald). "Trying to constrain her contentious spirit is as impossible as trying to pick up a handful of oil. She is both unsteady and slippery" (Buzzell). "Such a woman cannot be tamed" (JFB). "When wholly unrestrained, she becomes her husband's torment and her own shame" Bridges).

A contentious wife is a constant irritation like a leaking roof on a rainy day, and trying to restrain her is as impossible as trying to restrain the wind or pick up a handful of oil.

Proverbs 27:17 "*As* iron sharpens iron, so a man sharpens the countenance of his friend." Some commentators take the word "countenance" literally as a reference to the face. "Conversation promotes intelligence, which the face exhibits" (JFB). "In the sympathies of friendship, when the mind is dull and the countenance overcast, a word from a friend puts an edge upon the blunted energy and exhilarates the countenance" (Bridges).

Kidner says the word "countenance" "almost equals 'personality' here." He goes on to say that "it can stand for the man himself." Many commentators seem to take it figuratively with no reference to the face. "Two minds, thus acting on each other, become more acute" (Barnes). "The interchange of ideas among people makes them more acute in their thinking" (MacDonald). "People can help each other improve by their discussions, criticisms, suggestions, and ideas" (Buzzell). "One friend may be the means of exciting another to reflect, dive deeply into, and illustrate a subject" (Clarke).

As a piece of iron is sharpened by rubbing against another piece of iron, so are one's ideas sharpened by interacting with other people.

"Man was framed not for solitude, but for society. It is only as a social being that his powers and affections are fully expanded" (Bridges). "There is a general principle here. It is—that all individual and solitary application has a tendency to languish: whereas social exertion keeps up its life and spirit, by the influence of mutual excitement" (Wardlaw).

Proverbs 27:18 "Whoever keeps the fig tree will eat its fruit; so he who waits on his master will be honored." Fruit in the first line corresponds to honor in the second (Delitzsch). As those who faithfully care for a fig tree reap the fruit, so those who faithfully serve their master will reap honor. Faithfulness will be honored (Bridges).

Barnes says, "As the fig tree requires constant care but yields abundant crops, so the ministrations of a faithful servant will not be without their due reward." "In other words, working well at one's job brings favorable results" (Buzzell). "Diligence secures a reward, even for the humble servant" (JFB).

Those who faithfully care for a fig tree will be rewarded with figs to eat, so those who faithfully serve their boss will be honored.

Jesus said, "If anyone serves Me, him *My* Father will honor" (Jn. 12:26).

Proverbs 27:19 "As in water face *reflects* face, so a man's heart *reveals* the man." The Hebrew text is obscure. Literally translated, it reads, "Like water face to face, so is the heart of man to a man" (Buzzell).

Some commentators say this proverb means: As water reflects the face, so the heart of people reveals who they really are. "As a man sees his face perfectly reflected by the water when looking into it; so the wise and penetrating man sees generally what is in the heart of another by considering the general tenor of his words and actions" (Clarke).

Most commentators, however, understand this to mean that as people see their faces reflected in the water, so they see themselves in others. When we look "in every heart of man, we may see our own likeness" (Barnes). "As you look into a clear pool, you see your face reflected in the water. Even so, as you study other people, you see much that you find in yourself—the same emotions, temptations, ambitions, thoughts, strengths, and weaknesses" (MacDonald). "We may see our characters in the developed tempers of others" (JFB). "Just as in the reflection of the water face answers to face so in another heart we see the reflection of our own" (Bridges). "There are certain principles and feelings in our nature common to all mankind" (Wardlaw).

Just as looking in water (a mirror) reflects our face, so in looking at the heart of others we see a reflection of our own heart.

Parents know how other parents feel. Widows know how other widows feel.

Proverbs 27:20 "Hell and Destruction are never full; so the eyes of man are never satisfied." The Hebrew word translated "hell" is *sheol*, which means "underworld" (BDB), "the grave" (Buzzell), "the world of the dead" (Barnes; Wardlaw). Destruction is death. In this proverb, death and the grave are personified. They have an insatiable appetite. They receive countless millions and yawn for more (Bridges).

The lust of the eyes is that craving of that which it sees. "The lust of power, riches, and splendor is never satisfied. Out of this ever unsatisfied desire spring all the changing fashions, the varied amusements, and the endless modes of getting money, prevalent in every age, and in every country" (Clarke). "The insatiable eyes of desires are always requiring new gratification" (Bridges).

"The desires of men are insatiable. They set their hearts on some particular object and long for its attainment. They fix in their mind some point of advancement in the acquisition of the world—some measure of wealth or of power which they think, if once realized, would satisfy them to the full. They get what they want, but they still long as before. There is ever something unattained. Having gained the summit of one eminence, they see another above it; as they mount, their views widen, their conceptions and wishes amplify, and still more is required to fill them" (Wardlaw).

As death and the grave have an insatiable appetite that is never full, people with the lust of the eye that craves what they see are never satisfied.

Some people shop until they drop and the next day go shopping again. They fill their lives with things and are never satisfied.

Russian author Leo Tolstoy told of a farmer who had a lust for more and more land. Finally, he heard of cheap land among the Bashkirs. He sold all he had, made a long journey to their territory, and arranged a deal with them. He could buy all the land he could walk around in one day for one thousand rubles. The next morning, he set out, walked far in one direction, and then turned left. He made many detours to include extra areas of good soil. By the time he made his last turn, he realized he had gone too far. He ran as fast as possible to get back to the starting point before sunset. Faster and faster, he ran, finally staggered, and fell across the starting point just as the sun set. He lay there dead. They buried him in a small hole, all the land he needed (Tolstoy, as told by Arthur G. Gish, cited by MacDonald).

The solution is to be satisfied with the Lord (Heb. 13:8). As the song says, "Turn your eyes upon Jesus. Look full in His wonderful face, and the things of earth will grow strangely dim in the light of His glory and grace." The soul is satisfied, having found something better.

Proverbs 27:21 "The refining pot *is* for silver and the furnace for gold, and a man *is valued* by what others say of him." The first line of this proverb is identical to Proverbs 17:3. Some commentators take this proverb to mean that as fire purifies silver and gold, so people should purify praise "from all the alloy of flattery and baseness with which it is too probably mixed up" (Barnes; see MacDonald). The most common explanation is that silver and gold are tried by fire, so people are tried by praise (NASB; NIV).

"Praise tests a person in a similar way (as silver and gold) in that his reaction to it shows what he is really like. If he gloats over it, he shows himself to be arrogant; he 'knows' he is good. But if he modestly accepts the praise, he shows humility" (Buzzell). "A man is tested by how he reacts to praise. Does it go to his head and ruin him, or does he accept it calmly and humbly?" (MacDonald). "A man's heart (is tried) by the praise he receives. If he feels it not, he deserves it; if he is puffed up by it, he is worthless" (Clarke). "Praise tests character. Vain men seek it; weak men are inflated by it; wise men disregard it, etc." (JFB).

Pointing out that Proverbs 17:3 says the Lord tries the heart, Kidner says this proverb shows one of the ways He does so. Bridges agrees, adding that praise is the "most searching furnace."

<u>As refiners put silver and gold in the furnace to test them, so people are tried by praise.</u>

Proverbs 27:22 "Though you grind a fool in a mortar with a pestle along with crushed grain, *yet* his foolishness will not depart from him." "The mortar is a bowl-shaped object. The pestle is a short, thick rod with a globular end and is used for pounding or pulverizing things in the mortar. You have probably seen a mortar and pestle on display in a drug store." It was used to "separate the wheat from the chaff" (MacDonald).

There are three different words for a fool in Proverbs. According to Buzzell, the one that appears in this proverb means to be "arrogant, hardened." Kidner says it suggests "stupidity and stubbornness" (Kidner, p. 41). Solomon says, "Fools despise wisdom and instruction" (1:7).

The point of this proverb is that you can separate wheat from the chaff by pounding wheat, but no amount of pounding will separate a fool from his folly. "Folly has become to the fool as a second nature, and he is not to be delivered from it by the sternest discipline, the severest means that may be tried" (Delitzsch). "All discipline, teaching, experience seem to be wasted on him" (Barnes). "Folly is too much a part of a fool to take it from him" (MacDonald). "A fool and his folly are so inseparable that if he is punished repeatedly, like grinding… grain with a pestle, he still remains foolish" (Buzzell). "No parental admonitions and chastisements,—no pains and penalties of human infliction,—no divine judgments,—will radically and permanently change the heart" (of a fool) (Wardlaw).

<u>By pounding wheat, the wheat can be separated from the chaff, but no amount of pounding will separate a fool from his folly.</u>

Pointing out that "foolishness *is* bound up in the heart of a child; the rod of correction will drive it far from him," Kidner says that "unless it is knocked out of him early, (foolishness) is virtually ineradicable" (Kidner, p. 41).

Proverbs 27:23-27 "Be diligent to know the state of your flocks, *and* attend to your herds; for riches *are* not forever, nor does a crown *endure* to all generations. *When* the hay is removed, and the tender grass shows itself, and the herbs of the mountains are gathered in, the lambs *will provide* your clothing, and the goats the price of a field; *you shall have* enough goats' milk for your food, for the food of your household, and the nourishment of your maidservants." Proverbs 27:23-27 consists of five verses that are "a brief treatise on life in an agricultural society" (Buzzell).

The rancher/farmer is urged to be diligent in tending his livestock (27:23; 24:30-34 are five verses that discuss the consequences of laziness). The reason for the attention (see "for" at the beginning of verse 24) is riches do not last forever and even a royal crown does not last to all generations. In other words, riches and royalty are contrasted with livestock that multiply through their offspring (Barnes; Buzzell). When properly cared for, livestock are "multiplied and continued from generation to generation" (Clarke). Livestock are "a more permanent form of wealth" (Bridges).

Furthermore, when the hay is harvested and the lambs are fed, they provide clothing (27:25-26a). On top of that, the goats will provide enough money to buy an additional field (23:26b) and enough goat's milk for the whole household, including the servants (23:27).

In short, the rancher/farmer should be diligent to care for his flocks and fields because they are a better investment than many other things. Beyond the rancher/farmer, the point is that it is "important to care for one's resources, to work hard, and to recognize God's provisions through nature" (Buzzell).

<u>As the rancher/farmer should be diligent in taking care of his resources that last from generation to generation, we should give attention to what will last: the permanent, not the passing; the eternal, not the temporal.</u>

Lessons learned from this passage: Be diligent. Pay attention (see "know" in verse 23). Work hard. Put your time and effort into that which will last from generation to generation, such as supporting some work of the Lord.

Proverbs 28

Proverbs 28:1 "The wicked flee when no one pursues, but the righteous are bold as a lion." The first half of this proverb assumes that wicked people have a guilty conscience (Delitzsch; JFB; MacDonald; Buzzell; et al.). Because of their wicked conscience, the wicked flee "even when no external danger threatens." They "run from imagined pursuers" (Buzzell). They fear getting caught. They "jump at the slightest noise;" they "drive with one eye on the rearview mirror" (MacDonald). They are constantly looking over their shoulder (see Kidner).

The assumption of the second half of this proverb is that the righteous do not have a guilty conscience (Bridges; Wardlaw; MacDonald; Clarke, et al.). Because of their clear conscience, they remain "even where external danger really threatens" (Delitzsch). They are fearless (Bridges). They are courageous as a lion because they feel "strong in God, and (feel) assured of (their) safety through Him" (Delitzsch; see Rom. 8:31). Since "God gives them courage; they have no fear of reprisal from wrongdoing" (Buzzell).

<u>Wicked people flee when there is no need to do so, but the righteous stand their ground and are as bold as a lion.</u>

An innocent conscience inspires confidence (Wardlaw) and courage.

Proverbs 28:2 "Because of the transgression of a land, many *are* its princes; but by a man of understanding *and* knowledge right will be prolonged." The transgression spoken of in this verse is not just of an individual's transgression toward God; it is the "transgression of a land." Commentators render it "rebellion." When there is rebellion in the land, there are many rulers, meaning there is a frequent change in rulers (Delitzsch; Barnes; MacDonald). "Rebellion in a nation results in turnover of leadership. For example, the Northern Kingdom had many rulers, 20 kings in nine dynasties" (Buzzell). "Anarchy producing contending rulers shortens the reign of each" (JFB).

On the other hand, if the ruler is a man of understanding and knowledge, righteousness will prevail for a long time. There is political stability where there is a wise ruler (Barnes; MacDonald).

<u>Rebellion results in a frequent change of rulers, but wise rulers produce political stability.</u>

Paul says, "Therefore I exhort first of all that supplications, prayers, intercessions, *and* giving of thanks be made for all men, for kings and all who are in authority, that we may lead a quiet and peaceable life in all godliness and reverence" (1 Tim. 2:1-2).

Proverbs 28:3 "A poor man who oppresses the poor *is like* a driving rain which leaves no food." You would think that poor people would understand poverty and thus be kind to the poor. This proverb speaks of poor people oppressing poor people! When poor people oppress poor people, it is like a driving rain that destroys the crops instead of nourishing the crops. Sweeping rains were frequent, "sometimes carrying flocks, crops, and houses away with them" (Clarke). In other words, when it comes to oppression, the poor are harder on the poor than the rich. They are "the worst oppressors of all, plundering them to their last morsels" (Barnes). "A poor man who rises to a position of wealth and power is often more oppressive on the poor than people from a higher income level would be" (MacDonald).

Bridges says, "A poor man suddenly raised to power, instead of sympathizing with grievances familiar to his former recollections, is usually pre-eminently distinguished by selfishness." He goes on to say, "Some of the Rulers in the French Revolution were raised from the lowest ranks. And their oppression was indeed a sweeping rain, leaving no food in fertile districts."

<u>When poor people oppress poor people, they are really hard on them, like a driving rain that harms the crops.</u>

Jesus told a parable that illustrates this proverb. He said, "Therefore, the kingdom of heaven is like a certain king who wanted to settle accounts with his servants. And when he had begun to settle accounts, one was brought to him who owed him ten thousand talents. But as he was not able to pay, his master commanded that he be sold, with his wife and children and all that he had, and that payment be made. The servant therefore fell down before him, saying, 'Master, have patience with me, and I will pay you all.' Then the master of that servant was moved with compassion, released him, and forgave him the debt. But that servant went out and found one of his fellow servants who owed him a hundred denarii; and he laid hands on him and took *him* by the throat, saying, 'Pay me what you owe!' So his fellow servant fell down at his feet and begged him, saying, 'Have patience with me, and I will pay you all.' And he would not, but went and threw him into prison till he should pay the debt" (Mt. 18:23-30).

Jesus told this parable in response to a question Peter had asked. "Then Peter came to Him and said, 'Lord, how often shall my brother sin against me, and I forgive him? Up to seven times?' Jesus said to him, 'I do not say to you, up to seven times, but up to seventy times seven'" (Mt. 18:21-22). Then Jesus told the parable.

Now hear the rest of the story. After Jesus told the parable, He said, "So when his fellow servants saw what had been done, they were very grieved, and came and told their master all that had been done. Then his master, after he had called him, said to him, 'You wicked servant! I forgave you all that debt because you begged me. Should you not also have had compassion on your fellow servant, just as I had pity on you?' And his master was angry and delivered him to the torturers until he should pay all that was due to him. So My heavenly Father also will do to you if each of you, from his heart, does not forgive his brother his trespasses" (Mt. 18:31-35).

Don't be so hard on others. Consider what God has done for you.

Proverbs 28:4 "Those who forsake the law praise the wicked, but such as keep the law contend with them." Lawbreakers praise lawbreakers. MacDonald suggests that those who throw off the restraints of God's Law often praise the wicked "in an attempt to justify themselves." At any rate, "Wrongdoers encourage one another" (JFB).

Law-keepers contend with lawbreakers. The Hebrew word translated "contend" means "to be stirred up, to engage in strife." Delitzsch says the law-keepers are "aroused against" the lawbreakers; they are deeply moved by their conduct. They cannot remain silent and let their wickedness go unpunished." Law-keepers "speak out for the cause of righteousness'" (MacDonald).

<u>Lawbreakers praise lawbreakers; law-keepers contend with lawbreakers.</u>

Proverbs 28:5 "Evil men do not understand justice, but those who seek the LORD understand all." People who are evil become confused concerning morality (Delitzsch). "By refusing to practice it (justice), they lose the power to understand it" (MacDonald). When people disobey the Lord, their sense of what is right is perverted; they find it difficult to even understand justice (Buzzell). They have no true standard of right and wrong (Bridges). Wickedness corrupts "a man's reasoning, gives him false principles, and (an) evil measuring of things (Taylor, cited by Bridges). Their conscience loses its discernment (see Wardlaw).

Those who seek the Lord see things from His perspective and, consequently, understand what is moral and what is not. They have discernment (MacDonald). They have a keen sense of justice (Buzzell). "All things are plain to them; both the truths and precepts of God" (Wardlaw).

<u>Evil people lose an understanding of justice, but those who seek the Lord understand all that pertains to justice.</u>

Men love darkness rather than light because their deeds are evil (Jn. 3:19). Evil people call darkness light and light darkness. They call evil good and good evil (see Isa. 5:20).

Proverbs 28:6 "Better *is* the poor who walks in his integrity than one perverse *in his* ways, though he *be* rich." This proverb is similar to Proverbs 19:1. In Proverbs 19:1, the perverse man is "perverse in his lips and is a fool." In this proverb, the perverse are living perverse lives.

The Hebrew word translated "integrity" means "completeness, integrity, moral innocence." It has been explained as "clean, honest" (MacDonald), "honest, blameless, morally whole" (Buzzell). People who live lives with integrity do not pretend to be moral; they are moral.

The Hebrew word rendered "perverse" means "twisted, perverted, devious." It has been explained as "crooked" (Kidner) and "falsehood" (Delitzsch). Perverse people pretend to live good lives, but they are deceivers who live evil lives (Delitzsch). They pretend to be living a good life while all the time practicing deceit and treachery (MacDonald).

Thus, it is better to be poor and honest than to be rich and wicked (Buzzell).

<u>It is better to be poor and live a moral life than to be rich and live a morally perverted life, pretending to live a morally good life while actually living a morally wicked life.</u>

Bridges puts it like this: "A man may walk in his uprightness and yet be poor. He may be perverse in his ways and be rich. And yet the poor man, with all his external disadvantages, is really better, more honorable, more happy, (and) more useful than the rich with all his earthly splendor."

Wardlaw makes an interesting suggestion. He says, "The sentiment *may be* understood of the poor man who remains poor because he will not have recourse to any improper means for bettering his condition, and to the rich man who by such means has made his wealth" (Wardlaw, italics added). Then he asks, "Who is better, the man who forfeits wealth for principle or the man who sacrifices principle for wealth?" He also says, "But the sentiment may be taken generally, and was probably so meant by Solomon, as referring to the poor good man and the ungodly rich man. He is better in real excellence and estimableness of character. He is better in regard to his influence in society."

Righteousness is better than riches in this life and certainly before the Judgment Seat of Christ.

Proverbs 28:7 "Whoever keeps the law *is* a discerning son, but a companion of gluttons shames his father." The discerning son is a law-keeper. The law here is the law of God (Wardlaw). The second half of this proverb implies that the law-abiding son brings joy to his father (Buzzell).

A son who lacks discernment is a companion of "gluttons." The Hebrew word translated "gluttons" means "worthless, make light of, squander, insignificant." It is used of gluttony. Delitzsch say it refers to people who "squander their means and destroy their health." "Associating with gluttons is foolish and shows lack of insight, for it can start a person on the path of drunkenness, laziness, and, ironically, even poverty" (Buzzell). Bridges puts it like this: "The depraved son bent upon his own gratification chooses the companionship of the ungodly and shortly becomes one with them!"

<u>A discerning son keeps the law and delights his father, but a son who lacks discernment keeps company with worthless people and disgraces his father.</u>

A word to parents: "Let us more diligently, more prayerfully, cultivate that wise and holy training of our children, which is God's appointed ordinance; and which however long or severely he may try our faith he will not fail to honor in his own best time" (Bridges).

A word to sons (and daughters): Don't be dumb. When choosing companions, use discernment.

Proverbs 28:8 "One who increases his possessions by usury and extortion gathers it for him who will pity the poor." The Mosaic Law forbids one Hebrew from charging usury (interest) to another Hebrew (Lev. 25:35-37), like a doctor charging "his own children for treatment" (Kidner). The Hebrews could, however, charge Gentiles interest (Deut. 23:20).

This proverb talks about *excessive* interest (JFB). Delitzsch explains, "Wealth increased by covetous plundering of a neighbor does not remain with him who has scraped it together in so relentless a manner, and without considering his own advantage; but it goes finally into the possession of one who is merciful towards the poor." Buzzell puts it like this, "A person who charged exorbitant interest of others and thus became rich would eventually lose his wealth which would be distributed to the poor."

<u>Those who gain wealth by charging excessive interest gather wealth that will someday go to people who pity the poor.</u>

Implications of the proverb include: "Ill-gotten gains do not prosper" (Barnes). "Covetousness is a curse" (Bridges). "God's providence directs the proper use of wealth" (JFB). "Justice eventually overtakes injustice" (Buzzell).

Proverbs 28:9 "One who turns away his ear from hearing the law, even his prayer *is* an abomination." In Proverbs 15:8, "the sacrifice of the wicked *is* an abomination to Jehovah." Here prayer is an abomination. The Hebrew word translated "abomination" means "repugnant, abhorrent, disgusting." When the disobedient pray, their prayer is disgusting to the Lord.

It is not only the evil that people do, but even their "apparent good" is an abomination to God (Delitzsch). If people do not hear God's Word, God not only does not hear their prayer, their prayer is hateful to Him (MacDonald).

<u>When those who do not hear the Word, and, therefore, do not obey it, pray, their prayers are repugnant to the Lord.</u>

Those who pray must first obey.

> I may as well kneel down
> And worship gods of stone
> As offer to the Living God
> A prayer of words alone.
>
> —*John Burton*

Proverbs 28:10 "Whoever causes the upright to go astray in an evil way, he himself will fall into his own pit; but the blameless will inherit good." Some people lead upright people into evil, causing them to go astray. Perhaps this is done by deception (Delitzsch). The success of the deceiver is suicidal (Barnes). They fall into the destruction they prepared for others (Delitzsch). As Proverbs 26:27 says, "Whoever digs a pit will fall into it, and he who rolls a stone will have it roll back on him." The upright deserve better treatment; the fact that the tempter did this to someone who is upright, heightens his guilt (Delitzsch).

On the other hand, the blameless, those who "refuse to be victimized by solicitations to sin" (MacDonald) will avoid the pit and will "inherit good." The Hebrew word translated "good" means "a good thing, benefit, welfare," even "happiness."

<u>Those who cause the upright to sin are destroyed by the destruction they plan for others, but the blameless, who do not follow the tempter, will be enriched.</u>

Proverbs 28:11 "The rich man *is* wise in his own eyes, but the poor who has understanding searches him out." The rich and the poor are contrasted in Proverbs 10:15 and in Proverbs 28:6.

People who are rich tend to think they are clever, priding themselves on their financial acumen; they confuse riches and wisdom (MacDonald). In their self-delusion, they think they are smart (see Delitzsch). People who are "purse-proud" put the weight of their purse into every word they utter (Wardlaw).

People who are poor, but have understanding, can see through the conceited rich. Buzzell puts it like this: "A discerning poor person can see through the pretentious facade of a conceited rich person who thinks he knows it all."

Wardlaw's comments on the poor in this proverb are insightful. Here is an edited version of what he has to say: Many poor people are blessed with sound judgment. They discern the true character of the proud rich. They see that wisdom and wealth do not always go together; "that a full purse is quite compatible with an empty head." They see that people's wisdom is not to be estimated by their opinion of themselves. They see abundant reasons for not making the rich an example to imitate.

<u>Rich people tend to think they are smart, but discerning poor people see through such conceited rich people.</u>

Commenting on this proverb, commentators have concluded: "Having money does not mean a person is wise" (Buzzell). "Wisdom is a gift not depending on any earthly possession" (Delitzsch). "Wealth blunts, poverty sharpens, the critical power of intellect" (Barnes). It is Wardlaw who puts this proverb in perspective. He reminds us that there are rich people who are humble and poor people who are conceited. He is right, of course. Proverbs are not absolute laws; there can be an exception to a proverb.

Proverbs 28:12 "When the righteous rejoice, *there is* great glory; but when the wicked arise, men hide themselves." The phrase "when the wicked arise" is repeated in Proverbs 28:28 and the point of this proverb is similar to Proverbs 29:2.

The Hebrew word translated "rejoice" means "rejoice, exalt." The first part of this proverb is talking about the righteous being exalted to power. Some translations render the opening words "when the righteous triumph" (NASB; NIV). Commentators say: "When the righteous rise to power" (MacDonald), "when a righteous leader rules a nation" (Buzzell), "when the righteous are "put at the head of civil affairs" (Clarke), etc. In contrast to the first half of this proverb, the second half says "when the wicked arise." The Hebrew word rendered "arise" was used of "elevation to places of power" (Wardlaw). Thus, this proverb talks about righteous versus wicked rulers.

When the righteous rule, there is glory. Glory has been taken to mean "men array themselves in festive apparel and show their joy conspicuously" (Barnes), "bright prosperity is increased" (Delitzsch), "there is great elation" (NIV), "the people are happy, (Prov. 11:10), for there is order (Prov. 28:2) and justice" (Buzzell),

When the wicked rise to power, people hide themselves. They are discouraged, intimidated, and fearful (Wardlaw). "They shrink and cower for fear" (Barnes; also MacDonald). Thus, they "try to escape a wicked rule" (JFB).

<u>When the righteous rule, the people are happy, but when the wicked rise to power, the people hide in fear.</u>

"When the wicked arise, men hide themselves; but when they perish, the righteous increase" (28:28). "When the righteous are in authority, the people rejoice; but when a wicked *man* rules, the people groan" (29:2).

Proverbs 28:13 "He who covers his sins will not prosper, but whoever confesses and forsakes *them* will have mercy." The Hebrew word translated "cover" means "cover, clothe, conceal." People conceal their sins from *themselves* by putting them out of mind, "banishing (them from) all serious thoughts" (Bridges), and using "self-deceiving excuses" (Delitzsch). People conceal their sins from *others* by refusing to acknowledge them, denying them, and lying about them. They also clothe themselves with good deeds to hide their sins from people. People cannot conceal their sins from *God*. Fig leaves do not work with Him.

People who do not properly deal with their sins do not prosper. "Hiding sin does not pay off" (Buzzell). "The door of access to God is barred. The covering of the disease precludes the possibility of the cure" (Bridges). "Sin buried is sin kept" (Kidner).

People who properly deal with their sins confess them (1 Jn. 1:9) and forsake them. Those who do that find mercy.

Bridges points out, "The contrast is not between great sins and small, but between sins covered and sins confessed and forsaken. Who covers the smallest sin, shall not prosper. Who confesses and forsakes the greatest shall find mercy."

<u>Those who conceal their sins do not prosper, but those who admit they have sinned and forsake their sin will find mercy.</u>

As theologians point out, there are two kinds of forgiveness, judicial and parental. When people recognize they are sinners and trust Jesus Christ, who died for sin and rose from the dead, they are forgiven the penalty of sins, which is death; that is judicial forgiveness. At that point, God declares them saints. But saints still sin. That is where Proverbs 28:13 comes into practice. "If we (believers) confess our sins, He is faithful and just to forgive us our sins" (1 Jn. 1:9). That is God's parental forgiveness.

Proverbs 28:14 "Happy *is* the man who is always reverent, but he who hardens his heart will fall into calamity." The Hebrew word translated "reverent" means "dread, be in dread, in awe" (see "fears" in NASB; NIV).

Who or what is feared? The NIV adds the words "the Lord," but those words are not in the Hebrew text (see also Wardlaw; Clarke; JFB). The highly respected Hebrew lexicon by Brown, Driver, and Briggs (BDB) suggests the meaning here is deeply dreading sin. Delitzsch says this proverb is talking about "anxious concern with which one has to guard against the danger of evil coming upon his soul; sin is the object, for while the truly pious is one who 'fears God,' he is at the same time one that 'fears evil.'" Buzzell concludes this refers to "fear or dread of the consequences of sin."

Those who fear falling into sin are happy. The comparison in the second half of the proverb implies that the reason they are happy is that they do not fall into trouble.

Those who harden their hearts fall into calamity. The Hebrew word translated "hard" means "hard, severe, stubborn." It is used figuratively of obstinacy (BDB). The comparison with the first half of this proverb indicates this is stubbornness concerning sin. Some people will not listen to the warnings in the Word. They steel their hearts against it (Delitzsch). They make themselves "insensible to sin, and so will not repent" (JFB). They are brazen (Kidner). The Hebrew word translated "calamity" means "evil, distress, misery, injury, calamity." Obstinate people fall into sin and misery (Barnes).

<u>Those who fear the consequences of sin are happy, but those who are stubborn about sin fall into it and are miserable.</u>

Proverbs 28:15 "*Like* a roaring lion and a charging bear *is* a wicked ruler over poor people." In this chapter, the wicked ruler is introduced in verse 12. A wicked ruler is a selfish tyrant, who is "intoxicated with power" (Wardlaw). For him, there is no "Higher Power." He fancies that the people under his rule are made for him; he is "a brutal monster without principle, and without heart" (Wardlaw).

Pity the poor under such rule. They have no resources to feed this hungry beast. So he roars at them like a roaring lion about to pounce on his prey. The roar terrorizes the weak and helpless poor. He charges them like a hungry bear. The charge traumatizes the defenseless poor. Such a ruler is cruel (JFB; Buzzell) and inhumane (MacDonald). "Resistance kindles his unfeeling heart into savage fury;" the poor might as well live among "the savage wild beasts of the forest" (Bridges). Because the poor do not fill his treasures, "he grinds, oppresses, and wastes them" (Wardlaw). He is an "insatiable oppressor" (Pool). No wonder they hide (28:12).

<u>A wicked ruler roars like a hungry lion and charges, like a hungry bear at the poor people who are not able to satisfy his hunger.</u>

Proverbs 28:16 "A ruler who lacks understanding *is* a great oppressor, *but* he who hates covetousness will prolong *his* days." Kidner calls a ruler without understanding a "mindless" tyrant. Based on the contrast in the second half of the proverb, the ruler who lacks understanding is a covetous person and since "covetousness often produces oppression" (JFB), mindless rulers are great oppressors. A ruler without wisdom seeks to enrich himself at all costs, trampling on others to get richer (MacDonald). He abuses his power for personal gain (Buzzell). He plunders the people (Delitzsch).

Also, the contrast "implies that a tyrannical leader will not live long" (Buzzell). Such a ruler "shortens his life as a man and his position as a ruler" (Delitzsch). In other words, a mindless ruler is stupid and short-lived (Kidner).

On the other hand, rulers who hate covetousness prolong their days. They hate defrauding people and consequently attain old age (Delitzsch). Those who live unselfishly for the good of their people prolong their days (MacDonald). A person who refuses to abuse his power for personal gain will enjoy the blessing of a long life (Buzzell). "A considerate ruler hating covetousness and living only for the good of his people shall usually prolong his days" (Bridges).

Wardlaw elaborates, "He who hates covetousness, who establishes himself in the affections and confidence of his people by justice and mercy, and by every liberal and generous endeavor to promote their best interests, identifying himself with them, making their honor and their happiness his own; he shall prolong his days."

<u>Because rulers who lack understanding are covetous, they are great oppressors who do not live long, but wise rulers hate covetousness and, as a result, live long lives.</u>

As Wardlaw wisely points out, "The maxims here are, in the spirit of them, applicable to all power and influence, and especially to authority over the poor and the dependent."

Proverbs 28:17 "A man burdened with bloodshed will flee into a pit; let no one help him." To say that a man is burdened with bloodshed is another way of saying he is a murderer. He is guilty of willful murder, not just manslaughter (Barnes).

The Hebrew word translated "burdened" means "oppressed." Delitzsch, the German scholar, says it "signifies the anguish of a guilty conscience." The willful murderer, who is oppressed with guilt, flees to a pit. The Hebrew word translated "pit" means "pit, cistern, well" and is used here "pit of the grave" (BDB). Delitzsch suggests that driven by guilt, the murderer "flees and finds no rest, till at last the grave receives him." Buzzell puts it like this: "A murderer's guilty conscience hounds him, tormenting him and causing him to try to escape punishment. His only escape is death."

In the meantime, Solomon says, no one should help the "fugitive" (MacDonald). The Hebrew word translated "help" means "grasp, support." Delitzsch says that no one should support him, or provide any refuge for him, nor rescue him from the arm of justice.

Many commentators agree that "help" means to help the criminal escape justice. "No one should seek to obstruct or interfere with justice" (MacDonald). "One who tries to console or rescue him is out of line; to aid a criminal is wrong" (Buzzell). "Let none give him protection. The law demands his life because he is a murderer; and let none deprive justice of its claim" (Clarke). People "must simply stand aloof and let God's judgments fulfill themselves" (Barnes).

<u>A willful murderer, who is oppressed with guilt, will try to flee until the day he (or she) dies and no one should help him (or her) escape justice.</u>

To aid a fugitive is a crime. Delitzsch goes a step further, saying, "no one should give him any assistance that would save him clandestinely and thereby become a partaker of his sin."

Proverbs 28:18 "Whoever walks blamelessly will be saved, but *he who is* perverse *in his* ways will suddenly fall." The salvation spoken of in this proverb is not salvation from damnation (MacDonald). That kind of salvation is by faith in Jesus Christ, who died for the sins of the world and rose from the dead; it is not by works (Eph. 2:8-9). The Hebrew word translated "saved" means "deliver, deliverance." In fact, commenting on this verse, the Hebrew lexicon says it means saved "from external evils" (BDB). Here salvation is deliverance from damage (MacDonald; see "kept safe" in the NIV).

Those who live blameless lives are delivered from many of the "snares of life" (MacDonald). Proverbs 10:9 says, "He who walks with integrity walks securely."

Those who live perverse lives suddenly fall. The Hebrew word translated "perverse" means "twist, crooked." It is the opposite of living blamelessly. The Hebrew word translated "suddenly" means "in one" (BDB; Kidner; see "at once" in the KJV; "will fall all at once" in the NASB; but "suddenly fall" in the NIV). MacDonald says they "will go down in one fell swoop." One event will cause them to fall and it will be sudden.

<u>Those who live blameless lives will be delivered from many of the dangers and damages of life, but those who live morally crooked lives fall suddenly—all at once.</u>

Those who have nothing to hide have nothing to fear (Kidner).

Proverbs 28:19 "He who tills his land will have plenty of bread, but he who follows frivolity will have poverty enough!" This proverb is similar to Proverbs 12:11, which says, "He who tills his land will be satisfied with bread, but he who follows frivolity *is* devoid of understanding." As in Proverbs 12:11, the contrast is between the industrious and the idle. Here there is also the contrast between plenty of food and plenty of poverty (MacDonald). One is filled with food; the other is filled with poverty (Buzzell). "One shall have plenty of bread and the other plenty of want" (Wardlaw).

The first fellow is a hardworking farmer who diligently works his farm. As a result, he will have plenty.

The second fellow is frivolous. The Hebrew word translated "frivolity" means "empty, vain, and worthless" and is used of unprofitable things (BDB). Because he is "devoid of understanding" (12:11) and "engages in empty, non-productive activities" (MacDonald; 28:19), instead of plenty of food, he will have plenty of poverty.

<u>Those who work have plenty to eat, but those who pursue worthless activities have plenty of poverty.</u>

"The blessing comes not by miracle, to encourage sloth; but in the use of means, to stimulate exertion" (Bridges).

Proverbs 28:20 "A faithful man will abound with blessings, but he who hastens to be rich will not go unpunished." As compared to people who hasten to be rich, faithful people who diligently work are richly blessed. They do not covet wealth (MacDonald).

Those who hasten to be rich will be punished. The fact that they are punished indicates they did something wrong. They hasten to be rich "at the expense of faithfulness" (Bridges). Punished implies "deceit or fraud" (JFB). Delitzsch says they who hasten to be rich are not only "unblessed," they are guilty and, therefore, punished. MacDonald says they are punished because they tried to get rich "quickly by unscrupulous means." Buzzell points out, "Being eager to get rich often leads to devious, dishonest ways resulting in the person being punished either by the courts or by poverty or both."

<u>Faithful people are richly blessed, but those who hasten to be rich by dishonest ways will be punished.</u>

Proverbs 28:22 says, "A man with an evil eye hastens after riches, and does not consider that poverty will come upon him."

Proverbs 28:21 "To show partiality *is* not good, because for a piece of bread a man will transgress." This is the last of six proverbs with the words "is not good" (17:26; 18:5; 19:2; 24:23; 25:27; 28:21). Although stated slightly differently, the first part of this proverb is repeated in Proverbs 24:23.

The first half of this proverb refers to judges and the second half to a bribe (Buzzell). At the time this was written, a "piece of bread" was proverbial "as the most extreme point of poverty" (Barnes). In other words, an unjust judge will accept a bribe "for the most trifling considerations" (MacDonald). "Justice can be so easily perverted" (Buzzell). It does not take much. The "slightest motive" will do (JFB). Imagine being "bribed by a bit of bread" (Moffatt, cited by Kidner).

It is not good for a judge to be partial because of a bribe of any price, yet some judges can be bribed for the most trifling amount of money.

Wardlaw observes that this proverb "assures us, in striking terms, that there is hardly anything that can come before a judge or an arbitrator, in which there may not be some consideration fitted to sway him, if he does not set himself, with decidedness of purpose, against 'respect of persons.'"

Proverbs 28:22 "A man with an evil eye hastens after riches, and does not consider that poverty will come upon him." The Hebrew word translated "evil" means "bad, evil." The Hebrew lexicon also says that in this verse, it means "unkind, vicious in disposition or temper." Delitzsch says it means "the jealous, envious, grudging, and at the same time (a) covetous man." Barnes says, "The covetous temper leads not only to dishonesty but to the 'evil eye' of envy." The evil eye describes a covetous person (JFB). Thus, the expression "evil eye" indicates covetousness with willingness to be evil to get what is desired.

Covetous people, who hasten to get rich by unscrupulous means, do not consider their end. Proverbs 28:20 says, "He who hastens to be rich will not go unpunished." This proverb says such people end up poor instead of rich. They race after riches, "little realizing that poverty will soon overtake them" (MacDonald). Buzzell puts it like this: "Ironically, a person who greedily tries to get rich quickly will end up in poverty, the opposite of his goal."

Covetous people, who hasten to get rich by unscrupulous means, do not consider the poverty that will come upon them.

Bridges makes two observations worthy of note: "The evil eye fixed on earth, can never look above" and "Abraham was rich without haste, with God's blessing."

Proverbs 28:23 "He who rebukes a man will find more favor afterward than he who flatters with the tongue." This proverb assumes that the one who is rebuked will, at some point, hear and heed the needed rebuke.

By this point in the book of Proverbs, Solomon assumes you know who to rebuke and who not to rebuke. Do not rebuke a scoffer. "A scoffer does not listen to rebuke" (13:1). "Do not correct a scoffer, lest he hate you" (9:8).). "He who corrects a scoffer gets shame for himself, and he who rebukes a wicked *man only* harms himself" (9:7). Rather, rebuke the wise. "Rebuke is more effective for a wise *man*" (17:10). "Rebuke one who has understanding, *and* he will discern knowledge" (19:25). "Rebuke a wise *man,* and he will love you" (9:8).

Even if the right kind of person is rebuked, the one issuing the rebuke might not find favor at first. In fact, at first, the one who flatters might receive more favor, but in the long run, the one who delivers a needed rebuke will find more favor than the flatterer.

Bridges says, "Few people have the wisdom to like reproofs that would do them good, better than praises that do them hurt. And yet a candid man, notwithstanding the momentary struggle of wounded pride, will afterward appreciate the purity of the motive and the value of the discovery. He that cries out against his surgeon for hurting him, when he is searching his wound, will yet pay him well and thank him too, when he has cured it."

Wardlaw puts his finger on the pulse of this proverb: "We should not look for immediate confession, or fancy we have failed because our 'rebuke' has at the time produced even anger. Let our friend have the leisure to think, to consider, to cool."

Those who deliver a needed rebuke might not find favor at first, but later they will have more favor than the flatterer.

Proverbs 28:24 "Whoever robs his father or his mother, and says, '*It is* no transgression,' the same *is* companion to a destroyer." This proverb is about a son (see "his") who robs his parents. In this case, perhaps he regards taking what belongs to his parents as "no particular sin because he will, at last, come to inherit it all" (Delitzsch). He says, "It is no big deal."

Such a son may think that robbing his parent is not wrong, but he is no different than being a companion with a destroyer. He, like the destroyer, destroys. He destroys "their (his parents) honorable reputation and peace of mind" (Buzzell). "He who mistreats *his* father *and* chases away *his* mother *is* a son who causes shame and brings reproach" (19:26). To all of that could be added, a son who steals from his parents is not only a destroyer, he is disrespectful, disobedient, dishonest, deceitful, and disgraceful. Shame, shame, shame on you, son, for bringing shame on your parents.

Bridges says, "To rob a stranger, a neighbor, a friend is evil; how much more a father and mother. The filial obligation of cherishing care is broken. Ingratitude is added to injustice. What length of wickedness will such a hardened sinner stop at! Could we wonder to see him the companion of a destroyer?"

<u>The son who robs his parents and says it is not wrong to do so is really no different than being a companion with a destroyer; they both destroy themselves and others.</u>

Proverbs 28:25 "He who is of a proud heart stirs up strife, but he who trusts in the LORD will be prospered." The first half of this proverb is a variation of Proverbs 15:18 and the second half is a variation of Proverbs 16:20 and Proverbs 29:25.

The Hebrew word translated "proud" means "wide, broad." Strong says it means "roomy." Buzzell says it means "large of soul." Figuratively, it can mean either "proud" (Strong; see "arrogant" in the NASB) or "greedy" (BDB; NIV; Kidner). It is translated "proud" in Proverbs 21:4 and, in Proverbs, another Hebrew word is translated "greedy."

Proud people stir up strife. The second half of this proverb implies that proud people do not trust the Lord. Bridges says, "The contrast between the proud and him that trusts in the Lord is very remarkable. It shows that pride is the root of unbelief." The proud trust themselves. They are "self-confident, and hence overbearing and litigious" (JFB). MacDonald suggests they stir up strife "by pushing everyone else aside in a futile race for riches or power or preeminence." Hatred (10:12), wrath (15:18), perversity (16:28), and anger (29:22) can also stir up strife.

Those who trust in the Lord prosper. The first half of this proverb implies that those who trust in the Lord do not stir up strife. They "enjoy the two-fold blessing of abundance and tranquility" (Barnes). God-fearing people succeed "in finding peace and satisfaction" (MacDonald). Wardlaw says those who trust the Lord have "comfort and peace and happiness in all situations; an inward satisfaction, a heart-feast, a prosperity of soul." Luther says faith is a precious thing. It rolls away all disquieting care. Our cause is with him, and we are at rest (Luther, cited by Bridges).

<u>Proud people stir up strife, but those who trust the Lord have peace and prosperity of soul.</u>

Some commentators say this proverb is about being greedy. Buzzell says it refers to those who have "an uncontrolled, avaricious appetite for material things. Because greed is selfish, it results in dissension or strife."

Wardlaw says this proverb refers to people with "aspiring ambition, full of large and grasping desires after the honor, wealth, and power of the world, and thus rendered discontented, haughty, and imperious. These are the men who have been the disturbers of the world's peace, ever restless, dissatisfied, envious, quarrelsome,—unhappy themselves, and the causes of unhappiness to others." He goes on to call them people with a "proud heart." He adds, "They fret and fume and are exasperated by whatever comes in their way. Hence strife—personal, domestic, and national feuds. And their pride is associated with high-minded self-confidence. They look to their own devices, their own resources, and their own power, for success."

Proverbs 28:26 "He who trusts in his own heart is a fool, but whoever walks wisely will be delivered." Those who trust themselves are fools. Their heart is "deceitful and desperately wicked, will infallibly deceive (them)" (Clarke). Those who put their "confidence in a detected and known deceiver; and of all deceivers on earth the human heart is the least to be trusted" are justly esteemed foolish (Wardlaw). Bridges says, "Our confidence determines our state. To trust an impostor, who has deceived us a hundred times, or a traitor, who has proved himself false to our most important interests, is surely to deserve the name of fool." They cast their "anchor inside the boat, and thus will drift incessantly" (MacDonald).

Bridges forcefully describes the foolishness of trusting ourselves. First, he quotes Bishop Wilson: "There is no sin, which a man ought not to fear, or to think himself capable of committing since we have in our corrupt will the seeds of every sin." Then Bridges adds, "None of us can safely presume that his heart may not hurry him into abominations, which he cannot now contemplate without horror. If Eve in a state of innocence, could believe a serpent before her maker; if 'the saint of the Lord' could worship the golden calf; if a 'the man after God s own heart' could wallow in adultery, murder, and deceit; if the wisest of men, and the warm-hearted disciple just referred to, could sink so low—what may not we do? Surely 'all men are liars,' the best of men, when left to themselves, are mournful spectacles of weakness and instability." Bridges concludes, "Yet in the blindness of our folly, we are ever ready to trust again if the Lord prevent not to our ruin."

Those who live wisely do not trust themselves. They trust the Lord (28:25; 22:17-19). Consequently, they are delivered. They "escape dangers to which one is exposed who walks in foolish confidence in his own heart and its changeful feelings, thoughts, imaginations, delusions" (Delitzsch).

<u>Those who trust themselves are fools, who will not be delivered from all kinds of trouble, but those who trust the Lord will be delivered from the snares of life.</u>

Understanding our utter sinfulness helps us to trust the Lord. Again Bridges nails it. He says, "We value than a deep knowledge of our indwelling weakness and corruption. Painful and humbling as it is, it establishes our faith and grounds us in the gospel far better than walking over the mere surface. This study of the heart strengthens the principle of that holy fear, which enables us to walk wisely, and thus delivers us from the evils of a self-confident state. Indeed, in a path where every step is strewed with snares, and beset with enemies, what need of the caution 'Walk circumspectly, looking on all sides' not as fools, but as wise! Sound confidence is proof of wisdom. Let it then be a standing maxim in religion to cultivate self-distrust: never to trust ourselves with our own keeping. We are too weak and, thus, needlessly to expose ourselves to danger. We cannot pray 'Lead us not into temptation' when we are rushing headlong into it, 'Deliver us from evil' when we seem to invite its approach."

Proverbs 28:27 "He who gives to the poor will not lack, but he who hides his eyes will have many curses." Although He is not mentioned, this proverb assumes the Lord is at work. He who gives to the poor will not lack, because "God's blessing reimburses him richly for what he bestows" (Delitzsch). "God will reward those who show mercy to the poor" (MacDonald).

On the other hand, instead of giving to people experiencing poverty in need, some people "hide" their eyes; they turn away, disregarding the poor (Barnes). They look the other way; they walk on the other side of the street. They roll up their car windows at the red light.

God will curse those who hide their eyes when they see the poor in need. In other words, they will have "all kinds of misfortunes" (Delitzsch), many sorrows (MacDonald).

God rewards those who give to the poor in need, but He curses those who disregard the poor in need with many sorrows.

The way to avoid lack is not to hoard money; it is to give to the poor in need! Reason says that you should hold on to what you have to avoid poverty, but reason fails to take God into account. "Covetousness indeed combines with reason to contradict the word of God" (Bridges). Earlier, Solomon wrote, "He who has pity on the poor lends to the Lord, and He will pay back what he has given" (19:17).

The problem with giving money to the poor on the street is that they may buy liquor instead of food. The solution is to take them to a restaurant and buy them a meal.

Proverbs 28:28 "When the wicked arise, men hide themselves; but when they perish, the righteous increase." The first part of this proverb is identical to the last half of Proverbs 28:12 (see also 29:2).

When the wicked rise to a place of political power, people hide themselves "for fear" (MacDonald). "The elevation of the wicked to power drives men to seek refuge from tyranny" (JFB).

When wicked political rulers are overthrown or are out of office, the righteous increase. They do not have to hide; they thrive (Buzzell). "They prosper, multiply, and increase as do plants, when the worms, caterpillars, and the like are destroyed" (Fleischer, cited by Delitzsch). "The power of the wicked even here, however, is but for a moment; and *when they perish*—as perish they will—*the righteous shall increase*" (Bridge, italics his).

When the wicked rise to power, people hide in fear, but when the wicked are out of office, the righteous thrive.

Proverbs 29

Proverbs 29:1 "He who is often rebuked, *and* hardens *his* neck, will suddenly be destroyed, and that without remedy." The second half of this proverb is repeated in Proverbs 6:15.

Some people just do not listen to wisdom, even when they are repeatedly warned. Rather than heed needed wisdom, they harden their necks. "The hardening of the neck is a metaphor derived from obstinate animals who will not submit to the yoke" (*Pulpit Commentary*). The oxen stiffen their necks, refusing the yoke of obedience (see Jer. 27:8). People who stiffen their necks become "stubborn" (Clarke). They "obstinately" refuse counsel (JFB). They put their hands over their ears! They stiffen their necks, harden their hearts (28:14), and steel their wills.

People who repeatedly reject rebuke will be destroyed. The Hebrew word translated "destroyed" means "break, break in pieces." It is translated "broken" in Proverbs 6:15 ("utterly broken to pieces" by JFB). It is used of breaking something like a vase (Judges 7:20).

People who repeatedly reject rebuke will be *suddenly* destroyed. The emphasis of the proverb is on the suddenness of the destruction (Barnes). There will be no time to turn around; it will be too late for that.

Thus, the sudden destruction will come without remedy. A remedy will no longer be available (Buzzell). There will be no "hope of any further opportunity" (MacDonald). They will be beyond remedy, repair, or restoration. The destruction will be "swift and final" (NKJV Study Bible).

<u>Refusal to hear repeated rebuke will result in sudden ruin without remedy.</u>

The door of opportunity to listen to wisdom will not always remain open. Those "who with stiff-necked persistence in sin and in self-delusion" set themselves in opposition to all endeavors to save them, shall one day suddenly be destroyed "without the prospect and possibility of restoration" (Delitzsch). "The people who lived before the flood refused to listen to Noah. The flood came and they were destroyed" (MacDonald). "Pharaoh grew more stubborn under the rod and rushed madly upon his *sudden* ruin" (Bridges, italics his).

There are parents who educate, entreat, encourage, exhort, reprimand, reprove, and rebuke a child to no avail. Those kinds of children will not listen to their parents, peers, or the police. They become more callous and, consequently, more careless, as they speed headlong toward calamity (28:14). Then, suddenly, they find their lives broken into pieces, like a vase fallen on the floor. Look at those pieces on the floor and learn before it is your life. In the words of Moses, "Therefore circumcise the foreskin of your heart, and be stiff-necked no longer" (Deut. 10:16). A circumcised heart is one that obeys.

Proverbs 29:2 "When the righteous are in authority, the people rejoice; but when a wicked *man* rules, the people groan." Proverbs 28:28 is similar. It says, "When the wicked arise, men hide themselves; but when they perish, the righteous increase" and the first half of Proverbs 28:28 is identical to the last half of Proverbs 28:12.

When the righteous rule, the people are happy (Delitzsch). They are "glad because they are more secure and prosperous" (Buzzell). "The robes of honor to *the righteous* are the garments of gladness to *the people*" (Bridges, italics his).

When the wicked come to power, the people sigh (Delitzsch). There is "widespread mourning" (MacDonald).

<u>When the righteous rule, the people are glad, but when the wicked rule, the people are sad.</u>

If the truths of Proverbs 28:12, 28:28, and 29 2 are summarized together, the result is that when the righteous rule, the people are happy (28:12; 29:2) and they thrive (28:28), but when the wicked are in power, the people moan, groan, and hide in fear. "The character of a nation's rulers affects the morale of the country" (MacDonald).

Character counts. When deciding which candidate to vote for, character should be a consideration.

Proverbs 29:3 "Whoever loves wisdom makes his father rejoice, but a companion of harlots wastes *his* wealth." The first half of this proverb is a variation of Proverbs 10:1 and the second half is similar to Proverbs 28:7 (see also 13:20). The son in the first half of this proverb is not only wise, he *loves* wisdom, which indicates he is eager to listen to it, learn from it, and live by it. One of the things wisdom teaches such a son is to avoid prostitutes (2:16; 5:1-14; 6:24-35; 7:1-27). A wise son is a delight to his father and, no doubt, to his mother (see also 10:1; 15:20; 23:15, 24; 27:11).

A foolish son is not only grief to his father; he wastes his father's money on prostitutes (Barnes; Bridges; Buzzell). This proverb speaks specifically about how the foolish son wastes his father's money. Some commentators, however, suggest that there is a general principle here that goes beyond the specific issue of wasting money on prostitutes. They say it applies to a "spendthrift" son (Wardlaw), to a "profligate" son (Barnes), to a "prodigal" son who squanders his father's substance in riotous living (MacDonald). "It is not the loss of the substance, but the loss of the son, that rends with agony the godly parent's heart" (Wardlaw). "The father of a fool has no joy" (17:21).

Sons who love wisdom make their fathers glad, but foolish sons, who waste their father's money on prostitutes, make their fathers grieve.

"Deep indeed is the anxiety—the joy or the sorrow—connected with children" (Bridges).

Proverbs 29:4 "The king establishes the land by justice, but he who receives bribes overthrows it." If a ruler governs with justice, the country is established. He "brings his country to a position of strength" (MacDonald). "Justice brings a nation stability and joy" (Buzzell; see 14:34; 16:12; 29:2; 29:14). The Magna Carta says, "We will sell justice to none" (Magna Carta, cited by Bridges).

On the other hand, if a ruler accepts bribes in making decisions, which means he or she is not ruling justly, the country is overthrown. The Hebrew word translated "overthrown" means "throw down, break or tear down." A ruler "who accepts bribes to pervert justice is undermining the stability of the government" (MacDonald). "A greedy leader contributes to the nation's downfall" (Buzzell).

Rulers who rule with justice establish a strong, stable government, but rulers who accept bribes and who do not make just decisions produce a weak government that will eventually break down.

Again, character counts (see 29:2).

It should be pointed out that some commentators take the word "bribes" to mean taxes. Technically, the Hebrew word translated "bribes" means "contribution, offering." According to Delitzsch, it refers to "a man of gifts," that is, either "one who lets gifts be made to him" or "a man of taxes, meaning one who imposes them." He says, "Both interpretations are possible" and adds, "A man on the throne, covetous of such gifts, brings the land to ruin by exacting contributions; on the contrary, a king helps the land to a good position, and an enduring prosperity, by the exercise of right, and that in appointing a well-proportioned and fit measure of taxation." Buzzell translates "bribes" as "a man of offerings or contributions" and goes on to say, "The Hebrew word for "bribes" usually refers to sacred offerings; here it may refer to taxes." Those who take "bribes" to mean taxes do so, because it is used elsewhere of taxes (Delitzsch cites Ezek. 45:13-16).

So which interpretation is correct? Keep in mind, the Hebrew word rendered "bribes" simply means "contribution, offering." Delitzsch renders the Hebrew text here as "a man of gifts," Buzzell as "a man of offerings or contributions," and Kidner as "man of offerings" (see "gifts" in the KJV, ASV, and RSV). Frankly, both "bribes" and "taxes" are interpretations. Those who explain the Hebrew word translated "bribes" as taxes do so because of the way it is used elsewhere. Those who understand it as a "bribes" do so because of the context of this proverb. For example, Lange argues that since the first part of this proverb is talking about justice, the "man of gifts (bribes)" is naturally the unjust ruler who as Bertheau says "perverts justice from love of gifts'" Kidner says "bribes" literally means "a man of offerings," that is, "one whose interest lies there" and he cites Proverbs 15:27, which is about bribes. "Bribes" ("offerings") is the preferred explanation.

"Your honor, it was not a bribe; it was a political contribution." No joke. A campaign "contribution" can be a bribe. In 2006, Alabama Governor Don Siegelman was convicted of bribery for accepting $500,000 in contributions for a state lottery campaign in exchange for a political appointment. King Solomon understood how bribery works; it is a "contribution."

Proverbs 29:5 "A man who flatters his neighbor spreads a net for his feet." The Hebrew word translated "flatters" means "smooth, slippery" and is used figuratively of the tongue, that is, of flattery (BDB, the Hebrew lexicon). Flatterers are smooth talkers.

Not all flattery is given with the intention to harm, but the second half of this proverb suggests that, in this case, flattery is used to trap someone. As Wardlaw says, spreading a net to trap is only done with mischief in mind. Thus, this proverb is talking about people who heap praise on others, not to please them, but to deceive them and profit from them (Clarke; see also Buzzell). People who use flattery to trap others fall into their own trap. Such a maneuver may work for a while, but eventually, flatterers are caught in the net they spread for others (see 28:10).

People who use flattery to deceive and trap others so they can profit set a trap in which they get caught.

Immoral women (and men) use flattery to seduce (2:16; 7:21).

Proverbs 29:6 "By transgression an evil man is snared, but the righteous sings and rejoices." Evil people are trapped by their transgression. They are "often snared in the net of their own sin" (MacDonald). Once trapped, they are in no mood to sing and rejoice.

If the second half of this proverb is taken apart from the first half, it might mean the righteous prosper and so sing and rejoice (Delitzsch; JFB). If the second half of this proverb is treated as a contrast to the first half, the righteous rejoice because they are not in "danger of falling into the snare" (see Barnes).

"Knox supplies the implicit comparison: 'innocence goes singing and rejoicing on its way'" (Kidner). The righteous are happy because they do not have to fear the consequences of transgression (MacDonald). They live carefree lives because "they need not worry that their actions might boomerang on them" (Buzzell).

Evil people are trapped by their transgression and, consequently, do not rejoice, but the righteous avoid the pitfalls of the evil and, consequently, they can sing and rejoice.

Proverbs 29:7 "The righteous considers the cause of the poor, *but* the wicked does not understand *such* knowledge." The basic meaning of the Hebrew word translated "considers" is "know." That is the way it is translated repeatedly in the Old Testament. It can, however, be rendered "consider" (Judges 18:14). The Hebrew word translated "cause" means "judgment, cause, plea, strife." Consequently, there are two different ways to understand the first half of this proverb.

The first possibility is that the righteous consider the *cause* of the poor. In fact, the Hebrew lexicon says the meaning the Hebrew here is "consider the cause" (BDB). The ASV translates it, "The righteous taketh knowledge of the cause of the poor." In a footnote, the NASB says this statement literally means "knows the cause." Based on the contrast with the second half of the proverb, it is safe to assume that the result of the righteous considering the cause of the poor is knowledge of their situation.

The second possibility is that the righteous consider *justice* for the poor. Bridges says, "The original gives to the Proverb a judicial aspect." Buzzell says, "Righteous people want to see justice rather than oppression extended to the poor" The NASB translates this part of the proverb, "The righteous is concerned for the rights of the poor" and the NIV, "The righteous care about justice for the poor."

In the final analysis, the meaning is more likely the meaning is that the righteous consider the cause of the poor. According to the standard Hebrew lexicon, that is the way it should be translated. Bridges says, "The maxim, however obviously applies more generally to the *considerate regard of the righteous*" (Bridges, italics his). Perhaps the point is that the righteous consider the plea of the poor, or even the struggle of the poor.

Wicked people do not consider the cause of the poor and, consequently, they do not even understand the knowledge of those who do! The wicked are not interested in showing any concern for the cause of the poor (MacDonald). Selfishness, not truth, justice, or mercy, is their standard (Bridges).

The righteous consider the cause of the poor; thus, they know their situation, but the wicked do not even understand the knowledge of those who consider the poor.

Wardlaw says, "Consideration of the cause of the poor is a part of the character of 'the righteous'" and "Disregard of the cause of the poor is part of the character of the wicked; and is itself wickedness." Bridges says, "*Consideration of the poor* is the true spirit of Christian sympathy; putting ourselves as far as may be in their place" (Bridges, italics his). On one of his visits to Jerusalem, Paul discussed justification by faith without the deeds of the Law with leaders there, which probably means the apostles and elders. The leaders agreed with Paul. He reports, "They desired only that we should remember the poor, the very thing which I also was eager to do" (Gal. 2:10). "One's relationship to God shows up in his attitude toward the needy" (Buzzell).

Earlier in this collection of the Proverbs of Solomon, he said, "A righteous *man* regards the life of his animal, but the tender mercies of the wicked *are* cruel" (12:10). Righteous people are sensitive toward the weak, helpless, and poor.

Proverbs 29:8 "Scoffers set a city aflame, but wise *men* turn away wrath." Delitzsch defines the scoffers as those "to whom nothing is holy, and who despise all authority." Clarke says they "contemptuously disregard God's law." Buzzell says they are those who "laugh at moral restrictions." The fact that they inflame a city suggests that they not only disregard God's law, they also despise civil authority.

Scoffers inflame a city. They "inflame the minds of the people against the powers that be" (Bridges). "They create turmoil by arousing tempers, agitating the people, and creating divisions" (MacDonald). "By the dissolution of the bonds of mutual respect and of piety, by the letting loose of passion, they disturb the peace and excite the classes of the community and individuals against each other" (Delitzsch). Mockers stir up trouble, keeping things in an uproar; "these troublemakers get others angry and incite rebellion" (Buzzell).

The wise turn away wrath. They "help calm a city by averting anger" (Buzzell). They "seek to avert discord and promote peace" (MacDonald).

In short, scoffers are trouble-makers and the wise are peacemakers (Kidner). Bridges says, "The one is a public injury; the other a public blessing. The one raises a tumult; the other quell it." He adds, "Proud and foolish men kindle the fire, which wise and good men must extinguish."

Scoffers, those who disregard God's law and despise human authority, can inflame a whole city by arousing anger, but the wise seek to prevent anger and promote peace.

Proverbs 29:9 "*If* a wise man contends with a foolish man, whether *the fool* rages or laughs, *there is* no peace." The Hebrew word translated "contends" means "judge, to enter into controversy." This proverb is about a wise person arguing with a fool.

Notice that the words "the fool" are in italics, indicating that they are not in the Hebrew text. Some old translators supplied "the wise" instead of "the fool" (Jerome; Luther). If the subject of the second half of the proverb is the wise, the meaning is that when a wise man argues with a foolish man, whether *the wise man* uses severity or humor, it doesn't make any difference. Nothing works with a fool. Barnes says, "All modes of teaching - the stern rebuke or the smiling speech - are alike useless with the 'foolish' man; there is 'no rest.' The ceaseless caviling goes on still" (also Clarke; JFB).

Kidner says, "The general sense is clear: there is no arguing calmly with a fool. But it is uncertain whether the subject of line 2 is the wise man (whose tactics are all unavailing) or, as seems more probable, the fool (who will adopt any approach but the quietly objective)."

All major translations supply "fool" instead of "wise" (KJV; NKJV; NASB; NIV; RSV). Most commentators conclude that is the meaning. The point of this proverb is that when the wise argue with a fool, the fool will either rage or laugh and keep on arguing so that there is no peace. The fool "becomes boisterous and laughs, and shows himself incapable of quietly listening to his opponent and of appreciating his arguments" (Delitzsch). "He will never be persuaded, and there will be no peace" (MacDonald).

Barnes describes the situation well: "*If a wise man contends* with the wise, he can make himself understood, and there is some hope of bringing the debate to a good issue. But to *contend with a fool, there is no rest*, no peace or quiet. It will go on without end. He will neither listen to reason nor yield to the argument. So intractable is he, that he will either *rage or laugh;* either vent upon us the fury of an ungoverned temper, or *laugh* us to scorn" (Bridges, italics his).

<u>If a wise person gets into an argument with a fool, the fool may rage or laugh, but he or she will not stop arguing; there will be no peace.</u>

Conclusion: Arguing with a fool and thinking you will get somewhere is foolish. Wardlaw explains that the fool "may often be found abundantly fond of disputation—eager to get into an argument. But there is no comfort or satisfaction in it, no end to it, and no good from it. In all discussions, the one object of the 'wise man' is truth. He will not think of contending for anything else. But the 'foolish man' cares not for this. He is confident he has truth already. He makes nothing but a dispute." Wardlaw goes on to say, "There is no silencing a fool. There is no end to either his heated and impetuous or to his scornful and laughing talk," and "the object of that man is an argument—an argument for the argument's sake; he has the fondness of a fool for fighting."

Proverbs 29:10 "The bloodthirsty hate the blameless, but the upright seek his well-being." The bloodthirsty are those who wish to shed blood; they are murderers (JFB). They hate the blameless. This has been taken to mean the bloodthirsty kill honest people so they cannot testify against them in court (Buzzell).

There are two possible interpretations of the second half of this proverb. Translated literally, the last phrase text reads, "seeks his soul." Thus the second line can mean *the upright seek the well-being* of the blameless (NKJV; NASB; Barnes; Bridges; JFB) or *the bloodthirsty seek to kill* the upright (NIV; Delitzsch; Kidner).

In the Old Testament, "to seek a man's life (or soul) is regularly used as a hostile expression" (1 Kings 19:10; Kidner). In other words, the bloodthirsty both hate and seek to kill.

<u>The bloodthirsty hates and seeks to kill innocent people.</u>

Is anger and hatred the explanation of mass murder? That is a problem in at least some situations.

Proverbs 29:11 "A fool vents all his feelings, but a wise *man* holds them back."

The Hebrew translated "vents" means "go, come out, bring forth words, that is, to speak." The one rendered "feelings" basically means "breath, wind, breath." The Hebrew lexicon says it also means "spirit," as in breathing quickly, "animation, agitation = temper, disposition" and used here of "temper, especially anger" (BDB). Fools talk about all their feelings, especially anger.

The Hebrew word translated "holds" means "soothe, still, stills anger." It was used of stilling the roaring sea. The one rendered "back" means "hinder, back." The Hebrew lexicon says here it means a wise man stills anger when it would break forth." Buzzell says the two words together mean "calms it back," liking stilling a storm, in other words, they keep themselves under control. Wise people control their feelings, especially anger.

The fool lets loose anger, but the wise do not give it unbridled course; rather, the wise hush it in the background, that is, in the heart (Delitzsch). "The idea of allowing anger to break out in an undisciplined manner by saying or doing whatever comes into mind without weighing the consequences, without counting ten, without holding it back and quieting it, without hearing the whole story, is totally wrong" (Adams, cited by MacDonald).

<u>Fools talk about all their feelings, especially anger, but wise people control their feelings, including anger.</u>

Because the Hebrew word translated "feelings" is "spirit," which is used of "mind," some commentators say the meaning in this proverb concerns the mind. For example, Bridges says, "It is sometimes thought a proof of honesty to *utter all our mind*. But it is rather a proof of *folly*. For how many things it would be far better never to speak; indeed to suppress the very thought!" (Bridges, italics his). He adds, "Take care that we speak nothing but the truth. But the whole truth may sometimes be legitimately restrained."

Proverbs 29:12 "If a ruler pays attention to lies, all his servants *become* wicked." If a ruler likes lies, his servants will become like him; they will be wicked. If a ruler takes "the advice of liars, he encourages wickedness in the people around him" (Buzzell). The thought seems to be, "His servants imitate him" (JFB).

Bridges put his finger on the pulse of this proverb: "The influence of the *ruler's* personal character upon his people involves a fearful responsibility. A wicked prince makes a wicked people.... Lies will be told to those that are ready to *hearken to them*" (Bridges, italics his).

Some commentators suggest that the lies the ruler likes are lies about himself! Delitzsch puts it like this: Since the ruler does not wish to hear the truth, his servants "seek to gain his favor by deceitful flatteries, misrepresentations, exaggerations, falsehoods." MacDonald says that if the ruler wants to be "pampered flattered, and comforted by pleasant news, " all his servants will treat him exactly that way. They will lie and flatter."

If a ruler listens to lies, all who serve him become wicked.

On the other hand, if a ruler rewards honesty, it will be encouraged (Buzzell). Hence, Bridges advises "all in authority (to) learn a lesson of responsibility." He goes on to quote English clergyman Robert South, who said, "Many kings have been destroyed by poison; but none has been so efficaciously mortal, as that drunk in by the ear" and he adds, "Massillon well taught his young prince, that the flattery of the courtier was little less dangerous than the rebellion of the traitor."

Proverbs 29:13 "The poor *man* and the oppressor have this in common: the LORD gives light to the eyes of both." This proverb is a variation of Proverbs 22:2, which says, "The rich and the poor have this in common, the LORD *is* the maker of them all."

From a human point of view, there is a difference between the poor and oppressors (MacDonald). They are opposites, morally (Buzzell).

From a divine point of view, the poor and the oppressor "meet on a common level before God" (MacDonald). The Lord gives both "light to the eyes," which means He gives "life" to both (see "O LORD my God; enlighten my eyes, lest I sleep the *sleep of* death" in Ps. 13:3). As Proverbs 22:2 says, the Lord created both of them. Delitzsch says both "owe the light of life to God, the creator and ruler of all things" (Wardlaw; Barnes; Clarke).

Poor people and oppressors are different, but they are alike in that God creates both.

Pointing out that there is one sky overall, Kidner says all have a common origin (Prov. 22:2), a common blessing (Mt. 5:44-45), and a common departure (Job 3:19).

Bridges puts it like this: "Both these classes, so distinct in their relative condition, *meet together* on the same level before God. However, *men* may differ; however, one may oppress and despise, and the other envy or hate; however the poor may be tempted to murmur because of the oppressions of his richer neighbor; however, the rich, by *usury* or unjust gain may take advantage of the necessities of the poor—*the LORD enlightens both their eyes*— 'He is no respecter of persons' (Acts 10:34). Both are partakers of his providential blessings (Mt. 5:45)" (Bridges, italics his).

Wardlaw says there are two lessons here: 1) a motive for the poor to put their trust in Him who is "the God of their life and the length of their days" and 2) a motive for oppressors to consider what they are doing.

Proverbs 29:14 "The king who judges the poor with truth, his throne will be established forever." The king who judges the poor with truth is the ruler who treats the poor "considerately and without prejudice" (MacDonald). He judges righteously.

What is the meaning of "his throne will be established forever"? Some commentators say this means the king's throne will be secure (NIV; Buzzell). Several other proverbs speak of a king's throne being established by righteousness (16:12; 25:5; 29:4). "God blesses rulers who are concerned about the poor and people appreciate such rulers" (Buzzell). "The test of a man in power, and his hidden strength, is the extent to which he keeps faith with those who can put the least pressure on him" (Kidner).

The king who will judge righteously and rule forever is the King of kings (JFB; MacDonald).

The ruler who rules righteously will establish his rule, but the King of kings will judge righteously and His reign will be forever.

Proverbs 29:15 "The rod and rebuke give wisdom, but a child left *to himself* brings shame to his mother." The rod is physical punishment and rebuke is verbal correction. Both forms of parental discipline impart wisdom. Use rebuke first. If that does not work, use the rod (Bridges also warns against using the rod without rebuke). The rod drives foolishness from children (22:15; see also 23:13-14).

Some children are left to themselves without parental discipline and guidance. While both parents are responsible (see "he" in 13:24), the remainder of this proverb says the problem is more the mother than the father in this case. Bridges suggests that only the mother is mentioned because she is the "chief superintendent of the early discipline" and, perhaps, because she is the most susceptible to this error.

A mother's "tender love often degenerates into a fond indulgence" (Delitzsch). Thus, the children are "pampered and indulged" (Barnes). Children who are allowed to do as they please and have whatever they want become unruly (Buzzell). "The restive (unruly) horse, with his rein loosened, full of his own spirit, plunges headlong down the precipice. The child, without government, rushes on under the impetuous impulse of his own will" (Bridges).

Undisciplined children will bring shame to their mothers. Barnes puts it like this: "The mother who yields weakly is as guilty of abandoning the child she spoils as if she cast him forth; and for her evil neglect, there shall fall upon her the righteous punishment of shame and ignominy." This is not to say that undisciplined children do not bring shame to the father, as Bridges points out, "so far as she (mother) yields to mistaken indulgence, she bears the greater share of the punishment."

Bridges also says the shame will be "too public to be concealed;" children left to themselves "will mingle the bitterest cup that man can ever have to drink, and stir up the saddest tears, that ever eyes can have to weep" and "either the child's will or the parent's heart, must be broken. Without wise and firm control, the parent is miserable; the child is ruined."

The disciplines of verbal rebuke and physical punishment impart wisdom to children, but children without discipline bring shame, especially to the mother.

Two verses later, Solomon says, "Correct your son, and he will give you rest; yes, he will give delight to your soul" (29:17).

Bridges applies this proverb to God's children. He says, "God's own children grow wiser under correction. They see their folly and in genuine shame turn from it, blessing him for his rod of faithfulness and love and teaching us the folly of rejecting medicines because they are bitter."

Proverbs 29:16 "When the wicked are multiplied, transgression increases; but the righteous will see their fall." The first part of this proverb "seems almost like a truism" (Wardlaw). Some commentators say the wicked in this proverb are those who are in power. Hence, they say it is when the wicked grow in number *and in power*, that wickedness increases (Delitzsch; Buzzell). MacDonald says the crime rate rises.

As Delitzsch points out, wickedness "carries judgment in itself" so that the righteous will see the wicked cast down from "power and influence." Bridges cites Noah, who saw the death of the wicked in the flood (Gen. 7:23), Abraham, who witnessed the destruction of Sodom and Gomorrah (Gen. 19:28), and Moses, who watched the devastation of the Egyptian army (Ex. 14:30) as illustrations. He also mentions the Babel-builders (Gen. 11:8).

Transgressions increase when the wicked grow in number and power, but the righteous will see their downfall.

Some interesting observations include: "Of course, there are exceptions, but they are the exceptions that prove the rule" (MacDonald). Were it not so, righteousness would be banished from the earth in the process of time. This will account for many of the numerous instances in which whole families fail (Clarke). "This proverb is like a motto to Psalm 12:1-8" (Delitzsch).

Bridges cites Bishop Patrick, who said, "The faithful Minister, conscious of his inability to stem the ever-flowing torrent of iniquity, would sink in despair, but for the assured confidence, that he is on the conquering side; that his cause, as the cause of his Lord, must eventually prevail. Yes—though now sin seems to triumph, and Satan boasts of his victories; yet 'the kingdoms of this world,' with all their vast population, shall 'become the kingdoms of our Lord and his Christ, and he shall reign forever and ever' (Rev. 11:15)."

Proverbs 29:17 "Correct your son, and he will give you rest; yes, he will give delight to your soul." (For similar proverbs on child discipline, see 10:1, 15:20, 29:3.) A few verses earlier, Solomon taught that an undisciplined child is a shame to his mother (29:15). Now Solomon says a disciplined son will bring rest and delight to parents. MacDonald remarks that proper discipline brings rest and delight, "instead of anxiety and heartache." Buzzell states that a disciplined son gives the parents peace and joy because their "son will behave and grow wiser." Discipline now; delight later (Kidner).

If parents correct (properly discipline) their son, he will bring them rest and delight.

Reminding us that the book of Proverbs is not out of date, Bridges expands on this proverb. He observes, "The measure and mode of *correction* indeed must depend upon the age, sex, temper of the child, the character, the aggravation, or the mitigating circumstances of the fault. But let it be, like our gracious Father's discipline, never more than can be borne. Make due allowance for any marks of ingenuous confession. Yet, with a wise application of the principle, there must be no exception to the rule. Different tempers, like different soils, require a corresponding difference of treatment. But discipline there must be; not relaxed in fondness, not pushed on in harshness; but authority tempered with love. If a gentle hand cannot control, a stronger hand must be applied" (Bridges, italics).

Proverbs 29:18 "Where *there is* no revelation, the people cast off restraint; but happy *is* he who keeps the law." The Hebrew word translated "revelation" means "vision, divine communication in a vision, prophecy" (see "vision" in the KJV). In the Old Testament, God communicated to the prophets by giving them a vision (Isa. 1:1). That is why the prophets are called "seers" (2 Sam. 24:7; etc.). In this proverb, "revelation" means the Word of God." First, Samuel 3:1 says, "The word of the LORD was rare in those days; *there was* no widespread revelation." No revelation means no "divine instruction" (Bridges), "no instruction in God's truth" (JFB), no "divine teaching" (Delitzsch). "The law, the prophets and the wisdom literature meet in this verse" (*The New Bible Commentary*, cited by Kidner).

This proverb is about not having the Word of God. Some do not have the Word because they do not hear it proclaimed. Others do hear the Word, but they do not know the Word. To borrow (and slightly change) words from Bridges, their ears are stopped up, their eyes are shut up, their hearts are bound up and they are tied up captives of Satan.

When the Word of God is not known, people cast off restraint. The Hebrew word translated "restraint" means "let go, let loose, lack restraint." "Without God's Word, people abandon themselves to their own sinful ways" (Buzzell). They "are let loose;" they are "left to run wild" (Barnes; MacDonald).

On the other hand, those individuals who keep the law, that is, obey God's Word, are happy. People "are only truly happy when they earnestly and willingly subordinate themselves to the word of God" (Delitzsch). It is not having the Word; it is obeying the Word. It is not hearing the Word; it is doing the Word. Those who trust the Lord will prosper (28:25). As the song says, "Trust and obey, for there is no other way to be happy in Jesus but to trust and obey."

Public morality (see "people'") and personal happiness (see "he'") are dependent on the obedience to the Word of God and on trust in the God of the Word.

<u>When the Word of God is not known, people lack its restraint, but those who obey the Word are happy.</u>

This proverb has suffered preacher abuse. The KJV translates the first part of it as "where there is no vision, the people perish." Preachers use that translation to proclaim, "Where there is no vision on the part of Christians to reach the lost, people perish in their sins." In the first place, "vision is not the "vision" people have of reaching the lost; it is the revelation God gives to the prophets. It is the word of God. In the second place, as Buzzell points out, this proverb "does not refer to unsaved people dying in sin." It is saying that "without God's Word people abandon themselves to their own sinful ways." This proverb is not about winning people to Christ, but there are verses in the New Testament that are (Mk. 16:15).

Proverbs 29:19 "A servant will not be corrected by mere words; for though he understands, he will not respond."

This proverb is obviously about a servant, but an analysis of the rest of the proverb indicates that Solomon does not have all servants in mind (see also 17:2). Solomon is thinking about a stubborn, unresponsive servant. This type of servant has been called "reluctant" (Barnes), "unreasonable" (Delitzsch), "stubborn," "irresponsible" (Kidner), "obstinate, intractable" (MacDonald), self-willed and unsubdued (Bridges).

Such a servant will not be corrected by mere word. Just talking to him will not do. "Oral orders are not always enough" (MacDonald; Buzzell).

The tendency is to think that such a servant does not understand. So more explanation is given, but even though he understands, he will not respond. Some commentators say that he will not respond with words; he will remain silent (Delitzsch; Bridges) and sullen (MacDonald). Others say he will not respond with obedience (Barnes; JFB). Either way, the point is, "He may 'understand' the words, but they produce no good effect" (Barnes).

<u>Some servants are so stubborn that they will not be corrected or respond with mere words or even with an explanation.</u>

So what should be done? When words are insufficient, Buzzell says, "other forms of correction are needed." Bridges suggest, "It were better to dismiss him than to lower our authority and countenance evil by yielding to his waywardness."

This proverb is about some servants, but perhaps it applies to some sons (13:1; 15:5).

Proverbs 29:20 "Do you see a man hasty in his words? *There is* more hope for a fool than for him." The second half of the proverb is repeated in Proverbs 26:12.

"The mouth of the fool pours forth foolishness" (15:2) and "the mouth of the wicked pours forth evil" (15:28). Some people's mouths just pour forth. They have no self-control over their tongue. They speak before they think (MacDonald). They blurt out thoughtless, insensitive remarks (Buzzell).

There is more hope for fools than for people who cannot control their tongues. The book of Proverbs does not hold out much hope for fools. For example, it says, "A fool's mouth *is* his destruction, and his lips *are* the snare of his soul" (18:7; see also 17:10). In other words, the words of fools ensnare them, eventually resulting in their destruction. There is more hope, however, for fools headed to destruction than for people who cannot control their tongues! People with uncontrolled tongues are worse off than fools! (Buzzell).

When you see people who have no self-control over their tongue, remember there is more hope for fools than for them (and is not much hope for fools).

Some people think they are wiser than everyone else. You cannot talk and listen at the same time. If you are always talking or thinking about what *you* will say next, you will never learn anything. There is not much hope for people like that.

Proverbs 29:21 "He who pampers his servant from childhood will have him as a son in the end." The Hebrew word translated "son" only appears here in the Old Testament. Therefore the meaning is not certain (Buzzell; see Kidner for an explanation of the problem with defining this Hebrew word). Most translations and commentators render the Hebrew word "son" (KJV; NKJV; NASB; Barnes; MacDonald; Delitzsch; Clarke; JFB; etc.; the NIV, however, translates it: "If a man pampers his servant from youth, he will bring grief in the end").

The backdrop of this proverb is a master who has not just a servant but a servant with a family (Wardlaw). The master pampers the child of his servant, who is destined in that day to be a servant. This is "clearly a warning to the indulgent master" (Kidner).

If a master pampers his servant's child, when the child grows older, he will expect to be treated as a son. The spoiled child of a servant "will forget his proper position and will soon expect you to treat him like a son" (MacDonald). When he has petted from "boyhood, (he) will claim at last the privilege, perhaps the inheritance, of sonship" (Barnes).

Clarke says, "Such persons are generally forgetful of their obligations, assume the rights and privileges of children, and are seldom good for anything."

Bridges says, "The greatest kindness to servants is to 'give to them that which is just and equal' (Col. 4:1)—*but no more*. Any defect in this rule will be sure to bring (as in the case referred to) future trouble" (Bridges, italics his).

Wardlaw says, "In the Scriptures, everything said on the duties of masters and servants is full of equity, propriety, and kindness. But the most righteous, honorable, and affectionate treatment of a servant must not be considered as implying such indulgence as would prove to the injury of a child or as would even unfit the servant for the situation which he or she is destined to fill, or is actually filling.

The master who pampers his servant's child will end up with an adult who expects to be treated as a son.

In his book *Advancement of Learning*, Francis Bacon's advice for handling servants is: "1. That we promote them by steps, not by leaps. 2. That we occasionally deny their wishes. Sudden elevation induces insolence. The constant granting of their wishes makes them only more imperative in demand" (Bacon, cited by Bridges).

Wardlaw suggests, "It applies to all cases in which persons are brought up in a way that does not accord with the prospects in life that are before them—with the situations they are destined, or are even in providence likely, to fill."

MacDonald applies this to employees. He says, "Undue familiarity in the employer-employee relationship often breeds contempt."

Proverbs 29:22 "An angry man stirs up strife, and a furious man abounds in transgression." The first half of this proverb is a variation of the first line of Proverbs 15:18 and Proverbs 28:25. Some commentators say this proverb is referring to two different people (MacDonald), but most say that both parts are about the same person. Both halves are also describing a general disposition, not a temporary state (Kidner).

Anger is not necessarily sinful. Paul commanded, "Be angry and do not sin" (Eph. 4:26). There is a righteous indignation, but there are angry people who stir up strife. They stir up all kinds of trouble (MacDonald). This is the anger that "quarrels even upon trifles or matters, which a forbearing consideration might have satisfactorily explained" (Bridges). A "hot temper is the cause of many a sin" (Moffatt, cited by Kidner).

People who are furious abound in sin, being controlled by passion instead of wisdom. Quick-tempered people act foolishly (14:17). They have lost self-control, perhaps committing such sins as "cursing or insulting others, misusing God's name, being rude, lacking kindness, being cruel or oppressive, and being proud (Buzzell; Bridges includes blasphemy and even murder). Their furious spirit carries them to extremes (Clarke). People filled with angry passions are prone to excess and prone to find excuses for their excess (Wardlaw).

People who are filled with passionate anger commit all kinds of sins and stir up strife.

Paul commands, "Do not let the sun go down on your wrath" (Eph. 4:26). "The short period of the day is abundantly sufficient to express right motives and to accomplish holy purposes" (Bridges).

Proverbs 29:23 "A man's pride will bring him low, but the humble in spirit will retain honor." Proud people tend to elevated themselves. Ironically, pride actually results in being brought low (Buzzell). "Pride *goes* before destruction and a haughty spirit before a fall" (16:18; see also 18:12). The proud are "universally despised" (Clarke). God hates pride (6:17), "because it influences a person to live independently of Him" (Buzzell).

Humble people are lowly in spirit, but others elevate them to a position of honor (Buzzell). They obtain honor without seeking it, honor before God and before others, which would be of no worth were it not connected with the honor before God (Delitzsch). "Before honor is humility" (15:33; see also 18:12). Best of all, God gives grace to the humble (3:34) and "Blessed are the poor in spirit; for theirs is the kingdom of heaven" (Mt. 5:3, 18:4).

"Whosoever shall exalt himself shall be abased; and he that shall humble himself shall be exalted" (Mt. 23:12; Lk. 14:11; 18:13).

Proud people, who elevate themselves, will be brought low, but those lowly in spirit will be elevated by others to a position of honor.

Conclusion: "Better *to be* of a humble spirit with the lowly, than to divide the spoil with the proud" (16:19).

Proverbs 29:24 "Whoever is a partner with a thief hates his own life; he swears to tell the truth, but reveals nothing." The partner to a thief is the accomplice (Barnes). In this case, the accomplice is put under oath. In other words, he is in court before a judge. He takes the oath, swearing to tell the truth. He has two options. He can tell the truth, or he can lie. There was no "pleading the Fifth Amendment" (MacDonald). Instead of telling the truth, he reveals nothing of what he knows. He lies. What is to be said of such a fellow? He has definitely perjured himself (Buzzell; Kidner). He has no reverence for an oath or for the court (Clarke, who adds, nor fear of God). He is now guilty before the judge (Lev. 5:1), risking punishment (JFB).

While all of that and more may be true, Solomon says such a fellow hates his own life. If he tells what he knows, he will be guilty of thief (see "partner with a thief). By lying, he has now committed two crimes, making things worst for himself. Instead of helping himself, he is hurting himself, which means he hates himself. If he loved himself, he would do what is best for himself, namely tell the truth, take his punishment, and do what is right next time.

If an accomplice in a thief swears to tell the truth and reveals nothing, he hates himself; he is not doing what is best for himself.

Proverbs 29:25 "The fear of man brings a snare, but whoever trusts in the LORD shall be safe." The reason that the fear of man brings a snare is that the fear of man results in refraining from doing what is right or yielding to the pressure to do what is wrong (MacDonald). It results in "one's actions (being) controlled or confined by the person who is dreaded" (Buzzell). Because of the fear of other people, Peter denied the Lord (Clarke). William Gurnall said, "We fear man so much because we fear God so little" (Gurnall, cited by MacDonald).

The Hebrew word translated "safe" means "to be high, to set (securely) on high" (BDB). The idea is being high makes someone unacceptable and unattainable and, therefore, is in a safe place. Kidner says it means "set on high," that is, "beyond man's reach." Those who trust in the Lord are safe and secure from the snares brought on by the fear of man. Trust in the Lord removes intimidation by man (Buzzell). "By the fear of the Lord, one departs from evil" (16:6).

The fear of man results in a snare, but faith in the Lord results in safety.

"If fear makes the giant tremble before the worm, *trust in the LORD* makes the worm stronger than the giant" (Bridges).

Proverbs 29:26 "Many seek the ruler's favor, but justice for man *comes* from the LORD." The first half of this proverb is a variation of Proverbs 19:6 (1 Kings 10:24).

When seeking justice, many seek the favor of earthly rulers. In the first place, to curry favor or influence or to gain justice from a ruler is no guarantee that justice will be done. The real problem with that line of thinking is, it is not the ruler who finally decides the fate of a man (Delitzsch). So, "to trust in the favor of princes is to build upon the sands" (Barnes).

In the final analysis, justice comes from the Lord. "The judgment which will set right all wrong will come from the Lord. It is better to wait for that than to run here and there, canvassing, bribing, flattering" (Barnes). The Lord will make all things right in the end; therefore, trust Him (Buzzell).

When seeking justice, many seek the favor of rulers, but justice comes from the Lord.

Proverbs 29:27 "An unjust man *is* an abomination to the righteous, and *he who is* upright in the way *is* an abomination to the wicked." At this point in the book of Proverbs, the proverbs of Solomon end. The last two chapters contain proverbs written by other people.

The Hebrew word rendered "abomination" means "repugnant, abhorrent, disgusting." It is used throughout the book of Proverbs of things that are repugnant to God (3:32; 6:16; 11:1, 20; 12:20; 15:8, 9, 26; 16:5; 17:15; 20:10, 23; 21:27; 28:9). In Deuteronomy 12:31, it is used of God's attitude toward idolatry and the sacrifice of children.

Unrighteous people are an abomination to righteous people, and the unrighteous feel the same way about the righteous. There is no rapport between the two (MacDonald). There is antagonism (Barnes). "The righteous are so concerned for honesty that they, like God, hate what is dishonest. And the distaste of the wicked for the upright reveals their perverse values" (Buzzell). "Common interests and mutual attraction at various levels may mask this enmity; nothing can mend it" (Kidner).

The righteous and the unrighteous detest each other.

Proverbs 30

Proverbs 30:1 "The words of Agur the son of Jakeh, *his* utterance. This man declared to Ithiel—to Ithiel and Ucal." This verse serves as the title for this chapter (Delitzsch; JFB), which contains the proverbs of Agur. All that is known about Agur comes from this chapter. He was the son of Jakeh; nothing is known about Jakeh. Buzzell suggests that Agur seems to have been humble (30:2-3), observant, and inquisitive (30:5-33; Buzzell; see also Kidner).

The Hebrew word translated "utterance" means "utterance, declaration, revelation." It was used of prophets in an ecstatic state (BDB), that is, "of the utterance of a divine oracle" (Barnes). The words of Agur were delivered by prophecy (Clarke). This material is "divine instruction" (Bridges; JFB).

Agur's words are addressed to Ithiel and Ucal. Nothing is known about them except that they were the recipients of Agur's wisdom. Some commentators suggest that Agur was a teacher and Ithiel and Ucal were his students (Bridges; Clarke; JFB). Wardlaw suggests that what is recorded here may have been in response to questions the students asked.

<u>An unknown (to us) prophet named Agur delivered divine instructions to two of his students.</u>

Bridges reminds us that "it is vain to speculate, where God is silent. Far better is it to give the full interest of our mind and heart to the matter of instruction than to indulge unprofitable curiosity respecting the writers. Our ignorance of the writers of many of the Psalms in no degree hinders their profit to us. We know their author, when the penmen are hidden. It is enough for us to be assured that they were "holy men of God, who wrote '*as they were moved by the Holy Spirit*' (2 Pet. 2:1)" (Bridges, italics his).

We have a word from God delivered through men, but in some cases, we know little or nothing of the mailman. Learn all you can about the mailman, but focus on the mail.

Proverbs 30:2 "Surely I *am* more stupid than *any* man, and do not have the understanding of a man." Proverbs 30:2-4 are a unit. The Hebrew word translated "stupid" means "brutishness." The idea is that to be like a beast means you are dull-minded (Buzzell), stupid in the sense of being ignorant. It is a "confession of ignorance" (Barnes), ignorance of God (Buzzell; see the next verse, which explains this verse in more detail). The psalmist said, "I *was* so foolish and ignorant; I was *like* a beast before You" (Ps. 73:22). Thus, Agur begins with a statement of humility, which is the "proper attitude for anyone who would inquire into the works and ways of God" (MacDonald).

<u>When it comes to the knowledge of God, the humble thing to do is begin with an admission of ignorance</u>.

"Genuine humility is the only path of wisdom. Unless a man stoops, he can never enter the door" (Bridges).

Proverbs 30:3 "I neither learned wisdom nor have knowledge of the Holy One." In verse 2, Agur humbly confesses his ignorance. Now he gives two details that explain exactly what he means. First, he says he has not learned wisdom, an expression that means he had not gone to the school of the wise men (Delitzsch; Clarke; see Amos 7:14-15). Second, he says he did not have knowledge of God. To understand what he means, the context must be taken into consideration (verses 2-4 are a unit). In verse 1, he says he spoke as a prophet, one who receives revelation from God (he knew God). In verse 5, he says, "every word of God is pure" (he knew God's Word). So what does he mean when he says in verse 3 that he had no knowledge of God? Verse 4 indicates that what he is really talking about is that he does not know the name of God. In reference to the next verse, Bridges says what Agur means is that he did not have a revelation of God's name. It would be more precise to say that Agur is saying that he does not have a revelation of the name of God's Son! (see the next verse).

<u>Those in the Old Testament, even those who went to the school of the prophets, did not know the name of God's Son.</u>

The Old Testament definitely says God has a Son. For example, Psalm 2 says, "Yet I have set My King On My holy hill of Zion. I will declare the decree: The LORD has said to Me, 'You *are* My Son, today I have begotten You. Ask of Me, and I will give *You* The nations *for* Your inheritance, And the ends of the earth *for* Your possession'" (Ps. 2:6-8). God declares that He sets His King on Zion. History makes no mention of a king of Israel being anointed in Zion. So this does not refer to David or Solomon. The Messiah, however, will rule the earth from Zion's holy hill. Then the King speaks, declaring that God says, "You are my Son." In other words, this is not just any ordinary representative sitting on the throne; it is the Sovereign's Son. The Heavenly Father has given His Son the nations, yea the whole earth, as His possession and inheritance. This passage cannot be about David because David was never given authority over the whole earth. Ancient Rabbis said this passage is Messianic. So does the New Testament (see Acts 13:33; Heb. 1:5).

Proverbs 30:4 "Who has ascended into heaven, or descended? Who has gathered the wind in His fists? Who has bound the waters in a garment? Who has established all the ends of the earth? What *is* His name, and what *is* His Son's name, if you know?" The context makes it clear that the subject is God. Agur says, "Surely I *am* more stupid than *any* man and do not have the understanding of a man. I neither learned wisdom nor have knowledge of the Holy One" (30:2-3). So when Agur asks the questions recorded in verse 4, he is obviously talking about God (Buzzell). Only God can ascend into heaven and descend from heaven. Only God can gather the winds in His hands, that is, control the wind. Only God can contain the waters, either the clouds or the ocean. Only God can establish the land masses (MacDonald). Thus, the last question is, "What is God's name and the name of His Son?" The Old Testament reveals that God has a Son (Ps. 2). What is not revealed is His name.

"At this point, the riddle has no answer. The OT would answer that 'His name' is the Lord God but did not have a name for His Son. This riddle was to remain unsolved until Jesus answered it for Nicodemus (Jn. 3:13). These verses form one of the most straightforward messianic texts in the Bible" (NKJV Study Bible). "From this verse, OT believers could understand that God has a Son" (MacDonald). Commenting on this verse, Bridges says, "There is a Son in the Eternal Godhead."

"What is his name, and what is his son's name? The speaker seeks the answer to the riddle of the universe in words reminiscent of God's challenge to Job in Job 38:4-9. He seeks God. The question about God's son is peculiar. Greenstone denies that the name applies to Israel or Moses or the Logos but gives no positive suggestion to explain it. Delitzsch suggests that it refers to the mediator in creation, revealed at last as God's Son. He well remarks, 'He would not have ventured this question if he did not suppose that God was not a unity who was without manifoldness in Himself'" (*The Wycliffe Bible Commentary*).

<u>Nature reveals some things about God, but nature does not reveal the name of God or God's Son.</u>

Another suggested interpretation is the notion that the question really has to do with God's nature. "The question, 'What is His name?' asks what His true character is like. The inquiry, 'What is the name of His son?' suggests the question, 'Has He imparted His nature or attributes to any other who may in any sense be called His 'Son'?" (Perowne, p. 180). "Tell me if you know reflects Agur's desire to know the nature of God" (Buzzell). At least that explanation recognizes that the Son is God's Son. Constable thinks that the son is Agur's son and Clarke makes son plural and says the son is "the holy angels, called his saints or holy ones." Waltke argues that the son is the privilege of a student because in the book of Proverbs, son always refers to a student who listens to his father, who is also his teacher (Waltke, *An Old Testament Theology*, pp. 918-919). The context indicates that the subject is God (30:3). So any interpretation that does not conclude that this verse is about God and His Son is ignoring the context.

Proverbs 30:5 "Every word of God *is* pure; He *is* a shield to those who put their trust in Him." This proverb is almost identical to Psalm 18:30. Since this verse and the next one both speak about the Word of God, they form a small unit.

Agur turns from the revelation of God in nature (30:4) to the revelation of God in His Word (MacDonald). The Hebrew word translated "pure" means "smelt, refine, test." The idea is refining a metal so that it is without dross (Buzzell; Kidner). The Word has been "tried. It has stood the trial and no dross has been found in it" (Bridges). The Word of God is without error (Wardlaw; Clarke), flawless (Kidner), infallible (MacDonald; Buzzell).

Agur learned two things from the Word. First, although not stated, clearly assumed, is that he knew God. As Buzzell says, "Man can know God only because He has revealed Himself through the written Word."

Second, from God's Word, Agur learned that when he trusted the God of the Word, God was a shield to him. It is with "the shield of faith with which you will be able to quench all the fiery darts of the wicked one" (Eph. 6:16). "The aim of revelation is to promote trust, not bare knowledge" (Kidner).

<u>Knowing that every word in God's Word is tried, tested, and true, people trust the God of the Word and find Him to be their shield.</u>

Bridges says, "If *every word of God is pure*, take care that no word is slighted" (Bridges, italics his). He adds, "Favoritism, however, is a besetting snare in the sacred study. How few range over the whole Revelation of God! To take a whole view of the universe, we should embrace not only the fruitful gardens but its barren deserts, coming equally from the hand of God, and none of them made for naught. To take a similarly comprehensive view of the sacred field, we must study the apparently barren, as well as the more manifestly fruitful, portions. Meat will be gathered from the detailed code of laws, from the historical annals of the kings, and from the 'wars and fightings'—the prolific results of 'the lusts of men' (Jas. 4:1). The whole Scripture is Scripture, and 'all Scripture is profitable' (1 Tim. 3:16)."

Proverbs 30:6 "Do not add to His words, lest He rebuke you (H3198), and you be found a liar." The previous verse spoke about the words of God. Since this verse and the previous one both speak about God's words, the two verses form a small unit.

Do not add to God's words. Do not mingle God's truth with your "imaginations and traditions" (Barnes) or even your "thoughts and speculations" (MacDonald). God's Word is sufficient (Buzzell). There is no room left for improvement of God's flawless revelation (Kidner). "You can no more increase their value by any addition than you can that of gold by adding any other metal to it" (Clarke).

If people add anything to God's Word, two things will happen. First, they will be rebuked. "God rebukes those who think they can know more of God than what He has revealed about Himself" (Buzzell).

The second thing that will happen to those to add to God's words is they will be found to be liars. Those who add "human speculation to divine revelation" are "often so far off base that God calls them liars" (Buzzell). "God reproves by manifesting its falsehoods" (Barnes). Be sure your falsehood about God's truth will find you out.

<u>Do not add anything to God's words because if you do, God will rebuke you, and you will be found a liar.</u>

In Jesus's day, the Jews added their oral law and traditions to the Hebrew Scriptures. The Roman Catholic Church added apocryphal writings and tradition to the inspired canon. The cults add their own "scripture" to God's sufficient Word.

Peter says believers should desire the sincere milk of the Word (1 Pet. 2:2). The Greek word translated "sincere" means "pure" (see "every word of God *is* pure" in verse 5).

Proverbs 30:7-9 "Two *things* I request of You (deprive me not before I die): remove falsehood and lies far from me; give me neither poverty nor riches— feed me with the food allotted to me; lest I be full and deny *You,* and say, 'Who *is* the LORD?' Or lest I be poor and steal, and profane the name of my God." Proverbs 30:7-9 is unit, a mini-paragraph. Delitzsch calls it a "brief discourse." This is the first of six proverbs in this chapter that contains lists of things ("two things;" 30:7-9, 15-16, 18-19, 21-23, 24-28, 29-31). This unit is the only prayer in the book of Proverbs. There are two requests here: protection from lying and provision for daily needs. The phrase "before I die" means "until I die" (Wardlaw).

The first request is that God would remove falsehood and lies from Agur, the author. "He didn't want to deceive others or to be deceived" (MacDonald).

The second request is that God would give him neither poverty nor riches. Many pray to be delivered from poverty, but not many people pray to be delivered from wealth. Only spiritually-minded people, aware of the temptation involved, would pray such a prayer.

In being rich, the temptation is to forget the Lord ("Who is the Lord?"). "Too often, the more we receive from God, the less he receives from us" (Bridges). In poverty, the peril is to steal and to deny the Lord by saying under oath that you did not do it (MacDonald).

Hence the prayer is to be preserved in the middle state between riches and poverty. In other words, he prayed, "Give me this day my daily bread" (see Mt. 6:11). When he dies, he wants to be able to look back on the life he spent "without the reproaches of an accusing conscience" (Delitzsch). In the meantime, he prays for contentment (Wardlaw).

<u>A spiritually-minded prayer is to ask the Lord that, until the day you die, He would protect you from lying and provide your daily needs, delivering you from the temptation of wealth because wealthy people tend to forget the Lord, and delivering you from the temptation of poverty because people in poverty tend to steal and profane God's name.</u>

We should pray for the grace to glorify the Lord in either poverty or plenty. Bishop Joseph Hall (1574-1656) said, "Whatsoever God gives, I am most thankful and indifferent; so while I am rich in estate, I may be poor in spirit and while I am poor in estate, I may be rich in grace" (Hall, cited by Bridges).

Proverbs 30:10 "Do not malign a servant to his master, lest he curse you, and you be found guilty." The Hebrew word translated "malign" means "use of the tongue," but more specifically, "slander." "Hurt not with your tongue" (Wardlaw). The command is to not "slander" a servant to the servant's master. Do not bring a "false accusation" against another man's servant (Clarke; Wardlaw). Slander and false accusation are always bad, but they are especially bad when the "subject of the slander is an inferior, and the charge against him (is) to his superior on whom he depends" (Wardlaw). Exaggeration of the actual facts puts the servant under suspicion and generally makes the person suspect (Kidner).

The reason given is that the servant will curse the slanderer (Clarke; JFB) and being guilty, the curse will come to pass because "God is the Defender of the oppressed" (MacDonald). Wardlaw concurs with that assessment. He says, "If the accuser is thus 'found guilty' in the sight of God, He will prove himself the friend of the oppressed, and will vindicate his cause, and avenge the wrong." Kidner also agrees, saying, "If the servant is innocent, his curse will count (see 26:2), for there is a Judge."

<u>Do not slander a servant to his master lest the servant curse you and you are found guilty because God will avenge the wrong.</u>

Barnes says the rule may be more generally applied. He says, "Those who take the most eager pleasure in finding fault are usually those, who can least bear the retort upon themselves" and "Should not this remembrance constrain us to "speak evil" *needlessly* 'of no man'?" (Bridges, italics his).

Proverbs 30:11 "*There is* a generation *that* curses its father, and does not bless its mother." Proverbs 30:11-14 mentions four kinds of generations. The English word "generation" conveys the concept of a period of time that includes all kinds of people. Does Agur mean that there is a *whole* generation of people who curse their fathers and do not bless their mothers? That depends on the meaning of the Hebrew word translated "generation." The basic meaning is "period, generation," but like all words, it has a "field of meaning." This particular Hebrew word "was used of a class of men" [BDB; see "There is a kind of *man*" in the NASB and "There are those who" in the NIV; also see Wardlaw; Buzzell ("four kinds of people"); Bridges ("race of men")]. Wardlaw says this Hebrew word is used repeatedly in Scripture of classes of people or a description of people.

The four things Agur mentions have been called "four kinds of vices" (Delitzsch), "four grand evils" (Clarke), "four kinds of hateful persons" (JFB), "four facets of arrogance," that is, the "arrogance prayed against in 7–9" (Kidner).

Here to "not bless" one's mother is "to curse" her (Delitzsch; Wardlaw explains that because of the parallelism, the two clauses may be regarded as much alike). These kinds of people not only do not honor their parents, they "evil-treated their parents" (Clarke). They "practiced brutality" (Kidner).

Commentators called such children "disrespectful" (MacDonald; Buzzell) or ungrateful (Delitzsch; Wardlaw). Wardlaw traces the root of their problem to a proud self-will, stubborn spirit, or to a spirit of covetousness and eagerness to obtain possessions and, therefore, wishing their parents dead, cursing them from living so long.

<u>There is a class of people who curse their fathers and do not bless their mothers.</u>

Proverbs 20:20 says, "Whoever curses his father or his mother, his lamp shall be put out in deep darkness," which means those who curse their father or mother will suffer dire consequences, including death. Bridges points out that cursing a parent was visited with the same punishment as blaspheming of God (compare Lev. 20:9 with Lev. 24:11-16), so near does the one sin approach to the other.

Proverbs 30:12 "*There is* a generation *that is* pure in its own eyes, *yet* is not washed from its filthiness." In this proverb, a "generation" is a "class of people" (see notes on verse 11). This verse describes people who think they are morally pure when they are morally filthy. They have been called blind concerning the judgment of themselves (Delitzsch), self-deceived (Wardlaw; Bridges). Nothing is so much hidden from them as themselves.

They have also been labeled as self-righteous (Delitzsch; Clarke; MacDonald) and as "hypocrites" (JFB; Buzzell). MacDonald says these self-righteous people are "vile and unclean, yet they have no sense of shame."

<u>A class of people think they are morally pure, but they are morally impure; they are self-deceived.</u>

It is possible to be justified in one's own eyes and not justified in the eyes of others or the eyes of God.

The Pharisees were "devoted to the externals of religion, and to them exclusively; 'washing the outside of the cup and platter,' while the inward part was wholly *unwashed from its filthiness*" (Bridges, italics his).

Proverbs 30:13 "*There is* a generation—oh, how lofty are their eyes! And their eyelids are lifted up." In this proverb, a "generation" is a "class of people" (see notes on verse 11). The lofty eyes and lifted-up eyelids are figures of speech for the "astonishing height of arrogance" (Delitzsch), "pride and arrogance" (MacDonald), "haughtiness" (Buzzell; Wardlaw). These people are full of "vanity, pride, and insolence" (Clarke).

<u>There is a class of people who are arrogant.</u>

Wardlaw suggests that these people "carry their heads high and look disdainfully down on all." He describes some groups of people who have "arrogance of learning" and some who have "the haughtiness of self-righteousness" (the "holier than thou" crowd).

Remember, God resists the proud (Jas. 4:6; 1 Pet. 5:5).

Proverbs 30:14 "*There is* a generation whose teeth *are like* swords, and whose fangs *are like* knives, to devour the poor from off the earth, and the needy from *among* men." In this proverb, a "generation" is a "class of people" (see notes on verse 11). The Hebrew word translated "devour" means "eat, devour, consume, destroy." It is a figure of speech for oppression. Using several figures of speech, Agur describes oppressors of the poor and needy, who can be said to be "fiercely oppressive" (MacDonald). The poor are helpless and defenseless (Delitzsch).

The instruments of oppression and destruction include teeth and fangs. Their teeth are like swords. They devour the poor and needy "as one eats bread" (Delitzsch; see Ps. 14:4). Perhaps this figure suggests that this is not an occasional indulgence, but "as they eat bread" daily, this is their daily activity (Bridges). Their fangs are like knives. These people are cruel (Bridges; Wardlaw).

Wardlaw says slavery and "some departments of business, in which griping and grasping avarice—that "love of money which is the root of all evil'" are illustrations. MacDonald says oppressors of the poor devour them "by long hours, low wages, miserable working conditions, and other forms of social injustice."

There is a class of people who oppress the poor and needy.

What is their problem? Delitzsch says these people have an "insatiable covetousness" (see also Bridges). MacDonald traces the root of the problem to "insatiable greed" (see also Clarke). Wardlaw says, "They are persons who, whether to gratify their avarice, or their profligate ambition, or their love of pleasure and dissipation and extravagance, make no account of the property, the liberty, the peace, the comfort, the enjoyment, the very lives of others,—and especially of the poor,—when they stand in the way of their own gratification."

To sum up, verses 11-14 describe four classes of people: the haters of parents, the self-deceived, the arrogant, and the cruel oppressors of the poor. Delitzsch calls these four vices "blackest ingratitude, loathsome self-righteousness, arrogant presumption, and unmerciful covetousness." Kidner calls them four facets of arrogance. He also suggests "there may be a sequence traceable from impious childhood (11) to practiced brutality (14); at all events pride is seen corrupting a person's attitude to his superiors (11), himself (12), the world at large (13), and his supposed inferiors (14)."

That last comment just may put its finger on the pulse of this passage. There is an arrogance that corrupts people's attitude toward their superiors, themselves, people in general, and their perceived inferiors.

Proverbs 30:15-16 "The leech has two daughters— Give *and* Give! There are three *things that* are never satisfied, four never say, 'Enough!': the grave, the barren womb, the earth *that* is not satisfied with water— and the fire never says, 'Enough!'" These two verses form a single proverb about a "voracious appetite" (Barnes), "insatiable desires" (Buzzell), "insatiable appetites" (Wardlaw). Some commentators use the word "greed" to describe what is going on here (Barnes; Delitzsch; Buzzell).

The bloodsucking leech has two daughters (a leech has a two-forked tongue, says Bridges) and both are named "Give" (MacDonald; Wardlaw; Kidner). Some commentators take the words "Give and Give" as the ceaseless *cry* of the daughters, not their names (Barnes; Buzzell; JFB; Bridges). There is very little, if any, difference between the two explanations. There are people who are never satisfied; they never say, "Enough." They always say, "Give me more."

The expression "There are three…four" is a literary device that conveys movement toward a climax (Barnes). Agur uses this formula four times (30:15, 30:18; 30:21, 30:29).

Four things are never satisfied; they never say, "Enough." They are never content (Clarke). They always want more. "The grave never says 'No vacancy.' Death never takes a holiday, and the tomb never fails to accommodate its victims" (MacDonald). "The barren womb is never willing to accept its sterility but hopes continually for motherhood" (MacDonald). No matter how much rain falls, the earth can take more. As long as fuel is supplied, fire never ceases to burn.

Like the grave, the barren womb, the earth taking in rain, and the continually burning fire, some people are never satisfied; they never say, "Enough:" they incessantly cry, "Give me, give me, give me more."

This proverb applies to people with excessive covetousness and greed (Clarke), people with "measureless ambition" (Kidner), and people with an insatiable appetite for possessions, sex, alcohol, etc. You would think that after a while, people would learn. Most don't.

Only the Lord totally satisfies. 'Let your conduct *be* without covetousness; *be* content with such things as you have. For He Himself has said, 'I will never leave you nor forsake you'" (Heb. 13:5).

Proverbs 30:17 "The eye *that* mocks *his* father, and scorns obedience to *his* mother, the ravens of the valley will pick it out, and the young eagles will eat it." The fact that the word "eye" is singular, not plural, indicates the reference is primarily to "mental activity" (Delitzsch). Perhaps it also indicates that not a word was spoken (Bridges), like the rolling of the eyes that speaks volumes without saying a word. The Hebrew word translated "mock" means to "mock, deride" and the one rendered "scorns" means "despise" (the noun means "contempt").

In vivid terms, this proverb describes the disgusting attitude of a child who goes beyond disrespecting and disobeying his (or her) parents to despising and deriding them (see 30:11). Imagine a child with contempt and ridicule for his (or her) parents.

There are dire consequences for despising one's parents. Ravens plucking out the eye is a figurative way of describing a "violent death" (MacDonald). Eagles eating a dead body indicates the corpse remains unburied (Buzzell). For Jews, an unburied body was a disgrace (MacDonald) and a sign of divine judgment (Bridges; Wardlaw). "The fate of the wayward son is for his carcass to be devoured by vultures" (MacDonald).

A son (or daughter) who has the disgusting attitude of deriding his father and despising his mother will experience dire consequences, divine judgment, a violent death, and a disgraceful burial.

Wardlaw, who lived in the 19th century, speaks of criminals who come to the gallows acknowledging that the "commencement of their career of vice was contempt for their parents." Bridges says, "Even where there is no such literal fulfillment, the curse is not the less sure."

"Let the young take warning,—and beware of every rising emotion of disrespect, and of every word, or look, or act of contempt and insubordination:—'Honor thy father and mother, which is the first commandment with promise'" (Wardlaw).

Proverbs 30:18 "There are three *things which* are too wonderful for me, Yes, four *which* I do not understand: the way of an eagle in the air, the way of a serpent on a rock, the way of a ship in the midst of the sea, and the way of a man with a virgin." The expression "There are three…four" is a literary device that conveys movement toward a climax (30:15). In this case, the main point is the way of a man with a virgin.

What is the common thread that ties together a flying eagle, a slithering snake, a moving ship, and the way of a man with a virgin? Buzzell lists the possible explanations as four mysterious things, four untraceable things, four seemingly difficult things (Kidner), or four things that go where there is no path.

Most commentators say the common element is that these four things leave no trace behind them (Delitzsch; Barnes; Bridges). Many commentators also say that verse 20 (about the adulterous woman) is an attachment that explains the way of a man with a virgin (Delitzsch; Bridges; Wardlaw), but the Hebrew word translated "virgin" here is the same one that is translated "virgin" in Isaiah 7:14. The adulterous woman of verse 20 is not the virgin of verse 19.

The Hebrew word translated "wonderful" means "surpassing, extraordinary." It is used here of something "difficult to understand" (BDB). The point of this passage is the wonder of four things (Delitzsch, who takes the untraceable interpretation, concedes that "the wonderfulness of the event" is the other possible explanation).

A large bird soaring high in the sky is a marvel. "The gracefulness and speed of the eagle are proverbial" (MacDonald). A snake slithering across a smooth rock, which has nothing on which to hold, is a wonder. It moves "without the benefit of legs, arms, or wings" (MacDonald). A heavy ship floating on the sea is amazing. Heavy objects sink! The way a man woos a young lady is a wonder to behold. The intricacies are fascinating to watch.

<u>As there is wonder in watching a large bird fly, a snake slither across a smooth rock, and a heavy ship float, there is a mystery as to how a young man woos a young lady.</u>

Eagles in the air and snakes on the ground do what they do naturally. They follow their instincts. Young man, use your head in selecting the woman you woo (see the next verse). Then, study her and follow your instincts.

Proverbs 30:20 "This *is* the way of an adulterous woman: She eats and wipes her mouth, and says, 'I have done no wickedness.'" As was pointed out in the comments on the previous verse, many commentators say that this verse is an attachment to verse 19 to explains the way of a man with a virgin (Delitzsch; Bridges; Wardlaw), but the Hebrew word translated "virgin" in verse 19 is the same one that is translated "virgin" in Isaiah 7:14. The virgin of verse 19 is not the adulterous woman of verse 20. This verse is not the way of a man with a woman; it is the way of an immoral woman with a man (Buzzell).

After her adulterous act, the adulterous woman eats, wipes her mouth, and proclaims her "complete innocence" (MacDonald). She feels no shame. She treats her sinful act as casually as eating a meal (Buzzell). It is "as unremarkable to her as a meal" (Kidner). She hides the evidence ("wipes her mouth;" JFB; Clarke; Bridges). If suspected, she admits no guilt.

Wardlaw describes what is happening: "Assuming the air of perfect composure—of one completely at her ease;—her conscience, if not actually seared, brought under sufficient coercive control to cover all emotion. She sits down as usual to her meal with her husband and family—with full self-possession and indifference of manner—just as if nothing had happened; eating, and wiping her mouth, and saying, 'I have done no evil'—telling tales perhaps of the guilt of others, affecting to shudder at them, and comparing her own innocence with their shameful conduct." Kidner simply says she is "utterly at ease."

<u>The way of the adulterous woman is to treat her wickedness as if it were no more than eating a meal and, if suspected, to proclaim that she has not done anything wicked.</u>

Proverbs 30:21-23 "For three *things* the earth is perturbed, yes, for four it cannot bear up: for a servant when he reigns, a fool when he is filled with food, a hateful *woman* when she is married, and a maidservant who succeeds her mistress." The word "earth" here means the "inhabitants of the earth" (Delitzsch; Buzzell). The Hebrew word translated "perturbed" means "agitated, perturbed" and the one rendered "bear" means "lift, carry, take, endure."

This proverb is about four things that agitate people, four things that are hard to endure. Two concern men and two are about women. When these four things happen, people tremble, feel "oppressed as by an insufferable burden (an expression similar to Amos 7:10)," and "society is shattered" (Delitzsch). These four insufferable things throw the earth into turmoil (MacDonald).

The first is a servant who reigns (see 19:10). He is unable to rise above the habits he had as servant (Delitzsch). Thus, he is "unprepared to rule" (Buzzell). He becomes "arrogant and overbearing, drunk with his new position" (MacDonald). He will abuse his power (Wardlaw). He becomes an "unprincipled tyrant" (Clarke).

The second is a fool who is filled with food. "This undeserved living without care and without want makes him only so much the more arrogant, troublesome, and dangerous" (Delitzsch).

The third is a hateful woman who is married. "An unmarried lady, an old spinster is meant, (one) who no one desired because she had nothing attractive and was only repulsive" (Delitzsch). The hateful woman is one who is unlovable, who, when she gets married, makes herself and others miserable (Barnes). "Her wretched disposition would normally have kept her single, but by some fluke, she lands a husband. Then she becomes imperious and haughty, taunting those who are still unmarried" (MacDonald)

The fourth is a maid who succeeds her mistress. Like the servant mentioned above, she does not know how to direct others (Buzzell). "She doesn't know how to act with refinement and grace but is coarse, rude, and vulgar" (MacDonald). "She quarrels with all around her. Her ungoverned tongue and temper are an unceasing source of agitation" (Bridges).

"The people tremble because social turmoil follows the sudden elevation of inexperienced, unqualified people to positions of power and success" (Buzzell).

A ruling servant, an overfed fool, a hateful married woman, and a ruling maid are four types of people who agitate people, making it hard to endure them.

The Peter Principle, a book by Dr. Laurence J. Peter and Raymond Hull (1969), contends that when an organization promotes its people based on achievement, those promoted will be promoted beyond their ability. In popular terms, "Employees tend to rise to their level of incompetence." Agur says when that happens, those who were promoted aggravate other people.

In this regard, it should be remembered that "The Bible delights in fruitful reversals of fortune (17:2; the Magnificat), but has no use for upstarts (19:10; Isa. 3:4, 5) who become too big for their boots" (Kidner).

To state the point of this proverb positively, "Harmony in society is encouraged when people maintain their proper roles and do not assume positions they are incapable of handling" (Buzzell).

Proverbs 30:24-28 "There are four *things which* are little on the earth, but they *are* exceedingly wise: The ants *are* a people not strong, yet they prepare their food in the summer. The rock badgers are a feeble folk, yet they make their homes in the crags. The locusts have no king, yet they all advance in ranks. The spider skillfully grasps with its hands, and it is in kings' palaces." Four things are wise out of all proportion to their size (MacDonald).

Ants are so small and weak that thousands are crushed by one shoe that steps on them (Bridges). Most species of ants do not provide for the winter; they cluster together and sleep, but the "harvester ant is an exception, however, since it stores food in warm, dry seasons for later use during cold times" (MacDonald). Clarke says ants store food for autumn and spring. At any rate, they are not strong, but they survive because of their foresight (Buzzell; 6:6-8).

Rock badgers are small, the size of rabbits, and defenseless, but they wisely live in the clefts of rocks, which provide them protection (Buzzell; the hymn says, "Rock of Ages, cleft for me").

Locusts do not have visible leaders but advance as a group. Wardlaw describes how they do it. They rise. They fly. They keep rank. They halt. They settle. They do everything with one consent for the common good.

Spiders (Heb. "a kind of lizard") are skillful and smart, managing to get into unlikely and important places (MacDonald). Is this referring to a spider (Gill; JFB) or a lizard (NASB; NIV; ESV; Barnes; Perowne; *Pulpit Commentary*)? "The expression [spider] wavers in a way that is with difficulty determinable between שְׂמָמִית and שְׂמָמִית. What kind of a beast is meant here is a question. The swallow is at once to be set aside. Only the lizard (lxx, Jerome) and the spider (Luther) remain to be considered.... Aruch testifies that the explanation is divided between spider and lizard in two places in the Talmud. Accordingly, and after the lxx and Jerome, it may be regarded as a confirmed tradition that שממית means not the spider, for which the name עֲכָבִישׁ is coined, but the lizard, and particularly the stellion (spotted lizard). The Arab. also confirms this name as applicable to the lizard.... So the sense is the lizard thou canst catch with the hand, and yet it is in kings' palaces, *i.e.*, it is a little beast, which one can grasp with his hand, and yet it knows how to gain an entrance into palaces, by which in its nimbleness and cunning this is to be thought of, that it can scale the walls even to the summit" (Delitzsch).

As a group, these creatures teach us that wisdom can triumph over size and strength. What they lack in strength, they make up in wisdom (Bridges). Individually, they teach us to plan for the future (ant), provide a safe dwelling (rock badger), work together (locust), and get into unlikely places.

Ants, rock badgers, locusts, and spiders are small and weak, but they are exceedingly wise in planning for the future, providing a safe residence, working together, and getting into unlikely places.

Ants prepare for the future and so should we (retirement by saving money and heaven by being saved, not by work, but by faith).

Kidner says these four teach provision, sanctuary, order, and audacity. Wardlaw puts it together like this: The lesson taught us by the ants is diligence, discretion, and foresight. The lesson from the rock badger is prudence with regard to residence and security for ourselves and our families against discomfort and danger, against all enemies and invaders. From the locust, we learn the importance and benefit of order, union, and cooperation, for the accomplishment of objects of common interest, whether civil or sacred. From the spider, we learn the advantage of skill, ingenuity, and industry in all the arts and occupations of life.

Wardlaw applies this to young men contemplating marriage: "We may apply the emblematic lessons to domestic life. Before a man can prudently marry and have a family, he should have some suitable provision made and something like a fair prospect of being able to support them. Next, a suitable dwelling adapted to his circumstances and convenience is to be found. Then, when settled, there must be harmony, union, and cooperation in all household departments. And lastly, there must be the diligent, constant, persevering application of his skill and labor to his worldly calling."

Proverbs 30:29-31 "There are three *things which* are majestic in pace, yes, four *which* are stately in walk: a lion, *which is* mighty among beasts and does not turn away from any; a greyhound, a male goat also, and a king *whose* troops *are* with him." In contrast to the four lowly creatures in verses 25-28, here are four who have a majestic walk. They have "graceful movement" (MacDonald).

The lion is "majestic and unruffled as it walks" (BBC). "Nothing can be more majestic than the walk of the lion. It is deliberate, equal, firm, and in every respect becoming the king of the forest" (Clarke). People and animals retreat from the lion because of its strength (Buzzell).

The Hebrew word translated "greyhound" does not appear anywhere else in the Old Testament. It means "one with loins girded." Various explanations have been given, such as the stripes of the zebra, the war-horse (see Bridges), the strutting rooster (NASB; NIV), and the greyhound (NKJV). "All these fit the description of lofty dignity, but perhaps the graceful greyhound is the best choice" (MacDonald). In the East, "scarcely anything can be conceived to go with greater fleetness, in full chase, than a greyhound with its prey in view: it seems to swim over the earth" Clarke).

The male goat has an "arrogant appearance" (Buzzell). It "is a picture of noble bearing as it strides at the head of a flock" (MacDonald).

The king, who has the support of his troops, "marches with regal dignity" (MacDonald). He "may strut with pride as he is seemingly invincible with his army in his presence" (Buzzell). His "troops are so firmly united to him as to render all hopes of successful conspiracy against him utterly vain. He walks boldly and majestically about, being safe in the affections of his people" (Clarke).

<u>Like a mighty lion who does not retreat from anyone, the graceful greyhound and the male goat are majestically at the head of the flock, so a king who has the support of his troops and people walks majestically.</u>

Like many others, this proverb leaves application to the reader (see JFB). "There is no moralizing or philosophizing. The theological implications (the Creator's power and wisdom—verses 1-5; Job 38–42:6) are left implicit, enriching the observer's delight, if he has eyes to see, but not intruding upon it" (Kidner).

Here is the way Wardlaw applies it: "We are not for a moment to suppose that the intention of Agur is merely to invite us to admire the gait of the 'lion,' the king of beasts, who marches on in the nobility of his might, in courageous consciousness of his power, altering not his pace, and fearless of whatever comes in his way:—or the grace and elegance of the 'greyhound,' and the nimble fleetness of his course,—or the portly dignity of the leader of the flock, that walks at their head, conducting and caring for them:—or the majesty of royal authority and honor, of a king maintaining his dignity, bearing his crowned head with the stateliness of office. In the peculiarities of the three animals, the characteristics of the king's character are figured:—his courage and undaunted intrepidity by the lion;—his readiness for activity and speed in the pursuit of every legitimate object,—as well as fit elegance and gracefulness, by the grey-hound;—and his becoming example set before his people, leading them in right ways, and caring for their safety, by the he-goat."

Proverbs 30:32-33 "If you have been foolish in exalting yourself, or if you have devised evil, *put your* hand on *your* mouth. For *as* the churning of milk produces butter, and wringing the nose produces blood, so the forcing of wrath produces strife." Putting your hand to your mouth is another way of saying, "Be silent" (Delitzsch). "Restrain the expression" (Bridges). This proverb gives two occasions when you should be silent and the reason for the silence.

If you have been foolish in exalting yourself, be silent. In this case, putting your hands over your mouth "expresses the silence of humiliation and repentance after the sin has been committed" (Barnes).

If you devise evil, be silent. In this case, putting your hands over your mouth expresses "self-restraint, which checks the haughty or malignant thought before it has passed even into words" (Barnes).

Agur gives the reason for being silent (see "for"). He talks about churning milk, wringing the nose, and forcing wrath. The Hebrew words translated "churning," "wringing," and "forcing" are the same word and it only appears here in the Old Testament. The basic meaning of the word is "squeezing or pressing." According to the Hebrew lexicon, when used of anger in this verse, it means "pressured insistence" (BDB). So speaking, when exalting yourself or devising evil has results. "Words increase the sin, show more of its power, and are more hurtful to others" (Bridges).

As the result of churning of milk is butter, the wringing the nose is blood, and the insisting on expressing anger is strife, so there will be results if you speak to exalt yourself or when you devise evil.

Proverbs 31

Proverbs 31:1 "The words of King Lemuel, the utterance which his mother taught him." The last chapter of Proverbs does not contain the proverbs of Solomon or Agur. The closing chapter records the words of King Lemuel. Actually, they are the utterance his mother taught him. The Hebrew word translated "utterance" means "utterance, declaration, revelation." It was used of prophets in an ecstatic state (BDB; see 30:1). Here, it is a reference to "divine revelation" (Wardlaw; Clarke). When Lemuel says his mother taught him the "utterance" and he wrote them here, he means she taught him the Word of God.

Who was King Lemuel? Some Jewish and Christian commentators think that Lemuel is another name for Solomon, but there is no evidence of that (Wardlaw). Lemuel was not a king in Israel. Ancient versions say he was king of Massa (Kidner).

All that is known about King Lemuel is what is recorded in this verse. His name means "dedicated to God" or "belonging to God" (MacDonald). His godly mother gave him a God-honoring name and taught him the Word of God (1:18 and 6:20 also speak of a mother instructing her son). He was a king.

<u>The godly mother of a king dedicated her son to the Lord and taught him the Word of God.</u>

What Lemuel's mother taught him is recorded in verses 2-9. Buzzell says it includes "the dangers of wayward women (31:3; 23:26-28) and wine (31:4-7; 23:29-35), and reminded him of his responsibility to champion the cause of justice." She taught him about immorality, intoxication, and injustice.

Proverbs 31:2 "What, my son? And what, son of my womb? And what, son of my vows?" Using the word "son" each time, the mother asks her son three questions. The repetition has been explained in several different ways. "The repetitions are emphatic; expressive of anxious love" (Barnes). "Repetitions denote earnestness" (JFB).

The first question simply addresses her son as "my son." "The question, which is at the same time a call, is like a deep sigh from the heart of the mother concerned for the welfare of her son" (Delitzsch).

The second question addresses her son as "son of my womb." "She wanted him to know that he was special to her" (Buzzell). This is a term of "special affection" (JFB).

The third question addresses her son as "son of my vows." The vows she speaks are not her marriage vows but those concerning her son (Delitzsch). Like Hannah, she no doubt prayed for his son and vowed to dedicate him to the Lord. "Then she (Hannah) made a vow and said, 'O LORD of hosts, if You will indeed look on the affliction of Your maidservant and remember me, and not forget Your maidservant, but will give Your maidservant a male child, then I will give him to the LORD all the days of his life, and no razor shall come upon his head'" (1 Sam. 1:11). "A child born after vows made for offspring is called the child of a person's vows" (Clarke; see also Delitzsch; Barnes; JFB; Buzzell). "If there were more Hannahs, would there not be more Samuels?" (Bridges).

These words express an earnest desire for the well-being of her son. The thought is, "What shall I say to you, my son?—the son of my womb? The son of my vows? What advice shall a mother give to the son she loves so dearly." "She then admonishes her son against those vices which she knew to be a special source of danger: and she does so in a manner calculated to interest, impress, and melt his heart,—appealing, with the tenderness of maternal to the tenderness of filial love" (Wardlaw).

<u>With words of deeply felt affection and special connection, a mother asks what advice she should give her son.</u>

Proverbs 31:3 "Do not give your strength to women, nor your ways to that which destroys kings." Lemuel's mother warns her son about immorality. The book of Proverbs contains a number of warnings about sexual immorality (2:16-19; 5:1-23; 6:24-29; 7:1-27; 22:14; 23:17; 29:3).

Immorality will drain a king's strength. "Adultery has a debilitating effect on one's mind and body" (Buzzell). "The strength of body, soul, and substance is destroyed" (Clarke).

Immorality will destroy the king and his kingdom. "The temptations of the harem were then, as now, the curse of all Eastern kingdoms" (Barnes). Moses warned future kings about this problem. "Neither shall he multiply wives for himself, lest his heart turn away" (Deut. 17:17).

Solomon is an example. To accommodate his wives, he built pagan temples for them to burn incense and sacrifice to their gods (1 Kings 11:7-8). 'Therefore the LORD said to Solomon, 'Because you have done this, and have not kept My covenant and My statutes, which I have commanded you, I will surely tear the kingdom away from you and give it to your servant. Nevertheless, I will not do it in your days, for the sake of your father David; I will tear it out of the hand of your son" (1 Kings 11:11-12). "Did not Solomon, king of Israel, sin by these things? Yet among many nations, there was no king like him, who was beloved of his God; and God made him king over all Israel. Nevertheless, pagan women caused even him to sin" (Neh. 13:26).

<u>Immorality will drain a king's strength and destroy him and his kingdom.</u>

Proverbs 31:4-5 "*It is* not for kings, O Lemuel, *It is* not for kings to drink wine, nor for princes intoxicating drink; lest they drink and forget the law, and pervert the justice of all the afflicted." Lemuel's mother warns her son about intoxication (see 20:1; 23:20-21; 23:29-35). She is not saying do not drink at all. This is a plea to refrain from excessive wine and strong drink (MacDonald). She warns about the dangers of alcoholism (Buzzell).

Lemuel's mother tells her son, a king, that wine is not for kings. The Hebrew word translated "wine" is the usual word for wine. It almost invariably denotes the fermented juice of the grape and, of course, when consumed in excess, is an intoxicating beverage.

Intoxicating drink is not for a prince. The Hebrew word translated "intoxicating drink" (translated "strong drink" in 20:1) is an intoxicating drink from a source other than grapes. It was distilled from barley, honey, or dates (Barnes).

A king or a prince should not drink to excess because he will forget the law and pervert justice. "They might forget the standards of justice demanded by the law" (MacDonald). If they are a "slave to drink," they may "handle falsely the facts of the case and give judgment contrary to them" (Delitzsch).

Such perversion of justice is particularly cruel on the afflicted. The Hebrew word translated "afflicted" means "affliction, poverty." Delitzsch says here it refers to the "whole class of the poorer people, suffering humanity." MacDonald calls them the "downtrodden" and Buzzell "the oppressed."

<u>Rulers, who have to make just decisions, should not drink in excess because when they do, they forget the law and pervert justice for the afflicted.</u>

"A woman wrongly condemned by Philip of Macedon, when drunk, boldly exclaimed, 'I appeal to Philip, but it shall be when he is sober.' Roused by the appeal, the monarch examined the cause and gave a righteous judgment" (Bridges).

Proverbs 31:6-7 "Give strong drink to him who is perishing, and wine to those who are bitter of heart. Let him drink and forget his poverty, and remember his misery no more." There is an improper (31:4-5) and a proper use (31:6-7) of wine. The abuse of wine should not destroy its proper use (Bridges, who calls it a gift of God).

Lemuel's mother tells her son that wine and strong drink are for those who are perishing and for those with a bitter heart. Wine was to be given to the dying and the despondent because it would relieve their pain. "It is all right for people like these to drink to forget their need and their misery" (MacDonald). It is an acceptable an anesthetic "to deaden physical pain or deep emotional bitterness" (Buzzell).

<u>One of the uses of wine is to relieve the pain of the dying and the despondent.</u>

Based on this proverb, noble women in Jerusalem prepared such a portion for those condemned to death (Delitzsch). On the cross, Jesus was offered it and refused it (Mk. 15:23). Barnes says it was the Jewish practice to give a cup of wine to mourners.

According to the psalmist, wine "makes glad the heart of man" (Ps. 104:15). It cheers people (Judges 9:13). The Samaritan gave it to the wounded traveler (Lk.10:34); Paul prescribed it for the infirmities of Timothy (1 Tim. 5:23).

Proverbs 31:8-9 "Open your mouth for the speechless, in the cause of all *who are* appointed to die. Open your mouth, judge righteously, and plead the cause of the poor and needy." Lemuel's mother warns her son about injustice. She wants her son to be a righteous king in his function as judge. So she exhorts him to speak up for those who cannot speak for themselves. It is pleading the cause for those appointed to die, for the poor, and for the needy. Delitzsch says this includes those who suffer from dumbness, blindness, and lameness and those who, on account of their youth, ignorance, or fear, cannot speak before the tribunal for themselves.

A righteous king uses his function as a judge to be an advocate for the helpless (Delitzsch). His great duty is to give help to those who had no other helper (Barnes). He is "to judge fairly, regardless of a person's social status" (Buzzell). "No case of distress, when coming to his knowledge, should be below his attention" (Bridges).

<u>A righteous ruler will speak up for those who cannot speak for themselves, such as those appointed to death, the poor, and the needy.</u>

Proverbs 31:10 "Who can find a virtuous wife? For her worth *is* far above rubies." Proverbs 31 contains the words of Lemuel, which his godly mother taught him (31:1). Prior to this, Lemuel's mother warned her son about the adulterous woman (31:3). Now, in great detail, she extols the virtuous wife. Perhaps as if to say, "Son, this is the kind of woman you should marry."

The Hebrew word rendered "virtuous" is difficult to translate. A brief word study will explain the nuances within this word (as with all words, the meaning of a word is determined by its context). The Hebrew lexicon lists its meanings as "strength, efficiency, ability, often involving moral worth" (BDB). Strong says it means "powerful." The root idea is "bodily vigor" (Delitzsch). It is translated "strength" (31:3), "mighty" (see "mighty men of valor" in Jos. 2:14; etc.), and "able" (Ex. 18:21).

In the book of Ruth, it is used of Boaz and of Ruth. Boaz is described as "a man of great wealth" (Ruth 2:1). That exact Hebrew expression is elsewhere translated "a mighty man of valor" (Judges 11:1). Of Ruth, it is said that all the people in town knew she was a "virtuous" woman (Ruth 3:11). Does that mean she was a "strong woman?"

What is the meaning of this Hebrew word in this passage? Clarke says it means "a woman of power and strength, a strong or virtuous wife." Jamieson, Fausset, and Brown say it literally means "of strength," that is, "moral courage." Wardlaw says in different contexts, it denotes "strength, wealth, ability." It is translated "excellent wife" in Proverbs 12:4 (NKJV; the NASB renders it "excellent wife" in this verse). Wardlaw concludes, "The word here is very comprehensive. It is to be interpreted from the description."

Thus, the meaning of this Hebrew word indicates that this is a strong, capable, virtuous wife. Such a wife is "capable, diligent, worthy, and good" (MacDonald). Perhaps the word "excellent," which is the way it is translated in Proverbs 12:4, could be used to include all of the nuances in this word (NASB; see Kidner). She is called the "ideal wife" (MacDonald), "a truly lovely wife" (JFB), a "noble wife" (Buzzell), and "a wife of noble character" (NIV).

The question indicates the difficulty in finding such a wife; not everyone finds her, only a few (Delitzsch). "So rare is this treasure, that the challenge is given 'who can find a virtuous woman?'" (Bridges; Warfield; Buzzell; see also 31:29).

An excellent wife is more valuable than rubies. She is a "rare treasure, a good excelling all earthly possession" (Delitzsch). She is invaluable (Clarke). "Her worth cannot be measured in terms of costly jewels" (MacDonald). "He who gets such a wife gets what is, in its own intrinsic worth, incomparably better than the greatest amount of wealth, than the richest precious stones and jewels" (Wardlaw).

<u>Finding an excellent (strong, able, virtuous) wife is difficult because they are so rare, but such a wife is worth more than can be measured in costly jewels.</u>

Wardlaw says, "The forming of the marriage union should be a matter of serious deliberation and inquiry, not a matter of hasty, capricious thoughtless resolution."

Her Husband

Proverbs 31:11 "The heart of her husband safely trusts her; so he will have no lack of gain." The husband of an excellent wife is mentioned three times in this section (31:11, 31:23, and 31:28; see also "him" in 31:12). For her, "To live for him is her highest happiness" (Bridges).

The heart of the husband of an excellent wife trusts her. As is obvious from the second half of this verse, he can trust to his wife "the entire management of his domestic affairs" (Wardlaw, who also says, "He can put his purse into her hands"). He can rely on her "prudence and skill" (JFB).

Her husband is confident he will not lack gain. The Hebrew word translated "gain" means "plunder, booty, spoil of war, gain." Hence, some commentators take this statement to mean that the husband of an excellent wife "*has no need of spoil*, no temptation to unjust gain; *no need* to leave his happy home, in order to enrich himself with the soldier's *spoils*" (Bridges, italics his; see also JFB; Clarke). Other commentators, however, conclude that the meaning here is simple "lack of gain, lack of honest gain" (Barnes; Delitzsch; Buzzell; MacDonald).

Thus, the husband of an excellent wife can rest assured that his wife will keep "the family possessions scrupulously together and increases them by her laborious and prudent management" (Delitzsch). "Her careful household management enhances their family's wealth" (Buzzell). In other words, the husband of such a wife will not be worried that his wife will be extravagance, contract debts, squander money, disgrace him, or ruin him (Wardlaw).

<u>The heart of the husband of an excellent wife confidently trusts her to manage the household in such a way that he will not lack material gain.</u>

Luther said of his wife, "The greatest gift of God is a pious amiable spouse, who fears God, loves his house, and with whom one can live in perfect confidence."

Proverbs 31:12 "She does him good and not evil all the days of her life." The excellent wife does her husband good. She is faithful to fulfill her role of helping her husband (Buzzell). The excellent wife does not do her husband evil. "Her good is unmixed; she will do him good and not evil" (Clarke).

The excellent wife does her husband good *all* her days. She does him good every day, all the days she is alive. "Her good is not capricious; it is constant and permanent while she and her husband live. This is her general character" (Clarke). "She never fails to cooperate" (MacDonald).

<u>The excellent wife does her husband good to the day she dies.</u>

Wardlaw elaborates. He says, "She studies his character; she makes herself aware of his peculiar tempers and humors, his likings and his dislikings—in order that she may, as far as possible from ability and from principle, accommodate herself to them; seeking in all things to please and gratify him. She devotes herself to the advancement of her husband's honor and reputation—his health of body and of mind,—his substantial interests,—his temporal and spiritual benefit, and, of course, the benefit of his family."

Her Clothes

Proverbs 31:13 "She seeks wool and flax, and willingly works with her hands." The excellent wife does not buy clothes already made. She seeks the raw materials of wool and flax, probably from her own flock and her own field (Clarke). She "willingly" makes clothes with her own hands. The Hebrew word translated "willingly" means "delight, pleasure." She enjoys her work (Buzzell; MacDonald). "All her labor is a cheerful service" (Clarke).

Among the Greeks, Romans, and Israelites, "the women, even of the highest ranks, worked with their hands at every kind of occupation necessary for the support of the family. This kind of employment was not peculiar to the virtuous woman in the text" (Clarke; JFB). "Manual labor, even menial service, in olden times was the employment of females in the highest ranks" (Bridges).

In this passage, Lemuel's mother is addressing her son, the king! This is the kind of wife the king should seek to be a queen. "The mother of Lemuel does not regard manual labor as beneath respectability and high station of the wife of a king" (Wardlaw).

<u>The excellent wife seeks the raw materials of wool and flax and enjoys making clothes with her own hands.</u>

"It may be necessary to retouch the lines of the picture that have been obscured by the length of years, to explain some parts of the description, which relate to ancient manners and customs, and to show how they may be usefully applied to those of our own age and country" (Horne, cited by Bridges). For one thing, as Bridges points out, she is not "a religious recluse, shut up from active obligations, under the pretense of greater sanctity and consecration to God. Here are none of those habits of monastic asceticism." He adds that she is full of energy.

Her Food

Proverbs 31:14 "She is like the merchant ships, she brings her food from afar." The excellent wife is like a merchant ship. The statement specifically mentions food from afar. She brings home, not just the local produce but also different foods from other countries.

Perhaps the figure implies other ideas. For example, MacDonald says as the ship is *laden* with produce, her shopping cart is loaded with the best bargains when she goes to the supermarket. Buzzell says when she goes shopping, she brings home interesting, unusual, and fascinating merchandise from other places. Clarke says, "She acts like merchants. If she buys anything for her household, she sells sufficient of her own manufactures to pay for it; if she imports, she exports: and she sends articles of her own manufacturing or produce to distant countries; she traffics with the neighboring tribes."

Delitzsch says, as "such ships as sail away and bring wares from a distance, are equipped, sent out, and managed by an enterprising spirit; so the prudent, calculating look of the brave wife, directed towards the care and the advancement of her house, goes out beyond the nearest circle; she (finds) also distant opportunities of advantageous purchase and profitable exchange, and brings in from a distance what is necessary for the supply of her house."

<u>The excellent wife does not settle for local produce; she brings home different foods from different places.</u>

Proverbs 31:15 "She also rises while it is yet night, and provides food for her household, and a portion for her maidservants." The excellent wife rises before the sun rises. Although she has household help (maidservants), she helps prepare food for her family (Buzzell). This could be more than breakfast. Clarke says, "To those who are going to the fields and to the flocks, she gives the food necessary for the day" (see also Buzzell). This is like the mother who cooks breakfast and prepares lunches for her school-age children.

The Hebrew word translated "portion" means "something prescribed." It can be a prescribed task (see "task" in Ex. 5:14) or a prescribed allotment of food (30:8). Some commentators take this to mean that the wife prepared food for her maidservants (Delitzsch, who cites 30:8 as proof). Other commentators say this means she delegates the day's work assignments to the maidservants (Buzzell). Either explanation is possible (Kidner). There are commentators who think the wife does both; she prepares breakfast for her maidservants and assigns them their work for the day (Barnes; MacDonald).

<u>The excellent wife rises before sunrise to help prepare the day's food for her family and delegate the day's work assignments to her maidservants.</u>

This statement indicates that the excellent woman is organized as well as industrious.

Her Business

Proverbs 31:16 "She considers a field and buys it; from her profits she plants a vineyard." The excellent wife buys a field. After considering its value (Bridges), and estimating its worth, she purchases it at a good bargain (Clarke). Buzzell says, this has caused some to question the validity of this statement because in those days, women were not permitted to invest. He goes on to say that she was able to purchase a field out of her earnings from other activities (verses 18 and 24). She had money to invest (see also Clarke; JFB).

After making a profit on her purchase, the excellent wife plants a vineyard. "She does not restrict herself to the bare necessaries of life; she is able to procure some of its comforts. She plants a vineyard that she may have wine for a beverage, for medicine, and for sacrifice" (Clarke).

This description shows that the excellent woman works hard and has a business mind (Buzzell). It also indicates that her industry extends household wealth (Delitzsch).

<u>The excellent wife carefully considers a field, buys it and from the profit on her purchase, she buys a vineyard.</u>

Proverbs 31:17 "She girds herself with strength, and strengthens her arms." The excellent wife is a woman of strength. She girds herself with strength, which means she works energetically (Buzzell), or perhaps that she takes on her task "with great vigor and enthusiasm" (MacDonald). She also strengthens her arms. Doing all that she does indicates that she has some degree of physical strength. She is ready and able to do most any work (see Bridges).

All of this indicates that an excellent wife "has a healthy attitude toward work" (Buzzell). "She is not afraid of strenuous work" (MacDonald). It may also imply that she "takes care of her own health and strength, not only by means of useful labor but by healthy exercise" (Clarke). This much is for sure: she is "ever active" (Clarke).

<u>The excellent wife is a woman of strength who energetically, enthusiastically, and eagerly goes about her work.</u>

Proverbs 31:18 "She perceives that her merchandise *is* good, and her lamp does not go out by night." The excellent wife perceives that her merchandise *is* good, that is, that it is profitable (BDB), because of the sale of the grapes and the wine (31:16; see Delitzsch).

The second half of this statement is connected to the first half (see "and"). In other words, because her endeavor has been profitable, she stays up at night. Her success spurs her to redouble her effort (Delitzsch). She stays up "planning ahead" (Buzzell). Perhaps she is working on her other business (Delitzsch, who points to the next verse).

<u>When the excellent wife makes a profit from her business, she does not slow down; she works at night.</u>

This wife's work is never done. She gets up before sunrise (verse 15) and works into the night (verse 18). Most wives can identify with that.

Proverbs 31:19 "She stretches out her hands to the distaff, and her hand holds the spindle." The excellent wife works at spinning. Until they were replaced by the spinning wheel, the distaff and the spindle were "the most ancient of all instruments used for spinning or making thread" (Clarke; Delitzsch, who says, "The spinning wheel is a German invention of the 16th century). The distaff was a staff that held the unspun flax, wool, etc. With one hand, she holds the staff, and with the other hand, she holds the spindle, which is what she had to do to spin wool and flax into yarn and thread (MacDonald).

Clarke describes the process. "She takes the distaff, that on which the wool or flax was rolled, and the spindle, that by twisting of which she twisted the thread with the right hand, while she held the distaff in the guard of the left arm, and drew down the thread with the fingers of the left hand."

Clearly, she is willing to work with her hands (31:13). She does not disdain manual labor or menial task (JFB). "She counts it no shame to be employed at the spindle and distaff" (Bridges).

<u>The excellent wife makes clothes, beginning with the spinning of the thread.</u>

Proverbs 31:20 "She extends her hand to the poor, yes, she reaches out her hands to the needy." The excellent wife helps the poor and needy. The labor mentioned in the previous verses (31:16-19) was not selfish (Delitzsch; Barnes). It was not for just herself (31:22) or her family (31:21; Bridges). It was to help others outside her immediate family. Given that the surrounding verses are about making clothes (31:19, 21, 22), this verse probably means that she gives clothes she has made (Buzzell).

The mention of hands (first singular and then plural) could indicate that she gives that which she made with her own hands. It also implies that she did not give gifts from a distance (Delitzsch). She was personally involved.

<u>The excellent wife not only makes clothes for herself (31:22) and her family (31:21), she makes clothes she can give to the poor and needy.</u>

In this regard, the excellent wife is an example of a principle that applies to all men and women, married and singles, young and old. Paul puts it like this: "Let him who stole steal no longer, but rather let him labor, working with *his* hands what is good, that he may have something to give him who has need" (Eph. 4:28). Also, in this regard, this hard-working woman not only pleases her husband; she pleases God (Delitzsch).

Proverbs 31:21 "She is not afraid of snow for her household, for all her household *is* clothed with scarlet." The excellent wife is not afraid of the snow because all in her family will be clothed with scarlet. Snow is not rare in Palestine and can sometimes be accompanied with "intense cold" (Delitzsch). The cold weather does not cause the excellent wife to fear (Delitzsch) or panic (Buzzell). "She does not dread the approach of winter because there is plenty of warm clothing in the closets" (MacDonald).

The problem is the meaning of the word "scarlet." The color scarlet does not keep people warm. Moreover, in this verse, the Hebrew word translated "scarlet" is plural, which is "abnormal" (Kidner). Several solutions have been suggested.

One explanation is that the Hebrew word translated "scarlet" could possibly mean "double," indicating "double thickness" (Septuagint, the Greek translation of the Old Testament; Jerome; Luther; Wardlaw; Bridges; Clarke). In order for "scarlet" to be translated "double" the Hebrew word has to be amended.

Of course, there is the view that the correct reading is scarlet and that the point is the color. Translations render the Hebrew word "scarlet" (NKJV; NASB; NIV; ESV). Scarlet would make the clothes "at once conspicuous" (Barnes). Delitzsch says the scarlet clothing is wool, which preserves warmth, and, at the same time, the color makes the clothing appear dignified. The dyes used indicate the "best fabrics" and also "a matter of taste" (JFB).

Another interpretation is that scarlet indicates "expensive garments" (Buzzell). It "denotes high cost. She can afford the best, and by implication, the fully adequate" (Kidner). "She spares no cost in protecting her family from the cold" (Buzzell). Saul is said to have clothed the daughters of Israel "in scarlet, with the luxury" and that he put "ornaments of gold" on their apparel (2 Sam. 1:24; see "luxuriously in scarlet" in the NASB and "in scarlet and finery" and the NIV).

<u>The excellent wife ensures that her family is clothed in the finest, warm, and colorful clothing when it snows.</u>

Although this verse does not say so, the surrounding verses seem to indicate that these are clothes she made (31:19, 22, 24).

Proverbs 31:22 "She makes tapestry for herself; her clothing *is* fine linen and purple." The excellent wife makes tapestry for her house and clothing for herself. The Hebrew word translated "tapestry" means "spread." It is used of a bedspread in Proverbs 7:16, which says, "I have spread my bed with tapestry, colored coverings of Egyptian linen" (Clarks, JFB; Buzzell; ESV translation). The phrase "for herself" does not mean "she prepares such pillows for her own bed, but that she herself (*i.e.*, for the wants of her house) prepares them" (Delitzsch).

The excellent wife wears clothes made of fine linen and purple. The linen is made from flax (31:13) and the purple is a dye made from a shellfish (Buzzell). In other words, she "clothes herself in costly attire" (Delitzsch; JFB says it was the "most costly goods"). The excellent wife is a queen (31:1; see comments on 31:10 and 31:13; Wardlaw). Therefore, her clothes fit her position (Bridges; Buzzell). She probably makes them herself (see 31:19 and 31:24; Wardlaw).

<u>The excellent wife makes tapestry for the beds in her house and wears expensive, colorful clothing.</u>

Proverbs 31:23 'Her husband is known in the gates, when he sits among the elders of the land." The excellent wife's husband is known in the gates. In ancient Israel, the "gates" are where the affairs of the city were deliberated (Delitzsch). It was like a modern City Hall. Her husband is not only a member of the city council, he is *known* there. He has "a well-known, reputable name; for there he sits, along with the elders of the land, who are chosen into the council of the city as the chief place of the land, and has a weighty voice among them" (Delitzsch).

This proverb indicates that an excellent wife is part of her husband's success. "She advances the estimation and the respect in which her husband is held" (Delitzsch). She "enhances her husband's standing among those who transact legal and judicial affairs at the city gate" (Buzzell).

Commentators offer explanations of how the wife helps her husband succeed. Barnes says, "The industry of the wife leaves the husband free to take his place among the elders that sit in councils." MacDonald suggests, "He can devote himself to public affairs without worrying about conditions at home." Buzzell puts it like this: "Though she is obviously aggressive and competent, she functions in a way that honors her husband's leadership rather than denigrates it. She respects him and builds him up." Clarke states He is respected "because he is the husband of a woman who is justly held in universal esteem. And her complete management of household affairs gives him full leisure to devote himself to the civil interests of the community."

<u>The excellent wife has a husband who is a well-known and respected leader in the community.</u>

Proverbs 31:24 "She makes linen garments and sells *them,* and supplies sashes for the merchants." The excellent wife makes and sells linen garments and sashes. She not only makes clothes for herself, but she is also such a good seamstress that she makes enough garments to sell (Buzzell; 31:22, where a different Hebrew word for linen is used). She not only makes garments, she makes sashes (belts, Buzzell). The linen garments were expensive (Buzzell) and the sashes were "often costly and highly valued" (JFB)

<u>The excellent wife makes and sells expensive garments and sashes.</u>

Her Character

Proverbs 31:25 "Strength and honor *are* her clothing; she shall rejoice in time to come." The excellent wife is clothed with strength, honor, and joy. The figure of clothing is used to convey her outward appearance (Buzzell), but her appearance is a reflection of her inner person (Bridges).

The excellent wife appears strong. This is not just her appearance; she is a strong woman (see comments on 31:10). She has "power over the changes of temporal circumstances, which easily shatter and bring to ruin a household resting on less solid foundations" (Delitzsch). She has "moral character" (JFB).

The excellent wife appears dignified (Delitzsch). The Hebrew word translated "honor" means splendor, honor, dignity." She appears honorable (JFB).

The excellent wife appears confident (Delitzsch; JFB; Buzzell; MacDonald). She "looks forward to the future, not with anxious care, but with confident gladness" (Barnes). She is not overburdened with care (Bridges). Buzzell notes that Proverbs 27:1 "cautions against boasting about tomorrow," that "does not do away with preparing for it (as ants do, 6:6-8; 30:25)."

<u>The excellent wife has an appearance of strength, dignity, and confidence.</u>

Proverbs 31:26 "She opens her mouth with wisdom, and on her tongue *is* the law of kindness." The excellent wife speaks wisdom and kindness.

The excellent wife speaks words of wisdom to her children, maidservants (31:15), and all others. "She says nothing that is foolish" (Bridges). Her words are not a display of knowledge to impress others; they are words of wisdom designed to benefit others.

The excellent wife speaks according to the law of kindness. The Hebrew word translated "kindness" means "goodness, kindness, loving-kindness," especially to the needy and miserable (BDB), "devoted love, fidelity" (Kidner). It is translated "mercy" in Proverbs 21:21. Her speech is not sarcastic or sanctimonious but sane and sensible (Wardlaw). "Her conversation is wise and gentle" (JFB).

Furthermore, her words are not just kind once in a while. With her, speaking kindly is a law that is consistently applied. She uses a principle "at all times, in all places, and in all companies" (Wardlaw).

Clarke says, "This is the most distinguishing excellence of this woman. Very few of those are called managing women who are not lords over their husbands, tyrants over their servants, and insolent among their neighbors. But this woman, with all her eminence and excellence, was of a meek and quiet spirit."

<u>The excellent wife speaks words of wisdom and consistently utters words of kindness.</u>

Proverbs 31:27 "She watches over the ways of her household, and does not eat the bread of idleness." The excellent wife manages the household and is not idle.

The excellent wife watches the activity of the family and servants. "Her eyes are turned everywhere; she is at one time here, at another there, to look after all with her own eyes; she does not suffer the day's work, according to the instructions given, to be left undone" (Delitzsch). It is said that mothers have eyes in the back of their heads. The excellent wife is involved in the management of the households (Buzzell). She "keeps in close touch with the affairs of her household" (MacDonald).

Bridges puts it like this: "Nothing is neglected that belongs to order, sobriety, economy, or general management. Does she understand the exact work of each under her care and their different abilities, when they need to be directed, and when they may be left to their own responsibility; what belongs to, and what is beyond, her own province of superintendence."

The excellent wife does not eat the bread of idleness. She is not inactive, lazy, or apathetic. She is engaged and energetic. "She does not waste time or engage in shallow, unproductive activity" (MacDonald).

<u>The excellent wife is actively overseeing the household affairs; she is not idle.</u>

Her praise

Proverbs 31:28-29 "Her children rise up and call her blessed; her husband *also*, and he praises her: 'Many daughters have done well, but you excel them all.'" The excellent wife (mother) is praised by both her children and her husband.

Her children call her blessed. They realize she is an "outstanding mother" (MacDonald). "They call her blessed; she is positive and optimistic and enjoys her role in life" (Buzzell). "She has brought the house and them to such prosperity, such a position of respect, and to a state where love reigns" (Delitzsch).

Her husband praises her. The Hebrew word translated "done well" is the same one that is rendered virtuous in verse 10. As was noted, it is difficult to translate because it contains a number of nuances. The most basic idea is "strength," which leads to the concept of "ability." The title "excellent wife" was chosen in order to incorporate both concepts. Thus in Proverbs 31:29, the husband of an excellent wife tells her that there are many excellent wives, but she is the "greatest" (Buzzell).

"Her husband is so satisfied with her conduct towards himself, his household, his business, and their children that he praises her. He shows himself sensible of her excellence, and encourages her, in her work, by the commendations he bestows" (Clarke).

"She is honored by those who best know her" (JFB).

<u>The excellent wife is praised by her children and her husband says she is the greatest of the excellent wives.</u>

Concerning Susanna Wesley, the mother of John and Charles Wesley, Clarke said, "She was a woman of great learning and information, and of a depth of mind, and reach of thought, seldom to be found among the daughters of Eve, and not often among the sons of Adam."

Proverbs 31:30 "Charm *is* deceitful and beauty *is* passing, but a woman *who* fears the LORD, she shall be praised." The excellent wife is praised because she fears the Lord. The previous verse says the excellent wife is praised by her children and her husband. This verse gives the basic reason she is praised (Delitzsch).

Charm can be deceitful. External appearance can deceive (Delitzsch). A woman may have charm and no common sense (MacDonald).

Beauty is passing. The beauty of the body fades away (Delitzsch). A woman may be beautiful but be impractical (MacDonald).

The woman who fears the Lord will be praised. The Hebrew word translated "fear" means 1) to be afraid, terrified, 2) to stand in awe, 3) to reverence, 4) to honor. In the Old Testament, the expression "the fear of the Lord" includes several concepts. The use of the word "Lord," instead of God, indicates that the fear of the Lord includes *knowing* the Lord because "LORD" is the covenant, personal name of God (see also 9:10, where the synonymous parallelism indicates that the fear of the Lord and the knowledge of the Lord are synonymous). The fear of the Lord also includes *reverence* for the Lord, which is the definition of the word "fear" (see also Ps. 33:8, where the parallelism indicates that the fear of the Lord and standing in awe are synonymous). And, yes, the fear of the Lord includes *fear* of the Lord, when you disobey Him.

The woman who fears the Lord will be praised, because the foundation of her life is her relationship to the Lord. The fear of the Lord is "the productive germ and pervading principle of (her) whole character" (Wardlaw). She may be "physically charming and beautiful, but those qualities may not last" (Buzzell). Inner beauty is "unfading beauty" (Clarke). Her true value is measured by that which is enduring (Delitzsch).

<u>The excellent wife is praised not because of her external charm or beauty but because of her internal fear of the Lord.</u>

"The last lesson of the book is the same as the first. The fear of the Lord is the condition of all womanly, as well as of all manly, excellence" (Barnes; Buzzell).

Beveridge says, "If I choose her for her *beauty*, I shall love her no longer than while that continues; and then farewell at once both duty and delight. But if I love her for her virtues; then, though all other sandy foundations fail, yet will my happiness remain entire" (Beveridge, cited by Bridges).

Proverbs 31:31 "Give her of the fruit of her hands, and let her own works praise her in the gates." The excellent wife will be praised because of the work of her hands.

Give the excellent wife her due. "The fruit of her hands" is "the blessing which she has secured for others" (and) "for her own enjoyment" (Delitzsch). "May she long enjoy the fruit of her labors! May she see her children's children, and peace upon Israel!" (Clarke). "If tongues were silent, her works would speak for her" (Wardlaw).

Let the excellent wife be praised for her work "in the gates." The expression "in the gates" is a reference to "the place where the representatives of the people come together, and where the people are assembled" (Delitzsch). "When the town fathers meet at the civic center, let them praise her outstanding accomplishments" (MacDonald). She "should be honored publicly. Honoring a *woman* was not normally done in Israel. But an unusual woman called for unusual recognition" (Buzzell, italics his).

It should be pointed out that the kind of woman described in this passage would not seek the praise of men. She would be "content to be known and loved within her own circle, she never presses herself into notice" (Bridges). Nevertheless, "Let what she has done be spoken of for a memorial of her; let her bright example be held forth in the most public places. Let it be set before the eyes of every female, particularly of every wife, and especially of every mother; and let them learn from this exemplar" (Clarke).

English theologian Simon Patrick wrote, "Let everyone extol her virtue. Let her not want the just commendation of her pious labors. But while some are magnified for the nobleness of the stock, from whence they sprung; others for their fortune; others for their beauty; others for other things; let the good deeds, which she herself hath done, be publicly praised in the greatest assemblies; where, if all men should be silent, her own works will declare her excellent worth" (Patrick, cited by Bridges).

<u>Let the excellent wife be publicly praised for her accomplishments.</u>

So Proverbs ends. Buzzell sums it up well when he says, "The virtues of a noble wife are those that are extolled throughout the Book of Proverbs: hard work, wise investments, good use of time, planning ahead, care for others, respect for one's spouse, ability to share godly values with others, wise counsel, and godly fear (worship, trust, service, obedience). As Proverbs has stated repeatedly, these are qualities that lead to honor, praise, success, personal dignity and worth, and enjoyment of life. In the face of the adulteress' temptations mentioned often in Proverbs, it is fitting that the book concludes by extolling a virtuous wife. Young men and others can learn from this noble woman. By fearing God, they can live wisely and righteously. *That* is the message of Proverbs" (Buzzell, italics his).

BIBLIOGRAPHY

Barnes, Albert. *Barnes' Notes on the Old Testament.* e-sword.net.
Baxter, J. Sidlow. *Explore the Book.* 6 vols. London: Marshall, Morgan, and Scott, 1965.
Bridges, Charles. *An Exposition of Proverbs.* 1846; reprint ed., London: Banner of Truth, 1960.
Brown, Francis, Samuel Rolles Driver, and Charles Augustus Briggs. *A Hebrew and English* Lexicon *of the Old Testament.* Oxford: Clarendon, 1962.
Buzzell, Sid S. "Proverbs," *The Bible Knowledge Commentary*: Old Testament, pp. 901-74. Edited by John F. Walvoord and Roy B. Zuck. Wheaton: Scripture Press Publications, Victor Books, 1985.
Clarke, Adam. *Adam Clarke's Bible Commentary.* e-sword.net.
Delitzsch, Franz. *Biblical Commentary on the Proverbs of Solomon.* 2 vols. Translated by M. G. Eason. Biblical Commentary on the Old Testament. Reprint ed., Grand Rapids: Wm. B. Eerdmans Publishing Co., n.d.
Jamieson, Robert, A. R. Fausset and David Brown. A *Commentary Critical and Explanatory on the Whole Bible.* e-sword.net.
Kidner, Derek. *The Proverbs.* Tyndale Old Testament Commentaries series. Leicester, Eng.: Tyndale Press, 1964; reprint ed., Downers Grove, Ill.: InterVarsity Press, 1978.
Lange, John Peter, ed. *Commentary on the Holy Scriptures.* 12 vols. Reprint ed., Grand Rapids: Zondervan Publishing House, 1960. Vol. 4: Psalms—Song of Solomon, by Carl Bernhard Moll and Otto Zockler. Translated and edited by Charles A.
MacDonald, William. *The Bible Believers Commentary.* e-sword.net.
Perowne, T. T. Proverbs. *Cambridge Bible for Schools and Colleges.* Cambridge: Universoty Press, 1899, e-word.net.

Waltke, Bruce K. *An Old Testament Theology.* Grand Rapids: Zondervan, 2007.
Wardlaw, Ralph, *Lectures on the book of Proverbs.* Minneapolis, Minn.: Klock & Klock Christian Publishers, 1981.

www.ingramcontent.com/pod-product-compliance
Lightning Source LLC
Chambersburg PA
CBHW081441070526
44586CB00019B/2198

9781948474108